AGNES KEFELI

religions of the
WORLD
PAST AND PRESENT

Kendall Hunt
publishing company

Front cover image courtesy Anne Clay; back cover image courtesy of author.

Kendall Hunt
publishing company

www.kendallhunt.com
Send all inquiries to:
4050 Westmark Drive
Dubuque, IA 52004-1840

Contents

Greetings vii
Introduction to the Study of Religion viii
Create Your Own Timeline xiv

PART 1

Religions Originating in Southeast Asia: The Myth of Liberation 1
Map 1 Harappan Civilization.. 2
Map 2 Jainism 3
Map 3 Sikhism 4
Map 4 Spread of Buddhism in Asia 5

    Hinduism 7
    Lecture Notes 8
    Video Questions 27
    Quiz (The Vedic Age) 33
    Crossword Puzzle 35
    Pictures Recognition 41
    Readings:
        Text 1 "Hymns from the Rig Veda" 46
        Text 2 "The Bhagavad Gita".. 49
        Text 3 "Gandhi's Reading of the Gita" 56
        Text 4 "The Laws of Manu" 59
        Text 5 "Kali" 81

    Buddhism.. 83
    Lecture Notes 85
    Video Questions 103
    Crossword Puzzle 111
    Pictures Recognition.. 117
    Readings:
        Text 6 "Sacred Biography of the Buddha Shakyamuni" 120
        Text 7 "The Path to Enlightenment" 135
        Text 8 "The Bodhisattva Vow" 139
        Text 9 "Satomi Myodo's Autobiography" 143

Jainism 155
Lecture Notes 156
Crossword Puzzle 161
Readings:
    Text 10 "Is There a Creator God?" 164
    Text 11 "Can Women Attain Liberation?" 165
Sikhism 167
Lecture Notes 168
Video Questions 173
Crossword Puzzle 175
Readings:
    Text 12 "The Hymns of Guru Nanak" 178

PART 2

Religions Originating in East Asia: The Myth of Harmony 185
Map: Asia 186
Shinto 187
Lecture Notes 188
Video Questions 193
In-Class Exercise 195
Crossword Puzzle 197
Readings:
    Text 13 "The Japanese Creation Myth" 200
Taoism (Daoism) 203
Lecture Notes 205
Video Questions 215
In-Class Reaction Paragraph on Taoism 217
Crossword Puzzle 219
Readings:
    Text 14 "Daodejing" 223
    Text 15 "Women in Taoism (Daoism)" 227
Confucianism 239
Lecture Notes 241
Crossword Puzzle 245
Readings:
    Text 16 "The Analects" 248
    Text 17 "Pan Chao: A Female Confucian Scholar" 253

PART 3

Religions Originating in the Middle East: The Myth of History 257
Maps: Middle Eastern Religions 258
Zoroastrianism 261
Lecture Notes 262
Crossword Puzzle 267

Readings:
Text 18 "The Battle Between Ahura Mazda and Angra Mainyu" 271

Judaism 273
Lecture Notes 274
Video Questions 287
Crossword Puzzle 295
Readings:
1. Mesopotamian Myths
Text 19 "The Flood in Mesopotamian Mythology: The Epic of Gilgamesh" 299
2. The Hebrew Bible
Reading Questions 301
Text 20 "Genesis" (chapters 1-18) 302
Text 21 "Joseph's Story in Genesis" (chapters 37-50) 313
Text 22 "Exodus" (chapters 1-22) 325
Text 23 "The Prophet Isaiah" 341
3. The Oral Torah
Reading Questions 343
Text 24 "The Oral Torah and the Practices of the Torah" 344
Text 25 "The Hereafter" 351

Christianity 375
Lecture Notes 377
Video Questions 387
The Life of Jesus Portrayed in the Stained Glass Windows in the Cathedral of Brussels 394
Crossword Puzzle 397
Readings:
1. The New Testament
Reading Questions 399
Text 26 "The Gospel According to Mark" 400
Text 27 "The Gospel According to Matthew" (chapters 1-3) 415
Text 28 "The Gospel of John" (chapters 13-21) 417
Text 29 "Paul's Letter to the Galatians" 424
Text 30 "Revelation" (chapter 1) 428
2. Protestantism (16th century)
Reading Questions 429
Text 31 "Martin Luther: The Reformation" 430

Islam 433
Lecture Notes 435
Video Questions 443
Matching Game: Let's Learn Arabic in One Day 449
Crossword Puzzle 451
Readings:
1. The Qur'an
Reading Questions 455
Text 32 "Surah 1: Al-Fatiha or the Opening" 456

Text 33 "Surah 2: Al-Baqara or the Heifer" 457

Text 34 "Surah 12: Yusuf or Joseph" 473

Text 35 "Surah 19: Maryam or Mary" 479

Text 36 "Surah 71: Nuh or Noah"..481

2. Hadith Sample

Reading Questions 482

Text 37 "The Night Journey in the Hadith"..483

Reading Glossary 485

References 489

Greetings

Dear Students:

Welcome to the *Religions of the World*! This class surveys the global range of human spiritual and religious experience. It examines various worldwide patterns of religious beliefs and practices, and then investigates particular faiths, communities, and traditions. My main goal is twofold. First, to help you develop a general understanding of the roles religion has played over time in individual and collective life in various geographical, historical, and cultural contexts; second, to give you a framework to ask further questions in other classes. Take it as a journey throughout the world. You will learn basic geography, history, and many languages in a very short time, and get a sense of what researchers do in Religious Studies.

This workbook is divided into three units: 1) an introduction to religions originating in India (Hinduism, Jainism, Buddhism, and Sikhism); 2) an introduction to religions originating in East Asia (Confucianism, Taoism, and Shinto); and finally, 3) an overview of the Abrahamic traditions of Judaism, Christianity, and Islam which originated in the Middle East.

Please bring your workbook every time you come to class. There you will find blank maps, crosswords, questions on short documentary films, pictures of religious art works, and an anthology of scriptures and scholarly articles with discussion questions. One part of the assignments will be done in class; another will be done on Blackboard.

Always check Blackboard for your weekly assignment and complementary course material (PowerPoints, lecture notes, study guides, quizzes).

Enjoy this trip around the world and have a wonderful semester!

Dr. Agnes Kefeli
Principal Lecturer
School of Historical, Philosophical, and Religious Studies
Arizona State University

Introduction to the Study of Religion

RELIGION

- = in Latin, "to tie back, to tie again"
- = ties people back to a greater reality
- = ties people together in a community

Why is the Study of Religion important in 21st c.?

- Religion plays a role in politics, arts, economics
- The study of religion develops greater tolerance

What is Religious Studies?

- Religious Studies take religion as an object of study
- Theologians versus Scholars of Religion
- Theologians want to prove that their religion is the true one
- Scholars or scientists of Religious Studies compare different customs, beliefs, rituals

What Will We Study this Semester?

- Religions of South Asia (Hinduism, Buddhism, Jainism, Sikhism)
- Religions of East Asia (Taoism, Confucianism, Shinto)
- Religions of the Middle East (Judaism, Christianity, Islam)

Religions of South Asia and the Myth of Liberation

- Life is seen as suffering.
- Why? Life always ends in old age, sickness, and death
- Humans are caught in endless cycle of suffering, death, and rebirth
- The goal of religion is to free oneself from wheel of death and rebirth (samsara)
- Once freed humans will experience ultimate reality

Religions of East Asia and the Myth of Harmony

- Tao (Dao) = mysterious source and ordering principle of the universe
- All of creation works via the opposites of yin and yang
- The ideal of life is balance
- Problem of existence is disharmony
- Taoism, Confucianism, and Shinto offer different means to reestablish harmony

The Religions of the Middle East and the Myth of History
- God is creator of all things
- God acts in time
- The story begins with initial harmony
- Then sin disrupts harmony
- Judaism, Christianity, Islam trace themselves back to Patriarch Abraham.
- In all three, goal = restoring harmony with will of God so that death can be overcome

How Will We Study the Religions of the World?
- We will use Bruce Lincoln's definition of religion
- Religion is:
  - a discourse
  - a set of practices
  - a community
  - an institution

We Will Ask the Following Questions
- What does it mean to be human?
- What is the basic human problem?
- What is the cause of the problem?
- What is the end or goal of transformation?
- What are the means of transformation?

Where, When, and Why did the Science of Religion Arise?
- In 16th c. religion was basic foundation of life
- In Europe Christianity was dominant
- New discoveries (People managed to build great civilizations without ever knowing Jesus Christ!)
- Religious wars (Time of Reformation)

The Enlightenment (18th c.)
- Religion became an object of study
- Would it be possible to find a new form of religion, beyond the quarrels of churches?
- A single religion, shared by the entire human race?

Deism
- Often called natural religion
- Belief in a creator God
- Belief in a moral code given to guide the conduct of human beings
- Belief in the promise of an afterlife
- The goal was peace

Result of the Enlighteners' Approach
- Scholars developed a scientific view of religion

- They asked questions:
  - What is religion?
  - Why does it exist? What is the source of religion?
  - What explains its variety?
  - Why are people religious?

Development of the Study of Religion (19th-20th c.)

- Materialistic Perspective
- Intellectualist Perspective
- Idealist or Faith Perspective
- Functional Perspective
- Semiotic Perspective

THE MATERIALISTIC PERSPECTIVE

- Humans Invented Religion
- Hostile to religion
- Religion = superstition, untrue
- Only the material world exists
- Religion will disappear as the world embraces scientific rationalism

Ludwig Feuerbach (19th c)

- German philosopher
- Gods are FALSE
- The origin of religion is FEAR
- Gods = projections of people's fears and desires
- Gods = the most fearsome natural elements of nature
- Religion is ALIENATION

Sigmund Freud (19th c.)

- Austrian psychoanalyst
- Religion = neurosis
- Religion = TOTEM and TABOO
- Religion = repressed sexuality and repressed violence
- = replaying of the loving and fearful relationships children with parents
- God (= father) can punish or reward for obedience or non-obedience to social norms.

Freud's Main Contribution

- Religion is more than a collection of beliefs
- Deep, hidden motivations shape religion in ways that must be examined

Karl Marx (19th c.)

- German socialist philosopher
- Religion = product of the mode of production
- Mode of production = economic base of society

- Economy determines everything else about society (politics, art, culture)
- The ruling class controls the economy, thus the cultural and religious systems.
- Religion = TOOL OF OPPRESSION

Marx's Contribution to the Study of Religion
- What do religious beliefs do for people socially?

The Materialistic Perspective and its downsides
- Religions are reduced to product of hidden neurosis, social need, or economic conflict
- If religion is untrue why study it?

THE INTELLECTUALIST PERSPECTIVE
- Religion = matter of belief + FORM OF KNOWLEDGE
- is a rational attempt to explain how nature works
- religion will disappear as the world embraces scientific rationalism

Edward Tylor (19th c.)
- English anthropologist
- First religion = ANIMISM = belief in spirits or anima in Latin
- Spiritual beings = personal powers behind all things
- Religious teaching arose from a rational effort to explain the world
- Animistic beliefs developed into ideas of gods, then to one god

James Frazer (19th c.)
- a Scottish anthropologist.
- First there was magic = pseudoscientific attempt to confront and control natural forces
- But magic does not always work
- Religious conceptions (prayers, pleading) replaced magic
- Ultimately, rational scientific thinking replaces religion when people finally understand the laws of nature

The Intellectualist Perspective and its downsides
- Most aspects rejected by modern critics
- This perspective was culturally biased

IDEALIST OR FAITH PERSPECTIVE (19TH AND 20TH C.)
- Religion = the experience and the true reflection of the sacred
- The sacred = realm of the extraordinary and supernatural, the source of the universe and its values

Rudolph Otto
- German professor of theology
- Religion emerges when people experience "the mystery that causes trembling and fascination"

Mircea Eliade

- Rumanian scholar of comparative religion
- Profane versus Sacred
- The profane is unimportant, the sacred is significant
- Divine models contained in cosmogonic myths show how life ought to be lived

Myths

- Historically untrue? NO
- Myths = symbolic or foundational stories about the origins and destiny of human beings and their world
- They express the religious beliefs of a group

Myths Answer the Important Questions

- how did the universe come into existence?
- what should be our relationship with the world of nature?
- why do human beings exist?
- why is there suffering in the world?
- how should we deal with it?
- what happens when we die?

Every Religion has Myths

- For Judaism and Christianity, the first chapters of the Book of Genesis constitute a myth of origins (cosmogonic myth)
- Eschatological myths deal with the end of times
- One of the critical aspects in the study of a religion is to ask: what are its myths?

Problem with Mircea Eliade

- Tended to present religious beliefs, myths, and symbols as timeless
- More contextual and historical perspective needed

FUNCTIONAL PERSPECTIVE

- Religion is useful
- Main representative: Emile Durkheim (1858-1917)
- French sociologist
- Humans cannot live without organized social structures
- Religion is a glue that holds a society together
- Religious rituals are occasions for individuals to renew their commitment to the community

Durkheim and Today

- This kind of thinking about religion persists today
- Problem: religions may be reduced to the product of social need

THE SEMIOTIC PERSPECTIVE (20TH C.)

- Religion = System of Symbols

- Seeks to understand religion in its own context in a more subjective fashion
- Religion = a system of symbols that needs to be deciphered

The Representatives of the Semiotic Perspective
- Have learned the necessary languages to conduct their research
- Have lived among the people they study
- No more single Islam, Christianity, or Buddhism

Clifford Geertz
- American anthropologist (1926-2006).
- Religion = cultural fact, NOT mere expression of social needs or economic tensions
- Culture is understood as a pattern of meanings or ideas carried in symbols that needs interpretation
- "thick description" = describes rituals and their exact and varied meanings for practitioners

Advantages and Limitations
- Geertz = a particularist. Opposed scripturalist religion and local religion
- True. Religious experiences will differ from one place to another
- Problem: can an outsider be truly objective?

Create Your Own Timeline

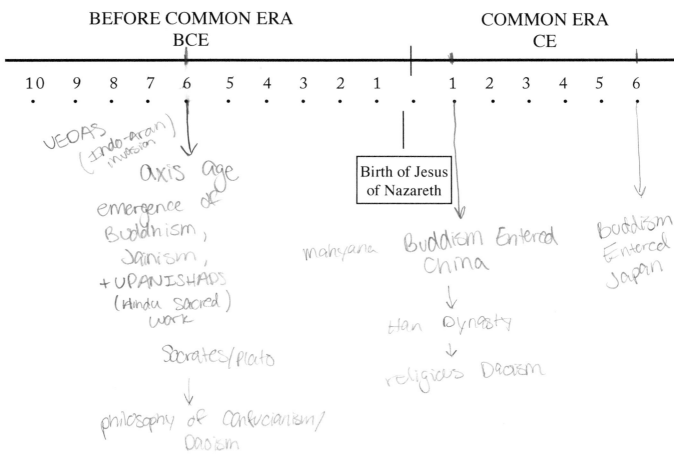

BEFORE COMMON ERA
BCE

COMMON ERA
CE

10 9 8 7 6 5 4 3 2 1   1 2 3 4 5 6

VEDAS
(Indo-Aryan
invasion)

axis age

emergence of
Buddhism,
Jainism,
+ UPANISHADS
(Hindu sacred)
work

Socrates/Plato

philosophy of Confucianism/
Daoism

Birth of Jesus
of Nazareth

mahayana Buddism Entered
China

Han Dynasty

religious Daoism

Buddhism
Entered
Japan

Create Your Own Timeline

COMMON ERA
CE

7   8   9   10   11   12   13   14   15   16   17   18   19   20

Buddism Entered
Tibet

emergence
of Islam

Part 1

RELIGIONS ORIGINATING IN SOUTH-EAST ASIA: THE MYTH OF LIBERATION

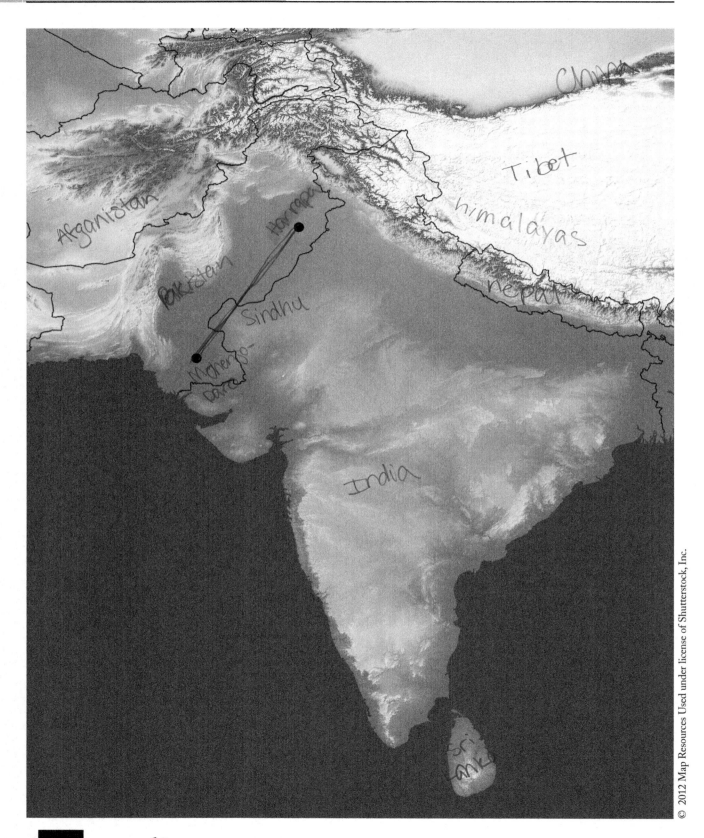

Part 1: RELIGIONS ORIGINATING IN SOUTHEAST ASIA: THE MYTH OF LIBERATION

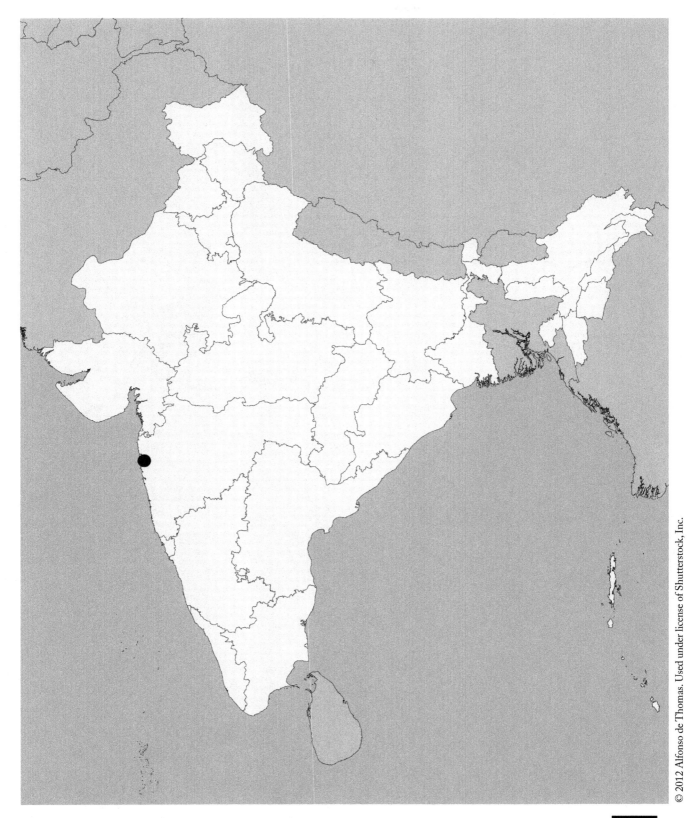

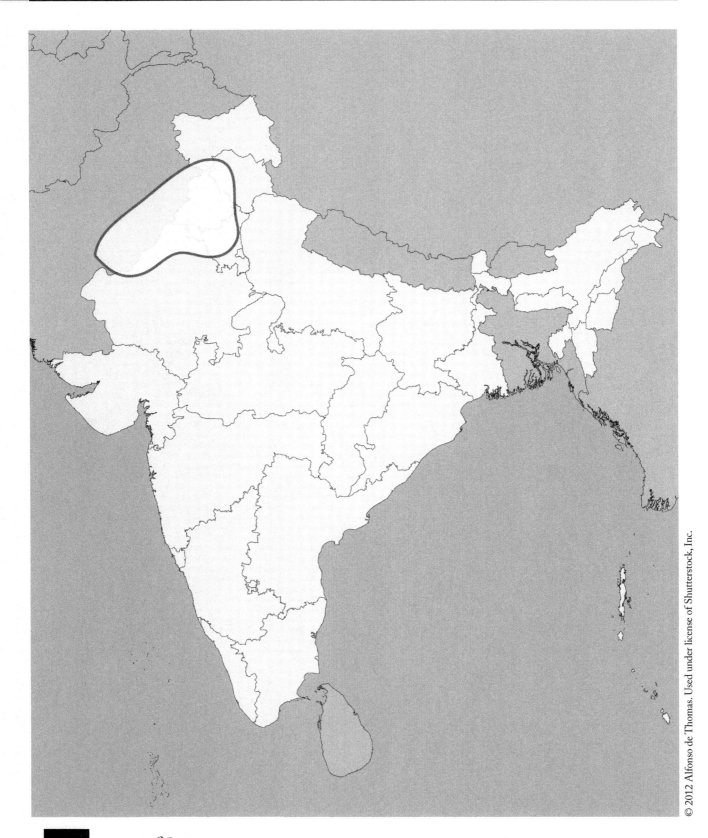

Part 1: RELIGIONS ORIGINATING IN SOUTHEAST ASIA: THE MYTH OF LIBERATION

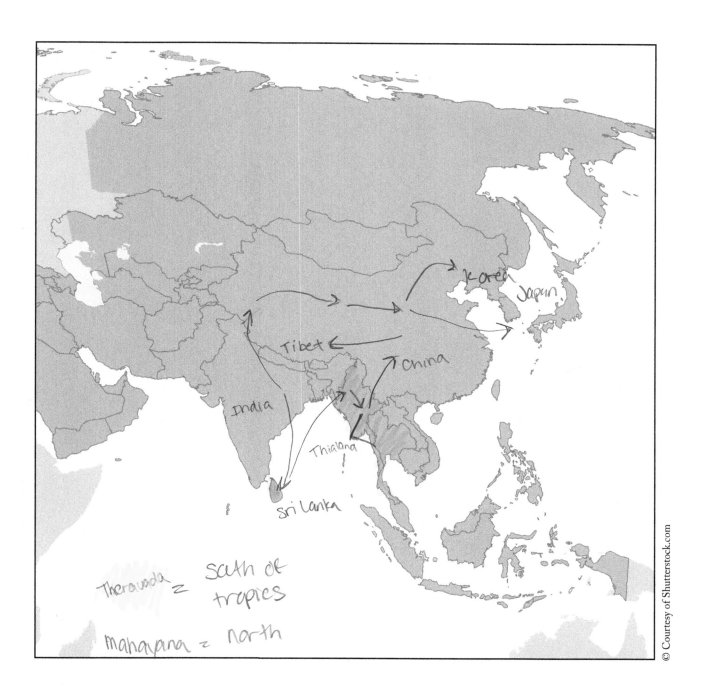

Korea

Japan

Tibet

China

India

Thialand

Sri Lanka

Theravada = South of tropies

Mahayana = North

© Courtesy of Shutterstock.com

Hinduism

Sadhu (Hindu Ascetic) in Udaipur, India

Part 1: **RELIGIONS ORIGINATING IN SOUTHEAST ASIA: THE MYTH OF LIBERATION**

TRADITIONAL TIME LINE
- BC = Before Christ
- AD = Anno Domini (in the year of our Lord)
- Problem: this time line is based on the birth of Jesus Christ
- And this course is about many different religions

TIME LINE IN RELIGIOUS STUDIES
- Instead of BC = Before Christ
  we use BCE = Before the Common Era
  [Both terms represent years before birth of Jesus]
- Instead of AD = Anno Domini (in the year of our Lord)
  we use CE = Common Era
  [Both terms represent years after birth of Jesus]

HINDUISM
- Third largest religion today after Christianity and Islam
- Second fastest growing religion after Islam
- Amalgam of spiritual traditions originating in South Asia
- Unites
  – Worship of many gods
  – Belief in a single divine reality

Origins of the Term Hinduism
- Comes from Sindhu
- Sindhu = great Indus River in Sanskrit
- 8th century CE: Muslim administrators/traders/scholars used Hindu to designate people who lived east of Indus River
- 19th-century British used Hindu to designate non-Muslim natives in census-taking

Hinduism is falsely singular
- Some traditions might justify
  – Caste
  – Social inequality
- Others might argue
  – For reform of society
  – For "God-given" egalitarianism
- Some practice animal sacrifices
  – But others are non violent ascetics

**Contrary to Christianity and Islam, Hinduism
DOES NOT HAVE**

- An identifiable founder
- A single canonical text accepted by all followers
- A religious elite or single priestly group
- A strong organizational structure to spread influence

How do Hindus Name their Religion?

Dharma (in Sanskrit)

- Duty
- The ways things are intended to be
- Law
- Way of life and thought

Where do Hindus Live?

- Mainly on the South Asian subcontinent
- India
- Nepal
- Pakistan and Bangladesh
- Buddhist Sri Lanka
- Burma, Malaysia, Indonesia, Fiji, and the Caribbean

Demography

- About 800 million Hindus in the world
- In North America over one million
- There are Euro-American converts to Hinduism (through Hare Krishna movement)

Brief History of India

- Two major ethnic groups in India:
  - Indo-Aryans in northern India
  - Dravidians in southern India
- Dravidians = aboriginal people of India
- The Indo-Aryans = invaders or migrants?

Dravidian Harappa or Indus Valley Civilization

- When? From about 2500 BCE to 1500 BCE
- Where? In the Indus Valley (in modern-day Pakistan)
- Significance: Religious symbols found at Harappa still appear in contemporary Indian culture

The Aryans Are Coming!

- When? About 1500 BCE
- From where? Central Asia — *mainly male gods*
- Did they force the Dravidians into southern India? Probably migration

Shiva can be recognized by a cobra around neck

Who were these Aryans?
- "Aryan" = noble in Sanskrit
- A nomadic people
- Language: Sanskrit
- Sacred writings = the Vedas

  brought by Aryans

Vedas
- Knowledge in Sanskrit
- Most venerated writings in Hinduism

Aryan Influence
- The Aryan class system came to dominate all of India
- Became basis of later caste system
- A priestly class known as **Brahmins** dominated late Aryan religion
- These Brahmins sought an esoteric knowledge

Axis Age (6th century BCE)
- Great changes occurred
- Older Aryan religion
  - Was polytheistic
  - Performed sacrifices

The Axis Age
- New thinkers sought
  - A single divine reality that might be the source of everything
  - Some came to reject religious ritual
  - Others abandoned social and family life to live alone in the forests
  - Others experimented new meditation techniques to seek the divine reality
  - People of any social class could experiment these techniques, not just priests
- Buddhism and Jainism came to be

A New Invader!
Alexander the Great
- 326 BCE
- The great civilizations of Greece and India came into contact

The Maurya Empire (ca. 322 BCE until 185 BCE)
- Named after its founder
- Maurya united almost all of India for the first time
- The most successful ruler was Ashoka (232 BCE). He became a Buddhist
- Time of *Bhagavad-Gita* (Song of the Blessed Lord), most famous text of Hinduism

So-Called Golden Age of India
- Gupta dynasty
- Northern India
- 4th century CE
- Was a time of revival for Hinduism and Aryan culture

Islam in India
- Entered in 8th century CE
- A century after the death of the Prophet Muhammad in 632
- 16th century: the Mughal Empire

Europeans in India
- Arrived in India in the 1500s
- Great Britain = dominant European power in the 18th century
- British East India Company
- Great Britain became the principal political power in 1757
- 1858 India became part of British Empire

Indian Independence Movement
- The Hindu Indian National Congress (1885)
- Muslim League (1906)
- 1920 Mohandas K. Gandhi became leader of the Indian National Congress

Mohandas Gandhi (1869-1948)
- Challenged British rule through a campaign of non-violent resistance
- Demanded benevolent behavior from high castes toward lower castes
- Was a mediator between Hindus and Muslims

1947, Independence!
- Historic India partitioned by the British into
  – the Hindu nation of India
  – the Muslim nation of Pakistan (divided into two parts: West and East Pakistan)
- Bangladesh was formed in 1971
- India = largest democratic nation in the world

EARLY HINDUISM OR THE RELIGION OF THE VEDIC AGE (1500 TO 6TH CENTURY BCE)

Before the Axis Age!!
Our knowledge of early Indic religion comes from the four Vedas

The Four Vedas
- Vedas = knowledge
- Earliest sacred books of Hinduism
- ca. 1500 to 400 BCE
- Liturgical handbook of early Aryan (Vedic) priests
- First existed orally
- 11th century CE earliest written manuscripts

Four Basic Sacred Collections of Vedas
- Rig Veda ("hymn knowledge") = most important, oldest
- Yajur Veda ("ceremonial knowledge") = sacrificial manual (prayers)
- Sama Veda ("chant knowledge") = collection of chants for priests at sacrifices
- Atharva Veda ("knowledge from the teacher") = magical spells and curses

Rig Veda
- "Hymn knowledge"
- Oldest of the four Vedas
- Over 1,000 hymns addressed to a single or to two or more Aryan deities called devas (deus, in Latin)
- Probably for the elite

What do we learn about early Indic religion in the Vedas?
- No temples
- Worship centered on fire sacrifices under the open sky

Brahmins (priests)
- Led sacrifices to Aryan (Vedic) deities
- Chanted the Vedic hymns
- Brahman
  = holy word, sacred knowledge, incantation, mystic utterance
  = stanzas of the Rig Veda
- Brahmins = the ones who recited *brahman* the [*not word*]
- To become a Brahmin, initiation needed

Sacrifices to the Gods
- Gods had to be kept happy
- Priests
  - Chanted Vedic hymns
  - Offered grain, animal flesh, and melted butter into a fire
- Each priest had a special function:
  - Altar builder
  - Libation pourer and invoker of the gods
  - Another was the fire kindler

Cosmogonic Myth
- Primordial being Purusha sacrificed
- His mouth became the priests
- His arms the warriors
- His thighs the producers
- His feet the workers
- First allusion to the four-fold class (varna) system (caste system)

Vedic Deities
- Major deities of the Vedic world = all male
- Connected to
  - Sacrifice
  - Martial conquest
  - Mystical experience
  - Maintenance of moral order
- Two kinds of deities:
  - Deities of earth and skies
  - Liturgical deities (= deified elements of ritual)

Deities of Earth and Skies
- **INDRA** = a warrior atmospheric god — *Storm god, rides white elephant*
- **VARUNA** = sky god and sustainer of the cosmic order
- **RUDRA-SHIVA**
  - = the dread mountain god
  - = destroyer or healer?
  - = worshipers asked him to be auspicious (shiva)
  - = significance: early form of Hinduism's great god Shiva, the Destroyer and Reviver

Liturgical Deities
AGNI
  - = fire god
  - = cleansed
  - = removed sin and guilt
  - = drove away demons
  - = protected homes

Shiva = god
cobra around neck

SOMA

- = a god (the lord of the plants)
- = a hallucinogen used in many Vedic rituals
- = the divine presence in the juice of the soma plant
- = produced insight and immortality
- = milk of cows associated with Soma

BRIHASPATI

- = a subtle blending of prayer, the priest, and the power of prayer personified
- = without him, ritual would be empty

Main Characteristics of Vedic Tradition

- Polytheistic system — *many gods*
- Did not elevate one deity above the others
- During prayers, they spoke of each of their divinities as being supreme (henotheism)
- Henotheism = temporary elevation of one of many gods to the highest rank that can be accorded, verbally or ritualistically

The Upanishads (Time of Axis Age) — *seek immortality, lots of experiments*
(beg. ca. 600 - 400 BCE?)

Definition of Upanishads

- Four Vedas end with later works, the Upanishads
- Upanishad = "to sit near by"
- Upanishads = religious dialogues
- Literature for the elite
- Main theme: relationship between the individual self and the underlying support of all

Significance of Upanishads

- Emphasis placed on inner experience
- Goals:
  - To seek intuitive knowledge of that which is the source of all reality
  - To reach spiritual immortality
- In Vedic religion, emphasis placed on outward ritual performances
  Goal = long life, wealth, good health

Shift from Outer to Inner Sacrifice

- Trend to asceticism
  - Goal: seek emancipation from the world's illusion and pain (moksha)
- Trend away from external ritualism

New Emphasis on the Soul

- Soul = one's inner Self (Atman)
- ATMAN is not jiva
- Jiva = observable, empirical self with a small "s"

Salvation through Meditation
- Upanishads distinguished between
  - *Atman*, the nonmaterial inner Self
  - *Prakriti* or matter, i.e. the natural world
- Matter is of an inferior order
- To be content with the natural world can only result in suffering
- Salvation is best attained by breaking away from the natural world
- Meditation will help to free the soul from the body

New Experiments in Mystical Techniques
- Could be done by people of all classes, not just the priests
- Did this change occur because some castes rebelled against the rigid Brahmin control of all life?

Important Concepts of Upanishads *After 6th c. BCE (Axis Age)*
- Brahman *— the ultimate reality of the universe, the source, impersonal*
- Atman *— inner most, unseen, true, trancendental Self of a person*
- Maya *— illusion, we live here, inadequate world view*
- Karma *— action / conceguense of action*
- Samsara *— wheel of birth, death, rebirth*
- Moksha *— liberation, escape from wheel / physical world*

Brahman
- The holy power of prayer in Vedic literature
- The ultimate reality of the world in the Upanishads
- Usually Brahman pictured as impersonal reality
- How can Brahman be known? It can be known by meditation through Atman *ocean ↑ drops of water*

Atman
- Brahman became subdivided into myriad individual Atmans
- Atman = the innermost, unseen, transcendental Self of a person
- It is different from jiva, the observable, empirical self with a small "s"

Maya
- Maya = illusion; the world viewed inadequately
- In truth, Atman, the eternal soul, is one with Brahman
- The basic human problem is ignorance
- Because of our ignorance, we do not know the true, spiritual reality of Atman/Brahman
- We believe that our true nature is the self (jiva) that does act *lower case 's'*

Karma
- To experience the joining of Atman and Brahman, the devotees have to free themselves from the self that acts (that is the Karmic self or jiva)
- *karma* = action and consequences of an action in Sanskrit

Upanishands path → detatch yourself from actions

Samsara
- Wheel of birth, death, and rebirth
- Because of our ignorance, the Atman, the true Self is trapped in the cycle of rebirth

Moksha
- The ultimate goal is NOT creation of good lives by good deeds
- The goal is to escape from Samsara (cycle of rebirth)
- How? Seek true knowledge
- True knowledge involves an experience of Oneness
- It is done through self-discipline and meditation

lotus flower represents moksha

The Upanishad Revolution
- Interiorization of religiosity
- Individual's struggle to free the inner Self (Atman) from matter replaced communal sacrificial rites

Classical Period of Hinduism (500 BCE-1000 CE)
- The Way of Works (Code of Manu)
- The Way of Devotion
- The Way of Knowledge (or the path to Meditation)

The Upanishad Enigma
How can one escape Samsara (cycle of rebirth) and experience true reality?

Three Ways of Salvation
- A way of works (called Karma Marga or Karma yoga)
- A way of devotion (called bhakti yoga)
- A way of knowledge (called jnana yoga, "the way of wisdom")

The Way of Works (Karma Marga) — *fulfill darma, duties of your own caste*
- The way of ritual, especially domestic ritual
- By performing domestic rituals one can acquire enough merit to be reborn in the highest caste (Brahmin)

The Code of Manu *main book of karma yoga*
- Manu = "a thinking being" or "mankind"
- Provides a good illustration of what the Way of Works is about
- Collection of ethical and religious guidelines for individuals and society
- Written by priests between 200 BCE and 200 CE
- Still influential today, especially in the countryside
- Explains
  - The dharma (duty) of the four principal castes (already introduced in the Vedas)
  - The four stages of life for Indian men of the upper classes

Caste System
- In the Vedas four basic castes (varna in Sanskrit = color)
- Caste system = division of society into social classes that are determined by birth or occupation
- Prevalent social system of the Aryans

The Four Basic Castes are
- The brahmins (priests and sages) ✳
- The kshatriyas (warriors) ✳
- Vaishyas (producers, that is merchants, bankers, farmers)
- Shudras (workers or servants)

Rules To Be Fulfilled
- Whoever fulfils his or her dharma in one life will experience a higher birth in the next
- Rules:
  - One should not marry outside of his/her caste
  - Sacramental rites should be performed at every important stage of life
  - Deities of the household should be worshiped each day and before each meal
  - Ancestors should be offered memorial prayers and food

The Duties of Women
- Are to serve their husbands unconditionally
- At no stage of her life can a woman be independent
- A husband is to be worshiped as a god (even if he is immoral)

Untouchables
- Cremation worker, street sweepers, tanners
- Are considered polluting
- Are considered to be outside the four classes
- Today the term "untouchable' is not used (discriminatory)
- They are called dalit, the "oppressed"
- Gandhi called them "harijan" (children of God)

Four Stages of Life
- Only for young men of the three higher varna
- Student – learn to chant vedas / study upanishards
- Householder – married / family
- Forest dweller – give up everything
- Renunciant (sannyasin)

What about women?
- What is their duty (dharma)?
- They do not pass through the four stages
- They marry, serve their husband, and perform the household duties
- They may take the vow of sannyasin

Part 1: RELIGIONS ORIGINATING IN SOUTHEAST ASIA: THE MYTH OF LIBERATION

The Way of Devotion or Bhakti Yoga — *turning to gods for help*

- Bhakti = devotion to a particular deity in grateful recognition of aid received
- Responded to the needs of ordinary people

How do you find out about the Way of Devotion?

- Read Mahabharata, "great epic of the descendants of Bharata" (5th century BCE - 5th century CE)
- In particular Bhagavad Gita (Song of the Blessed Lord) — 1st century BCE

Main Characteristics

- Open to all without restriction as caste (Not the case of Vedas)
- Vehicle of religious instruction for most people
- Inspired popular series on Indian TV

Mahabharata (5th century BCE - 5th century CE)

long epic poem about bharata dynasty

- Deals with the exploits of Aryan clans
- Tells how the sons of Pandu (Pandavas) conquered their cousins, the Kauravas, with the help of the god Krishna

Bhagavad Gita

song of god

- Written in dialogue form
- Two main figures:
  – Arjuna, the great warrior of the family of Pandavas
  – God Krishna, Arjuna's charioteer and advisor, an avatar (alternate form) of Vishnu Arjuna's Dilemma
- Should he fight to restore his throne or should he accept his relatives' rule to avoid violence and family bloodshed?

Vishnu – recognized by big conch. shell in hand

Krishna's Answer

- Fight!
- Why? Arjuna belongs to the warrior class
- Arjuna should carry on his social duty (dharma), otherwise social chaos will follow

Why?

- Since human beings cannot avoid acting, acts must be guided by class dharma
- Any action (karma) that is motivated by desire results in bondage to a universal round of reincarnations (samsara)
- Karma represents a universal cause-effect continuum

The Key to Escape the Cycle of Rebirth (Samsara)

- Act in such a way that you are not attached to the results of your actions (karma)
- If we can overcome attachment to the results of our actions, we can identify ourselves with our eternal Self (atman)

According to Krishna, how can such detachment from karmic self (jiva) be obtained?

- One needs to carry on caste duty without thought of reward (all desire for success, all greed should be rooted out)
- Another way is to surrender oneself and all one's actions to a god (here himself, Krishna)

Krishna in Bhagavad Gita

- Underlying reality of all
- Brahman taught by the Upanishads
- Krishna is a personal form of Brahman

Main Contribution of Bhagavad Gita

- Anyone, regardless of class, gender, or age, can practice devotional service to the Supreme deity
- God loves humans and is concerned about them, taking various forms (avatars) to express compassion

The Bhakti Way

Puranas (Ca. 400 through 900 CE)

- Stories about the exploits of three gods and their consorts
- The gods are
    - Brahma (the creator) — *4 heads*
    - Vishnu (the preserver) — *conch in hand*
    - Shiva (the destroyer) — *cobra around neck*
- Called as a group = the trimurti (Three Forms of the Divine)

Brahma, the Creator

- Least important of three deities
- No devotional movements focusing on Brahma developed
- Creative force that made the universe
- No longer active on earth
- Special patron of the priestly class
- With four faces (= all-knowing nature)
- With four arms (= power of deity)

wife = Sarasvati — portrayed w/ instrument (goddess of learning, music, arts)

Shiva, the Destroyer

- Most popular of all the gods
- In Vedas, Rudra-Shiva (Shiva = "lucky")
- Antithetical character
- Destroyer god of regeneration
- Erotic lover AND renouncer
- Male AND female
- In him all energies are united
- How is Shiva portrayed?
    - Dancing (speeding the cycles of birth and death)
    - A cobra around his neck

Kali, Shiva's first wife
Destroyer of universe
- necklace of skulls
- skirt of severed hands
- dark skin, tongue out
Parvati, Shiva's second wife

Symbols Associated with Shiva
- *Lingam*, stylized representation of the male sexual organ
- *Yoni*, stylized representation of the female sexual organ
- = objects of worship at home or in temples

Gods Associated with Shiva
- Shiva's consort is Parvati
- Ganesh, Shiva's and Parvati's elephant-headed son

Ganesh
- Worshiped as a god who overcomes obstacles and upholds dharma
- Ganesh can be found in the entryways of Hindu homes

elephant head

Shaivism
- Religious movement focusing on devotion to Shiva
- Developed in 2nd century CE

Vishnu, the Preserver
- In Vedas, minor nature god, associated with sun
- In classical Hinduism = god of love, compassion, and forgiveness
- He is the light that destroys darkness
- Purpose is to sustain a just dharmic order (dharma = order that holds the universe together)

Vishnu's Avataras (or Avatars)
- Avataras = earthly incarnations of deity (to help humanity in times of trouble)
- Krishna (draws humans to the Divine by the power of Love)
- Siddartha Gautama, founder of Buddhism
- Rama (god and mythical king)

Hindu Epic Ramayana (400 BCE?)
- Tells the story of Rama and Sita
- Rama wins his wife, Sita, who has been abducted by a demon-king
- Rama is the ideal man and his wife, the ideal woman
- Birthplace of Rama = Ayodhya (focus of religious conflict between Hindus and Muslims)

Vaishnavism
- Religious movement focusing on devotion to Vishnu (12th century CE onward)
- Today Vishnu and his various forms is the most important object of devotion in India

Female Deities
- 50 million Hindus worship some form of the goddess (Devi, general term for Goddess)
- These worshipers are called shaktas
- Shakti = the active energy or power of the Goddess
- Erotic images are frequently used to symbolize the Goddess's abundant creativity

Male and Female Deities
- Share same aspects:
  - creating
  - preserving
  - destroying
- Destruction = merciful act. It allows the continuation of the cosmic cycles.

Main Female Deities
- Devi
- Durga
- Kali

Goddess Devi
- Worshiped as a mother who always desires the well-being of her children
- Appears as a gracious, nurturing spouse:
  - as the lovely Parvati, Shiva's spouse and daughter of the mountain Himalaya
  - as the goddess of fortune, Vishnu's spouse, Lakshmi
  - as the goddess of wisdom and learning, Sarasvati

Durga, "the Unapproachable"
- Beautiful woman with a gentle face
- But with ten arms holding weapons
- Vanquishes demons who threaten the dharma
- Rides a lion

Kali, "the Black"
- Wears human skulls around her neck
- Rips the flesh of her victims
- Drinks blood — *fangs at*
- Necklace of skulls = she is the destroyer of evil

Ganges River
- Sacred
- Mother Ganga
- Waters flow down from the Himalayas
- Karma and sins are washed away

PUJA AT HOME
- Daily worship of a deity image
- Images worshiped may be iconic (four-armed Vishnu) or non iconic (Shiva lingam)
- Domestic worship in room apart or an alcove
- Altar with images of deities, pictures of the family members' gurus and souvenir items from pilgrimages
- Possible offerings: flowers, food, personal prayers and chanting, incense, light
- Ritual purity is important. Times for prayer are after the morning or evening bath.

Worship in a Temple
- Far more elaborate
- Carried out (but not always) by Brahmin priests
- Deity treated as a living king or queen

Darshan
- Visual contact with the divine
- Devotee sees the deity and is, in turn, seen by the deity

Festivals
Partially on a lunar calendar

Holi
- Spring festival
- Commemorates a myth
- The son of a demon king is spared from a fire. To his father's dismay, the son has taken refuge in Lord Vishnu.
- Social distinctions are broken down
- People throw colorful paints on one another

Ganesh Chaturthi
- March, April, May, or June
- Honors Lord Ganesh, the remover of obstacles
- Includes the carrying of large images of Ganesh into bodies of water

Diwali
- Autumn festival of lights
- Fireworks are common
- Honors Lakshmi, the goddess of wealth
- In North of India, the New Year begins with Diwali

Kumbha Mela
- Every few years
- Held alternately at four sacred spots (sacred river sites in Northern India)
- Drops of the holy nectar of eternity are said to have fallen

Varanasi (or Benares)
- Ganges river
- City devoted to Shiva
- The body's cremation at Varanasi brings freedom from rebirth

The Way of Knowledge
(or The Path of Meditation)
- Jnana Yoga
- Knowledge = highest form of spiritual attainment
- Basic Human Problem: ignorance
- Ignorance: we believe that our selves are separate from the Absolute

Code of Manu
- The final stage, that of the homeless wanderer (sannyasin), pictured as a means of completing the Way of Knowledge
- Way of Knowledge particularly appropriate for priestly caste

Hindu Philosophy
- Took shape from 500 BCE to 500 CE
- Most important philosophical systems are
  – Sankhya ("Analysis" "count")
  – Raja Yoga ("Royal Yoga")
  – Advaita Vedanta

Commonalities
- Deep roots in the Vedas + other Hindu scriptures
- Direct personal experiences of the truth through meditation
- Hold ethics to be central to orderly social life
- Ultimate cause of suffering is peoples' ignorance of their true nature, the Self (Atman)

The Sankhya System
- Oldest in India
- Founder: Kapila (semi-mythical sage, 7th century BCE)
- Explains the universe without gods
- Dualistic. There are 2 realities:
  – Prakriti is matter (real and not an illusion)
  – Soul
- Purpose of Sankhya = free souls from bondage to matter

Krishna = Blue

Rama & Sita
- photo
- story

The Raja Yoga or "Royal Yoga"
- Way of Physical Discipline
- Yoga system of mental discipline first mentioned in the Upanishads
- Founder: Pantajali, a yogin of 2nd century CE
- Borrowed from Sankhya system

Goal
- Training the physical body so that the soul can be free
- Body = microcosm of the universe
- All bodily energies can be harnessed
- They can produce transformative religious experience

Eight Steps for Perfection of Meditation

- Ahimsa (not harming living things), no deceit, no stealing + sexual restraint
- Cleanliness, calm, study, and prayer
- Lotus posture
- Breath control + repetition of mantra (word recited with each breath to clear the mind)
- Control of senses
- Steadying of the mind by concentrating on a single object
    - candle flame
    - picture of a saint or guru
    - yantras, that is linear images with complex cosmic symbolism
    - OM symbol, representing the original sound of creation – it is topped by the sun and the moon
- Meditation (dyana)
- Samadhi (mental stage achieved by deep meditation): oneness with Brahman, and therefore liberation (moksha), is experienced

EXTRA NOTES

Before 6th c. BCE = VEDAS = sacrifices to
gods + polytheism / henotheism + caste
<u>inequality</u>

6c. BCE = AXIS AGE = time of the Upishads (new sacred writing)
    = search for single reality thragh meditation
    = <u>any one can do it</u>

HINDUISM

HINDUISM: An Ancient Path in the Modern World

1. Who were the Dravidians? Whom did they worship?

   aboriginal people of India — mother goddess & the bull

2. Who were the Aryans?

   Invaders from Southern Russia & Central Asia

3. What were the Vedas? Who wrote them? When?

   ⭐ *sacred writings — Indo-Aryan — 1500-450 BCE*

4. How many gods are there in Hinduism?

   millions

5. According to the film, the gods of Hinduism are all aspects of what?

   Brahman

6. Explain the phrase, "Atman (self) is Brahman."

   The Brahman is split into millions of Atman like drops of water that form an ocean

7. What are the Brahmins? What do they do?

   ⭐ *Priests — conduct rituals / sacrifices*

8. What is the doctrine of the transmigration of souls?

   Upanishads

9. Hindus follow the "proper path" or __*Dharma*__

10. How can a Hindu attain release from the endless cycle of rebirth?

    moksha

11. What is puja?

    form of worship

12. What inspired the Indian nationalist movement?

    salt tax — non violent protest

13. How did Mahatma Gandhi resist British rule over India?

    nonviolent movement

14. Which Indian river is particularly holy according to the film?

    Ganges river

15. Which Indian city is particularly holy? What happens to someone who dies there?

Vernasi (or Benaras)

16. How do Hindus ritually dispose of their dead?

Cremation

17. What is a guru?

a Spiritual teacher

18. What is an ashram?

a Spiritual center

19. What did the guru give his disciple?

20. Who is Lakshmi?

Vishnu's spouse- goddess of fortune

21. Who is Hanuman? Which animals run freely through his temples?

22. How are images treated in Hindu temples? Why?

23. What is the spring festival? What is it characterized by?

Holi

24. What is raga?

songs performed using the sitar and tabla at certain times in the day

25. When is a particularly auspicious time to chant?

26. What is one way Hindus purify themselves?

ritual bathing

27. Explain the caste system. When did the caste system develop?

4 main, social structure

28. Who are the Untouchables? What did Gandhi call them?

lowest caste — children of god

29. What are the main differences between Islam and Hinduism?

Puja

1. What is puja?

an ancient and personal ritual, form of worship

2. Where and when is it performed?

3. Who is Brahma? How can he be recognized in pictures?

creator — four faces

4. When do people pray to Lord Ganesh?

over com obsticals

5. Who is Vishnu? Who is Krishna? What is attractive about Krishna? How do you recognize Krishna's worshipers?

→ god of love - avatar of vishnu - humoras

6. Name the main female deities in Hinduism.

durga , Kali

7. What is darshan?

visual contact w/ divine

8. What is the purpose of puja?

9. Who is Shiva? How is he represented? What objects of worship are linked with Shiva?

the creator & destroyer

10. What does fire symbolize?

the presence of the divine contained w/in oneself

11. What does water symbolize?

the elixir of life that sustains life

12. How do Hindus view their religion? Is Hinduism polytheistic or monotheistic?

*monothestic
→ many gods -
one brahma*

Ganesh: Elephant God

1. What is the largest city in India? What is its former name? How many people live there? What is the dominant religion?

2. What are the preparations made for the festival?

3. What is offered during puja?

4. What is Ganesh the god of?

   over coming obsticles

5. Ganesh is often depicted with which animal?

6. Why did Parvati create Ganesh? How?

7. What did Ganesh do to Shiva? How did Shiva react?

8. What did Parvati demand of Shiva?

9. How did Ganesh come to have an elephant head?

10. What is the supreme god of Hinduism?

11. What is Ganesh the god of according to the boy?

12. What does the family buy the night before the festival?

13. On the morning of the festival, what does the father do?

14. Who guides the father in his worship?

15. How does puja transform the image?

16. Most Hindus worship where?

17. Why is a bell rung in the temple?

18. How many stages in life are there according to Hindus?

4

19. What is atman?

innermost Self

20. What is samsara?

wheel of birth, death, rebirth

21. What is the ultimate goal of life? How can it be attained?

Moksha — way of works
way of devotion   way of knowledge

22. What do Hindus do with their statues of Ganesh at the end of the festival?

23. What happens to the communal statues?

THE VEDIC AGE

1. Vedic temples were elaborate permanent complexes where priests lived and performed Vedic rites
   a.) True
   b.) False

2. _____ is the temporary elevation of one of many gods to the highest rank.
   a.) henotheism
   b.) monotheism
   c.) polytheism
   d.) agnosticism

3. The early form of classical Hinduism's great god Shiva (the Destroyer and God of Regeneration) was _____.
   a.) Brihaspati
   b.) Vishnu
   c.) Agni
   d.) Rudra

4. Women played an important role in the performance of Vedic sacrifices
   a.) True
   b.) False

5. The Vedas are
   a.) read in silence
   b.) chanted through the repetition of syllables
   c.) read aloud but not chanted

HINDUISM

TEXT 1. HYMNS FROM THE RIG VEDA

1. On the basis of these hymns, who are the Vedic gods? What are their qualities?

2. What facilitates the relationship between gods and human beings?

3. Why is sacrifice central to the Vedic worldview?

4. Why do you think it could be difficult to challenge the Hindu caste system?

5. Compare the creation myth in the Rig Veda and the Shinto myth of creation [TEXT 13]. What is similar? What is different? According to the Rig Veda, can human beings know how everything began?

Please turn to your reading glossary at the end of your workbook for unknown vocabulary.

Text One

Hymns from the Rig Veda

TRANSLATED BY WENDY DONIGER O'FLAHERTY

1 I PRAY TO AGNI

1 I pray to Agni, the household priest who is the god of the sacrifice, the one who chants and invokes and brings most treasure.

2 Agni earned the prayers of the ancient sages, and of those of the present, too; he will bring the gods here.

3 Through Agni one may win wealth, and growth from day to day, glorious and most abounding in heroic sons.

4 Agni, the sacrificial ritual that you encompass on all sides--only that one goes to the gods.

5 Agni, the priest with the sharp sight of a poet, the true and most brilliant, the god will come with the gods.

6 Whatever good you wish to do for the one who worships you, Agni, through you, O Angiras, that comes true.

7 To you, Agni, who shine upon darkness, we come, day after day, bringing our thoughts and homage to you, the king over sacrifices, the shining guardian of the Order, growing in your own house.

8 Be easy for us to reach, like a father to his son. Abide with us, Agni, for our happiness.

8.48 WE HAVE DRUNK THE SOMA

1 I have tasted the sweet drink of life, knowing that it inspires good thoughts and joyous expansiveness to the extreme, that all the gods and mortals seek it together, calling it honey.

2 When you penetrate inside, you will know no limits, and you will avert the wrath of the gods. Enjoying Indra's friendship, O drop of Soma, bring riches as a docile cow brings the yoke.

3 We have drunk the Soma; we have become immortal; we have gone to the light; we have found the gods. What can hatred and the malice of a mortal do to us now, O immortal one?

4 When we have drunk you, O drop of Soma, be good to our heart, kind as a father to his son, thoughtful as a friend to a friend. Far-famed Soma, stretch out our life-span so that we may live.

5 The glorious drops that I have drunk set me free in wide space. You have bound me together in my limbs as thongs bind a chariot. Let the drops protect me from the foot that stumbles and keep lameness away from me.

6 Inflame me like a fire kindled by friction; make us see far; make us richer, better. For when I am intoxicated with you, Soma, I think myself rich. Draw near and make us thrive.

7 We would enjoy you, pressed with a fervent heart, like riches from a father. King Soma, stretch out our life-spans as the sun stretches the spring days.

8 King Soma, have mercy on us for our well-being. Know that we are devoted to your laws. Passion and fury are stirred up. O drop of Soma, do not hand us over to the pleasure of the enemy.

9 For you, Soma, are the guardian of our body; watching over men, you have settled down in every limb. If we break your laws, O god, have mercy on us like a good friend, to make us better.

10 Let me join closely with my compassionate friend so that he will not injure me when I have drunk him. O lord of bay

horses, for the Soma that is lodged in us I approach Indra to stretch out our life-span.

11 Weaknesses and diseases have gone; the forces of darkness have fled in terror. Soma has climbed up in us, expanding. We have come to the place where they stretch out life-spans.

12 The drop that we have drunk has entered our hearts, an immortal inside mortals. O fathers, let us serve that Soma with the oblations and abide in his mercy and kindness.

13 Uniting in agreement with the fathers, O drop of Soma, you have extended yourself through sky and earth. Let us serve him with an oblation; let us be masters of riches.

14 You protecting gods, speak out for us. Do not let sleep or harmful speech seize us. Let us, always dear to Soma, speak as men of power in the sacrificial gathering.

15 Soma, you give us the force of life on every side. Enter into us, finding the sunlight, watching over men. O drop of Soma, summon your helpers and protect us before and after.

10.90 PURUSA-SUKTA, OR THE HYMN OF MAN

1 The Man has a thousand heads, a thousand eyes, a thousand feet. He pervaded the earth on all sides and extended beyond it as far as ten fingers.

2 It is the Man who is all this, whatever has been and whatever is to be. He is the ruler of immortality, when he grows beyond everything through food.

3 Such is his greatness; and the Man is yet more than this. All creatures are a quarter of him; three quarters are what is immortal in heaven.

4 With three quarters the Man rose upwards, and one quarter of him still remains here. From this he spread out in all directions, into that which eats and that which does not eat.

5 From him Viraj was born, and from Viraj came the Man. When he was born, he ranged beyond the earth behind and before.

6 When the gods spread the sacrifice with the Man as the offering, spring was the clarified butter, summer the fuel, autumn the oblation.

7 They anointed the Man, the sacrifice born at the beginning, upon the sacred grass. With him the gods, Sadhyas, and sages sacrificed.

8 From that sacrifice in which everything was offered; the melted fat was collected, and he made it into those beasts who live in the air, in the forest, and in villages.

9 From that sacrifice in which everything was offered, the verses and chants were born, the metres were born from it, and from it the formulas were born.

10 Horses were born from it, and those other animals that

have two rows of teeth; cows were born from it, and from it goats and sheep were born.

11 When they divided the Man, into how many parts did they apportion him? What do they call his mouth; his two arms and thighs and feet?

12 His mouth became the Brahmin; his arms were made into the Warrior, his thighs the People, and from his feet the Servants were born.

13 The moon was born from his mind; from his eye the sun was born. Indra and Agni came from his mouth, and from his vital breath the Wind was born.

14 From his navel the middle realm of space arose; from his head the sky evolved. From his two feet came the earth, and the quarters of the sky from his ear. Thus they set the worlds in order.

15 There were seven enclosing-sticks for him, and thrice seven fuel-sticks, when the gods, spreading the sacrifice, bound the Man as the sacrificial beast.

16 With the sacrifice the gods sacrificed to the sacrifice. These were the first ritual laws. These very powers reached the dome of the sky where dwell the Sadhyas, the ancient gods.

10.129 CREATION HYMN (NASADIYA)

1 There was neither non-existence nor existence then; there was neither the realm of space, nor the sky which is beyond. What stirred? Where? In whose protection? Was there water, bottomlessly deep?

2 There was neither death nor immortality then. There was no distinguishing sign of night nor of day. That one breathed, windless, by its own impulse. Other than that there was nothing beyond.

3 Darkness was hidden by darkness in the beginning; with no distinguishing sign, all this was water. The life force that was covered with emptiness, that one arose through the power of heat.

4 Desire came upon that one in the beginning; what was the first seed of mind. Poets seeking in their heart with wisdom found the bond of existence in non-existence.

5 Their cord was extended across. Was there below? Was there above? There were seed-placers; there were powers. There was impulse beneath; there was giving-forth above.

6 Who really knows? Who will here proclaim it? When was it produced? Whence is this creation? The god came afterwards, with the creation of this universe. Who then knows whence it has arisen?

7 Whence this creation has arisen--perhaps it formed itself, or perhaps it did not--the one who looks down on it, in the highest heaven, only he knows--or perhaps he does not know.

HINDUISM

TEXT 2. THE BHAGAVAD GITA

1. Summarize Arjuna's main dilemma.

2. Why did Krishna urge Arjuna to fight?

3. According to the twelfth teaching, how can one escape *samsara*?

Please turn to your reading glossary at the end of your workbook for unknown vocabulary.

Text Two

The Bhagavad-Gita

PHILOSOPHY AND SPIRITUAL DISCIPLINE

1 *Sanjaya* [narrates an events on battlefield to blind king]
Arjuna sat dejected,
[warrior] filled with pity,
his sad eyes blurred by tears.
Krishna gave him counsel.

2 *Lord Krishna* — [avater of vishnu]
Why this cowardice
in time of crisis, Arjuna?
The coward is ignoble, shameful,
foreign to the ways of heaven.

3 Don't yield to impotence!
it is unnatural in you!
banish this petty weakness from your heart.
rise to the fight, Arjuna!

4 *Arjuna*
Krishna, how can I fight
against Bhishma and Drona [teacher]
with arrows [his grandfather]
when they deserve my worship?

THE SECOND TEACHING
5 It is better in this world
to beg for scraps of food
than to eat meals

smeared with the blood
or elders I killed
at the height of their power
while their goals
were still desires.

6 We don't know which weight
is worse to bear—
our conquering them
or their conquering us.
we will not want to live
if we kill
the sons of Dhritarashtra
assembled before us.

7 The flaw of pity
blights my very being;
conflicting sacred duties
confound my reason.
I ask you to tell me
decisively—Which is better?
I am your pupil.
Teach me what I seek!

8 I see nothing
that could drive away
the grief
that withers my senses;
even if I won kingdoms
of unrivaled wealth
on earth
and sovereignty over gods.

SANJAYA

9 Arjuna told this
To Krishna—then saying,
"I shall not fight,"
He fell silent.

10 Mocking him gently,
Krishna gave this counsel
as Arjuna sat dejected,
between the two armies.

Lord Krishna

11 You grieve for those beyond grief,
and you speak words of insight;
but learned men do not grieve
for the dead or the living.

12 Never have I not existed,
nor you, nor these kings;
and never in the future
shall we cease to exist.

13 Just as the embodied self
centers childhood, youth, and old age,
so does it enter another body;
this does not confound a steadfast man.

14 Contacts with matter make us feel
heat and cold, pleasure and pain.
Arjuna, you must learn to endure
fleeting things—they come and go!

15 When these cannot torment a man,
when suffering and joy are equal
for him and he has courage,
he is fit for immortality.

16 Nothing of nonbeing comes to be,
nor does being cease to exist;
the boundary between those two
is seen by men who see reality.

17 Indestructible is the presence
that pervades all this;
no one can destroy
this unchanging reality.

18 Our bodies are known to end,
but the embodied self is enduring,
indestructible, and immeasurable;
therefore, Arjuna, fight the battle!

19 He who thinks this self a killer
and he who thinks it killed,
both fail to understand;
it does not kill, nor is it killed.

20 It is not born,
it does not die;
having been,
it will never not be;
unborn, enduring,
constant, and primordial,
it is not killed
when the body is killed.

21 Arjuna, when a man knows the self
to be indestructible, enduring, unborn,
unchanging, how does he kill
or cause anyone to kill?

22 As a may discards
worn-out clothes
to put on new
and different ones,
so the embodied self
discards
its worn-out bodies
to take on other new ones.

23 Weapons do not cut it,
fire does not burn it,
waters do not wet it,
wind does not wither it.

24 It cannot be cut or burned;
tt cannot be wet or withered;
it is enduring, all-pervasive,
fixed, immovable, and timeless.

25 It is called unmanifest,
inconceivable, and immittable;
since you know that to be so,
you should not grieve!

26 If you think of its birth
and death as ever-recurring,
then, too, Great Warrior,
you have no cause to grieve!

27 Death is certain for anyone born,
and birth is certain for the dead;
since the cycle is inevitable,
you have no cause to grieve!

28 Creatures are unmanifest in origin,
manifest in the midst of life,
and unmanifest again in the end.
since this is so, why do you lament?

29 Rarely someone
sees it,
rarely another
speaks it,
rarely anyone
hears it—
even hearing it,
no one really knows it.

30 The self embodied in the body
of every being is indestructible;
you have no cause to grieve
for all these creatures, Arjuna!

31 Look to your own duty;
do not tremble before it;
Nothing is better for a warrior
than a battle of sacred duty.

32 The doors of heaven open
for warriors who rejoice
to have a battle like this
thrust on them by chance.

33 If you fail to wage this war
of sacred duty,
you will abandon your own duty
and fame only to gain evil.

34 People will tell
of your undying shame,
and for a man of honor
shame is worse than death.

35 The great chariot warriors will think
you deserted in fear of battle;
you will be despised
by those who held you in esteem.

36 Your enemies will slander you,
scorning your skill
in so many unspeakable ways—
could any suffering be sores?

37 If you are killed, you win heaven;
if you triumph, you enjoy the earth;
therefore, Arjuna, stand up
and resolve to fight the battle!

38 Impartial to joy and suffering,
gain and loss, victory and defeat,
arm yourself for the battle,
lest you fall into evil.

39 Understanding is defined in terms of philosophy;
now hear it in spiritual discipline.
armed with this understanding, Arjuna,
you will escape the bondage of action.

40 No effort in this world
is lost or wasted;
a fragment of sacred duty
saves you from great fear.

41 This understanding is unique
in its inner core of resolve;
diffuse and pointless are the ways
irresolute men understand.

42 Undiscerning men who delight
in the tenets of ritual lore
utter florid speech, proclaiming,
"There is nothing else!"

43 Drive by desire, they strive after heaven
and contrive to win powers and delights,
but their intricate ritual language
bears only the fruit of action in rebirth.

44 Obsessed with powers and delights,
their reason lost in words,
they do not find in contemplation
this understanding of inner resolve.

45 Arjuna, the realm of sacred love
is nature—beyond its triad of qualities,
dualities, and mundane rewards,
be forever lucid, alive to your self.

46 For the discerning priest,
all of sacred lore
has no more value than a well
when water flows everywhere.

47 Be intent on action,
not on the fruits of action;
avoid attraction to the fruits
and attachment to inaction!

48 Perform actions, firm in discipline,
relinquishing attachment;
be impartial to failure and success—
this equanimity is called discipline.

49 Arjuna, action is far inferior
to the discipline of understanding;
so seek refuge in understanding—pitiful
are men drawn by fruits of action.

50 Disciplined by understanding,
one abandons both good and evil deeds;
so arm yourself for discipline—
discipline is skill in actions.

51 Wise men disciplined by understanding
relinquish the fruit born of action;
freed from these bonds of rebirth,
they reach a place beyond decay.

52 When your understanding passes beyond
the swamp of delusion,
you will be indifferent to all
that is heard in sacred lore.

53 When your understanding turns
from sacred lore to stand fixed,
immovable in contemplation,
then you will reach discipline.

54 *Arjuna*
Krishna, what defines a man
deep in contemplation whose insight
and thought are sure? How would he speak?
how would he sit? How would he move?

55 *Lord Krishna*
When he give up desires in his mind,
is content with the self within himself,
then he is said to be a man
whose insight is sure, Arjuna.

56 When suffering does not disturb his mind,
when his craving for pleasures has vanished,
when attraction, far, and anger are gone,
he is called a sage whose thought is sure.

57 When he shows no preference
in fortune or misfortune
and neither exults nor hates,
his insight is sure.

58 When like a tortoise retracting
its limbs, he withdraws his senses
completely from sensuous objects,
his insight is sure.

59 Sensuous objects fade
when the embodied self abstains from food;
the taste lingers, but it too fades
in the vision of higher truth.

60 Even when a man of wisdom
tries to control them, Arjuna,
the bewildering senses
attack his mind with violence.

61 Controlling them all,
with discipline he should focus on me;
when his senses are under control,
his insight is sure.

62 Brooding about sensuous objects
makes attachment to them grow;
from attachment desire arises,
from desire anger is born.

63 From anger comes confusion;
from confusion memory lapses;
from broken memory understanding is lost;
from loss of understanding, he is ruined.

64 But a man of inner strength
whose senses experience objects
without attraction and hatred,
in self-control, finds serenity.

65 In serenity, all his sorrows
dissolve;
his reason becomes serene,
his understanding sure.

66 Without discipline,
he has no understanding or inner power;
without inner power, he has no peace;
and without peace where is joy?

67 If his mind submits to the play
of the senses,
they drive away insight,
as wind drives a ship on water.

68 So, Great Warrior, when withdrawal
of the senses
from sense objects is complete,
discernment is firm.

69 When it is might for all creatures,
a master of restraint is awake;
when they are awake, it is night
for the sage who sees reality.

70 As the mountainous depths
Of the ocean
Are unmoved when waters
Rush into it,
So the men unmoved
When desires center him
Attains a peace that eludes
The man of many desires.

71 When he renounces all desires
And acts without craving,
Possessiveness,
Or individuality, he finds peace.

72 This is the place of the infinite spirit;
Achieving it, one is freed from delusion;
Abiding in it even at the time of death,
One finds the pure calm of infinity.

THE TWELFTH TEACHING
DEVOTION

1 *Arjuna*
Who best knows discipline:
men who worship you with devotion,
ever disciplined, or men who worship
the imperishable, unmanifest?

2 *Lord Krishna*
I deem most disciplined
men of enduring discipline
who worship me with true faith,
entrusting their minds to me.

3 Men reach me too who worship
what is imperishable, ineffable, unmanifest,
omnipresent, inconceivable,
immutable at the summit of existence.

4 Mastering their senses,
with equanimity toward everything,
they reach me, rejoicing
in the welfare of all creatures.

5 It is more arduous when their reason
clings to my unmanifest
for men constrained by bodies,
the unmanifest way is hard to attain.

6 But men intent on me
renounce all actions to me
and worship me, meditating
with singular discipline.

7 When they entrust reason to me,
Arjuna, I soon arise
to rescue them from the ocean
of death and rebirth.

8 Focus your mind on me,
let your understanding enter me;
then you will dwell
in me without doubt.

9 If you cannot concentrate
your thought firmly on me,
then seek to reach me, Arjuna,
by discipline in practice.

10 Even if you fail in practice,
dedicate yourself to action;
performing actions for my sake,
you will achieve success.

11 If you are powerless to do
even this, rely on my discipline,
be self-controlled,
and reject all fruit of action.

12 Knowledge is better than practice,
meditation better than knowledge,
rejecting fruits of action
is better still—it brings peace.

13 One who bears hate for no creature
is friendly, compassionate, unselfish,
free of individuality, patient,
the same in suffering and joy.

14 Content always, disciplined,
self-controlled, firm in his resolve,
his mind and understanding dedicated to me,
devoted to me, he is dear to me.

15 The world does not flee from him,
nor does he flee from the world;
free of delight, rage, fear,
and disgust, he is dear to me.

16 Disinterested, pure, skilled,
indifferent, untroubled,
relinquishing all involvements,
devoted to me, he is dear to me.

17 He does not rejoice or hate,
grieve or feel desire;
relinquishing fortune and misfortune,
the man of devotion is dear to me.

18 Impartial to foe and friend,
honor and contempt,
cold and heat, joy and suffering,
he is free from attachment.

19 Neutral to blame and praise,
silent, content with his fate,
unsheltered, firm in thought,
the man of devotion is dear to me.

20 Even more dear to me are devotees
who cherish this elixir of sacred duty
as I have taught it,
intent on me in their faith.

HINDUISM

TEXT 3. GANDHI'S READING OF THE GITA

Gandhi is well-known for having used non-violent means to oppose Western colonialism. How did he reinterpret Krishna's call to fight? What is the real battlefield for human beings?

Please turn to your reading glossary at the end of your workbook for unknown vocabulary.

Text Three

Gandhi's Reading of the Gita

4.13.4 ON THE GITA

QUESTIONER: I am told you recite the Bhagavadgita daily?

GANDHI: Yes, we finish the entire Gita reading once every week.

QUESTIONER: But at the end of the Gita Krishna recommends violence.

GANDHI: I do not think so. I am also fighting. I should not be fighting effectively if I were fighting violently. The message of the Gita is to be found in the second chapter of the Gita where Krishna speaks of the balanced state of mind, of mental equipoise. In nineteen verses at the close of the second chapter of the Gita, Krishna explains how this state can be achieved. It can be achieved, he tells us, after killing all your passions. It is not possible to kill your brother after having killed all your passions. I should like to see that man dealing death--who has no passions, who is indifferent to pleasure and pain, who is undisturbed by the storms that trouble mortal man. The whole thing is described in language of beauty that is unsurpassed. These verses show that the fight Krishna speaks of is a spiritual fight.

QUESTIONER: To the common mind it sounds as though it was actual fighting.

GANDHI: You must read the whole thing dispassionately in its true context. After the first mention of fighting, there is no mention of fighting at all. The rest is a spiritual discourse.

QUESTIONER: Has anybody interpreted it like you?

GANDHI: Yes. The fight is there, but the fight as it is going on within. The Pandavas and Kauravas are the forces of good and evil within. The war is the war between Jekyll and Hyde, God and Satan, going on in the human breast. The internal evidence in support of this interpretation is there in the work itself and in the Mahabharata of which the Gita is a minute part. It is not a history of war between two families, but the history of man--the history of the spiritual struggle of man.

QUESTIONER: Is the central teaching of the Gita selfless action or non-violence?

GANDHI: I have no doubt that it is *anasakti*--selfless action. Indeed I have called my little translation of the Gita Anasaktiyoga. And anasakti transcends ahimsa. He who would be *anasakta* (selfless) has necessarily to practise non-violence in order to attain the state of selflessness. Ahimsa is, therefore, a necessary preliminary, it is included in *anasakti*, it does not go beyond it.

QUESTIONER: Then does the Gita teach himsa and ahimsa both?

GANDHI: I do not read that meaning in the Gita. It is quite likely that the author did not write it to inculcate ahimsa, but as a commentator draws innumerable interpretations from a poetic text, even so I interpret the Gita to mean that if its central theme is anasakti, it also teaches ahimsa. Whilst we are in the flesh and tread the solid earth, we have to practise ahimsa. In the life beyond there is no himsa or ahimsa.

"Gandhi's Reading of the Gita" (editor's title, originally titled "On the Gita") by M. K. Gandhi from *Hindu Dharma*, Navajivan Trust. Reprinted by permission.

QUESTIONER: But Lord Krishna actually counters the doctrine of ahimsa. For Arjuna utters this pacifist resolve:

Better I deem it, if my kinsmen strike,
To face them weaponless, and bear my breast
To shaft and spear, than answer blow with blow

And Lord Krishna teaches him to 'answer blow with blow.'

GANDHI: There I join issue with you. Those words of Arjuna were words of pretentious wisdom. 'Until yesterday,' says Krishna to him, 'you fought your kinsmen with deadly weapons without the slightest compunction. Even today you would strike if the enemy was a stranger and not your own kith and kin!' The question before him was not of non-violence but whether he should slay his nearest and dearest.

TEXT 4. THE LAWS OF MANU

1. What kind of idealized society do the laws of Manu portray?

2. What is the perfect king?

3. What is the perfect wife?

4. What is the servant's duty?

5. How does this document legitimize social and gender hierarchy?

Please turn to your reading glossary at the end of your workbook for unknown vocabulary.

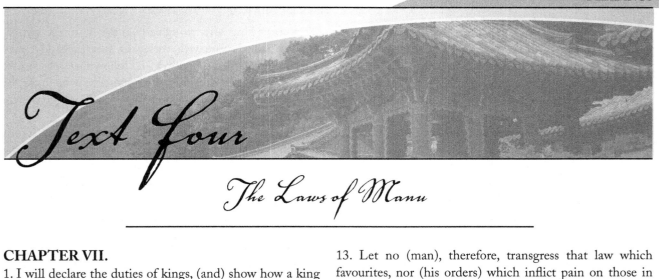

Text Four
The Laws of Manu

CHAPTER VII.

1. I will declare the duties of kings, (and) show how a king should conduct himself, how he was created, and how (he can obtain) highest success.

2. A Kshatriya, who has received according to the rule the sacrament prescribed by the Veda, must duly protect this whole (world). warrior

3. For, when these creatures, being without a king, through fear dispersed in all directions, the Lord created a king for the protection of this whole (creation),

4. Taking (for that purpose) eternal particles of Indra, of the Wind, of Yama, of the Sun, of Fire, of Varuna, of the Moon, and of the Lord of wealth (Kubera).

5. Because a king has been formed of particles of those lords of the gods, he therefore surpasses all created beings in lustre;

6. And, like the sun, he burns eyes and hearts; nor can anybody on earth even gaze on him.

7. Through his (supernatural) power he is Fire and Wind, he Sun and Moon, he the Lord of justice (Yama), he Kubera, he Varuna, he great Indra.

8. Even an infant king must not be despised, (from an idea) that he is a (mere) mortal; for he is a great deity in human form.

9. Fire burns one man only, if he carelessly approaches it, the fire of a king's (anger) consumes the (whole) family, together with its cattle and its hoard of property.

10. Having fully considered the purpose, (his) power, and the place and the time, he assumes by turns many (different) shapes for the complete attainment of justice.

11. He, in whose favour resides Padma, the goddess of fortune, in whose valour dwells victory, in whose anger abides death, is formed of the lustre of all (gods).

12. The (man), who in his exceeding folly hates him, will doubtlessly perish; for the king quickly makes up his mind to destroy such (a man).

13. Let no (man), therefore, transgress that law which favourites, nor (his orders) which inflict pain on those in disfavour.

14. For the (king's) sake the Lord formerly created his own son, Punishment, the protector of all creatures, (an incarnation of) the law, formed of Brahman's glory.

15. Through fear of him all created beings, both the immovable and the movable, allow themselves to be enjoyed and swerve not from their duties.

16. Having fully considered the time and the place (of the offence), the strength and the knowledge (of the offender), let him justly inflict that (punishment) on men who act unjustly.

17. Punishment is (in reality) the king (and) the male, that the manager of affairs, that the ruler, and that is called the surety for the four orders' obedience to the law.

18. Punishment alone governs all created beings, punishment alone protects them, punishment watches over them while they sleep; the wise declare punishment (to be identical with) the law.

19. If (punishment) is properly inflicted after (due) consideration, it makes all people happy; but inflicted without consideration, it destroys everything.

20. If the king did not, without tiring, inflict punishment on those worthy to be punished, the stronger would roast the weaker, like fish on a spit;

21. The crow would eat the sacrificial cake and the dog would lick the sacrificial viands, and ownership would not remain with any one, the lower ones would (usurp the place of) the higher ones.

22. The whole world is kept in order by punishment, for a guiltless man is hard to find; through fear of punishment the whole world yields the enjoyments (which it owes).

23. The gods, the Danavas, the Gandharvas, the Rakshasas, the bird and snake deities even give the enjoyments (due

from them) only, if they are tormented by (the fear of) punishment.

24. All castes (varna) would be corrupted (by intermixture), all barriers would be broken through, and all men would rage (against each other) in consequence of mistakes with respect to punishment.

25. But where Punishment with a black hue and red eyes stalks about, destroying sinners, there the subjects are not disturbed, provided that he who inflicts it discerns well.

26. They declare that king to be a just inflicter of punishment, who is truthful, who acts after due consideration, who is wise, and who knows (the respective value of) virtue, pleasure, and wealth.

27. A king who properly inflicts (punishment), prospers with respect to (those) three (means of happiness); but he who is voluptuous, partial, and deceitful will be destroyed, even through the (unjust) punishment (which he inflicts).

28. Punishment (possesses) a very bright lustre, and is hard to be administered by men with unimproved minds; it strikes down the king who swerves from his duty, together with his relatives.

29. Next it will afflict his castles, his territories, the whole world together with the movable and immovable (creation), likewise the sages and the gods, who (on the failure of offerings) ascend to the sky.

30. (Punishment) cannot be inflicted justly by one who has no assistant, (nor) by a fool, (nor) by a covetous man, (nor) by one whose mind is unimproved, (nor) by one addicted to sensual pleasures.

31. By him who is pure (and) faithful to his promise, who acts according to the Institutes (of the sacred law), who has good assistants and is wise, punishment can be (justly) inflicted.

32. Let him act with justice in his own domain, with rigour chastise his enemies, behave without duplicity towards his friends, and be lenient towards Brahmanas.

33. The fame of a king who behaves thus, even though he subsist by gleaning, is spread in the world, like a drop of oil on water.

34. But the fame of a king who acts in a contrary manner and who does not subdue himself, diminishes in extent among men like a drop of clarified butter in water.

35. The king has been created (to be) the protector of the castes (varna) and orders, who, all according to their rank, discharge their several duties.

36. Whatever must be done by him and by his servants for the protection of his people, that I will fully declare to you in due order.

37. Let the king, after rising early in the morning, worship Brahmanas who are well versed in the threefold sacred science and learned (in polity), and follow their advice.

38. Let him daily worship aged Brahmanas who know the Veda and are pure; for he who always worships aged men, is honoured even by Rakshasas.

39. Let him, though he may already be modest, constantly learn modesty from them; for a king who is modest never perishes.

40. Through a want of modesty many kings have perished, together with their belongings; through modesty even hermits in the forest have gained kingdoms.

41. Through a want of humility Vena perished, likewise king Nahusha, Sudas, the son of Pigavana, Sumukha, and Nemi.

42. But by humility Prithu and Manu gained sovereignty, Kubera the position of the Lord of wealth, and the son of Gadhi the rank of a Brahmana.

43. From those versed in the three Vedas let him learn the threefold (sacred science), the primeval science of government, the science of dialectics, and the knowledge of the (supreme) Soul; from the people (the theory of) the (various) trades and professions.

44. Day and night he must strenuously exert himself to conquer his senses; for he (alone) who has conquered his own senses, can keep his subjects in obedience.

45. Let him carefully shun the ten vices, springing from love of pleasure, and the eight, proceeding from wrath, which (all) end in misery.

46. For a king who is attached to the vices springing from love of pleasure, loses his wealth and his virtue, but (he who is given) to those arising from anger, (loses) even his life.

47. Hunting, gambling, sleeping by day, censoriousness, (excess with) women, drunkenness, (an inordinate love for) dancing, singing, and music, and useless travel are the tenfold set (of vices) springing from love of pleasure.

48. Tale-bearing, violence, treachery, envy, slandering, (unjust) seizure of property, reviling, and assault are the eightfold set (of vices) produced by wrath.

49. That greediness which all wise men declare to be the root even of both these (sets), let him carefully conquer; both sets (of vices) are produced by that.

50. Drinking, dice, women, and hunting, these four (which have been enumerated) in succession, he must know to be the most pernicious in the set that springs from love of pleasure.

51. Doing bodily injury, reviling, and the seizure of property, these three he must know to be the most pernicious in the set produced by wrath.

52. A self-controlled (king) should know that in this set of seven, which prevails everywhere, each earlier-named vice is more abominable (than those named later).

53. (On a comparison) between vice and death, vice is declared to be more pernicious; a vicious man sinks to the nethermost (hell), he who dies, free from vice, ascends to heaven.

54. Let him appoint seven or eight ministers whose ancestors have been royal servants, who are versed in the sciences, heroes skilled in the use of weapons and descended from (noble) families and who have been tried.

55. Even an undertaking easy (in itself) is (sometimes) hard to be accomplished by a single man; how much (harder is it for a king), especially (if he has) no assistant, (to govern) a kingdom which yields great revenues.

56. Let him daily consider with them the ordinary (business, referring to) peace and war, (the four subjects called) sthana, the revenue, the (manner of) protecting (himself and his kingdom), and the sanctification of his gains (by pious gifts).

57. Having (first) ascertained the opinion of each (minister) separately and (then the views) of all together, let him do what is (most) beneficial for him in his affairs.

58. But with the most distinguished among them all, a learned Brahmana, let the king deliberate on the most important affairs which relate to the six measures of royal policy.

59. Let him, full of confidence, always entrust to that (official) all business; having taken his final resolution with him, let him afterwards begin to act.

60. He must also appoint other officials, (men) of integrity, (who are) wise, firm, well able to collect money, and well tried.

61. As many persons as the due performance of his business requires, so many skilful and clever (men), free from sloth, let him appoint.

62. Among them let him employ the brave, the skilful, the high-born, and the honest in (offices for the collection of) revenue, (e.g.) in mines, manufactures, and storehouses, (but) the timid in the interior of his palace.

63. Let him also appoint an ambassador who is versed in all sciences, who understands hints, expressions of the face and gestures, who is honest, skilful, and of (noble) family.

64. (Such) an ambassador is commended to a king (who is) loyal, honest, skilful, possessing a good memory, who knows the (proper) place and time (for action, who is) handsome, fearless, and eloquent.

65. The army depends on the official (placed in charge of it), the due control (of the subjects) on the army, the treasury and the (government of) the realm on the king, peace and

its opposite (war) on the ambassador.

66. For the ambassador alone makes (kings') allies and separates allies; the ambassador transacts that business by which (kings) are disunited or not.

67. With respect to the affairs let the (ambassador) explore the expression of the countenance, the gestures and actions of the (foreign king) through the gestures and actions of his confidential (advisers), and (discover) his designs among his servants.

68. Having learnt exactly (from his ambassador) the designs of the foreign king, let (the king) take such measures that he does not bring evil on himself.

69. Let him settle in a country which is open and has a dry climate, where grain is abundant, which is chiefly (inhabited) by Aryans, not subject to epidemic diseases (or similar troubles), and pleasant, where the vassals are obedient and his own (people easily) find their livelihood.

70. Let him build (there) a town, making for his safety a fortress, protected by a desert, or a fortress built of (stone and) earth, or one protected by water or trees, or one (formed by an encampment of armed) men or a hill-fort.

71. Let him make every effort to secure a hill-fort, for amongst all those (fortresses mentioned) a hill-fort is distinguished by many superior qualities.

72. The first three of those (various kinds of fortresses) are inhabited by wild beasts, animals living in holes and aquatic animals, the last three by monkeys, men, and gods respectively.

73. As enemies do not hurt these (beings, when they are) sheltered by (their) fortresses, even so foes (can) not injure a king who has taken refuge in his fort.

74. One bowman, placed on a rampart, is a match in battle for one hundred (foes), one hundred for ten thousand; hence it is prescribed (in the Sastras that a king will posses) a fortress.

75. Let that (fort) be well supplied with weapons, money, grain and beasts of burden, with Brahmanas, with artisans, with engines, with fodder, and with water.

76. Let him cause to be built for himself, in the centre of it, a spacious palace, (well) protected, habitable in every season, resplendent (with whitewash), supplied with water and trees.

77. Inhabiting that, let him wed a consort of equal caste (varna), who possesses auspicious marks (on her body), and is born in a great family, who is charming and possesses beauty and excellent qualities.

78. Let him appoint a domestic priest (purohita) and choose officiating priests (ritvig); they shall perform his domestic rites and the (sacrifices) for which three fires are required.

79. A king shall offer various (Srauta) sacrifices at which liberal fees (are distributed), and in order to acquire merit, he shall give to Brahmanas enjoyments and wealth.

80. Let him cause the annual revenue in his kingdom to be collected by trusty (officials), let him obey the sacred law in (his transactions with) the people, and behave like a father towards all men.

81. For the various (branches of business) let him appoint intelligent supervisors; they shall inspect all (the acts) of those men who transact his business.

82. Let him honour those Brahmanas who have returned from their teacher's house (after studying the Veda); for that (money which is given) to Brahmanas is declared to be an imperishable treasure for kings.

83. Neither thieves nor foes can take it, nor can it be lost; hence an imperishable store must be deposited by kings with Brahmanas.

84. The offering made through the mouth of a Brahmana, which is neither spilt, nor falls (on the ground), nor ever perishes, is far more excellent than Agnihotras.

85. A gift to one who is not a Brahmana (yields) the ordinary (reward; a gift) to one who calls himself a Brahmana, a double (reward); a gift to a well-read Brahmana, a hundred-thousandfold (reward); (a gift) to one who knows the Veda and the Angas (Vedaparaga, a reward) without end.

86. For according to the particular qualities of the recipient and according to the faith (of the giver) a small or a great reward will be obtained for a gift in the next world.

87. A king who, while he protects his people, is defied by (foes), be they equal in strength, or stronger, or weaker, must not shrink from battle, remembering the duty of Kshatriyas.

88. Not to turn back in battle, to protect the people, to honour the Brahmanas, is the best means for a king to secure happiness.

89. Those kings who, seeking to slay each other in battle, fight with the utmost exertion and do not turn back, go to heaven.

90. When he fights with his foes in battle, let him not strike with weapons concealed (in wood), nor with (such as are) barbed, poisoned, or the points of which are blazing with fire.

91. Let him not strike one who (in flight) has climbed on an eminence, nor a eunuch, nor one who joins the palms of his hands (in supplication), nor one who (flees) with flying hair, nor one who sits down, nor one who says 'I am thine;'

92. Nor one who sleeps, nor one who has lost his coat of mail, nor one who is naked, nor one who is disarmed, nor one who looks on without taking part in the fight, nor one who is fighting with another (foe);

93. Nor one whose weapons are broken, nor one afflicted (with sorrow), nor one who has been grievously wounded, nor one who is in fear, nor one who has turned to flight; (but in all these cases let him) remember the duty (of honourable warriors).

94. But the (Kshatriya) who is slain in battle, while he turns back in fear, takes upon himself all the sin of his master, whatever (it may be);

95. And whatever merit (a man) who is slain in flight may have gained for the next (world), all that his master takes.

96. Chariots and horses, elephants, parasols, money, grain, cattle, women, all sorts of (marketable) goods and valueless metals belong to him who takes them (singly) conquering (the possessor).

97. A text of the Veda (declares) that (the soldiers) shall present a choice portion (of the booty) to the king; what has not been taken singly, must be distributed by the king among all the soldiers.

98. Thus has been declared the blameless, primeval law for warriors; from this law a Kshatriya must not depart, when he strikes his foes in battle.

99. Let him strive to gain what he has not yet gained; what he has gained let him carefully preserve; let him augment what he preserves, and what he has augmented let him bestow on worthy men.

100. Let him know that these are the four means for securing the aims of human (existence); let him, without ever tiring, properly employ them.

101. What he has not (yet) gained, let him seek (to gain) by (his) army; what he has gained, let him protect by careful attention; what he has protected, let him augment by (various modes of) increasing it; and what he has augmented, let him liberally bestow (on worthy men).

102. Let him be ever ready to strike, his prowess constantly displayed, and his secrets constantly concealed, and let him constantly explore the weaknesses of his foe.

103. Of him who is always ready to strike, the whole world stands in awe; let him therefore make all creatures subject to himself even by the employment of force.

104. Let him ever act without guile, and on no account treacherously; carefully guarding himself, let him always fathom the treachery which his foes employ.

105. His enemy must not know his weaknesses, but he must know the weaknesses of his enemy; as the tortoise (hides its limbs), even so let him secure the members (of his government against treachery), let him protect his own weak points.

106. Let him plan his undertakings (patiently meditating) like a heron; like a lion, let him put forth his strength; like

a wolf, let him snatch (his prey); like a hare, let him double in retreat.

107. When he is thus engaged in conquest, let him subdue all the opponents whom he may find, by the (four) expedients, conciliation and the rest.

108. If they cannot be stopped by the three first expedients, then let him, overcoming them by force alone, gradually bring them to subjection.

109. Among the four expedients, conciliation and the rest, the learned always recommend conciliation and (the employment of) force for the prosperity of kingdoms.

110. As the weeder plucks up the weeds and preserves the corn, even so let the king protect his kingdom and destroy his opponents.

111. That king who through folly rashly oppresses his kingdom, (will), together with his relatives, ere long be deprived of his life and of his kingdom.

112. As the lives of living creatures are destroyed by tormenting their bodies, even so the lives of kings are destroyed by their oppressing their kingdoms.

113. In governing his kingdom let him always observe the (following) rules; for a king who governs his kingdom well, easily prospers.

114. Let him place a company of soldiers, commanded (by a trusty officer), the midst of two, three, five or hundreds of villages, (to be) a protection of the kingdom.

115. Let him appoint a lord over (each) village, as well as lords of ten villages, lords of twenty, lords of a hundred, and lords of a thousand.

116. The lord of one village himself shall inform the lord of ten villages of the crimes committed in his village, and the ruler of ten (shall make his report) to the ruler of twenty.

117. But the ruler of twenty shall report all such (matters) to the lord of a hundred, and the lord of a hundred shall himself give information to the lord of a thousand.

118. Those (articles) which the villagers ought to furnish daily to the king, such as food, drink, and fuel, the lord of one village shall obtain.

119. The ruler of ten (villages) shall enjoy one kula (as much land as suffices for one family), the ruler of twenty five kulas, the superintendent of a hundred villages (the revenues of) one village, the lord of a thousand (the revenues of) a town.

120. The affairs of these (officials), which are connected with (their) villages and their separate business, another minister of the king shall inspect, (who must be) loyal and never remiss;

121. And in each town let him appoint one superintendent of all affairs, elevated in rank, formidable, (resembling) a planet among the stars.

122. Let that (man) always personally visit by turns all those (other officials); let him properly explore their behaviour in their districts through spies (appointed to) each.

123. For the servants of the king, who are appointed to protect (the people), generally become knaves who seize the property of others; let him protect his subjects against such (men).

124. Let the king confiscate the whole property of those (officials) who, evil-minded, may take money from suitors, and banish them.

125. For women employed in the royal service and for menial servants, let him fix a daily maintenance, in proportion to their position and to their work.

126. One pana must be given (daily) as wages to the lowest, six to the highest, likewise clothing every six months and one drona of grain every month.

127. Having well considered (the rates of) purchase and (of) sale, (the length of) the road, (the expense for) food and condiments, the charges of securing the goods, let the king make the traders pay duty.

128. After (due) consideration the king shall always fix in his realm the duties and taxes in such a manner that both he himself and the man who does the work receive (their due) reward.

129. As the leech, the calf, and the bee take their food little by little, even so must the king draw from his realm moderate annual taxes.

130. A fiftieth part of (the increments on) cattle and gold may be taken by the king, and the eighth, sixth, or twelfth part of the crops.

131. He may also take the sixth part of trees, meat, honey, clarified butter, perfumes, (medical) herbs, substances used for flavouring food, flowers, roots, and fruit;

132. Of leaves, pot-herbs, grass, (objects) made of cane, skins, of earthen vessels, and all (articles) made of stone.

133. Though dying (with want), a king must not levy a tax on Srotriyas, and no Srotriya, residing in his kingdom, must perish from hunger.

134. The kingdom of that king, in whose dominions a Srotriya pines with hunger, will even, ere long, be afflicted by famine.

135. Having ascertained his learning in the Veda and (the purity of) his conduct, the king shall provide for him means of subsistence in accordance with the sacred law, and shall protect him in every way, as a father (protects) the lawful son of his body.

136. Whatever meritorious acts (such a Brahmana) performs under the full protection of the king, thereby the king's length of life, wealth, and kingdom increase.

137. Let the king make the common inhabitants of his realm who live by traffic, pay annually some trifle, which is called a tax.

138. Mechanics and artisans, as well as Sudras who subsist by manual labour, he may cause to work (for himself) one (day) in each month.

139. Let him not cut up his own root (by levying no taxes), nor the root of other (men) by excessive greed; for by cutting up his own root (or theirs), he makes himself or them wretched.

140. Let the king, having carefully considered (each) affair, be both sharp and gentle; for a king who is both sharp and gentle is highly respected.

141. When he is tired with the inspection of the business of men, let him place on that seat (of justice) his chief minister, (who must be) acquainted with the law, wise, self-controlled, and descended from a (noble) family.

142. Having thus arranged all the affairs (of) his (government), he shall zealously and carefully protect his subjects.

143. That (monarch) whose subjects are carried off by robbers (Dasyu) from his kingdom, while they loudly call (for help), and he and his servants are (quietly) looking on, is a dead and not a living (king).

144. The highest duty of a Kshatriya is to protect his subjects, for the king who enjoys the rewards, just mentioned, is bound to (discharge that) duty.

145. Having risen in the last watch of the night, having performed (the rite of) personal purification, having, with a collected mind, offered oblations in the fire, and having worshipped Brahmanas, he shall enter the hall of audience which must possess the marks (considered) auspicious (for a dwelling).

146. Tarrying there, he shall gratify all subjects (who come to see him by a kind reception) and afterwards dismiss them; having dismissed his subjects, he shall take counsel with his ministers.

147. Ascending the back of a hill or a terrace, (and) retiring (there) in a lonely place, or in a solitary forest, let him consult with them unobserved.

148. That king whose secret plans other people, (though) assembled (for the purpose), do not discover, (will) enjoy the whole earth, though he be poor in treasure.

149. At the time of consultation let him cause to be removed idiots, the dumb, the blind, and the deaf, animals, very aged men, women, barbarians, the sick, and those deficient in limbs.

150. (Such) despicable (persons), likewise animals, and particularly women betray secret council; for that reason he must be careful with respect to them.

151. At midday or at midnight, when his mental and bodily fatigues are over, let him deliberate, either with himself alone or with his (ministers), on virtue, pleasure, and wealth,

152. On (reconciling) the attainment of these (aims) which are opposed to each other, on bestowing his daughters in marriage, and on keeping his sons (from harm),

153. On sending ambassadors, on the completion of undertakings (already begun), on the behaviour of (the women in) his harem, and on the doings of his spies.

154. On the whole eightfold business and the five classes (of spies), on the goodwill or enmity and the conduct of the circle (of neighbours he must) carefully (reflect).

155. On the conduct of the middlemost (prince), on the doings of him who seeks conquest, on the behaviour of the neutral (king), and (on that) of the foe (let him) sedulously (meditate).

156. These (four) constituents (prakriti, form), briefly (speaking), the foundation of the circle (of neighbours); besides, eight others are enumerated (in the Institutes of Polity) and (thus) the (total) is declared to be twelve.

157. The minister, the kingdom, the fortress, the treasury, and the army are five other (constituent elements of the circle); for, these are mentioned in connexion with each (of the first twelve; thus the whole circle consists), briefly (speaking, of) seventy-two (constituent parts).

158. Let (the king) consider as hostile his immediate neighbour and the partisan of (such a) foe, as friendly the immediate neighbour of his foe, and as neutral (the king) beyond those two.

159. Let him overcome all of them by means of the (four) expedients, conciliation and the rest, (employed) either singly or conjointly, (or) by bravery and policy (alone).

160. Let him constantly think of the six measures of royal policy (guna, viz.) alliance, war, marching, halting, dividing the army, and seeking protection.

161. Having carefully considered the business (in hand), let him resort to sitting quiet or marching, alliance or war, dividing his forces or seeking protection (as the case may require).

162. But the king must know that there are two kinds of alliances and of wars, (likewise two) of both marching and sitting quiet, and two (occasions for) seeking protection.)

163. An alliance which yields present and future advantages, one must know to be of two descriptions, (viz.) that when one marches together (with an ally) and the contrary (when the allies act separately).

164. War is declared to be of two kinds, (viz.) that which is undertaken in season or out of season, by oneself and for

one's own purposes, and (that waged to avenge) an injury done to a friend.

165. Marching (to attack) is said to be twofold, (viz. that undertaken) by one alone when an urgent matter has suddenly arisen, and (that undertaken) by one allied with a friend.

166. Sitting quiet is stated to be of two kinds, (viz. that incumbent) on one who has gradually been weakened by fate or in consequence of former acts, and (that) in favour of a friend.

167. If the army stops (in one place) and its master (in another) in order to effect some purpose, that is called by those acquainted with the virtues of the measures of royal policy, the twofold division of the forces.

168. Seeking refuge is declared to be of two kinds, (first) for the purpose of attaining an advantage when one is harassed by enemies, (secondly) in order to become known among the virtuous (as the protege of a powerful king).

169. When (the king) knows (that) at some future time his superiority (is) certain, and (that) at the time present (he will suffer) little injury, then let him have recourse to peaceful measures.

170. But when he thinks all his subjects to be exceedingly contented, and (that he) himself (is) most exalted (in power), then let him make war.

171. When he knows his own army to be cheerful in disposition and strong, and (that) of his enemy the reverse, then let him march against his foe.

172. But if he is very weak in chariots and beasts of burden and in troops, then let him carefully sit quiet, gradually conciliating his foes.

173. When the king knows the enemy to be stronger in every respect, then let him divide his army and thus achieve his purpose.

174. But when he is very easily assailable by the forces of the enemy, then let him quickly seek refuge with a righteous, powerful king.

175. That (prince) who will coerce both his (disloyal) subjects and the army of the foe, let him ever serve with every effort like a Guru.

176. When, even in that (condition), he sees (that) evil is caused by (such) protection, let him without hesitation have recourse to war.

177. By all (the four) expedients a politic prince must arrange (matters so) that neither friends, nor neutrals, nor foes are superior to himself.

178. Let him fully consider the future and the immediate results of all undertakings, and the good and bad sides of all past (actions).

179. He who knows the good and the evil (which will result from his acts) in the future, is quick in forming resolutions for the present, and understands the consequences of past (actions), will not be conquered.

180. Let him arrange everything in such a manner that no ally, no neutral or foe may injure him; that is the sum of political wisdom.

181. But if the king undertakes an expedition against a hostile kingdom, then let him gradually advance, in the following manner, against his foe's capital.

182. Let the king undertake his march in the fine month Margasirsha, or towards the months of Phalguna and Kaitra, according to the (condition of his) army.

183. Even at other times, when he has a certain prospect of victory, or when a disaster has befallen his foe, he may advance to attack him.

184. But having duly arranged (all affairs) in his original (kingdom) and what relates to the expedition, having secured a basis (for his operations) and having duly dispatched his spies;

185. Having cleared the three kinds of roads, and (having made) his sixfold army (efficient), let him leisurely proceed in the manner prescribed for warfare against the enemy's capital.

186. Let him be very much on his guard against a friend who secretly serves the enemy and against (deserters) who return (from the enemy's camp); for such (men are) the most dangerous foes.

187. Let him march on his road, arraying (his troops) like a staff (i.e. in an oblong), or like a waggon (i.e. in a wedge), or like a boar (i.e. in a rhombus), or like a Makara (i.e. in two triangles, with the apices joined), or like a pin (i.e. in a long line), or like a Garuda (i.e. in a rhomboid with far-extended wings).

188. From whatever (side) he apprehends danger, in that (direction) let him extend his troops, and let him always himself encamp in an array, shaped like a lotus.

189. Let him allot to the commander-in-chief, to the (subordinate) general, (and to the superior officers) places in all directions, and let him turn his front in that direction whence he fears danger.

190. On all sides let him place troops of soldiers, on whom he can rely, with whom signals have been arranged, who are expert both in sustaining a charge and in charging, fearless and loyal.

191. Let him make a small number of soldiers fight in close order, at his pleasure let him extend a large number in loose ranks; or let him make them fight, arranging (a small

number) in the needle-array, (and a large number) in the thunderbolt-array.

192. On even ground let him fight with chariots and horses, in water-bound places with boats and elephants, on (ground) covered with trees and shrubs with bows, on hilly ground with swords, targets, (and other) weapons.

193. (Men born in) Kurukshetra, Matsyas, Pankalas, and those born in Surasena, let him cause to fight in the van of the battle, as well as (others who are) tall and light.

194. After arranging his troops, he should encourage them (by an address) and carefully inspect them; he should also mark the behaviour (of the soldiers) when they engage the enemy.

195. When he has shut up his foe (in a town), let him sit encamped, harass his kingdom, and continually spoil his grass, food, fuel, and water.

196. Likewise let him destroy the tanks, ramparts, and ditches, and let him assail the (foe unawares) and alarm him at night.

197. Let him instigate to rebellion those who are open to such instigations, let him be informed of his (foe's) doings, and, when fate is propitious, let him fight without fear, trying to conquer.

198. He should (however) try to conquer his foes by conciliation, by (well-applied) gifts, and by creating dissension, used either separately or conjointly, never by fighting, (if it can be avoided.)

199. For when two (princes) fight, victory and defeat in the battle are, as experience teaches, uncertain; let him therefore avoid an engagement.

200. (But) if even those three before-mentioned expedients fail, then let him, duly exerting himself, fight in such a manner that he may completely conquer his enemies.

201. When he has gained victory, let him duly worship the gods and honour righteous Brahmanas, let him grant exemptions, and let him cause promises of safety to be proclaimed.

202. But having fully ascertained the wishes of all the (conquered), let him place there a relative of the (vanquished ruler on the throne), and let him impose his conditions.

203. Let him make authoritative the lawful (customs) of the (inhabitants), just as they are stated (to be), and let him honour the (new king) and his chief servants with precious gifts.

204. The seizure of desirable property which causes displeasure, and its distribution which causes pleasure, are both recommendable, (if they are) resorted to at the proper time.

205. All undertakings (in) this (world) depend both on the ordering of fate and on human exertion; but among these two (the ways of) fate are unfathomable; in the case of man's work action is possible.

206. Or (the king, bent on conquest), considering a friend, gold, and land (to be) the triple result (of an expedition), may, using diligent care, make peace with (his foe) and return (to his realm).

207. Having paid due attention to any king in the circle (of neighbouring states) who might attack him in the rear, and to his supporter who opposes the latter, let (the conqueror) secure the fruit of the expedition from (the prince whom he attacks), whether (he may have become) friendly or (remained) hostile.

208. By gaining gold and land a king grows not so much in strength as by obtaining a firm friend, (who), though weak, (may become) powerful in the future.

209. A weak friend (even) is greatly commended, who is righteous (and) grateful, whose people are contented, who is attached and persevering in his undertakings.

210. The wise declare him (to be) a most dangerous foe, who is wise, of noble race, brave, clever, liberal, grateful, and firm.

211. Behaviour worthy of an Aryan, knowledge of men, bravery, a compassionate disposition, and great liberality are the virtues of a neutral (who may be courted).

212. Let the king, without hesitation, quit for his own sake even a country (which is) salubrious, fertile, and causing an increase of cattle.

213. For times of need let him preserve his wealth; at the expense of his wealth let him preserve his wife; let him at all events preserve himself even by (giving up) his wife and his wealth.

214. A wise (king), seeing that all kinds of misfortunes violently assail him at the same time, should try all (the four) expedients, be it together or separately, (in order to save himself.)

215. On the person who employs the expedients, on the business to be accomplished, and on all the expedients collectively, on these three let him ponder and strive to accomplish his ends.

216. Having thus consulted with his ministers on all these (matters), having taken exercise, and having bathed afterwards, the king may enter the harem at midday in order to dine.

217. There he may eat food, (which has been prepared) by faithful, incorruptible (servants) who know the (proper) time (for dining), which has been well examined (and hallowed) by sacred texts that destroy poison.

218. Let him mix all his food with medicines (that are) antidotes against poison, and let him always be careful to

wear gems which destroy poison.

219. Well-tried females whose toilet and ornaments have been examined, shall attentively serve him with fans, water, and perfumes.

220. In like manner let him be careful about his carriages, bed, seat, bath, toilet, and all his ornaments.

221. When he has dined, he may divert himself with his wives in the harem; but when he has diverted himself, he must, in due time, again think of the affairs of state.

222. Adorned (with his robes of state), let him again inspect his fighting men, all his chariots and beasts of burden, the weapons and accoutrements.

223. Having performed his twilight-devotions, let him, well armed, hear in an inner apartment the doings of those who make secret reports and of his spies.

224. But going to another secret apartment and dismissing those people, he may enter the harem, surrounded by female (servants), in order to dine again.

225. Having eaten there something for the second time, and having been recreated by the sound of music, let him go to rest and rise at the proper time free from fatigue.

226. A king who is in good health must observe these rules; but, if he is indisposed, he may entrust all this (business) to his servants.

CHAPTER IX.

1. I will now propound the eternal laws for a husband and his wife who keep to the path of duty, whether they be united or separated.

2. Day and night woman must be kept in dependence by the males (of) their (families), and, if they attach themselves to sensual enjoyments, they must be kept under one's control.

3. Her father protects (her) in childhood, her husband protects (her) in youth, and her sons protect (her) in old age; a woman is never fit for independence.

4. Reprehensible is the father who gives not (his daughter in marriage) at the proper time; reprehensible is the husband who approaches not (his wife in due season), and reprehensible is the son who does not protect his mother after her husband has died.

5. Women must particularly be guarded against evil inclinations, however trifling (they may appear); for, if they are not guarded, they will bring sorrow on two families.

6. Considering that the highest duty of all castes, even weak husbands (must) strive to guard their wives.

7. He who carefully guards his wife, preserves (the purity of) his offspring, virtuous conduct, his family, himself, and his (means of acquiring) merit.

8. The husband, after conception by his wife, becomes an embryo and is born again of her; for that is the wifehood of a wife (gaya), that he is born (gayate) again by her.

9. As the male is to whom a wife cleaves, even so is the son whom she brings forth; let him therefore carefully guard his wife, in order to keep his offspring pure.

10. No man can completely guard women by force; but they can be guarded by the employment of the (following) expedients:

11. Let the (husband) employ his (wife) in the collection and expenditure of his wealth, in keeping (everything) clean, in (the fulfilment of) religious duties, in the preparation of his food, and in looking after the household utensils.

12. Women, confined in the house under trustworthy and obedient servants, are not (well) guarded; but those who of their own accord keep guard over themselves, are well guarded.

13. Drinking (spirituous liquor), associating with wicked people, separation from the husband, rambling abroad, sleeping (at unseasonable hours), and dwelling in other men's houses, are the six causes of the ruin of women.

14. Women do not care for beauty, nor is their attention fixed on age; (thinking), '(It is enough that) he is a man,' they give themselves to the handsome and to the ugly.

15. Through their passion for men, through their mutable temper, through their natural heartlessness, they become disloyal towards their husbands, however carefully they may be guarded in this (world).

16. Knowing their disposition, which the Lord of creatures laid in them at the creation, to be such, (every) man should most strenuously exert himself to guard them.

17. (When creating them) Manu allotted to women (a love of their) bed, (of their) seat and (of) ornament, impure desires, wrath, dishonesty, malice, and bad conduct.

18. For women no (sacramental) rite (is performed) with sacred texts, thus the law is settled; women (who are) destitute of strength and destitute of (the knowledge of) Vedic texts, (are as impure as) falsehood (itself), that is a fixed rule.

19. And to this effect many sacred texts are sung also in the Vedas, in order to (make) fully known the true disposition (of women); hear (now those texts which refer to) the expiation of their (sins).

20. 'If my mother, going astray and unfaithful, conceived illicit desires, may my father keep that seed from me,' that is the scriptural text.

21. If a woman thinks in her heart of anything that would pain her husband, the (above-mentioned text) is declared (to be a means for) completely removing such infidelity.

22. Whatever be the qualities of the man with whom a woman is united according to the law, such qualities even she assumes, like a river (united) with the ocean.

23. Akshamala, a woman of the lowest birth, being united to Vasishtha and Sarangi, (being united) to Mandapala, became worthy of honour.

24. These and other females of low birth have attained eminence in this world by the respective good qualities of their husbands.

25. Thus has been declared the ever pure popular usage (which regulates the relations) between husband and wife; hear (next) the laws concerning children which are the cause of happiness in this world and after death.

26. Between wives (striyah) who (are destined) to bear children, who secure many blessings, who are worthy of worship and irradiate (their) dwellings, and between the goddesses of fortune (sriyah, who reside) in the houses (of men), there is no difference whatsoever.

27. The production of children, the nurture of those born, and the daily life of men, (of these matters) woman is visibly the cause.

28. Offspring, (the due performance on religious rites, faithful service, highest conjugal happiness and heavenly bliss for the ancestors and oneself, depend on one's wife alone.

29. She who, controlling her thoughts, speech, and acts, violates not her duty towards her lord, dwells with him (after death) in heaven, and in this world is called by the virtuous a faithful (wife, sadhvi)

30. But for disloyalty to her husband a wife is censured among men, and (in her next life) she is born in the womb of a jackal and tormented by diseases, the punishment of her sin.

31. Listen (now) to the following holy discussion, salutary to all men, which the virtuous (of the present day) and the ancient great sages have held concerning male offspring.

32. They (all) say that the male issue (of a woman) belongs to the lord, but with respect to the (meaning of the term) lord the revealed texts differ; some call the begetter (of the child the lord), others declare (that it is) the owner of the soil.

33. By the sacred tradition the woman is declared to be the soil, the man is declared to be the seed; the production of all corporeal beings (takes place) through the union of the soil with the seed.

34. In some cases the seed is more distinguished, and in some the womb of the female; but when both are equal, the offspring is most highly esteemed.

35. On comparing the seed and the receptacle (of the seed), the seed is declared to be more important; for the offspring of all created beings is marked by the characteristics of the seed.

36. Whatever (kind on seed is sown in a field, prepared in due season, (a plant) of that same kind, marked with the peculiar qualities of the seed, springs up in it.

37. This earth, indeed, is called the primeval womb of created beings; but the seed develops not in its development any properties of the womb.

38. In this world seeds of different kinds, sown at the proper time in the land, even in one field, come forth (each) according to its kind.

39. The rice (called) vrihi and (that called) sali, mudga-beans, sesamum, masha-beans, barley, leeks, and sugar-cane, (all) spring up according to their seed.

40. That one (plant) should be sown and another be produced cannot happen; whatever seed is sown, (a plant of) that kind even comes forth.

41. Never therefore must a prudent well-trained man, who knows the Veda and its Angas and desires long life, cohabit with another's wife.

42. With respect to this (matter), those acquainted with the past recite some stanzas, sung by Vayu (the Wind, to show) that seed must not be sown by (any) man on that which belongs to another.

43. As the arrow, shot by (a hunter) who afterwards hits a wounded (deer) in the wound (made by another), is shot in vain, even so the seed, sown on what belongs to another, is quickly lost (to the sower).

44. (Sages) who know the past call this earth (prithivi) even the wife of Prithu; they declare a field to belong to him who cleared away the timber, and a deer to him who (first) wounded it.

45. He only is a perfect man who consists (of three persons united), his wife, himself, and his offspring; thus (says the Veda), and (learned) Brahmanas propound this (maxim) likewise, 'The husband is declared to be one with the wife.'

46. Neither by sale nor by repudiation is a wife released from her husband; such we know the law to be, which the Lord of creatures (Pragapati) made of old.

47. Once is the partition (of the inheritance) made, (once is a maiden given in marriage, (and) once does (a man) say,' I will give;' each of those three (acts is done) once only.

48. As with cows, mares, female camels, slave-girls, buffalo-cows, she-goats, and ewes, it is not the begetter (or his owner) who obtains the offspring, even thus (it is) with the wives of others.

49. Those who, having no property in a field, but possessing seed-corn, sow it in another's soil, do indeed not receive the grain of the crop which may spring up.

50. If (one man's) bull were to beget a hundred calves on another man's cows, they would belong to the owner of the cows; in vain would the bull have spent his strength.

51. Thus men who have no marital property in women, but sow their seed in the soil of others, benefit the owner of the woman; but the giver of the seed reaps no advantage.

52. If no agreement with respect to the crop has been made between the owner of the field and the owner of the seed, the benefit clearly belongs to the owner of the field; the receptacle is more important than the seed.

53. But if by a special contract (a field) is made over (to another) for sowing, then the owner of the seed and the owner of the soil are both considered in this world as sharers of the (crop).

54. If seed be carried by water or wind into somebody's field and germinates (there), the (plant sprung from that) seed belongs even to the owner of the field, the owner of the seed does not receive the crop.

55. Know that such is the law concerning the offspring of cows, mares, slave-girls, female camels, she-goats, and ewes, as well as of females of birds and buffalo-cows.

56. Thus the comparative importance of the seed and of the womb has been declared to you; I will next propound the law (applicable) to women in times of misfortune.

57. The wife of an elder brother is for his younger (brother) the wife of a Guru; but the wife of the younger is declared (to be) the daughter-in-law of the elder.

58. An elder (brother) who approaches the wife of the younger, and a younger (brother who approaches) the wife of the elder, except in times of misfortune, both become outcasts, even though (they were duly) authorised.

59. On failure of issue (by her husband) a woman who has been authorised, may obtain, (in the) proper (manner prescribed), the desired offspring by (cohabitation with) a brother-in-law or (with some other) Sapinda (of the husband).

60. He (who is) appointed to (cohabit with) the widow shall (approach her) at night anointed with clarified butter and silent, (and) beget one son, by no means a second.

61. Some (sages), versed in the law, considering the purpose of the appointment not to have been attained by those two (on the birth of the first), think that a second (son) may be lawfully procreated on (such) women.

62. But when the purpose of the appointment to (cohabit with) the widow bas been attained in accordance with the

law, those two shall behave towards each other like a father and a daughter-in-law.

63. If those two (being thus) appointed deviate from the rule and act from carnal desire, they will both become outcasts, (as men) who defile the bed of a daughter-in-law or of a Guru.

64. By twice-born men a widow must not be appointed to (cohabit with) any other (than her husband); for they who appoint (her) to another (man), will violate the eternal law.

65. In the sacred texts which refer to marriage the appointment (of widows) is nowhere mentioned, nor is the re-marriage of widows prescribed in the rules concerning marriage.

66. This practice which is reprehended by the learned of the twice-born castes as fit for cattle is said (to have occurred) even among men, while Vena ruled.

67. That chief of royal sages who formerly possessed the whole world, caused a confusion of the castes (varna), his intellect being destroyed by lust.

68. Since that (time) the virtuous censure that (man) who in his folly appoints a woman, whose husband died, to (bear) children (to another man).

69. If the (future) husband of a maiden dies after troth verbally plighted, her brother-in-law shall wed her according to the following rule.

70. Having, according to the rule, espoused her (who must be) clad in white garments and be intent on purity, he shall approach her once in each proper season until issue (be had).

71. Let no prudent man, after giving his daughter to one (man), give her again to another; for he who gives (his daughter) whom he had before given, incurs (the guilt of) speaking falsely regarding a human being.

72. Though (a man) may have accepted a damsel in due form, he may abandon (her if she be) blemished, diseased, or deflowered, and (if she have been) given with fraud.

73. If anybody gives away a maiden possessing blemishes without declaring them, (the bridegroom) may annul that (contract) with the evil-minded giver.

74. A man who has business (abroad) may depart after securing a maintenance for his wife; for a wife, even though virtuous, may be corrupted if she be distressed by want of subsistence.

75. If (the husband) went on a journey after providing (for her), the wife shall subject herself to restraints in her daily life; but if he departed without providing (for her), she may subsist by blameless manual work.

76. If the husband went abroad for some sacred duty, (she) must wait for him eight years, if (he went) to (acquire)

learning or fame six (years), if (he went) for pleasure three years.

77. For one year let a husband bear with a wife who hates him; but after (the lapse of) a year let him deprive her of her property and cease to cohabit with her.

78. She who shows disrespect to (a husband) who is addicted to (some evil) passion, is a drunkard, or diseased, shall be deserted for three months (and be) deprived of her ornaments and furniture.

79. But she who shows aversion towards a mad or outcast (husband), a eunuch, one destitute of manly strength, or one afflicted with such diseases as punish crimes, shall neither be cast off nor be deprived of her property.

80. She who drinks spirituous liquor, is of bad conduct, rebellious, diseased, mischievous, or wasteful, may at any time be superseded (by another wife).

81. A barren wife may be superseded in the eighth year, she whose children (all) die in the tenth, she who bears only daughters in the eleventh, but she who is quarrelsome without delay.

82. But a sick wife who is kind (to her husband) and virtuous in her conduct, may be superseded (only) with her own consent and must never be disgraced.

83. A wife who, being superseded, in anger departs from (her husband's) house, must either be instantly confined or cast off in the presence of the family.

84. But she who, though having been forbidden, drinks spirituous liquor even at festivals, or goes to public spectacles or assemblies, shall be fined six krishnalas.

85. If twice-born men wed women of their own and of other (lower castes), the seniority, honour, and habitation of those (wives) must be (settled) according to the order of the castes (varna).

86. Among all (twice-born men) the wife of equal caste alone, not a wife of a different caste by any means, shall personally attend her husband and assist him in his daily sacred rites.

87. But he who foolishly causes that (duty) to be performed by another, while his wife of equal caste is alive, is declared by the ancients (to be) as (despicable) as a Kandala (sprung from the) Brahmana (caste).

88. To a distinguished, handsome suitor (of) equal (caste) should (a father) give his daughter in accordance with the prescribed rule, though she have not attained (the proper age).

89. (But) the maiden, though marriageable, should rather stop in (the father's) house until death, than that he should ever give her to a man destitute of good qualities.

90. Three years let a damsel wait, though she be marriageable; but after that time let her choose for herself a bridegroom (of) equal (caste and rank).

91. If, being not given in marriage, she herself seeks a husband, she incurs no guilt, nor (does) he whom she weds.

92. A maiden who choses for herself, shall not take with her any ornaments, given by her father or her mother, or her brothers; if she carries them away, it will be theft.

93. But he who takes (to wife) a marriageable damsel, shall not pay any nuptial fee to her father; for the (latter) will lose his dominion over her in consequence of his preventing (the legitimate result of the appearance of) her enemies.

94. A man, aged thirty years, shall marry a maiden of twelve who pleases him, or a man of twenty-four a girl eight years of age; if (the performance of) his duties would (otherwise) be impeded, (he must marry) sooner.

95. The husband receives his wife from the gods, (he does not wed her) according to his own will; doing what is agreeable to the gods, he must always support her (while she is) faithful.

96. To be mothers were women created, and to be fathers men; religious rites, therefore, are ordained in the Veda to be performed (by the husband) together with the wife.

97. If, after the nuptial fee has been paid for a maiden, the giver of the fee dies, she shall be given in marriage to his brother, in case she consents.

98. Even a Sudra ought not to take a nuptial fee, when he gives away his daughter; for he who takes a fee sell his daughter, covering (the transaction by another name).

99. Neither ancients nor moderns who were good men have done such (a deed) that, after promising (a daughter) to one man, they have her to another;

100. Nor, indeed, have we heard, even in former creations, of such (a thing as) the covert sale of a daughter for a fixed price, called a nuptial fee.

101. 'Let mutual fidelity continue until death,' this may be considered as the summary of the highest law for husband and wife.

102. Let man and woman, united in marriage, constantly exert themselves, that (they may not be) disunited (and) may not violate their mutual fidelity.

103. Thus has been declared to you the law for a husband and his wife, which is intimately connected with conjugal happiness, and the manner of raising offspring in times of calamity; learn (now the law concerning) the division of the inheritance.

104. After the death of the father and of the mother, the brothers, being assembled, may divide among themselves in

equal shares the paternal (and the maternal) estate; for, they have no power (over it) while the parents live.

105. (Or) the eldest alone may take the whole paternal estate, the others shall live under him just as (they lived) under their father.

106. Immediately on the birth of his first-born a man is (called) the father of a son and is freed from the debt to the manes; that (son), therefore, is worthy (to receive) the whole estate.

107. That son alone on whom he throws his debt and through whom he obtains immortality, is begotten for (the fulfilment of) the law; all the rest they consider the offspring of desire.

108. As a father (supports) his sons, so let the eldest support his younger brothers, and let them also in accordance with the law behave towards their eldest brother as sons (behave towards their father).

109. The eldest (son) makes the family prosperous or, on the contrary, brings it to ruin; the eldest (is considered) among men most worthy of honour, the eldest is not treated with disrespect by the virtuous.

110. If the eldest brother behaves as an eldest brother (ought to do), he (must be treated) like a mother and like a father; but if he behaves in a manner unworthy of an eldest brother, he should yet be honoured like a kinsman.

111. Either let them thus live together, or apart, if (each) desires (to gain) spiritual merit; for (by their living) separate (their) merit increases, hence separation is meritorious.

112. The additional share (deducted) for the eldest shall be one-twentieth (of the estate) and the best of all chattels, for the middlemost half of that, but for the youngest one-fourth.

113. Both the eldest and the youngest shall take (their shares) according to (the rule just) stated (each of) those who are between the eldest and the youngest, shall have the share (prescribed for the) middlemost.

114. Among the goods of every kind the eldest shall take the best (article), and (even a single chattel) which is particularly good, as well as the best of ten (animals).

115. But among (brothers) equally skilled in their occupations, there is no additional share, (consisting of the best animal) among ten; some trifle only shall be given to the eldest as a token of respect.

116. If additional shares are thus deducted, one must allot equal shares (out of the residue to each); but if no deduction is made, the allotment of the shares among them shall be (made) in the following manner.

117. Let the eldest son take one share in excess, the (brother) born next after him one (share) and a half, the younger ones

one share each; thus the law is settled.

118. But to the maiden (sisters) the brothers shall severally give (portions) out of their shares, each out of his share one-fourth part; those who refuse to give (it), will become outcasts.

119. Let him never divide (the value of) a single goat or sheep, or a (single beast) with uncloven hoofs; it is prescribed (that) a single goat or sheep (remaining after an equal division, belongs) to the eldest alone.

120. If a younger brother begets a son on the wife of the elder, the division must then be made equally; this the law is settled.

121. The representative (the son begotten on the wife) is not invested with the right of the principal (the eldest brother to an additional share); the principal (became) a father on the procreation (of a son by his younger brother); hence one should give a share to the (son begotten on the wife of the elder brother) according to the rule (stated above).

122. If there be a doubt, how the division shall be made, in case the younger son is born of the elder wife and the elder son of the younger wife,

123. (Then the son) born of the first wife shall take as his additional share one (most excellent) bull; the next best bulls (shall belong) to those (who are) inferior on account of their mothers.

124. But the eldest (son, being) born of the eldest wife, shall receive fifteen cows and a bull, the other sons may then take shares according to (the seniority of) their mothers; that is a settled rule.

125. Between sons born of wives equal (in caste) (and) without (any other) distinction no seniority in right of the mother exists; seniority is declared (to be) according to birth.

126. And with respect to the Subrahmanya (texts) also it is recorded that the invocation (of Indra shall be made) by the first-born, of twins likewise, (conceived at one time) in the wombs (of their mothers) the seniority is declared (to depend) on (actual) birth.

127. He who has no son may make his daughter in the following manner an appointed daughter (putrika, saying to her husband), 'The (male) child, born of her, shall perform my funeral rites.'

128. According to this rule Daksha, himself, lord of created beings, formerly made (all his female offspring) appointed daughters in order to multiply his race.

129. He gave ten to Dharma, thirteen to Kasyapa, twenty-seven to King Soma, honouring (them) with an affectionate heart.

130. A son is even (as) oneself, (such) a daughter is equal to a son; how can another (heir) take the estate, while such (an appointed daughter who is even) oneself, lives?

131. But whatever may be the separate property of the mother, that is the share of the unmarried daughter alone; and the son of an (appointed) daughter shall take the whole estate of (his maternal grandfather) who leaves no son.

132. The son of an (appointed) daughter, indeed, shall (also) take the estate of his (own) father, who leaves no (other) son; he shall (then) present two funeral cakes to his own father and to his maternal grandfather.

133. Between a son's son and the son of an (appointed) daughter there is no difference, neither with respect to worldly matters nor to sacred duties; for their father and mother both sprang from the body of the same (man).

134. But if, after a daughter has been appointed, a son be born (to her father), the division (of the inheritance) must in that (case) be equal; for there is no right of primogeniture for a woman.

135. But if an appointed daughter by accident dies without (leaving) a son, the husband of the appointed daughter may, without hesitation, take that estate.

136. Through that son whom (a daughter), either not appointed or appointed, may bear to (a husband) of equal (caste), his maternal grandfather (has) a son's son; he shall present the funeral cake and take the estate.

137. Through a son he conquers the worlds, through a son's son he obtains immortality, but through his son's grandson he gains the world of the sun.

138. Because a son delivers (trayate) his father from the hell called Put, he was therefore called put-tra (a deliverer from Put) by the Self-existent (Svayambhu) himself.

139. Between a son's son and the son of a daughter there exists in this world no difference; for even the son of a daughter saves him (who has no sons) in the next world, like the son's son.

140. Let the son of an appointed daughter first present a funeral cake to his mother, the second to her father, the funeral to his father's father.

141. Of the man who has an adopted (Datrima) son possessing all good qualities, that same (son) shall take the inheritance, though brought from another family.

142. An adopted son shall never take the family (name) and the estate of his natural father; the funeral cake follows the family (name) and the estate, the funeral offerings of him who gives (his son in adoption) cease (as far as that son is concerned).

143. The son of a wife, not appointed (to have issue by another), and he whom (an appointed female, already) the mother of a son, bears to her brother-in-law, are both unworthy of a share, (one being) the son of an adulterer and (the other) produced through (mere) lust.

144. Even the male (child) of a female (duly) appointed, not begotten according to the rule (given above), is unworthy of the paternal estate; for he was procreated by an outcast.

145. A son (legally) begotten on such an appointed female shall inherit like a legitimate son of the body; for that seed and the produce belong, according to the law, to the owner of the soil.

146. He who takes care of his deceased brother's estate and of his widow, shall, after raising up a son for his brother, give that property even to that (son).

147. If a woman (duly) appointed bears a son to her brother-in-law or to another (Sapinda), that (son, if he is) begotten through desire, they declare (to be) incapable of inheriting and to be produced in vain.

148. The rules (given above) must be understood (to apply) to a distribution among sons of women of the same (caste); hear (now the law) concerning those begotten by one man on many wives of different (castes).

149. If there be four wives of a Brahmana in the direct order of the castes, the rule for the division (of the estate) among the sons born of them is as follows:

150. The (slave) who tills (the field), the bull kept for impregnating cows, the vehicle, the ornaments, and the house shall be given as an additional portion to the Brahmana (son), and one most excellent share.

151. Let the son of the Brahmana (wife) take three shares of the (remainder of the) estate, the son of the Kshatriya two, the son of the Vaisya a share and a half, and the son of the Sudra may take one share.

152. Or let him who knows the law make ten shares of the whole estate, and justly distribute them according to the following rule:

153. The Brahmana (son) shall take four shares, son of the Kshatriya (wife) three, the son of the Vaisya shall have two parts, the son of the Sudra may take one share.

154. Whether (a Brahmana) have sons or have no sons (by wives of the twice-born castes), the (heir) must, according to the law, give to the son of a Sudra (wife) no more than a tenth (part of his estate).

155. The son of a Brahmana, a Kshatriya, and a Vaisya by a Sudra (wife) receives no share of the inheritance; whatever his father may give to him, that shall be his property.

156. All the sons of twice-born men, born of wives of the same caste, shall equally divide the estate, after the others have given to the eldest an additional share.

157. For a Sudra is ordained a wife of his own caste only (and) no other; those born of her shall have equal shares, even if there be a hundred sons.

158. Among the twelve sons of men whom Manu, sprung from the Self-existent (Svayambhu), enumerates, six are kinsmen and heirs, and six not heirs, (but) kinsmen.

159. The legitimate son of the body, the son begotten on a wife, the son adopted, the son made, the son secretly born, and the son cast off, (are) the six heirs and kinsmen.

160. The son of an unmarried damsel, the son received with the wife, the son bought, the son begotten on a re-married woman, the son self-given, and the son of a Sudra female, (are) the six (who are) not heirs, (but) kinsmen.

161. Whatever result a man obtains who (tries to) cross a (sheet of) water in an unsafe boat, even that result obtains he who (tries to) pass the gloom (of the next world) with (the help of) bad (substitutes for a real) son.

162. If the two heirs of one man be a legitimate son of his body and a son begotten on his wife, each (of the two sons), to the exclusion of the other, shall take the estate of his (natural) father.

163. The legitimate son of the body alone (shall be) the owner of the paternal estate; but, in order to avoid harshness, let him allow a maintenance to the rest.

164. But when the legitimate son of the body divides the paternal estate, he shall give one-sixth or one-fifth part of his father's property to the son begotten on the wife.

165. The legitimate son and the son of the wife (thus) share the father's estate; but the other tell become members of the family, and inherit according to their order (each later named on failure of those named earlier).

166. Him whom a man begets on his own wedded wife, let him know to be a legitimate son of the body (Aurasa), the first in rank.

167. He who was begotten according to the peculiar law (of the Niyoga) on the appointed wife of a dead man, of a eunuch, or of one diseased, is called a son begotten on a wife (Kshetraga).

168. That (boy) equal (by caste) whom his mother or his father affectionately give, (confirming the gift) with (a libation of) water, in times of distress (to a man) as his son, must be considered as an adopted son (Datrima).

169. But he is considered a son made (Kritrima) whom (a man) makes his son, (he being) equal (by caste), acquainted with (the distinctions between) right and wrong, (and) endowed with filial virtues.

170. If (a child) be born in a man's house and his father be not known, he is a son born secretly in the house (Gudhotpanna), and shall belong to him of whose wife he was born.

171. He whom (a man) receives as his son, (after he has been) deserted by his parents or by either of them, is called a son cast off (Apaviddha).

172. A son whom a damsel secretly bears in the house of her father, one shall name the son of an unmarried damsel (Kanina, and declare) such offspring of an unmarried girl (to belong) to him who weds her (afterwards).

173. If one marries, either knowingly or unknowingly, a pregnant (bride), the child in her womb belongs to him who weds her, and is called (a son) received with the bride (Sahodha).

174. If a man buys a (boy), whether equal or unequal (in good qualities), from his father and mother for the sake of having a son, that (child) is called a (son) bought (Kritaka).

175. If a woman abandoned by her husband, or a widow, of her own accord contracts a second marriage and bears (a son), he is called the son of a re-married woman (Paunarbhava).

176. If she be (still) a virgin, or one who returned (to her first husband) after leaving him, she is worthy to again perform with her second (or first deserted) husband the (nuptial) ceremony.

177. He who, having lost his parents or being abandoned (by them) without (just) cause, gives himself to a (man), is called a son self-given (Svayamdatta).

178. The son whom a Brahmana begets through lust on a Sudra female is, (though) alive (parayan), a corpse (sava), and hence called a Parasava (a living corpse).

179. A son who is (begotten) by a Sudra on a female slave, or on the female slave of his slave, may, if permitted (by his father), take a share (of the inheritance); thus the law is settled.

180. These eleven, the son begotten on the wife and the rest as enumerated (above), the wise call substitutes for a son, (taken) in order (to prevent) a failure of the (funeral) ceremonies.

181. Those sons, who have been mentioned in connection with (the legitimate son of the body), being begotten by strangers, belong (in reality) to him from whose seed they sprang, but not to the other (man who took them).

182. If among brothers, sprung from one (father), one have a son, Manu has declared them all to have male offspring through that son.

183. If among all the wives of one husband one have a son, Manu declares them all (to be) mothers of male children through that son.

184. On failure of each better (son), each next inferior (one) is worthy of the inheritance; but if there be many (of) equal (rank), they shall all share the estate.

185. Not brothers, nor fathers, (but) sons take the paternal estate; but the father shall take the inheritance of (a son) who leaves no male issue, and his brothers.

186. To three (ancestors) water must be offered, to three the funeral cake is given, the fourth (descendant is) the giver of these (oblations), the fifth has no connection (with them).

187. Always to that (relative within three degrees) who is nearest to the (deceased) Sapinda the estate shall belong; afterwards a Sakulya shall be (the heir, then) the spiritual teacher or the pupil.

188. But on failure of all (heirs) Brahmanas (shall) share the estate, (who are) versed the in the three Vedas, pure and self-controlled; thus the law is not violated.

189. The property of a Brahmana must never be taken by the king, that is a settled rule; but (the property of men) of other castes the king may take on failure of all (heirs).

190. (If the widow) of (a man) who died without leaving issue, raises up to him a son by a member of the family (Sagotra), she shall deliver to that (son) the whole property which belonged to the (deceased).

191. But if two (sons), begotten by two (different men), contend for the property (in the hands) of their mother, each shall take, to the exclusion of the other, what belonged to his father.

192. But when the mother has died, all the uterine brothers and the uterine sisters shall equally divide the mother's estate.

193. Even to the daughters of those (daughters) something should be given, as is seemly, out of the estate of their maternal grandmother, on the score of affection.

194. What (was given) before the (nuptial) fire, what (was given) on the bridal procession, what was given in token of love, and what was received from her brother, mother, or father, that is called the sixfold property of a woman.

195. (Such property), as well as a gift subsequent and what was given (to her) by her affectionate husband, shall go to her offspring, (even) if she dies in the lifetime of her husband.

196. It is ordained that the property (of a woman married) according to the Brahma, the Daiva, the Arsha, the Gandharva, or the Pragapatya rite (shall belong) to her husband alone, if she dies without issue.

197. But it is prescribed that the property which may have been given to a (wife) on an Asura marriage or (one of the) other (blamable marriages, shall go) to her mother and to her father, if she dies without issue.

198. Whatever property may have been given by her father to a wife (who has co-wives of different castes), that

the daughter (of the) Brahmani (wife) shall take, or that (daughter's) issue.

199. Women should never make a hoard from (the property of) their families which is common to many, nor from their own (husbands' particular) property without permission.

200. The ornaments which may have been worn by women during their husbands' lifetime, his heirs shall not divide; those who divide them become outcasts.

201. Eunuchs and outcasts, (persons) born blind or deaf, the insane, idiots and the dumb, as well as those deficient in any organ (of action or sensation), receive no share.

202. But it is just that (a man) who knows (the law) should give even to all of them food and raiment without stint, according to his ability; he who gives it not will become all outcast.

203. If the eunuch and the rest should somehow or other desire to (take) wives, the offspring of such among them as have children is worthy of a share.

204. Whatever property the eldest (son) acquires (by his own exertion) after the father's death, a share of that (shall belong) to his younger (brothers), provided they have made a due progress in learning.

205. But if all of them, being unlearned, acquire property by their labour, the division of that shall be equal, (as it is) not property acquired by the father; that is a settled rule.

206. Property (acquired) by learning belongs solely to him to whom (it was given), likewise the gift of a friend, a present received on marriage or with the honey-mixture.

207. But if one of the brothers, being able (to maintain himself) by his own occupation, does not desire (a share of the family) property, he may be made separate (by the others) receiving a trifle out of his share to live upon.

208. What one (brother) may acquire by his labour without using the patrimony, that acquisition, (made solely) by his own effort, he shall not share unless by his own will (with his brothers).

209. But if a father recovers lost ancestral property, he shall not divide it, unless by his own will, with his sons, (for it is) self-acquired (property).

210. If brothers, (once) divided and living (again) together (as coparceners), make a second partition, the division shall in that case be equal; in such a case there is no right of primogeniture.

211. If the eldest or the youngest (brother) is deprived of his share, or if either of them dies, his share is not lost (to his immediate heirs).

212. His uterine brothers, having assembled together, shall equally divide it, and those brothers who were reunited (with him) and the uterine sisters.

213. An eldest brother who through avarice may defraud the younger ones, shall no (longer hold the position of) the eldest, shall not receive an (eldest son's additional) share, and shall be punished by the king.

214. All brothers who habitually commit forbidden acts, are unworthy of (a share of) the property, and the eldest shall not make (anything his) separate property without giving (an equivalent) to his younger brothers.

215. If undivided brethren, (living with their father,) together make an exertion (for gain), the father shall on no account give to them unequal shares (on a division of the estate).

216. But a son, born after partition, shall alone take the property of his father, or if any (of the other sons) be reunited with the (father), he shall share with them.

217. A mother shall obtain the inheritance of a son (who dies) without leaving issue, and, if the mother be dead, the paternal grandmother shall take the estate.

218. And if, after all the debts and assets have been duly distributed according to the rule, any (property) be afterwards discovered, one must divide it equally.

219. A dress, a vehicle, ornaments, cooked food, water, and female (slaves), property destined for pious uses or sacrifices, and a pasture-ground, they declare to be indivisible.

220. The division (of the property) and the rules for allotting (shares) to the (several) sons, those begotten on a wife and the rest, in (due) order, have been thus declared to you; hear (now) the laws concerning gambling.

221. Gambling and betting let the king exclude from his realm; those two vices cause the destruction of the kingdoms of princes.

222. Gambling and betting amount to open theft; the king shall always exert himself in suppressing both (of them).

223. When inanimate (things) are used (for staking money on them), that is called among men gambling (dyuta), when animate beings are used (for the same purpose), one must know that to be betting (samahvaya).

224. Let the king corporally punish all those (persons) who either gamble and bet or afford (an opportunity for it), likewise Sudras who assume the distinctive marks of twice-born (men).

225. Gamblers, dancers and singers, cruel men, men belonging to an heretical sect, those following forbidden occupations, and sellers of spirituous liquor, let him instantly banish from his town.

226. If such (persons who are) secret thieves, dwell in the realm of a king, they constantly harass his good subjects by their forbidden practices.

227. In a former Kalpa this (vice of) gambling has been seen to cause great enmity; a wise man, therefore, should not practise it even for amusement.

228. On every man who addicts himself to that (vice) either secretly or openly, the king may inflict punishment according to his discretion.

229. But a Kshatriya, a Vaisya, and a Sudra who are unable to pay a fine, shall discharge the debt by labour; a Brahmana shall pay it by installments.

230. On women, infants, men of disordered mind, the poor and the sick, the king shall inflict punishment with a whip, a cane, or a rope and the like.

231. But those appointed (to administer public) affairs, who, baked by the fire of wealth, mar the business of suitors, the king shall deprive of their property.

232. Forgers of royal edicts, those who corrupt his ministers, those who slay women, infants, or Brahmanas, and those who serve his enemies, the king shall put to death.

233. Whenever any (legal transaction) has been completed or (a punishment) been inflicted according to the law, he shall sanction it and not annul it.

234. Whatever matter his ministers or the judge may settle improperly, that the king himself shall (re-) settle and fine (them) one thousand (panas).

235. The slayer of a Brahmana, (A twice-born man) who drinks (the spirituous liquor called) Sura, he who steals (the gold of a Brahmana), and he who violates a Guru's bed, must each and all be considered as men who committed mortal sins (mahapataka).

236. On those four even, if they do not perform a penance, let him inflict corporal punishment and fines in accordance with the law.

237. For violating a Guru's bed, (the mark of) a female part shall be (impressed on the forehead with a hot iron); for drinking (the spirituous liquor called) Sura, the sign of a tavern; for stealing (the gold of a Brahmana), a dog's foot; for murdering a Brahmana, a headless corpse.

238. Excluded from all fellowship at meals, excluded from all sacrifices, excluded from instruction and from matrimonial alliances, abject and excluded from all religious duties, let them wander over (this) earth.

239. Such (persons) who have been branded with (indelible) marks must be cast off by their paternal and maternal relations, and receive neither compassion nor a salutation; that is the teaching of Manu.

240. But (men of) all castes who perform the prescribed penances, must not be branded on the forehead by the king, but shall be made to pay the highest amercement.

241. For (such) offences the middlemost amercement shall be inflicted on a Brahmana, or he may be banished from the realm, keeping his money and his chattels.

242. But (men of) other (castes), who have unintentionally committed such crimes, ought to be deprived of their whole property; if (they committed them) intentionally, they shall be banished.

243. A virtuous king must not take for himself the property of a man guilty of mortal sin; but if he takes it out of greed, he is tainted by that guilt (of the offender).

244. Having thrown such a fine into the water, let him offer it to Varuna, or let him bestow it on a learned and virtuous Brahmana.

245. Varuna is the lord of punishment, for he holds the sceptre even over kings; a Brahmana who has learnt the whole Veda is the lord of the whole world.

246. In that (country), where the king avoids taking the property of (mortal) sinners, men are born in (due) time (and are) long-lived,

247. And the crops of the husbandmen spring up, each as it was sown, and the children die not, and no misshaped (offspring) is born.

248. But the king shall inflict on a base-born (Sudra), who intentionally gives pain to Brahmanas, various (kinds of) corporal punishment which cause terror.

249. When a king punishes an innocent (man), his guilt is considered as great as when he sets free a guilty man; but (he acquires) merit when he punishes (justly).

250. Thus the (manner of) deciding suits (falling) under the eighteen titles, between two litigant parties, has been declared at length.

251. A king who thus duly fulfils his duties in accordance with justice, may seek to gain countries which he has not yet gained, and shall duly protect them when he has gained them.

252. Having duly settled his country, and having built forts in accordance with the Institutes, he shall use his utmost exertions to remove (those men who are nocuous like) thorns.

253. By protecting those who live as (becomes) Aryans and by removing the thorns, kings, solely intent on guarding their subjects, reach heaven.

254. The realm of that king who takes his share in kind, though he does not punish thieves, (will be) disturbed and he (will) lose heaven.

255. But if his kingdom be secure, protected by the strength of his arm, it will constantly flourish like a (well)- watered tree.

256. Let the king who sees (everything) through his spies, discover the two sorts of thieves who deprive others of their property, both those who (show themselves) openly and those who (lie) concealed.

257. Among them, the open rogues (are those) who subsist by (cheating in the sale of) various marketable commodities, but the concealed rogues are burglars, robbers in forests, and so forth.

258. Those who take bribes, cheats and rogues, gamblers, those who live by teaching (the performance of) auspicious ceremonies, sanctimonious hypocrites, and fortune-tellers,

259. Officials of high rank and physicians who act improperly, men living by showing their proficiency in arts, and clever harlots,

260. These and the like who show themselves openly, as well as others who walk in disguise (such as) non-Aryans who wear the marks of Aryans, he should know to be thorns (in the side of his people).

261. Having detected them by means of trustworthy persons, who, disguising themselves, (pretend) to follow the same occupations and by means of spies, wearing various disguises, he must cause them to be instigated (to commit offences), and bring them into his power.

262. Then having caused the crimes, which they committed by their several actions, to be proclaimed in accordance with the facts, the king shall duly punish them according to their strength and their crimes.

263. For the wickedness of evil-minded thieves, who secretly prowl over this earth, cannot be restrained except by punishment.

264. Assembly-houses, houses where water is distributed or cakes are sold, brothels, taverns and victualler's shops, cross-roads, well-known trees, festive assemblies, and play-houses and concert-rooms,

265. Old gardens, forests, the shops of artisans, empty dwellings, natural and artificial groves,

266. These and the like places the king shall cause to be guarded by companies of soldiers, both stationary and patrolling, and by spies, in order to keep away thieves.

267. By the means of clever reformed thieves, who associate with such (rogues), follow them and know their various machinations, he must detect and destroy them.

268. Under the pretext of (offering them) various dainties, of introducing them to Brahmanas, and on the pretence of (showing them) feats of strength, the (spies) must make them meet (the officers of justice).

269. Those among them who do not come, and those who suspect the old (thieves employed by the king), the king

Text Four: THE LAWS OF MANU

shall attack by force and slay together with their friends, blood relations, and connexions.

270. A just king shall not cause a thief to be put to death, (unless taken) with the stolen goods (in his possession); him who (is taken) with the stolen goods and the implements (of burglary), he may, without hesitation, cause to be slain.

271. All those also who in villages give food to thieves or grant them room for (concealing their implements), he shall cause to be put to death.

272. Those who are appointed to guard provinces and his vassals who have been ordered (to help), he shall speedily punish like thieves, (if they remain) inactive in attacks (by robbers).

273. Moreover if (a man), who subsists by (the fulfilment of) the law, departs from the established rule of the law, the (king) shall severely punish him by a fine, (because he) violated his duty.

274. Those who do not give assistance according to their ability when a village is being plundered, a dyke is being destroyed, or a highway robbery committed, shall be banished with their goods and chattels.

275. On those who rob the king's treasury and those who persevere in opposing (his commands), he shall inflict various kinds of capital punishment, likewise on those who conspire with his enemies.

276. But the king shall cut off the hands of those robbers who, breaking into houses, commit thefts at night, and cause them to be impaled on a pointed stake.

277. On the first conviction, let him cause two fingers of a cut-purse to be amputated; on the second, one hand and one foot; on the third, he shall suffer death.

278. Those who give (to thieves) fire, food, arms, or shelter, and receivers of stolen goods, the ruler shall punish like thieves.

279. Him who breaks (the dam of) a tank he shall slay (by drowning him) in water or by (some other) (mode of) capital punishment; or the offender may repair the (damage), but shall be made to pay the highest amercement.

280. Those who break into a (royal) storehouse, an armoury, or a temple, and those who steal elephants, horses, or chariots, he shall slay without hesitation.

281. But he who shall take away the water of a tank, made in ancient times, or shall cut off the supply of water, must be made to pay the first (or lowest) amercement.

282. But he who, except in a case of extreme necessity, drops filth on the king's high-road, shall pay two karshapanas and immediately remove (that) filth.

283. But a person in urgent necessity, an aged man, a pregnant woman, or a child, shall be reprimanded and clean the (place); that is a settled rule.

284. All physicians who treat (their patients) wrongly (shall pay) a fine; in the case of animals, the first (or lowest); in the case of human beings, the middlemost (amercement).

285. He who destroys a bridge, the flag (of a temple or royal palace), a pole, or images, shall repair the whole (damage) and pay five hundred (panas).

286. For adulterating unadulterated commodities, and for breaking gems or for improperly boring (them), the fine is the first (or lowest) amercement.

287. But that man who behaves dishonestly to honest (customers) or cheats in his prices, shall be fined in the first or in the middlemost amercement.

288. Let him place all prisons near a high-road, where the suffering and disfigured offenders can be seen.

289. Him who destroys the wall (of a town), or fills up the ditch (round a town), or breaks a (town)- gate, he shall instantly banish.

290. For all incantations intended to destroy life, for magic rites with roots (practised by persons) not related (to him against whom they are directed), and for various kinds of sorcery, a fine of two hundred (panas) shall be inflicted.

291. He who sells (for seed-corn that which is) not seed-corn, he who takes up seed (already sown), and he who destroys a boundary (-mark), shall be punished by mutilation.

292. But the king shall cause a goldsmith who behaves dishonestly, the most nocuous of all the thorns, to be cut to pieces with razors.

293. For the theft of agricultural implements, of arms and of medicines, let the king award punishment, taking into account the time (of the offence) and the use (of the object).

294. The king and his minister, his capital, his realm, his treasury, his army, and his ally are the seven constituent parts (of a kingdom); (hence) a kingdom is said to have seven limbs (anga).

295. But let him know (that) among these seven constituent parts of a kingdom (which have been enumerated) in due order, each earlier (named) is more important and (its destruction) the greater calamity.

296. Yet in a kingdom containing seven constituent parts, which is upheld like the triple staff (of an ascetic), there is no (single part) more important (than the others), by reason of the importance of the qualities of each for the others.

297. For each part is particularly qualified for (the accomplishment of) certain objects, (and thus) each is declared to be the most important for that particular purpose which is effected by its means.

298. By spies, by a (pretended) display of energy, and by carrying out (various) undertakings, let the king constantly ascertain his own and his enemy's strength;

299. Moreover, all calamities and vices; afterwards, when he has fully considered their relative importance, let him begin his operations.

300. (Though he be) ever so much tired (by repeated failures), let him begin his operations again and again; for fortune greatly favours the man who (strenuously) exerts himself in his undertakings.

301. The various ways in which a king behaves (resemble) the Krita, Treta, Dvapara, and Kali ages; hence the king is identified with the ages (of the world).

302. Sleeping he represents the Kali (or iron age), waking the Dvapara (or brazen) age, ready to act the Treta (or silver age), but moving (actively) the Krita (or golden) age.

303. Let the king emulate the energetic action of Indra, of the Sun, of the Wind, of Yama, of Varuna, of the Moon, of the Fire, and of the Earth.

304. As Indra sends copious rain during the four months of the rainy season, even so let the king, taking upon himself the office of Indra, shower benefits on his kingdom.

305. As the Sun during eight months (imperceptibly) draws up the water with his rays, even so let him gradually draw his taxes from his kingdom; for that is the office in which he resembles the Sun.

306. As the Wind moves (everywhere), entering (in the shape of the vital air) all created beings, even so let him penetrate (everywhere) through his spies; that is the office in which he resembles the Wind.

307. As Yama at the appointed time subjects to his rule both friends and foes, even so all subjects must be controlled by the king; that is the office in which he resembles Yama.

308. As (a sinner) is seen bound with ropes by Varuna, even so let him punish the wicked; that is his office in which he resembles Varuna.

309. He is a king, taking upon himself the office of the Moon, whose (appearance) his subjects (greet with as great joy) as men feel on seeing the full moon.

310. (If) he is ardent in wrath against criminals and endowed with brilliant energy, and destroys wicked vassals, then his character is said (to resemble) that of Fire.

311. As the Earth supports all created beings equally, thus (a king) who supports all his subjects, (takes upon himself) the office of the Earth.

312. Employing these and other means, the king shall, ever untired, restrain thieves both in his own dominions and in (those of) others.

313. Let him not, though fallen into the deepest distress, provoke Brahmanas to anger; for they, when angered, could instantly destroy him together with his army and his vehicles.

314. Who could escape destruction, when he provokes to anger those (men), by whom the fire was made to consume all things, by whom the (water of the) ocean was made undrinkable, and by whom the moon was made to wane and to increase again?

315. Who could prosper, while he injures those (men) who provoked to anger, could create other worlds and other guardians of the world, and deprive the gods of their divine station?

316. What man, desirous of life, would injure them to whose support the (three) worlds and the gods ever owe their existence, and whose wealth is the Veda?

317. A Brahmana, be he ignorant or learned, is a great divinity, just as the fire, whether carried forth (for the performance of a burnt-oblation) or not carried forth, is a great divinity.

318. The brilliant fire is not contaminated even in burial-places, and, when presented with oblations (of butter) at sacrifices, it again increases mightily.

319. Thus, though Brahmanas employ themselves in all (sorts of) mean occupations, they must be honoured in every way; for (each of) them is a very great deity.

320. When the Kshatriyas become in any way overbearing towards the Brahmanas, the Brahmanas themselves shall duly restrain them; for the Kshatriyas sprang from the Brahmanas.

321. Fire sprang from water, Kshatriyas from Brahmanas, iron from stone; the all-penetrating force of those (three) has no effect on that whence they were produced.

322. Kshatriyas prosper not without Brahmanas, Brahmanas prosper not without Kshatriyas; Brahmanas and Kshatriyas, being closely united, prosper in this (world) and in the next.

323. But (a king who feels his end drawing nigh) shall bestow all his wealth, accumulated from fines, on Brahmanas, make over his kingdom to his son, and then seek death in battle.

324. Thus conducting himself (and) ever intent on (discharging) his royal duties, a king shall order all his servants (to work) for the good of his people.

325. Thus the eternal law concerning the duties of a king has been fully declared; know that the following rules apply in (due) order to the duties of Vaisyas and Sudras.

326. After a Vaisya has received the sacraments and has taken a wife, he shall be always attentive to the business whereby he may subsist and to (that of) tending cattle.

327. For when the Lord of creatures (Pragapati) created cattle, he made them over to the Vaisya; to the Brahmana, and to the king he entrusted all created beings.

328. A Vaisya must never (conceive this) wish, I will not keep cattle; and if a Vaisya is willing (to keep them), they must never be kept by (men of) other (castes).

329. (A Vaisya) must know the respective value of gems, of pearls, of coral, of metals, of (cloth) made of thread, of perfumes, and of condiments.

330. He must be acquainted with the (manner of) sowing of seeds, and of the good and bad qualities of fields, and he must perfectly know all measures and weights.

331. Moreover, the excellence and defects of commodities, the advantages and disadvantages of (different) countries, the (probable) profit and loss on merchandise, and the means of properly rearing cattle.

332. He must be acquainted with the (proper), wages of servants, with the various languages of men, with the manner of keeping goods, and (the rules of) purchase and sale.

333. Let him exert himself to the utmost in order to increase his property in a righteous manner, and let him zealously give food to all created beings.

334. But to serve Brahmanas (who are) learned in the Vedas, householders, and famous (for virtue) is the highest duty of a Sudra, which leads to beatitude.

335. (A Sudra who is) pure, the servant of his betters, gentle in his speech, and free from pride, and always seeks a refuge with Brahmanas, attains (in his next life) a higher caste.

336. The excellent law for the conduct of the (four) castes (varna), (when they are) not in distress, has been thus promulgated; now hear in order their (several duties) in times of distress.

HINDUISM

TEXT 5. KALI

Who is Kali? Why is she so popular?

Please turn to your reading glossary at the end of your workbook for unknown vocabulary.

Text Five

Kali

From *Classical Hindu Mythology: A Reader in the Sanskrit Puranas,* edited and mandated by Cornelia Dimmitt and J. A. B. van Buitenen, pp. 238-240. Reprinted by permission of Temple University Press. 1978 by Temple University. All Rights Reserved.

The Birth of Kali and the Final Battle

As they had been commanded, the Daityas, led by Canda and Munda, formed a fourfold army and sallied forth, their weapons raised aloft. They saw the goddess, smiling slightly, positioned on her lion atop the great golden peak of a mighty mountain. When they saw her, they made zealous efforts to seize her, while other demons from the battle approached her with bows and swords drawn. Then Ambika became violently angry with her enemies, her face growing black as ink with rage. Suddenly there issued forth from between her eyebrows Kali, with protruding fangs, carrying a sword and a noose, with a mottled, skull-topped staff, adorned with a necklace of human skulls, covered with a tiger-skin, gruesome with shriveled flesh. Her mouth gaping wide, her lolling tongue terrifying, her eyes red and sunken, she filled the whole of space with her howling. Attacking and killing the mighty demons, she devoured the armed force of the enemies of the gods. Seizing with one hand the elephants with their back-riders, drivers, warriors and bells, she hurled them into her maw. In the same way she chewed up warriors with their horses, harlots and charioteers, grinding them up most horribly with her teeth. One she grabbed by the hair of the head, another by the nape of the neck, another she trod underfoot while another she crushed against her chest. The mighty striking and throwing weapons loosed by those demons she caught in her mouth and pulverised in fury. She ravaged the entire army of powerful evil-souled Asuras; some she devoured while others she trampled; some were slain by the sword, others bashed by her skull-topped club, while other demons went to perdition crushed by the sharp points of her teeth.

Seeing the sudden demise of the whole Daitya army, Canda rushed to attack that most horrendous goddess Kali. The great demon covered the terrible-eyed goddess with a shower of arrows while Munda hurled discuses by the thousands. Caught in her mouth, those weapons shone like myriad orbs of the sun entering the belly of the clouds. Then howling horribly, Kali laughed aloud malevolently, her maw gaping wide, her fangs glittering, awful to behold. Astride her huge lion, the goddess rushed against Canda; grabbing his head by the hair, she decapitated him with her sword. When he saw Canda dead, Munda attacked, but she threw him too to the ground, stabbing him with her sword in rage. Seeing both Canda and the mighty Munda felled, the remains of the army fled in all directions, overcome with fear.

Grabbing the heads of the two demons, Kali approached Candikä and shrieked, cackling with fierce, demoniac laughter, "I offer you Canda and Munda as the grand victims in the sacrifice of battle. Now you yourself will kill Sumbha and Nisumbha!" Witnessing this presentation of the two great Asuras, the eminent Candika spoke graciously to Kali, "Since you have captured Canda and Munda and have brought them to me, O goddess, you will be known as Camunda!" . . .

So speaking, the honorable goddess Candikä of fierce mettle vanished on the spot before the eyes of the gods. And all the gods, their enemies felled, performed their tasks without harassment and enjoyed their shares of the sacrifices. When Sumbha, enemy of the gods, world-destroyer, of mighty

Text Five: **KALI**

power and valor, had been slain in battle and the most valiant Nisumbha had been crushed, the rest of the Daityas went to the netherworld.

In such a way, then, does the divine goddess, although eternal, take birth again and again to protect creation. This world is deluded by her; it is begotten by her; it is she who gives knowledge when prayed to and prosperity when pleased. By Mahäkali is this entire egg of Brahma pervaded, lord of men. At the awful time of dissolution she takes on the form of Mahämari, the great destructress of the world. She is also its unborn source; eternal, she sustains creatures in time. As Laksmi, or Good Fortune, she bestows wealth on men's homes in times of prosperity. In times of disaster she appears as Misfortune for their annihilation. When the goddess is praised and worshiped with flowers, incense, perfume and other gifts, she gives wealth, sons, a mind set upon Dharma, and happiness to all mankind.

Buddhism

Buddha at Seoraksan National Park, South Korea

Photo Courtesy Anne Clay

Sinheungsa Temple, Korea

Photo Courtesy Anne Clay

The Guardians of Sinheungsa Temple, Korea

Part 1: RELIGIONS ORIGINATING IN SOUTHEAST ASIA: THE MYTH OF LIBERATION

BUDDHISM

Dharma
- Buddhists use term "dharma" to refer to their religion *teachings of the Budda*
- Norm, that which is true
- Way of life and thought
- + refers specifically to teachings of Gautama Buddha

Buddhism, a Nontheistic Religion. Why?
- No personal God
- No creator God
- No unchanging reality
- No belief in Hindu Brahman
- Buddha = human being who attained full enlightenment through meditation

✱ men of Kshitria cast wear big earrings = long eartubes

Time and Place of Emergence
- Northeast India (today's Nepal)
- 6th century BCE
- Spread to Southeast and East Asia
- 12th century CE declined in India (after Muslim invasion)

Axis Age (6th century BCE)
- Turning century in history of India
- Religious system controlled by Brahmins + Aryan caste system met resistance
- Emergence of Buddhism and Jainism

Varna = caste, color
nir vana = moksha
ahimsa = non-violence

Buddhism and Jainism— Commonalities
- Originated in India —
- Liberation of self from suffering
- Sprang from Kshatriya caste
- Denied saving efficacy of Vedas
- Denied Vedic ritual observances
- Challenged Brahmin priesthood

✱ Buddhism rejects varna

Influence of Indian Thought
Did founder of Buddhism intend to begin new religion?

YES!
Early Buddhist literature shows that Buddhism rejected
- Vedas
- Vedic practice
- Vedic reliance on priests

- Caste system
- Gender and social limitations
- Belief in any permanent spiritual reality

+ no Brahman (no permenance) in Buddhism   *+ no Atman! (anatman)*

Elements of Indian thought are still visible
- Notion of ahimsa (non harm)
- Notion of rebirth called samsara — *gods are also subjected to*
- Notion of karma (actions and consequences of actions)
- Moksha = nirvana in Buddhism (release from suffering and inner peace beyond consciousness)
  ↳ only human beings can experience

Internal Divisions
- 1. Theravada ("The Way of the Elders")
- 2. Mahayana ("Large Vehicle")

Theravada
- Called Hinayana by Mahayana Buddhists (Hina = small) [derogatory term]
- In basic Indian worldview
  − "River" = cycle of rebirth
  − Far bank of the river = liberation from the cycle
- Each person must row to opposite shore in small raft that holds only that person
- Buddha had no external assistance

Theravada
Shakya= Budda's clan   *↳ South of Tropics Budda*   *ONE guide – Siddartha Gutama or Shakyamuni ↳ enlightenment*

The surest way to reach enlightenment
- Most conservative
- Sri Lanka (formerly Ceylon)
- Stresses ideal of reaching nirvana through detachment and meditation
- Life of monk offers sure path to nirvana
- Buddha was above all a man *= awakened one*
- Many lay people spend some period of life in monastic discipline

= attend sangha or monastery

Most Important Missionary of Theravada Buddhism:
King Ashoka of Mauryan Empire   *— Responsible for spread of Hinduism beyond India*
- 3rd century BCE (Northern India)
- Renounced violence after conquering most of India and converted to Buddhism
- Condemned slaughter of animals
- Sent missionaries beyond India, in particular Sri Lanka + Central Asia

Mahayana
- "Large vehicle of raft" (Maha = large; yana = means)
- A large vessel, with a pilot, carries many persons to liberation
- Reached China through Central Asia on silk routes

Mahayana
- Mainly China, Korea, and Japan
- Enlightenment is possibility for everyone (NOT just for monks)
- Buddha has almost divine character
- Emphasis on his wonders and miracles
- There are many other Buddhas, enlightened beings who can help each generation
- Everyone is potential Buddha *emphasizes salvation for all*

Place and Numbers
- About 350 million (= number of Protestant Christians)
- Fourth largest world religion after Christianity, Islam, and Hinduism
- Over 98 percent live in Asia
- 62 percent are Mahayana followers (north of tropics)
- 38 percent are Theravada followers (south of tropics)

Name of very first Buddhist Scriptures Tripitaka.

Buddhists are majority in
- Sri Lanka
- Myanmar (formerly Burma)
- Thailand
- Laos
- Cambodia
- Japan

Siddhartha Gautama (6th century BCE)
- Born in northern India at Lumbini grove, about 100 miles from Benares
- Gautama (family name) was from Shakya clan
- In Chinese, he is known as Shakyamuni (sage of Shakyas)
- Miraculous birth
- Father made sure that Gautama would be raised in luxury
- Moved through Brahmanic (Hindu) steps as student and then as householder

Tree of enlightenment = Bodhi Tree

Four Passing Sights
- Sorrowful old man
- Man racked by illness
- Corpse on funeral pyre
- Monk, calmly walking in yellow robe

Great Renunciation
- Gautama = sannyasin
- He studied with famous Brahmin teachers
- Disturbed by priests' animal sacrifices
- Why try to atone for misdeeds by destroying life?
- During six years, he pursued asceticism to attain moksha
- But no release or spiritual fulfillment

most significant result of karma (both Hinduism & Buddhism) - rebirth

Enlightenment
- Practiced a form of meditation that did not cause such bodily pain
- Under Bodhi tree (tree of enlightenment) he became a Buddha
- Buddha = "awakened one" = enlightened being
- Realized cause of suffering (DESIRE) and means for ending it (STOP CRAVING)

Deer Park Sermon at Sarnath
- Taught five ascetics
  - Four Noble Truths about suffering
  - Eightfold Path for liberation from suffering
- Middle path = path between two extremes
  - Brahmins who practiced Vedic rituals in temples and homes (too worldly)
  - Wandering ascetics (too much suffering)

Formation of Order of Buddhist Monks and Nuns
- Sangha = literally "community" or "assembly"
- Laymen of good families (brahmins, kshatriya) and his own family joined
- Buddha traveled in northern India
- Made many converts among men of all castes

What about women?
- First Buddha denied women access to sangha
- Women's presence would bring improper sexual activity
- Buddha's aunt and stepmother organized first group of women ascetics

} Theravada Buddhism

Buddha Said Yes to Female Sangha!
- Revolutionary. Women can achieve enlightenment!
- Separate monastic orders for men and women
- But number of regulations placed on women's behavior was DOUBLE

Buddha's Death
- Died quietly near Varanasi at age of 80
- Buddha's Teachings or Dharma
- Dharma = total sum of Buddhist teachings about how to view world and how to live properly
- Buddha did not write down his teachings
- Passed on in various languages
- Pali, a language related to Sanskrit

Buddha, the Healer of Suffering
- What are symptoms?
- What causes suffering?
- Can anything be done about patient's distress?
- What is treatment?

Four Noble Truths in Deer Park of Sarnath

- Life is suffering (dukkha)
- Cause of suffering is desire (tanha)
  - This desire makes us believe that there is something permanent in life
- There is release from suffering
- Way to find release is to follow Eightfold Path

Eightfold Path

1. Right View
2. Right Aim
3. Right Speech
4. Right Action
5. Right Living
6. Right Effort
7. Right Mindfulness
8. Right Concentration

1+2 = Wisdom (Bodhi Tree)

3+ 4+5 = morality

6 + 7+8 = meditation

7th step = meditation = Dhyana

★Chan & Zen come from dyana

How could the Buddha make the claim that his method was superior to other paths he had experienced himself?

Hindu Beliefs and the Buddha

- For Hindus, all living beings possess an immutable Self or soul (Atman)
- For the Buddha, there is no self or no permanent identity (anatman)

Anatman, Revolutionary Concept

- No separate, permanent, or immortal self
- Human being = a composite of constantly changing states of being (skandhas in Sanskrit)

Skandhas ("aggregates") *— states of being*

1. Body
2. Perception
3. Feelings
4. Predispositions, generated by past existences *— consciousness*
5. Reasoning
- Each skandha is in permanent flux

Consciousness is NOT soul

What holds these forces together?

- Karma
- Accounts for seeming permanence of the skandhas
- When hold of karma disappears, all skandhas will dissipate

consciousness is a process subject to change; soul is permanent

☞ when law of karma disappears, forces dissipate

What a Buddhist strives for is the recognition of

- Suffering
- Impermanence
- Anatman (no self)

nothing to cling to (Shunyata)

what is left is emptiness (Shunyata)

Chain of Causation
- Every event depends on a cause
- Central cause is karma – our acts of will
- These acts (good or bad) influence our personality-developing process
- After death, process continues
- Candle metaphor

Gods
- = Humans
- Imperfect and impermanent
- Finite, subject to death and rebirth
- Need to be reborn as human beings to experience enlightenment

stuck in samsara

Goal of Buddhist practice
- To escape "the chain of causation" and attain nirvana
- Nirvana = extinguishing of a flame from lack of fuel
- Nirvana = cessation of all conditioned thoughts, that is karma

What allows law of karma to be effective?
- Desire
- The only way to end suffering is to end all cravings
- A passion-free life has NO karmic consequences

Nirvana
- "Quietude of heart"
- Deathless, peaceful, unchanging state that cannot be described
- Possible to reach enlightenment during one's lifetime
- No more rebirth (caste does not matter)

Early Development of Buddhism
- Buddhist monks spread across the Gangetic plain
- Several conferences of monks on monastic orthopraxy

Tripitaka ("three baskets")
- First Buddhist scriptures
- Written down in India about 80 BCE on palm leaves and stored in baskets
- Divided according to their subject into 3 groups
- In Pali language

Three sections
- Vinaya Pitaka or "the basket of disciplinary regulations" (monastic guidelines: rules on begging, eating, relations between monks and lay people)
- Sutta Pitaka or "the basket of Discourses" (basic teachings of the Buddha in form of dialogue or sermon)
- Abidhamma Pitaka or "the basket of higher philosophy" (analysis of the nature of existence)

Theravada Buddhism: The Way of the Elders
- Vada = the way
- Thera = elders

Main Characteristics
- Conservative and traditional
- Study of Tripitaka
- Buddha was just a man (cannot help or intervene in human world)
- GOAL is to imitate Buddha in monasticism or asceticism + to become an ARHAT ("perfect being," "worthy") , i.e. a person who has reached nirvana through own effort

Can the Buddha help others reach Nirvana?
- NO
- Salvation is through self-effort rather than through intervention of heavenly beings
- Monk must achieve nirvana for himself in own solitary meditation

Practice
- Meditation exercises
- Breathing exercises
- Let emotions pass away without attachment
- Mind detaches itself from likes and dislikes

Goal of a Theravadin Buddhist
- Become an arhat ("perfect being," "worthy"), a person who has reached nirvana through own effort
- Glorification of example of the monk – bhikshu
- Monks imitate way of the Buddha

What about lay people?
- Lay people build up merit, so in later life they may have better chance to become enlightened
- By supporting the monks through their offering
- Doing good works
- Spending some period of life in monastic discipline

Monasteries
- Center of village life
- Run schools
- Meditation centers
- Medical clinics
- Care for stray animals

What about women?
- About 1000 years ago, orders of nuns disappeared in Theravadin countries
- There are now attempts to revive fully ordained orders of nuns

Lay Devotional Practices
- People give alms and food to the monks
- They venerate relics thought to be from Buddha (it can be a tooth, a tiny bone chip, a begging bowl)

Stupas
- Shrine in shape of a dome
- Contains sacred relics of Buddha or remains of famous monks
- Marks sacred sites
- Built by the laity as act of special merit

Why Make Offerings to the Shrines?
- Purpose is NOT to worship the Buddha
- The Buddha was just a man
- Purpose is
  - To pay respect to ideas of Buddhahood and Nirvana
  - To dedicate oneself to the quest for spiritual liberation

Mahayana Buddhism: The "Big Vehicle"
Principal form of Buddhism in China, Korea, and Japan

Spread of Mahayana Buddhism into China
- Entered China through Central Asia in 1st century CE
- Gained prominence in 7th century CE
- First Chinese rejected Theravada Buddhism
- WHY?
- Chinese ancestor worship made essential the continuation of male heirs

Why did Mahayana Buddhism Spread Successfully?
- Allowed many pre-Buddhist beliefs and practices to survive
- Indigenous gods became heavenly Buddhas
- Recognizes that people find themselves at different stages of spiritual maturity

Mahayana Buddhism spread
- To Korea through China, 4th century CE
- To Japan through Korea, 6th century
  - In competition with Shinto
  - Buddhism brought aspects of Chinese culture, writing, literature, and art
- To Tibet through Nepal, 7th century
  - In competition with Bon (indigenous animistic religion)
  - Large monasteries established by Indian monks

Mahayana Buddhist Texts of India
- Most written in Sanskrit during first five centuries CE
- Later freely translated into Chinese and Tibetan

"Lotus Sutra"— 100 BCE-100 CE?
- Most popular
- Contains sayings of the Buddha
- Reveals that historical Buddha is but a manifestation of the real Buddha
- Real Buddha = Cosmic Buddha who wants to show compassion for all beings
- Came to earth in form of man because he loved mankind and wished to help
- Buddha did not die

Buddhism = can't replace wish w/ another higher wish (ie wish for nirvana)

☆ all people can become Buddha

Main Goal of Mahayana Buddhism
- To become like the Buddha by seeking enlightenment for the sake of saving others
- We are not called just to individual liberation but to save all

= become Bodhisattva

Mahayana Goal – Theravada Goal
- In Theravada, goal is to become an ARHAT ("perfect being," "worthy")
- In Mahayana, goal is to become a BODHISATTVA

Bodhisattva
- Literally = "a being intended for enlightenment" or "future Buddha"
- Postponed entrance to nirvana in order to help other beings
- Bodhisattvas accumulate store of merit that they can share with others

3 Major Concepts of Mahayana Buddhism
- TRIKAYA
- KARUNA — *compassion for all + liberation for all*
- SHUNYATA

TRIKAYA or the Mahayana Cosmos
Three Bodies or Aspects of the Buddha *in Lotus Sutra*
1. THE COSMIC BODY or nature of the Buddha
2. THE HEAVENLY BODY of the Buddha
- Dhyani Buddhas (Contemplative Buddhas) *– est. own kingdom w/ good karma* *enagh*
  - Amitabha Buddha *– land of Bliss, originally prince*
- Bodhisattvas *– human being, taken vow*
  - Avalokiteshvara
3. THE BODY OF THE BUDDHA or earthly manifestation of the Buddha (Siddartha)

↳ Historical Buddha

Does NOT apply to Theravada

Bodhisattva in Theravada and Mahayana Buddhism
- Theravada = future Buddha
- Mahayana = saviors + primary objects of devotion
- Serve humanity by offering
  – compassionate intervention
  – means to salvation

LOTUS SUTRA= main book of mahayana buddhism

How do You Become a Bodhisattva?

- Any person is potentially a bodhisattva
- It takes many lives to become one
- Should develop spiritual insight and take Great Vow of Compassion for all living beings

The Bodhisattva Path— Avalokiteshvara

- Most popular bodhisattva
- Bodhisattva of Compassion (KARUNA)
  – "The Lord Who Looks Down from Above"
- Can shift form
  – Female Guanyin ("hears all cries") in China
  – Female Kannon in Japan
- Chenrizi in Tibet (Dalai Lama is Chenrizi's incarnation)

Dalai lama

Shunyata

- Emptiness (of any permanent individual essence)
- Lack of distinction of all things
- Indian philosopher Nagarjuna (2nd-3rd century CE)
- Everything is in constant change
- Even the teachings of the Buddha + samsara + nirvana are products of mental construction
- To join cosmic Buddha, one needs to free oneself from ALL mental constructs

Still Unclear?

- Everything becomes zero. There is nothing to cling to.
- Reality can be experienced directly without hindrance (without words or mind constructs)
- + You can be compassionate without attachment

Major Mahayana Schools in China and Japan

- Pure Land Schools
- Meditative Schools
- Rationalist Schools
- Esoteric or Mystery Schools
- Political-Social School

Pure Land Schools

- Jing-tu in China or Jodo in Japan
- Faith in Amitaba Buddha and his Western paradise (not works)
- Appeal to common people = They do not demand meditation, ceremony, scripture study or even literacy
- Devout repetition of his name are all sufficient to enter Amitabha's paradise

Meditative School

Chan (in Chinese) or Zen (in Japanese) comes from Dhyana
  – meditation
  – seventh step of Noble Eightfold Path

ZAZEN – seated position of meditation

KOAN – word puzzle the answer is beyond words

Think in a different way

Tibetan Buddhism

FOUNDER = Bodhidharma (500 CE)

(Bodhi Tree of enlightenment)

- Indian monk
- Shocked Chinese emperor
- Studying sacred Buddhist scriptures and building monasteries are worthless acts
- Reading, works, rituals <u>are of little merit</u>
- Mind-to-mind direct transmission of enlightenment with no dependence on words

Main Characteristics

- Goal = immediate enlightenment such as Gautama achieved under Bo-tree after meditation
- Salvation = private, personal experience
- Every individual has nature of the Buddha
- Doctrine of shunyata (= emptiness – that is emptiness of any permanent individual essence)

compassion
10,000 arms

Guanyin – female
avalokiteshvara

Kannon – Japanease name

Chenrizi = same

Enlightenment

- Sudden
- Brings awareness of unity of oneself with universe
- No duality between oneself and the world, the Buddha and I
- All are the Buddha

Meditation techniques

- Goal = stop distinguishing, separating, defining, analyzing, and describing
- Seated meditation (zazen)
- Word puzzles (koan)
- Manual labor in kitchen and garden

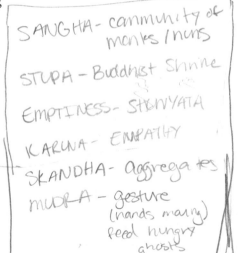

SANGHA – community of monks / nuns

STUPA – Buddhist Shrine

EMPTINESS – SHUNYATA

KARUNA – EMPATHY

SKANDHA – aggregates

MUDRA – gesture (hands many) feed hungry ghosts

Transmission of Knowledge

- From master to disciple
- Mind to mind
- Private sessions with master

Great Influence on Japanese Culture

- Code of behavior of the samurai warrior
- Serving of tea
  – Reveals Tathata, the "thatness of life," its unconditioned reality
- Ink calligraphy and painting
- Haiku poetry (short poem of three lines)
- Garden design
- Flower arrangement

TENDAI RATIONALIST SCHOOL

empty present

past → future

- Tian-tai in China or Tendai in Japan
- Rejection of Meditative Schools
- Equal weight given to meditation and study
- In China, tried to reconcile Theravada and Mahayana paths
- In Japan, the Tendai school made Buddhism a Japanese religion

Focus on Pure Land, Zen, Tibet Buddhism

TENDAI RATIONALIST SCHOOL
- Too many Buddhist texts (confusing)
- They look contradictory
- Order is necessary
- Categorized all teachings of Buddha as a ladder of steps leading to Enlightenment

SHINGON SCHOOL or Esoteric or Mystery schools
= Mystical School
- Shingon in Japanese (9th century CE)
- Founder: a monk named Kukai
- Strongly mystical
- Possible to attain Buddha-hood in this life
- All phenomena of universe = manifestations of the "body, voice, and mind" of Buddha Vairocana, also known as Dainichi (Buddha of Ultimate knowledge)

Buddha Vairocana, also known as Dainichi
- Solar Buddha or Buddha of Ultimate Knowledge
- Gautama Buddha is his historical earthly manifestation

GOAL = BE ONE WITH SOLAR BUDDHA

Nature of the Esoteric School
- Elitist
- Master is necessary
- Devotees need to ascend a ladder of ten spiritual (intellectual and moral) degrees

NICHIREN (Sun Lotus) SCHOOL

= Political-Social School
- Japanese National School
- Founded in 13th century CE
- Founder: young monk who called himself Nichiren

Nichiren
- Called for a return to Lotus Sutra
- Nichiren = earthly manifestation of Jogyo, a bodhisattva
- Rejected teachings of Pure Land Schools
- Addressed the evils of the present world (corruption of the authorities)

Rituals
- Chant "Nam myoho renge kyo" ("Hail to the wonderful truth of the Lotus Sutra!")
- Why?
- To connect with divine power of universe
- To activate Buddha nature
- To lead to moral uplift of individual and society

Missionary and Political Buddhism

- If Japanese carry the truth Nichiren taught to the world, the world will find peace
- 30 percent of Japanese Buddhists are in Nichiren tradition
- Organize long peace walks
- Peace Pagodas arose in U.S. and Europe

Tibetan Buddhism: Vajrayana Buddhism (The Tantric School) ("Diamond Vehicle" or "Vehicle of the Lightning Bolt")

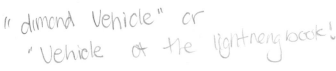

Historical Development

- Unique elements
  - Pre-Buddhist Tibetan religion (Bon religion)
  - Indian Mahayana (Tantric) Buddhism
- Buddhism was late in coming to Tibet
- Entered in 7th century CE but strong opposition
- Took firmer root in 8th century

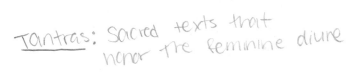

Bon = Animism and Shamanism

- Animism = sees all elements of nature as being filled with spirits
- Shaman = human being who contacts and attempts to manipulate the power of spirits for group
- Bon = "murmuring spells"
- Belief in demons was incorporated from Bon animism
- Demons became guardians of Dharma

Prayer Wheels in Bon Religion and Buddhism

- In Bon religion, they drove off demons
- In Buddhism, they contain carved mantras
- These mantras invoke help of Avalokiteshvara (Chenrizi) in developing compassion (= being less self-centered)

Tantrism

- Refers to "unorthodox" movements of Hinduism, Jainism, and Buddhism
- Invites human males and females to experience, through disciplined sexual energy, cosmic forces
- Cosmic reality is understood as interplay of male and female forces

Tantric Manuals in Hinduism

- Discussions between Shiva and his consorts
- Include dialogues about ritual, discipline, and meditation

Buddhist Tantric School

- Originated in India but took root in Tibet
- Padma-Sambhava from India brought the Buddhist teaching called Vajrayana ("Diamond" or "Thunderbolt Vehicle") [late 8th century]

Buddhist Tantric School
- Buddhas and bodhisattvas are provided with spouses and consorts
- Union of male and female Buddhas is thought to overcome duality of life present in world
- In sexual union, nonduality and nothingness (shunyata) can be experienced momentarily
- There is erasure of distinction between male and female

Male and Female Buddhas
- Male Buddhas = dynamic, active
- Female Buddhas = contemplative and wise
- Together they represent union of wisdom and compassion
- This union is key to enlightenment

Buddhist Pantheon
- 5 celestial self-born (dhyani) Buddhas (among them, Amitabha), with one at each of the cardinal directions and one in the center (Vairocana)
- Are all paired off and have Buddha offspring
- All emerge from the Adi-Buddha, the Buddha essence

Savior Beings under Feminine Names
- Tara, consort of Avalokiteshvara
- Emanation of Amitabha
- Brought Buddha Gautama into existence
- Feminine principle of wisdom or higher insight

many eyes on her body, she can see everything

Goal of Worship
- Identify oneself with Buddhas and consorts
- How?
  - By fasting
  - Meditation on mandalas, visual aids
  - Repetition of mantras
  - Visual evocation

Objects of Meditation
- Mandalas (chart-like representations of the Cosmic Buddha)
- Thangkas (Thankas) = paintings on cloth of the Buddhas

Recipe for Enlightenment
1. Begin identifying yourself with the Buddha on Thangka
2. Tap his or her energies
3. Find yourself at center of mandala
4. Let your ego dissolve itself into emptiness (shunyata)
5. You are finally liberated from ego attachment

Result: Vajrayana Experience
(Vajra = Thunderbolt)
- One's identity is merged with the Buddhas
- This leads to the Vajrayana experience
- Enlightenment comes like a thunderbolt (vajra)

Lamas
- One who is superior
- Teachers   *= teacher*
- Until 14th century could take a spouse
- Abbots of monasteries = hereditary position

Reaction: the Yellow Hat School
- 14th century
- Stricter monastic discipline
- No meat, less alcohol, more praying, and reintroduction of celibacy

Problem
- Abbots had no sons
- New theory arose
- Abbots of monasteries = incarnations of the bodhisattva Avalokiteshvara (Chenrizi)
- After their deaths, were reborn in another human form

Search for New Abbot
- Goal: find a young child, born forty-nine days after the abbot's death
- Child had to
  – demonstrate clear familiarity with abbot's belongings
  – have magical marks of abbot on his body
- Child taken from his family, raised in the monastery, and installed as abbot

Historical Development
- Yellow Hat school spread to Mongolia and Siberia, in Russia
- 16th century, Grand Lama of the monastery at Lhasa (the incarnation of Avalokita) acquired title of Dalai Lama
- Dalai = "ocean" of wisdom
- 17th century Dalai Lama = temporal and religious leader of Tibet
- One-fifth of the population lived in monasteries

Tenzin Gyatzo
- Present Dalai Lama
- Chinese took control of Tibet in 1951
- 1959 Chinese destroyed monasteries in Tibet and Mongolia
- Dalai Lama fled to northern India, Dharamsala
- Dharamsala = center for preservation of Tibetan culture

mandala = chart like representation of cosmic Budda
Tangkasz paintings on a cloth of the Buddahs

Bardo Thodol

- "The between state in which there is liberation through hearing"
- Most famous Buddhist text
- In the West, known as "Tibetan Book of the Dead"
- Focuses on
  - Liberation of person during the 49-day period between moment of death and next incarnation
  - This period is the "bardo" – "the time between"

EXTRA NOTES

Amitaba is represented w/ hands together
representing meditation

amitaba
to someone sitting in hair up

Avalokiteshuara
- most popular bodhisattva
- probably, "The Lord who looks down from above"
- can shift form
    > = Guanyin "hears all cries" in China — female, multiple arms
      = Kannon in Japan
      = Chenrizi in Tibet - dali lama reincarnation of

Vairocana   - four heads
Buddha of Ultimate knowledge   or   Solar Buddha
                                       (Dainichi in Japanese)

Guan Yin   1,000 arms

Mitreya Buddha of the future
         overweight, joyful

Manjustri - Boddhisva of knowledge
            uses sword to fight ignorance

BUDDHISM

BUDDHISM: The Middle Way of Compassion

1. Retell the story of the Buddha (Prince Siddhartha Gautama). Where and when was he born? What was his social background? What did fortune-tellers predict about his future life? How was Gautama raised? Why did he leave home? What kind of life did he lead? What happened under the Bo tree?

2. What is the Buddhist middle way?

3. What is karma? How did Buddha see the cycle of rebirth?

4. What is the end of suffering?

5. What happened in the famous Deer Park at Sarnath?

6. What are the Four Noble truths?

7. What are the components of the Eightfold Path?

8. What is the Tripitaka?

9. What is thangka painting?

10. What is a stupa?

11. How many people in the world are Buddhists?

12. What are the two main branches of Buddhism?

13. Who follows Theravada Buddhism? What does this word mean?

14. What is the sangha?

15. How do Theravada Buddhists view the Buddha?

16. How do lay people gain merit in Theravada Buddhism?

17. Where is Mahayana Buddhism practiced? What does the word Mahayana mean?

18. How do Mahayana Buddhists view the Buddha?

19. Do Mahayana Buddhists believe in supernatural Buddhas?

20. How are people saved in Mahayana Buddhism?

21. What happens when Buddhists turn prayer wheels?

22. In Nepal how do Hindus view the Buddha?

23. Who is Amitabha Buddha? What did he create? What is the purpose of this place?

24. What kind of life do Zen Buddhists have?

25. Where do you find the Tantric School of Buddhism? What are its main characteristics?

26. What does it mean to be a Buddhist?

THE PURE LAND SCHOOL OF MAHAYANA BUDDHISM

To the Land of Bliss

1. Where does the film take place?

    maht Emil – 8w china

2. What effect did the Chinese Cultural Revolution (1966-1976) have on the practice of Buddhism?

3. Describe the funerary rituals performed on behalf of the abbot.

4. How did Shakyamuni view life and death?

    as a happy event

5. What did the Buddha seek?

6. What happens after death?

7. What is Buddha nature?

8. What is the significance of "Releasing the Burning Mouths"?

    feed/nourish hungry ghosts

9. What do mourners do? What is the purpose of their chanting?

    Chant – forms a cosmic bond w/ master
    focus on "good"

10. Do Buddhists believe in the soul?

11. What defines an individual?

conesciousness

12. What happens to consciousness after death?

— a transitional body — ug finds where
— 7 days 2nd trans body   its rebon

13. Is the old man certain about what will happen to the abbot after death? Why or why not?

14. Who is Amitabha?

Buddha
    infinite light/life

15. Describe the Land of Bliss. How do you get there? Is it far away? Is it describable? Is going to the Land of Bliss automatic?

one-hundred -billion
            buddha lands away

depends on good karma

16. What are the obstacles to reaching the Land of Bliss? How can one overcome such obstacles?

bad karma
  — evil relms

17. How do the mourners talk about their master? Are there many Buddhas and bodhisattvas in the world?

18. What is done to the body?

19. What does the master do after his death?

20. What happens to the relics?

TIBETAN Buddhism: Tantra of Gyüto

1. What is a mandala?

2. What is unique about the Tibetan monks' throat singing?

3. When and where was the monastery of Gyüto founded?

4. Why did the Gyüto College move to India?

5. How are children trained in Tantra?

6. Describe the daily life of the monks.

7. What happens to the mandala during ceremonies?

8. What was the name of the pre-Buddhist religion of Tibet?

9. What did the Indian Buddhist teacher Padmasambhava do for Tibet? When did he do it?

10. What role did the monasteries play in the history of Buddhism?

11. When did the Chinese Communists invade Tibet?

12. How was the Dalai Lama inaugurated in 1958?

13. Where did the Dalai Lama go in 1959? Why?

BUDDHISM

TEXT 6. SACRED BIOGRAPHY OF THE BUDDHA SHAKYAMUNI

1. What supernatural elements do you see in the Buddha's life story as presented here by the 1st-century Indian poet Ashvaghosba?

2. Based on this story, what can you tell of the religious culture into which the Buddha was born? Do you think Buddhism was created from scratch or was it an innovation based on earlier practices and beliefs?

3. What does it mean to be enlightened? How is enlightenment described in this text?

Please turn to your reading glossary at the end of your workbook for unknown vocabulary.

Text Six
Sacred Biography Of The Buddha Shakyamuni

1. THE BIRTH OF THE BODHISATTVA

There lived once upon a time a king of the Shakyas, a scion of the solar race, whose name was Shuddhodana. He was pure in conduct, and beloved of the Shakyas like the autumn-moon. He had a wife, splendid, beautiful, and steadfast, who was called the Great Maya, from her resemblance to Maya the Goddess. These two tasted of love's delights, and one day she conceived the fruit of her womb, but without any defilement, in the same way in which knowledge joined to trance bears fruit. Just before her conception she had a dream. A white king elephant seemed to enter her body, but without causing her any pain. So Maya, queen of that god-like king, bore in her womb the glory of his dynasty. But she remained free from the fatigues, depressions, and fancies which usually accompany pregnancies. Pure herself, she longed to withdraw into the pure forest, in the loneliness of which she could practise trance. She set her heart on going to Lumbini, a delightful grove, with trees of every kind, like the grove of Citraratha in Indra's Paradise. She asked the king to accompany her, and so they left the city, and went to that glorious grove.

When the queen noticed that the time of her delivery was approaching, she went to a couch overspread with an awning, thousands of waiting-women looking on with joy in their hearts. The propitious, constellation of Pushya shone brightly when a son was born to the queen, for the weal of the world. He came out of his mother's side, without causing her pain or injury. His birth was as miraculous as that of Aurva, Prithu, Mandhatri, and Kakshivat, heroes of old who were born respectively from the thigh, from the hand, the head or the armpit. So he issued from the womb as befits a Buddha. He did not enter the world in the usual manner, and he appeared like one descended from the sky. And since he had for many aeons been engaged in the practice of meditation, he now was born in full awareness, and not thoughtless and bewildered as other people are. When born, he was so lustrous and steadfast that it appeared as if the young sun had come down to earth. And yet, when people gazed at his dazzling brilliance, he held their eyes like the moon. His limbs shone with the radiant hue of precious gold, and lit up the space all around. Instantly he walked seven steps, firmly and with long strides. In that he was like the constellation of the Seven Seers. With the bearing of a lion he surveyed the four quarters, and spoke these words full of meaning for the future: 'For enlightenment I was born, for the good of all that lives. This is the last time that I have been born into this world of becoming.'

2. ASITA'S VISIT

Then Asita, the great seer, came to the palace of the ruler of the Shakyas, thirsting for the true Dharma. He knew of the birth of him who would put an end to birth, for in his trance he had perceived the miraculous signs which had attended it. In wonderment he looked upon the wondrous royal babe, and noticed that the soles of his feet were marked with wheels, that his fingers and toes were joined by webs, that a circle of soft down grew between his eyebrows, and that his testicles were withdrawn like those of an elephant. Lying on his nurse's lap the child seemed to Asita to be like Skanda, son of Agni, on the lap of his divine mother. With tears flickering on his eyelashes the seer sighed, and looked up to the highest heaven.

He then explained his agitation to the king in these words: 'It is not for him that I am perturbed, but I am alarmed because disappointed for myself. For the time has come when I must pass away, just when he is born who shall discover the extinction of birth, which is so hard to win. Uninterested in worldly affairs he will give up his kingdom. By strenuous efforts he will win that which is truly real. His gnosis will blaze forth like the sun, and remove the darkness of delusion from this world. The world is carried away in distress on the flooded river of suffering, which the foam of disease over-sprays, which has old age for its surge and rushes along with the violent rush of death: across this river he will ferry the world with the mighty boat of gnosis. The stream of his most excellent Dharma shall flow along with the current of wisdom, banked in by firm morality, cooled by Transic concentration, and holy works shall cover it like melodious ducks: the world of the living, tormented with the thirst of its cravings, will drink from this stream. To those who are tormented with pains and hemmed in by their worldly concerns, who are lost in the desert tracks of Samson, he shall proclaim the path which leads to salvation, as to travellers who have lost their way. Creatures are scorched by the fire of greed, which feeds on sense-objects as its fuel: he will refresh them with the rain of the Dharma, which is copious like the rain from a mighty cloud when the summer's burning heat is over. With the irresistible hammer of the most excellent true Dharma he will break down the door which imprisons living beings with the bolt of craving and the panels of dark delusion, and thus he will enable them to escape. The world is entangled in the snares of self-delusion, it is overwhelmed by suffering, it has no refuge: after he has won full enlightenment this boy, then. a king of Dharma, will free the world from its bonds.

'You, O king, have no reason to grieve for him. In this world of men we should grieve for those only who cannot bear this perfect Dharma, usually either because they are too deluded, or too intoxicated with sensuous pleasures. I myself fall short of the perfection required, and the final goal still eludes me. Through my proficiency in the trances I can take up my abode in the highest heaven. But even that I must regard as a misfortune, since I shall not be able to hear this Dharma.'

3. THE BODHISATTVA'S YOUTH AND MARRIAGE

Queen Maya could not bear the joy which she felt at the sight of her son's majesty, which equalled that of the wisest seers. So she went to heaven, to dwell there. Her sister, his aunt, then brought up the prince as if he were her own son. And the prince grew up, and became more perfect every day. His childhood passed without serious illness, and in due course he reached maturity. In a few days he acquired the knowledge appropriate to his station in life, which normally it takes years to learn. Since the king of the Shakyas had, however, heard from Asita, the great seer, that the supreme beatitude would be the prince's future goal, he tried to tie him down by sensual pleasures, so that he might not go away into the forest. He selected for him from a family of long-standing unblemished reputation a maiden, Yashodhara by name, chaste and outstanding for her beauty, modesty, and good breeding, a true Goddess of Fortune in the shape of a woman. And the prince, wondrous in his flashing beauty, took his delight with the bride chosen for him by his father, as it is told of Indra and Shad in the Ramayana.

The monarch, however, decided that his son must never see anything that could perturb his mind, and he arranged for him to live in the upper storeys of the palace, without access to the ground. Thus he passed his time in the upper part of the palace, which was as brilliantly white as rain clouds in autumn, and which looked like a mansion of the Gods shifted to the earth. It contained rooms suited to each season, and the melodious music of the female attendants could be heard in them. This palace was as brilliant as that of Shiva on Mount Kailasa. Soft music came from the gold-edged tambourines which the women tapped with their finger-tips, and they danced as beautifully as the choicest heavenly nymphs. They entertained him with soft words, tremulous calls, wanton swayings, sweet laughter, butterfly kisses, and seductive glances. Thus he became a captive of these women who were well versed in the subject of sensuous enjoyment and indefatigable in sexual pleasure. And it did not occur to him to come down from the palace to the ground, just as people who in reward for their virtues live in a palace in heaven are content to remain there, and have no desire to descend to the earth.

In the course of time the fair-bosomed Yashodhara bore to the son of Shuddhodana a son, who was named Rahula. It must be remembered that all the Bodhisattvas, those beings of quite incomparable spirit, must first of all know the taste of the pleasures which the senses can give. Only then, after a son has been born to them, do they depart to the forest. Through the accumulated effects of his past deeds the Bodhisattva possessed in himself the root cause of enlightenment, but he could reach it only after first enjoying the pleasures of the senses.

4. THE AWAKENING

In the course of time the women told him how much they loved the groves near the city, and how delightful they were. So, feeling like an elephant locked up inside a house, he set his heart on making a journey outside the palace. The king heard of the plans of his dearly beloved son, and arranged a pleasure excursion which would be worthy of his own affection and royal dignity, as well as of his son's youth. But he gave orders that all the common folk with any kind of affliction should be kept away from the royal road, because he feared that they might agitate the prince's sensitive mind. Very gently all cripples were driven away, and all those who were crazy, aged, ailing, and the like, and also all wretched beggars. So the royal highway became supremely magnificent.

The citizens jubilantly acclaimed the prince. But the Gods of the Pure Abode, when they saw that everyone was happy as if in Paradise, conjured up the illusion of an *old man*, so as to induce the king's son to leave his home. The prince's charioteer explained to him the meaning of old age. The prince reacted to this news like a bull when a lightning-flash crashes down near him. For his understanding was purified by the noble intentions he had formed in his past lives and by the good deeds he had accumulated over countless aeons. In consequence his lofty soul was shocked to hear of old age. He sighed deeply, shook his head, fixed his gaze on the old man, surveyed the festive multitude, and, deeply perturbed, said to the charioteer: 'So that is how old age destroys indiscriminately the memory, beauty, and strength of all! And yet with such a sight before it the world goes on quite unperturbed. This being so, my son, turn round the horses, and travel back quickly to our palace! How can I delight to walk about in parks when my heart is full of fear of ageing?' So at the bidding of his master's son the charioteer reversed the chariot. And the prince went back into his palace, which now seemed empty to him, as a result of his anxious reflections.

On a second pleasure excursion the same gods created a *man with a diseased body*. When this fact was explained to him, the son of Shuddhodana was dismayed, trembled like the reflection of the moon on rippling water, and in his compassion he uttered these words in a low voice: 'This then is the calamity of disease, which afflicts people! The world sees it, and yet does not lose its confident ways.

Greatly lacking in insight it remains gay under the constant threat of disease. We will not continue this excursion, but go straight back to the palace! Since I have learnt of the danger of illness, my heart is repelled by pleasures and seems to shrink into itself.'

On a third excursion the same gods displayed a *corpse*, which only the prince and his charioteer could see being borne along the road. The charioteer again explained the meaning of this sight to the prince. Courageous though he was, the king's son, on hearing of death, was suddenly filled with dismay. Leaning his shoulder against the top of the chariot rail, he spoke these words in a forceful voice: 'This is the end which has been fixed for all, and yet the world forgets its fears and takes no heed! The hearts of men are surely hardened to fears, for they feel quite at ease even while travelling along the road to the next life. Turn back the chariot! This is no time or place for pleasure excursions. How could an intelligent person pay no heed at a time of disaster, when he knows of his impending destruction?'

5. WITHDRAWAL FROM THE WOMEN

From then onwards the prince withdrew from contact with the women in the palace, and in answer to the reproaches of Udayin, the king's counsellor, he explained his new attitude in the following words: 'It is not that I despise the objects of sense, and I know full well that they make up what we call the "world." But when I consider the impermanence of everything in this world, then I can find no delight in it. Yes, if this triad of old age, illness, and death did not exist, then all this loveliness would surely give me great pleasure. If only this beauty of women were imperishable, then my mind would certainly indulge in the passions, though, of course, they have their faults. But since even women attach no more value to their bodies after old age has drunk them up, to delight in them would clearly be a sign of delusion. If people, doomed to undergo old age, illness, and death, are carefree in their enjoyment with others who are in the same position, they behave like birds and beasts. And when you say that our holy books tell us of gods, sages, and heroes who, though high- minded, were addicted to sensuous passions, then that by itself should give rise to agitation, since they also are now extinct. Successful high-mindedness seems to me incompatible with both extinction and attachment to sensory concerns, and appears to require that one is in full control of oneself. This being so, you will not prevail upon me to devote myself to ignoble sense pleasures, for I am afflicted by ill and it is my lot to become old and to die.

Text Six: **SACRED BIOGRAPHY OF THE BUDDHA SHAKYAMUNI**

How strong and powerful must be your own mind, that in the fleeting pleasures of the senses you find substance! You cling to sense-objects among the most frightful dangers, even while you cannot help seeing all creation on the way to death. By contrast I become frightened and greatly alarmed when I reflect on the dangers of old age, death, and disease. I find neither peace nor contentment, and enjoyment is quite out of the question, for the world looks to me as if ablaze with as all-consuming fire. If a man has once grasped that death is quite inevitable, and if nevertheless greed arises in his heart, then he must surely have an iron will not to weep in this great danger, but to enjoy it.' This discourse indicated that the prince had come to a final decision and had combated the very foundations of sensuous passion. And it was the time of sunset.

6. THE FLIGHT

Even amidst the allure of the finest opportunities for sensuous enjoyment the Shakya king's son felt no contentment, and he could not regain a feeling of safety. He was, in fact, like a lion hit in the region of the heart by an arrow smeared with a potent poison. In the hope that a visit to the forest might bring him some peace, he left his palace with the king's consent, accompanied by as escort of ministers' sons, who were chosen for their reliability and their gift for telling entertaining stories. The prince rode out on the good horse Kanthaka, which looked splendid, for the bells of its bit were of fresh gold and its golden trappings beautiful with waving plumes. The beauties of the landscape and his longing for the forest carried him deep into the countryside. There he saw the soil being ploughed, and its surface, broken with the tracks of the furrows, looked like rippling water. The ploughs had torn up the sprouting grass, scattering tufts of grass here and there, and the land was littered with tiny creatures who had been killed and injured, worms, insects, and the like. The sight of all this grieved the prince as deeply as if he had witnessed the slaughter of his own kinsmen. He observed the ploughmen, saw how they suffered from wind, sun, and dust, and how the oxen were worn down by the labour of drawing. And in the supreme nobility of his mind he performed an act of supreme pity. He then alighted from his horse and walked gently and slowly over the ground, overcome with grief. He reflected on the generation and the passing of all living things, and in his distress he said to himself: 'How pitiful all this!'

His mind longed for solitude, he withdrew from the good friends who walked behind him, and went to a solitary spot at the foot of a rose-apple tree. The tree's lovely leaves were in constant motion, and the ground underneath it salubrious and green like beryl. There he sat down, reflected on the origination and passing away of all that lives, and then he worked on his mind in such a way that, with this theme as a basis, it became stable and concentrated. When he had won through to mental stability, he was suddenly freed from all desire for sense-objects and from cares of any kind. He had reached the first stage of trance, which is calm amidst applied and discursive thinking. In his case it had already at this stage a supramundane purity. He had obtained that concentration of mind which is born of detachment, and is accompanied by the highest rapture and joy, and in this state of trance his mind considered the destiny of the world correctly, as it is: 'Pitiful, indeed, that these people who themselves are helpless and doomed to undergo illness, old age, and destruction, should, in the ignorant blindness of their self-intoxication, show so little respect for others who are likewise victims of old age, disease, and death! But now that I have discerned this supreme Dharma, it would be unworthy and unbecoming if I, who am so constituted, should show no respect for others whose constitution is essentially the same as mine.' When he thus gained insight into the fact that the blemishes of disease, old age, and death vitiate the very core of this world, he lost at the same moment all self-intoxication, which normally arises from pride in one's own strength, youth, and vitality. He now was neither glad nor grieved; all doubt, lassitude, and sleepiness disappeared; sensuous excitements could no longer influence him; and hatred and contempt for others were far from his mind.

7. THE APPARITION OF A MENDICANT

As this understanding, pure and dustless, grew farther in his noble soul, he saw a man glide towards him, who remained invisible to other men, and who appeared in the guise of a *religious mendicant*. The king's son asked him: 'Tell me who you are,' and the answer was: 'O Bull among men, I am a recluse who, terrified by birth and death, have adopted a homeless life to win salvation. Since all that lives is to extinction doomed, salvation from this world is what I wish, and so I search for that most blessed state in which extinction is unknown. Kinsmen and strangers mean the same to me, and greed and hate for all this world of sense have ceased to be. Wherever I may be, that is my home--the root of a tree, a deserted sanctuary, a hill or wood. Possessions I have none, no expectations either. Intent on the supreme goal I wander about, accepting any alms I may receive.' Before the prince's very eyes he then flew up into the sky. For he was a denizen of the heavens, who had seen other Buddhas in the past, and who had come to him in this form so as to remind him of the task before him.

When that being had risen like a bird into the sky, the best of men was elated and amazed. Then and there he intuitively perceived the Dharma, and made plans to leave his palace for the homeless life. And soon after returning to his palace he decided to escape during the night. The gods knew of his intention, and saw to it that the palace doors were open. He descended from the upper part of the palace, looked with disgust upon the women lying about in all kinds of disorderly positions, and unhesitatingly went to the stables in the outermost courtyard. He roused Chandaka, the groom, and ordered him quickly to bring the horse Kanthaka. 'For I want to depart from here today, and win the deathless state!'

8. THE DISMISSAL OF CHANDAKA

They rode off, till they came to a hermitage, where the prince took off his jewels, gave them to Chandaka and dismissed him with this message to his father, king Shuddhodana: 'So that my father's grief may be dispelled, tell him that I have gone to this penance grove for the purpose of putting an end to old age and death, and by no means because I yearn for Paradise, or because I feel no affection for him, or from moody resentment. Since I have left for the homeless life with this end in view, there is no reason why he should grieve for me. Some day in any case all unions must come to an end, however long they may have lasted. It is just because we must reckon with perpetual separation that I am determined to win salvation, for then I shall no more be torn away from my kindred. There is no reason to grieve for me who have left for the homeless life so as to quit all grief. Rather should one grieve over those who greedily cling to those sensuous passions in which all grief is rooted. My father will perhaps say that it was too early for me to leave for the forest. But then there is no such thing as a wrong season for Dharma, our hold on life being so uncertain. This very day therefore I will begin to strive for the highest good--that is my firm resolve! Death confronts me all the time--how do I know how much of life is still at my disposal?'

The charioteer once more tried to dissuade the prince, and received this reply: 'Chandaka, stop this grief over parting from me! All those whom birth estranged from the oneness of Dharma must one day go their separate ways. Even if affection should prevent me from leaving my kinsfolk just now of my own accord, in due course death would tear us

apart, and in that we would have no say. Just think of my mother, who bore me in her womb with great longing and with many pains. Fruitless proves her labour now. What am I now to her, what she to me? Birds settle on a tree for a while, and then go their separate ways again. The meeting of all living beings must likewise inevitably end in their parting. Clouds meet and then they fly apart again, and in the same light I see the union of living beings and their parting. This world passes away, and disappoints all hopes of everlasting attachment. It is therefore unwise to have a sense of ownership for people who are united with us as in a dream--for a short while only, and not in fact. The colouring of their leaves is connate to trees, and yet they must let it go; how much more must this apply to the separation of disparate things! This being so, you had better go away now, and cease, my friend, from grieving! But if your love for me still holds you back, go now to the king, and then return to me. And, please, give this message to the people in Kapilavastu who keep their eyes on me: "Cease to feel affection for him, and bear his unshakeable resolve: 'Either he will extinguish old age and death, and then you shall quickly see him again; or he will go to perdition, because his strength has failed him and he could not achieve his purpose'."

9. THE PRACTICE OF AUSTERITIES

From then onwards the prince led a religious life, and diligently studied the various systems practised among ascetics and yogins. After a time the sage, in search of a lonely retreat, went to live on the bank of the river Nairanjana, the purity of which appealed to that of his own valour. Five mendicants had gone there before him to lead a life of austerity, in scrupulous observance of their religious vows, and proud of their control over the five senses. When the monks saw him there, they waited upon him in their desire for liberation, just as the objects of sense wait upon a lordly man to whom the merits of his past lives have given wealth, and the health to enjoy them. They greeted him reverently, bowed before him, followed his instructions, and placed themselves as pupils under his control, just as the restless senses serve the mind. He, however, embarked on further austerities, and particularly on starvation as the means which seemed most likely to put an end to birth and death. In his desire for quietude he emaciated his body for six years, and carried out a number of strict methods of fasting, very hard for men to endure. At mealtimes he was content with a single jujube fruit, a single sesamum seed, and a single grain of rice--so intent he was on winning the further, the unbounded, shore of Samsara. The bulk of his body was greatly reduced by this self-torture, but by way of compensation his psychic power grew correspondingly more and more. Wasted away though he was, his glory and majesty remained unimpaired, and his sight gladdened the eyes of those who looked upon him. It was as welcome to them as the full moon in autumn to the white lotuses that bloom at night. His fat, flesh, and blood had all gone. Only skin and bone remained. Exhausted though he was, his depth seemed exhausted like that of the ocean itself.

After a time, however, it became clear to him that this kind of excessive self-torture merely wore out his body without any useful result. Impelled both by his dread of becoming and by his longing for Buddhahood, he reasoned as follows: 'This is not the Dharma which leads to dispassion, to enlightenment, to emancipation. That method which some time ago I found under the rose-apple tree, that was more certain in its results. But those meditations cannot be carried out in this weakened condition; therefore I must take steps to increase again the strength of this body. When that is worn down and exhausted by hunger and thirst, the mind in its turn must feel the strain, that mental organ which must reap the fruit. No, inward calm is needed for success! Inward calm cannot be maintained unless physical strength is constantly and intelligently replenished. Only if the body is reasonably nourished can undue strain on the mind be avoided. When the mind is free from strain and is serene, then the faculty of Transic concentration can arise in it. When thought is joined to Transic concentration, then it can advance through the various stages of trance. We can then win the dharmas which finally allow us to gain that highest state, so hard to reach, which is tranquil, ageless, and deathless. And without proper nourishment this procedure is quite impossible.'

10. NANDABALA'S GIFT

His courage was unbroken, but his boundless intellect led him to the decision that from now on again he needed proper food. In preparation for his first meal he went into the Nairanjana river to bathe. Afterwards he slowly and painfully worked his way up the river bank, and the trees on the slope reverently bent low their branches to give him a helping hand. At the instigation of the deities, Nandabala, daughter of the overseer of the cowherds, happened to pass there, her heart bursting with joy. She looked like the foamy blue waters of the Yamuna river, with her blue dress, and her arms covered with blazing white shells. When she saw him,

faith further increased her joy, her lotus eyes opened wide, she prostrated herself before him, and begged him to accept milk-rice from her. He did, and his meal marked the most fruitful moment of her life. For himself, however, he gained the strength to win enlightenment. Now that his body had been nourished, the Sage's bodily frame became fully rounded again. But the five mendicants left him, because they had formed the opinion that he had now quite turned away from the holy life--just as in the Samkhya system the five elements leave the thinking soul once it is liberated. Accompanied only by his resolution, he proceeded to the root of a sacred fig-tree, where the ground was carpeted with green grass. For he was definitely determined to win full enlightenment soon.

The incomparable sound of his footsteps woke Kala, a serpent of high rank, who was as strong as a king elephant. Aware that the great Sage had definitely determined on enlightenment, he uttered this eulogy: 'Your steps, O Sage, resound like thunder reverberating in the earth; the light that issues from your body shines like the sun: No doubt that you today will taste the fruit you so desire! The flocks of blue jays which are whirling round up in the sky show their respect by keeping their right sides towards you; the air is full of gentle breezes: It is quite certain that today you will become a Buddha.'

The Sage thereupon collected fresh grass from a grass cutter, and, on reaching the foot of the auspicious great tree, sat down and made a vow to win enlightenment. He then adopted the cross-legged posture, which is the best of all because so immovable, the limbs being massive like the coils of a sleeping serpent. And he said to himself: 'I shall not change this my position so long as I have not done what I set out to do!' Then the denizens of the heavens felt exceedingly joyous, the herds of beasts, as well as the birds, made no noise at all, and even the trees ceased to rustle when struck by the wind: for the Lord had seated himself with his spirit quite resolved.

11. THE DEFEAT OF MARA

Because the great Sage, the scion of a line of royal seers, had made his vow to win emancipation, and had seated himself in the effort to carry it out, the whole world rejoiced--but Mara, the inveterate foe of the true Dharma, shook with fright. People address him gladly as the God of Love, the one who shoots with flower-arrows, and yet they dread this Mara as the one who rules events connected with a life of passion, as one who hates the very thought of freedom. He had with him his three sons--Hurry, Gaiety, and Sullen Pride--and his three daughters--Discontent, Delight, and Thirst. These asked him why he was so disconcerted in his mind. And he replied to them with these words: 'Look over there at that sage, clad in the armour of determination, with truth and spiritual virtue as his weapons, the arrows of his intellect drawn ready to shoot! He has sat down with the firm intention of conquering my realm. No wonder that my mind is plunged in deep despondency! If he should succeed in overcoming me, and could proclaim to the world the way to final beatitude, then my realm would be empty today, like that of the king of Videha of whom we hear in the Epics that he lost his kingdom because he misconducted himself by carrying off a Brahmin's daughter. But so far he has not yet won the eye of full knowledge. He is still within my sphere of influence. While there is time I therefore will attempt to break his solemn purpose, and throw myself against him like the rush of a swollen river breaking against the embankment!'

But Mara could achieve nothing against the Bodhisattva, and he and his army were defeated, and fled in all directions--their elation gone, their toil rendered fruitless, their rocks, logs, and trees scattered everywhere. They behaved like a hostile army whose commander had been slain in battle. So Mara, defeated, ran away together with his followers. The great seer, free from the dust of passion, victorious over darkness' gloom, had vanquished him. And the moon, like a maiden's gentle smile, lit up the heavens, while a rain of sweet-scented flowers, filled with moisture, fell down on the earth from above.

12. THE ENLIGHTENMENT

Now that he had defeated Mara's violence by his firmness and calm, the Bodhisattva, possessed of great skill in Transic meditation, put himself into trance, intent on discerning both the ultimate reality of things and the final goal of existence. After he had gained complete mastery over all the degrees and kinds of trance:

1. In the *first watch* of the night he recollected the successive series of his former births. 'There was I so and so; that was my name; deceased from there I came here'--in this way he remembered thousands of births, as though living them over again. When he had recalled his own births and deaths in all these various lives of his, the Sage, full of pity, turned his compassionate mind towards other living beings, and he thought to himself: 'Again and again they must leave the people they regard as their own, and must go on elsewhere, and that without ever stopping. Surely this world is unprotected and helpless, and like a wheel it turns round and round.' As he continued steadily to recollect the past thus, he came to the definite conviction that this world of Samsara is as unsubstantial as the pith of a plantain tree.

2. Second to none in valour, he then, in the second watch of the night, acquired the supreme heavenly eye, for he himself was the best of all those who have sight. Thereupon with the perfectly pure heavenly eye he looked upon the entire world, which appeared to him as though reflected in a spotless mirror. He saw that the decease and rebirth of beings depend on whether they have done superior or inferior deeds. And his compassionateness grew still further. It became clear to him that no security can be found in this flood of Samsaric existence, and that the threat of death is ever-present. Beset on all sides, creatures can find no resting place. In this way he surveyed the five places of rebirth with his heavenly eye. And he found nothing substantial in the world of becoming, just as no core of heartwood is found in a plantain tree when its layers are peeled off one by one.

3. Then, as the third watch of that night drew on, the supreme master of trance turned his meditation to the real and essential nature of this world: 'Alas, living beings wear themselves out in vain! Over and over again they are born, they age, die, pass on to a new life, and are reborn! What is more, greed and dark delusion obscure their sight, and they are blind from birth. Greatly apprehensive, they yet do not know how to get out of this great mass of ill.' He then surveyed the twelve links of conditioned co-production, and saw that, beginning with ignorance, they lead to old age and death, and, beginning with the cessation of ignorance, they lead to the cessation of birth, old age, death, and all kinds of ill.

When the great seer had comprehended that where there is no ignorance whatever, there also the karma-formations are stopped--then he had achieved a correct knowledge of all there is to be known, and he stood out in the world as a Buddha. He passed through the eight stages of Transic insight, and quickly reached their highest point. From the summit of the world downwards he could detect no self anywhere. Like the fire, when its fuel is burnt up, he became tranquil. He had reached perfection, and he thought to himself: 'This is the authentic Way on which in the past

Text Six: SACRED BIOGRAPHY OF THE BUDDHA SHAKYAMUNI

so many great seers, who also knew all higher and all lower things, have travelled on to ultimate and real truth. And now I have obtained it!'

4. At that moment, in the *fourth watch* of the night, when dawn broke and all the ghosts that move and those that move not went to rest, the great seer took up the position which knows no more alteration, and the leader of all reached the state of all-knowledge. When, through his Buddhahood, he had cognized this fact, the earth swayed like a woman drunken with wine, the sky shone bright with the Siddhas who appeared in crowds in all the directions, and the mighty drums of thunder resounded through the air. Pleasant breezes blew softly, rain fell from a cloudless sky, flowers and fruits dropped from the trees out of season--in an effort, as it were, to show reverence for him. Mandarava flowers and lotus blossoms, and also water lilies made of gold and beryl, fell from the sky on to the ground near the Shakya sage, so that it looked like a place in the world of the gods. At that moment no one anywhere was angry, ill, or sad; no one did evil, none was proud; the world became quite quiet, as though it had reached full perfection. Joy spread through the ranks of those gods who longed for salvation; joy also spread among those who lived in the regions below. Everywhere the virtuous were strengthened, the influence of Dharma increased, and the world rose from the dirt of the passions and the darkness of ignorance. Filled with joy and wonder at the Sage's work, the seers of the solar race who had been protectors of men, who had been royal seers, who had been great seers, stood in their mansions in the heavens and showed him their reverence. The great seers among the hosts of invisible beings could be heard widely proclaiming his fame. All living things rejoiced and sensed that things went well. Mara alone felt deep displeasure, as though subjected to a sudden fall.

For seven days He dwelt there--his body gave him no trouble, his eyes never dosed, and he looked into his own mind. He thought: 'Here I have found freedom,' and he knew that the longings of his heart had at last come to fulfilment. Now that he had grasped the principle of causation, and finally convinced himself of the lack of self in all that is, he roused himself again from his deep trance, and in his great compassion he surveyed the world with his Buddha-eye, intent on giving it peace. When, however, he saw on the one side the world lost in low views and confused efforts, thickly covered with the dirt of the passions, and saw on the other side the exceeding subtlety of the Dharma of

emancipation, he felt inclined to take no action. But when he weighed up the significance of the pledge to enlighten all beings he had taken in the past, he became again more favourable to the idea of proclaiming the path to Peace. Reflecting in his mind on this question, he also considered that, while some people have a great deal of passion, others have but little. As soon as India and Brahma, the two chiefs of those who dwell in the heavens, had grasped the Sugata's intention to proclaim the path to Peace, they shone brightly and came up to him, the weal of the world their concern. He remained there on his seat, free from all evil and successful in his aim. The most excellent Dharma which he had seen was his most excellent companion. His two visitors gently and reverently spoke to him these words, which were meant for the weal of the world: 'Please do not condemn all those that live as unworthy of such treasure! Oh, please engender pity in your heart for beings in this world! So varied is their endowment, and while some have much passion, others have only very little. Now that you, O Sage, have yourself crossed the ocean of the world of becoming, please rescue also the other living beings who have sunk so deep into suffering! As a generous lord shares his wealth, so may also you bestow your own virtues on others! Most of those who know what for them is good in this world and the next, act only for their own advantage. In the world of men and in heaven it is hard to find anyone who is impelled by concern for the weal of the world.' Having made this request to the great seer, the two gods returned to their celestial abode by the way they had come. And the sage pondered over their words. In consequence he was confirmed in his decision to set the world free.

Then came the time for the alms-round, and the World-Guardians of the four quarters presented the seer with begging-bowls. Gautarna accepted the four; but for the sake of his Dharma he turned them into one. At that time two merchants of a passing caravan came that way. Instigated by a friendly deity, they joyfully saluted the seer, and, elated in their hearts, gave him alms. They were the first to do so.

After that the sage saw that Arada and Udraka Ramaputra were the two people best equipped to grasp the Dharma. But then he saw that both had gone to live among the gods in heaven. His mind thereupon turned to the five mendicants. In order to proclaim the path to Peace, thereby dispelling the darkness of ignorance, just as the rising sun conquers the darkness of night, Gautama betook himself to the blessed city of Kashi, to which Bhimaratha gave his love, and which is adorned with the Varanasi river and with many splendid forests. Then, before he carried out his wish to go into the region of Kashi, the Sage, whose eyes were like those of a bull, and whose gait like that of an elephant in rut, once more fixed his steady gaze on the root of the Bodhi-tree, after he had turned his entire body like an elephant.

13. THE MEETING WITH THE MENDICANT

He had fulfilled his task, and now, calm and majestic, went on alone, though it seemed that a large retinue accompanied him. A mendicant, intent on Dharma, saw him on the road, and in wonderment folded his hands and said to him. "The senses of others are restless like horses, but yours have been tamed. Other beings are passionate, but your passions have ceased. Your form shines like the moon in the night-sky, and you appear to be refreshed by the sweet savour of a wisdom nearly tasted. Your features shine with intellectual power, you have become master over your senses, and you have the eyes of a mighty bull. No doubt that you have achieved your aim. Who then is your teacher, who has taught you this supreme felicity?' But he replied: 'No teacher have I. None need I venerate, and none must I despise. Nirvana have I now obtained, and I am not the same as others are. Quite by myself, you see, have I the Dharma won. Completely have I understood what must be understood, though others failed to understand it. That is the reason why I am a Buddha. The hostile forces of defilement I have vanquished. That is the reason why I should be known as one whose self is calmed. And, having calmed myself, I now am on my way to Varanasi, to work the weal of fellow-beings still oppressed by many ills. There shall I beat the deathless Dharma's drum, unmoved by pride, not tempted by renown. Having myself crossed the ocean of suffering, I must help others to cross it. Freed myself, I must set others free. This is the vow which I made in the past when I saw all that lives in distress.' In reply the mendicant whispered to himself, 'Most remarkable, indeed!' and he decided that it would be better not to stay with the Buddha. He accordingly went his way, although repeatedly he looked back at Him with eyes full of wonderment, and not without some degree of longing desire.

14. THE MEETING WITH THE FIVE MENDICANTS

In due course the Sage saw the city of Kashi, which resembled the interior of a treasury. It lies where the two rivers Bhagirathi and Varanasi meet; and, like a mistress, they hold it in their embrace. Resplendent with majestic power, shining like the sun, he reached the Deer Park. The clusters of trees resounded with the calls of the cuckoos and great seers frequented it. The five mendicants--he of the Kaundinya clan, Mahanaman, Vashpa, Ashvajit, and Bhadrajit--saw him from afar, and said to one another: 'There is our pleasure-loving friend, the mendicant Gautama, who gave up his austerities! When he comes to us, we must certainly not get up to meet him, and he is certainly not worth saluting. People who have broken their vows do not deserve any respect. Of course, if he should wish to talk to us, let us by all means converse with him. For it is unworthy of saintly people to act otherwise towards visitors, whoever they may be.' Although they had thus decided what to do, the mendicants, when the Buddha actually moved towards them, soon went back on their plans. The nearer he came, the weaker was their resistance. One of them took his robe, another with folded hands reached out for his alms-bowl, the third offered him a proper seat, and the two remaining ones presented him with water for his feet. By these manifold tokens of respect they all treated him as their teacher. But, as they did not cease calling him by his family name, the Lord, in his compassion, said to them: 'To an Arhat, worthy of reverence, you should not speak, O mendicants, in the same way as you did formerly, omitting the special veneration due to him! As for myself, praise and contempt are surely the same. But in your own interest you should be warned against behaving in a manner which will bring you harm. It is for the weal of the world that a Buddha has won enlightenment, and the welfare of all that lives has been his aim. But the Dharma is cut off for those who slight their teacher by addressing him with his family name, for that is like showing disrespect for one's parents.' So spoke the great seer, the best of all speakers, filled with compassion. But, led astray by delusion and a deficiency in spiritual solidity, they answered him with a slight smile on their faces: 'Gautama, so far the supreme and most excellent austerities have not led you to an understanding of true reality! Only by them can the goal be achieved, but you dwell in sensuous comfort! What is your ground for saying to us that you have seen the truth?'

15. TURNING THE WHEEL OF DHARMA

Since the mendicants thus refused to believe in the truth found by the Tathagata, He, who knew the path to enlightenment to be different from the practice of austerities, expounded to them the path from his direct knowledge of it: 'Those foolish people who torment themselves, as well as those who have become attached to the domains of the senses, both these should be viewed as faulty in their method, because they are not on the way to deathlessness. These so-called austerities but confuse the mind which is overpowered by the body's exhaustion. In the resulting stupor one can no longer understand the ordinary things of life, how much less the way to the Truth which lies beyond the senses. The minds of those, on the other hand, who are attached to the worthless sense- objects, are overwhelmed by passion and darkening delusion. They lose even the ability to understand the doctrinal treatises, still less can they succeed with the method which by suppressing the passions leads to dispassion. So I have given up both these extremes, and have found another path, a middle way. It leads to the appeasing of all ill, and yet it is free from happiness and joy.'

The Buddha then expounded to the five mendicants the holy eightfold path, and the four holy truths.

'And so I came to the conviction that suffering must be comprehended, its cause given up, its stopping mastered, and this path developed. Now that I have comprehended suffering, have given up its cause, have realized its stopping, and have developed this path--now I can say that my organ of spiritual vision has been opened. As long as I had not seen these four divisions of the holy real truth, so long did I not claim to be emancipated, so long did I not believe I had done what was to be done. But when I had penetrated the holy truths, and had thereby done all that had to be done: then I did claim to be emancipated, then I did see that I had reached my goal.' And when the great seer, full of compassion, had thus proclaimed the Dharma, he of the Kaundinya clan, and hundreds of gods with him, obtained the insight which is pure and free from dust.

16. THE MEETING OF FATHER AND SON

In due course the Buddha went to Kapilavastu, and preached the Dharma to his father. He also displayed to him his proficiency in wonderworking power, thereby making him more ready to receive his Dharma. His father was overjoyed by what he heard, folded his hands, and said to him: 'Wise and fruitful are your deeds, and you have released me from great suffering. Instead of rejoicing at the gift of the earth, which brings nothing but sorrow, I will now rejoice at having so fruitful a son. You were right to go away and give up your prosperous home. It was right of you to have toiled with such great labours. And now it is right of you that you should

have compassion on us, your dear relations, who loved you so dearly, and whom you did leave. For the sake of the world in distress you have trodden the path to supreme reality, which could not be found even by those seers of olden times who were gods or kings. If you had chosen to become a universal monarch, that could have given me no more joy than I have now felt at the sight of your miraculous powers and of your holy Dharma. If you had chosen to remain bound up with the things of this world, you could as a universal monarch have protected mankind. Instead, having conquered the great ills of the Sanasaric world, you have become a Sage who proclaims the Dharma for the weal of all. Your miraculous powers, your mature intellect, your definite escape from the countless perils of the Samsaric world--these have made you into the sovereign master of the world, even without the insignia of royalty. That you could not have done if you had remained among the things of this world, and you would have been truly powerless, how ever much you had thrived as a king.'

17. FURTHER CONVERSIONS

After that the Buddha visited Shravasti, accepted the gift of the Jetavana Grove, admonished king Prasenajit, and exhibited his miraculous powers to confute the disputants of other schools. His miracles caused the people of Shravasti greatly to honour and revere him. He, however, departed from them, and rose in glorious majesty miraculously above the Triple world, reached the heaven of the Thirty-three where his mother dwelt, and there preached the Dharma for her benefit. His cognition enabled the Sage to educate his mother. He passed the rainy season in that heaven, and accepted alms in due form from the king of the gods who inhabit the ether. Then, descending from the world of the Gods, he came down in the region of Samkashya. The Gods, who by his presence had gained spiritual calm, stood in their mansions and followed him with their eyes. And the kings on earth raised their faces to the sky, bowed low, and received him respectfully.

After in heaven he had instructed his mother and those gods who desired to be saved, the Sage travelled over the earth, converting those who were ripe for conversion.
Devadatta, his cousin, and a member of the order of monks, saw His greatness and success, and was offended in his pride. His mind, so proficient in the trances, whirled round in a kind of delirium, he became quite frenzied and did many despicable things. He created a schism in the Sage's community, and the resulting separation further increased his ill-will. It was through him that on Vulture Peak a huge rock rolled down on the Sage with great force, but, though

aimed at Him, it did not hit Him, but broke into two pieces before it could reach Him. On the royal highway he let loose a king elephant who rushed towards the Tatbagata, with a noise like the thundering of the black clouds at the end of the world, and with the force of the wind in the sky on a dark moonless night. So the elephant rushed towards the Lord, murder in his heart, and the people wept and held up their arms. But without hesitating the Lord went on, collected and unmoved, and without any feeling of ill-will. His friendliness made him compassionate towards all that lives, and in addition he was protected, by the gods who with devoted love followed close behind him. So even that great elephant could not touch the Sage, who calmly advanced on his way. The monks who followed the Buddha fled in haste even while the elephant was a long way off. Ananda alone stayed with the Buddha. But when the elephant had come quite near, the Sage's spiritual power soon brought him to his senses, inducing him to lower his body and place his head on the ground, like a mountain, the sides of which have been shattered by a thunderbolt. With the well-formed webbed fingers of his hand, beautiful and soft as a lotus, the Sage stroked the elephant's head, as the moon touches a cloud with its rays. But Devadatta, after he had in his malice done many wicked and evil deeds, fell to the regions below, detested by all alike, whether they were kings or citizens, Brahmins or sages.

19. THE DESIRE FOR DEATH

Years later, the Lord was at Vaisali, on the bank of Markata's pool. He sat there under a tree, in shining majesty. Mara appeared in the grove, and said to him: 'Formerly, on the bank of the Nairanjana river, when I spoke to you immediately after your enlightenment, I said to you, O Sage: "You have done what there was to be done. Now enter the final Nirvana!" But you replied: "I shall not enter the final Nirvana until I have given security to the afflicted and made them get rid of their defilements." Now, however, many have been saved, others desire to be saved, others again will be saved. It is right therefore that now you should enter the final Nirvana.' On hearing these words, the supreme Arhat replied: 'In three months' time I shall enter the final Nirvana. Do not be impatient, and wait a while!' This promise convinced Mara that his heart's desire would soon be fulfilled. Jubilant and exulting, he disappeared.

Tathagatas have the power to live on to the end of the aeon. But the great Seer now entered into a trance with such a force of Yoga, that he gave up the physical life which was

still due to him, and after that he continued to live on in a unique way for a while by the might of his miraculous psychic power. And at the moment that he gave up his claim to live to the end of the aeon, the earth staggered like a drunken woman, and in all directions great firebrands fell from the sky. Indra's thunderbolts flashed unceasingly on all sides, pregnant with fire and accompanied by lightning. Everywhere flames blazed up, as if the end of the world with its universal conflagration had come. Mountain tops toppled down and shed heaps of broken trees. There was the terrible sound of the heavenly drums thundering in the sky, like that of a cavern filled to the brim with wind. During this commotion which affected alike the world of men, the heavens and the sky, the great Sage emerged from his deep trance, and uttered these words: 'Now that I have given up my claim to live up to the end of the aeon, my body must drag itself along by its own power, like a chariot when the axle has been taken out. Together with my future years I have been set free from the bonds of becoming, as a bird which, on hatching, has broken through its shell.'

When Ananda saw the commotion in the world, his hair stood on end, he wondered what it might be, trembled and lost his habitual serenity. He asked the omniscient one, who is experienced in finding causes, for the cause of this event. The Sage replied: This earthquake indicates that I have given up the remaining years of life still due to me. For three months only, reckoned from today, will I sustain my life.' On hearing this Ananda was deeply moved, and his tears flowed, as gum flows from a sandal tree when a mighty elephant breaks it down.

20. THE LEAVE-TAKING FROM VAISA, THE FINAL COUCH, INSTRUCTIONS TO THE MALLAS

Three months later the great Sage turned his entire body round like an elephant, looked at the town of Vaisali, and uttered these words: 'O Vaisali, this is the last time that I see you. For I am now departing for Nirvana!' He then went to Kusinagara, bathed in the river, and gave this order to Ananda: 'Arrange a couch for me between those twin Sal trees! In the course of this night the Tathagata will enter Nirvana!' When Ananda had heard these words, a film of tears spread over his eyes. He arranged the Sage's last resting place, and then amid laments informed him that he had done so. In measured steps the rest of Men walked to his final resting place no more return in store for him, no

Text Six: SACRED BIOGRAPHY OF THE BUDDHA SHAKYAMUNI

further suffering. In full sight of his disciples he lay down on his right side, rested his head on his hand, and put one leg over the other. At that moment the birds uttered no sound, and, as if in trance, they sat with their bodies all relaxed. The winds ceased to move the leaves of the trees, and the trees shed wilted flowers, which came down like tears.

In his compassion the All-knowing, when he lay on his last resting place, said to Ananda, who was deeply disturbed and in tears: 'The time has come for me to enter Nirvana. Go, and tell the Mallas about it. For they will regret it later on if they do not now witness the Nirvana.' Nearly fainting with grief; Ananda obeyed the order, and told the Mallas that the Sage was lying on his final bed.

The Mallas, their faces covered with tears, came along to see the Sage. They paid homage to Him, and then, anguish in their minds, stood around Him. And the Sage spoke to them as follows: 'In the hour of joy it is not proper to grieve. Your despair is quite inappropriate, and you should regain your composure! The goal, so hard to win, which for many aeons I have wished for, now at last it is no longer far away. When that is won--no earth, or water, fire, wind or ether present; unchanging bliss, beyond all objects of the senses, a peace which none can take away, the highest thing there is; and when you hear of that, and know that no becoming mars it, and nothing ever there can pass away--how is there room for grief then in your minds? At Gaya, at the time when I won enlightenment, I got rid of the causes of becoming, which are nothing but a gang of harmful vipers; now the hour comes near when I get rid also of this body, the dwelling place of the acts accumulated in the past. Now that at last this body, which harbours so much ill, is on its way out; now that at last the frightful dangers of becoming are about to be extinct; now that at last I emerge from the vast and endless suffering--is that the time for you to grieve?'

So spoke the Sage of the Shakya tribe, and the thunder of his voice contrasted strangely with the deep calm with which He faced his departure. All the Mallas felt the urge to reply, but it was left to the oldest among them to raise his voice, and to say: 'You all weep, but is there any real cause for grief? We should look upon the Sage as a man who has escaped from a house on fire! Even the gods on high see it like that, how much more so we men! But that this mighty man, that the Tathagata, once He has won Nirvana, will pass beyond our ken--that is what causes us grief! When those who travel in a dreadful wilderness

lose their skilful guide, will they not be deeply disturbed? People look ridiculous when they come away poor from a goldmine; likewise those who have seen the great Teacher and Sage, the All-seeing himself, in his actual person, ought to have some distinctive spiritual achievement to carry away with them!' Folding their hands like sons in the presence of their father, the Maas thus spoke much that was to the point. And the Best of Men, aiming at their welfare and tranquillity, addressed to them these meaningful words: 'It is indeed a fact that salvation cannot come from the mere sight of Me. It demands strenuous efforts in the practice of Yoga. But if someone has thoroughly understood this my Dharma, then he is released from the net of suffering, even though he never cast his eyes on Me. A man must take medicine to be cured; the mere sight of the physician is not enough. Likewise the mere sight of Me enables no one to conquer suffering; he will have to meditate for himself about the gnosis I have communicated. If self-controlled, a man may live away from Me as far as can be; but if he only sees my Dharma then indeed he sees Me also. But if he should neglect to strive in concentrated calm for higher things, then, though he live quite near Me, he is far away from Me. Therefore be energetic, persevere, and try to control your minds! Do good deeds, and try to win mindfulness! For life is continually shaken by many kinds of suffering, as the flame of a lamp by the wind.' In this way the Sage, the Best of All those who live, fortified their minds But still the tears continued to pour from their eyes, and perturbed in their minds they went back to Kusinagara. Each one felt helpless and unprotected, as if crossing the middle of a river all on his own.

21. PARINIRVANA

Thereupon the Buddha turned to his Disciples, and said to them: 'Everything comes to an end, though it may last for an aeon. The hour of parting is bound to come in the end. Now I have done what I could do, both for myself and for others. To stay here would from now on be without any purpose. I have disciplined, in heaven and on earth, all those whom I could discipline, and I have set them in the stream. Hereafter this my Dharma, O monks, shall abide for generations and generations among living beings. Therefore, recognize the true nature of the living world, and do not be anxious; for separation cannot possibly be avoided. Recognize that all that lives is subject to this law; and strive from today onwards that it shall be thus no more! When the light of gnosis has dispelled the darkness of ignorance, when all existence has been seen as without substance, peace ensues when life draws to an end, which seems to cure a long sickness at last. Everything, whether stationary or movable, is bound to perish in the end. Be ye therefore mindful and vigilant! The time for my entry into Nirvana has now arrived! These are my last words!'

Thereupon, supreme in his mastery of the trances, He at that moment entered into the first trance, emerged from it and went on to the second, and so in due order he entered all of them without omitting one. And then, when he had ascended through all the nine stages of meditational attainment, the great Seer reversed the process, and returned again to the first trance. Again he emerged from that, and once more he ascended step by step to the fourth trance. When he emerged from the practice of that, he came face to face with everlasting Peace.

And when the Sage entered Nirvana, the earth quivered like a ship struck by a squall, and firebrands fell from the sky. The heavens were lit up by a preternatural fire, which burned without fuel, without smoke, without being fanned by the wind. Fearsome thunderbolts crashed down on the earth, and violent winds raged in the sky. The moon's light waned, and, in spite of a cloudless sky, an uncanny darkness spread everywhere. The rivers, as if overcome with grief, were filled with boiling water. Beautiful flowers grew out of season on the Sal trees above the Buddha's couch, and the trees bent down over him and showered his golden body with their flowers. Like as many gods the five-headed Nagas stood motionless in the sky, their eyes reddened with grief; their hoods closed and their bodies kept in restraint, and with deep devotion they gazed upon the body of the Sage. But, well-established in the practice of the supreme Dharma, the gathering of the gods round king Vaishravana was not grieved and shed no tears, so great was their attachment to the Dharma. The Gods of the Pure Abode, though they had great reverence for the Great Seer, remained composed, and their minds were unaffected; for they hold the things of this world in the utmost contempt. The kings of the Gandharvas and Nagas, as well as the Yakshas and the Devas who rejoice in the true Dharma--they all stood in the sky, mourning and absorbed in the utmost grief. But Mara's hosts felt that they had obtained their heart's desire. Overjoyed they uttered loud laughs, danced about, hissed like snakes, and triumphantly made a frightful din by beating drums, gongs and tom-toms. And the world, when the Prince of Seers had passed beyond, became like a mountain whose peak has been shattered by a thunderbolt; it became like the sky without the moon, like a pond whose lotuses the frost has withered, or like learning rendered ineffective by lack of wealth.

22. THE RELICS

Those who had not yet got rid of their passions shed tears. Most of the monks lost their composure and felt grief. Those only who had completed the cycle were not shaken out of their composure, for they knew well that it is the nature of things to pass away. In due course the Mallas heard the news. Like cranes pursued by a hawk they quickly streamed forth under the impact of this calamity, and cried in their distress, 'Alas, the Saviour!' In due course the weeping Malin, with their powerful arms, placed the Seer on a priceless bier of ivory inlaid with gold. They then performed the ceremonies which befitted the occasion, and honoured Him with many kinds of charming garlands and with the finest perfumes. After that, with zeal and devotion they all took hold of the bier. Slender maidens, with tinkling anklets and copper-stained finger-nails, held a priceless canopy over it, which was like a cloud white with flashes of lightning. Some of the men held up parasols with white garlands, while others waved white yaks' tails set in gold. To the accompaniment of music the Mallas slowly bore along the bier, their eyes reddened like those of bulls. They left the city through the Naga Gate, crossed the Hiranyavati river, and then moved on to the Mukuta shrine, at the foot of which they raised a pyre. Sweet-scented barks and leaves, aloewood, sandalwood, and cassia they heaped on the pyre, sighing with grief all the time. Finally they placed the Sage's body on it. Three times they tried to light the pyre with a torch, but it refused to burn. This was due to Kashyapa the Great coming along the road, Kashyapa whose mind was meditating pure thoughts. He longed to see the remains of the holy body of the departed Hero, and it was his magical power which prevented the fire from flaring up. But now the monk approached with rapid steps, eager to see his Teacher once more, and immediately he had paid his homage to the Best of Sages the fire blazed up of its own. Soon it had burnt up the Sage's skin, flesh, hair and limbs. But although there was plenty of ghee, fuel, and wind, it could not consume His bones. These were in due time purified with the finest water, and placed in golden pitchers in the city of the Mallas. And the Manes chanted hymns of praise over them: 'These jars now hold the relics great in virtue, as mountains hold their jewelled ore. No fire harms these relics great in virtue; like Brahma's realm when all else is burned up. These bones, His friendliness pervades their tissue; the fire of passion has no strength to burn them; the power of devotion has preserved them; cold though they are, how much they warm our hearts!'

For some days they worshiped the relics in due form and with the utmost devotion. Then, however, one by one, ambassadors from the seven neighbouring kings arrived in the town, asking for a share of the relics. But the Mallas, a proud people and also motivated by their esteem for the relics, refused to surrender any of them. Instead, they were willing to fight. The seven kings, like the seven winds, then came up with great violence against Kusinagara, and their forces were like the current of the flooded Ganges.

Wiser counsels prevailed, and the Mallas devotedly divided into eight parts the relics of Him who had understood Life. One part they kept for themselves. The seven others were handed over to the seven kings, one to each. And these rulers, thus honoured by the Mallas, returned to their own kingdoms, joyful at having achieved their purpose. There, with the appropriate ceremonies, they erected in their capital cities Stupas for the relics of the Seer.

23. THE SCRIPTURES

In due course the five hundred Arhats assembled in Raja-griha, on the slope of one of its five mountains, and there and then they collected the sayings of the great Sage, so that his Dharma might abide. Since it was Ananda who had heard Him speak more often than anyone else, they decided, with the agreement of the wider Buddhist community, to ask him to recite His utterances. The sage from Vaideha then sat down in their midst, and repeated the sermons as they had been spoken by the Best of All speakers. And each one he began with, 'Thus have I heard,' and with a statement of the time, the place, the occasion, and the person addressed. It is in this way that he established in conjunction with the Arhats the Scriptures which contain the Dharma of the great Sage. They have in the past led to Nirvana those who have made the effort fully to master them. They still today help them to Nirvana, and they will continue to do so in the future.

BUDDHISM

TEXT 7. THE PATH TO ENLIGHTENMENT

1. This text is an excerpt from the *Foundations of Mindfulness*, an important sutra of the Theravada canon. Who was this text written for? What was its purpose?

2. How is the human body described in this text? Why do you think this attitude is adopted?

Please turn to your reading glossary at the end of your workbook for unknown vocabulary.

Text Seven

The Path to Enlightenment

Thus have I heard. On one occasion the Blessed One was living in the Kuru country at a town of the Kurus named Kammasadhamma. There he addressed the *bhikkhus* thus: 'Bhikkhus.' 'Venerable sir,' they replied. The Blessed One said this:

Bhikkhus, this is the direct path for the purification of being, for the surmounting of sorrow and lamentation, for the disappearance of pain and grief, for the attainment of the true way, for the realization of *nibbana*--namely, the four foundations of mindfulness.

'What are the four? Here, *bhikkhus*, a *bhikkhu* abides contemplating the body as a body, ardent, fully aware and mindful, having put away covetousness and grief for the world. He abides contemplating feelings as feelings, ardent, fully aware and mindful, having put away covetousness and grief for the world. He abides contemplating mind as mind, ardent, fully aware and mindful, having put away covetousness and grief for the world. He abides contemplating mind-objects as mind-objects, ardent, fully aware and mindful, having put away covetousness and grief for the world.

'And how, *bhikkhus*, does a *bhikkhu* abide contemplating the body as a body? Here a *bhikkhu*, gone to the forest or to the root of a tree or to an empty hut, sits down; having folded his legs crosswise, set his body erect and established in mindfulness in front of him, ever mindful he breathes in, mindful he breathes out. Breathing in long, he understands: "I breathe in long"; or breathing out long, he understands: "I breathe out long."

Breathing in short, he understands: "I breathe in short"; or breathing out short, he understands: "I breathe out short." He trains thus: "I shall breathe in experiencing the whole body [of breath]"; he trains thus: "I shall breathe out experiencing the whole body of breath]." He trains thus: "I shall breathe in tranquillizing the bodily formation"; he trains thus: "I shall breathe out tranquillizing the bodily formation." Just as a skilled turner or his apprentice, when making a long turn, understands: "I make a long turn"; or, when making a short turn, understands: "I make a short turn"; so too, breathing in long, a *bhikkhu* understands: "I breathe in long" . . . he trains thus: "I shall breathe out tranquillizing the bodily formation."

'In this way he abides contemplating the body as a body internally, or he abides contemplating the body as a body externally, or he abides contemplating the body as a body both internally and externally. Or else he abides contemplating in the body its arising factors, or he abides contemplating in the body its vanishing factors, or he abides contemplating in the body both its arising and vanishing factors. Or else mindfulness that "there is a body" is simply established in him to the extent necessary for bare knowledge and mindfulness. And he abides independent, not clinging to anything in the world. That is how a *bhikkhu* abides contemplating the body as a body.

'Again, *bhikkhus*, when walking, a *bhikkhu* understands: "I am walking"; when standing, he understands: "I am standing"; when sitting, he understands: "I am sitting"; when lying down, he understands: "I am lying down"; or he understands accordingly however his body is disposed.

'In this way he abides contemplating the body as a body internally, externally, and both internally and externally . . . And he abides independent, not clinging to anything in the world. That too is how a *bhikkhu* abides contemplating the body as a body.

'Again, *bhikkhus*, a *bhikkhu* is one who acts in full awareness when going forward and returning; who acts in full awareness when looking ahead and looking away; who acts in full awareness when flexing and extending his limbs; who acts in full awareness when wearing his robes and carrying his outer robe and bowl; who acts in full awareness when eating, drinking, consuming food and tasting; who acts in full awareness when defecating and urinating; who acts in full awareness when walking, standing, sitting, falling asleep, waking up, talking and keeping silent.

'In this way he abides contemplating the body as a body internally, externally, both internally and externally . . . And he abides independent, not clinging to anything in the world. That too is how a *bhikkhu* abides contemplating the body as a body.

'Again, *bhikkhus*, a *bhikkhu* reviews this same body up from the soles of the feet and down from the top of the hair, bounded by skin, as full of many kinds of impurity thus: "In this body there are head-hairs, body-hairs, nails, teeth, skin, flesh, sinews, bones, bone-marrow, kidneys, heart, liver, diaphragm, spleen, lungs, large intestines, small intestines, contents of the stomach, faeces, bile, phlegm, pus, blood, sweat, fat, tears, grease, spittle, snot, oil of the joints and urine." Just as though there were a bag with an opening at both ends full of many sorts of grain, such as hill rice, red rice, beans, peas, millet and white rice, and a man with good eyes were to open it and review it thus: "This is hill rice, this is red rice, these are beans, this is millet, this is white rice"; so too, a *bhikkhu* reviews this same body . . . as full of many kinds of impurity thus: "In this body there are head-hairs . . . and urine."

'In this way he contemplates the body as a body internally, externally, and both internally and externally . . . And he abides independent, not clinging to anything in the world. That too is how a *bhikkhu* abides contemplating the body as a body.

'Again, *bhikkhus*, a *bhikkhu* reviews this same body, however it is placed, however disposed, as consisting of elements thus: "In this body there are the earth element, the water element, the fire element and the air element." Just as though a skilled butcher or his apprentice had killed a cow and was seated at the crossroads with it cut up into pieces; so too, a *bhikkhu* reviews this same body . . . as consisting of elements thus: "In this body there are the earth element, the water element, the fire element and the air element."

'In this way he abides contemplating the body as a body internally, externally, and both internally and externally . . . And he abides independent, not clinging to anything in the world. That too is how a *bhikkhu* abides contemplating the body as a body.

'Again, *bhikkhus*, as though he were to see a corpse thrown aside in a charnel ground, one, two, or three days dead, bloated, livid and oozing matter, a *bhikkhu* compares this same body with it thus: "This body too is of the same nature, it will be like that, it is not exempt from that fate."

'In this way he abides contemplating the body as a body internally, externally, and both internally and externally . . . And he abides independent, not clinging to anything in .the world. That too is how a *bhikkhu* abides contemplating the body as a body.

'Again, as though he were to see a corpse thrown aside in a charnel ground, being devoured by crows, hawks, vultures, dogs, jackals, or various kinds of worms, a *bhikkhu* compares this same body with it thus: "This body too is of the same nature, it will be like that, it is not exempt from that fate."

'. . . That too is how a *bhikkhu* abides contemplating the body as a body.

'Again, as though he were to see a corpse thrown aside in a charnel ground, a skeleton with flesh and blood, held together with sinews . . . a fleshless skeleton smeared with blood held together with sinews . . . a skeleton without flesh and blood, held together with sinews . . . disconnected bones scattered in all directions--here a hand-bone, there a foot-bone, here a shin-bone, there a thigh-bone, here a hip-bone, there a backbone, here a rib-bone, there a breast-bone, here an arm-bone, there a shoulder-bone, here a neck-bone, there a jaw-bone, here a tooth, there the skull--a *bhikkhu* compares this same body with it thus: "This body too is of the same nature, it will be like that, it is not exempt from that fate."

'. . . That too is how a *bhikkhu* abides contemplating the body as a body.

'Again, as though he were to see a corpse thrown aside in a charnel ground, bones bleached white, the colour of shells . . . bones heaped up, more than a year old . . . bones rotted and crumbled to dust, a *bhikkhu* compares this same body with it thus: "This body too is of the same nature, it will be like that, it is not exempt from that fate."

'In this way he abides contemplating the body as a body internally, or he abides contemplating the body as a body externally, or he abides contemplating, the body as a body both internally and externally. Or else he abides contemplating in the body its arising factors, or he abides contemplating in the body its vanishing factors, or he abides contemplating in the body both its arising and vanishing factors. Or else mindfulness that "there is a body" is simply established in him to the extent necessary for bare knowledge and mindfulness. And he abides independent, not clinging to anything in the world. That is how a *bhikkhu* abides contemplating the body as a body.' [Instructions on the other three foundations of mindfulness--feelings, mind and mind-objects--follow.]

'*Bhikkhus*, if anyone should develop these four foundations of mindfulness in such a way for seven years, one of two fruits could be expected for him: either final knowledge here and now, or, if there is a trace of clinging left, non-return.

'Let alone seven years, *bhikkhus*. If anyone should develop these four foundations of mindfulness in such a way for six years . . . for five years . . . for three years . . . for two years . . . for one year, one of two fruits could be expected for him: either final knowledge here and now, or, if there is a trace of clinging left, non-return.

'Let alone one year, *bhikkhus*. If anyone should develop these four foundations of mindfulness in such a way for seven months . . . for six months . . . for five months . . . for four months . . . for three months . . . for two months . . . for one month . . . for half a month, one of two fruits could be expected for him: either final knowledge here and now, or, if there is a trace of clinging left, non-return.

'Let alone half a month, *bhikkhus*. If anyone should develop these four foundations of mindfulness in such a way for seven days, one of two fruits could be expected for him: either final knowledge here and now, or, if there is a trace of clinging left, non-return.

'So it was with reference to this that it was said: "*Bhikkhus*, there is a direct path for the purification of beings, for the surmounting of sorrow and lamentation, for the disappearance of pain and grief, for the attainment of the true way, for the realization of *nibbana*--namely the four foundations of mindfulness."'

BUDDHISM

TEXT 8. THE BODHISATTVA VOW

1. This text comes from an important Mahayana work called *Ornament for the Sage's Mind* (11th or 12th century CE). After reading this excerpt, describe briefly what a Bodhisattva is and why, from a Buddhist perspective, one would want to become a Bodhisattva.

2. What does taking the Bodhisattva vow entail? What ethical commandments and proscriptions are involved?

Please turn to your reading glossary at the end of your workbook for unknown vocabulary.

Text Eight

The Bodhisattva Vow

It is certain that sentient beings have not lost the good fortune to abandon the two obstructions. Yet, because they lack a virtuous guide, they are mistakenly attached to things that lack intrinsic existence, and as a result, they do not understand the three thoroughly afflicted things--afflictions such as ignorance, action and birth--before, later or in the middle. They naturally descend into the depths of the well of *samsara*, from the peak of existence to the final Avici. No matter how they rise through toil, they are saddened each day by the suffering of pain and the suffering of change. They are absorbed in actions and afflictions that are like reflections, and they fall, made destitute by momen tary inpermanence and by objects whose foundation is like the reflection of the moon in swiftly moving water.

Due to the power of compassion, *bodhisattvas* who have understood the emptiness of intrinsic nature feel destitute themselves [because sentient beings] are made destitute by impermanence. They wish to attain buddhahood, the cause of the arising of the perfect essence of the ambrosia of the excellent doctrine--antidote to all mistaken conceptions--whose nature is one of friendship to all beings. Inspired by that [wish] and not thinking of themselves, they seek only to benefit others. As a result, they undergo great hardship and become completely exhausted in amassing the collections [of merit and wisdom] over a long time.

It is said, 'Through engaging in hardship, they completely amass the collections over a long time and are certain to attain the state of omniscience.' Therefore, it is said, 'Completely gripped by compassion and great compassion--the root of the qualities of a buddha--the blessed buddhas find omniscience and act for the welfare of all beings.' Therefore it is great compassion alone that causes the blessed ones not to abide in *nirvana*. As [the *Madhyarnakavatara* I.2.] says: 'Just mercy is seen as the seed, as water for growth, and as the ripening to a state of enjoyment for a long time.' The *Pramanavarttika* [11.199] says: 'Those with great mercy act only on behalf of others.'

Furthermore, through becoming constantly familiar with all sentient beings who abide in three realms, it [i.e., compassion] will increase. Thus, through the power of cultivating great compassion, you will promise to rescue all sentient beings, thus creating the aspiration to enlightenment [*bodhicitta*]. 'Because *bodhisattvas*, endowed with great compassion and possessing the lineage of complete, perfect enlightenment, suffer at the suffering of others, Ananda, I say that whoever goes for refuge to the Buddha, *dharma* and *sangha* and correctly maintains and fully protects the five bases of practice [not to kill, steal, lie, engage in sexual misconduct, or use intoxicants], the merit of that virtue is inconceivable and immeasurable. I say that *sravakas* and *pratyekabuddhas*, even to the point of nirvana, are unable to take its measure.' By hearing of such benefits, great joy is created. 'By saying, "I go for refuge until enlightenment to the Buddha, the dharma and the supreme community," one is saying, "Relying on refuge in the form-body, the truth-body and community of irreversible *bodhisattvas*, I will become a complete and perfect buddha; having extricated everyone in this world from suffering, I will place them in complete and perfect buddhahood." With this brief [statement], those of the sharpest faculties create the nature of the *bodhisattva* vow.

"The Bodhisattva Vow" translated by Donald S. Lopez, Jr., from *Munimatalamkara* by *Abhayakaragupta*, in Donald S. Lopez, Jr., Buddhist Scriptures, (London: Penguin Classics, 2004) pp. 389-393. Reprinted by permission of Donald S. Lopez, Jr.

Regarding this vow, beginners and those who follow the customs of laypeople should take the vow from a guru who knows the rite for taking the vow properly. In his absence, one should imagine oneself to be in the presence of the buddhas and *bodhisattvas* and take [the vow]. If it is done in full form, place an image of the *Tathagata* in front, 'Ananda, whosoever, with a mind most clear, makes a *mandala* for the *Tathagata* in the shape of a square or a half-moon, in the shape of a circle or a chariot, will, in accordance with the number [of offerings] become the lord of Kuru in the north, Videha in the east, Godaniya in the west, and Jambudvipa in the south. At death, in accordance with the number, one will be born in the heavens of Thirty-Three, Free from Combat, Joyous and Liking Emanation.' By following such statements in the *Katagara Sutre*; anoint the *mandala* and properly offer the five offerings, 'O Ananda, I will protect completely any sentient beings whosoever who join their palms and make obeisance, saying, "I bow down to the blessed *Tathagata*."' Such benefits are set forth.

Properly create great clarity towards the buddhas and *bodhisattvas* of the ten directions and bow down. Then make a *mandala* and so forth in front of the guru and then humble yourself by sitting or kneeling and joining your palms and then request three times, "Son of good lineage before me, I wish to receive the *bodhisattva* vow. Therefore, if I am worthy to receive it, because of your mercy for me, please bestow the vow of the *bodhisattva's* ethics.' To this, the guru says three times, 'Do you aspire to enlightenment?' 'In my presence, will you receive the foundation of training in the ethics of the *bodhisattvas*?' Promise saying, 'I will maintain them.' Repeat after the guru: 'I beseech the blessed buddhas and *bodhisattvas* gathered from the realms of the ten directions to consider me. I beseech the master to consider me. I, so and so, confess all of the sins, no matter how small, that I have performed, ordered others to perform, or admired, with my body, speech and mind, against the buddhas and *bodhisattvas*, my parents, and other sentient beings, in this lifetime or in another existence. I am aware of them, remember them, and do not conceal them.' Say this three times.

Then say three times: 'I, so-and-so, from this day until the essence of enlightenment, go for refuge to the best of bipeds, the blessed Buddha, endowed with great compassion, the all-knowing, the all-teaching, who has transcended all enemies and all fear, the great being, endowed with an immutable body, endowed with an unsurpassed body. I go for refuge to the *dharma*, the supreme peace of those who are freed

from desire. I go for refuge to the supreme of assemblies, the community of irreversible *Bodhisattvas*.' 'Just as *bodhisattvas* in the past, present, and future create the aspiration to enlightenment and have gone, go, and will go to buddhahood in order to liberate, rescue, and completely protect limitless realms of sentient beings from the sufferings of *sansara* and in order to establish them in the unsurpassed knowledge of omniscience, and just as all the buddhas know and see with the knowledge of a buddha and the eye of a buddha, which is unobstructed, and just as they have understood and continue to understand the reality of phenomena, so I, so-and-so, through this rite, in the presence of the master so-and-so and in the presence of all the buddhas and *bodhisattvas* create the aspiration to unsurpassed, complete, perfect enlightenment.' Say that three times.

'I dedicate the roots of virtue produced from my confession of sins, going for refuge to the three, and creating the aspiration to enlightenment to unsurpassed, complete, perfect enlightenment. In a world without protection, without refuge, without a home, without friends and without a haven, I will be a protector, a refuge, a home, a friend and a haven. I will free all those sentient beings who have not crossed the ocean of existence. I will take completely beyond sorrow those who have not passed completely beyond sorrow by leading them beyond sorrow to the unobstructed *dharmadhatu*. I will quell the suffering of those whose suffering has not been quelled.' Say that three times. 'I, so-and-so, by creating the aspiration to enlightenment in that way, will hold each in the realm of limitless sentient beings to be my mother, father, sister, brother, son, daughter, relative, or half-brother or sister. Holding them in that way, I will begin to multiply roots of virtue to the limit of my ability, my power and my capacity. From this day forward, no matter how small, I will give gifts, guard ethics, enhance patience, work with effort, enter into concentration, analyse with wisdom and study skilful methods, all for the sake of the welfare, benefit and happiness of all sentient beings. I will follow, in accordance with the Mahayana, those endowed with great compassion who, beginning with [the aspiration to] unsurpassed, complete, perfect enlightenment, entered into the great [*bodhisattva*] levels. Therefore, I will train to be a *bodhisattva*. From this day forward, I, called "*bodhisattva*," ask to be cared for by the master.' Say that three times. Thus, in the presence of the image of the *Tathagata*, bow down and ask all the buddhas and *bodhisattvas* to be aware of your earlier dedication of merit, of your holding beings [to be family members], of

Text Eight: THE BODHISATTVA VOW

your amassing of the collections in order to protect them, and of your following of the Mahayana. [The guru] says, 'In my presence, this person has correctly received and holds the vow of the ethics of the *bodhisattva*.'

If you take it yourself without such a guru, leave out, 'I beseech the master to consider me' and in the presence of the master named so-and-so' and [instead of saying, 'From this day forward I, the *bodhisattva* so and so, beseech the master to care for me' say, 'From this day forward I, the *bodhisattva* so-and-so, beseech the blessed buddhas and *bodhisattvas* to care for me.' Immediately upon beseeching them, one is praised by the buddhas and *bodhisattvas*. Think about this constantly in order to increase virtue.

BUDDHISM

TEXT 9. SATOMI MYODO'S AUTOBIOGRAPHY

1. In your opinion, how did Satomi's early life experiences and hardships shape her religious perspective and practice?

2. Who guided Satomi through her religious training? How did that person foster her training?

3. What was Satomi's goal in pursuing her religious vocation? Describe her experience in struggling to achieve it.

4. How would you qualify Satomi's religious practice?

Please turn to your reading glossary at the end of your workbook for unknown vocabulary.

Text Nine

Satomi Myodo's Autobiography

Lies and Deception

When I was young--until the age of twenty or so--I was no good at all. I was a real devil! Why was I like that? Of course this was the result of my karma, but what additionally spurred on that bad karma was, first and foremost, the contradiction between my elementary school's curriculum in ethics and the everyday life of the adults around me. During ethics period in school we were made to listen to all sorts of lectures in "moral education" and were prevailed upon to "be good" and "tell the truth," and so on.

When 1 went home, however, I found lies and deception. One moment a guest would arrive and my parents would say sweet words to his face and play up to him, but when he left, instantly, like a hand turning over, they would bad-mouth and ridicule him. Such events were not unusual. I wondered if this went on only in my home; but no, whatever home, whatever adult--even my respected schoolteacher--all were the same. I didn't know what to make of it. "What is this all about?" I asked myself. "Oh, I get it! As a subject of study, the morality we learn in school is best just drummed into the head, like a recording. But life and morality are two absolutely different things. The reality of everyday life is built on lies." It got to the point where the question of truth and falsehood ceased to enter my mind.

With these attitudes, I entered Girls' High School. I went to the Public Girls' School, which took as its motto "Good Wives and Wise Mothers." Every Monday morning the principal would assemble all the students in the auditorium and give a talk. It was always bound to be scrupulous and exhaustive instruction for the benefit of the future good wives and wise mothers. At the conclusion of the talk he invariably added a word of advice: be careful with members of the opposite sex. According to this advice, the male of the species is nothing but a fearful wild beast with gnashing fangs that will swoop down upon any young girl he fancies. How could a girl concerned with her future prospects sacrifice herself to this beast? Don't be careless! Don't go near them! Don't look them in the face! Such were his stern words.

I absolutely couldn't stand men! A man to me was some kind of disgusting jet-black panther. What was marriage? What was a good wife and wise mother? Wasn't she the prey of that despicable panther? Was there ever such a contradiction? Was there ever a speech so degrading to us? Was he saying that right now men were like wild animals to us, but that later--when we married--they would become blessed, godlike beings on whom we should rely? How absurd! I felt very indignant toward the principal's speeches. At the same time, a fierce resentment blazed up in me toward "them"--those beasts who gobbled up the pure virgins. I was especially disgusted with charming men; I imagined that their charm would cause even greater injury to the virgins. I cursed those men as the bitterest enemy: "I put the evil eye on you! I wish you would drop dead!" My heart's desire was to directly approach this dreadful beast, twist him around my little finger, and toss him over my shoulder. I wanted to deliver a shattering blow.

At that time, my life revolved around the world of literature. After graduation from Girls' High School, I went to Tokyo, dreaming of becoming a writer. I stayed at my uncle's house and became the student of a certain novelist who was famous at the time. But my feelings toward men had not changed. I selected a target, devised a plan of attack, and steadily began to carry it out. My chances of victory were quite good, I thought. "He's bound to fall for it!" I told myself, thinking it would be easy for me to knock him speechless. I had faith in myself.

Climbing Again

But what a mistake! At the critical moment, bang! the bottom fell through. The one whose luck gave out was not he but I: I got pregnant. At that time, unlike now, abortion was a terrible thing. I was afraid of being punished if I had one. My future prospects were pitch black. What could I do? I didn't want to hold on to him just to finish him off. Since things had turned out like this, I no longer cared about his state of mind. He was in love with me, but that was not at issue for me. It was unnecessary even to think of marriage.

My studies meant a lot to me. But I was pregnant. I returned to my parents' home, alone and without purpose. My parents were poor farmers in a mountain village in Hokkaido. I was an only child. My parents' sole desire was to make something of me, with their limited means. To do this, they had sent me to an exclusive girls' school and had even gone so far as to send me to Tokyo to advance their desire. But this parental love had never once gotten through to me and touched my heart.

Meanwhile, I just grew more and more fretful. But since in this case I certainly reaped what I had sowed, I couldn't complain. My parents seemed to have vague suspicions about my extraordinary bodily condition but deliberately avoided referring to it. I wanted to be severely scolded, condemned and thrown out, or told to go kill myself. But I was going to have to be the one to bring the subject up, somehow or other. I too kept silent.

Every day the three of us silently arose, and silently we went to work in the fields. As for me--with my body, which couldn't be more shameful, and my face, which one could hardly bear to look at--I just wanted to crawl into a hole and disappear. Looking like a barrel whose hoops were about to burst, and in a condition of utter despair, I was incapable even of dying. I could do nothing but sit back and watch my shame grow. I felt wretched, miserable, ashen--as if I were traveling alone at night through an endless wilderness, wearily dragging one foot after the other.

One day I went as usual to the fields, working and getting covered with dirt. From a distance, my father urgently called my name. I went to see what he wanted and found Father squatting at the edge of the field, gazing intently at something. A moment passed. I felt a little strange squatting quietly by my father's side. Absently, my eye caught his line, of vision. There was nothing but a single weed growing there. Softly, Father began to speak.

"I've been watching this for some time . . . it's quite interesting. . . . Look! A winged ant is crawling up the weed. It climbs up, little by little . . . it seems to want to reach the top. Oh, it fell! There--it's climbing again! For some time now it's been doing this over and over again." Just as he said, a winged ant was climbing up the weed and falling, falling and climbing up again.

"Here! Climbing again! Look, it must be tired now. When it's tired, it stretches its legs and beats its little wings up and down like that. That's how it restores its energy. Then, when it's rested, it starts climbing again."

Father continued to speak without taking his eyes off the brave little insect. I too inadvertently became intrigued. I stared at it intently for quite a while. Suddenly, it hit me--I understood what my father was getting at! It was unbearable! I quickly got up and left his side. I ran to the shady side of the field where no one could see me and fell down wailing. I cried and cried in anguish.

"Oh, Father, I understand; I really understand! Do you love me so much? I'm so unfilial! Do you still cherish such hope for me, when I am so disgusted with myself? How unworthy I am! But how grateful! I'm sorry! Oh, Father, from now on I promise to be a filial daughter! I promise to make you happy!" I determined to repay my father's love, no matter what. Just then, an iron shackle was broken and at once a broad expanse of light burst upon the world.

Superiority Complex

As I looked back at the mass of immorality I had been, I saw what a gloomy and anxious state of being it was. I couldn't help pitying those who had not yet awakened to sincerity. What a miserable way to live! Somehow or other, I felt, those people must be made to comprehend sincerity. Somehow or other, they must be drawn into its realm. Thus I immediately resolved, "From now on I will dive right into the midst of those people, maintaining sincerity to the end. I'll even die for their sake!"

I was prepared to meet rejection. Ridicule, misunderstanding, abuse, even physical attack--did any of it matter? My mind was made up. "Even into a blazing fire, brandishing the single word *sincerity*--onward!" I believed without a doubt that sincerity could raise the dead. I danced with joy! I felt like running around in circles, shouting, "There is such a thing as sincerity! Honestly there is! Please believe me! I beg you!" But could I get people to believe me?

Certainly there was such a thing as sincerity. I believed in it. "But what is sincerity? What is its true nature?" I asked myself. Though it was fainthearted of me, I knew I couldn't give a definite answer to the question. "I'm no good at that kind of thing. For that you need someone who has mastered the Way and penetrated sincerity. Such a person can give a satisfactory answer to anyone," I thought. To clarify the true nature of sincerity would be the first step in my search for the Way.

I realized that until this time I had been impure and cold-hearted. I had never shed so much as one tear for truth. I had never thought of others nor felt the need to do so. Self-centered and capricious, I had thought I could play with others in any way I wanted. I had thought "honest person" was another term for "great fool." I had cherished the superiority complex of an evil person. I was haughty, but in truth I was an insignificant nobody. The moment I was struck by my father's sincerity, though, I truly turned around 180 degrees.

I gave birth to my elder daughter in December of the year I returned home. The baby's father had come to my home about two months before. The son of a Hokkaido stationmaster, he had gone to Tokyo to study but quit school to come live with me. He was a handsome man, steadfast and pure-hearted. My parents immediately announced the wedding party and invited the people of the village.

My husband did all sorts of unfamiliar work--chopping wood, caring for horses, anything and everything. The next year I gave birth to my second daughter. But even though I was the mother of two children, I didn't feel like a wife to him, and the husband-wife love never developed. I did not want to get a divorce, though. Why? For the sake of the children. I couldn't burden the innocent children with the unhappiness brought on by my immorality. I felt there could be no excuse for making them orphans, come what may. The atmosphere at home, however, began to move in

the opposite direction of these intentions. A chasm was gradually opening up between my husband and my parents. I was in a predicament. If I spoke, I would make the bad feelings between the two sides worse. So I held my peace. Finally, one night, my father and my husband quarreled over an insignificant thing. In the end, my husband stormed out of the house in the middle of the night.

I lived on with my parents in our Hokkaido mountain village, gathering firewood and cultivating the fields. Until now my mental energy had been dissipated in the delusory condition of the sixth consciousness. But starting from the time my husband left and lasting for about two years, my mental condition was in a very strange spiritual stage. Was it some kind of bizarre mysticism? Was it lunacy? Often, while remaining in this same body, I leaped over the world of humanity and ascended to the distant world of beginningless eternity. There I was completely enfolded in the heart of God. I lost my form and became one with God, the solitary Light, which peacefully, truly peacefully, shone out all around. It was indescribable, blissful fulfillment. This condition progressed until I stumbled into the world of absolute nothingness and lapsed into unconsciousness. From this state I again advanced until hallucinations began to appear.

Hallucinating

My first hallucination occurred right after the children's father left me. It was a day in late spring. I say "late spring," but this was the north country and, moreover, a village deep in the mountains. The cuckoo had finally begun to sing and the farmers breathed a sigh of relief, as that was the signal that the last frost had passed. It was planting season. I went, as usual, into the fields. I worked alone.

As I gazed out over the broad expanse of gently sloping mountain fields, brilliant flecks of sunlight sparkled like scattered gold dust. Heat waves shimmered from the surface of the freshly plowed mounds of earth. I had finished a section of the work and was rather tired, so I sat down on a pile of chaff between the fields. In an instant, before I knew what hit me, I fell into a trance.

I don't know how much time passed then, but suddenly, from out of nowhere, I heard a grave voice calling out my name, "Matsuno! Matsuno!" I blinked my eyes open and again heard the voice, saying, "Look over there!"

I peered over suspiciously, and . . . how strange! A moment ago a field of plain dirt had been there, but now the field was bursting with peas in full bloom. I looked more closely and . . . what?! The pea field was crawling with green caterpillars. The rustling sound they made as they devoured the leaves, stems, and flowers made me choke.

"The human world is decimated like this, too!" This was simultaneously the message of the voice and my own intuition.

Then *pop*! In an instant the pea field vanished and the place became a dense forest, "Huh?" I wondered for an instant.

"The roots are already cut"--that voice again!--I strained my ears. . . . "The roots of the rampant evil of this world are already cut in the invisible world. Matsuno, stand up and fight!" This was the stern command.

"I will!" I vowed. "I'll just have to give a push and that'll finish it off!" I danced for joy with my sense of mission. In that moment, I returned to my usual self. The vision vanished; the voice ceased. But the psychological effect continued vividly, guiding me forcibly and casting a definite hue over every aspect of my daily life.

My mind was abnormally strained. I felt a thrill of adventure in embracing this "sacred mystery," as if I were soaring to the peak of a distant, towering mountain. The "sacred mystery" was the "vow to the *kami* that I must not betray. I felt that if so much as one word of this leaked out, the demonic powers would instantly profit, the vow would lose all efficacy and I would plunge headlong into hell!

From then on, I kept seeing these visions and dreams, and at the same time I became so impatient to carry out my vow that I couldn't keep still. I burned with the feeling that I must soon go to Tokyo to proceed with my sworn objective. But I could not formulate a concrete plan to accomplish it:

I came to wonder whether I really needed such a plan. "Anything would be all right; the important thing is to get going. Strike out! Forward! Hup, two, three, four! That's the way! No need to worry about the next moment, just press ahead! Step by step, hurling myself against all obstacles!"

One day I stood before my father and mother and made a formal request. "Please send me to Tokyo again." This was three months after my husband had left home.

"What do you want to do in Tokyo?"

"Study."

"Studying is fine, but what on earth would you study?"

"I can't say."

"Why not?"

I kept silent. I couldn't tell anyone. The divine secret must not be revealed!

My mother burst out, "You probably want to go to your husband's place. Well that's understandable--"

Father broke in, "Well, if you want to go, all right, but I--"

"No, it's not that," I cut him off. I knew what he was going to say. I appreciated his grandmotherly heart, but what was that to the new me?

I advanced one step: "Really, it's selfish, but I'd like to ask you to take care of the children for a little while."

Both parents stared at me in bewilderment for a moment, and then Father asked, "You want to leave both children with us?"

"Yes! Please, will you?"

"We can't do it. Take one along with you!" Father quickly replied.

I was defeated. "All right." There was nothing I could do about it, I thought. "Well, I have one more request." I rallied myself for my second approach.

"Go ahead."

"I need about a hundred yen." This took death-defying courage.

"What would you do with a hundred yen? Thirty yen is plenty. I'll give you that, all right?"

"All right." There was nothing I could do about that either.

Thus, with a nursing child on my back and thirty yen in my pocket, I left immediately for Tokyo. I say thirty yen, but the thirty yen of that day was worth more than ten thousand of today's yen. Anyway, for less than five yen, I was able to go from Sapporo to Ueno Station, Tokyo.

Going Insane

Myodo travels to Tokyo and begins to study philosophy of religion at Toyo University. Her husband's aunt becomes distressed with Myodo because the aunt thinks Myodo is neglecting her baby in order to keep up with schoolwork. Myodo's father comes, assesses the situation, and agrees with the woman. Myodo's baby is taken from her, and Myodo is crushed: "Surely the child cried for my breast, she writes. She composes a poem that denigrates herself while expressing deep longing for her baby, Sumiko:

> This mother is worse than a demon.
> If I die of insanity
> Don't grieve, my Sumiko.

It was several months later, a snowy February night. As I lay on my bed between sleeping and waking, my mind drifted off to a garden with alpine flowers in bloom, the likes of which I had never seen. In a little while, a lacquer-black darkness seemed to fall like a curtain before my eyes. In the midst of this darkness, a huge, round, blood-red flower suddenly burst open. It looked like fireworks bursting in the sky. Just then my whole body was seized by a violent and uncontrollable trembling.

Suddenly, in my delirium, I saw a sword in the ceiling just above where I was lying. It was pointing down at me, piercing through the ceiling boards as if it would drop right onto my windpipe. I saw it as if I were looking through a pane of glass. "It's there to kill me," I thought. "It's the landlady. There's something evil about her. She thinks I suspect something and is afraid I'll expose her. She's scheming with her accomplice to do away with me! But the *kami* will stand by me! I have nothing to fear! I'll fix them --I'll get the jump on them!"

I got up quietly and slipped my coat on over my nightgown. Thus dressed, I escaped from the house through the second-floor window, running from roof to roof. I walked briskly away, letting my bare feet guide me. I was not cold nor was I even chilled. I finally reached a place that I thought was a beach. As I gazed out over the dark surface of the ocean, my thoughts ran like this: "I've got to cross the ocean and get to the Kegon Waterfall at Nikko. In the pool below the waterfall, someone is crying out, 'Life is incomprehensible!' it's the young philosopher Fujimura Misao! He has thrown himself into the water and he hasn't come up yet! I'll jump in and save him!" When, as I believed, I did so, he floated lightly to the surface, though he had been down there a long time.

Suddenly, a voice cried, "Halloooo!"

"Yah! It's the accomplice! The rat!" I was frightened and tried to run away, but that guy grabbed the sleeve of my coat. Spinning around, I slipped out of the coat, leaving it in his hand, and ran away. He chased after me again and grabbed my nightgown. Once more I spun around and left him holding it." Wearing just my underpants, I dashed away as fast as I could. From here and there people came running and surrounded me. I looked and saw that they were all policemen. It was the dead of night. I spent that night in a detention cell and was carried forcibly the next morning in a rickshaw to a mental hospital. I had finally gone insane.

> When I speak
> My lips are cold.
> The autumn wind . . .

Goto-san

One day the nurse came to summon me, saying I had a visitor. When I entered the reception room, I was surprised to see my father standing there alone. He had come all the way from Hokkaido to pick me up. For a moment I was startled and at a loss: must I leave this pleasant hospital and return to the world of corruption? The painful memories of the past that I had utterly forgotten came flooding back all at once. "What an evil woman I am. I abandon my children, separate from my husband, and cause my parents such worry. . . . Was my first insight into sincerity wrong somehow? Was I deluded? What on earth is karma anyway?" Thinking such thoughts, I put my beloved hospital behind me and walked out with my father.

Father abruptly asked, "Well, what do you want to do now?" I had no idea. Unlike before, my mind was all foggy and indecisive. For now, at least, I had no desire to go to school. I suddenly remembered an uncle named Tetsumei on my father's side who was chief priest at a temple in Hakodate.

"Please send me to Tetsumei's."

"Nonsense." Father would not hear of it. He said, as if to himself, "It's no good taking her back to Hokkaido. Maybe I should talk it over with Goto-san." Goto-san was the landlady at the newspaper shop.

Goto-san spoke kindly, "I have an acquaintance who is a master of physiognomy. Go see him and you'll be able to settle on a good plan."

I was soon taken to the home of this so-called master by Goto-san. He gave this appraisal: "By nature, this woman is extremely imitative; therefore, if she were to be an actress, she would certainly succeed. Within that field, if she were to be a *kageki* actress, her success would be all the greater."

Goto-san made up her mind quickly. "Any occupation would do; if you could even be a success, it would be wonderful. If you were successful, you'd make your father very happy. If you were to go to school or something, it would take a long time, and who knows whether or not you would succeed. Why not become an actress instead?"

Father, too, was inclined to go along with this. I was reluctant, but I couldn't help being moved by his ardent parental love and his desire to help me. For me to succeed according to his desire--even if only for a while--would make him happy, and this I wanted very much. "To be sincere is to forget myself and serve others, to abandon all of my own desires and fulfill my father's expectations." Thus I admonished myself. . . .

Receiving the Koan

Myodo becomes a kageki actress and meets with modest success in her profession. Unfortunately, her success does not satisfy her, and she begins to visit temples, seeking out religious teachers. Over the next twenty years, she investigates many different traditions and attends many spiritual meetings but here, as in her professional career, she does not find what she is looking for. Finally, she turns to Zen.

There is a Soto Zen temple in Sapporo called Chuoji Temple. Its chief priest was a renowned monk, proficient in both learning and virtue; soon he was to become abbot of the Soto headquarters temple. Every week at Chuoji, there was a meeting on Zen doctrine with lectures primarily on koans. I had joined this group some time ago. I felt that the priest's learned talks were truly jewels taken from an infinite storehouse. He was far superior to the ordinary religious

person. I was deeply impressed by his sermons and admired the personal character that shone through his words. I occupied a seat at Chuoji for a long time, feeling that under this priest's influence, someday even my cloud of delusion would clear up. I heard talks on koans from the *Mumonkan*, the *Hekigan*, and the *Shoyoroku*. But my mental condition was as usual, and I went around and around in the same old circles. "This won't do!" I thought. Thus, for the first time, I became seriously interested in doing *zazen*.

In the Maruyama district, not far from Sapporo Jinja, there is a Rinzai Zen temple called Zuiryuji. Joten Roshi, then of Zuiganji Temple in Matsushima, was a former resident at Zuiryuji who, I understand, had restored the temple and painted a picture of Bodhidharma. In his day, they say, there were a considerable number of practicing monks there. Every year at the spring and fall equinoxes, Joten Roshi came to Zuiryuji and presided over a week-long *zazen sesshin*. I decided to attend. As I arrived, I saw a large stone signpost inscribed with "Hokkaido Dojo" standing next to the main temple gate. With the idea that this would be the final and decisive battle, I walked through those gates. It was about the time of the start of World War II.

In the room designated as the Zendo, about thirty men and women who appeared to be laypersons were sitting in rows before a statue of the Buddha. All of us received the koan *Mu* from Joten Roshi. I felt that at any moment I could realize awakening and silently and earnestly repeated "*Mu, Mu*" at the bottom of my *hara*. I thought I could surely awaken within the one week. Presently a bell was rung. The participants began to line up in front of the gong and, stiff as I was, I had to go too. So, imitating everyone else, I entered the room. I was completely ignorant of the proper behavior for the room, though. As I bowed to the Roshi, who was sitting inside, I screwed up all the courage in my body and suddenly, from twelve feet away, let out with, "The Mind is the Way!" This was an intuition I had had once when I was doing *misogi*. I thought that this kind of thing was satori.

"Such a theory is all wrong," replied Roshi. "It's not a theory," I thought, though I was unable to reply.

Reaching Saari

Day after day, in this manner, I rushed on blindly. Then, in the last meditation period, I dimly realized how to fix the direction of my mind. With this boost to my self-confidence, I thought, "Great! I'll certainly realize satori by

Text Nine: SATOMI MYODO'S AUTOBIOGRAPHY

the next spring equinox! Then I'll be sure to receive Roshi's endorsement! Satan isn't a very easy thing, though. . . ."

In order to practice meditation, I quickly left my family ("severing all karmic bonds") and moved into a hut attached to the back of that Kannon shrine by the waterfall where, until the previous year, an old charcoal maker had lived. I was accompanied by Chimpe-san, a little dog that the charcoal maker had left behind. Inside, the hut was gloomy. The coarse tatami mats were sooty and laid out loosely, unattached to anything. In a large, built-in hearth in a corner of the room, a jet-black, soot-covered pothook dangled down. While living in this hut with Chimpe-san, helped out with the charcoal making and found work in the fields. Living the most meager of lives, I continued with *zazen*.

At first I felt I would reach satori within a week. Then the spring equinox came and went, then the fall equinox, and the spring equinox repeated, until finally the fifth fall equinox approached. I had still not achieved satori! I didn't intend to meet Roshi personally until I achieved satori; I thought it would be useless. In truth, I thought I would easily attain satori and then meet him. But the more I practiced *zazen*, the less things turned out the way I expected.

"What is this all about?" I asked myself. "It must be because I've got some impurity left in a corner of my heart. The first thing I've got to do is find it and get rid of it." I had probably heard a talk at a temple once about the six perfections." Knowing that one perfection completes the other five perfections, I had made a Hinayana-type giving vow." I had tried to fulfill it, but I thought that at some time I must have fallen short and that that failure must be what was blocking my achievement of satori. Something occurred to me.

I had recently visited Mr. K_____, who had returned not long ago from Manchuria and lived in the neighborhood. Mr. K_____ and his wife were living in a worn-out charcoal kiln that looked like a mud hut. The inside was empty. There were hardly any household goods; of bedding, I could see nothing but two blankets. It was one room without a closet, just like my hut. In this place, and approaching the last month of pregnancy, Mrs. K_____ was sleeping, covered with her blanket, when I visited.

"You must be cold."

"No, we've got a Korean stove," she replied.

The three futon quilts I was using popped into my mind then, and I thought of giving one of them to this woman who would soon be a mother. But when I returned to my hut I felt stingy. In spite of myself, I had hesitated up to that moment.

"This is terrible! I've got to knock out this impure nature once and for all!" I thought. So, quickly adding some old clothes to the futon, I returned with them secretly, late at night, to the K_____s' place.

"Great! Now I'll realize satori! Surely by this equinox satori will open up and--though a little on the late side--I will have to meet Roshi!" I was enthusiastic and, rousing my spirits, I repeated "*Mu, Mu*" doggedly. Thus, at last, the anticipated fall equinox arrived.

But without satori.

Beyond the Spheres

And once again the equinox passed.

And yet, still no satori. Thus it became late fall, and even then I couldn't break through.

"Oh, I'm no good! I can't achieve satori no matter what I do! What deep crimes I must have committed! And what a dunce I am! Maybe I could wipe out my crimes with religious practice, but my stupidity . . . no matter what I do, it isn't going to improve! Why should a stupid creature like me expect to attain a wonderful thing like satori?" A flood of emotions forced their way into my heart. Tears fell from my eyes, and I cried out loud. A spray of rain suddenly hit the small window of my hut. The night deepened.

> I can't die
> With my heart full of longing.
> The autumn rain.

I would have liked to die! But I thought thus: "Even if I die, this suffering won't end." Besides, I'm not the only one; somewhere in this world there may be one or two other dull-witted people like me, suffering like me. Well, I'll keep on living! And, along with people I've never met, I'll probably keep on suffering. But I only hope that I am one of those who will awaken to satori at the end of this life. No, I emphatically do not say 'this life.' Even the next life, or the following one, would be fine. And, all right, it's fine even if I am eternally unable to achieve satori! This is my vow! Now that I have made it, it can never in the future be changed!" Thus I vowed firmly in my heart.

In that moment, my tenacious grasping onto satori was suddenly cut off.

As I thought this, I lost consciousness. I don't know how long I remained unconscious, but I awoke suddenly, as if from a dream. In that moment, strange things began to happen. First--and I admit it was hazy--what seemed like a life-soul made of a gaseous substance spontaneously came into being and swelled up and up until it became, in the next moment, some kind of strange and unknown animal-like creature. Like a monkey climbing up a branch, it ascended quickly and agilely. In a moment it reached the top and bumped its head on the sky. Just then, myself unmistakably became Amenominakanushino-Okami. This went a step beyond the spheres of *kami* possession or "oneness of *kami* and person" that I had hitherto known. In the next moment, the room shrank and the universe was transformed into its essence and appeared at my feet. "Ah! The beginning of the universe--right now! . . . Ah, there is no beginning!"

The next moment, the whole world became a deep blue, glowing and rippling, magnificent whole. "Ah! I gave birth to Buddha and Christ! . . . The unborn, first parent . . . that's me! I gave birth to me! I was what I am before my parents were born!"

These strange, intuitive worlds unfolded instantaneously one after another, as if boldly resolving great issues in huge strokes and with dazzling speed.

"Satori! It's satori! I've awakened! It must be satori!" I snatched Chimpe-san, who was sleeping nearby, up into my arms and walked around the room saying, "Thank you, Chimpe-san! Thank you, Chimpe-san!" I felt as if the whole world had all at once been turned upside down.

> Dew drops, even dust--
> Nothing is unclean.
> The own-nature is pure, the own-nature
> is pure
> Kami and Buddha--
> I've searched for you everywhere.
> But you are here, you are here!

Not-Self

The mental world had stagnated in me for a long time without the slightest stirring. Now it sprang abruptly into life. There is absolutely no comparison between so-called ESP, psychic powers, and so forth, and the special mental phenomena that occurs when one forgets about the world accessible to the senses. The latter is the vivid activity of the total self.

I spent many days dancing gratefully with the joy of one who has come upon a prolific and eternally inexhaustible spring. Still, I wondered if this was the real thing. I wanted to get explicit certification as soon as possible, but Joten Roshi wouldn't be coming until next spring. So I went to see him.

> My unborn parent,
> How dear, how beloved.
> My parent is here!
> My parent is me! Me!

I set out with this and the two *waka* poems in my pocket. Fortunately, I caught the Roshi at the entrance, just as he was going out.

"I met you five years ago at the fall equinox *zazen* meeting," I said, skipping the formalities.

"Is that so?" the Roshi replied, carefully scrutinizing my face. "You've become quite an old woman, haven't you?"

"Yes. You've become quite old, too." The Roshi smiled and stroked the top of his head. I quickly took the sheet of poems out of my pocket and showed it to him. After a moment, the Roshi said, "You've come to quite a good level, but . . ."

"But what haven't I reached yet? And how do I get there?" The Roshi closed his mouth and said nothing.

"I keep hearing that I must cut off all thoughts and become 'not-self,' but are all the things that come up in the mind evil thoughts that must be severed?" I asked.

"Not necessarily."

"But how can you tell the difference between the good and the evil ones?"

One after another, things I wanted to ask came flooding out. But this was just a standing chat with the Roshi, whom I had caught on his way out, and I had to restrain my overabundant questioning. I asked a question on the run: "What's the point of so strenuously repeating '*Mu, Mu*'?"

"Yes, that's just like putting a heavy stone on top of a pickle barrel."

"I get it! The moment you take off that heavy stone, the passions and delusions pop up from the bottom, yelling 'Nyaah!' just like a jack-in-the-box, eh?" I said half to myself.

With the parting words "Yes, that's right," the Roshi left hurriedly. He was quite noncommittal. So was my satori all right or not? Afterward, I went twice to pay a call, but both times I was turned away at the door. With things having come to this pass, the vivid mental life of that time gradually faded; the turning wheels slowed. Simultaneously, my happiness and inspiration cooled and finally were completely extinguished.

I became rather sick and tired of working so hard for satori and wondered, "Isn't the suffering inherent in the three poisons and the passions itself each individual's process of religious practice? Aren't the pain and pleasure of the ten worlds--just as they are--one great state of religious practice? Self-realization or no self-realization, when one considers that all things are always treading the one path of religious practice, it's clear that there is nowhere outside this from which to intervene. It's fine, just as it is! It's precious, just like this! It's wonderful! Such a thing as the 'salvation of all sentient beings' is a lot of uncalled-for meddling!" I felt dispirited and desolate, like still water gradually turning stagnant. "What a strange place you've fallen to!" I thought. "This can't be the right track!" But I did not have the means to get myself out of that place.

The following year, in early February, I went to Zuiganji Temple in Matsushima seeking Joten Roshi's guidance, as I couldn't wait for him to come to Hokkaido. But here, too, it ended in ambiguity because I couldn't express myself adequately and formulate the right questions.

It was the period before the end of the war when food was extremely difficult to get. In the waiting room at the station, below the seat, were the bodies of two people who had starved to death, stretched out and covered with mats.

Starving people, half dead and half alive, were tottering about on both sides of the platform, looking as if they would collapse right then and there. Either they were resigned or their minds were gone, because their faces had carefree expressions as if nothing were wrong at all. "Ah! To collapse and die where you fall! How simple!" I envied those people.

Roshi did not come to Hokkaido for the March equinox. I was desolate. Before long, my wonderful experience sank into the deep shadows of my subconscious. . . .

The Power of Sincerity

When Myodo arrives at Mitaka Convent from Hokkaido she has another setback; the prioress will not admit her. Instead, Myodo visits the Roshi who lives with his wife in Taiheiji, near the convent.

"Please do stay here. The Roshi should be back soon," the Roshi's wife consented cheerfully.

"Thank goodness! Thank you so much!" I thought.

When the Roshi returned, he showed me to the public bath, where I relaxed and unwound. When I left the bath, the Roshi was waiting for me at the entrance. I was very grateful. "What a kind person!" I thought.

I expected to take my leave early the next morning, but Roshi asked, "Why not stay here until things are settled at the convent?" I was happy to hear him say that, but I couldn't help thinking it over. There was no reason to believe I would ever be able to repay this kindness, even partially, and that troubled me. I hesitated for some time, but in the end I accepted the offer.

Four days later word came from the convent, and I quickly went there.

The prioress was gentle and kind, yet she also possessed great mental power, unmarred by the tiniest flaw. Once the greetings were dispensed with, she said, "I have thought a great deal about you. . . . I think it would be best if you were to live in a believing layperson's home and travel from there back and forth to the convent for religious training. I'm looking for such a home for you now."

"Oh no!" I thought. "That's terrible! That might be all right for somebody else, but for me it's no good. I've got to be admitted!" I well understood that the prioress was concerned about me. But really, the dilemma of my double life had given me no end of trouble for many years. I had finally come to feel that I absolutely had to stop straddling the fence--I must be either laywoman or nun. If I couldn't practice Buddhism in the convent, so be it! But to practice like that, going back and forth, would be no practice at all!

I concentrated my resolve. "Don't underestimate the power of sincerity!" I thought. "As long as I have breath, even if 'like dew at the edge of a field, I vanish,' I will push straight ahead, despite mountains, despite rivers! If I fall down, get up again! If I stumble, I'll right myself! Just advance! Just advance! To either life or death!"

"I want to practice *takuhotsu*, but it's not right to do so as a laywoman," I said as I had planned.

"Do you have any relative hereabouts, or someone who could guarantee you?"

"No." I guarantee myself! But I suppose that insofar as I am my own guarantee, there is no assurance.

"If you became ill, it would be a problem, wouldn't it?"

"Please don't concern yourself over that!" I thought there was no need to worry about such things before they happened.

"You shouldn't say that. In such a case, you become a problem to those around you."

"Yes, you're right. . . ." I gave in.

After we had gone back and forth with several questions and answers, the prioress said, "We have an age limit at this convent; only women in their twenties or thirties may enter."

"Aha, the trump card! Did I fail the test? Well, I guess there's no point in further discussion," I thought. Nonetheless, I kept trying. I asked her, "Can't something be done about that?"

"No. We can't break the rules of the convent just for you."

"Of course. So here, too, I am defeated," I thought. I tried one last approach. "If you cannot consent to have me as a practitioner, can't you find some kind of use for me? Anything at all, I won't mind! I'll do anything, anything! But please

just let me stay in some corner. I beg you!" Unexpectedly, a teardrop rolled off my face. I bowed down. There was nothing more to say. My ammunition was exhausted.

In the end, the convent doors would not open for me. Once again I had exhausted the bottommost depths of my heart. I had tried my best, there was nothing to be done about it! There was no karmic tie. Thus I was satisfied and felt no regrets.

I returned to Taiheiji to tell the Roshi of the poor outcome at the convent. "Well, what will you do?" he asked.

"Go back to Hokkaido, I suppose." I was thinking of going to see Zen master Suga.

"But you went to so much trouble to come here from Hokkaido to practice Buddhism."

"Yes," I said, feeling a sudden tightness in my chest.

Roshi said, "Maybe you could stay here. . . ." After a pause he added, "Well, think it over carefully." I was pierced to the marrow by this compassion. However, since this was something I couldn't very well decide with my heart, I postponed the reply until the next morning. I had two problems. First, I considered, I would feel bad if I couldn't give Zen master Suga an account of the whole course of events. And second, I wondered if I could really presume upon the kindness of the Roshi and his wife like this. But, I thought, besides practicing Zen, I could help out the wife for a month or two and then return home. Thus I stayed on.

Zazen and Teisho

The Roshi took me to the Zen meetings at Soseiji Temple in Nakano. There for the first time I heard *teisho*. It was brusque and plain yet had a wonderful power. I listened with intense concentration, holding my breath. But in fact, I didn't understand well. Again, the Roshi spoke to me in detail about *zazen*--the right way to do it, things to watch for, and so forth. This too was something I was happy to hear at last. I was deeply impressed by this meticulous guidance, which exhausted the limits of kindness. Finally, I made up my mind to engage in really thorough practice with Roshi.

Though I didn't neglect my other duties for my own individual practice, I felt I must first and foremost sit in *zazen*. Thus I rose early every morning and meditated, facing a wall in the corner of the kitchen. While doing *zazen*, various important but previously overlooked questions frequently came to mind. At such times I always asked Roshi about them and received an explanation. In other cases too, whenever problems arose, I always received guidance. I tried never to let questions linger in my mind. Thus, after a month in Tokyo, I received permission to join a five-day *sesshin* at Shinkoji Temple.

At the first *dokusan*, Roshi examined my mental state. Even there I couldn't help speaking of the baggage of past experiences that I lugged around.

Roshi said, "That is *makyo*. Please try to start all over again."

"Really?" I thought. "All right, if that's the case, I will get a fresh start." Thus making up my mind, I sat enthusiastically with *Mu*. But all of a sudden--were the old experiences of sinking into *kami* possession working their mischief?--I slipped into a state of blankness, as though drunk. When I came to my senses, I thought, "This is no good!" and tried to have another go at it. But no matter how many times I started over, each time I was captivated before I knew it and drawn into the lair. Thus the *sesshin* came to an end in this indefinite state.

Again, Roshi took me to the Zen meetings at Tokorozawa's Raikoji Temple. There, once a month, there was *zazen* and *teisho*. This time the teisho was on the *Mumonkan's* "Kasho and the Flagpole." The tatami mats of the main hall at Raikoji were worn at the edges and tattered. When I saw that, I found myself thinking, "When I worked as a *miko*, business really thrived; I could have easily had these mats fixed. Maybe I should become a *miko* again! Even that isn't altogether useless in the work of liberating the dead who have lost their way."

Just then--"Aha!"--I caught myself. "You fool! That's the flagpole! Yes--when the merest glance casts a reflection in your mind, that's the flagpole! Knock over that flagpole in your mind! One after another, knock them down!" This is how I took "Kasho and the Flagpole." Until now my *zazen* practice had been grasping at clouds. Now I had discovered a principle to guide my practice. I thought to myself that I must never lessen the tension in my *hara*.

Five Eons of Practice

There was no August *sesshin* at Shinkoji Temple, so I'll go on to the September *sesshin*.

It was the second day of the *sesshin*. I was working very hard with my hara, saying, "*Mu, Mu,*" when all of a sudden-- "Unh!"--it was as if three people had pulled me over backward. "Oh no!" I thought. I repulsed this with effort, straightened my posture, and resumed, "*Mu, Mu.*" Then again "Unh!"--I was dragged down.

"This is awful!" I thought. I kept trying to pull myself together, but no matter how many times I tried, it was no use. "What now?" I thought. I wonder if I'm dozing off." When the walking meditation was over, I thought to myself, "Okay, now!" and sat, hardening my *hara* all the more. As I did so, once again it started. "Very strange," I thought. "I know! It's a possessing spirit! The spirit of a dead person." (In possession by spirits of the dead, one is thrown onto one's back, facing up; in the case of spirits of the living, one is pushed over onto one's face.) "I don't know if it's a good spirit or a bad spirit, but there's more than one of them, anyway! . . . Okay. . . ."

"Hey! Everybody!" I said silently to the spirits. 'Wait a minute, please! When I attain *kensho*, I will without fail perform a memorial service for you. Until then, please be patient and wait quietly on the spirit shelf." With this statement to free me of their presence, I sat with all the more intense effort.

After that, I was not dragged over as badly as before, but if my effort slackened even a little, I was instantly pulled down. This continued all day.

I was dead tired. That evening when I tried to settle down to sleep, the instant I laid my head on the pillow, I saw: "Ah! This out-breath is *Mu*!" Then: "The in-breath too is *Mu*!" Next breath, too: *Mu*! Next breath: *Mu, Mu*! "*Mu*, a whole sequence of *Mu*! Croak, croak; meow, meow--these too are *Mu*! The bedding, the wall, the column, the sliding door-- these too are *Mu*! This, that and everything is *Mu*! Ha ha! Ha ha ha ha ha! That Roshi is a rascal! He's always tricking people with his '*Mu, Mu, Mu*'! . . . Hmm. I wonder if, after this, I should rush to Roshi's room for *dokusan*. No, that would be childish. . . ."

I felt as if a chronic disease of forty years had been cured in an instant. I slept soundly that night.

Very early the next morning was *dokusan*. Abruptly, I said, "Roshi, I saw *Mu*." At least I was able to say that much clearly. Then Roshi examined me in a number of ways, and *kensho* was confirmed.

"You slept soundly last night, eh?" asked Roshi. "Yes, I slept well," I answered truthfully. They say that the night after *kensho*, you can't sleep for joy, but that wasn't the case for me; my mood wasn't particularly affected. "For some reason, I feel quite calm," I thought. I felt as if I had finally gulped down some big thing that had been stuck in my throat a long time. And the fog in my mind had all at once lifted. I thought, "So this is *kensho*, eh? If even a dull person like me is able to see *Mu*--albeit ever so slightly then in the whole world there isn't a single person who can't attain *kensho*! 'Seek and you will find. Look and you will see. Knock and it will be opened to you.' That's right! That's true!"

"Visiting Zenkoji Temple, drawn by an ox." I had been drawn by a mind that sought. It seemed as if I had been going around and around in circles, repeating the same mistakes over and over for forty years. But now that I have awakened from the dream and can see dearly, I know that the saying "You don't have the same experience twice" is really true. Not a single step is given to repeating the past or to useless efforts. I can see now that things which seemed redundant or insignificant at the time were all necessary conditions for what followed.

It is also clear to me that the return of this lost child to the original home for which she has longed is a gift. I have returned home thanks to the compassion and skill of the buddhas and bodhisattvas. "Amida's five eons of practice was for me, Shinran, alone." Ah, thank you! Thank you! All things in the universe have together nurtured small and insignificant me. They have given their very lifeblood for my sake.

> Ah, hardship--more and more it
> accumulates.
> I have my limits, but I will try
> with all my might.
> Pressure makes you into a jewel.

These verses [written by my teacher] have been with me constantly since beginning Buddhist practice. They always spur me on and arouse feelings of aspiration and gratitude. They are the words of an enlightened person--my beloved teacher. Today, let me return them to him to express my gratitude for his kindness:

> To exist is to accumulate hardship.
> Only thus can my life continue to flow.
> *--Gassho*

Jainism

Jain Priest Praying at the Temple of Lodruva Jaisalmer in Rahastha State in India

JAINISM

Central Problem of Indian Religious Life
How to find release from karma and escape the continual round of rebirth?

Origin of Name
- Jain = one who follows a jina
- Jina = "conqueror" in Sanskrit = has been victorious over the obstacles to liberation
- Jainism calls for life of self-denial and renunciation
- This life will lead to liberation

Buddhism and Jainism – Commonalities
- Originated in India during Axis Age (6th century BCE) — *The time of Buddha*
- Looked toward liberation of the self
- Sprang from Kshatriya caste (warrior-chieftain class)
- Denied the saving efficacy of the Vedas
- Objected to the ritual observances based upon them
- Challenged authority of Brahmin priesthood

Jainism vs. Buddhism
- Jain adherents mainly in India
- Jainism has 4 to 6 million adherents, mainly in Bombay (Mumbai)
- Jainism affirms the substantiality of individual selves, as jivas
- Jiva = the individual's higher consciousness or soul

Jainism vs. Hinduism
- Jainism = religion of self-reliance
- Gods cannot help. They too are working out their own liberation.
- Priests cannot invoke any special powers
- Jainism does not accept the Vedas
- In Jainism, women can be nuns

Impact
- Ahimsa (non violence) embraced by Gandhi
- Big role in global environmental and animal rights movements

The Founder: Mahavira
- Was a contemporary of the Buddha
- Died in ca. 527 BCE — *An naked*
- Prince of a kshatriya clan
- At 30 started wandering as spiritual seeker
- Meditated and wandered naked

- Practiced strict ahimsa (non-injury)
- Reached liberation after 12 years of meditation, silence, and extreme fasting
- Taught the path; followers came from all castes
- Left no writings
- Considered the last of 24 savior beings called Tirthankaras   *NOT GODS*
- Tirthankaras (ford-makers) are those who escaped the cycle of rebirth

→ place where the river is the lowest and one can wade across

Divisions Jain Community
- Should monks wear clothes or go naked?
- Two groups
  – Digambara ("sky-clad") go naked
  – Shvetambara ("white-clad") wear white robes

= EXTREME
- acetic path
- giving away everything

Jain Texts
- Agamas ("tradition")
- Contain the teachings of sages + sermons of Mahavira

liberation of the self + jiva

Jain Cosmology
- Every living being has a jiva
- Jiva = living substance, soul, all good, all perfect, all-knowing
- Opposite is ajiva (body, matter, lifeless things in the universe, evil)

Problem
- Jivas are "weighed down" by karma
- Karma is a glue that sticks the jiva to the ajiva
- What causes karma?
- All actions, well intentioned or not, produce karma and burden jiva

Jiva as true self distinguishes Jainism from Buddhism & Hinduism

Is there a solution? Can you unstick the jiva from the ajiva?
- Yes
- HOW?
- Only a commitment to inactivity or to activity that focuses on liberating the jiva will STOP further accumulation of karmic matter

What Happens to the Soul, Once unstuck?
- Rises to top of universe
- Dwells in full consciousness, knowledge, and bliss
- The liberated soul is an "all-knowing one" (kevalin) ← *goal*
- No ultimate communion with Brahman (like Hinduism)
- Individual souls remain separate

Jinas and Tirthankaras
- Jinas = victors
- The tirthankaras = jinas who serve as models for others
- Appear at each downward cycle to regenerate the world

Spiritual Practices for the Monks and Nuns
- Ascetic path
- Monks and Nuns practice Five Great Vows

Five Great Vows
- Non violence
- Non lying
- Non stealing
- Chastity
- Non attachment

The Twelve Vows for Lay Folk
- Never to take life
- Never to lie
- Never to steal
- Never to be unchaste
- No greed (give away any excess)
- Avoid temptation to sin
- Limit number of things in daily use
- Be on guard against evils that can be avoided
- Keep stated periods for meditation
- Observe special periods of self-denial
- Spend occasional days as monk
- Give alms in support of ascetics

Moral Restrictions
- No gambling
- No eating meat
- No drinking alcohol
- No adultery
- No hunting
- No thieving
- No debauchery

Practice

- Meditation – about an hour twice a day
- Praise the Tirthankaras
- Venerate teachers
- Hold particular position for length of time to show indifference to body
- Perform daily puja (worship) at home in front of images
- Fast as monks at least once a year
- Give up certain foods and activities for a length of time

Jains in Everyday Life

- Diet strictly vegetarian
- Homes scrupulously clean
- Jains take careers in business
- Known for their philanthropy

World Jainism

- 20th century = Jain meditation centers in Europe, America, Brazil, and Africa
- New order of semi-monks and semi-nuns (samans and samanis) developed in 1980

EXTRA NOTES

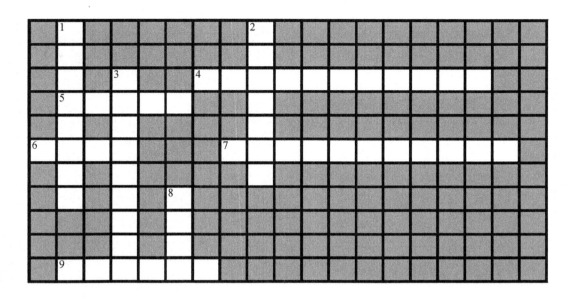

ACROSS

4. "White-clad," a Jain community which wears white robes
5. Body, matter, lifeless things, evil in the universe (opposite of jiva)
6. "Conqueror," one who is perfect and has been victorious over the obstacles to liberation
7. "Crossing maker" or Jina who helped others find their way (there are 24)
9. "Tradition," the Jain texts, the teachings of sages such as the sermons of Mahavira

DOWN

1. "Great man," "Hero" (or Nataputta Vardhamana), most recent Tirthankara
2. "All-knowing one," the liberated soul in Jainism
3. "Sky-clad," a highly ascetic community of Jain monks who go naked
8. Spirit, soul

JAINISM

TEXTS 10 & 11.

1. What is the Jain argument against the idea of a creator god? [See TEXT 10]

2. What are the arguments for and against women's liberation from *samsara*? What impact could these arguments have on women's place and function in society? [See TEXT 11]

Text Ten

Is There a Creator God?

Some foolish men declare that a Creator made the world.

The doctrine that the world was created is ill-advised, and should be rejected. If God created the world, where was he before creation?

If you say he was transcendent then, and needed no support, where is he now? No single being had the skill to make this world--For how can an immaterial god create that which is material?

How could God have made the world without any raw material?

If you say he made this first, and then the world, you are faced with an endless regression.

If you say that this raw material arose naturally you fall into another fallacy, For the whole universe might thus have been its own creator and have arisen naturally in the same way.

If God created the world by an act of his own will, without any raw material, Then it is just his will and nothing else-- and who will believe this nonsense? If he is ever perfect and complete, how could the will to create have arisen in him?

If, on the other hand, he is not perfect, he could no more create the universe than a potter could.

If he is formless, actionless, and all-embracing, how could he have created the world?

Such a soul, devoid of all modality, would have no desire to create anything. If he is perfect, he does not strive for the three aims of humanity,

So what advantage would be gained by creating the universe?

If you say that he created for no purpose, because it was his nature to do so, then God is pointless.

If he created in some kind of sport, it was the sport of a foolish child, leading to trouble. . . .

If out of love for living things and need of them he made the world,

Why did he not make creation wholly blissful, free from misfortune?

If he were transcendent he would not create, for he would be free;

Nor if involved in transmigration, for then he would not be almighty.

So the doctrine that the world was created by God makes no sense at all.

And God commits great sin in killing the children that he himself created.

If you say that he kills only to destroy evil beings, why did he create such beings in the first place? . . .

Good men should combat the believer in divine creation, maddened by an evil doctrine.

Know that the world is uncreated, as time itself is, without beginning and end. . . .

Uncreated and indestructible, it endures through the compulsion of its own nature,

Divided into three sections--hell, earth, and heaven.

Text Eleven

Can Women Attain Liberation?

WOMEN CANNOT ATTAIN LIBERATION

10. [Going] without clothes and [using] the hands as a bowl for receiving alms have been taught by the supreme lords of the Jinas [as] the sole path to liberation (*moksa*); all other [ways of mendicant behavior] are not [valid] paths. . . .

19. [Worldly behavior,] the outward sign of which is the accepting possessions--be they small or great--is condemned in the teaching of the Jinas; [only] one without possessions is free from household life.

20. One endowed with the five great vows (*mahavrata*) and the three protections (*gupti*) is restrained [i.e., is a mendicant]. He [alone] is on the path to liberation free from bonds and is worthy of praise.

21. The second outward sign is said to be that of the higher and lower "listeners" [i.e., lay people]: the lower, holding the bowl, wanders for alms silently, with well-controlled movement and speech.

22. The [third] outward sign is that of women: a nun eats food only once per day and wears one piece of cloth [while a female novice who wears two pieces of clothing] eats wearing [only] one.

23. In the teaching of the Jina no person who wears clothes attains [liberation], even if he is a Tirthankara. The path to liberation is that of nakedness, and all other [paths] are wrong paths.

24. It is taught [in the scriptures] that in the genital organs of women, in the area between their breasts, and in their navels and armpits are extremely small living beings, so how can women be ordained [since their bodies make them unable to keep the first vow of non-violence]?

25. If there is purity because of right-view, then she too is said to be associated with the path. [However, even if] she has practiced severe [ascetic] practices it is said in the teaching that there is no ordination for women.

26. Women do not have purity of mind, and by nature their minds are slack, women get their period each month, [and therefore] they have no meditation free from anxiety.

WOMEN CAN ATTAIN LIBERATION

2. There is liberation for women, because women possess all the causes [necessary for liberation]. The cause of liberation is fulfillment of the three jewels (*ratna-traya*), and this is not incompatible [with womanhood].

[Commentary:] The cause of liberation from the sickness of cyclic existence is the non-deficiency of the [three jewels:] correct view, knowledge, and conduct. There is liberation from cyclic existence for those who perfect them. Furthermore, because women do not lack the causes of nirvana, it is not reasonable [to assert] that any of the three jewels are incompatible with womanhood, and so it is not the case that there is no liberation for women. . . .

4. Nuns are able to understand the Jina's words, have faith in them, and practice them faultlessly.

[Commentary:] Correct knowledge is the proper understanding of the Jina's words. Correct view is faith in [the Jina's words] . . . Correct conduct involves applying them appropriately. And this is just what the three jewels are

Source: "Can Women Attain Liberation?" (editor's title, originally titled "Women Cannot Attain Liberation" from *Kundakunda, Sutraprabhrta*, and "Women Can Obtain Liberation" from *Strinirvana-pariccheda*) translated by Royce Wiles. Reprinted by permission of Royce Wiles.

said to be. Release [from cyclic existence] is characterized by complete freedom from all karmas, [which occurs when the three jewels] are perfected. . . . All of these are found in women.

[A Digambara opponent] might assert that women cannot attain release because they have clothes. People like householders, who are bound by possessions, cannot attain release. If it were not the case [that people who own clothes have possessions], then even male [monks] could wear clothes, and renouncing them would be irrelevant [to the attainment of release]. . . .

If [as the opponent claims] liberation cannot be attained by those who [wear] clothes, and if one could attain liberation by renouncing them, then certainly it would be acceptable for [women] to renounce [clothing]. Clothes are not necessary for life, and since even life itself may be abandoned [in order to attain liberation], then it goes without saying that [one may renounce] mere clothes! If release were attained simply due to the absence of those [clothes], then what fool seeking release would lose it just through wearing clothes?

The Lord Arhats, the guides for the path to release, taught that women must wear clothes and prohibited them from renouncing clothes, and so it follows that clothes are necessary for release, like a whisk broom [that is used to sweep away small creatures]. . . . If women were to give up clothing, this would result in their abandoning the whole corpus of monastic rules. As is well known, women are overpowered by [men who] are excited due to seeing their naked bodies and limbs, in the one way that mares--who naturally have clothing--are overpowered by stallions. . . . Furthermore, women from good families are naturally very shy, and if they [were required to] abandon clothing [in order to become nuns], then they would refuse to do so.

Clothes are a possession, and so there is some demerit in wearing them, but still by this all of the monastic rules are maintained. Therefore, having ascertained that there is greater benefit and lesser demerit in wearing clothes, rather than renouncing them, the holy Arhats declared that nuns must wear clothes and prohibited them from abandoning them.

Sikhism

Golden Temple, the Main Sanctuary of Sikhs, Amritsar, India

SIKHISM

Overview
- Fifth largest of all world religions
- Emerged in the 16th century CE as a religious movement in northwest India
- Sikhism = syncretism of Hinduism and Islam or a new revelation?

Guru Nanak (1469-ca. 1539)
- Founder
- Sikhs = disciples, students, seekers of truth
- Nine gurus succeeded Nanak (the last one being Guru Gobind Singh, 17th century)

Guru Nanak – Central Beliefs
- Believed in the One, the formless and transcendent God
- God = creator
- To God one owes absolute submission in love
- Love is expressed in community singing, NOT through temple ritual and asceticism

Guru Nanak Rejected:
- Caste divisions and hierarchy
- Shrines, asceticism
- Competing religious identities of Hindu and Muslim

Sikhs Today
- 2 percent of the Indian population (30 million)
- Located in the Punjab
- Partition in 1947 was dramatic
- Fight for Sikh regional autonomy or independent Khalistan
- Form diaspora in Europe and especially in the U.S.
- Do not seek converts

Hinduism versus Islam—Differences

In Hinduism
- MANY gods
- Religious images
- Vegetarianism

In Islam
- ONE God
- No religious images
- Killing of cows allowed

Commonalities
- Mystical path
- Sufism (mystical Islam) and Hinduism recognize important role of a spiritual master
  - guru for Hindus
  - sheikh for Sufis

Kabir (15th century CE)
- Son of Muslim parents and disciple of a Hindu guru, Ramananda
- Poet + weaver
- Tried to build bridges between the two religions
- Emphasis on devotion to the Beloved (the Ultimate Reality)

Themes in Kabir's Poetry
- Kabir attacked both Brahmin and Islamic ritualism
- An end to reincarnation could be brought only through complete love of God
- Emphasis on teacher

Nanak's Biography
- Born in 1469
- Came from a Hindu business family in Punjab region
- Businessman + had family
- Left family and devoted himself to spiritual life
- Mardana, a Muslim minstrel, joined him in quest for truth
- At age 30, turning point
- While bathing, Nanak disappeared in the water
- Had been taken into the presence of God

God commissioned him
- To go and repeat the Divine Name
- Tell others to do likewise
- To practice charity, ritual bathing, service, and meditation
- "There is no Hindu; there is no Muslim."
- Mocked Hindu and Muslim rituals
- Wore a combination of Hindu and Muslim garments
- Even in death, Nanak reconciled Hindus and Muslims

Nanak's Teaching
Close to Islam
- Nanak's God ("Nam" = True Name is ONE, merciful)
- Lower creatures serve the highest of the creatures, the human being. Meat eating is OK.
- Equality of all humans

Close to Hinduism
- Maya (illusion)
- Transmigration of souls
- Law of Karma
- A God-centric life will lead to nirvana

How can one reach liberation?
- Through devotion to one God
- Through repetition of the name of God
- Through singing praises to God
- Through social mission

Political History of Sikhism
- Initially Nanak's creed was peaceful
- Because of persecution, Sikhism changed into self-defensive faith

Second Guru Angad (1504-1552)
- Compiled a collection of Nanak's and his own hymns
- Established "langar," communal feast for disciples

Fifth Guru Arjan (1563-1606)
- Compiled the Guru Granth Sahib ("Book of the Lord"), also called the Adi Granth ("Original Collection")
- Built Amritsar (The Pool of Immortality)
- Killed for his faith

Sixth Guru Har Gobind (1606-1645)
- Created first Sikh army
- Adopted practice of wearing a sword
- Fought against Muslim Mughals

The Tenth and Last Guru Gobind Singh (1675-1708)
- Created a military fraternity
- Fraternity is called khalsa ("pure ones")
- Members become singhs ("lions") through initiation
- Initiation = Baptism of the sword
- Traditionally for boys
- More recently for girls as well

The Five K's or Distinguishing Marks of the Singhs
- Uncut hair (in association with the lion and its power)
- Comb (to hold the hair)
- Short pants (for modesty)
- Steel bracelet (to symbolize strength and service to God)
- Sword (for defense)

Adi ("first") Granth (Sikh Scripture)
- After the last Guru was assassinated, Sikh Scripture succeeded as Guru
- 6,000 hymns

Private Sikh Practices
- Prayer before dawn and in evening (2 hours per day)
- Bathe and recite the japji (a poem by Guru Nanak that begins the Adi Granth). Jap means "recitation."
- Continual repetition of the Name of God

Congregational Practices
- Gurdwaras ("house or gateway of the Guru")
- No priestly class
- No caste and gender differences for kirtan (congregational worship)
- Guru Granth Sahib treated like a king
- Langar = communal meal open to all
- Charity = one-tenth of one's income

Women in Sikhism
- Traditionally men read the scriptures
- Guru Gobind Singh initiated women into the Khalsa
- In 1996, women allowed to perform sacred services
- Guru Gobind Singh forbade female infanticide
- In 2001 condemnation of female foeticide

EXTRA NOTES

SIKHISM

THE GOLDEN TEMPLE

1. Describe the festivities at Guru Nanak's Birthday Festival.

   turban tying competition

2. Where is Harsimran Kaur from? Why is this place an important holy place for the Sikhs?

3. Who was Guru Nanak?

   founder of Sikhism

4. What are the basic teachings of Sikhism?

5. Is there a guru today? What replaced the guru?

   no - The guru Granth Sahib

6. What is the Guru Granth Sahib?

   most sacred writing in Sikhism
   teachings of 10 gurus

7. Describe the evening prayer at the Kaur's home.

   fan holy book chants
   clean hands

8. What is the holiest place of Sikhism? Describe its inside and outside.

   The Golden temple
   surrounded by lake
   copy kept there & adorn walls of temple 200yr old

9. How many Sikhs are there in the world?

   30 million

10. What are the 5 symbols of faith?

kesh

dont cut hair

kangha

comb - keep hair tity

kachha

shorts - moral restraint

kara

steel bracelet - unity w/ god

kirpan

sword/dagger - self sacrafice/ courage

11. Nanak's creed was peaceful. Why did Sikhism change into a self-defensive faith?

had to fight for religious freedom

12. How do Sikhs differ from Hindus in their beliefs?

no chanting/ sacred fires

13. What do boys do during the celebration of Nanak's birthday?

14. Describe the marriage ceremony.

arranged   age   appearance   character   simple   coupe willing

15. What is a langar?

10:43

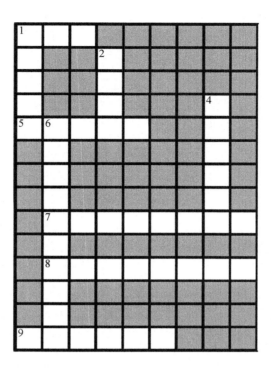

ACROSS

1. The Holy Name of God
5. He was a famous Muslim weaver who drew his spirituality from Hinduism and Islam
7. Sikh house of worship ("house or gateway of the Guru")
8. The holy city of Sikhism
9. Literally the "pure ones" (a military fraternity)

DOWN

1. Founder of Sikhism (born in 15th century CE)
2. Muslim mystic
4. Communal meal open to all
6. Sacred book of the Sikhs and current guru of the Sikh community

SIKHISM

TEXT 12. THE HYMNS OF GURU NANAK

1. What is the Sikh argument for the idea of a creator god?

2. On the basis of these hymns, what can you tell of the religious culture into which Guru Nanak was born? Do you think Sikhism was created from scratch or was it an innovation based on earlier practices and beliefs?

3. What is God's nature and what are humans' responsibilities toward God and the world?

4. On the basis of these hymns, how can one escape *samsara*?

Please turn to your reading glossary at the end of your workbook for unknown vocabulary.

Text Twelve

The Hymns of Guru Nanak

One Universal Creator God. The Name Is Truth. Creative Being Personified. No Fear. No Hatred. Image Of The Undying, Beyond Birth, Self-Existent. By Guru's Grace ~ Chant And Meditate:
True In The Primal Beginning. True Throughout The Ages. True Here And Now. O Nanak, Forever And Ever True.

By thinking, He cannot be reduced to thought, even by thinking hundreds of thousands of times.
By remaining silent, inner silence is not obtained, even by remaining lovingly absorbed deep within.
The hunger of the hungry is not appeased, even by piling up loads of worldly goods.
Hundreds of thousands of clever tricks, but not even one of them will go along with you in the end.
So how can you become truthful? And how can the veil of illusion be torn away?
O Nanak, it is written that you shall obey the Hukam of His Command, and walk in the Way of His Will.

By His Command, bodies are created; His Command cannot be described.
By His Command, souls come into being; by His Command, glory and greatness are obtained.
By His Command, some are high and some are low; by His Written Command, pain and pleasure are obtained.
Some, by His Command, are blessed and forgiven; others, by His Command, wander aimlessly forever.
Everyone is subject to His Command; no one is beyond His Command.
O Nanak, one who understands His Command, does not speak in ego.

Some sing of His Power-who has that Power?
Some sing of His Gifts, and know His Sign and Insignia.
Some sing of His Glorious Virtues, Greatness and Beauty.

Some sing of knowledge obtained of Him, through difficult philosophical studies.
Some sing that He fashions the body, and then again reduces it to dust.
Some sing that He takes life away, and then again restores it.
Some sing that He seems so very far away.

SECTION 01 - JUP - PART 002

Some sing that He watches over us, face to face, ever-present.
There is no shortage of those who preach and teach.
Millions upon millions offer millions of sermons and stories.
The Great Giver keeps on giving, while those who receive grow weary of receiving.
Throughout the ages, consumers consume.
The Commander, by His Command, leads us to walk on the Path.
O Nanak, He blossoms forth, Carefree and Untroubled.

True is the Master, True is His Name-speak it with infinite love.
People beg and pray, "Give to us, give to us," and the Great Giver gives His Gifts.
So what offering can we place before Him, by which we might see the Darbaar of His Court?
What words can we speak to evoke His Love?
In the Amrit Vaylaa, the ambrosial hours before dawn, chant the True Name, and contemplate His Glorious Greatness.
By the karma of past actions, the robe of this physical body is obtained. By His Grace, the Gate of Liberation is found.
O Nanak, know this well: the True One Himself is All.

He cannot be established, He cannot be created.
He Himself is Immaculate and Pure.
Those who serve Him are honored.

O Nanak, sing of the Lord, the Treasure of Excellence.
Sing, and listen, and let your mind be filled with love.
Your pain shall be sent far away, and peace shall come to your home.
The Guru's Word is the Sound-current of the Naad; the Guru's Word is the Wisdom of the Vedas; the Guru's Word is all-pervading.
The Guru is Shiva, the Guru is Vishnu and Brahma; the Guru is Paarvati and Lakhshmi.
Even knowing God, I cannot describe Him; He cannot be described in words.
The Guru has given me this one understanding:
there is only the One, the Giver of all souls. May I never forget Him!

If I am pleasing to Him, then that is my pilgrimage and cleansing bath. Without pleasing Him, what good are ritual cleansings?
I gaze upon all the created beings: without the karma of good actions, what are they given to receive?
Within the mind are gems, jewels and rubies, if you listen to the Guru's Teachings, even once.
The Guru has given me this one understanding:
there is only the One, the Giver of all souls. May I never forget Him!

Even if you could live throughout the four ages, or even ten times more,
and even if you were known throughout the nine continents and followed by all,
with a good name and reputation, with praise and fame throughout the world-
—still, if the Lord does not bless you with His Glance of Grace, then who cares? What is the use?
Among worms, you would be considered a lowly worm, and even contemptible sinners would hold you in contempt.
O Nanak, God blesses the unworthy with virtue, and bestows virtue on the virtuous.
No one can even imagine anyone who can bestow virtue upon Him.

Listening—the Siddhas, the spiritual teachers, the heroic warriors, the yogic masters.
Listening—the earth, its support and the Akaashic ethers.
Listening—the oceans, the lands of the world and the nether regions of the underworld.
Listening—Death cannot even touch you.
O Nanak, the devotees are forever in bliss.
Listening—pain and sin are erased.

Listening—Shiva, Brahma and Indra.
Listening—even foul-mouthed people praise Him.
Listening—the technology of Yoga and the secrets of the body.
Listening—the Shaastras, the Simritees and the Vedas.
O Nanak, the devotees are forever in bliss.

SECTION 01 - JUP - PART 003

Listening—pain and sin are erased.

Listening—truth, contentment and spiritual wisdom.
Listening—take your cleansing bath at the sixty-eight places of pilgrimage.
Listening—reading and reciting, honor is obtained.
Listening—intuitively grasp the essence of meditation.
O Nanak, the devotees are forever in bliss.
Listening—pain and sin are erased.

Listening—dive deep into the ocean of virtue.
Listening—the Shaykhs, religious scholars, spiritual teachers and emperors.
Listening—even the blind find the Path.
Listening—the Unreachable comes within your grasp.
O Nanak, the devotees are forever in bliss.
Listening—pain and sin are erased.

The state of the faithful cannot be described.
One who tries to describe this shall regret the attempt.
No paper, no pen, no scribe
can record the state of the faithful.
Such is the Name of the Immaculate Lord.
Only one who has faith comes to know such a state of mind.

The faithful have intuitive awareness and intelligence.
The faithful know about all worlds and realms.
The faithful shall never be struck across the face.
The faithful do not have to go with the Messenger of Death.
Such is the Name of the Immaculate Lord.
Only one who has faith comes to know such a state of mind.

The path of the faithful shall never be blocked.
The faithful shall depart with honor and fame.
The faithful do not follow empty religious rituals.
The faithful are firmly bound to the Dharma.
Such is the Name of the Immaculate Lord.
Only one who has faith comes to know such a state of mind.

The faithful find the Door of Liberation.
The faithful uplift and redeem their family and relations.

The faithful are saved, and carried across with the Sikhs of the Guru.
The faithful, O Nanak, do not wander around begging.
Such is the Name of the Immaculate Lord.
Only one who has faith comes to know such a state of mind.

The chosen ones, the self-elect, are accepted and approved.
The chosen ones are honored in the Court of the Lord.
The chosen ones look beautiful in the courts of kings.
The chosen ones meditate single-mindedly on the Guru.
No matter how much anyone tries to explain and describe them,
the actions of the Creator cannot be counted.
The mythical bull is Dharma, the son of compassion;
this is what patiently holds the earth in its place.
One who understands this becomes truthful.
What a great load there is on the bull!
So many worlds beyond this world—so very many!
What power holds them, and supports their weight?
The names and the colors of the assorted species of beings
were all inscribed by the Ever-flowing Pen of God.
Who knows how to write this account?
Just imagine what a huge scroll it would take!
What power! What fascinating beauty!
And what gifts! Who can know their extent?
You created the vast expanse of the Universe with One Word!
Hundreds of thousands of rivers began to flow.
How can Your Creative Potency be described?
I cannot even once be a sacrifice to You.
Whatever pleases You is the only good done,
You, Eternal and Formless One!

Countless meditations, countless loves.
Countless worship services, countless austere disciplines.
Countless scriptures, and ritual recitations of the Vedas.
Countless Yogis, whose minds remain detached from the world.

SECTION 01 - JUP - PART 004
Countless devotees contemplate the Wisdom and Virtues of the Lord.
Countless the holy, countless the givers.
Countless heroic spiritual warriors, who bear the brunt of the attack in battle (who with their mouths eat steel).
Countless silent sages, vibrating the String of His Love.
How can Your Creative Potency be described?
I cannot even once be a sacrifice to You.
Whatever pleases You is the only good done,
You, Eternal and Formless One.

Countless fools, blinded by ignorance.
Countless thieves and embezzlers.
Countless impose their will by force.
Countless cut-throats and ruthless killers.
Countless sinners who keep on sinning.
Countless liars, wandering lost in their lies.
Countless wretches, eating filth as their ration.
Countless slanderers, carrying the weight of their stupid mistakes on their heads.
Nanak describes the state of the lowly.
I cannot even once be a sacrifice to You.
Whatever pleases You is the only good done,
You, Eternal and Formless One.

Countless names, countless places.
Inaccessible, unapproachable, countless celestial realms.
Even to call them countless is to carry the weight on your head.
From the Word, comes the Naam; from the Word, comes Your Praise.
From the Word, comes spiritual wisdom, singing the Songs of Your Glory.
From the Word, come the written and spoken words and hymns.
From the Word, comes destiny, written on one's forehead.
But the One who wrote these Words of Destiny—no words are written on His Forehead.
As He ordains, so do we receive.
The created universe is the manifestation of Your Name.
Without Your Name, there is no place at all.
How can I describe Your Creative Power?
I cannot even once be a sacrifice to You.
Whatever pleases You is the only good done,
You, Eternal and Formless One.

When the hands and the feet and the body are dirty,
water can wash away the dirt.
When the clothes are soiled and stained by urine,
soap can wash them clean.
But when the intellect is stained and polluted by sin,
it can only be cleansed by the Love of the Name.
Virtue and vice do not come by mere words;
actions repeated, over and over again, are engraved on the soul.
You shall harvest what you plant.
O Nanak, by the Hukam of God's Command, we come and go in reincarnation.

Pilgrimages, austere discipline, compassion and charity
—these, by themselves, bring only an iota of merit.

Listening and believing with love and humility in your mind,

cleanse yourself with the Name, at the sacred shrine deep within.

All virtues are Yours, Lord, I have none at all.

Without virtue, there is no devotional worship.

I bow to the Lord of the World, to His Word, to Brahma the Creator.

He is Beautiful, True and Eternally Joyful.

What was that time, and what was that moment? What was that day, and what was that date?

What was that season, and what was that month, when the Universe was created?

The Pandits, the religious scholars, cannot find that time, even if it is written in the Puraanas.

That time is not known to the Qazis, who study the Koran.

The day and the date are not known to the Yogis, nor is the month or the season.

The Creator who created this creation—only He Himself knows.

How can we speak of Him? How can we praise Him? How can we describe Him? How can we know Him?

SECTION 01 - JUP - PART 005

O Nanak, everyone speaks of Him, each one wiser than the rest.

Great is the Master, Great is His Name. Whatever happens is according to His Will.

O Nanak, one who claims to know everything shall not be decorated in the world hereafter.

There are nether worlds beneath nether worlds, and hundreds of thousands of heavenly worlds above.

The Vedas say that you can search and search for them all, until you grow weary.

The scriptures say that there are 18,000 worlds, but in reality, there is only One Universe.

If you try to write an account of this, you will surely finish yourself before you finish writing it.

O Nanak, call Him Great! He Himself knows Himself.

The praisers praise the Lord, but they do not obtain intuitive understanding

—the streams and rivers flowing into the ocean do not know its vastness.

Even kings and emperors, with mountains of property and oceans of wealth

—these are not even equal to an ant, who does not forget God.

Endless are His Praises, endless are those who speak them.

Endless are His Actions, endless are His Gifts.

Endless is His Vision, endless is His Hearing.

His limits cannot be perceived. What is the Mystery of His Mind?

The limits of the created universe cannot be perceived.

Its limits here and beyond cannot be perceived.

Many struggle to know His limits,

but His limits cannot be found.

No one can know these limits.

The more you say about them, the more there still remains to be said.

Great is the Master, High is His Heavenly Home.

Highest of the High, above all is His Name.

Only one as Great and as High as God

can know His Lofty and Exalted State.

Only He Himself is that Great. He Himself knows Himself.

O Nanak, by His Glance of Grace, He bestows His Blessings.

His Blessings are so abundant that there can be no written account of them.

The Great Giver does not hold back anything.

There are so many great, heroic warriors begging at the Door of the Infinite Lord.

So many contemplate and dwell upon Him, that they cannot be counted.

So many waste away to death engaged in corruption.

So many take and take again, and then deny receiving.

So many foolish consumers keep on consuming.

So many endure distress, deprivation and constant abuse.

Even these are Your Gifts, O Great Giver!

Liberation from bondage comes only by Your Will.

No one else has any say in this.

If some fool should presume to say that he does,

he shall learn, and feel the effects of his folly.

He Himself knows, He Himself gives.

Few, very few are those who acknowledge this.

One who is blessed to sing the Praises of the Lord,

O Nanak, is the king of kings.

Priceless are His Virtues, Priceless are His Dealings.

Priceless are His Dealers, Priceless are His Treasures.

Priceless are those who come to Him, Priceless are those who buy from Him.

Priceless is Love for Him, Priceless is absorption into Him.

Priceless is the Divine Law of Dharma, Priceless is the Divine Court of Justice.

Priceless are the scales, priceless are the weights.
Priceless are His Blessings, Priceless is His Banner and Insignia.
Priceless is His Mercy, Priceless is His Royal Command.
Priceless, O Priceless beyond expression!
Speak of Him continually, and remain absorbed in His Love.
The Vedas and the Puraanas speak.
The scholars speak and lecture.
Brahma speaks, Indra speaks.

SECTION 01 - JUP - PART 006

The Gopis and Krishna speak.
Shiva speaks, the Siddhas speak.
The many created Buddhas speak.
The demons speak, the demi-gods speak.
The spiritual warriors, the heavenly beings, the silent sages, the humble and serviceful speak.
Many speak and try to describe Him.
Many have spoken of Him over and over again, and have then arisen and departed.
If He were to create as many again as there already are, even then, they could not describe Him.
He is as Great as He wishes to be.
O Nanak, the True Lord knows.
If anyone presumes to describe God,
he shall be known as the greatest fool of fools!

Where is that Gate, and where is that Dwelling, in which You sit and take care of all?
The Sound-current of the Naad vibrates there, and countless musicians play on all sorts of instruments there.
So many Ragas, so many musicians singing there.
The praanic wind, water and fire sing; the Righteous Judge of Dharma sings at Your Door.
Chitr and Gupt, the angels of the conscious and the subconscious who record actions, and the Righteous Judge of Dharma who judges this record sing.
Shiva, Brahma and the Goddess of Beauty, ever adorned, sing.
Indra, seated upon His Throne, sings with the deities at Your Door.
The Siddhas in Samaadhi sing; the Saadhus sing in contemplation.
The celibates, the fanatics, the peacefully accepting and the fearless warriors sing.
The Pandits, the religious scholars who recite the Vedas, with the supreme sages of all the ages, sing.
The Mohinis, the enchanting heavenly beauties who entice hearts in this world, in paradise, and in the underworld of the subconscious sing.
The celestial jewels created by You, and the sixty-eight holy places of pilgrimage sing.
The brave and mighty warriors sing; the spiritual heroes and the four sources of creation sing.
The planets, solar systems and galaxies, created and arranged by Your Hand, sing.
They alone sing, who are pleasing to Your Will. Your devotees are imbued with the Nectar of Your Essence.
So many others sing, they do not come to mind. O Nanak, how can I consider them all?
That True Lord is True, Forever True, and True is His Name.
He is, and shall always be. He shall not depart, even when this Universe which He has created departs.
He created the world, with its various colors, species of beings, and the variety of Maya.
Having created the creation, He watches over it Himself, by His Greatness.
He does whatever He pleases. No order can be issued to Him.
He is the King, the King of kings, the Supreme Lord and Master of kings. Nanak remains subject to His Will.

Make contentment your ear-rings, humility your begging bowl, and meditation the ashes you apply to your body.
Let the remembrance of death be the patched coat you wear, let the purity of virginity be your way in the world, and let faith in the Lord be your walking stick.
See the brotherhood of all mankind as the highest order of Yogis; conquer your own mind, and conquer the world.
I bow to Him, I humbly bow.
The Primal One, the Pure Light, without beginning, without end. Throughout all the ages, He is One and the Same.

Let spiritual wisdom be your food, and compassion your attendant. The Sound-current of the Naad vibrates in each and every heart.
He Himself is the Supreme Master of all; wealth and miraculous spiritual powers, and all other external tastes and pleasures, are all like beads on a string.
Union with Him, and separation from Him, come by His Will. We come to receive what is written in our destiny.

SECTION 01 - JUP - PART 007

I bow to Him, I humbly bow.
The Primal One, the Pure Light, without beginning,

without end. Throughout all the ages, He is One and the Same.

The One Divine Mother conceived and gave birth to the three deities.
One, the Creator of the World; One, the Sustainer; and One, the Destroyer.
He makes things happen according to the Pleasure of His Will. Such is His Celestial Order.
He watches over all, but none see Him. How wonderful this is!
I bow to Him, I humbly bow.
The Primal One, the Pure Light, without beginning, without end. Throughout all the ages, He is One and the Same.

On world after world are His Seats of Authority and His Storehouses.
Whatever was put into them, was put there once and for all.
Having created the creation, the Creator Lord watches over it.
O Nanak, True is the Creation of the True Lord.
I bow to Him, I humbly bow.
The Primal One, the Pure Light, without beginning, without end. Throughout all the ages, He is One and the Same.

If I had 100,000 tongues, and these were then multiplied twenty times more, with each tongue,
I would repeat, hundreds of thousands of times, the Name of the One, the Lord of the Universe.
Along this path to our Husband Lord, we climb the steps of the ladder, and come to merge with Him.
Hearing of the etheric realms, even worms long to come back home.
O Nanak, by His Grace He is obtained. False are the boastings of the false.

No power to speak, no power to keep silent.
No power to beg, no power to give.

No power to live, no power to die.
No power to rule, with wealth and occult mental powers.
No power to gain intuitive understanding, spiritual wisdom and meditation.
No power to find the way to escape from the world.
He alone has the Power in His Hands. He watches over all.
O Nanak, no one is high or low.

Nights, days, weeks and seasons;
wind, water, fire and the nether regions
—in the midst of these, He established the earth as a home for Dharma.
Upon it, He placed the various species of beings.
Their names are uncounted and endless.
By their deeds and their actions, they shall be judged.
God Himself is True, and True is His Court.
There, in perfect grace and ease, sit the self-elect, the self-realized Saints.
They receive the Mark of Grace from the Merciful Lord.
The ripe and the unripe, the good and the bad, shall there be judged.
O Nanak, when you go home, you will see this.

This is righteous living in the realm of Dharma.
And now we speak of the realm of spiritual wisdom.
So many winds, waters and fires; so many Krishnas and Shivas.
So many Brahmas, fashioning forms of great beauty, adorned and dressed in many colors.
So many worlds and lands for working out karma. So very many lessons to be learned!
So many Indras, so many moons and suns, so many worlds and lands.
So many Siddhas and Buddhas, so many Yogic masters. So many goddesses of various kinds.
So many demi-gods and demons, so many silent sages. So many oceans of jewels.
So many ways of life, so many languages. So many dynasties of rulers.

Part 2

RELIGIONS ORIGINATING IN EAST ASIA: THE MYTH OF HARMONY

Scale 1:48,000,000

Azimuthal Equal-Area Projection

0 — 800 Kilometers

0 — 800 Miles

Boundary representation is
not necessarily authoritative.

Source: Central Intelligence Agency

803537AI (G00543) 6-12

Part 2: RELIGIONS ORIGINATING IN EAST ASIA: THE MYTH OF HARMONY

Shinto

© 2012 Arttila JANDI. Used under license of Shutterstock, Inc.

SHINTO

Main Commonalities between Religions Originating in East Asia
- The world really exists. It is NOT an illusion (*maya*).
- Goal = live in harmony with universe. There is no conception of *moksha* (escaping the universe).
- Ancestor Veneration: Many gods are ancestors and the dead are still living
- Religious Pluralism

Two Major Concepts to Understand Japanese and Chinese Religious Traditions
- Harmony
  Example: In ancestor worship, the descendants must establish harmonious relations with the dead
- Virtue = Moral excellence; goodness; righteousness

TAO (DAO)
- Tao (or Dao)
- "Way" or "path" = "the Way of all things"
- Mysterious source and ordering principle of universe
- Potential for all things

SHINTO
- Japanese ethnic religion
- Shinto = "way of the spirits"
  – Shen (spirits)
  – To (way)
- Goal of life = harmony with the Kami

What causes disharmony?
- Individualism
- View of nature as lifeless material
- Forgetting ancestors and heroes
- Loss of national pride

Who are the Kami?
- Powers in natural phenomena
- Energies that can animate nature
- Family ancestors, dead leaders, national or local heroes
- Kami can become humans; humans could become Kami
- Worship is communion with the Kami

Historical Development

Shinto vs. Buddhism
- Introduction of Buddhism into Japan (6th c. CE)
- This led to development of Shinto as a separate religion
- Written texts of oral Shinto emerged in 8th c.

Shinto Texts
- Kojiki (712, "Chronicles of Ancient Events")
- Nihongi (720, "Chronicles of Japan")

Period of Adjustment (Shinto vs. Buddhism)
- 8th century Emperor expanded influence of Buddhism
  - Kami became Bodhisattvas
- 17th century each family was required to belong to Buddhist temple
- 18th century scholars called for return to Ancient ways
  - Buddha and Confucius became Kami

State Shinto
- 19th century
  - Western imperialist challenge (Emperor Meiji = modernizer)
  - Meiji purified Shinto of many Buddhist influences
  - Places of worship had to decide whether they would be Shinto or Buddhist
  - All citizens required to register at Shinto shrine
  - No more state patronage of Buddhism
- 20th century—after defeat—Emperor Hirohito denied his divinity
- Beginning of privately funded Shrine Shinto

Creation Story from Kojiki
- Izanagi (He Who Invites) AND Izanami (She Who Invites) created Japanese islands
- After the production of the islands, the couple produced many Kami

Death of Izanami
- The birth of the fire god killed Izanami
- She went to the land of the dead
- Izanagi sought her in the corrupt land of the dead
- Izanagi polluted himself
- Ceremonial cleansing was required for him
- From this act of cleansing, other (Kami) were created

Most Important Kami

- Amaterasu, the sun goddess
- Amaterasu's grandson ruled islands
- First human emperor = Jimmu Tenno (660 BCE)
  - Amaterasu's great-grandson
  - Ancestor of all imperial houses
  - Human with Kami nature
  - Able to communicate with the sun goddess

Shrine of Amaterasu at Ise

- Simple structure of unpainted cedar
- Symbols of Amaterasu
  - mirror
  - sword
  - string of stone jewels
- Shrine is rebuilt every 20 years

Shrines

- 100,000 shrines in Japan
- Every village shrine and guardian Kami
- Torii = Sacred gateway entrance
  - Basins for washing mouth and hands before entering torii
- Priests and priestesses conduct rites in offering hall
- In Shinto there are few images of deity

EXTRA NOTES

SHINTO

1. What is the creation story of Japan?

2. Who are the Kami? How many are there?

3. What does the word Shinto mean?

4. What does the film say about Mt. Tachi and the Island Okinoshima?

5. Who lives on the island of Okinoshima?

6. What role do priests fulfill in Shinto?

7. What is the Imperial Shrine? How does it remain permanent while at the same time being permanently renewed?

8. How is the shrine at Izumo different from the shrine at Ise?

9. What do the Shinto priests offer to the Kami?

10. What is the relationship between Buddhism and Shinto?

SHINTO

What influence did Buddhism have on Shinto? Provide 3 concrete examples.

1.

2.

3.

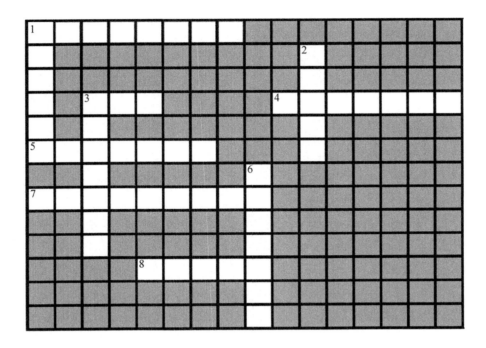

ACROSS

1. Shelf or home altar for the veneration of Japanese spirits
3. Major shrine to the Sun goddess
4. Second Chronicles of Japanese history
5. He Who Invites, the male principle, a deity in the earliest chronicles of Japanese history
7. The Sun goddess
8. Gatelike structure. It marks the territory of a Shinto shrine

DOWN

1. Earliest chronicles of Japanese history from the creation down to the middle of the 7th century.
2. Emperor who modernized Japan in the last quarter of the 19th century
3. She Who Invites, the female principle, a deity in the earliest chronicles of Japanese history
6. Code of honor for Japanese warriors

SHINTO

TEXT 13. THE JAPANESE CREATION MYTH

1. Describe the central conflict of this myth. How do you interpret the ending?

2. How different is this myth from the creation story in Genesis? [See Text 20]

Text Thirteen

The Japanese Creation Myth

OF OLD, Heaven and Earth were not yet separated, and the In and Yo (feminine and masculine principles) not yet divided. They formed a chaotic mass like an egg which was of obscurely defined limits and contained germs.

The purer and clearer part was thinly drawn out, and formed Heaven, while the heavier and grosser element settled down and became Earth.

The finer element easily became a united body, but the consolidation of the heavy and gross element was accomplished with difficulty.

Heaven was therefore formed first, and Earth was established subsequently.

Thereafter Divine Beings were produced between them.

Hence it is said that when the world began to be created, the soil of which lands were composed floated about in a manner which might be compared to the floating of a fish sporting on the surface of the water.

At this time a certain thing was produced between Heaven and Earth. It was in form like a reed-shoot. Now this became transformed into a God, and was called Kuni-toko-tachi no Mikoto [Land-eternal-stand-of-August-thing].

Next there was Kuni no sa-tsuchi no Mikoto [Land-of-right-soil-of-Augustness] and next Toyo-kumu-nu no Mikoto, [Rich-form-plain-of-Augustness] in all three deities.

These were pure males spontaneously developed by the operation of the principle of Heaven.

The next Deities who came into being were Uhiji-ni no Mikoto and Suiji-ni no Mikoto, also called Uhiji-ne no Mikoto [Mud-earth] and Suhiji-ne no ikoto [Sand-earth].

The next Deities which came into being were Oho-to nochi no Mikoto [Great-after-door] and Oho-to mahe no Mikoto [Great-before-door].

The next Gods which came into being were Omo-taru no Mikoto [Face- leasing] and Kashiko-ne no Mikoto [awful], also called Aya-kashiko-ne no Mikoto, Imi kashiki no Mikoto, or Awo-kashiki-ne no Mikoto, or Aya-kashiki no Mikoto.

The next Deities which came into being were Izanagi no Mikoto [Male-who-invites] and Izanami no Mikoto [Female-who-invites].

These make eight Deities in all. Being formed by the mutual action of the Heavenly and Earthly principles, they were made male and female. From Kuni no toko-tachi no Mikoto to Izanagi no Mikoto and Izanami no Mikoto are called the seven generations of the age of the Gods.

Izanagi no Mikoto and Izanami no Mikoto stood on the floating bridge of Heaven, and held counsel together, saying: "Is there not a country beneath?"

Thereupon they thrust down the jewel-spear of Heaven, and groping about therewith found the ocean. The brine which dripped from the point of the spear coagulated and became an island which received the name of Ono-goro-jima [Spontaneously-congealed-island].

The two Deities thereupon descended and dwelt in this island. Accordingly they wished to become husband and wife together, and to produce countries.

So they made Ono-goro-jima the pillar of the centre of the land.

Now the male deity turning by the left, and the female deity by the right, they went round the pillar of the land separately. When they met together on one side, the female deity spoke first and said:--"How delightful! I have met with a lovely youth." The male deity was displeased, and said:--"I am a man, and by right should have spoken first. How is it that on the contrary thou, a woman, shouldst have been the first to speak? This was unlucky. Let us go round again." Upon this the two deities went back, and having met anew, this time the male deity spoke first, and said:--"How delightful! I have met a lovely maiden."

Then he inquired of the female deity, saying:--"In thy body is there aught formed?" She answered, and said:--"In my body there is a place which is the source of femininity." The male deity said:--"In my body again there is a place which is the source of masculinity. I wish to unite this source-place of my body to the source-place of thy body." Hereupon the male and female first became united as husband and wife.

Now when the time of birth arrived, first of all the island of Ahaji was reckoned as the placenta, and their minds took no pleasure in it. Therefore it received the name of Ahaji no Shima [the island which is unsatisfactory].

Next there was produced the island of Oho-yamato no Toyo-aki-tsushima [rich-harvest-of-island].

Next they produced the island of Iyo no futa-na, and next the island of Tsukushi. Next the islands of Old and Sado were born as twins. This is the prototype of the twin-births which sometimes take place among mankind.

Next was born the island of Koshi, then the island of Oho-shima, then the island of Kibi no ko.

Hence first arose the designation of the Oho-ya-shima country [great-eight-island country].

Then the islands of Tsushima and Iki, with the small islands in various parts, were produced by the coagulation of the foam of the salt-water.

They next produced the sea, then the rivers, and then the mountains. Then they produced Ku-ku-no-chi, the ancestor of the trees, and next the ancestor of herbs, Kaya no hime.

After this Izanagi no Mikoto and Izanami no Mikoto consulted together, saying:--"We have not produced the Great-eight-island country, with the mountains, rivers, herbs, and trees. Why should we not produce someone who shall be lord of the universe? They then together produced the Sun-Goddess, who was called Oho-hiru-me no muchi [Great-noon-female-of-possessor].

The resplendent luster of this child shone throughout all the six quarters [North, East, South, West, Above and Below]. Therefore the two Deities rejoiced, saying:--"We have had many children, but none of them have been equal to this wondrous infant. She ought not to be kept long in this land, but we ought of our own accord to send her at once to Heaven, and entrust to her the affairs of Heaven."

At this time Heaven and Earth were still not far separated, and therefore they sent her up to Heaven by the ladder of Heaven.

They next produced the Moon.

His radiance was next to that of the Sun in splendour. This God was to be the consort of the Sun-Goddess, and to share in her government. They therefore sent him also to Heaven.

Next they produced the leech-child, which even at the age of three years could not stand upright. They therefore placed it in the rock-camphor-wood boat of Heaven, and abandoned it to the winds.

Their next child was Sosa no wo no Mikoto [Impetuous One].

This God had a fierce temper and was given to cruel acts. Moreover he made a practice of continually weeping and wailing. So he brought many of the people of the land to an untimely end. Again he caused green mountains to become withered. Therefore the two Gods, his parents, addressed Sosa no wo no Mikoto, saying:--"Thou art exceedingly wicked, and it is not meet that thou shouldst reign over the world. Certainly thou must depart far away to the Netherland" [Hades]. So they at length expelled him.

Their next child was Kagu tsuchi [god of fire].

Now Izanami no Mikoto was burnt by Kagu tsuchi, so that she died. When she was lying down to die, she gave birth to the Earth-Goddess, Hani- yama-hime, and the Water-Goddess, Midzu-ha-no-me. Upon this Kagu tsuchi took to wife Hani-yama-hime, and they had a child named Waka-musubi [young growth]. On the crown of this Deity's head were produced the silkworm and the mulberry tree, and in her navel the five kinds of grain.

Thereafter, Izanagi no Mikoto went after Izanami no Mikoto, and entered the land of Yomi [Hades]. When he reached her they conversed together, and Izanami no Mikoto said: "My lord and husband, why is the coming so late? I have already eaten of the cooking-furnace of Yomi. Nevertheless, I am about to lie down to rest. I pray thee, do not thou look on me." Izanagi no Mikoto did not give ear to her, but secretly took his many-toothed comb and, breaking off its end tooth, made of it a torch, and looked at her. Putrefying matter had gushed up, and maggots swarmed. This is why people at the present day avoid using a single light at night, and also avoid throwing away a comb at night. Izanagi no Mikoto was greatly shocked, and said: "Nay! I have come unawares to a hideous and polluted land." So he speedily ran away back again. Then Izanami no Mikoto was angry, and said: "Why didst thou not observe that which I charged thee? Now am I put to shame." So she sent the eight Ugly Females of Yomi to pursue and slay him. Izanagi no Mikoto therefore drew his sword, and, flourishing it behind him, ran away. Then he took his black head-dress and flung it down. It became changed into grapes, which the Ugly Females seeing, took and ate. When they had finished

eating them, they again pursued Izanagi no Mikoto. Then he flung down his many-toothed comb, which forthwith became changed into bamboo-shoots. The Ugly Females pulled them up and ate them, and when they had done eating them, again gave chase. Afterwards, Izanami no Mikoto came herself and pursued him. By this time Izanagi no Mikoto had reached the Even Pass of Yomi.

But, having visited in person the Land of Yomi, he had brought on himself ill-luck. In order, therefore, to wash away the defilement, he visited the Aha gate [a strait famous for its rapid tides] and the Haya-sufu-na [Quick-suchname] gate. But the tide in these two gates was exceeding strong. So he returned and, took his way towards Wodo [little gate) in Tachibana. There he did his ablutions. At this time, entering the water, he blew out and produced Iha-tsu-tsu no Mikoto [Rock-of-Elder); coming out of the water, he blew forth and produced Oho-nawo-bi no Kami [Great Remedy Person]. Entering a second time, he blew out and produced Sokotsutsu, no Mikoto [Bottom-elder]; coming out he blew forth and produced Oho-aya-tsu-bi no Kami [Great-Pattern-of-Person]. Entering again, he blew forth and produced Aka-tsutsu no Mikoto [Red Elder], and coming out he blew out and produced the various deities of Heaven and Earth, and of the Sea-plain.

After this, Izanagi no Mikoto, his divine task having been accomplished, and his spirit-career about to suffer a change, built himself an abode of gloom in the island of Ahaji, where he dwelt for ever in silence and concealment.

Taoism (Daoism)

Ying Yang Symbol of Harmony

Giant Joss Pot with Dragon in Chinese Temple

Part 2: RELIGIONS ORIGINATING IN EAST ASIA: THE MYTH OF HARMONY

TAOISM (DAOISM)

Two Major Concepts to Understand Chinese Religious Traditions
- Harmony
- Virtue (DE in Chinese): moral excellence, goodness, righteousness

What is the Tao (Dao)?
- "Way" or "path" = "the Way of all things"
- Mysterious source and ordering principle of universe

Major Dynasties and Periods of Chinese History
- Shang Dynasty (ca. 1600-1122 BCE) — *before axis age (6ᵗʰ BCE)*
  - First identifiable Chinese state
  - Cult of Shang Di
- Chou (Zhou) Dynasty (1122-221 BCE) — *6ᵗʰ c. BCE, time of axis age*
  - Time of chaos
  - Philosophical Daoism in 6th century BCE   *Time of chaos/war*
- Ch'in dynasty (221-206 BCE)
  - China united for the first time
- Han dynasty (206 BCE-220 CE)
  - Religious Daoism in 1st-2nd century CE — *Buddhism entered China*
  - Confucian ideas prevailed in administration   *1 c. common era*

Daoism
- Philosophical Daoism emerged between 6th and 3rd century BCE under the Chou (Zhou) dynasty before first unification of China
- Time of major political and social chaos
- How to restore virtue (DE)?

Three Schools of Philosophy
- Legalist (or Authoritarian): human beings are basically selfish and materialistic. Clearly defined laws must be enforced to maintain order [power comes from military might].
- Confucian: virtue exists. Human beings need structure and rules in order to learn to love. Family training. *— Optimistic about human nature*
- Daoist school exalts nature over society. Virtue is understanding and conforming to the Dao.

Development of Daoism
- Started as a mystical philosophy of life (no focus on gods and no use of rituals)
- WHEN? 6th-3rd century BCE
- Developed into a popular religious system with many deities and many rituals
- WHEN? 1st-2nd century CE

Daoism Today
- In recent past, persecuted in mainland China
- Resurgence in popularity

Daoism Practiced
- Taiwan
- Hong Kong
- Chinese communities of Malaysia, Thailand, Singapore
- U.S. (San Francisco)

A Taste of Daoist Worldview
- No god-creator. There is the Dao.
- Dao (the Way) = mysterious source and ordering principle of the universe
- It is "zero" (that is the pure potential)
- Source of gods
- Neither positive nor negative
- No command; no judgment
- Experienced as female because Dao sustains and nurtures

Liz doing the right thing at the right time = propriety

How does the Dao produce the world?
- Self-generation or gestation; the Dao grows itself into the universe
- The universe is the body of the Dao

Stages of Cosmic Gestation
Dao as primal chaos moved around until in its center was formed a "drop" of primordial breath
- Primordial breath or energy (qi or ch'i) divided itself
- Yin (femaleness) and Yang (maleness) interacted and formed
- Heaven, earth, and humanity
- The Four seasons
- The Five directions (four directions plus the center) and the Five phases [4 and 5 are the basic structure of universe]

Qi (Ch'i)
- Dao generated qi (ch'i)
- Qi (ch'i) = "the One" = primordial energy, the breath of life
- Each human being has this qi
- Daoist practice is based on how humans nurture qi

Yin and Yang
- Qi developed two complementary patterns of energy or energy modes
- YIN = dark, heavy, obscure, passive, earth, death, and feminine
- YANG = light, warm, airy, active, life, heaven, and masculine
- The whole universe can be understood as yin, yang, or a combination of the two in flux and interaction
- Both energies harmonized and formed human beings

- Human body = microcosm of world
- Cosmic connections can be found between body parts, seasons, planets, divinities, and the elements

Five Phases
- Metal, Wood, Fire, Water, Earth
- They are linked with the five directions: east, south, west, north, and solstices
- They are linked with body parts
- They are linked with planets, names of gods, and basic colors
- In short, they are patterns or modes of activity that repeat themselves in nature and human body

Daoist Practice
- Learn how to control qi
- Goal is to ally oneself to the yang pattern of light-male-heaven
- But also cultivate yin quality of femaleness; female-yin energies nurture and vitalize male-yang energies
- Powerful divinities may be called down to revitalize us

T'ai-chi ch'uan
- Developed in 18th century CE as a training for martial arts
- Helps to channel qi to body organs and revitalize them
- Practiced by Chinese at dawn and dusk for their health

Ancient Folk Tradition during the Shang dynasty
- Were incorporated into Daoism, Confucianism, and Buddhism
- Beliefs and practices typical of everyday life passed down from generation to generation

Major Features of Folk Tradition during the Shang dynasty
- Veneration of ancestors
  – Sacred rituals are called li
- Veneration of deities and nature spirits
- Belief in an underlying order in the cosmos, nature, and human societies
  – Shang Ti, the Lord-on-High, ruler of the universe

Laozi = founder of philosophical Taoism

Shang Ti (Di)
- Shang dynasty (1600-1122 BCE) – *ancestor*
- Ruler of the Universe
- NOT a Creator-God
- Supreme ancestor of the Chinese + ancestor of ruling Shang family
- Guarantor of moral order
- Emperor = chief priest and diviner *→ predict future*

★ Yin went down & formed earth

★ Yang went up & formed heaven

Mandate of Heaven (T'ien Ming) Under Chou (Zhou) Dynasty
- Zhou dynasty overthrew Shang dynasty *6th c. BCE*
- Needed justification for rebellion
- Mandate of Heaven = Dao of Heaven or Order of Heaven

- Heaven
   = deity, supreme reality (but not embodied)
   = divine order of universe
   = Self-existing moral law of virtue
- Heaven will choose a virtuous family to rule
- Special relationship based on merit, not birth

Emperor = Son of Heaven
- Title held until 1906
- Heaven, earth, and the emperor linked together
- Ruler conducted rituals to maintain harmony between Earth and Heaven

More Features of Folk Tradition
- Belief in keeping harmony
- How can one keep harmony in the world?
   – Maintain worship of gods and ancestors + respect for elders
   – Divination
     • reading cracks on heated bones and shells
     • sticks or coins dropped on the ground to form trigrams and hexagrams
     • "I Ching" (Yijing) ("Book of Changes")

Daoism = Ambiguous Designation
- Came to distinguish itself from Confucianism
- Refers to
   – Philosophical tradition or Dao jia ("the Philosophy of the Dao")   *the old baby, old portrayed old*
     • Traced to legendary sage Laozi (Lao-tzu or Lao-tse)
     • Expressed in Daodejing ("The Classic of the Way and its Power")
   – Religious tradition or Dao jiao (Teaching of the Dao) [1st-2nd century CE]
     • Worship of deities through rituals. Human Laozi becomes Cosmic Laozi (the world is the body of Laozi = body of the Dao)

Philosophical Daoism
- Scripture = Daodejing ("The Classic of the Way and its Power")   *political manual How the king should rule*
- Author Laozi
- 350 and 275 BCE?
- Systematized previous beliefs about Dao
- Main concern: how can individuals experience Dao and let their lives flow in harmony with it
- Book originally conceived as political manual:

To Be in Harmony with the Dao. What does this mean concretely?
   • Live a simple, natural life
   • Experience the unity of all things, rather than separation
   • Accept and cooperate with things as they are
   • Be receptive and quiet

A Life Based on Wu Wei

- Wu wei = "non-action," "inaction," "non-purposiveness"
    - Refraining from overly aggressive action
    - Refraining from taking an intentional action contrary to natural flow of things
- Action without ego-assertion, concretely it means:
    - Having no ambitions, no desires for fame and power
    - Having no need to dominate others
    - Leading a contemplative life
    - Loving nature
    - Virtue (de) will be natural, NOT contrived (vs. Confucianism)

In politics, Wu wei = non-interference

- The ruler plays a passive role
- The ruler is hardly noticed
- The ruler takes feelings and opinions of his people as his own
- If the government imposes strict laws, it will cause resentment and crime
- If it stresses morality, the people will act artificially

In Education

- Be passively open and receptive

Zhuang Zi (Master Chuang) (4th century BCE)   = lao zi

- Less political than Daodejing
- Focused mainly on the individual path
- Total detachment from society and civilization
- Judgments are relative
- Life is a delusion?

humorous

Religious Daoism

- Developed in 1st-2nd century CE   - when Buddhism entered China
- Daodejing and Zhuang Zi speak of eternal Dao
- The two books seem to suggest that whoever is in harmony with the Dao may live forever

Pursuit of Immortality and Well-Being

- If balance can be restored between yin and yang, humans can avoid death
- How?
    - Alchemy
    - Hygienic and dietary regime
    - Sorcery
    - Breath control techniques and physical exercises
    - Sexual practices involving suppression of orgasm
    - Living a life of virtue
    - Worship in temples and petition to a deity or an immortal for assistance

Daoist Societies
- Emerged in 2nd century CE
- Had a political and religious dimension
- Responded to decline of Han dynasty (206 BCE-220 CE)
- Present unjust order had to be replaced by new Daoist imperium

Response to Buddhism
- Buddhism entered China in 1st century CE
- Production of sacred books
- Opening of Daoist temples
- Groups of ascetics got together

Messianic Character
- 1st century CE, Laozi = immortal
- 2nd century CE = deity = Taishang Laojun, "Lord Lao on High"
- Laozi will manifest himself to save mankind from the Han rule
- Rebellions occurred, led by faith healers, advocating egalitarian ideas

Institutionalization of Ancient Practices
- Folk religion expressed itself orally
- Daoist societies regulated worship of deities and ancestors
- Liturgy came to be written down in literary Chinese

Religious Daoism
The Way of the Celestial Masters (1st-2nd century CE in Western China)
- Founder: Zhang Daoling (healer)
- Group still exists today in Taiwan
- Secret society + strict hierarchy
- Goal: attain longevity through faith healing, meditative trance, and alchemy
- Accepted minorities and women in the ranks of parish leadership

Celestial Master Zhang Daoling
- Personally ordained by Laozi, who appeared to him out of the spirit world
- Discovered formula for potion of immortality
- Ascended alive to heaven
- Successors Also Called Celestial Masters
- Line of hereditary "Celestial Masters"

Libationers
- Ones who make an offering
- Leaders of dioceses
- Of both sexes and trained to exorcize illness by prescribing confession of sin
- Teachers of social ethics
- Administered justice
- Collected family contributions

Political Impact
- Led revolts against government
- Thanks to this group, Daoism received imperial recognition

Yellow Turbans (The Way of Great Peace)
- Founder: Zhang Jue
- 2nd century CE conquered the whole of the Yellow River in eastern China
- Yin and yang were no longer in balance in heaven and on earth
- A new "Yellow Heaven" mandate was to replace the Han dynasty mandate

Religious Daoist Pantheon
- Organized on bureaucratic model of Han dynasty
- At the top unmanifest Dao
- Then, Qi = primordial chaos or breath
- First category of deities (emanations of the Dao)
  - Three Purities — heaven, earth, humanity
  - Jade Emperor
  - Three Officials
- They hold courts in celestial paradises

(handwritten annotations: DAO; heaven ↑ yang (Qi) — yin ↓ earth; combine; humanity; laozi = lord of humanity)

The Three Purities
- = Emanations of the Dao
- Lord of Heaven, Lord of Earth, and Lord of Humanity

Three Purities and Correlates
- The priest can invoke them to ward off negative energies
- Have microcosmic correlates in the head, heart, and abdomen of human beings
  Ex: The Lord of Humanity (Laozi) has his microcosmic power seated in the abdomen of each person.

The Jade Emperor
- Huang Di, the Jade Emperor identified with Shang Di, ruler of Heaven
- Jade Emperor = mythical emperor of ancient China
- Governed popular pantheon of regional gods

The Three Officials (Officials of Heaven, Earth, and Water)
- Ancient deities
- Keep records of human deeds on earth
- Control each person's life span and fate after death
- Stern
- When a Daoist falls sick, priest would submit petitions to the Three Officials

Second Category of Daoist Deities

- Human beings who have become immortals and gods
- Eight immortals
- Queen Mother of the West
- Still lower in hierarchy are the spirits of demons, humans, ancestors, and animals
- "Shen," God of the stove

Internal Gods

- 36,000 gods inside our body
- Just as the macrocosm of the universe contains gods, so does the human body

EXTRA NOTES

Confucianism →
can be trained to
be virtuos

virtue = De
propriety = Li
God of State = Shen

Taoism →
if you have
rules you will
rebel

Analects - teachings of confucius

Laozi and Confucius were deified (1-2 centure CE)
at the time when Buddhism entered China

Shu (reciprocity) = a confucian virtue, do onto others as
you would have
them do to you

Religious Daoism developed 1st-2nd c. CE
- time Buddhism entered China

★ gods &
priests wear
exact same
robe

clouds/smoke in Daoist art = the Dao
"temples" and altars are all temporary

turtle, cranes, peaches = immortality

★ Zhang Guolaa → recognized carrying peach
↳ immortal

TAOISM / CONFUCIANISM

1. When did Communism take over in China?

2. Who was the leader of the Communist Revolution?

3. When did Buddhism enter China?

4. When did anti-religious policies relax in China?

5. What is the Tao (Dao)?

6. What do Taoists believe in?

7. How can longevity be achieved?

8. What is the Taoist view of nature?

9. Who was Confucius?

10. What was Confucius' model of society?

11. What was destroyed during the Cultural Revolution in China?

12. Where is the temple of the Jade Emperor?

13. What do people do at the top of Taishan Mountain?

TAOISM (DAOISM)

TEXT 14. DAODEJING

Describe the characteristics of an ideal Daoist ruler.

Text Fourteen

Daodejing

One
As to a Dao--
      if it can be specified as a Dao,
      it is not a permanent Dao.
As to a name--
      if it can be specified as a name,
      it is not a permanent name.

Having no name
      is the beginning of the ten thousand things.
Having a name
      is the mother of the ten thousand things.

Thus,
to be permanently without desires
      in order to see the subtleties.
to permanently have desires
      in order to see that which is yearned for.

The two--
      together they come to the fore,
      differently they are named.
Together they are called:
Darker even than darkness--
Gate of multiple subtleties.

Two
Everybody in the world knows the beautiful as being beautiful.
      Thus there is already ugliness.

Everybody knows what is good.
      Thus there is that which is not good.

That

      presence and nonpresence generate each other,
      difficult and easy complement each other,
      long and short give each other shape,
      above and below fill each other,
      tones and voices harmonize with each other,
      before and after follow each other,
is permanent.

Therefore the sage
      resides with the task of nonaction,
      practices the teaching of nonspeaking.

The ten thousand things--
      he makes them work, but does not initiate them,
      he makes them act, but does not depend on them,
      he makes them complete their tasks and does not
        reside with them.

Well,
      only because he does not reside with them,
      they do not depart.

Twenty-five
There is a thing--
      it came to be in the undifferentiated,
      it came alive before heaven and earth.

What stillness! What emptiness!
Alone it stands fast and does not change.
It can be mother to heaven and earth.

I do not know its name.
It is called Dao.
If I was forced to name it,
        I would say "Greatness."
"Greatness" means "to proceed."
"To proceed" means "distance."
"Distance" means "return."

The Dao is great.
Heaven is great.
The earth is great.
The king is also great.
In the land there are four greats--
        and the king positions himself where they are one.
Humans follow the earth as a rule.
The earth follows heaven as a rule.
Heaven follows the Dao as a rule.
The Dao follows its self-so as a rule.

Twenty-nine
If one wants to take hold of the world,
        and act on it--
I see that he will not succeed.
Well,
        the world is a sacred vessel,
        and not something that can be acted on.
Those who act on things will be defeated by them.
Those who take things in their hands will lose them.

The things:
        some go, some follow,
        some burn, some break,
        some rise, some fall.
Therefore the sage
        discards the excessive,
        discards the great,
        discards the extraordinary.

Thirty
When the ruler of people is assisted by the Dao
        then the force of weapons is not used in the world.

Such affairs like to turn around:
        Where armies were placed
        grow thorns and brushes.

The one who is good has success--
        that is all.
He does not use force to get it.
He has success and is not proud.
He has success and is not arrogant.
He has success and does not brag.
He has success and does not get anything with which he
        would abide.
This is called: "He has success without using force."

If a thing grows up and then gets old,
        this is called "not the Dao."
"Not the Dao" ends early.

Thirty-one
Weapons are the tools of ill omen.
Generally they are loathed.
Thus one who has intentions will not reside with them.
When the noble man is at his residence
        he esteems the left.
When the noble man makes use of the military
        he esteems the right.

Thus,
weapons are not the tools of the noble man.
Weapons are the tools of ill omen.
When he cannot do otherwise, he uses them—
        to him staying calm is the best.
Do not regard them with delight.
To regard them with delight--
        this is to enjoy the killing of people.
Well, by enjoying the killing of people
        one is unable to get what one wants in the world.
Therefore
        in auspicious matters the left is in highest regard,
        in matters of mourning the right is in highest regard.
Therefore
        the lieutenant general stands to the left
        and the supreme commander stands to the right.
That is to say:
        they are positioned in accordance with funeral rites.
When masses of people are killed,
        this is faced with grief and sorrow.
When a war is won,
        the occasion is treated—with funeral rites.

Thirty-four
The Dao--
> How it flows!
> Left and right it can be.

The task is completed,
the duty is fulfilled,
> but it is without name.
The ten thousand things return to it,
> but it does not act as their ruler,
> so that it is constantly without desire.
It can be named with the small.
The ten thousand things return to it,
> but it does not act as their ruler.
It can be mandated with the great.

Therefore
> the sage can accomplish the great
> by his not acting on the great.
Thus he can accomplish the great.

Forty-nine
The sage is constantly without a heart;
> he takes the heart of the common people as the heart.

That which is good
> he holds to be good.
That which is not good
> he also holds to be good.
Thus he attains goodness.
That which is true
> he holds to be true.
That which is not true
> he also holds to be true.
Thus he attains truth.

When the sage resides in the world,
> he fuses himself with it.
For the world he merges hearts.
All the people fix ears and eyes on him,
> and the sage regards them as smiling children.

TEXT 15. WOMEN IN TAOISM (DAOISM)

1. How did Daoist philosophical literature relate to women?

2. The author (Barbara Reed) contends that Daoism is potentially feminist. How is this claim reflected in Daoist practice and belief?

3. In what way does the relationship between *yin* and *yang* reflect gender relationship?

4. The author interprets certain passages from the Tao te ching (Daodejing) as valuing the female or feminine traits. Do you feel that her interpretations are justified or does she infer too much on the basis of contemporary, western views of gender?

5. Who is the Queen Mother of the West (Hsi Wang Mu)? Why is she important?

Text Fifteen

Women in Daoism

TAOISM

> The Valley Spirit never dies.
> It is named the Mysterious Female.
> And the Doorway of the Mysterious Female
> Is the base from which Heaven and Earth sprang.
> It is there within us all the while;
> Draw upon it as you will, it never runs dry.
>   (Tao te ching VI, Waley 1958, 149)

ANY religious or philosophical tradition that symbolizes cosmic and personal creativity as the "Mysterious Female" has great potential for attracting women's participation. Taoism not only uses female images for creative powers, but also advocates the harmony and equality of all opposites, including male and female. Women's historical fate in Taoism is especially interesting because it developed within the extremely patriarchal culture of Confucian China.

Taoism is the native religious tradition of China. It has shaped Chinese culture along with the native philosophical tradition of Confucianism and the imported Buddhist religion. According to tradition, Taoism was founded by the legendary Lao tzu in the sixth century B.C.E. But its roots are traceable to ancient shamanistic practices, deities, and myths which were incorporated into a rich tradition of philosophy, ritual, and magic. The Taoist tradition has several interacting strands: the mystical and philosophical texts, such as the Tao te ching (compiled ca. third century

B.C.E.) and the Chuang tzu (fourth century B.C.E.), the Taoist religious sects dating from the second century C.E., and various techniques of exorcising malevolent spirits and attaining immortality.

WOMEN IN TAOIST PHILOSOPHICAL LITERATURE

The two great classics of Taoist philosophy, the Tao te ching and Chuang tzu, extol the way of nature as the path to happiness. The mysterious way of nature is called Tao. One can know Tao by yielding to and following nature. One should act spontaneously, naturally, without purpose. These two Taoist texts describe similar paths to simplicity and happiness, but they address themselves to different audiences and use radically different styles. The Tao te ching uses feminine imagery and traditional views of female roles to counter destructive male behavior. Chuang tzu illustrates the Tao by describing anecdotes in the lives of individuals who manifest the Tao.

The Tao te ching is a short, cryptic text addressed to the ruler. One who has the responsibility of rule could, it suggests, create a simple and happy society by allowing the Tao to govern. The mysterious Tao can transform all things spontaneously if the ruler does not intervene with obstructive behavior. The Sage Ruler says: "So long as I love quietude, the people will of themselves go straight. So long as I act only by inactivity the people will of themselves become prosperous" (Tao te ching LVII, Waley 1958, 211). To communicate the Tao, the path of quietude and inactivity, the Tao te ching relies heavily on female imagery. Ultimately, the Tao is ineffable: "The Way that can be told of is not an Unvarying Way" Waley 1958, 141). But the Tao manifests itself in creativity and in spontaneous, nonaggressive human behavior. The Tao te ching symbolizes this behavior in concrete images from nature: water, the uncarved block, the child, the female, the mother, the valley, the dark, the bellows, the door, the empty vessel, the mare, and the hen. Most of these symbols are explicitly female, and all of them point to the potentiality associated with female reproduction or the unqualified nature of motherly love. Ellen Chen has shown that in many ways the Tao represents the Great Mother, the creative power of the female (1969, 1973, 1974).

Creation in the Tao te ching is the production of all things from the womb of the Mother. The Tao is named the "Mother," the "dark," and the "mysterious." She is the "doorway" through which things enter the visible world (VI, Waley 1958, 149). All things were created by her and continue to rely on her for their sustenance. The creativity of the Tao depends on the womb of creation, on its emptiness, its potentiality. The Tao is nonbeing in the Taoist understanding of nonbeing as the potential for new being--not in the usual Western sense of the negation of being. The Tao as empty has unlimited potentiality.

> The Way is like an empty vessel
> That yet may be drawn from
> Without ever needing to be filled
> It is bottomless; the very progenitor of all things in
>   the world.
> (Tao te ching IV, Waley 1958, 146)

Tao as nonbeing is the beginning of all things and should also be that to which all things return. Unless one realizes that nonbeing is the sacred quality of female creative power, the return to the darkness of nonbeing appears to be a morbid search for annihilation (Chen 1974, 52-53). The return to original nonbeing is truly the return to authentic existence. Perhaps the goal of returning to the Tao is rooted in an earlier worship of the mother goddess (Chen 1974, 53). Because the cycle of return is grounded in the creative power of the Tao, it has none of the terror or meaninglessness associated with Hindu conceptions of life in continuing cycles. As Eliade (1959) has suggested, the terror of cyclical views of time occurs only when the sacred nature of the cosmos has been forgotten (107-109). The Tao te ching does not envision a primordial beginning

with specific gods and goddesses. The creative powers of the beginning are instead symbolized by the abstract Mother, the Tao. She provides the comfort and meaning for the return to the beginning.

Nonbeing and being are both described with female imagery. Tao as the nameless (nonbeing) is beyond categories, but in attempting to describe it the text uses images of the dark and mysterious female. Tao as the named (being) is the source of all things. In Ellen Chen's view, the creativity of the nameless Tao as Mother is based on her emptiness, and the creativity of the named Tao (being) is based on its potentiality. The Mother is nonbeing, and her child of unlimited potential is being (Chen 1973, 411).

The spirit and creativity of the Mother is also found within all her creatures.

> The Valley Spirit never dies.
> It is named the Mysterious Female.
> And the Doorway of the Mysterious Female
> Is the base from which Heaven and Earth sprang.
> It is there within us all the while;
> Draw upon it as you will, it never runs dry.
> (Tao te ching VI, Waley 1958, 149)

The Taoist follows the Tao by acting as a child and clinging to the Mother's breast (XX, Waley 1958, 169). The way to act in the world is to follow the role traditionally assigned to women in society--to be weak, flexible, and lowly. Creative power comes from these positions, not from positions of strength, hardness, or superiority. "He who knows the male, yet cleaves to what is female/Becomes like a ravine, receiving all things under heaven" (XXVIII, Waley 1958, 178). The lowly position is identified with women but is advocated for all--particularly for the ruler, to whom the entire text is addressed. If the ruler acts passively, all things spontaneously follow the creative principle within them.

The Tao te ching takes a negative view toward the achievements of traditionally male-dominant Chinese civilization--its books, laws, and travel (Chen 1974, 53). And it views the traditional love of the mother as the model for the relationship of the Tao to all creation. The Tao, like the love of a mother, makes no distinctions; it embraces both the "good" and the "bad" (LXII, Waley 1958, 218). One who follows Tao also refrains from judgments and accepts all things that come from the mother (XLIX, Waley 1958, 202). Traditional

Text Fifteen: WOMEN IN DAOISM

sex roles and biological differences are recognized but denied determinative status. All people (male or female) should take the role of the infant clinging to the Mother or of the female animal beneath the male in order to live in harmony in the world and to return to the Tao.

The Tao te ching uses both female biological characteristics and traditional socially defined characteristics to symbolize the Taoist path. The biological imagery of the womb and breast dominates images of the Tao; the social role of passivity dominates the images of the person who follows the Tao.

Chuang tzu does not use female imagery to communicate the Tao. Whereas the Tao te ching uses universal female images abstracted from nature to counter the normal way of perceiving and acting, Chuang tzu teaches in concrete anecdotes. The text illustrates Tao by describing people who have lived in harmony with it. Although women are mentioned, most of the characters are men. But all those who follow Tao act in the yielding and spontaneous way suggested by the Tao te ching. Chuang tzu expands the meaning of returning to the Tao by expressing a joyful acceptance of the mysterious transformation called "death." One should yield to all things brought about by the Tao, even death.

There are two items in Chuang tzu that are particularly interesting for this investigation of women in Taoism. First, Chuang tzu mentions a myth of a utopian matrilineal society in which people "knew their mothers, but not their fathers" (XX.DC, Watson 1968, 327). Second, Chuang tzu sees no sex restrictions for the immortal beings who are an important part of later popular legends and religious Taoism. Hsi Wang Mu, the Queen Mother of the West, appears as one who found Tao and became immortal (VI, Watson 1968, 82). And there is also an old woman with the complexion of a child who knew Tao and tried to teach it to a sage (VI, Watson 1968, 82-83).

The Tao te ching and Chuang tzu both reject the aggressive, highly structured societies of their times in favor of lives of simplicity close to nature. With no value placed on social hierarchy, there is no place for the denigration of women. In fact, in the Tao te ching women serve as models.

YIN AND YANG

The complementary principles of yin and yang are important in most of Chinese thought and religion. They are not unique to Taoism, but in Taoism they are fundamental. Yin is the dark side, the cold, the damp, the female. Yang is the sunny side, the hot, the dry, the male.

In Taoist thinking, yin and yang are the complementary principles of the cosmos. The ideal is balance, not the victory of one over the other. In the Tao te ching the balance is grounded in the yin, which has the lower position. In Chuang tzu the alternation of the two, such as life and death, is accepted as the transformation of the Tao. Neither is superior--the yin state of death is as acceptable as the yang state of life. One cannot exist without the other; they are both part of the wondrous Tao.

The yin-yang duality of balance is strikingly different from Western conceptions of conflict dualism. In Western dualism, the victory of good over evil is based on a conflict that separates everything and everyone into two opposing sides that cannot exist in peace. Violence, whether physical or mental, may be necessary for the victory of one side over the other. There is no room for compromise with the other side--"You are either for us or against us," as the saying goes. This conflict dualism gives great hope to those on the side of "good" because there is the assurance that good is stronger than evil. Good, usually represented as God, will win in the end. The closer the end, the more hope for the forces of good.

Taoist harmony is a radically different goal than the victory of good over evil. It is based on a complementary dualism rather than a conflict dualism. There are two sides, but they depend on each other for their existence. The goal is the balancing of the two sides, the mutual interaction of the two forces. This complementary dualism has been the core of much east Asian religion and philosophy. It is the yin-yang model that originated in ancient China. One attains harmony in society and nature through the balancing of the positive forces of yang and the negative forces of yin. The cooperative actions of male and female, summer and winter, the sun and rain are examples of this complementary dualism, in which neither side is better than nor independent of the other. Yin and yang are viewed as female and male principles or forces, but women and men contain both principles and need the harmony of the two for physical and mental health

The idea of the balance and relativity of yin and yang is difficult to maintain. In later Confucian thought and in some religious

Taoism, yang is evaluated as the superior. In the Taoist quest for immortality, the relativity of individual life and death is superseded by the development of techniques for holding off death by the accumulation of yang. Breathing exercises, special diets, laboratory alchemy, and sexual practices were all developed in the context of yin-yang theory to prolong life and to attain individual immortality.

Even though the desire for the yang principle of life dominates, however, the importance of the yin principle never dies. Taoist techniques for attaining immortality are based on the cooperation of yin and yang and maternal creativity. The union of yin and yang in sexual intercourse is one technique to produce an immortal body and serves as the paradigm for others. In laboratory alchemy, the crucible functions as the womb, the elements of cinnabar and lead as female and male sexual fluids, and the alchemic firing process as the sexual technique (van Gulik 1974, 80). The equal importance of yin and yang is central to most Taoist paths to immortality. Both yin and yang could be absorbed through the skin to further the Taoist's progress toward immortality. The Classic of the Five Sacred Talismans (Ling-pao wu fu ching) of the third or fourth century suggests that the adept "breathe" in yang from the light of the sun and yin from the light of the moon at midnight (Seidel 1983, 1039).

HISTORY OF RELIGIOUS TAOISM

The Taoist religion can be most narrowly defined as the religious organization that traces itself to the second century revelations to Chang Tao-ling. A deified form of Lao tzu, the legendary author of the Tao te ching, appeared to him. Chang Tao-ling became known as the first Celestial Master (t'ien-shih) after he ascended into the heavens. He received a new teaching that taught how to cure illness and how to create a new religious and political structure in China. This structure soon became based on patriarchal leadership, with his male descendants carrying out the religious administration as Celestial Masters. The leadership was not totally male, however. The basic position of ritual and moral leadership was the libationer (ch'i-chiu) who served small dioceses. Both women and men served as libationers. The twenty- four dioceses were to be presided over by twenty-four male and female officials. Kristofer Schipper (1978) has suggested two possible reasons for this equal participation of men and women: the Taoist cosmology, which is based on the balance of yin and yang; and the possibility that women were historically important in the development of the Taoist organization (375).

High-level participation of women in Taoist leadership does seem remarkable. The Taoist canon contains evidence of Taoist ordination for women. Michael Saso (1978) also has a copy of a Taoist text that lists eight grades of perfection for women Taoists (284, n.15). Maspero (1981) describes the ranks of ordination in the Way of the Celestial Masters as parallel for men and women: Sons and Daughters of the Tao (tao-nan, tao-nu), Man and Woman Wearing the Cap (nan-kuan, nu-kuan), and Father and Mother of the Tao (tao-fu, tao-mu). Only the highest rank of Divine Lord (shen-chun) has no parallel female rank (378).

Perhaps more important evidence of women's participation in Taoism is the mention of individual women in historical texts. Wei Hua-ts'un (251-334) is considered the spiritual founder of the Shang-ch'ing Mao Shan sect. She was the child and wife of classically educated scholars and was herself educated in reading Taoist texts. She was ordained as a libationer in the Meng-wei tradition of Taoism before she posthumously founded a new sect. From the perspective of this sect, her life is not as important as her spiritual activities after death. After she had been dead for thirty years she appeared to Yang Hsi in a vision and passed on to him the scriptures revealed to her by the Immortals (Saso 1978, 37).

The Taoist religion as a whole grew up in the context of shamanism. Women in China have always been important in contacting the world of the spirits, so there is nothing surprising in the role of women in a new organization based on communication with the Immortals. Many of the male Taoist leaders were influenced by shamanist women in their families. Chang Lu, the grandson of the legendary First Celestial Master, was successful in expanding the new religion and was well known for the "sorcery cult" that he received from his mother (Stein 1979, 60), who was an important priestess at the court of the Wei dynasty (Schipper 1978, 375). Chou Tzu-liang, who had a series of revelations in the sixth century, had two influential religious women in his family. His grandmother was a great shamaness, and the maternal aunt who raised him converted his father to the Taoist religion (Stein 1979, 54-55).

Individual Taoist women are also mentioned in Chinese texts as great laboratory alchemists. Alchemy of the laboratory was both a means of creating an elixir of immortality and a microcosm of the transformations of the universe. The fourth century text by Ko Hung describes the wife of a Han dynasty courtier who was an accomplished alchemist Ko Hung's own wife, Pao Ku, was also known as

Text Fifteen: **WOMEN IN DAOISM**

an alchemist from an influential Taoist family (Needham 1983, 76). A woman alchemist known as Teacher Keng was an attraction at the ninth century Tang imperial court. She entertained the emperor with her chemical procedures and magical tricks. According to the writer who records her life history, she may have been an Immortal herself (Needham 1983, 169-171). A twelfth century work by the poet Han Yen-thou gives a first hand account of the Taoist alchemy of Li Shao-yun, a widow determined to perfect the elixir of immortality. She wandered from one Taoist temple to another developing her process for transforming cinnabar into a potion that would turn her into an Immortal. The poet describes her extreme thinness, the precision of the weights and measures in her procedures, and her eventual death (Needham 1983, 191-92).

Saso's research on Taoism in contemporary Taiwan shows that active roles for women in official capacities have not completely disappeared. The Taoist Master Chuang keeps a picture of his dead mother, the ordained priestess Ch'en A-kuei, on his altar. She excelled in her Taoist training but could not perform public rituals because her family was of high social status (Saso 1978, 76-79). In a less official role, a married daughter of Master Chuang also carries on the family tradition by writing out the long ritual documents for her father's use in public ceremonies (Saso 1978, 112).

Women's widespread participation in the Taoist religion must be seen in the light of the status of religious Taoism in Chinese culture as a whole. Such high level participation of women in a long continuous tradition of Chinese civilization would be truly amazing if this tradition were the primary or elite tradition. Such is not the case with Taoism. The Taoists coexisted with the Buddhists and the elite Confucians, and they were always closest to the lower levels of popular religion. Even with intermittent imperial support, Taoists were at the bottom of the social hierarchy, along with women. Chinese histories confirm this status. As Saso has noted, "Since the men who wrote Chinese history were for the most part (at least publicly) Confucian, the Taoist was always relegated (with women) to the last place in the biographies of famous people in the dynastic histories" (Saso 1978, 4).

TAOISM, POPULAR CULTS, AND SHAMANISM

The three Chinese traditions of Confucianism, Buddhism and Taoism are difficult to separate into distinct strands because, unlike Western religions, they were seldom seen as mutually exclusive. It is even more difficult to separate organized Taoism from the diffuse, unorganized popular religion of the Chinese. Confucian historians have been quick to associate anything not strictly Confucian or purely Buddhist with the Taoist tradition. Religious practices considered immoral were often labeled "Taoist" by officials. Such is the fate of any religion that loses a struggle for dominance (Stein 1979, 53). Popular religion and Taoism strongly influenced each other, but the Taoists drew a clear line between themselves and what they considered excessive, immoral cults. Taoist adepts converted people in the local cults to the more highly organized Taoist religion--sometimes to encourage political rebellion and sometimes to lead them to more civilized rituals without the wild shamanist trances or animal sacrifice (Miyakawa 1979, 101). Taoism prohibited participation in the "excessive" cults but encouraged the masses to continue many popular communal and domestic rituals important to women and men--worship of ancestors, of the soil god, and of the god of the stove (Stein 1979, 77).

Taoist priests have not only encouraged much Chinese religion, but also have served as its ritual specialists. Taoist priests initiated into the esoteric literature and liturgy of Taoist sects have the unique role in Chinese religion of performing the elaborate rituals of cosmic renewal (*chiao*). The *chiao* is a ritual performed in the classical Chinese language to renew the community's relationship with the deities--especially at times of temple repair. Women who have participated in this esoteric ritual tradition have already been mentioned, but public ritual performance by women is now rare. Many more women serve religious functions outside this literary ritual tradition. In both traditional and modern Chinese societies, a large number of the shamans who serve on the margins of organized religion have been female. Shamanessea (*wu*) and female mediums predated Taoist sects, influenced them, and were rejected by them, but continued to operate on the periphery of the movement.

Shamanism, which was central to ancient Chinese religion, centered around women. The Chinese word for shaman--*wu*--originally referred exclusively to a woman. In the Chou dynasty (1122?-256 B.C.E.), she danced and sang in the fields to invoke the deities and thereby brought the needed rain and fertility for the crops (Chow 1978, 65-68). During this ancient period, she was a figure of great power who probably personified the great goddesses of rain and fertility. The official cults later rejected her, and she was left to perform her spiritual craft on the margins of Chinese society (Schafer 1951, 156-157).

Female shamanism influenced organized Taoism both through the families of Taoist leaders and through its belief in communication with the supernatural as a basis for Taoist revelations from Immortals. Shamanesses cannot perform the high liturgies of the initiated priesthood, but they can perform many of their ordinary functions of exorcism, healing, and communication with many deities and ghosts. They use many of the same deities and are associated with the same Taoist temples. Shamanesses, shamans, and Taoist priests function more at different levels in the same religion than in completely different religions. Initiated priests and priestesses are the educated functionaries of popular religion; modern shamanesses are the typically uneducated women who come to serve the same community, often after suffering psychological or social crises.

Research on contemporary Cantonese shamanesses yields valuable information on their careers and relationship to Taoism (Potter 1974, 207-231). The three shamanesses of Ping Shan in the New Territories of Hong Kong all began their work as intermediaries to the spirit world only after extreme crises. The most respected of them resigned herself to life as a medium only after her seven young children had died, her husband had died, and the spirits of her dead children continually possessed her and made her momentarily "die." She finally accepted the social and financial role of village medium with the help of an older spirit medium. The second Ping Shan woman became a shamaness after her four young children died and she was possessed by two of them, who fought over her fate. Her husband refused to let her become a shamaness until the possessing spirits caused her to "die" several times one evening. She entered the profession with the assistance of a Taoist priest. The priest helped her establish her own altar to the deities demanded by her children' spirits. He addressed the deities as follows: "Here is a woman who, with the aid of her children's spirits, wishes to become a spirit medium. Please help her" (Potter 1974, 227). The Taoist priest spoke to the same deities as the woman and encouraged her in her religious profession. The third woman became a shamaness after the death of her 9-year-old son and her subsequent illness of three years. She was apparently the only Ping Shan shamanist with a history of shamanism in her family. Her grandmother's sister was the spirit medium who taught her

the profession. This older woman was a respected medium who lived to be 120 years old (Potter 1974, 228).

These Cantonese women serve the religious, psychological, and social needs of their community. They communicate with the spirits of the dead from village families. They protect the health of children vulnerable to soul kidnapping or evil fates. They take care of the spirits of the unmarried girls of the village who are denied support and a place on their family altars (because women do not belong to their parents' family but are destined for the family of their husbands). And they even predict the future (Potter 1974, 207). Taoist priests may also serve in some of these roles, but they are not as available. A family of Ping Shan who had been plagued by a brother's spirit paid a famous Taoist priest from a nearby town to exorcise the spirit. The priest failed. Later during a seance with the shamaness the spirit told his brother that if he would hang a piece of silver paper with his name inscribed on it by the ancestral altar, then the spirit would bring the family good fortune. In this instance a shamaness and a Taoist priest attempted to accomplish the same task, and the shamaness alone succeeded (Potter 1974, 208-209).

In dealing with the guilt and fears associated with dead relatives, old women are in a better position to "exorcise" these demons. They know the village gossip and have become sensitive to others' emotions in the way required by people who live dependent on others. They must understand the feelings of the living and the dead. Most evil ghosts are female, and the reasons seem obvious (Potter 1974, 229). The frustrations; anger, and jealousy of Cantonese women mistreated by mother-in-laws, abused by husbands who take second wives, or ignored by families in preference to their brothers have few public outlets. Surely these emotions are felt by the community, especially by the women, and surface through their "spirits" or psyches.

In Taiwan today, women often serve as mediums for Redhead Taoist priests, who are so named because of the color of their caps. These priests are considered heterodox by the Blackhead priests, who can trace their lineage back to the founders of their sect and have received complete registers of deities to call on for formal rituals. The Redhead priests are less involved in the literary traditions and closer to popular religious practices. The popular San-nai (Three Sisters) Sect of Redhead priests trace their history back to three legendary women who practiced exorcism and spirit

Text Fifteen: **WOMEN IN DAOISM**

possession (Saso 1978, 60). In the Lu Shan sect, a female medium surnamed Wu is possessed every morning at 10 A.M. by the goddess Ch'en Nai-ma and serves as the intermediary to the spirit world for local Redhead priests. The priests interpret the illegible spirit writing she produces while in a trance. In this way Redhead priests remain closely tied to the spontaneous shamanism rejected by both elite Taoism and Confucianism in China.

VIEWS OF THE BODY

Religions often associate women more closely than men with the physical body. Whenever body is contrasted with spirit, this association means lower status for women. Fear and guilt about the body is then transferred to the female sex. Taoism does not have a body-spirit dualism. The complementary duality of yin and yang is within nature. The physical world is highly valued, and the physical human body in its most purified form is the Taoist's goal.

The natural universe is the transformation of yin and yang. It is the body of the Tao. The individual human body is a microcosm of the universe, and it undergoes the same transformations, is controlled by the same forces, and is of highest value. The goal of immortality in religious Taoism is not the immortality of a disembodied spirit; it is the prolongation of life in a purified physical body. Just as gold is the incorruptible and highest form of metal, the bodies of the highest Celestial Immortals are of the purest, most incorruptible substance.

The division of male and female in the body of the universe is most clearly the division of Heaven and Earth. Heaven and Earth are the father and mother of the macrocosm and are equally important. In the earliest Taoist scripture, the T'ai-p'ing ching, the Master says, "Father and mother are equally human beings, and Heaven and Earth are both 'celestial'" (Kaltenmark 1979, 37). The respect for Mother Earth is as important as that for Heaven, which traditionally had been associated with moral law and natural order. In this scripture, followers are prohibited from digging wells because it would be equivalent to wounding one's own mother. People must be content with the natural springs which serve as the nipples of Mother Earth (Kaltenmark 1979, 37). This Taoist vision of the world is clearly wholistic. Each being is part of the larger body of the universe, and to harm any part of the universe is to harm oneself, one's siblings, or one's own parents.

Taoism views even women's bodies and sexuality positively. Women's menstrual blood is powerful, not impure as in many religions. Menstrual blood is the essence (*ching*) of the woman, which she can use to increase her life span if she can nurture it; semen serves the same function for men. The bodily fluids of men and women are equally valuable as the sources of natural life and immortal life. Both menstrual blood and semen provide the raw material for creating an embryo for an immortal body (Needham 1983, 240). Human sexuality is valued as the obvious means of creation and is given religious and philosophical meaning. Sexual intercourse is the primary form of the interaction of yin and yang and thus represents the mysterious Tao.

The female body as symbol for creativity in the Tao te ching is not lost in the religious movement of Taoism. The Tao as the dark womb of creation is often given more mythological form. In a fifth century Taoist text (San-t'ien nei-chieh ching), creation proceeds from nonbeing, which produces the Three Breaths, which in turn produce the Jade Mother of Divine Mystery. The Jade Mother then gives birth to the legendary Lao tzu, who creates the world (Schipper 1978, 362-363). In this type of myth, the creativity of the Tao manifests itself as a specific woman--the mother of Lao tzu. Early birth legends of Lao tzu do not mention a father but only his mother, from whom he took the surname Li. Elsewhere Lao tzu himself is Mother Li and gives birth to himself (Schipper 1978, 363).

If the female body represents the creative power of the Tao, then it could be the model for all Taoists. In some instances, men apparently tried to imitate the physical characteristics of women. This imitation goes beyond the use of women's traditionally passive social role as a model. The Hsiang-erh commentary on the Tao te ching says that men should cultivate a female character, and modern lore tells of Taoist practices leading to the atrophy of male genitals or to old Taoist men urinating in a female position (Schipper 1978, 365). In Chuang tzu, when the Taoist character Lieh tzu reaches the highest level of understanding he takes the place of his wife in the kitchen (VII, Watson 1968, 97), but even more extreme is the case in the *Lu-chu chih* in which the man Lu Tung-pin actually claims he is pregnant (Schipper 1978, 364). Pregnancy is a basic Taoist model for attaining immortality. A Taoist, male or female, creates and nurtures an immortal embryo within the corruptible physical body. According to this model, males must become females, at least metaphorically, to achieve their goal of deathlessness.

Sometimes sexual transformation did go the other way in Taoism. A text from about the eighteenth century proposes Hsi Wang Mu's ethical and physiological path to immortality specifically to women Taoists, but the end of the path is the rejuvenated form of a young boy rather than a young girl (Needham 1983, 237).

FEMALE ADEPTS

Women such as Hsi Wang Mu attained the secret of Tao and thus immortality in legendary times. Chinese literature is full of women who have learned the secrets of Tao in historical times, either accidentally or through the study of alchemy or meditation. One source for these stories is Pao p'u-tzu, written by Ko Hung in the fourth century (Ware 1966). He was a scholar who defended the claims of esoteric Taoism, especially the belief that normal human beings can attain the status of Immortals through Taoist arts. He argues that just because some people have not seen Immortals is no proof that they do not exist; they do exist, because people have reported their existence. Some of the stories he offers as proof describe female adepts who have learned the secrets of immortality.

Ko Hung reports a second-hand story of a 4-year-old girl who learned the secret of prolonging life. Her father, Chan Kuang-ting, had to flee from disaster, but his young daughter was unable to make the difficult trip. He abandoned her in a tomb with a few months' supply of food and drink and then fled. After three years the father returned and went to the tomb to collect his daughter's bones for burial. At the tomb he found his daughter alive and well. She explained that at first she was hungry but that then she imitated a large tortoise in the corner of the tomb that stretched its neck and swallowed its own breath (Ware 1966, 57-58). This story is used to prove that tortoises, known for their longevity in China, possess specific techniques leading to long life. It also demonstrates that gender is not relevant to the ability to master the Taoist arts leading to extreme longevity.

Another story tells of an amazing 200-year-old woman captured by hunters during the Han dynasty (202 B.C.E.-220 C.E.). She was naked and covered with thick black hair. When questioned, she told her unusual story.

> I was originally a Ch'in concubine. Learning that with the arrival of bandits from the East the King of Ch'in would surrender and the palace would be burned, I became frightened and ran away to the mountains where I famished for lack of food. I was on the point of dying when an old man taught me how to eat the leaves and fruits of pines. At first it was bitter and unpleasant, but I gradually grew used to it until it produced lack of hunger and thirst. In the winter I suffered no cold, and in the summer I felt no heat (Ware 1966, 194).

Unfortunately this woman, who proved to be nearing immortality, was taken back to the court and fed a normal diet, whereupon she lost her hair and died. Ko Hung tells us that if left alone she would have become an Immortal.

The last story of a woman using Taoist arts in Pao p'u-tzu is that of a girl from a family who possessed the esoteric knowledge of Taoist alchemy. A Han courtier, Ch'eng Wei, married her but failed to convince her to give him the secrets. She believed her own efforts in the laboratory were successful because she was fated to master the Tao, but she did not believe that he was so fated. He harassed her to give him the secrets until she went crazy, fled, and later died (Ware 1966, 264-265).

A tale from the I-yuan gives further evidence of female adepts (Miyakawa 1979, 85-86). The tale tells of a shrine to a certain Lady Mei-ku in the third century B.C.E. Mei-ku was an accomplished Taoist master who could walk on water. She once broke the law of the Tao, and her husband killed her in rage and threw her body in a lake. A shaman placed her corpse in a lakeside shrine, and thereafter she would appear twice a month standing on the water. Fishing and hunting were then prohibited in this area because the shaman said that Lady Mei-ku hated to see animals suffer and die as she had (Miyakawa 1979, 85).

These four stories have one thing in common: all the women have experienced crises within a family relationship. The crisis that motivates or ends the practice of Taoist arts is caused by a male member of her family--father, husband, or patron/lover. These stories linking the practice of Taoist arts with family crises and the need for survival are similar to the stories of modern shamanesses who seek communication with the spirits only after family crises and financial necessity.

Not all women experienced crises in their search for the secrets of the Tao. The Taoist canon contains several texts that describe meditation techniques for any woman to follow. Women are important in these meditation texts as both practitioners and as representations of visualized deities.

The meditation techniques of religious Taoism demonstrate that the spiritual powers are not identified with one sex. The spirits that rule the internal world of the body and the external world of the universe are both male and female. Neither immortality nor spiritual powers are gender specific. The female spirits include various jade maidens, fairies, goddesses, and powerful spirit-generals who aid women and men in their meditation. These female spiritual beings are as diverse as the male spirits. Many are beautiful and even erotic maidens. Some are terrifying and ugly female spirits. An example of the diversity is found in Michael Saso's description of a ritual to counter black magic used by a contemporary Taoist priest (Saso 1978, 156-160). Of the six spirit-generals called on to fight the battle against evil, two are women. General Hsiao-lieh is a beautiful woman: "She is eight feet tall, and her face is white and clear complexioned, with pretty features and delicate eyes" (Saso 1978, 159). General Kang-Hsien is hideous: "She is ten feet tall, with the face of an ugly woman, yellow hair, and large protruding white teeth" (Saso 1978, 158). However, although differing in beauty, both women are courageous and strong. Here beauty is not associated with weakness.

Some meditation texts have separate spirits for women and men. The goals and techniques of the meditation are the same; only the register of spirits to be visualized differs. In the T'ai-p'ing ching women and men may both meditate on the Primordial one, or women may visualize the internal spirits that control the body as female and the men may visualize them as male (Kaltenmark 1979, 41-42). Another example of separate but equal participation in meditation requires marriage for the highest level of participation. When first initiated into the sect, young children receive a register of 1 or more spirit generals for meditation. At the second childhood initiation, they receive a register of 10 generals. At adolescence, sex distinctions begin, and women receive a register of 75 Superior Powers while the men receive 75 Superior Immortals. The highest station is not for the individual but for the married couple whose combined register amounts to 150 spirit generals (Schipper 1978, 377). This practice follows the model of the complementarity of male and female, yang and yin, in which both are equal and necessary.

Sexual techniques were also used to prolong life and sometimes even to form an incorruptible embryo for a new existence. The state of Taoist texts and current research make it difficult to fully understand women's participation in the sexual techniques or their understanding of them. Much literature focuses on male techniques of preventing ejaculation and using the yang semen and the yin essence absorbed from the female during intercourse. All people have an essence within them, and when it is exhausted, they die. The essence for the man is his semen; the essence for the woman is her menstrual blood (Maspero 1981, 518). Sexual intercourse is important for the nourishing of the essence, but only if it is done right. The Immortal P'eng-tsu recommends to men that they choose young women who do not know the techniques themselves because women who know the technique will seek to prolong their own lives and not give up their essence (Maspero 1981, 530). The physical techniques for women are not as clear as the suggested male techniques for preventing ejaculation. But women were obviously using these techniques for their own benefit, as they used other Taoist meditative disciplines. Lest these Taoists seem to be involved in continual sexual orgies, we must add that the texts contain many restrictions limiting when these practices could be performed. The restricted days, based on regular monthly and yearly prohibitions, number over two hundred a year. In addition, there are restrictions based on weather and personal circumstances that reduce the possible days to only a few per year (Maspero 1981, 532-533).

Taoist women found communal living most conducive to following these methods leading to immortality. Life in convents appealed even to high-ranking women during the Tang dynasty (618-907 C.E.). Daughters of Tang emperors Tai Tsung and Jui Tsung chose to become Taoist priestesses. A new convent was built for Jui Tsung's daughters, who took the Taoist titles "Jade Realized Princess" and "Golden Transcendent Princess" (Schafer 1978a, 7). Many Tang Taoist priestesses were known for their beauty and dressed in the same rich costumes worn by the immortal goddesses whom they sought to imitate. Tang poetry depicts them in their crowns and splendid cloaks as they seek their true love--immortality:

> To go off in search of transcendence--
> Halcyon filigrees and golden comb are discarded:
> She enters among the steep tors;
> Fog rolls up--as her yellow net-gauze cloak;
> Clouds sculptured--as her white jade crown.
> (Hsueh Chao-yun, Schafer 1978a, 45-46)

Sexual intercourse was one form of inner alchemy practiced in Taoist convents that created, not surprisingly, suspicion and hostility in outsiders. This form was later superceded by an inner alchemy for combining the yin and yang within a woman's own body without intercourse. A text written around 1798 by Liu I-ming explains that a woman's menstrual blood alone was enough to create an immortal body (Needham 1983, 240). By this time, Confucian and Buddhist influences had permeated Taoist communal life. A list of rules for Taoist nuns from the late eighteenth century requires them to abstain from wine and meat, remain celibate, and preserve their hymens if possible (Needham 1983, 237).

Even with the increased restrictions, some Chinese continued to see Taoist nuns as models of transcendence. Liu T'ieh-yun (1857-1909) in the last chapters of his novel *The Travels of Lao Ts'an* (translated as "A nun of Taishan" by Lin Yutang, 1950), depicted a young Taoist nun as the embodiment of the freedom, self-determination, and compassion that he sought in a new China.

FEMALE DEITIES
Taoist texts, Chinese mythology, and popular literature are filled with female divinities. Most have been related to Taoism at either the popular level or in the rituals. Ancient China was filled with powerful dragon women, river goddesses, and rain goddesses who lived on the cloudy peaks of mountains. Edward Schafer (1980) has shown how the state cult of medieval China turned these goddesses into abstract and asexual deities (58-61) and how T'ang prose and poetry depicted them as man-destroying evil creatures often disguised as beautiful women (187-189).

One example of a transformed creature is Nu-kua, a dragon goddess who, according to ancient Chinese mythology, created humanity and repaired the world. Huai-nan-tzu, the eclectic Taoist work of the second century B.C.E, contains the legend of her saving the world.

In very ancient times, the four pillars [at the compass points] were broken down, the nine provinces [of the habitable world] were split apart, Heaven did not wholly cover [Earth] and Earth did not completely support [Heaven]. Fires flamed without being extinguished, waters inundated without being stopped, fierce beasts ate people, and birds of prey seized the old and weak in their claws. Thereupon Nu-kua fused together stones of the five colors with which she patched together azure Heaven. She cut, off the feet of a

turtle with which she set up the four pillars. She slaughtered the Black Dragon in order to save the province of Chi [the present Hopei and Shansi provinces in North China]. She collected the ashes of reeds with which to check the wild waters (Bodde 1961, 386-387).

Nu-kua not only saved the world; in another myth, she also created humanity out of yellow mud (Bodde 1961, 388-389). The fate of this powerful and benevolent dragon was unkind. She was preserved primarily as one of the three emperors of the golden age--covered with robes and deprived of her serpentine and female characteristics.

Some early goddesses survived better. Hsi Wang Mu (Queen Mother of the West) was first mentioned in Chuang tzu, and a full mythology and cult devoted to her developed by about 100 C.E. (Loewe 1979, 88). Chinese artists depicted her with a royal headdress and seated on a half-dragon and half-tiger creature (Loewe 1979, 101-112). As symbols of yin and yang, the tiger and dragon represent the cosmic transformations over which Hsi Wang Mu reigns. Chinese worshippers believed her to be the source of immortality: she could provide the desired potion to eliminate death. Her gift of immortality was first mentioned in the third century B.C.E. text Mu t'ien tzu chuan, which describes the meeting between the divine Queen of the West and the earthly King Mu of Chou (Loewe 1979, 92-93). King Mu offered precious gifts, and she responded with the promise of immortality and marriage. Hsi Wang Mu's meetings with King Mu are part of a larger cycle of Chinese myths of seasonal meetings between rulers and goddesses or between stellar gods and goddesses (Loewe 1979, 112-126). These Myths also reflect the ancient Chinese fertility rites, Miring which young men and women celebrated the beginning of the new season with poetry contests and sexual intercourse (Granet 1932, 147ff.). The seasonal interaction of yin and yang brings both agricultural and human fertility.

The attraction and mythology of Hsi Wang Mu continued, and she became the Fairy Queen of all the Taoist Immortals. A biography of her from the fourth or fifth century describes her life and paradise in detail. Her paradise in the K'un-lun mountains is filled with magical beauty: jade towers, silk tents, charming music, and the youthful men and women who serve as attendants for the benevolent Queen (Bauer 1976, 180). Hsi Wang Mu was also known for her concern for women's problems: she was invoked in Taoist rituals to dispel the White Tiger deity who causes miscarriages

Text Fifteen: WOMEN IN DAOISM

in women (Hou 1979, 218). Hsi Wang Mu's cult did not survive, but she continues to exist in Chinese literature and art as the Queen of all Immortals who cultivates the peaches of immortality. She is one of the characters in the popular novel Journey to the West (Yu 1977-83).

Nature goddesses have also survived--the Mother of Lightning (Maspero 1981, 98), the Old Woman Who Sweeps Heaven Clear (97), the Woman in the Moon (96), and the Mother of the Pole Star. Stellar deities are central to Taoist rituals, and the Mother of the Pole Star, Tou-mu, is one of the most important. As patroness of the contemporary Taoist Master Chuang, she appears on his altar as an eight-armed, four-headed goddess--a deity of awesome power (Saco 1978, 121).

Chinese domestic rituals often involve goddesses, usually paired with a male god to reflect yin-yang duality. The kitchen god and his wife keep records of the deeds of the household to ensure that justice is done--his wife is responsible for the records of the women of the family (Maspero 1981, 113). Another couple, the Lord and Lady of the Bed, are worshipped for fertility and marital happiness (Maspero 1981, 118). A solitary goddess, the goddess of the latrine, is sometimes worshipped by girls seeking a good husband. Although Taoism has encouraged such domestic rituals, there is nothing in them unique to Taoism.

Two goddesses enshrined in Taoist temples continue to be important in providing protection for the individual. The Empress of Heaven (Tien-hou) protects sailors, aided by a deity who can see for one thousand *li* (Chinese mile) and one who can hear for one thousand li (Maspero 1981, 145-146). Her cult has been popular since the eleventh century. The Sacred Mother (Sheng-mu) or Lady Mother (Nai-nai niang-niang) protects women and children and is assisted by the popular goddess who brings children to women who worship her. These two Taoist goddesses avert disaster and send children just like the Buddhist *bonhisattva* Kuan-yin, who is given female form in China.

TAOISM TODAY

The Tao te ching and Chuang tzu have won their way into the world's canon of literary and philosophical classics.

They will surely influence future generations of Chinese and non-Chinese readers. The future of Taoism as an organized religion is not so clear Taoist activity in the People's Republic of China appears to be minimal. However, activity in Hong Kong, Taiwan, and other Chinese communities continues. After the arrival of the sixty-third Celestial Master in Taiwan in 1949 (who was succeeded by the sixty-fourth in 1970), Taiwan has seen increased participation and building of temples. Taoism in Taiwan has married priests from a diverse group of sects that recognize the authority of the present Celestial Master. Laywomen serve in various ways in the temples. At the Hsing T'ien Temple in Taipei, the temple courtyard is filled with blue-robed women carrying out the faith healing for which the temple has gained its reputation. They lay hands on the sick or on clothing brought by the families of those too sick to come in person. Women also serve on the margins of organized Taoism--as mediums for the Redhead priests or as independent mediums communicating with the spirits for the aid of their clients.

Organized Taoism in Hong Kong centers around the Lung-men lineage of the Ch'uan-chen order of celibate priests and priestesses living in convents (Strickmann 1979, 164). These women and men recognize the First Celestial Master Chang Tao-ling as the founder of their religion, but they are unconcerned with the man in Taiwan who claims descent from him Organized Taoism even continues in Honolulu, where there were three active Taoist priests when Saso surveyed the situation (Saso 1978, 61).

Religious Taoism today survives with a cosmology based on the power of the female and interdependence of male and female. The creative principle is symbolically female because the Tao, like an empty womb, is the origin of all things. Harmony in this world depends not on male domination of female, but on male-female mutuality symbolized by the balance of yin and yang principles. The contemporary Taoist pantheon still recognizes female representations of power, benevolence, and creativity. However, in their views of women's sexuality and public leadership, the earlier positive attitudes of Taoism have long since been modified by the Chinese Buddhist and Confucian traditions.

Confucianism

Chinese Representation of K'ung fu-tzu (Confucius)

CONFUCIANISM

- Confucianism is a Western term
  - Term coined by Jesuit missionaries to China in 16th century
- In China, Confucianism = *ru* tradition
  - [*Ru* = self-cultivation of moral virtue]
- Dominant tradition in education and politics in East Asia until early 20th century
- Confucianism is undergoing a current revival

How do Daoists and Confucians differ from one another?

Daoists

- Emphasized nature
- Harmony of individuals with Dao
- If humans let the Dao happen, virtue (DE) will come spontaneously

Confucians

- Emphasized better relationships
- Harmony between cosmos order and social order   *training/education*
- Humans make the Dao great by seeking virtue (DE)

The Founder: K'ung fu-tzu (Kong Fuzi)

- Great Master K'ung
- 551-479 BCE —— *time of chaos*
- Poor aristocrat
- At age of 50, served as official in Lu
  - His policies were rejected
  - He resigned
- Became a wandering teacher

Confucius, a Revolutionary?

- ⭐Did not question tradition. Accepted ⭐
  - The Lord on High (Shang Di)
  - Mandate of Heaven (T'ien Ming)
  [Heaven = power that rules universe. Determines what is right or wrong.]
  - Ancestor worship
  - Spirits
  - Efficacy of rituals
- Emphasized the cultivation of moral virtues
- Believed political involvement can transform present world

Confucius
- Challenged corrupt, autocratic leaders
- Argued for meritocracy
- Advocated education for all — *not girls*
- At age 67 he returned to Lu and spent the rest of his life teaching

Confucian Texts
- Four Books   *— used in schools*
- Five Classics

The Four Books
- Analects (Lun Yu)
  - Sayings and conversations of Confucius
  - Compiled after his death
- Great Learning (Da Xue) = first text read by school boys about education of future junzis
- Doctrine of the Mean (Chung Yung). What is relationship between humanity and world order?
- Book of Mencius (3rd century BCE)
  - Sayings of one of Confucius' principal disciples
  - Systematized the teachings of Confucius

Mencius ("Master Meng," 371-289 BCE)
- Humans are by nature good
- Natural goodness must be cultivated
- Emphasized family obligations
- Rulers must provide for all citizens
  - Just land distribution
- Right to revolt against a unjust ruler

The Five Classics
- Book of Poetry
- Book of Changes (Yijing or I Ching) [book of divination]
- Book of History
- Book of Rites
- Spring and Summer Annals

Confucius' Teachings
- Humans are not primarily individuals
- Humans are in relationships

Five Basic Relationships
- Parent and child
- Husband and wife
- Elder and younger brother
- Friend and friend
- Ruler and subject

Basic problem of humanity

- Social chaos (Remember Zhou/Chou dynasty!)
- Chaos is caused by a breakdown of virtue
  - Primary virtue = ren (benevolence) = will to seek the good of others
- Confucius aimed to restore social harmony
- Means of restoring harmony
  - Education in virtue (DE)
  - Virtuous or ideal person = gentleman (junzi)

Inner virtues

- HAVE TO BE CULTIVATED WITHIN YOU
- REN, also written as jen = benevolence; sympathy for people's suffering = will to seek good of others
- SHU = reciprocity
  - Do not do to others what you would not have them do to you
- Self-correcting wisdom (hsueh)

Outer virtues

- SHOULD BE APPLIED IN YOUR RELATIONSHIPS WITH OTHERS
- Li (propriety, good form)
  - Courtesy, respect
  - Right and proper order in family or social context
  - Religious rituals (ancestor veneration + worship of deities)
- HSIAO or XIAO = Filial piety (devotion for parents)
- Rectification of names (CHENG-MING) = give people right titles

Han dynasty (206 BCE–220 CE) adopted Confucianism

- Emperor sacrificed at Confucius' grave
- Confucius' grave became national shrine
- ☆ Temples of culture (wen miao)
  - Established in each province
  - Included images of Confucius
  - Sacrifices to Confucius
- ☆ Birthday of Confucius = holiday
- Five classics = core curriculum
- Civil service exam for officials

Confucianism / Ru

- dominate tradition of education
  & politics in China until beg. of 20th
- temples closed during
  Communist revolution

- end of 20th c. – 21st c
  = current revival

Cult of Confucius

- Confucius' descendants were ennobled
- Miracle stories about Confucius circulated
  - He could predict future
  - He was a god
  - He could perform miracles

EXTRA NOTES

Wu Wei is not important to Confucianism

The Gods' function in Daoism

- control shifts of energy
- teach the Dao
- control Human Beings' lifespan

Daoist view after life as Bureaucracy
w/ emperor

Junzi= ideal person

Kung Fu Tzu = Confucius

Ru= self cultivation of moral virtue

Cheng ming= rectification of names

wen miao= Confucian   wen= cultural
temple of culture   refinement

CONFUCIANISM

TEXT 16. The Analects

Define the characteristics of a gentleman (junzi).

Text Sixteen

The Analects

BOOK 1

1 The Master said, Studying, and from time to time going over what you've learned—that's enjoyable, isn't it? To have a friend come from a long way off—that's a pleasure, isn't it? Others don't understand him, but he doesn't resent it—that's the true gentleman, isn't it?

2 Master You said,[1] A man filial to his parents, a good brother, yet apt to go against his superiors—few are like that! The man who doesn't like to go against his superiors but likes to plot rebellion—no such kind exists! The gentleman operates at the root. When the root is firm, then the Way may proceed. Filial and brotherly conduct—these are the root of humaneness, are they not?

3 The Master said, Clever words and a pleasing countenance—little humaneness there!

4 Master Zeng said, Each day I examine myself on three matters. In making plans for others, am I being loyal to them? In my dealings with friends, am I being trustworthy? Am I passing on to others what I have not carefully thought about myself?

5 The Master said, Guiding a state of a thousand chariots,[2] be attentive to affairs and trustworthy, frugal in expenditures and sparing of others. Employ the common people only at proper times.[3]

6 The Master said, Young people should be filial at home, brotherly with others, circumspect, and trustworthy. Let them act kindly toward the populace in general and befriend those of humane character. If after that, they have energy left over, let them study the arts.[4]

7 Zixia said, If he treats worthy persons as worthy and is respectful to them, does all in his power to serve his father and mother, gives his best in the service of the ruler, and in dealings with friends is faithful to his word, though some may say he lacks learning, I would surely call him learned!

8 The Master said, If the gentleman lacks gravity, he won't command respect. If he studies he will avoid narrowmindedness. Put prime value on loyalty and trustworthiness, have no friends who are not your equal,[5] and, if you make mistakes, don't be afraid to correct them.

9 Master Zeng said, Tend carefully to death rites, and pay reverence to those long departed, and the people will in the end be rich in virtue.

10 Ziqin questioned Zigong, saying, When the Master goes to a particular state, he is certain to learn about its government. Does he seek such information? Or do others just give it to him?

Zigong said, The Master goes about it by being cordial, forthright, respectful, modest, and deferential. The Master's way of seeking is different from that of others.

11 The Master said, While his father is alive, observe his intentions. After his father is dead, observe his actions. If after three years he hasn't changed his father's way of doing things, then you can call him filial.

12 Master You said, What ritual values most is harmony. The Way of the former kings was truly admirable in this respect. But if in matters great and small one proceeds in this manner, the results may not always be satisfactory. You may understand the ideal of harmony and work for it, but if you do not employ ritual to regulate the proceedings, things will not go well.

13 Master You said, Trustworthiness is close to rightness—it ensures that people will live up to their word.

Courtesy is close to ritual decorum; it ensures that people will give wide berth to shame and disgrace. When one makes no mistakes in what he favors, he can serve as a leader.[6]

14   The Master said, A gentleman when he eats doesn't try to stuff himself, when he chooses a dwelling is not overly concerned about comfort. He is attentive to affairs, careful of his words, and looks to those who have the Way to correct himself. He's the kind who can be called a lover of learning.

15   Zigong said, Poor but free of obsequiousness, rich but free of arrogance—how would that do?

The Master said, All right. But not as good as poor but happy in the Way, rich but a lover of rites.

Zigong said, When the *Odes* says:

As something cut, something filed,
something ground, something polished[7]

is that what it's talking about?

The Master said, Si (Zigong), now I can begin to talk to you about the *Odes*. Someone tells you the first step, and you understand the step that comes after!

16   The Master said, Don't worry about whether other people understand you. Worry about whether you understand other people.[8]

NOTES

1. A few of Confucius' more distinguished disciples are addressed as "Master."
2. The domain of a feudal lord.
3. Call them up for forced labor or military service only when they are not busy with farm work.
4. Literature, rites, music, and so on.
5. That is, in moral character.
6. The sentence is obscure and open to widely differing interpretations.
7. *Book of Odes,* no. 55, which describes a man of elegant bearing. Zigong takes the lines to refer to moral training.
8. That is, judge them correctly.

BOOK 2

1   The Master said, Conduct government in accordance with virtue, and it will be like the North Star standing in its place, with all the other stars paying court to it.

2   The Master said, The three hundred poems of the *Book of Odes* may be summed up in a single phrase: Think nothing base.[1]

3   The Master said, Guide them with government orders, regulate them with penalties, and the people will seek to evade the law and be without shame. Guide them with virtue, regulate them with ritual, and they will have a sense of shame and become upright.

4   The Master said, At fifteen I set my mind on learning; by thirty I had found my footing; at forty I was free of perplexities; by fifty I understood the will of Heaven; by sixty I learned to give ear to others; by seventy I could follow my heart's desires without overstepping the line.

5   Meng Yi Zi asked about filial devotion. The Master replied, Never break the rules.

When Fan Chi was driving the carriage, the Master reported this to him, saying, Meng Sun (Meng Yi Zi) asked me about filial devotion. I told him, Never break the rules.

Fan Chi said, What did you mean by that?

The Master said, While they are alive, serve them according to ritual. When they die, bury them according to ritual, and sacrifice to them in accord with ritual.

6   Meng Wu Bo asked about filial devotion. The Master said, Your father and mother should have to worry only about your falling ill.

[Or, according to another interpretation of the last clause:] In the case of one's father and mother, one just worries about their falling ill.

7.   Ziyou asked about filial devotion. The Master said, Nowadays it's taken to mean just seeing that one's parents get enough to eat. But we do that much for dogs or horses as well. If there is no reverence, how is it any different?

8   Zixia asked about filial devotion. The Master said, The difficult part is the facial expression.[2] As for young people taking on the heavy work when there's something to be done, or older people going first when there's wine and food—can this be called filial devotion?

9   The Master said, I talk a whole day with Hui, and he never disagrees with me, as though he were stupid. But later, when I examine his private conduct, I see that it fully exemplifies my ideas. No, Hui is not stupid.

10   The Master said, Watch what he does, observe the path he follows, examine where he comes to rest—can any person then remain a mystery? Can any person remain a mystery?

11   The Master said, Be thoroughly versed in the old, and understand the new then you can be a teacher.

12   The Master said, The gentleman is not a utensil.[3]

13   Zigong asked about the gentleman. The Master said, First he puts his words into action. Only later does he follow up with explanations.

14   The Master said, The gentleman is fair-minded and not partisan. The petty man is partisan and not fair-minded.

15   The Master said, Learning without thought is pointless. Thought without learning is dangerous.

16   The Master said, To delve into strange doctrines can bring only harm.[4]

17   The Master said, You (Zilu), shall I teach you what it means to know something? When you know, to know you know. When you don't know, to know you don't know. That's what knowing is.

18   Zizhang was studying to gain an official position. The Master said, Hear much, put aside what's doubtful, and in your speech apply the rest with caution—then you'll make few mistakes. Observe much, put aside what's suspicious, and in your actions apply the rest with caution—then you'll have little to regret. Making few mistakes, having little to regret—the way to official position lies in this.

19   Duke Ai asked, saying, How can I make the common people submissive? Confucius replied, Promote the straight and let them oversee the crooked—then the common people will be submissive. Promote the crooked and let them oversee the straight— then the common people will not be submissive.

20   Ji Kangzi asked, How can I make the common people respectful, loyal, and diligent in their work?

The Master said, If you are strict in overseeing them, they will be respectful. If you are filial and compassionate, they will be loyal. If you promote persons of goodness and teach those who are incompetent, then the people will be diligent.

21   Someone questioned Confucius, saying, Why aren't you in government?

The Master said, *The Book of Documents* says: Filial, only be filial, a friend to elder and younger brothers—this contributes to government.[5] To do this is in fact to take part in government. Why must I be "in government"?

22   The Master said, Persons who lack trustworthiness—I don't know how they get by! Big carts that have no yoke-bar, little carts that have no collar-bar—how can you go anywhere in them?

23   Zizhang questioned the Master, saying, Can we know how things will be ten generations from now?

The Master said, Yin followed the rites of Xia, and we know in what ways it added to or subtracted from them. Zhou follows the rites of Yin, and we know in what ways it added to or subtracted from them. Whoever carries on from Zhou, we can know how things will be even a hundred generations from now.

24   The Master said, To sacrifice to those who are not one's ancestors is flattery. To see what is right and not do it is cowardly.

NOTES

1. Quoting a phrase from poem no. 297 and interpreting it out of context, Confucius stresses his view of the didactic import of the *Book of Odes*. In the poem, the words refer to carriage drivers and mean something like "Ah, never swerving!"

2. Watching the faces of one's parents to make certain how they are reacting. Or perhaps the meaning is keeping the proper expression on one's own face.

3. Not something to be used because he has some special knowledge or ability.

4. No one knows just what Confucius means by this. Perhaps the term *yiduan*, translated here as "strange doctrines," has some quite different meaning, though it suggests going off in an unusual direction.

5. From a lost section of the *Book of Documents*.

BOOK 4

1   The Master said, Humaneness is the beauty of the community. If you can choose but do not make humaneness your home, how can you be called wise?

2   The Master said, A person lacking in humaneness cannot endure straightened circumstances for long, nor can he enjoy favorable circumstances for long. The humane person rests in humaneness, the wise person profits from humaneness.

3   The Master said, Only the humane person is able to like others and is able to hate others.

4   The Master said, Truly set your mind on humaneness, and you will be without evil.

5   The Master said, Wealth and eminence are what people desire, but if one can't get them by means that accord with the Way, one will not accept them. Poverty and low position are what people hate, but if one can't avoid them by means that accord with the Way, one will not reject them.

If the gentleman rejects humaneness, how can he be worthy of the name of gentleman? The gentleman never departs from humaneness even for the space of a meal—in confusion and distress he holds fast to it stumbling, faltering, be holds fast to it.

6   The Master said, I have never seen a person who really loved humaneness or a person who really hated the lack of humaneness. A person who really loved humaneness

would have no one who surpassed him. A person who really hated the lack of humaneness would conduct himself humanely, never allowing those who lack humaneness to affect his behavior.

Is there someone who for a whole day is willing to use all his strength to achieve humaneness? I've never seen anyone who lacked the strength to do so—there may be such a person, but I've never seen one.[1]

7   The Master said, People's errors vary with the category they belong to. Look at the errors, and you know the degree of humaneness.

8   The Master said, Hear the Way in the morning, and it won't matter if you die that evening.

9   The Master said, A man of station whose will is set on the Way but who is ashamed of poor clothing and poor food—not worth talking to!

10   The Master said, With regard to worldly affairs, the gentleman has no strong likes and no strong dislikes—he sides with what is right.

11   The Master said, The gentleman has his mind fixed on virtue; the petty man has his mind fixed on land. The gentleman has his mind fixed on penalties; the petty man has his mind fixed on bounty.

12   The Master said, Act only with profit in mind, and you face much rancor.

13   The Master said, Can you govern the state with ritual and a deferential approach? Then you will have no difficulty. If you cannot govern the state with ritual and a deferential approach, then what use is ritual alone?

14   The Master said, Don't worry that you have no position[2]—worry about how you can qualify for one. Don't worry that people don't know you—look for some reason to become known.

15   The Master said, Shen (Master Zeng), my Way has one theme running throughout!

Master Zeng said, Yes.

After the Master left, the disciples asked, What did he mean?

Master Zeng said, The Master's Way consists of loyalty and reciprocity[3] alone.

16   The Master said, The gentleman is alert to what is right. The petty man is alert to what is profitable.

17   The Master said, When you see a worthy person, think about how you can equal him. When you see an unworthy person, reflect on your own conduct.

18   The Master said, In serving your father and mother, you may gently admonish them. But if you see they have no intention of listening to you, then be respectful as before and do not disobey them. You might feel distressed but should never feel resentful.

19   The Master said, While his father and mother are alive, a son should not go on distant journeys. If he travels, he must have a fixed destination.

20   The Master said, If after three years [a son] has not changed his father's way of doing things, then you can call him filial.

21   The Master said, You must not be ignorant of the age of your father and mother! For one thing, it is a cause for rejoicing; for another, a cause for fear.

22   The Master said, People in old times were sparing in their words. They were ashamed to think that their actions might not measure up.

23   The Master said, Those who go wrong by holding back are few.

24   The Master said, The gentleman desires to be hesitant in speech but prompt in action.

25   The Master said, Virtue is not alone. It invariably has neighbors.

26   Ziyou said, Be too censorious in serving the ruler, and you will end up in disgrace. Be that way with your friends, and you will lose them.

NOTES

1. What we lack is not the strength but the determination to do so.

2. Confucius probably means a position in government, but the saying has much broader implications.

3. Fellow feeling, doing to others as you would have them do to you.

TEXT 17. Pan Chao (ca. 48-ca. 112): A Female Confucian Scholar

1. Pan Chao was one of the most important historians of the Han dynasty. She also edited books on astronomy and wrote the following text for unmarried women of her family. According to her, what were the wife's responsibilities? How could a wife win her husband's love?

2. How did Pan Chao justify her normative claims with regard to gender roles?

3. Would you consider that Pan Chao's work is essentially conservative? Would you find any challenges to traditional gender roles in her writing?

4. After reading Pan Chao and Barbara Reed's article [see TEXT 15], would you conclude that Taoism (Daoism) has a more positive view of women than Confucianism or vice versa? Please provide examples from both texts to back up your position.

Text Seventeen

Pan Chao: A Female Confucian Scholar

LESSONS FOR WOMEN

Introduction

I, the unworthy writer, am unsophisticated, unenlightened, and by mature unintelligent, but I am fortunate both to have received not a little favor from my scholarly father, and to have had a (cultured) mother and instructresses upon whom to rely for a literary education as well as for training in good manners. More than forty years have passed since at the age of fourteen I took up the dustpan and the broom in the Ts'ao family. During this time with trembling heart I feared constantly that I might disgrace my parents, and that I might multiply difficulties for both the women and the men (of my husband's family). Day and night I was distressed in heart, (but) I labored without confessing weariness. Now and hereafter, however, I know how to escape (from such fears).

Being careless, and by nature stupid, I taught and trained (my children) without system. Consequently I fear that my son Ku may bring disgrace upon the Imperial Dynasty by whose Holy Grace he has unprecedentedly received the extraordinary privilege of wearing the Gold and the Purple, a privilege for the attainment of which (by my son, I) a humble subject never even hoped. Nevertheless, now that he is a man and able to plan his own life, I need not again have concern for him. But I do grieve that you, my daughters, just now at the age for marriage, have not at this time had gradual training and advice; that you still have not learned the proper customs for married women. I fear that by failure in good manners in other families you will humiliate both your ancestors and your clan. I am now seriously ill, life is uncertain. As I have thought of you all in so untrained a state, I have been uneasy many a time for you. At hours of leisure I have composed in seven chapters these instructions under the title, "Lessons for Women." In order that you may have something wherewith to benefit your persons, I wish every one of you, my daughters, each to write out a copy for yourself.

From this time on every one of you strive to practise these (lessons).

Chapter I
Humility

On the third day after the birth of a girl the ancients observed three customs: (first) to place the baby below the bed; (second) to give her a potsherd with which to play; and (third) to announce her birth to her ancestors by an offering. Now to lay the baby below limbed plainly indicated that she is lowly and week, and should regard it as her primary duty to humble herself before others. To give her potsherds with which to play indubitably signified that she should practise labor and consider it her primary duty to be industrious. To announce her birth before her ancestors clearly meant that she ought to esteem as her primary duty the continuation of the observance of worship in the home.

These three ancient customs epitomize a woman's ordinary way of life and the teachings of the traditional ceremonial rites and regulations. Let a woman modestly yield to others; let her respect others; let her put others first, herself last. Should she do something good, let her not mention it; should she do something bad, let her not deny it, Let her bear disgrace; let her even endure when others speak or do evil to her. Always let her seem to tremble and to fear.

"A Female Confucian Scholar" (editor's title, originally titled "Lessons for Women") from *Pan Chao: Foremost Woman Scholar of China* by Nancy Lee Swann, 1932. Used by permission of the East Asian Library and Gest Collection, Princeton University.

(When a woman follows each maxims as these,) then she may be said to humble herself before others.

Let a woman retire late to bed, but rise early to duties; let her not dread tasks by day or by night. Let her not refuse to perform domestic duties whether easy or difficult. That which must be done, let her finish completely, tidily, and systematically. (When a woman follows such rules as these,) then she may be said to be industrious.

Let a women be correct in manner and upright in character in order to serve her husband. Let her live in purity and quietness (of spirit), and attend to her own affairs. Let her love not gossip and silly laughter. Let her cleanse and purify and arrange in order the wine and the food for the offerings to the ancestors. (When a woman observes such principles as these,) then she may be said to continue ancestral worship.

No woman who observes these three (fundamentals of life) has ever had a bad reputation or has fallen into disgrace. If a woman fail to observe them, how can her name be honored; how can she but bring disgrace upon herself?

Chapter II
Husband and Wife

The Way of husband and wife is intimately connected with *Yin* and *Yang,* and relates to the individual to gods and ancestors. Truly it is the great principle of Heaven and Earth, and the great basis of human relationships. Therefore the "Rites" honor union of man and woman; and in the "Book of Poetry" the "First Ode" manifests the principle of marriage. For these reasons the relationship cannot but be an important one.

If a husband be unworthy then he possesses nothing by which to control his wife, if a wife be unworthy, then she possesses nothing with which to serve her husband. If a husband does not control his wife, then the rules of conduct manifesting his authority are abandoned and broken. If a wife does not serve her husband, then the proper relationship (between men and women) and the natural order of things are neglected and destroyed. As a matter of fact the purpose of these two (the controlling of women by men, and the serving of men by women) is the same.

Now examine the gentlemen of the present age. They only know that wives must be controlled, and that the husband's rules of conduct manifesting his authority must be established. They therefore teach their boys to read books and (study) histories. But they do not in the least understand that husbands and masters must (also) be served, and that the proper relationship and the rites should he maintained.

Yet only to teach men and not to teach women,—is that not ignoring the essential relation between them? According to the "Rites," it is the rule to begin to teach children to read at the age of eight years, and by the age of fifteen years they ought then to be ready for cultural training. Only why should it not be (that girls' education as well as boys' be) according to this principle?

Chapter III
Respect and Cautions

As *Yin* and *Yang* are not of the same nature, so man and woman have different characteristics. The distinctive quality of the *Yang* is rigidity; the function of the *Yin* is yielding. Man is honored for strength; a woman is beautiful on account of her gentleness. Hence there arose the autumn saying: "A man though born like a wolf may, it is feared, become a weak monstrosity; a woman though born like a mouse may, it is feared, become a tiger."

Now for self-culture nothing equals respect for others. To counteract firmness nothing equals compliance. Consequently it can be said that the Way of respect and acquiescence is woman's most important principle of conduct. So respect may be defined as nothing other than holding on to that which is permanent; and acquiescence nothing other than being liberal and generous. Those who are steadfast in devotion know that they should stay in their proper places; those who are liberal and generous esteem others, and honor and serve (them).

If husband and wife have the habit of staying together, never leaving one another, and following each other around within the limited space of their own rooms, then they will lust after and take liberties with one another. From such action improper language will arise between the two. This kind of discussion may lead to licentiousness. Out of licentiousness will be born a heart of disrespect to the husband. Such a result comes from not knowing that one should stay in one's proper place.

Furthermore, affairs may be either crooked or straight; words may be either right or wrong. Straightforwardness cannot but lead to quarreling; crookedness cannot but lead to accusation. If there are really accusations and quarrels, then undoubtedly there will be angry affairs. Such a result comes from not esteeming others, and not honoring and serving (them).

(If wives) suppress not contempt for husbands, then it follows (that such wives) rebuke and scold (their husbands). (If husbands) stop not short of anger, then they are certain to beat (their wives). The correct relationship between husband and wife is based upon harmony and intimacy, and (conjugal) love is grounded in proper union. Should actual blows be dealt, how could matrimonial relationship be preserved? Should sharp words be spoken, how could (conjugal) love exist? If love and proper relationship both be destroyed, then husband and wife are divided.

Chapter IV
Womanly Qualifications

A woman (ought to) have four qualifications: (1) womanly virtue; (2) womanly words; (3) womanly bearing; and (4) womanly work. Now what is called womanly virtue need not be brilliant ability, exceptionally different from others. Womanly words need be neither clever in debate nor keen in conversation. Womanly appearance requires neither a pretty nor a perfect face and form. Womanly work need not be work done more skillfully than that of others.

To guard carefully her chastity; to control circumspectly her behavior; in every motion to exhibit modesty; and to model each act on the best usage, this is womanly virtue.

To choose her words with care; to avoid vulgar language; to speak at appropriate times; and not to weary Where (with much conversation), may be called the characteristics of womanly words.

To wash and scrub filth away; to keep clothes and ornaments fresh and clean; to wash the head and bathe the body regularly, and to keep the person free from disgraceful filth, may be called the characteristics of womanly bearing.

With whole-hearted devotion to sew and to weave; to love not gossip and silly laughter; in cleanliness and order (to prepare) the wine and food for serving guests, may be called the characteristics of womanly work.

These four qualifications characterize the greatest virtue of a woman. No woman can afford to be without them. In fact they are very easy to possess if a woman only treasure them in her heart. The ancients had a saying; "Is Love afar off? If I desire love, then love is at hand!" So can it be said of these qualifications.

Chapter V
Whole-hearted Devotion

Now in the "Rites" is written the principle that a husband may marry again, but there is no Canon that authorizes a woman to be married the second time. Therefore it is said of husbands as of Heaven, that as certainty as people cannot run away from Heaven, so surely a wife cannot leave (a husband's bane).

If people in action or character disobey the spirits of Heaven and of Earth, then Heaven punishes them. Likewise if a woman errs in the rites and in the proper mode of conduct, then her husband esteems her lightly. The simian book, "A Pattern for Women," (*Nu Hsien*) says : "To obtain the love of one man is the crown of a woman's life; to lose the love of one man is to miss the aim in woman's life." For these reasons a woman cannot but seek to win her husband's heart. Nevertheless, the beseeching wife need not use Battery, coaxing words, and cheap methods to gain intimacy.

Decidedly nothing is better (to gain the heart of a husband) than whole-hearted devotion and correct manors. In accordance with the rites and the proper mode of conduct, (let a woman) live a pure life. Let her have cars that hear not licentiousness; and eyes that see not depravity. When she goes outside her own home, let her not be conspicuous in dress and manners. When at home let her not neglect her dress. Women should not ensemble in groups, nor gather together, (for gossip and silly laughter). They should not stand watching in the gateways. (If a woman follows) these rules, she may be said to have whole-hearted devotion and correct manners.

If all her actions, she is frivolous, she sees and hears (only) that which pleases herself. At home her hair is dishevelled, and her dress is slovenly. Outside the home she emphasizes her femininity to attract attention; she says what ought not to be said; and she looks at what ought not to be seen. (If a woman does such as) these, (she may be) said to be without whole-hearted devotion and correct manners.

Chapter VI
Implicit Obedience

Now "to win the love of one man is the crown of a woman's life; to lose the love of one man is her eternal disgrace." This saying advises a fixed will end a whole-hearted devotion for a woman. Ought she then to lose the hearts of her father and mother-in-law?

There are times when love may lead to differences of opinion (between individuals); there are times when duty size, lead to disagreement. Even should the husband say that he loves something. When the parents-in-law say "no," this is called a case of duty leading to disagreement. This being so, then what about the hearts of the parents-in-law? Nothing is better than an obedience which sacrifices personal opinion.

Whenever the mother-in-law says, "Do not do that," and if what she says is right, unquestionably the daughter-in-law obeys. Whenever the mother-in-law says, "Do that," even if what she says is wrong, still the daughter-in-law submits unfailingly to the command.

Let a woman not act contrary to the wishes and the opinions of parents-in-law about right and wrong; let her not dispute with than what is straight and what is crooked. Such (docility) may be called obedience which sacrifices personal opinion. Therefore the ancient book, "A Pattern for Women," says: "It a daughter-in-law (who follows the wishes of her parents-in-law) is like an echo and a shadow, how could she not be praised?"

Chapter VII
Harmony with Younger Brothers- and Sisters-in-law

In order for a wife to gain the love of her husband, she must win for herself the love of her parents-in-law. To win for herself the love of her parents-in-law, she must secure for herself the good will of Younger brothers- and sisters-in-law. For these reasons the right and the wrong, the praise and the blame of a woman alike depend upon younger brothers- and sisters-in-law. Consequently it will not do for a woman to lose their affection.

They are stupid both who know not that they must not lose (the hearts of) younger brothers- and sisters-in-law, and who cannot be in harmony with them in order to be intimate with them. Excepting only the Holy Men, few are able to be faultless. Now Yen Tau's, greatest virtue was that he was able to reform. Confucius praised him (for not committing a misdeal) the second time. (In comparison with him) a woman is the more likely (to make mistakes).

Although a woman possesses a worthy woman's qualifications, and is wise and discerning by nature, is she able to be perfect? Yet if a woman live in harmony with her immediate family, unfavorable criticism will be silenced (within the home, But) if a man and woman disagree, then this evil will be noised abroad. Such consequences are inevitable. The "Book of Changes" says:

"Should two hearts harmonise,
The united strength can cut gold.
Words from hearts which agree,
Give forth fragrance like the orchid."

This saying may be applied to (harmony in the home).

Though a daughter-in-law and her younger sisters-in-law are equal in rank, nevertheless (they should) respect (each other); though love (between them may be) sparse, their proper relationship should be intimate. Only the virtuous, the beautiful, the modest, and the respectful (young women) can accordingly rely upon the sense of duty to make their affection sincere, and magnify love to bind their relationships firmly.

Then the excellence and the beauty of such a daughter-in-law becomes generally known. Moreover, any flaws and mistakes are hidden and unreveeled. Parents-in-law toast of her good deeds; her husband is satisfied with her. Praise of her radiates, nuking her illustrious in district and in neighborhood; and her brightness readies to her own father and mother.

But a stupid and foolish person as an elder sister-in-law uses her rank to exalt herself; as a younger sister-in-law, because of parents' favor, she becomes filled with arrogance. If arrogant, how can a woman live in harmony with others? If love and proper relationships be perverted, how can praise be secured? In such instances the wife's good is hidden, and her faults are declared. The mother-in-law will be angry, and the husband will be indignant. Blame will reverberate and spread in and outside the home. Disgrace will gather upon the daughter-in-law's person, on the one hand to add humiliation to her own father and mother, and on the other to increase the difficulties of her husband.

Such than is the basis for both honor and disgrace; the foundation for reputation or for ill-repute. Can a woman be too cautious? Consequently to seek the hearts of young brothers- and sisters-in-law decidedly nothing can be esteemed better than modesty and acquiescence.

Modesty is virtue's handle; as acquiescence is the wilds (most refitted) characteristic. All who possess these two have sufficient for harmony with others. In the "Book of Poetry" it is written that "here is no evil; there is no dart." So it may be said of (these two, modesty and acquiescence).

Part 3

RELIGIONS ORIGINATING IN THE MIDDLE EAST: THE MYTH OF HISTORY

MIDDLE EAST

Scale 1:21,000,000

Lambert Conformal Conic Projection,
standard parallels 12°N and 38°N

0   300 Kilometers
0   300 Miles

Boundary representation is
not necessarily authoritative.

Golan Heights is Israeli-occupied Syria.

West Bank is Israeli-occupied with current status subject to the
Israeli-Palestinian Interim Agreement; permanent status to be
determined through further negotiation.

The status of the Gaza Strip is a final status issue to be resolved
through negotiations.

Israel proclaimed Jerusalem as its capital in 1950, but the US, like
nearly all other countries, maintains its Embassy in Tel Aviv-Yafo.

803513AI (G00412) 6-12

Source: Central Intelligence Agency

Game: What is missing on this map?

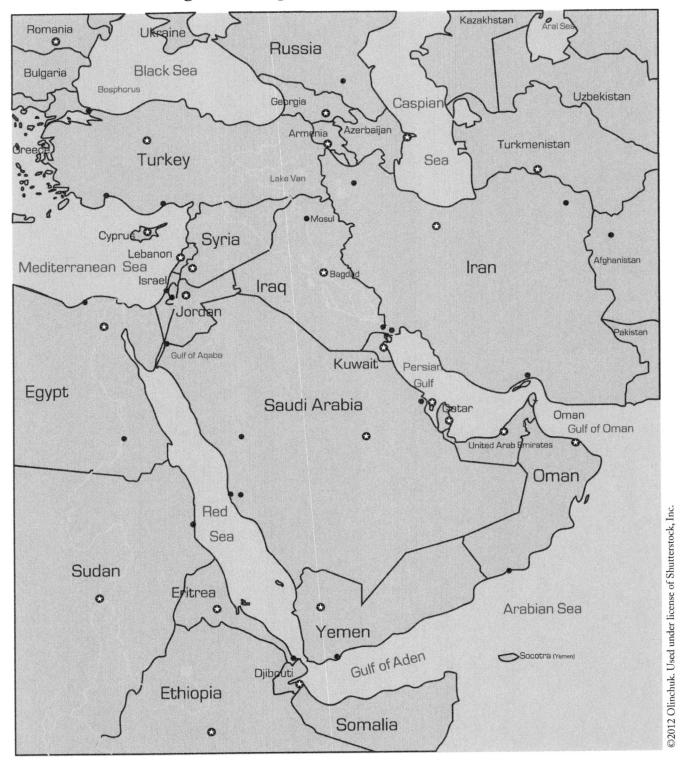

Zoroastrianism

Zoroastrian Fire Temple in Isfahan, Iran

INTRODUCTION TO MONOTHEISTIC RELIGIONS ORIGINATING IN MIDDLE EAST WITH SPECIAL EMPHASIS ON ZOROASTRIANISM

Judaism, Christianity, and Islam
- Originated in the Middle East
- Claim descent from Abraham
- God called Abraham, who
  - Renounced other gods
  - Lived by faith in the one true God

Zoroastrianism had some influence
- Judaism
- Christianity
- Islam – 7c CE

All four religions
- Believe in one all-powerful personal deity
- Monotheistic religions
- Good and evil

ZOROASTRIANISM (ORIGINS)
- Monotheistic
- Ancient Persia
- Challenged native Persian/Iranian animism — Axis Age
- Ahura Mazda (Wise God) spoke to Zarathustra (10th-6th century BCE?)

symbol is fire   (Zoroaster) → Bramin (highest class)
encounter w/ arc angel = one god

Center of Zoroastrianism Today
- Mumbai, India
- Zoroastrians immigrated to India
- Known as Parsis (Persians)
- Approximately 250,000 Zoroastrians in world today

God is
persa/Iran SAME AREA
- One
- Holy, righteous, immortal
- Creator
- Omniscient
- Omnipotent
- Has no equals
- Transcendent
- Personal
- Beyond gender

Humanity is central to creation
- Superior to other creatures
- Special relationship with God
- Special responsibility

Special human status   > free will

- Reason
- Freedom
- Moral choice
- Capacity for good and evil

Humanity and Creator
- Creator has revealed good path
- The path is revealed in scriptures
  – *Avesta* (Law) is sacred Zoroastrian liturgical text

Two eternal spirits of Zoroastrianism
- Spenta Mainyu (a good spirit)   court of Angels
- Angra Mainyu (an evil spirit, "the destructive spirit")   Satan, court of Devils
- Both spirits emanate from the one God, Ahura Mazda
- They exist in a balance and are both necessary for life

Why do Humans Choose Evil?
- Two possible explanations
  – Humans are free to make moral choice
  – Evil force (Angra Mainyu)

Only One Life to Live
- Zoroastrianism emphasizes human accountability
  – Good deeds are rewarded in paradise
  – Evil deeds punished in hell
- Soul is judged on the 4th day after death
- On 4th day the soul is judged
  – Deeds are weighed on scale

Zoroastrian Eschatology
- At end of time, Ahura Mazda will wipe away all evil
- Apocalyptic battle between good and evil
  – Resurrection of dead to fight for good or evil
- Angra Mainyu will be destroyed
  – New age will begin
  – No more evil, death, or disease

Tower of Silence = Dakhma

Restoration of the Relationship with God
- What brings about this restoration?
- Way revealed by God
- Sacred Writings
  – Reveal God's plan of salvation

In Zoroastrianism
- Good thought
- Good word
- Good Deed
- Nature = sacred
- Worship God
  – Sacred fire in Fire Temples symbolizes God's presence

Zoroastrian Funerary Rites in Past
- Corpses are impure
  – Corpses cannot be buried or burned
  – This would defile earth or fire
- Corpses are exposed to carrion birds
  – Corpse is bound in roofless dakhma (tower of silence)
  – Corpse eaten by vultures

Linear Time
- Zoroastrianism = 1st religion to propose linear concept of time
- Existence moves from its creation by God to a final culmination
- The world is real, not illusion
  – Proving ground for humans
- = Judaism, Christianity, Islam

For Judaism, Christianity, and Islam, Historical Events Become Myth
- Exodus (Moses) for Judaism
- Birth of Christ for Christianity
- Hijra for Islam (Migration of Muhammad from Mecca to Medina)

EXTRA NOTES

ZOROASTRIANISM

TEXT 18. THE BATTLE BETWEEN AHURA MAZDA AND ANGRA MAINYU

1. Compare/contrast Ahura Mazda and Angra Mainyu.

2. What is the relationship between the two?

Text Eighteen

The Battle Between Ahura Mazda and Angra Mainyu

CREATION AND THE MILLENNIA

In later Pahlavi Zoroastrian writings, Angra Mainyu has a more elevated role in cosmic history. The following selection from the Bundahishn, *a Pahlavi text on cosmogony and cosmic history, describes the initial confrontation between Ahura Mazda and Angra Mainyu and their ensuing 12,000-year battle. During the first 3,000 years, Ahura Mazda created the Beneficent Immortals and the world. Angra Mainyu responded by creating helper demons. They then agreed to limit the struggle to an additional 9,000 years.*

As revealed by the religion of the Mazda Worshipers (i.e., Zoroastrians), so it is declared that Ahura Mazda is supreme in omniscience and goodness, and unrivalled in splendor. The region of light is the place of Ahura Mazda, which they call "endless light," and the omniscience and goodness of the unrivalled Ahura Mazda is what they call "revelation."

Revelation is the explanation of both spirits together. One is he who is independent of unlimited time, because Ahura Mazda and the region, religion, and time of Ahura Mazda were and are and ever will be. Meanwhile, Angra Mainyu in darkness, with backward understanding and desire for destruction, was in the abyss, and it is he who will not be. The place of that destruction, and also of that darkness, is what they call the "endlessly dark." Between them was empty space, that is, what they call "air," in which is now their meeting.

Both are limited and unlimited spirits, for the supreme is that which they call endless light, and the abyss that which is endlessly dark, so that between them is a void, and one is not connected with the other, Again, both spirits are limited as to their own selves. Secondly, on account of the omniscience of Ahura Mazda, both things are in the creation of Ahura Mazda, the finite and the infinite. For, this they know is that which is in the covenant of both spirits. Again, the complete sovereignty of the creatures of Ahura Mazda is in the future existence, and that also is unlimited forever and everlasting. The creatures of Angra Mainyu will perish at the time when the Final Body occurs, and that also is eternity.

Ahura Mazda, through omniscience, knows that Angra Mainyu exists. And whatever he schemes he infuses with malice and greediness till the end. Because he accomplishes the end by many means, he also produced spiritually the creatures which were necessary for those means, and they remained three thousand years in a spiritual state, so that they were unthinking and unmoving, with intangible bodies.

The evil spirit, on account of backward knowledge, was not aware of the existence of Ahura Mazda. Afterwards, he arose from the abyss, and came in the light which he saw. Desirous of destroying, and because of his malicious nature, he rushed in to destroy that light of Ahura Mazda unassailed by fiends. He saw its bravery and glory were greater than his own, so he fled back to the gloomy darkness, and formed many demons and fiends. The creatures of the destroyer arose for violence.

Bundahishn, chapter 1, adapted from E. W. West, *Pahlavi Texts*, part 1 (Oxford: Clarendon Press, 1880)

Ahura Mazda examined the creatures of the Destructive Spirit, which were terrible, corrupt, and bad, and considered them not commendable. Afterwards, the evil spirit saw the creatures of Ahura Mazda. There appeared many creatures, and they seemed to him commendable. He commended the creatures and creation of Ahura Mazda. Then Ahura Mazda, with a knowledge of which way the end of the matter would be, went to meet the evil spirit, and proposed peace to him and spoke thus: "Evil sprit! Bring assistance to my creatures and offer praise, so that, in reward for it, you and your creatures may become immortal and undecaying, without hunger and thirst."

The evil spirit shouted, "I will not depart. I will not provide assistance for your creatures. I will not offer praise among your creatures, and I am not of the same opinion with you as to good things. I will destroy your creatures forever and everlasting. Moreover, I will force all your creatures into disaffection to you and affection for myself." The explanation for this is that the evil spirit reflected that Ahura Mazda was helpless as regarded him. Therefore, Ahura Mazda offered peace, and Angra Mainyu did not agree, but continued on even into conflict with him.

Ahura Mazda spoke: "You are not omniscient and almighty, oh evil spirit, so that it is not possible for you to destroy me. And it is not possible for you to force my creatures so that they will not return to my possession." Through omniscience, Ahura Mazda knew if he did not grant a period of contest, then it would be possible for Angra Mainyu to seduce his creatures. As even now there are many of the intermixture of humankind who practice wrong more than right. Ahura Mazda spoke to the evil spirit: "Appoint a period so that the intermingling of the conflict may be for nine thousand years." For he knew that by appointing this period the evil spirit would be undone. Then the evil spirit, unobservant and through ignorance, was content with that agreement, just like two men quarrelling together, who propose a time thus: Let us appoint such-and-such a day for a fight.

Through omniscience, Ahura Mazda also knew that, within these nine thousand years, for three thousand years everything proceeds by the will of Ahura Mazda. In the next three thousand years, there is an intermingling of the wills of Ahura Mazda and Angra Mainyu. In the last three thousand years the evil spirit is made powerless, and they keep the adversary away from the creatures.

Afterwards, Ahura Mazda recited the *Ahunvar* (the Zoroastrians' most sacred prayer). He also exhibited to the evil spirit his own triumph in the end, and the impotence of the evil spirit, the annihilation of the demons, and the resurrection and undisturbed future existence of the creatures forever and everlasting. The evil spirit, who perceived his own impotence and the annihilation of the demons, became confounded, and fell back to the gloomy darkness...He became confounded and impotent as to the harm he caused the creatures of Ahura Mazda, and he remained three thousand years in confusion.

Ahura Mazda created his creatures in the confusion of Angra Mainyu. First he produced Vohu Manah (Good thought), by whom the movement of the creatures of Ahura Mazda was advanced. The evil spirit first created Mitokht (Falsehood), and then Akoman (Evil Thought). The first of Ahura Mazda's creatures of the world was the sky, and his good thought, by good procedures, produced the light of the world, along with which was the good religion of the Mazda Worshipers. This was because the resurrection which happens to the creatures was known to him. Afterwards arose Ardavahist, then Shatvairo, then Spendarmad, then Horvadad, and then Amerodad (the Beneficent Immortals). From the dark world of Angra Mainyu were Akoman and Andar, then Sovar then Nakahed, and then Tairev and Zairik. Of Ahura Mazda's creatures of the world, the first was the sky, the second water, the third earth. The fourth plans, the fifth animals, and the sixth mankind.

Judaism

A Young Woman Lighting the Candles for Jewish Sabbath

JUDAISM

Judaism
- Small group; only 14 million
- No single founder
- No central authority

To be a Jew is to
- Be in continuing dialogue with God
- Be part of people Israel
  - Israel = "he who strives, wrestles with God"
- See history as shaped by special relationship with God
- Recognize God as the one source of righteous living
- Acknowledge scriptural obligations

Geography of Judaism
- Repeatedly dispersed over centuries
- After Holocaust (1938-1945) some Jews founded a homeland in Israel
- Israel became a Jewish state in 1948
- Other Jews live around the world

The Hebrew Bible (called Tanak)
- Torah (Teaching)
- Nevi'im (Prophets)
- Kethuvim (Writings)

T
A
N
A
K

Torah (5 Books of Moses)
- Genesis
- Exodus
- Leviticus
- Numbers
- Deuteronomy

The Torah includes
- Historical narrative
- Doctrine of God as
  - Creator
  - Redeemer
  - Revelator
  - Lawgiver
  - Judge

- Ethic of justice
- Ritual Prescriptions
- Law Code

Torah
- Written Torah = Books of Moses *Pentateuch*
- Torah also means more broadly all teachings revealed by God

Nevi'im
- Former Prophets
  – Includes Joshua, Judges, I-II Samuel
  – History of Israel
- Latter Prophets
  – Canonical Prophets
  – Writings of individual prophets
  – Includes Isaiah, Hosea, Ezekiel, Amos

Kethuvim
- Proverbs
- Reflections on life (Ecclesiastes)
- Hymns (Psalms)
- Lyrics (Song of Solomon)
- Poetry

Origins and Ancestors (Source: Genesis)
- Creation in 6 Days
  – Origin of Sabbath
- God = sole creator
- Creation = good
- Special place of humanity

Primal History of Mankind
- First man (Adam) and woman (Eve)
- Expulsion from paradise because of disobedience
- Great flood
  – Divine judgment for human wickedness
  – Noah and family and animals saved in ark
  – God promises not to destroy world with flood again
- Tower of Babel

Abraham and his Descendants
- Special Covenant with God
- Covenant = pacts between God and Israel

- Covenant often includes
  - God's promises
  - Specific stipulations Israel

God called Abraham
- Abraham migrated from Ur
- Made covenant with God in Haran
  - Abraham promised to worship God alone
  - God promised Abraham
    - Land of Canaan
    - Descendants
- The covenant would be sealed by circumcision

Abraham and Isaac
- Isaac born miraculously
- Sacrifice of Isaac
  - God tests Abraham
  - God demands sacrifice of Isaac
  - Abraham complies
  - At last moment, God provides an animal substitute
  - God rewards Abraham for his obedience

Patriarchs
- Abraham
- Isaac *(from Sarah)*
- Jacob

[handwritten diagram box:]
Abraham
↓   ↓
Ishmael   Isaac
↓   ↓
12 sons   Jacob (Israel)
(ancesters of   ↓
Arabs)   12 sons
              (ancesters of
              Israelite Tribes)

[handwritten right margin:]
in order
Abraham
↓
Isaac
↓
Jacob
↓
moses
↓
David

Jacob and Tribes of Israel
- Son of Isaac, Grandson of Abraham
- Jacob has 12 sons
  - Each one is ancestor of a tribe in Israel
- Jacob and sons flee to Egypt to escape famine
- Their descendants become slaves in Egypt

Moses and the Exodus
- Source: The Book of Exodus
- 1500-1280 BCE
- God called Moses to liberate Hebrews
- God sent 10 plagues on Egyptians
- Egyptians reluctantly allowed Israelites to leave
- Exodus = Going out from Egypt
- Pesach (Passover) = Annual Jewish celebration of Exodus

[handwritten bottom:]
Three covenants
1) flood - (Noah)
2) mosaic - 10 commandments
3)

Mosaic Covenant

- Moses led Hebrews to Mount Horeb or Sinai
- There Moses received Torah
  - Includes 10 Commandments
- Mosaic covenant extended Abrahamic covenant
  - God gave a systematic law at Sinai
  - Example: Sabbath observance

Torah

- Instruction given by God
- First Five Books
- May refer to the Tanak as a whole
- May also refer to total revelation from God
  - Tanak (the written Torah) + related authoritative commentary
- Orally passed down from Moses to disciples

↳ Talmud= oral Toran

Ark of Covenant and Tent of Meeting

- Ark of the Covenant
  - Contained tablets of 10 Commandments
  - Symbolic throne of the Lord (YHWH)
- Tent of Meeting
  - Meticulously described in Torah
  - Contained Ark
  - Prototype of later Temples

Davidic Monarchy

- Source: Prophetic Books

Need for Strong Monarch

- 10th century BCE—Philistines threaten Israel
  - Seafaring enemy
  - Migrated from Crete to Canaan
  - Armed with iron weapons
  - Made Israel recognize need for strong leader

Early Kings of Israel

- Saul
- David (ruled 1000-960 BCE)
- Solomon (960-922 BCE)
  - David's son

✶ Joshua entered the promised land

Israel under David and Solomon

- Golden Age
- Jerusalem = David's capital
- Solomon built temple to Yahweh

Civil War: Division into 2 Kingdoms

- 922 BCE—Israel was divided into two kingdoms:
- Israel in the north
  - 10 northern tribes
- Judah in the south
  - Davidic dynasty
  - Jerusalem
  - Temple

Fall of the Northern Kingdom (Israel)

- 722 BCE—Assyria conquered Israel
- Assyrians deported Israelites

Prophet (Navi) — explain what happened

- Emissary sent by God
- Receives words from God
- Speaks on behalf of God to Israel and Judah
- Interpreted these historical events

Prophetic Message

- God demands and rewards obedience
- God punishes disobedience
- God is God of all nations, not just the Israelites
- God uses other nations to punish Israel
- God will not give up easily on the people
- God will send a Messiah, or anointed one
  - Descendant of David
  - Messiah will restore Davidic kingdom in all its glory
- Restoration of Israel at end of world
- All nations will come to God thanks to Israel

Exile

- 586 BCE—Nebuchadnezzar II of Babylon
  - Destroyed Solomon's temple
  - Deported most of the population
- The people lost all that had defined them:
  - Independence
  - King
  - Temple
  - Land

main consequence of exile

Effects of Exile

- Diaspora
  - Babylon became a center of Jewish life → even after prince cyrus invited them back

- Synagogue *emergence*
  - Temple ritual was de-emphasized
  - Written word took on new importance
  - Sabbath service of worship, study, psalms
- Scriptures—Oral traditions were recorded
- Language
  - Hebrew declined, replaced by Aramaic

Return from Exile
- Persian king Cyrus conquered Babylon
- Allowed Jews to return to homeland
- Jews rebuilt 2nd Temple

Priestly Hegemony under Persians
- Priests developed 2nd Temple ritual
- Priests made final edition of Pentateuch
- Priests compiled prophetic books (Neviim)

Alexander the Great in 333 BCE
- Hellenistic culture
  - (From Hellas, Greece)
  - Major influence
- Alexandria, Egypt
  - Major Jewish center
  - Septuagint *— bible translated into greek*
- Judea
  - Hellenized upper class
  - Sought to transform Jerusalem into Greek city

Persecution by King Antiochus IV (2nd century BCE)
- Tried to destroy Judaism
- Forbade
  - Sabbath
  - Circumcision
  - Torah study
- Temple became shrine to Zeus

Maccabean Revolt
- Antiochus' policies provoked revolt
- Priestly Hasmonean family led revolt
  - Judas Maccabee (the Hammer) = charismatic leader
- 164 BCE—Rebels had regained temple
  - Feast of Hanukkah
  - Recalls the rededication of Second Temple

Canon of Scripture

- By 150 BCE the books that would eventually be accepted into the Hebrew canon were finished. They included:
  - Job
  - Daniel
  - Psalms

Roman Rule (63 BCE–638 CE)

- 63 BCE—Roman general Pompey conquered Jerusalem
- Roman Empire rules Judea until Muslim conquest in 638 CE

During Roman Rule

- Jews enjoyed some religious independence
- Led by priests
- Local government was entrusted to local princes, of whom Herod the Great (37 BCE-4 CE) was one
- Herod was ruler of Palestine at the time Jesus was born

Outside Influences in 1st century BCE

- Hellenistic culture
- Alien rule
  - Babylonian
  - Persian
  - Greek
  - Roman
- Diaspora

New questions had arisen

- What was authoritative scripture?
- Who could interpret Scriptures?

2nd temple destroyed 70 CE

Four Important Factions

- Sadducees (priestly families) *considered written torah (pentateuch) as authentic, priests interpret* *5 books of moses*
- Essenes (monastic community) *considered temple corrupt, celebate, "end of time"*
- Pharisees (teachers of the synagogues) *anyone interpret,*
- Zealots (rebels against Roman rule)

Destruction of 2nd Temple in 70 CE

- Ended power of priesthood
  - Sacrifice was no longer possible
  - Ritual was thus de-emphasized
- Judaism emphasized scripture interpretation
- Leadership passed from priest to rabbis
- Development of Rabbinical/Talmudic Judaism

Pharisees Provided New Leadership. Why?
- Politically reliable to Rome
- Pharisees established academy
  – Yavneh (or Jamnia)
- Pharisees = leaders of synagogue tradition

Reinterpretation of Judaism after Fall of Temple
- People of Israel are holy
- Every male head of Jewish household = priest
- Table in every Jewish house is an altar

Formation of the Talmud
- 200 CE—Rabbi Judah compiled Mishnah ("repetition")
  – Codification of Torah in 6 sections
- Gemara ("tradition," "completion")
  – Commentary of the Mishnah
  – Completed in 6th century
- Mishnah + Gemara = Talmud

Two Talmuds
- Palestinian (or Jerusalem) Talmud (about 400 CE) — *Smaller of the two*
- Babylonian Talmud (about 600 CE) = most authoritative
- 2 types of text
  – Halakhah ("direction"): legal material, commandments and rules for living
  – Haggadah ("tradition"): anecdotes, stories, tales

Jews in Roman Empire
- 4th century—Christianity became official religion of Roman empire
- Legal restrictions on Jews in Empire
  – Jews could not proselytize
  – Jews could not marry Christians
  – Jews could not own slaves

Jews in Muslim Caliphate
- By 712—Islamic caliphate
  – Stretched from India into Spain
- Under Muslim rule Jews prospered
- Muslim Spain became center of Jewish life

Septuagint – greek translation of Bible (Tanak) done in Alexandria Egypt

Moses Maimonides, 1135-1204
- Most important Medieval Jewish thinker
- Identified 13 basic beliefs of Judaism
- Tried to reconcile Greek philosophy and Judaism
- Judaism = rational religion

Jews in Western Europe, 800

- 9th century—Charlemagne encouraged Jews to settle
- But from 11th century—Jewish life became precarious
  - Jews lived in ghettos—separate sections of town
  - Jews excluded from guilds
  - Jews forbidden to own farmland
  - Jews were often moneylenders
- Resented by their clients
  - Jews suffered pogroms

Jews in Spain (Sepharads)

- 1492—Christian kingdoms defeated Muslims in Spain
- 1492—Jews expelled from Spain
- Many fled to Muslim Ottoman Empire

Kabbalah

- Mystical tradition
- Esoteric (secret meaning to Bible)
- Zohar (Book of Splendor)
  - Ca. 1300
  - Central work of Kabbalah
  - Provided a theory of redemption

Ashkenazi Judaism in 18th century

- 13th-16th century—Ashkenazim expelled from
  - England
  - France
  - Spain
- Jews fled to Poland
- Ashkenazi Jews
  - Spoke Yiddish
  - Lived in villages (shtetls)
  - Governed themselves
- 17th century—Jews suffered pogroms

Hasidism

- Hasid = pious
- Emphasized meditative prayer

- worship is festive / communal
- ecstatic singing & dancing

Israel ben Eliezer (1700-1760)

- Founder of Hasidism
- BESHT (Baal Shem Tov)
  - Master of the Good Name
- Ecstatic healer and miracle-worker

- Emphasized joy
  - Religious feeling = greater than scholarship
  - Festive and communal worship
  - Ecstatic singing, dancing
- Tzaddik (Righteous One)

Haskalah (Enlightenment)
- Secular universalism
- Moses Mendelssohn (1729-1786)

Judaism In 19th Century
- Reform Judaism
- Orthodox Judaism
- Conservative Judaism

Religious Practice
- Rites of Passage
- Daily Prayer
- Dietary restrictions
- Weekly Sabbath
- Annual Festivals

Rites of Passage
- Circumcision
- Bar Mitzvah

Daily Prayer
- Jews praise God three times a day
- Tefillin
- Tallith

Kosher (ritually correct) diet
- Kosher rules in Talmud determine which foods may be eaten
- How allowed foods are to be prepared
- Acceptable manner of consumption

Weekly Sabbath
- Begins Friday at sundown (and)
- Ends Saturday at sundown
- Reenactment of creation myth
- Home service
  - Sabbath candles are lighted
  - 2 loaves of Sabbath bread = Symbol of manna from heaven in wilderness
- Sabbath service on Saturday morning in synagogue

Napolean Bonaparte
- *Unlocked the ghettos*
- *When invaded muted jews to be equal citizens in his empire*
- *According to French revolutionaries*
- *All humans have reason in common*
- *religion is not an identity marker*

Religious Calendar
- Rosh Hashanah (New Year)
- Yom Kippur (Day of Atonement)
  - Abstinence from work
  - Prayers for forgiveness and reconciliation
- Pilgrim Festivals
  - Sukkot (Tabernacles, Booths)
  - Pesach (Passover)
  - Shavuot (Weeks)

major Cultural Centers

☆ Babylonia

☆ Egypt (Alexandria) — Septuagint =
     greek translation of (tanak) Bible

☆ Spain (under muslim rule) [Sepharads] — Jewish mysticism
                                              or Kabbalah

    - main book = Zohar
    - the language of the bible needs to be "decoded"

☆ Eastern Europe (Ashkenaz)

    — Pograms

EXTRA NOTES

Jesus and the Prophet muhammad are both
decendents of <u>Abraham</u>

<u>Saul</u> was the first king of Israel
    ↳ <u>David</u> succeeded him
       ↳ <u>Solomon</u> succeeded him (Built the temple)

The first temple was <u>**built**</u> at the time of soloman
  it was <u>destroyed</u> at the time of <u>Buddha</u> 6thc BCE
    destroyed by Babylonians

Transformed status of Jews & unlocked the ghettos
     French Revolution

Reform Judism
Ethies of the Torah are mae important than
rituals and kosher rules

JUDAISM

The Beginnings

1. What is the problem of defining Judaism?

it is more comprehensive than a religion; society

2. Is Judaism pluralistic?

today, some is religious some is cultural

3. When did Judaism begin?

Abram received divine call "I will make thee a great nation..."

4. Where did Abraham live? What happened to him?

Islam,

5. What was the greatest contribution of Judaism?

6. What is a covenant?

a pact / contract w god

7. What was the Abrahamic covenant?

his family will multiply and live in the land (Israel)

8. What happened to Israel in Egypt? How did they escape from Egypt?

They were enslaved, moses/miracals

9. What did Moses receive from God at Sinai?

10 commandments   code of laws/ethics

10. What does the word Torah mean?

The "instruction" specifically 1st 5 books of Hebrew bible

11. What did the twelve tribes do?

12. Who was the first king? Who succeeded him?

Saul — David

13. Who built the temple? When?

David- 960 BCE

14. What was the center of the cult?

    Sacraficial system

15. What was the promised land?

    Jereusiamem

16. What were the people of the united kingdom called?

    Children of Isral, Isnailites

17. After Solomon, what happened to Israel?

    seperated in two groups

18. How was the Northern Kingdom destroyed?

    concured by Cyrians

19. When did the Babylonians invade Judah?

    500 BCE

20. What did Cyrus do for the Jews?

    permited them to return

21. When did Jews build the second temple?

    after returned   end of 6th c BCE
    500 BCE

22. The repatriates canonized which part of the Bible?

    penteteuch - first 5 books

23. What are the three parts of the Hebrew scriptures?

24. What did the Maccabees do? When did they live?

    ruled the area

25. When did Romans conquer Jerusalem?

    63 BCE

26. What was Judaism's greatest crisis? What happened to Jerusalem and the temple? When?

    17ce
    Jews of Palastine rebelled against Roman empire - lost and sent into exile

After the Destruction of the Second Temple

1. Who destroyed the second temple? When was it destroyed?

2. What was the consequence of the destruction of the second temple?

3. Where did Jews live after the destruction of the temple?

4. Instead of being temple centered, Judaism became _____ centered. Which period of Jewish history does this remind you of?

5. When did Jews visit the temple previously?

6. What was the synagogue?

7. How was Yahweh worshiped before the destruction of the temple?

8. What is the Mishnah? When was it compiled?

9. What is the Talmud? When was it compiled?

10. How and where did Jews spread in the world?

11. When did Christianity arise? What was its consequence?

12. How did Jews cope with exile?

13. Who were the Hasidim?

14. What were the consequences of the American and French revolutions?

15. How do Reform Jews look at the Torah? How do they differ from the Orthodox Jews?

Festivals

1. How many times do Jews pray per day?

2. What is a minyan?

3. What is the Sabbath? When does it occur? What do people do or not do during the Sabbath?

   sunday - don't worry / work
   devote day to God / study

4. Passover (Pesach). When does it occur? What is the meaning of this festival?

   ancient - marked harvest   exile from exodus
   the Last supper was meal

5. Feast of Weeks (Shavuot or Pentecost). When does it occur? What did it celebrate in ancient times? What does it celebrate now?

   celebrated first fruits of summer
   giving of torah to moses

6. Feast of Booths or Tabernacles (Sukkot). What does it commemorate?

   fall - commemorated 40 year   - most joy ful
   isralutes

7. What is Rosh Hashanah?

   religious new year

8. Yom Kippur. What does it celebrate?   *> ask god to forgive sins*

9. What does Purim celebrate?

   minor - emancipation of jews

10. What does Hanukkah celebrate?

    pr religious victory

11. When does circumcision occur?

12. Define kosher.

13. What is a Bar Mitzvah? What is a Bat Mitzvah?

Bar Mitzvah Boys

1. What does Bar Mitzvah mean? When does it occur?

   right of passage age 13

2. How many commandments are there?

   630

3. What does Bar Mitzvah mean for the boys that undergo it?

   become responsible for keeping commandments himself

4. What is a tefillin? When are they worn? How are they put on? What do the boxes contain?

   sacred objects   during pray straps word 7 times

5. What are tefillin made of?

   kosher hides of animals

6. What do the scribes do to prepare and maintain the tefillin?

7. What is Torah? What is the meaning of Torah?

   Instruction/teaching written scriptures

8. What does the rabbi help Avi do?

   help read torah

9. What kind of food do Jews eat?

10. What is tallith?

11. What is minyan?

12. What is Talmud?

13. Where does Avi's family celebrate his Bar Mitzvah? What is the Western Wall?

14. Where is the Torah scroll kept?

15. What are the two main groups of Jews?

16. What does Avi's family throw at him? Why?

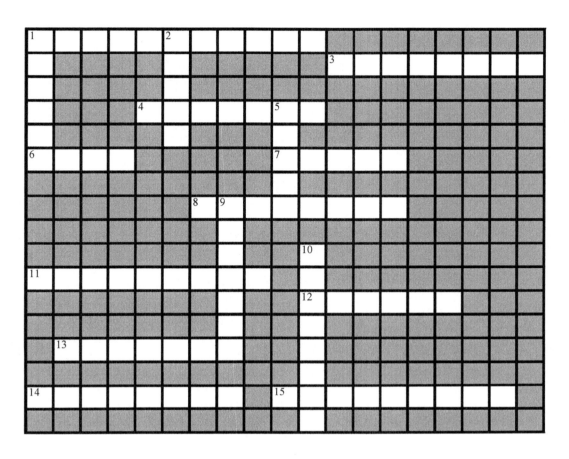

ACROSS

1. Doctrines about the end of times and the end of life
3. Festival that commemorates the Exodus
4. Day of prayer and rest (Saturday)
6. First king of Israel
7. Teacher of the Torah
8. The Writings (third part of the Hebrew Bible)
11. Jewish sect that believed in the authority of the Oral Torah and the resurrection of the dead
12. Prophets (second part of the Hebrew Bible)
13. First-century Jewish revolutionaries
14. Dispersed people. It began with the Babylonian exile.
15. Priestly families in charge of the temple

DOWN

1. The Hebrews' migration from Egypt under the leadership of Moses
2. Name for the Hebrew Bible
5. Refers to "law," "instruction," "teaching" based on divine revelation
9. Semi-monastic Jewish group usually associated with the Dead Sea scrolls
10. An early-winter Jewish Festival that recalls the rededication of the Second Temple

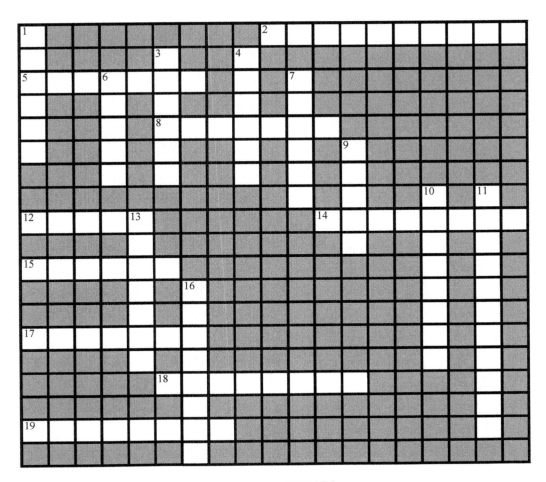

ACROSS

2. Day of Atonement
5. Code of law compiled by Rabbi Judah around 200 CE
8. Interpretation, commentary of scripture
12. Master of the Good Name, whose real name was Israel ben Eliezer (1700-1760), founder of Hasidism.
14. Literally, it means "received," "handed down." It has come to designate Jewish Mysticism.
15. Quorum for a prayer service in a synagogue (10)
17. Prayer shawl
18. Phylacteries (small boxes containing Biblical scriptures)
19. Mediterranean Jew

DOWN

1. Commentary on the Mishnah
3. Codified Oral Torah (Mishnah and its commentary together)
4. Attack against Jews
6. The mother of Ishmael
7. Ritually correct diet
9. Book of Splendor, a mystical commentary on the Torah, written in 13th-century Spain
10. Jewish religious movement that appeared in 18th-century Eastern Europe as a response to excessive Talmudic study and persecution
11. The coming-of-age ceremony for boys
13. Title meaning "Righteous Person" used for a wise master and leader of the Hasidim Haskalah
16. Jews of Northern and Eastern Europe

Text Nineteen

The flood in Mesopotamian Mythology

The Epic of Gilgamesh

Insight into a people's ideas about life and death can be gained by examining their myths and their literature. The Epic Gilgamesh, probably written in the latter part of the third millennium (2000s) B.C., was the great epic poem of Mesopotamia. Its hero Gilgamesh, ruled the Sumerian city-state of Uruk around 2700 B.C. The poem is about the mythical adventures this king part god himself, has struggling with life, the gods, and death. In one adventure, Gilgamesh faces death by embarking on a search for immortality. As part of that search he descends into the Netherworld to find Utnapishtim, a human who has been granted immortality by the gods. In the following selection, Gilgamesh questions Utnapishtim, who tells him the story of the flood.

"Oh, father Utnapishtim, you who have entered the assembly of the gods, I wish to question you concerning the living and the dead, how shall I find the life for which I am searching?"

Utnapishtim said, "There is no permanence. Do we build a house to stand for ever, do we seal a contract to hold for all time? Do brothers divide an inheritance to keep forever, does the flood time of rivers endure? It is only the nymph of the dragon-fly who sheds her larva and sees the sun in his glory. From the days of old there is no permanence. The sleeping and the dead, how alike they are, they are like a painted death. What is there between the master and the servant when both have fulfilled their doom? When the Annunaki, the judges, come together, and Mammetun the mother of destinies, together they decree the fates of men. Life and death they allot but he day of death they do not disclose."

Then Gilgamesh said to Utnapishtim the Faraway, "I look at you now, Utnapishtim, and your appearance is not different from mine there is nothing strange in your features. I thought I should find you like a hero prepared for battle, but you lie here taking your ease on your back. Tell me truly, how was it that you came to enter the company of the gods and to possess everlasting life?" Utnapishtim said to Gilgamesh, "I will reveal to you a mystery, I will tell you a secret of the gods."

"You know the city Shurrupak, it stands on the banks of Euphrates? That city grew old and the gods that were it in were old. There was Anu, lord of the firmament,. Their father, and warrior Enlil their counselor, Ninurta the helper, and Ejjugi watcher over canals; and with them also was Ea. In those days the world teemed. The people multiplied, the world bellowed like a wild bull, and the great god was aroused by the clamour. Enlil heard the clamour and he said to the gods in council, "The uproar of mankind is intolerable and sleep is no longer possible by reason of the babel." So the gods in their hearts were moved to let loose the deluge; but my lord Ea warned me in a dream. He whispered their words to my house of reeds, "Reed-house, reed house! Wall, O wall, hearken reed-house, wall reflect; O man of Shurrupak, son of Ubara-Tutu; tear down your house and build a boat, abandon possessions and look for life, despise worldly goods and save your soul alive. Tear down your house, I say, and build a boat."

"When I had understood I said to my lord, 'Behold, what you have commanded I will honour and perform,. But how shall I answer the people, the city, the elders?' Then Ea opened his mouth and said to me, his servant, 'Tell them this: I have learnt that Enlil is wrathful against me, I dare no longer walk in his land nor live in his city; I will go down to the Gulf to dwell with Ea my lord. But on you he will rain down abundance, rare fish and shy wild-fowl, a rich harvest-tide. In the evening the rider of the story will bring you wheat in torrents.'"...

"On the seventh day the boat was complete...

"I loaded into her all that I had of gold and of living things, my family, my kin, the beasts of the field both wild and tame, and all the craftsmen...

"For six days and six nights the winds blew, torrent and tempest and flood overwhelmed the world, tempest and flood raged together like warring hosts. When the seventh day dawned the storm from the south subsided, the sea grew calm, the flood was stilled; I looked at the face of the world and there was silence, all mankind was turned to clay. The surface of the sea stretched as flat as a rooftop; I opened a hatch and the light fell on my face. Then I bowed low, I sat down and I wept, the tears streamed down my face, for on every side was the waste of water. I looked for land in vain, but fourteen leagues distant there appeared a mountain, and there the boat grounded; on the mountain of Nisir the boat held fast, she held fast and did not budge... When the seventh day dawned I looked a dove and let her go. She flew away but finding no resting place, she returned. I loosed a raven, she saw that the waters had retreated, she ate, she flew around, she cased and she did not come back.

Then I threw everything open to the four winds, I made a sacrifice and poured out a libation on the mountain top. Seven and again seven cauldrons I set up on their stands, I heaped up wood and cane and cedar and myrtle. When the gods smelled the sweet savour, they gathered like flies over the sacrifice. Then, at last, Ishtar also came, she lifted her necklace with the jewels of heaven that once Anu had made to please her. 'O you gods here present, by the lapis lazuli round my neck I shall remember these days as I remember the jewels of my throat; these last days I shall not forget. Let all the gods gather round the sacrifice, except Enlil. He shall not approach this offering, for without reflection he brought the flood; he consigned my people to destruction.'

"When Enlil had come, when he saw the boat, he was wrath and swelled with anger at the gods, the host of heaven, 'Has any of these mortals escaped? Not one was to have survived the destruction.' Then the god of the wells and canals Ninurta opened his mouth and said to the warrior Enlil, 'Who is there of the gods that can devise without Ea? It is Ea alone who knows all things.' Then Ea opened his mouth and spoke to warrior Enlil, "Wisest of gods, here Enlil, how could you so senselessly bring down the flood?...

"Then Enlil went up into the boat, he took me by the hand and my wife and made us enter the boat and kneel down on either side, he standing between us. He touched our foreheads to bless us saying, 'In times past Utnapishtim was a mortal man; henceforth he and his wife shall live in the distance at the mouth of the rivers.' Thus it was that the gods took me and placed me here to live in the distance, at the mouth of the rivers."

Questions on the Bible

1. Some scholars argue that Genesis 1 and Genesis 2 have been written in two different contexts and times by different authors or editors. Do you think this is correct? To answer this question, consider the sequence of creation. Is it the same in Genesis 1 and 2? What does God look like in Genesis 1 and 2? Is He the same? [See TEXT 20]

2. Religious Studies scholars view myths as foundational stories that explain the main beliefs, rituals, and ethical values of a community. What did you learn from Genesis 1-3? [See TEXT 20]

3. How different is the Creation story in the Bible, in the Japanese Nihongi, and in the Hindu Rig Veda? In what way do the differences between these three myths shed the light on the main differences between Jewish, Shinto, and Hindu views of the world and the place of man and/or the divine in it? [See TEXTS 1, 13, and 20]

4. What are the main differences between the Gilgamesh epic, one of the best-known Mesopotamian myths, and the Great Flood in Genesis 5-9? Is the narrative structure the same? How different is the Mesopotamian and the Biblical understandings of the divine nature? [See TEXTS 19 and 20]

5. Compare the Great Flood in Genesis 5-9 and Noah in the Qur'an (Surah 71). How does the Qur'anic Noah differ from the Biblical Noah? What accounts for these differences? [See TEXTS 20 and 36]

6. Compare Joseph's story in Genesis and the Qur'an. How does the Qur'anic Joseph differ from the Biblical Joseph? Is the portrayal of Joseph always positive in the Biblical narrative? Did Joseph deserve his fate in the Qur'an? What does the portrayal of Joseph in the Qur'an say about Islam's understanding of "prophethood"? (Remember that in Islam, Adam, Abraham, Noah, Joseph, etc. are prophets.) [See TEXTS 21 and 34]

7. What is your impression of gender relationship in the Bible? What is the role of women in the domestic sphere and in the development of the Biblical narrative? What are their responsibilities? Do they have a separate or independent identity? What is their relationship with God? [See TEXTS 20, 21, and 22]

8. Would you consider Abraham's story as a typical biography? What kind of model of the faithful life does he offer? What is his relationship to God? Would you characterize this relationship as fixed or evolving? [See TEXT 20]

9. What is the big difference between the Abrahamic covenant and the Mosaic covenant? Do you think that the Ten Commandments can be regarded as ethical guidelines for all times and places? What about the laws on the treatment of slaves? [See TEXTS 20 and 22]

10. Who is the liberator in Exodus, God or Moses? Why? [See TEXT 22]

11. Would you consider Moses a hero? [See TEXT 22]

12. Read the Book of Isaiah. In 722 BCE, the Assyrians invaded the Northern kingdom of Israel. How did the Prophet Isaiah explain this tragedy? What was his message to the people of Judah? [See TEXT 23]

Text Twenty

Genesis

1

¹ In the beginning, God· created the heavens and the earth. ² The earth was formless and empty. Darkness was on the surface of the deep and God's Spirit was hovering over the surface of the waters.

³ God said, "Let there be light," and there was light. ⁴ God saw the light, and saw that it was good. God divided the light from the darkness. ⁵ God called the light "day", and the darkness he called "night". There was evening and there was morning, the first day.

⁶ God said, "Let there be an expanse in the middle of the waters, and let it divide the waters from the waters." ⁷ God made the expanse, and divided the waters which were under the expanse from the waters which were above the expanse; and it was so. ⁸ God called the expanse "sky". There was evening and there was morning, a second day.

⁹ God said, "Let the waters under the sky be gathered together to one place, and let the dry land appear;" and it was so. ¹⁰ God called the dry land "earth", and the gathering together of the waters he called "seas". God saw that it was good. ¹¹ God said, "Let the earth yield grass, herbs yielding seeds, and fruit trees bearing fruit after their kind, with their seeds in it, on the earth;" and it was so. ¹² The earth yielded grass, herbs yielding seed after their kind, and trees bearing fruit, with their seeds in it, after their kind; and God saw that it was good. ¹³ There was evening and there was morning, a third day.

¹⁴ God said, "Let there be lights in the expanse of the sky to divide the day from the night; and let them be for signs to mark seasons, days, and years; ¹⁵ and let them be for lights in the expanse of the sky to give light on the earth;" and it was so. ¹⁶ God made the two great lights: the greater light to rule the day, and the lesser light to rule the night. He also made the stars. ¹⁷ God set them in the expanse of the sky to give light to the earth, ¹⁸ and to rule over the day and over the night, and to divide the light from the darkness. God saw that it was good. ¹⁹ There was evening and there was morning, a fourth day.

²⁰ God said, "Let the waters abound with living creatures, and let birds fly above the earth in the open expanse of the sky." ²¹ God created the large sea creatures and every living creature that moves, with which the waters swarmed, after their kind, and every winged bird after its kind. God saw that it was good. ²² God blessed them, saying, "Be fruitful, and multiply, and fill the waters in the seas, and let birds multiply on the earth." ²³ There was evening and there was morning, a fifth day.

²⁴ God said, "Let the earth produce living creatures after their kind, livestock, creeping things, and animals of the earth after their kind;" and it was so. ²⁵ God made the animals of the earth after their kind, and the livestock after their kind, and everything that creeps on the ground after its kind. God saw that it was good.

²⁶ God said, "Let's make man in our image, after our likeness. Let them have dominion over the fish of the sea, and over the birds of the sky, and over the livestock, and over all the earth, and over every creeping thing that creeps on the earth." ²⁷ God created man in his own image. In God's image he created him; male and female he created them. ²⁸ God blessed them. God said to them, "Be fruitful, multiply, fill the earth, and subdue it. Have dominion over the fish of the sea, over the birds of the sky, and over every living thing that moves on the earth." ²⁹ God said, "Behold,† I have given you every herb yielding seed, which is on the surface of all the earth, and every tree, which bears fruit yielding seed. It will be your food. ³⁰ To every animal of the earth, and to every bird of the sky, and to everything that creeps on the earth, in which there is life, I have given every green herb for food;" and it was so.

³¹ God saw everything that he had made, and, behold, it was very good. There was evening and there was morning, a sixth day.

2

¹ The heavens, the earth, and all their vast array were finished. ² On the seventh day God finished his work which he had done; and he rested on the seventh day from all his work which he had done. ³ God blessed the seventh day, and made it holy, because he rested in it from all his work of creation which he had done.

⁴ This is the history of the generations of the heavens and of the earth when they were created, in the day that Yahweh˙ God made the earth and the heavens. ⁵ No plant of the field was yet in the earth, and no herb of the field had yet sprung up; for Yahweh God had not caused it to rain on the earth. There was not a man to till the ground, ⁶ but a mist went up from the earth, and watered the whole surface of the ground. ⁷ Yahweh God formed man from the dust of the ground, and breathed into his nostrils the breath of life; and man became a living soul. ⁸ Yahweh God planted a garden eastward, in Eden, and there he put the man whom he had formed. ⁹ Out of the ground Yahweh God made every tree to grow that is pleasant to the sight, and good for food, including the tree of life in the middle of the garden and the tree of the knowledge of good and evil. ¹⁰ A river went out of Eden to water the garden; and from there it was parted, and became the source of four rivers. ¹¹ The name of the first is Pishon: it flows through the whole land of Havilah, where there is gold; ¹² and the gold of that land is good. Bdellium† and onyx stone are also there. ¹³ The name of the second river is Gihon. It is the same river that flows through the whole land of Cush. ¹⁴ The name of the third river is Hiddekel. This is the one which flows in front of Assyria. The fourth river is the Euphrates. ¹⁵ Yahweh God took the man, and put him into the garden of Eden to cultivate and keep it. ¹⁶ Yahweh God commanded the man, saying, "You may freely eat of every tree of the garden; ¹⁷ but you shall not eat of the tree of the knowledge of good and evil; for in the day that you eat of it, you will surely die."

¹⁸ Yahweh God said, "It is not good for the man to be alone. I will make him a helper comparable to‡ him." ¹⁹ Out of the ground Yahweh God formed every animal of the field, and every bird of the sky, and brought them to the man to see what he would call them. Whatever the man called every living creature became its name. ²⁰ The man gave names to all livestock, and to the birds of the sky, and to every animal of the field; but for man there was not found a helper comparable to him. ²¹ Yahweh God caused the man to fall into a deep sleep.

As the man slept, he took one of his ribs, and closed up the flesh in its place. ²² Yahweh God made a woman from the rib which he had taken from the man, and brought her to the man. ²³ The man said, "This is now bone of my bones, and flesh of my flesh. She will be called 'woman,' because she was taken out of Man." ²⁴ Therefore a man will leave his father and his mother, and will join with his wife, and they will be one flesh. ²⁵ The man and his wife were both naked, and they were not ashamed.

3

¹ Now the serpent was more subtle than any animal of the field which Yahweh God had made. He said to the woman, "Has God really said, 'You shall not eat of any tree of the garden'?"

² The woman said to the serpent, "We may eat fruit from the trees of the garden, ³ but not the fruit of the tree which is in the middle of the garden. God has said, 'You shall not eat of it. You shall not touch it, lest you die.'"

⁴ The serpent said to the woman, "You won't really die, ⁵ for God knows that in the day you eat it, your eyes will be opened, and you will be like God, knowing good and evil."

⁶ When the woman saw that the tree was good for food, and that it was a delight to the eyes, and that the tree was to be desired to make one wise, she took some of its fruit, and ate. Then she gave some to her husband with her, and he ate it, too. ⁷ Their eyes were opened, and they both knew that they were naked. They sewed fig leaves together, and made coverings for themselves. ⁸ They heard Yahweh God's voice walking in the garden in the cool of the day, and the man and his wife hid themselves from the presence of Yahweh God among the trees of the garden.

⁹ Yahweh God called to the man, and said to him, "Where are you?"

¹⁰ The man said, "I heard your voice in the garden, and I was afraid, because I was naked; so I hid myself."

¹¹ God said, "Who told you that you were naked? Have you eaten from the tree that I commanded you not to eat from?"

¹² The man said, "The woman whom you gave to be with me, she gave me fruit from the tree, and I ate it."

¹³ Yahweh God said to the woman, "What have you done?"

The woman said, "The serpent deceived me, and I ate."

¹⁴ Yahweh God said to the serpent,
"Because you have done this,
you are cursed above all livestock,
and above every animal of the field.

You shall go on your belly
and you shall eat dust all the days of your life.
¹⁵ I will put hostility between you and the woman,
and between your offspring and her offspring.
He will bruise your head,
and you will bruise his heel."

¹⁶ To the woman he said,
"I will greatly multiply your pain in childbirth.
You will bear children in pain.
Your desire will be for your husband,
and he will rule over you."

¹⁷ To Adam he said,
"Because you have listened to your wife's voice,
and ate from the tree,
about which I commanded you, saying, 'You shall not eat of it,'
the ground is cursed for your sake.
You will eat from it with much labor all the days of your life.
¹⁸ It will yield thorns and thistles to you;
and you will eat the herb of the field.
¹⁹ You will eat bread by the sweat of your face until you return to the ground,
for you were taken out of it.
For you are dust,
and you shall return to dust."

²⁰ The man called his wife Eve because she would be the mother of all the living. ²¹ Yahweh God made garments of animal skins for Adam and for his wife, and clothed them.

²² Yahweh God said, "Behold, the man has become like one of us, knowing good and evil. Now, lest he reach out his hand, and also take of the tree of life, and eat, and live forever—" ²³ Therefore Yahweh God sent him out from the garden of Eden, to till the ground from which he was taken. ²⁴ So he drove out the man; and he placed cherubim* at the east of the garden of Eden, and a flaming sword which turned every way, to guard the way to the tree of life.

4

¹ The man knew* Eve his wife. She conceived,† and gave birth to Cain, and said, "I have gotten a man with Yahweh's help." ² Again she gave birth, to Cain's brother Abel. Abel was a keeper of sheep, but Cain was a tiller of the ground. ³ As time passed, Cain brought an offering to Yahweh from the fruit of the ground. ⁴ Abel also brought some of the firstborn of his flock and of its fat. Yahweh respected Abel and his offering, ⁵ but he didn't respect Cain and his offering. Cain was very angry, and the expression on his face fell. ⁶ Yahweh said to Cain, "Why are you angry? Why has the expression of your face fallen? ⁷ If you do well, won't it be lifted up? If you don't do well, sin crouches at the door. Its desire is for you, but you are to rule over it." ⁸ Cain said to Abel, his brother, "Let's go into the field." While they were in the field, Cain rose up against Abel, his brother, and killed him.

⁹ Yahweh said to Cain, "Where is Abel, your brother?"
He said, "I don't know. Am I my brother's keeper?"

¹⁰ Yahweh said, "What have you done? The voice of your brother's blood cries to me from the ground. ¹¹ Now you are cursed because of the ground, which has opened its mouth to receive your brother's blood from your hand. ¹² From now on, when you till the ground, it won't yield its strength to you. You will be a fugitive and a wanderer in the earth."

¹³ Cain said to Yahweh, "My punishment is greater than I can bear. ¹⁴ Behold, you have driven me out today from the surface of the ground. I will be hidden from your face, and I will be a fugitive and a wanderer in the earth. Whoever finds me will kill me."

¹⁵ Yahweh said to him, "Therefore whoever slays Cain, vengeance will be taken on him sevenfold." Yahweh appointed a sign for Cain, so that anyone finding him would not strike him.

¹⁶ Cain left Yahweh's presence, and lived in the land of Nod, east of Eden. ¹⁷ Cain knew his wife. She conceived, and gave birth to Enoch. He built a city, and named the city after the name of his son, Enoch. ¹⁸ Irad was born to Enoch. Irad became the father of Mehujael. Mehujael became the father of Methushael. Methushael became the father of Lamech. ¹⁹ Lamech took two wives: the name of the first one was Adah, and the name of the second one was Zillah. ²⁰ Adah gave birth to Jabal, who was the father of those who dwell in tents and have livestock. ²¹ His brother's name was Jubal, who was the father of all who handle the harp and pipe. ²² Zillah also gave birth to Tubal Cain, the forger of every cutting instrument of bronze and iron. Tubal Cain's sister was Naamah. ²³ Lamech said to his wives,
"Adah and Zillah, hear my voice.
You wives of Lamech, listen to my speech,
for I have slain a man for wounding me,
a young man for bruising me.
²⁴ If Cain will be avenged seven times,
truly Lamech seventy-seven times."

²⁵ Adam knew his wife again. She gave birth to a son, and named him Seth, saying, "for God has given me another child instead of Abel, for Cain killed him." ²⁶ A son was also born to Seth, and he named him Enosh. At that time men began to call on Yahweh's name.

5

¹ This is the book of the generations of Adam. In the day that God created man, he made him in God's likeness. ² He created them male and female, and blessed them. On the day they were created, he named them Adam.˙ ³ Adam lived one hundred thirty years, and became the father of a son in his own likeness, after his image, and named him Seth. ⁴ The days of Adam after he became the father of Seth were eight hundred years, and he became the father of other sons and daughters. ⁵ All the days that Adam lived were nine hundred thirty years, then he died.

⁶ Seth lived one hundred five years, then became the father of Enosh. ⁷ Seth lived after he became the father of Enosh eight hundred seven years, and became the father of other sons and daughters. ⁸ All of the days of Seth were nine hundred twelve years, then he died.

⁹ Enosh lived ninety years, and became the father of Kenan. ¹⁰ Enosh lived after he became the father of Kenan eight hundred fifteen years, and became the father of other sons and daughters. ¹¹ All of the days of Enosh were nine hundred five years, then he died.

¹² Kenan lived seventy years, then became the father of Mahalalel. ¹³ Kenan lived after he became the father of Mahalalel eight hundred forty years, and became the father of other sons and daughters ¹⁴ and all of the days of Kenan were nine hundred ten years, then he died.

¹⁵ Mahalalel lived sixty-five years, then became the father of Jared. ¹⁶ Mahalalel lived after he became the father of Jared eight hundred thirty years, and became the father of other sons and daughters. ¹⁷ All of the days of Mahalalel were eight hundred ninety-five years, then he died.

¹⁸ Jared lived one hundred sixty-two years, then became the father of Enoch. ¹⁹ Jared lived after he became the father of Enoch eight hundred years, and became the father of other sons and daughters. ²⁰ All of the days of Jared were nine hundred sixty-two years, then he died.

²¹ Enoch lived sixty-five years, then became the father of Methuselah. ²² After Methuselah's birth, Enoch walked with God for three hundred years, and became the father of more sons and daughters. ²³ All the days of Enoch were three hundred sixty-five years. ²⁴ Enoch walked with God, and he was not found, for God took him.

²⁵ Methuselah lived one hundred eighty-seven years, then became the father of Lamech. ²⁶ Methuselah lived after he became the father of Lamech seven hundred eighty-two years, and became the father of other sons and daughters. ²⁷ All the days of Methuselah were nine hundred sixty-nine years, then he died.

²⁸ Lamech lived one hundred eighty-two years, then became the father of a son. ²⁹ He named him Noah, saying, "This one will comfort us in our work and in the toil of our hands, caused by the ground which Yahweh has cursed." ³⁰ Lamech lived after he became the father of Noah five hundred ninety-five years, and became the father of other sons and daughters. ³¹ All the days of Lamech were seven hundred seventy-seven years, then he died.

³² Noah was five hundred years old, then Noah became the father of Shem, Ham, and Japheth.

6

¹ When men began to multiply on the surface of the ground, and daughters were born to them, ² God's sons saw that men's daughters were beautiful, and they took any that they wanted for themselves as wives. ³ Yahweh said, "My Spirit will not strive with man forever, because he also is flesh; so his days will be one hundred twenty years." ⁴ The Nephilim˙ were in the earth in those days, and also after that, when God's sons came in to men's daughters and had children with them. Those were the mighty men who were of old, men of renown.

⁵ Yahweh saw that the wickedness of man was great in the earth, and that every imagination of the thoughts of man's heart was continually only evil. ⁶ Yahweh was sorry that he had made man on the earth, and it grieved him in his heart. ⁷ Yahweh said, "I will destroy man whom I have created from the surface of the ground—man, along with animals, creeping things, and birds of the sky—for I am sorry that I have made them." ⁸ But Noah found favor in Yahweh's eyes.

⁹ This is the history of the generations of Noah: Noah was a righteous man, blameless among the people of his time. Noah walked with God. ¹⁰ Noah became the father of three sons: Shem, Ham, and Japheth. ¹¹ The earth was corrupt before God, and the earth was filled with violence. ¹² God saw the earth, and saw that it was corrupt, for all flesh had corrupted their way on the earth.

¹³ God said to Noah, "I will bring an end to all flesh, for the earth is filled with violence through them. Behold, I will destroy them and the earth. ¹⁴ Make a ship of gopher wood. You shall make rooms in the ship, and shall seal it inside and outside with pitch. ¹⁵ This is how you shall make it. The length of the ship shall be three hundred cubits,† its width fifty cubits, and its height thirty cubits. ¹⁶ You shall make a roof in the ship, and you shall finish it to a cubit upward. You shall set the door of the ship in its side. You shall make it with lower, second, and third levels. ¹⁷ I, even I, will bring the flood of waters on this earth, to destroy all flesh having the breath of life from under the sky. Everything that is in the earth will

die. ¹⁸ But I will establish my covenant with you. You shall come into the ship, you, your sons, your wife, and your sons' wives with you. ¹⁹ Of every living thing of all flesh, you shall bring two of every sort into the ship, to keep them alive with you. They shall be male and female. ²⁰ Of the birds after their kind, of the livestock after their kind, of every creeping thing of the ground after its kind, two of every sort will come to you, to keep them alive. ²¹ Take with you some of all food that is eaten, and gather it to yourself; and it will be for food for you, and for them." ²² Thus Noah did. He did all that God commanded him.

7

¹ Yahweh said to Noah, "Come with all of your household into the ship, for I have seen your righteousness before me in this generation. ² You shall take seven pairs of every clean animal with you, the male and his female. Of the animals that are not clean, take two, the male and his female. ³ Also of the birds of the sky, seven and seven, male and female, to keep seed alive on the surface of all the earth. ⁴ In seven days, I will cause it to rain on the earth for forty days and forty nights. I will destroy every living thing that I have made from the surface of the ground."

⁵ Noah did everything that Yahweh commanded him.

⁶ Noah was six hundred years old when the flood of waters came on the earth. ⁷ Noah went into the ship with his sons, his wife, and his sons' wives, because of the floodwaters. ⁸ Clean animals, unclean animals, birds, and everything that creeps on the ground ⁹ went by pairs to Noah into the ship, male and female, as God commanded Noah. ¹⁰ After the seven days, the floodwaters came on the earth. ¹¹ In the six hundredth year of Noah's life, in the second month, on the seventeenth day of the month, on that day all the fountains of the great deep burst open, and the sky's windows opened. ¹² It rained on the earth forty days and forty nights.

¹³ In the same day Noah, and Shem, Ham, and Japheth—the sons of Noah—and Noah's wife and the three wives of his sons with them, entered into the ship— ¹⁴ they, and every animal after its kind, all the livestock after their kind, every creeping thing that creeps on the earth after its kind, and every bird after its kind, every bird of every sort. ¹⁵ Pairs from all flesh with the breath of life in them went into the ship to Noah. ¹⁶ Those who went in, went in male and female of all flesh, as God commanded him; then Yahweh shut him in. ¹⁷ The flood was forty days on the earth. The waters increased, and lifted up the ship, and it was lifted up above the earth. ¹⁸ The waters rose, and increased greatly on the earth; and the ship floated on the surface of the waters. ¹⁹ The waters rose very high on the earth. All the high mountains that were under the whole sky were covered. ²⁰ The waters rose fifteen cubits* higher, and the mountains were covered. ²¹ All flesh died that moved on the earth, including birds, livestock, animals, every creeping thing that creeps on the earth, and every man. ²² All on the dry land, in whose nostrils was the breath of the spirit of life, died. ²³ Every living thing was destroyed that was on the surface of the ground, including man, livestock, creeping things, and birds of the sky. They were destroyed from the earth. Only Noah was left, and those who were with him in the ship. ²⁴ The waters flooded the earth one hundred fifty days.

8

¹ God remembered Noah, all the animals, and all the livestock that were with him in the ship; and God made a wind to pass over the earth. The waters subsided. ² The deep's fountains and the sky's windows were also stopped, and the rain from the sky was restrained. ³ The waters continually receded from the earth. After the end of one hundred fifty days the waters receded. ⁴ The ship rested in the seventh month, on the seventeenth day of the month, on Ararat's mountains. ⁵ The waters receded continually until the tenth month. In the tenth month, on the first day of the month, the tops of the mountains were visible.

⁶ At the end of forty days, Noah opened the window of the ship which he had made, ⁷ and he sent out a raven. It went back and forth, until the waters were dried up from the earth. ⁸ He himself sent out a dove to see if the waters were abated from the surface of the ground, ⁹ but the dove found no place to rest her foot, and she returned into the ship to him, for the waters were on the surface of the whole earth. He put out his hand, and took her, and brought her to him into the ship. ¹⁰ He waited yet another seven days; and again he sent the dove out of the ship. ¹¹ The dove came back to him at evening and, behold, in her mouth was a freshly plucked olive leaf. So Noah knew that the waters were abated from the earth. ¹² He waited yet another seven days, and sent out the dove; and she didn't return to him anymore.

¹³ In the six hundred first year, in the first month, the first day of the month, the waters were dried up from the earth. Noah removed the covering of the ship, and looked. He saw that the surface of the ground was dry. ¹⁴ In the second month, on the twenty-seventh day of the month, the earth was dry.

¹⁵ God spoke to Noah, saying, ¹⁶ "Go out of the ship, you, your wife, your sons, and your sons' wives with you. ¹⁷ Bring

out with you every living thing that is with you of all flesh, including birds, livestock, and every creeping thing that creeps on the earth, that they may breed abundantly in the earth, and be fruitful, and multiply on the earth."

[18] Noah went out, with his sons, his wife, and his sons' wives with him. [19] Every animal, every creeping thing, and every bird, whatever moves on the earth, after their families, went out of the ship.

[20] Noah built an altar to Yahweh, and took of every clean animal, and of every clean bird, and offered burnt offerings on the altar. [21] Yahweh smelled the pleasant aroma. Yahweh said in his heart, "I will not again curse the ground any more for man's sake because the imagination of man's heart is evil from his youth. I will never again strike every living thing, as I have done. [22] While the earth remains, seed time and harvest, and cold and heat, and summer and winter, and day and night will not cease."

9

[1] God blessed Noah and his sons, and said to them, "Be fruitful, multiply, and replenish the earth. [2] The fear of you and the dread of you will be on every animal of the earth, and on every bird of the sky. Everything that moves along the ground, and all the fish of the sea, are delivered into your hand. [3] Every moving thing that lives will be food for you. As I gave you the green herb, I have given everything to you. [4] But flesh with its life, that is, its blood, you shall not eat. [5] I will surely require accounting for your life's blood. At the hand of every animal I will require it. At the hand of man, even at the hand of every man's brother, I will require the life of man. [6] Whoever sheds man's blood, his blood will be shed by man, for God made man in his own image. [7] Be fruitful and multiply. Increase abundantly in the earth, and multiply in it."

[8] God spoke to Noah and to his sons with him, saying, [9] "As for me, behold, I establish my covenant with you, and with your offspring after you, [10] and with every living creature that is with you: the birds, the livestock, and every animal of the earth with you, of all that go out of the ship, even every animal of the earth. [11] I will establish my covenant with you: All flesh will not be cut off any more by the waters of the flood. There will never again be a flood to destroy the earth." [12] God said, "This is the token of the covenant which I make between me and you and every living creature that is with you, for perpetual generations: [13] I set my rainbow in the cloud, and it will be a sign of a covenant between me and the earth. [14] When I bring a cloud over the earth, that the rainbow will be seen in the cloud, [15] I will remember my covenant, which is between me and you and every living

creature of all flesh, and the waters will no more become a flood to destroy all flesh. [16] The rainbow will be in the cloud. I will look at it, that I may remember the everlasting covenant between God and every living creature of all flesh that is on the earth." [17] God said to Noah, "This is the token of the covenant which I have established between me and all flesh that is on the earth."

[18] The sons of Noah who went out from the ship were Shem, Ham, and Japheth. Ham is the father of Canaan. [19] These three were the sons of Noah, and from these the whole earth was populated.

[20] Noah began to be a farmer, and planted a vineyard. [21] He drank of the wine and got drunk. He was uncovered within his tent. [22] Ham, the father of Canaan, saw the nakedness of his father, and told his two brothers outside. [23] Shem and Japheth took a garment, and laid it on both their shoulders, went in backwards, and covered the nakedness of their father. Their faces were backwards, and they didn't see their father's nakedness. [24] Noah awoke from his wine, and knew what his youngest son had done to him. [25] He said,
"Canaan is cursed.
He will be a servant of servants to his brothers."
[26] He said,
"Blessed be Yahweh, the God of Shem.
Let Canaan be his servant.
[27] May God enlarge Japheth.
Let him dwell in the tents of Shem.
Let Canaan be his servant."
[28] Noah lived three hundred fifty years after the flood. [29] All the days of Noah were nine hundred fifty years, and then he died.

10

[1] Now this is the history of the generations of the sons of Noah and of Shem, Ham, and Japheth. Sons were born to them after the flood.

[2] The sons of Japheth were: Gomer, Magog, Madai, Javan, Tubal, Meshech, and Tiras. [3] The sons of Gomer were: Ashkenaz, Riphath, and Togarmah. [4] The sons of Javan were: Elishah, Tarshish, Kittim, and Dodanim. [5] Of these were the islands of the nations divided in their lands, everyone after his language, after their families, in their nations.

[6] The sons of Ham were: Cush, Mizraim, Put, and Canaan. [7] The sons of Cush were: Seba, Havilah, Sabtah, Raamah, and Sabteca. The sons of Raamah were: Sheba and Dedan. [8] Cush became the father of Nimrod. He began to be a mighty one in the earth. [9] He was a mighty hunter before

Yahweh. Therefore it is said, "like Nimrod, a mighty hunter before Yahweh". ¹⁰ The beginning of his kingdom was Babel, Erech, Accad, and Calneh, in the land of Shinar. ¹¹ Out of that land he went into Assyria, and built Nineveh, Rehoboth Ir, Calah,¹² and Resen between Nineveh and the great city Calah. ¹³ Mizraim became the father of Ludim, Anamim, Lehabim, Naphtuhim, ¹⁴ Pathrusim, Casluhim (which the Philistines descended from), and Caphtorim.

¹⁵ Canaan became the father of Sidon (his firstborn), Heth, ¹⁶ the Jebusites, the Amorites, the Girgashites,¹⁷ the Hivites, the Arkites, the Sinites, ¹⁸ the Arvadites, the Zemarites, and the Hamathites. Afterward the families of the Canaanites were spread abroad. ¹⁹ The border of the Canaanites was from Sidon—as you go toward Gerar—to Gaza—as you go toward Sodom, Gomorrah, Admah, and Zeboiim—to Lasha. ²⁰ These are the sons of Ham, after their families, according to their languages, in their lands and their nations.

²¹ Children were also born to Shem (the elder brother of Japheth), the father of all the children of Eber.²² The sons of Shem were: Elam, Asshur, Arpachshad, Lud, and Aram. ²³ The sons of Aram were: Uz, Hul, Gether, and Mash. ²⁴ Arpachshad became the father of Shelah. Shelah became the father of Eber. ²⁵ To Eber were born two sons. The name of the one was Peleg, for in his days the earth was divided. His brother's name was Joktan.²⁶ Joktan became the father of Almodad, Sheleph, Hazarmaveth, Jerah, ²⁷ Hadoram, Uzal, Diklah, ²⁸ Obal, Abimael, Sheba, ²⁹ Ophir, Havilah, and Jobab. All these were the sons of Joktan. ³⁰ Their dwelling extended from Mesha, as you go toward Sephar, the mountain of the east. ³¹ These are the sons of Shem, by their families, according to their languages, lands, and nations.

³² These are the families of the sons of Noah, by their generations, according to their nations. The nations divided from these in the earth after the flood.

11

¹ The whole earth was of one language and of one speech. ² As they traveled from the east, they found a plain in the land of Shinar, and they lived there. ³ They said to one another, "Come, let's make bricks, and burn them thoroughly." They had brick for stone, and they used tar for mortar. ⁴ They said, "Come, let's build ourselves a city, and a tower whose top reaches to the sky, and let's make a name for ourselves, lest we be scattered abroad on the surface of the whole earth."

⁵ Yahweh came down to see the city and the tower, which the children of men built. ⁶ Yahweh said, "Behold, they are one people, and they all have one language, and this is what they begin to do. Now nothing will be withheld from them, which they intend to do. ⁷ Come, let's go down, and there confuse their language, that they may not understand one another's speech." ⁸ So Yahweh scattered them abroad from there on the surface of all the earth. They stopped building the city. ⁹ Therefore its name was called Babel, because there Yahweh confused the language of all the earth. From there, Yahweh scattered them abroad on the surface of all the earth.

¹⁰ This is the history of the generations of Shem: Shem was one hundred years old when he became the father of Arpachshad two years after the flood. ¹¹ Shem lived five hundred years after he became the father of Arpachshad, and became the father of more sons and daughters.

¹² Arpachshad lived thirty-five years and became the father of Shelah. ¹³ Arpachshad lived four hundred three years after he became the father of Shelah, and became the father of more sons and daughters.

¹⁴ Shelah lived thirty years, and became the father of Eber. ¹⁵ Shelah lived four hundred three years after he became the father of Eber, and became the father of more sons and daughters.

¹⁶ Eber lived thirty-four years, and became the father of Peleg. ¹⁷ Eber lived four hundred thirty years after he became the father of Peleg, and became the father of more sons and daughters.

¹⁸ Peleg lived thirty years, and became the father of Reu. ¹⁹ Peleg lived two hundred nine years after he became the father of Reu, and became the father of more sons and daughters.

²⁰ Reu lived thirty-two years, and became the father of Serug. ²¹ Reu lived two hundred seven years after he became the father of Serug, and became the father of more sons and daughters.

²² Serug lived thirty years, and became the father of Nahor. ²³ Serug lived two hundred years after he became the father of Nahor, and became the father of more sons and daughters.

²⁴ Nahor lived twenty-nine years, and became the father of Terah. ²⁵ Nahor lived one hundred nineteen years after he became the father of Terah, and became the father of more sons and daughters.

²⁶ Terah lived seventy years, and became the father of Abram, Nahor, and Haran.

²⁷ Now this is the history of the generations of Terah. Terah became the father of Abram, Nahor, and Haran. Haran became the father of Lot. ²⁸ Haran died in the land of his birth, in Ur of the Chaldees, while his father Terah was still alive. ²⁹ Abram and Nahor married wives. The name of Abram's wife was Sarai, and the name of Nahor's wife was Milcah, the daughter of Haran, who was also the father of

Iscah. ³⁰ Sarai was barren. She had no child. ³¹ Terah took Abram his son, Lot the son of Haran, his son's son, and Sarai his daughter-in-law, his son Abram's wife. They went from Ur of the Chaldees, to go into the land of Canaan. They came to Haran and lived there. ³² The days of Terah were two hundred five years. Terah died in Haran.

12

¹ Now Yahweh said to Abram, "Leave your country, and your relatives, and your father's house, and go to the land that I will show you. ² I will make of you a great nation. I will bless you and make your name great. You will be a blessing. ³ I will bless those who bless you, and I will curse him who treats you with contempt. All the families of the earth will be blessed through you."

⁴ So Abram went, as Yahweh had told him. Lot went with him. Abram was seventy-five years old when he departed from Haran. ⁵ Abram took Sarai his wife, Lot his brother's son, all their possessions that they had gathered, and the people whom they had acquired in Haran, and they went to go into the land of Canaan. They entered into the land of Canaan. ⁶ Abram passed through the land to the place of Shechem, to the oak of Moreh. At that time, Canaanites were in the land.

⁷ Yahweh appeared to Abram and said, "I will give this land to your offspring." *

He built an altar there to Yahweh, who had appeared to him. ⁸ He left from there to go to the mountain on the east of Bethel and pitched his tent, having Bethel on the west, and Ai on the east. There he built an altar to Yahweh and called on Yahweh's name. ⁹ Abram traveled, still going on toward the South.

¹⁰ There was a famine in the land. Abram went down into Egypt to live as a foreigner there, for the famine was severe in the land. ¹¹ When he had come near to enter Egypt, he said to Sarai his wife, "See now, I know that you are a beautiful woman to look at. ¹² It will happen, when the Egyptians see you, that they will say, 'This is his wife.' They will kill me, but they will save you alive. ¹³ Please say that you are my sister, that it may be well with me for your sake, and that my soul may live because of you."

¹⁴ When Abram had come into Egypt, Egyptians saw that the woman was very beautiful. ¹⁵ The princes of Pharaoh saw her, and praised her to Pharaoh; and the woman was taken into Pharaoh's house. ¹⁶ He dealt well with Abram for her sake. He had sheep, cattle, male donkeys, male servants, female servants, female donkeys, and camels. ¹⁷ Yahweh afflicted Pharaoh and his house with great plagues because of

Sarai, Abram's wife. ¹⁸ Pharaoh called Abram and said, "What is this that you have done to me? Why didn't you tell me that she was your wife? ¹⁹ Why did you say, 'She is my sister,' so that I took her to be my wife? Now therefore, see your wife, take her, and go your way."

²⁰ Pharaoh commanded men concerning him, and they escorted him away with his wife and all that he had.

13

¹ Abram went up out of Egypt—he, his wife, all that he had, and Lot with him—into the South. ² Abram was very rich in livestock, in silver, and in gold. ³ He went on his journeys from the South as far as Bethel, to the place where his tent had been at the beginning, between Bethel and Ai, ⁴ to the place of the altar, which he had made there at the first. There Abram called on Yahweh's name. ⁵ Lot also, who went with Abram, had flocks, herds, and tents. ⁶ The land was not able to bear them, that they might live together; for their possessions were so great that they couldn't live together. ⁷ There was strife between the herdsmen of Abram's livestock and the herdsmen of Lot's livestock. The Canaanites and the Perizzites lived in the land at that time. ⁸ Abram said to Lot, "Please, let there be no strife between you and me, and between your herdsmen and my herdsmen; for we are relatives. ⁹ Isn't the whole land before you? Please separate yourself from me. If you go to the left hand, then I will go to the right. Or if you go to the right hand, then I will go to the left."

¹⁰ Lot lifted up his eyes, and saw all the plain of the Jordan, that it was well-watered everywhere, before Yahweh destroyed Sodom and Gomorrah, like the garden of Yahweh, like the land of Egypt, as you go to Zoar. ¹¹ So Lot chose the Plain of the Jordan for himself. Lot traveled east, and they separated themselves from one other. ¹² Abram lived in the land of Canaan, and Lot lived in the cities of the plain, and moved his tent as far as Sodom. ¹³ Now the men of Sodom were exceedingly wicked and sinners against Yahweh.

¹⁴ Yahweh said to Abram, after Lot was separated from him, "Now, lift up your eyes, and look from the place where you are, northward and southward and eastward and westward, ¹⁵ for I will give all the land which you see to you and to your offspring forever. ¹⁶ I will make your offspring as the dust of the earth, so that if a man can count the dust of the earth, then your offspring may also be counted. ¹⁷ Arise, walk through the land in its length and in its width; for I will give it to you."

¹⁸ Abram moved his tent, and came and lived by the oaks of Mamre, which are in Hebron, and built an altar there to Yahweh.

14

[1] In the days of Amraphel, king of Shinar; Arioch, king of Ellasar; Chedorlaomer, king of Elam; and Tidal, king of Goiim, [2] they made war with Bera, king of Sodom; Birsha, king of Gomorrah; Shinab, king of Admah; Shemeber, king of Zeboiim; and the king of Bela (also called Zoar). [3] All these joined together in the valley of Siddim (also called the Salt Sea). [4] They served Chedorlaomer for twelve years, and in the thirteenth year they rebelled. [5] In the fourteenth year Chedorlaomer came, and the kings who were with him, and struck the Rephaim in Ashteroth Karnaim, the Zuzim in Ham, the Emim in Shaveh Kiriathaim, [6] and the Horites in their Mount Seir, to El Paran, which is by the wilderness. [7] They returned, and came to En Mishpat (also called Kadesh), and struck all the country of the Amalekites, and also the Amorites, that lived in Hazazon Tamar. [8] The king of Sodom, and the king of Gomorrah, the king of Admah, the king of Zeboiim, and the king of Bela (also called Zoar) went out; and they set the battle in array against them in the valley of Siddim [9] against Chedorlaomer king of Elam, Tidal king of Goiim, Amraphel king of Shinar, and Arioch king of Ellasar; four kings against the five. [10] Now the valley of Siddim was full of tar pits; and the kings of Sodom and Gomorrah fled, and some fell there. Those who remained fled to the hills. [11] They took all the goods of Sodom and Gomorrah, and all their food, and went their way. [12] They took Lot, Abram's brother's son, who lived in Sodom, and his goods, and departed.

[13] One who had escaped came and told Abram, the Hebrew. At that time, he lived by the oaks of Mamre, the Amorite, brother of Eshcol and brother of Aner. They were allies of Abram. [14] When Abram heard that his relative was taken captive, he led out his three hundred eighteen trained men, born in his house, and pursued as far as Dan. [15] He divided himself against them by night, he and his servants, and struck them, and pursued them to Hobah, which is on the left hand of Damascus. [16] He brought back all the goods, and also brought back his relative Lot and his goods, and the women also, and the other people.

[17] The king of Sodom went out to meet him after his return from the slaughter of Chedorlaomer and the kings who were with him, at the valley of Shaveh (that is, the King's Valley). [18] Melchizedek king of Salem brought out bread and wine. He was priest of God Most High. [19] He blessed him, and said, "Blessed be Abram of God Most High, possessor of heaven and earth. [20] Blessed be God Most High, who has delivered your enemies into your hand." Abram gave him a tenth of all.

[21] The king of Sodom said to Abram, "Give me the people, and take the goods for yourself."

[22] Abram said to the king of Sodom, "I have lifted up my hand to Yahweh, God Most High, possessor of heaven and earth, [23] that I will not take a thread nor a sandal strap nor anything that is yours, lest you should say, 'I have made Abram rich.' [24] I will accept nothing from you except that which the young men have eaten, and the portion of the men who went with me: Aner, Eshcol, and Mamre. Let them take their portion."

15

[1] After these things Yahweh's word came to Abram in a vision, saying, "Don't be afraid, Abram. I am your shield, your exceedingly great reward."

[2] Abram said, "Lord· Yahweh, what will you give me, since I go childless, and he who will inherit my estate is Eliezer of Damascus?" [3] Abram said, "Behold, you have given no children to me: and, behold, one born in my house is my heir."

[4] Behold, Yahweh's word came to him, saying, "This man will not be your heir, but he who will come out of your own body will be your heir." [5] Yahweh brought him outside, and said, "Look now toward the sky, and count the stars, if you are able to count them." He said to Abram, "So your offspring will be." [6] He believed in Yahweh, who credited it to him for righteousness. [7] He said to Abram, "I am Yahweh who brought you out of Ur of the Chaldees, to give you this land to inherit it."

[8] He said, "Lord Yahweh, how will I know that I will inherit it?"

[9] He said to him, "Bring me a heifer three years old, a female goat three years old, a ram three years old, a turtledove, and a young pigeon." [10] He brought him all these, and divided them in the middle, and laid each half opposite the other; but he didn't divide the birds. [11] The birds of prey came down on the carcasses, and Abram drove them away.

[12] When the sun was going down, a deep sleep fell on Abram. Now terror and great darkness fell on him. [13] He said to Abram, "Know for sure that your offspring will live as foreigners in a land that is not theirs, and will serve them. They will afflict them four hundred years. [14] I will also judge that nation, whom they will serve. Afterward they will come out with great wealth; [15] but you will go to your fathers in peace. You will be buried at a good old age. [16] In the fourth generation they will come here again, for the iniquity of the Amorite is not yet full." [17] It came to pass that, when the sun went down, and it was dark, behold, a smoking furnace and

a flaming torch passed between these pieces. ¹⁸ In that day Yahweh made a covenant with Abram, saying, "I have given this land to your offspring, from the river of Egypt to the great river, the river Euphrates: ¹⁹ the land of the Kenites, the Kenizzites, the Kadmonites, ²⁰ the Hittites, the Perizzites, the Rephaim, ²¹ the Amorites, the Canaanites, the Girgashites, and the Jebusites."

16

¹ Now Sarai, Abram's wife, bore him no children. She had a servant, an Egyptian, whose name was Hagar.² Sarai said to Abram, "See now, Yahweh has restrained me from bearing. Please go in to my servant. It may be that I will obtain children by her." Abram listened to the voice of Sarai. ³ Sarai, Abram's wife, took Hagar the Egyptian, her servant, after Abram had lived ten years in the land of Canaan, and gave her to Abram her husband to be his wife. ⁴ He went in to Hagar, and she conceived. When she saw that she had conceived, her mistress was despised in her eyes. ⁵ Sarai said to Abram, "This wrong is your fault. I gave my servant into your bosom, and when she saw that she had conceived, she despised me. May Yahweh judge between me and you."

⁶ But Abram said to Sarai, "Behold, your maid is in your hand. Do to her whatever is good in your eyes." Sarai dealt harshly with her, and she fled from her face.

⁷ Yahweh's angel found her by a fountain of water in the wilderness, by the fountain on the way to Shur.⁸ He said, "Hagar, Sarai's servant, where did you come from? Where are you going?"

She said, "I am fleeing from the face of my mistress Sarai."

⁹ Yahweh's angel said to her, "Return to your mistress, and submit yourself under her hands." ¹⁰ Yahweh's angel said to her, "I will greatly multiply your offspring, that they will not be counted for multitude."¹¹ Yahweh's angel said to her, "Behold, you are with child, and will bear a son. You shall call his name Ishmael, because Yahweh has heard your affliction. ¹² He will be like a wild donkey among men. His hand will be against every man, and every man's hand against him. He will live opposed to all of his brothers."

¹³ She called the name of Yahweh who spoke to her, "You are a God who sees," for she said, "Have I even stayed alive after seeing him?" ¹⁴ Therefore the well was called Beer Lahai Roi.˙ Behold, it is between Kadesh and Bered.

¹⁵ Hagar bore a son for Abram. Abram called the name of his son, whom Hagar bore, Ishmael. ¹⁶ Abram was eighty-six years old when Hagar bore Ishmael to Abram.

17

¹ When Abram was ninety-nine years old, Yahweh appeared to Abram and said to him, "I am God Almighty. Walk before me and be blameless. ² I will make my covenant between me and you, and will multiply you exceedingly."

³ Abram fell on his face. God talked with him, saying, ⁴ "As for me, behold, my covenant is with you. You will be the father of a multitude of nations. ⁵ Your name will no more be called Abram, but your name will be Abraham; for I have made you the father of a multitude of nations. ⁶ I will make you exceedingly fruitful, and I will make nations of you. Kings will come out of you. ⁷ I will establish my covenant between me and you and your offspring after you throughout their generations for an everlasting covenant, to be a God to you and to your offspring after you. ⁸ I will give to you, and to your offspring after you, the land where you are traveling, all the land of Canaan, for an everlasting possession. I will be their God."

⁹ God said to Abraham, "As for you, you will keep my covenant, you and your offspring after you throughout their generations. ¹⁰ This is my covenant, which you shall keep, between me and you and your offspring after you. Every male among you shall be circumcised. ¹¹ You shall be circumcised in the flesh of your foreskin. It will be a token of the covenant between me and you. ¹² He who is eight days old will be circumcised among you, every male throughout your generations, he who is born in the house, or bought with money from any foreigner who is not of your offspring. ¹³ He who is born in your house, and he who is bought with your money, must be circumcised. My covenant will be in your flesh for an everlasting covenant. ¹⁴ The uncircumcised male who is not circumcised in the flesh of his foreskin, that soul shall be cut off from his people. He has broken my covenant."

¹⁵ God said to Abraham, "As for Sarai your wife, you shall not call her name Sarai, but her name will be Sarah. ¹⁶ I will bless her, and moreover I will give you a son by her. Yes, I will bless her, and she will be a mother of nations. Kings of peoples will come from her."

¹⁷ Then Abraham fell on his face, and laughed, and said in his heart, "Will a child be born to him who is one hundred years old? Will Sarah, who is ninety years old, give birth?" ¹⁸ Abraham said to God, "Oh that Ishmael might live before you!"

¹⁹ God said, "No, but Sarah, your wife, will bear you a son. You shall call his name Isaac.˙ I will establish my covenant with him for an everlasting covenant for his offspring after him. ²⁰ As for Ishmael, I have heard you. Behold, I have blessed him, and will make him fruitful, and will multiply

him exceedingly. He will become the father of twelve princes, and I will make him a great nation. ²¹ But I will establish my covenant with Isaac, whom Sarah will bear to you at this set time next year."

²² When he finished talking with him, God went up from Abraham. ²³ Abraham took Ishmael his son, all who were born in his house, and all who were bought with his money: every male among the men of Abraham's house, and circumcised the flesh of their foreskin in the same day, as God had said to him. ²⁴ Abraham was ninety-nine years old when he was circumcised in the flesh of his foreskin. ²⁵ Ishmael, his son, was thirteen years old when he was circumcised in the flesh of his foreskin. ²⁶ In the same day both Abraham and Ishmael, his son, were circumcised. ²⁷ All the men of his house, those born in the house, and those bought with money from a foreigner, were circumcised with him.

18

¹ Yahweh appeared to him by the oaks of Mamre, as he sat in the tent door in the heat of the day. ² He lifted up his eyes and looked, and saw that three men stood near him. When he saw them, he ran to meet them from the tent door, and bowed himself to the earth, ³ and said, "My lord, if now I have found favor in your sight, please don't go away from your servant. ⁴ Now let a little water be fetched, wash your feet, and rest yourselves under the tree. ⁵ I will get a piece of bread so you can refresh your heart. After that you may go your way, now that you have come to your servant."

They said, "Very well, do as you have said."

⁶ Abraham hurried into the tent to Sarah, and said, "Quickly prepare three seahs of fine meal, knead it, and make cakes." ⁷ Abraham ran to the herd, and fetched a tender and good calf, and gave it to the servant. He hurried to dress it. ⁸ He took butter, milk, and the calf which he had dressed, and set it before them. He stood by them under the tree, and they ate.

⁹ They asked him, "Where is Sarah, your wife?"

He said, "There, in the tent."

¹⁰ He said, "I will certainly return to you at about this time next year; and behold, Sarah your wife will have a son."

Sarah heard in the tent door, which was behind him. ¹¹ Now Abraham and Sarah were old, well advanced in age. Sarah had passed the age of childbearing. ¹² Sarah laughed within herself, saying, "After I have grown old will I have pleasure, my lord being old also?"

¹³ Yahweh said to Abraham, "Why did Sarah laugh, saying, 'Will I really bear a child when I am old?' ¹⁴ Is anything too hard for Yahweh? At the set time I will return to you,

when the season comes round, and Sarah will have a son."

¹⁵ Then Sarah denied it, saying, "I didn't laugh," for she was afraid.

He said, "No, but you did laugh."

¹⁶ The men rose up from there, and looked toward Sodom. Abraham went with them to see them on their way. ¹⁷ Yahweh said, "Will I hide from Abraham what I do, ¹⁸ since Abraham will surely become a great and mighty nation, and all the nations of the earth will be blessed in him? ¹⁹ For I have known him, to the end that he may command his children and his household after him, that they may keep the way of Yahweh, to do righteousness and justice; to the end that Yahweh may bring on Abraham that which he has spoken of him." ²⁰ Yahweh said, "Because the cry of Sodom and Gomorrah is great, and because their sin is very grievous, ²¹ I will go down now, and see whether their deeds are as bad as the reports which have come to me. If not, I will know."

²² The men turned from there, and went toward Sodom, but Abraham stood yet before Yahweh. ²³ Abraham came near, and said, "Will you consume the righteous with the wicked? ²⁴ What if there are fifty righteous within the city? Will you consume and not spare the place for the fifty righteous who are in it? ²⁵ May it be far from you to do things like that, to kill the righteous with the wicked, so that the righteous should be like the wicked. May that be far from you. Shouldn't the Judge of all the earth do right?"

²⁶ Yahweh said, "If I find in Sodom fifty righteous within the city, then I will spare the whole place for their sake." ²⁷ Abraham answered, "See now, I have taken it on myself to speak to the Lord, although I am dust and ashes. ²⁸ What if there will lack five of the fifty righteous? Will you destroy all the city for lack of five?"

He said, "I will not destroy it if I find forty-five there."

²⁹ He spoke to him yet again, and said, "What if there are forty found there?"

He said, "I will not do it for the forty's sake."

³⁰ He said, "Oh don't let the Lord be angry, and I will speak. What if there are thirty found there?"

He said, "I will not do it if I find thirty there."

³¹ He said, "See now, I have taken it on myself to speak to the Lord. What if there are twenty found there?"

He said, "I will not destroy it for the twenty's sake."

³² He said, "Oh don't let the Lord be angry, and I will speak just once more. What if ten are found there?"

He said, "I will not destroy it for the ten's sake."

³³ Yahweh went his way, as soon as he had finished communing with Abraham, and Abraham returned to his place.

Text Twenty-one

Joseph's Story in Genesis

37

¹ Jacob lived in the land of his father's travels, in the land of Canaan. ² This is the history of the generations of Jacob. Joseph, being seventeen years old, was feeding the flock with his brothers. He was a boy with the sons of Bilhah and Zilpah, his father's wives. Joseph brought an evil report of them to their father.³ Now Israel loved Joseph more than all his children, because he was the son of his old age, and he made him a tunic of many colors. ⁴ His brothers saw that their father loved him more than all his brothers, and they hated him, and couldn't speak peaceably to him.

⁵ Joseph dreamed a dream, and he told it to his brothers, and they hated him all the more. ⁶ He said to them, "Please hear this dream which I have dreamed: ⁷ for behold, we were binding sheaves in the field, and behold, my sheaf arose and also stood upright; and behold, your sheaves came around, and bowed down to my sheaf."

⁸ His brothers asked him, "Will you indeed reign over us? Will you indeed have dominion over us?" They hated him all the more for his dreams and for his words. ⁹ He dreamed yet another dream, and told it to his brothers, and said, "Behold, I have dreamed yet another dream: and behold, the sun and the moon and eleven stars bowed down to me." ¹⁰ He told it to his father and to his brothers. His father rebuked him, and said to him, "What is this dream that you have dreamed? Will I and your mother and your brothers indeed come to bow ourselves down to you to the earth?" ¹¹ His brothers envied him, but his father kept this saying in mind.

¹² His brothers went to feed their father's flock in Shechem. ¹³ Israel said to Joseph, "Aren't your brothers feeding the flock in Shechem? Come, and I will send you to them." He said to him, "Here I am."

¹⁴ He said to him, "Go now, see whether it is well with your brothers, and well with the flock; and bring me word again." So he sent him out of the valley of Hebron, and he came to Shechem. ¹⁵ A certain man found him, and behold, he was wandering in the field. The man asked him, "What are you looking for?"

¹⁶ He said, "I am looking for my brothers. Tell me, please, where they are feeding the flock."

¹⁷ The man said, "They have left here, for I heard them say, 'Let's go to Dothan.'"

Joseph went after his brothers, and found them in Dothan. ¹⁸ They saw him afar off, and before he came near to them, they conspired against him to kill him. ¹⁹ They said to one another, "Behold, this dreamer comes.²⁰ Come now therefore, and let's kill him, and cast him into one of the pits, and we will say, 'An evil animal has devoured him.' We will see what will become of his dreams."

²¹ Reuben heard it, and delivered him out of their hand, and said, "Let's not take his life." ²² Reuben said to them, "Shed no blood. Throw him into this pit that is in the wilderness, but lay no hand on him"—that he might deliver him out of their hand, to restore him to his father. ²³ When Joseph came to his brothers, they stripped Joseph of his tunic, the tunic of many colors that was on him; ²⁴ and they took him, and threw him into the pit. The pit was empty. There was no water in it.

²⁵ They sat down to eat bread, and they lifted up their eyes and looked, and saw a caravan of Ishmaelites was coming from Gilead, with their camels bearing spices and balm and myrrh, going to carry it down to Egypt. ²⁶ Judah said to his brothers, "What profit is it if we kill our brother and conceal his blood? ²⁷ Come, and let's sell him to the Ishmaelites, and not let our hand be on him; for he is our brother, our flesh." His brothers listened to him. ²⁸ Midianites who were merchants passed by, and they drew and lifted up Joseph out of the pit, and sold Joseph to the Ishmaelites for twenty pieces of silver. The merchants brought Joseph into Egypt.

²⁹ Reuben returned to the pit, and saw that Joseph wasn't in the pit; and he tore his clothes. ³⁰ He returned to his brothers, and said, "The child is no more; and I, where will I go?" ³¹ They took Joseph's tunic, and killed a male goat, and dipped the tunic in the blood. ³² They took the tunic of many colors, and they brought it to their father, and said, "We have found this. Examine it, now, and see if it is your son's tunic or not."

³³ He recognized it, and said, "It is my son's tunic. An evil animal has devoured him. Joseph is without doubt torn in pieces." ³⁴ Jacob tore his clothes, and put sackcloth on his waist, and mourned for his son many days. ³⁵ All his sons and all his daughters rose up to comfort him, but he refused to be comforted. He said, "For I will go down to Sheol˙ to my son, mourning." His father wept for him. ³⁶ The Midianites sold him into Egypt to Potiphar, an officer of Pharaoh's, the captain of the guard.

38

¹ At that time, Judah went down from his brothers, and visited a certain Adullamite, whose name was Hirah. ² There, Judah saw the daughter of a certain Canaanite man named Shua. He took her, and went in to her. ³ She conceived, and bore a son; and he named him Er. ⁴ She conceived again, and bore a son; and she named him Onan. ⁵ She yet again bore a son, and named him Shelah. He was at Chezib when she bore him. ⁶ Judah took a wife for Er, his firstborn, and her name was Tamar. ⁷ Er, Judah's firstborn, was wicked in Yahweh's sight. So Yahweh killed him. ⁸ Judah said to Onan, "Go in to your brother's wife, and perform the duty of a husband's brother to her, and raise up offspring for your brother." ⁹ Onan knew that the offspring wouldn't be his; and when he went in to his brother's wife, he spilled his semen on the ground, lest he should give offspring to his brother. ¹⁰ The thing which he did was evil in Yahweh's sight, and he killed him also. ¹¹ Then Judah said to Tamar, his daughter-in-law, "Remain a widow in your father's house, until Shelah, my son, is grown up;" for he said, "Lest he also die, like his brothers." Tamar went and lived in her father's house.

¹² After many days, Shua's daughter, the wife of Judah, died. Judah was comforted, and went up to his sheep shearers to Timnah, he and his friend Hirah, the Adullamite. ¹³ Tamar was told, "Behold, your father-in-law is going up to Timnah to shear his sheep." ¹⁴ She took off the garments of her widowhood, and covered herself with her veil, and wrapped herself, and sat in the gate of Enaim, which is on the way to Timnah; for she saw that Shelah was grown up, and she wasn't given to him as a wife. ¹⁵ When Judah saw her, he thought that she was a prostitute, for she had covered her face. ¹⁶ He turned to her by the way, and said, "Please come, let me come in to you," for he didn't know that she was his daughter-in-law.

She said, "What will you give me, that you may come in to me?"

¹⁷ He said, "I will send you a young goat from the flock."

She said, "Will you give me a pledge, until you send it?"

¹⁸ He said, "What pledge will I give you?"

She said, "Your signet and your cord, and your staff that is in your hand."

He gave them to her, and came in to her, and she conceived by him. ¹⁹ She arose, and went away, and put off her veil from her, and put on the garments of her widowhood. ²⁰ Judah sent the young goat by the hand of his friend, the Adullamite, to receive the pledge from the woman's hand, but he didn't find her. ²¹ Then he asked the men of her place, saying, "Where is the prostitute, that was at Enaim by the road?"

They said, "There has been no prostitute here."

²² He returned to Judah, and said, "I haven't found her; and also the men of the place said, 'There has been no prostitute here.'" ²³ Judah said, "Let her keep it, lest we be shamed. Behold, I sent this young goat, and you haven't found her."

²⁴ About three months later, Judah was told, "Tamar, your daughter-in-law, has played the prostitute. Moreover, behold, she is with child by prostitution."

Judah said, "Bring her out, and let her be burned." ²⁵ When she was brought out, she sent to her father-in-law, saying, "I am with child by the man who owns these." She also said, "Please discern whose these are—the signet, and the cords, and the staff."

²⁶ Judah acknowledged them, and said, "She is more righteous than I, because I didn't give her to Shelah, my son."

He knew her again no more. ²⁷ In the time of her travail, behold, twins were in her womb. ²⁸ When she travailed, one put out a hand, and the midwife took and tied a scarlet thread on his hand, saying, "This came out first." ²⁹ As he drew back his hand, behold, his brother came out, and she said, "Why have you made a breach for yourself?" Therefore his name was called Perez.˙ ³⁰ Afterward his brother came out, who had the scarlet thread on his hand, and his name was called Zerah.†

39

¹ Joseph was brought down to Egypt. Potiphar, an officer of Pharaoh's, the captain of the guard, an Egyptian, bought him from the hand of the Ishmaelites that had brought him down there. ² Yahweh was with Joseph, and he was a prosperous man. He was in the house of his master the

Egyptian. ³ His master saw that Yahweh was with him, and that Yahweh made all that he did prosper in his hand. ⁴ Joseph found favor in his sight. He ministered to him, and Potiphar made him overseer over his house, and all that he had he put into his hand. ⁵ From the time that he made him overseer in his house, and over all that he had, Yahweh blessed the Egyptian's house for Joseph's sake. Yahweh's blessing was on all that he had, in the house and in the field. ⁶ He left all that he had in Joseph's hand. He didn't concern himself with anything, except for the food which he ate.

Joseph was well-built and handsome. ⁷ After these things, his master's wife set her eyes on Joseph; and she said, "Lie with me."

⁸ But he refused, and said to his master's wife, "Behold, my master doesn't know what is with me in the house, and he has put all that he has into my hand. ⁹ No one is greater in this house than I am, and he has not kept back anything from me but you, because you are his wife. How then can I do this great wickedness, and sin against God?"

¹⁰ As she spoke to Joseph day by day, he didn't listen to her, to lie by her, or to be with her. ¹¹ About this time, he went into the house to do his work, and there were none of the men of the house inside. ¹² She caught him by his garment, saying, "Lie with me!"

He left his garment in her hand, and ran outside. ¹³ When she saw that he had left his garment in her hand, and had run outside, ¹⁴ she called to the men of her house, and spoke to them, saying, "Behold, he has brought a Hebrew in to us to mock us. He came in to me to lie with me, and I cried with a loud voice. ¹⁵ When he heard that I lifted up my voice and cried, he left his garment by me, and ran outside." ¹⁶ She laid up his garment by her, until his master came home. ¹⁷ She spoke to him according to these words, saying, "The Hebrew servant, whom you have brought to us, came in to me to mock me, ¹⁸ and as I lifted up my voice and cried, he left his garment by me, and ran outside."

¹⁹ When his master heard the words of his wife, which she spoke to him, saying, "This is what your servant did to me," his wrath was kindled. ²⁰ Joseph's master took him, and put him into the prison, the place where the king's prisoners were bound, and he was there in custody. ²¹ But Yahweh was with Joseph, and showed kindness to him, and gave him favor in the sight of the keeper of the prison. ²² The keeper of the prison committed to Joseph's hand all the prisoners who were in the prison. Whatever they did there, he was responsible for it. ²³ The keeper of the prison didn't look after anything that was under his hand, because Yahweh was with him; and that which he did, Yahweh made it prosper.

40

¹ After these things, the butler of the king of Egypt and his baker offended their lord, the king of Egypt. ² Pharaoh was angry with his two officers, the chief cup bearer and the chief baker. ³ He put them in custody in the house of the captain of the guard, into the prison, the place where Joseph was bound. ⁴ The captain of the guard assigned them to Joseph, and he took care of them. They stayed in prison many days. ⁵ They both dreamed a dream, each man his dream, in one night, each man according to the interpretation of his dream, the cup bearer and the baker of the king of Egypt, who were bound in the prison. ⁶ Joseph came in to them in the morning, and saw them, and saw that they were sad. ⁷ He asked Pharaoh's officers who were with him in custody in his master's house, saying, "Why do you look so sad today?"

⁸ They said to him, "We have dreamed a dream, and there is no one who can interpret it."

Joseph said to them, "Don't interpretations belong to God? Please tell it to me."

⁹ The chief cup bearer told his dream to Joseph, and said to him, "In my dream, behold, a vine was in front of me, ¹⁰ and in the vine were three branches. It was as though it budded, it blossomed, and its clusters produced ripe grapes. ¹¹ Pharaoh's cup was in my hand; and I took the grapes, and pressed them into Pharaoh's cup, and I gave the cup into Pharaoh's hand."

¹² Joseph said to him, "This is its interpretation: the three branches are three days. ¹³ Within three more days, Pharaoh will lift up your head, and restore you to your office. You will give Pharaoh's cup into his hand, the way you did when you were his cup bearer. ¹⁴ But remember me when it is well with you. Please show kindness to me, and make mention of me to Pharaoh, and bring me out of this house. ¹⁵ For indeed, I was stolen away out of the land of the Hebrews, and here also I have done nothing that they should put me into the dungeon."

¹⁶ When the chief baker saw that the interpretation was good, he said to Joseph, "I also was in my dream, and behold, three baskets of white bread were on my head. ¹⁷ In the uppermost basket there were all kinds of baked food for Pharaoh, and the birds ate them out of the basket on my head."

¹⁸ Joseph answered, "This is its interpretation. The three baskets are three days. ¹⁹ Within three more days, Pharaoh will lift up your head from off you, and will hang you on a tree; and the birds will eat your flesh from off you." ²⁰ On the third day, which was Pharaoh's birthday, he made a feast for all his servants, and he lifted up the head of the chief cup bearer and the head of the chief baker among his servants. ²¹ He restored

the chief cup bearer to his position again, and he gave the cup into Pharaoh's hand; ²² but he hanged the chief baker, as Joseph had interpreted to them. ²³ Yet the chief cup bearer didn't remember Joseph, but forgot him.

41

¹ At the end of two full years, Pharaoh dreamed, and behold, he stood by the river. ² Behold, seven cattle came up out of the river. They were sleek and fat, and they fed in the marsh grass. ³ Behold, seven other cattle came up after them out of the river, ugly and thin, and stood by the other cattle on the brink of the river. ⁴ The ugly and thin cattle ate up the seven sleek and fat cattle. So Pharaoh awoke. ⁵ He slept and dreamed a second time; and behold, seven heads of grain came up on one stalk, healthy and good. ⁶ Behold, seven heads of grain, thin and blasted with the east wind, sprung up after them. ⁷ The thin heads of grain swallowed up the seven healthy and full ears. Pharaoh awoke, and behold, it was a dream. ⁸ In the morning, his spirit was troubled, and he sent and called for all of Egypt's magicians and wise men. Pharaoh told them his dreams, but there was no one who could interpret them to Pharaoh.

⁹ Then the chief cup bearer spoke to Pharaoh, saying, "I remember my faults today. ¹⁰ Pharaoh was angry with his servants, and put me in custody in the house of the captain of the guard, with the chief baker. ¹¹ We dreamed a dream in one night, he and I. Each man dreamed according to the interpretation of his dream. ¹² There was with us there a young man, a Hebrew, servant to the captain of the guard, and we told him, and he interpreted to us our dreams. He interpreted to each man according to his dream. ¹³ As he interpreted to us, so it was. He restored me to my office, and he hanged him."

¹⁴ Then Pharaoh sent and called Joseph, and they brought him hastily out of the dungeon. He shaved himself, changed his clothing, and came in to Pharaoh. ¹⁵ Pharaoh said to Joseph, "I have dreamed a dream, and there is no one who can interpret it. I have heard it said of you, that when you hear a dream you can interpret it."

¹⁶ Joseph answered Pharaoh, saying, "It isn't in me. God will give Pharaoh an answer of peace."

¹⁷ Pharaoh spoke to Joseph, "In my dream, behold, I stood on the brink of the river; ¹⁸ and behold, there came up out of the river seven cattle, fat and sleek. They fed in the marsh grass; ¹⁹ and behold, seven other cattle came up after them, poor and very ugly and thin, such as I never saw in all the land of Egypt for ugliness. ²⁰ The thin and ugly cattle ate up the first seven fat cattle; ²¹ and when they had eaten them up, it couldn't be known that they had eaten them, but

they were still ugly, as at the beginning. So I awoke. ²² I saw in my dream, and behold, seven heads of grain came up on one stalk, full and good; ²³ and behold, seven heads of grain, withered, thin, and blasted with the east wind, sprung up after them. ²⁴ The thin heads of grain swallowed up the seven good heads of grain. I told it to the magicians, but there was no one who could explain it to me."

²⁵ Joseph said to Pharaoh, "The dream of Pharaoh is one. What God is about to do he has declared to Pharaoh. ²⁶ The seven good cattle are seven years; and the seven good heads of grain are seven years. The dream is one. ²⁷ The seven thin and ugly cattle that came up after them are seven years, and also the seven empty heads of grain blasted with the east wind; they will be seven years of famine. ²⁸ That is the thing which I have spoken to Pharaoh. God has shown Pharaoh what he is about to do. ²⁹ Behold, seven years of great plenty throughout all the land of Egypt are coming. ³⁰ Seven years of famine will arise after them, and all the plenty will be forgotten in the land of Egypt. The famine will consume the land, ³¹ and the plenty will not be known in the land by reason of that famine which follows; for it will be very grievous. ³² The dream was doubled to Pharaoh, because the thing is established by God, and God will shortly bring it to pass.

³³ "Now therefore let Pharaoh look for a discreet and wise man, and set him over the land of Egypt. ³⁴ Let Pharaoh do this, and let him appoint overseers over the land, and take up the fifth part of the land of Egypt's produce in the seven plenteous years. ³⁵ Let them gather all the food of these good years that come, and store grain under the hand of Pharaoh for food in the cities, and let them keep it. ³⁶ The food will be to supply the land against the seven years of famine, which will be in the land of Egypt; so that the land will not perish through the famine."

³⁷ The thing was good in the eyes of Pharaoh, and in the eyes of all his servants. ³⁸ Pharaoh said to his servants, "Can we find such a one as this, a man in whom is the Spirit of God?" ³⁹ Pharaoh said to Joseph, "Because God has shown you all of this, there is no one so discreet and wise as you. ⁴⁰ You shall be over my house. All my people will be ruled according to your word. Only in the throne I will be greater than you." ⁴¹ Pharaoh said to Joseph, "Behold, I have set you over all the land of Egypt." ⁴² Pharaoh took off his signet ring from his hand, and put it on Joseph's hand, and arrayed him in robes of fine linen, and put a gold chain about his neck. ⁴³ He made him ride in the second chariot which he had. They cried before him, "Bow the knee!" He set him over all the land of Egypt. ⁴⁴ Pharaoh said to Joseph, "I am Pharaoh. Without you, no man shall lift up his hand or his foot in all the land of Egypt." ⁴⁵ Pharaoh called Joseph's name Zaphenath-Paneah. He gave him Asenath, the daughter of

Potiphera priest of On as a wife. Joseph went out over the land of Egypt.

⁴⁶ Joseph was thirty years old when he stood before Pharaoh king of Egypt. Joseph went out from the presence of Pharaoh, and went throughout all the land of Egypt. ⁴⁷ In the seven plenteous years the earth produced abundantly. ⁴⁸ He gathered up all the food of the seven years which were in the land of Egypt, and laid up the food in the cities. He stored food in each city from the fields around that city. ⁴⁹ Joseph laid up grain as the sand of the sea, very much, until he stopped counting, for it was without number. ⁵⁰ To Joseph were born two sons before the year of famine came, whom Asenath, the daughter of Potiphera priest of On, bore to him.⁵¹ Joseph called the name of the firstborn Manasseh,* "For", he said, "God has made me forget all my toil, and all my father's house." ⁵² The name of the second, he called Ephraim:† "For God has made me fruitful in the land of my affliction."

⁵³ The seven years of plenty, that were in the land of Egypt, came to an end. ⁵⁴ The seven years of famine began to come, just as Joseph had said. There was famine in all lands, but in all the land of Egypt there was bread. ⁵⁵ When all the land of Egypt was famished, the people cried to Pharaoh for bread, and Pharaoh said to all the Egyptians, "Go to Joseph. What he says to you, do." ⁵⁶ The famine was over all the surface of the earth. Joseph opened all the store houses, and sold to the Egyptians. The famine was severe in the land of Egypt. ⁵⁷ All countries came into Egypt, to Joseph, to buy grain, because the famine was severe in all the earth.

42

¹ Now Jacob saw that there was grain in Egypt, and Jacob said to his sons, "Why do you look at one another?" ² He said, "Behold, I have heard that there is grain in Egypt. Go down there, and buy for us from there, so that we may live, and not die." ³ Joseph's ten brothers went down to buy grain from Egypt. ⁴ But Jacob didn't send Benjamin, Joseph's brother, with his brothers; for he said, "Lest perhaps harm happen to him."⁵ The sons of Israel came to buy among those who came, for the famine was in the land of Canaan. ⁶ Joseph was the governor over the land. It was he who sold to all the people of the land. Joseph's brothers came, and bowed themselves down to him with their faces to the earth. ⁷ Joseph saw his brothers, and he recognized them, but acted like a stranger to them, and spoke roughly with them. He said to them, "Where did you come from?"

They said, "From the land of Canaan, to buy food."

⁸ Joseph recognized his brothers, but they didn't recognize him. ⁹ Joseph remembered the dreams which he dreamed about them, and said to them, "You are spies! You have come to see the nakedness of the land."

¹⁰ They said to him, "No, my lord, but your servants have come to buy food. ¹¹ We are all one man's sons; we are honest men. Your servants are not spies."

¹² He said to them, "No, but you have come to see the nakedness of the land!"

¹³ They said, "We, your servants, are twelve brothers, the sons of one man in the land of Canaan; and behold, the youngest is today with our father, and one is no more."

¹⁴ Joseph said to them, "It is like I told you, saying, 'You are spies!' ¹⁵ By this you shall be tested. By the life of Pharaoh, you shall not go out from here, unless your youngest brother comes here. ¹⁶ Send one of you, and let him get your brother, and you shall be bound, that your words may be tested, whether there is truth in you, or else by the life of Pharaoh surely you are spies." ¹⁷ He put them all together into custody for three days.

¹⁸ Joseph said to them the third day, "Do this, and live, for I fear God. ¹⁹ If you are honest men, then let one of your brothers be bound in your prison; but you go, carry grain for the famine of your houses. ²⁰ Bring your youngest brother to me; so will your words be verified, and you won't die."

They did so. ²¹ They said to one another, "We are certainly guilty concerning our brother, in that we saw the distress of his soul, when he begged us, and we wouldn't listen. Therefore this distress has come upon us."²² Reuben answered them, saying, "Didn't I tell you, saying, 'Don't sin against the child,' and you wouldn't listen? Therefore also, behold, his blood is required." ²³ They didn't know that Joseph understood them; for there was an interpreter between them. ²⁴ He turned himself away from them, and wept. Then he returned to them, and spoke to them, and took Simeon from among them, and bound him before their eyes. ²⁵ Then Joseph gave a command to fill their bags with grain, and to restore each man's money into his sack, and to give them food for the way. So it was done to them.

²⁶ They loaded their donkeys with their grain, and departed from there. ²⁷ As one of them opened his sack to give his donkey food in the lodging place, he saw his money. Behold, it was in the mouth of his sack. ²⁸ He said to his brothers, "My money is restored! Behold, it is in my sack!" Their hearts failed them, and they turned trembling to one another, saying, "What is this that God has done to us?" ²⁹ They came to Jacob their father, to the land of Canaan, and told him all that had happened to them, saying, ³⁰ "The man, the lord of the land, spoke roughly with us, and took us for spies of the country. ³¹ We said to him, 'We are honest men. We are no spies. ³² We are twelve brothers, sons of our father; one is no more, and the youngest is today with our

father in the land of Canaan.' ³³ The man, the lord of the land, said to us, 'By this I will know that you are honest men: leave one of your brothers with me, and take grain for the famine of your houses, and go your way. ³⁴ Bring your youngest brother to me. Then I will know that you are not spies, but that you are honest men. So I will deliver your brother to you, and you shall trade in the land.' "

³⁵ As they emptied their sacks, behold, each man's bundle of money was in his sack. When they and their father saw their bundles of money, they were afraid. ³⁶ Jacob, their father, said to them, "You have bereaved me of my children! Joseph is no more, Simeon is no more, and you want to take Benjamin away. All these things are against me."

³⁷ Reuben spoke to his father, saying, "Kill my two sons, if I don't bring him to you. Entrust him to my care, and I will bring him to you again."

³⁸ He said, "My son shall not go down with you; for his brother is dead, and he only is left. If harm happens to him along the way in which you go, then you will bring down my gray hairs with sorrow to Sheol.' "

43

¹ The famine was severe in the land. ² When they had eaten up the grain which they had brought out of Egypt, their father said to them, "Go again, buy us a little more food."

³ Judah spoke to him, saying, "The man solemnly warned us, saying, 'You shall not see my face, unless your brother is with you.' ⁴ If you'll send our brother with us, we'll go down and buy you food; ⁵ but if you don't send him, we won't go down, for the man said to us, 'You shall not see my face, unless your brother is with you.' "

⁶ Israel said, "Why did you treat me so badly, telling the man that you had another brother?"

⁷ They said, "The man asked directly concerning ourselves, and concerning our relatives, saying, 'Is your father still alive? Have you another brother?' We just answered his questions. Is there any way we could know that he would say, 'Bring your brother down?' "

⁸ Judah said to Israel, his father, "Send the boy with me, and we'll get up and go, so that we may live, and not die, both we, and you, and also our little ones. ⁹ I'll be collateral for him. From my hand will you require him. If I don't bring him to you, and set him before you, then let me bear the blame forever; ¹⁰ for if we hadn't delayed, surely we would have returned a second time by now."

¹¹ Their father, Israel, said to them, "If it must be so, then do this: Take from the choice fruits of the land in your bags, and carry down a present for the man, a little balm, a little honey, spices and myrrh, nuts, and almonds; ¹² and take double money in your hand, and take back the money that was returned in the mouth of your sacks. Perhaps it was an oversight. ¹³ Take your brother also, get up, and return to the man. ¹⁴ May God Almighty give you mercy before the man, that he may release to you your other brother and Benjamin. If I am bereaved of my children, I am bereaved."

¹⁵ The men took that present, and they took double money in their hand, and Benjamin; and got up, went down to Egypt, and stood before Joseph. ¹⁶ When Joseph saw Benjamin with them, he said to the steward of his house, "Bring the men into the house, and butcher an animal, and prepare; for the men will dine with me at noon."

¹⁷ The man did as Joseph commanded, and the man brought the men to Joseph's house. ¹⁸ The men were afraid, because they were brought to Joseph's house; and they said, "Because of the money that was returned in our sacks the first time, we're brought in; that he may seek occasion against us, attack us, and seize us as slaves, along with our donkeys." ¹⁹ They came near to the steward of Joseph's house, and they spoke to him at the door of the house, ²⁰ and said, "Oh, my lord, we indeed came down the first time to buy food. ²¹ When we came to the lodging place, we opened our sacks, and behold, each man's money was in the mouth of his sack, our money in full weight. We have brought it back in our hand. ²² We have brought down other money in our hand to buy food. We don't know who put our money in our sacks."

²³ He said, "Peace be to you. Don't be afraid. Your God, and the God of your father, has given you treasure in your sacks. I received your money." He brought Simeon out to them. ²⁴ The man brought the men into Joseph's house, and gave them water, and they washed their feet. He gave their donkeys fodder. ²⁵ They prepared the present for Joseph's coming at noon, for they heard that they should eat bread there.

²⁶ When Joseph came home, they brought him the present which was in their hand into the house, and bowed themselves down to the earth before him. ²⁷ He asked them of their welfare, and said, "Is your father well, the old man of whom you spoke? Is he yet alive?"

²⁸ They said, "Your servant, our father, is well. He is still alive." They bowed down humbly. ²⁹ He lifted up his eyes, and saw Benjamin, his brother, his mother's son, and said, "Is this your youngest brother, of whom you spoke to me?" He said, "God be gracious to you, my son." ³⁰ Joseph hurried, for his heart yearned over his brother; and he sought a place to weep. He entered into his room, and wept there. ³¹ He washed his face, and came out. He controlled himself, and said, "Serve the meal."

³² They served him by himself, and them by themselves, and the Egyptians who ate with him by themselves, because

the Egyptians don't eat with the Hebrews, for that is an abomination to the Egyptians.[33] They sat before him, the firstborn according to his birthright, and the youngest according to his youth, and the men marveled with one another. [34] He sent portions to them from before him, but Benjamin's portion was five times as much as any of theirs. They drank, and were merry with him.

44

[1] He commanded the steward of his house, saying, "Fill the men's sacks with food, as much as they can carry, and put each man's money in his sack's mouth. [2] Put my cup, the silver cup, in the sack's mouth of the youngest, with his grain money." He did according to the word that Joseph had spoken. [3] As soon as the morning was light, the men were sent away, they and their donkeys. [4] When they had gone out of the city, and were not yet far off, Joseph said to his steward, "Up, follow after the men. When you overtake them, ask them, 'Why have you rewarded evil for good? [5] Isn't this that from which my lord drinks, and by which he indeed divines? You have done evil in so doing.'" [6] He overtook them, and he spoke these words to them.

[7] They said to him, "Why does my lord speak such words as these? Far be it from your servants that they should do such a thing! [8] Behold, the money, which we found in our sacks' mouths, we brought again to you out of the land of Canaan. How then should we steal silver or gold out of your lord's house? [9] With whomever of your servants it is found, let him die, and we also will be my lord's slaves."

[10] He said, "Now also let it be according to your words. He with whom it is found will be my slave; and you will be blameless."

[11] Then they hurried, and each man took his sack down to the ground, and each man opened his sack. [12] He searched, beginning with the oldest, and ending at the youngest. The cup was found in Benjamin's sack.[13] Then they tore their clothes, and each man loaded his donkey, and returned to the city.

[14] Judah and his brothers came to Joseph's house, and he was still there. They fell on the ground before him. [15] Joseph said to them, "What deed is this that you have done? Don't you know that such a man as I can indeed do divination?"

[16] Judah said, "What will we tell my lord? What will we speak? How will we clear ourselves? God has found out the iniquity of your servants. Behold, we are my lord's slaves, both we and he also in whose hand the cup is found."

[17] He said, "Far be it from me that I should do so. The man in whose hand the cup is found, he will be my slave; but as for you, go up in peace to your father."

[18] Then Judah came near to him, and said, "Oh, my lord, please let your servant speak a word in my lord's ears, and don't let your anger burn against your servant; for you are even as Pharaoh. [19] My lord asked his servants, saying, 'Have you a father, or a brother?' [20] We said to my lord, 'We have a father, an old man, and a child of his old age, a little one; and his brother is dead, and he alone is left of his mother; and his father loves him.' [21] You said to your servants, 'Bring him down to me, that I may set my eyes on him.' [22] We said to my lord, 'The boy can't leave his father, for if he should leave his father, his father would die.' [23] You said to your servants, 'Unless your youngest brother comes down with you, you will see my face no more.' [24] When we came up to your servant my father, we told him the words of my lord. [25] Our father said, 'Go again and buy us a little food.' [26] We said, 'We can't go down. If our youngest brother is with us, then we will go down: for we may not see the man's face, unless our youngest brother is with us.' [27] Your servant, my father, said to us, 'You know that my wife bore me two sons. [28] One went out from me, and I said, "Surely he is torn in pieces;" and I haven't seen him since. [29] If you take this one also from me, and harm happens to him, you will bring down my gray hairs with sorrow to Sheol." [30] Now therefore when I come to your servant my father, and the boy is not with us; since his life is bound up in the boy's life; [31] it will happen, when he sees that the boy is no more, that he will die. Your servants will bring down the gray hairs of your servant, our father, with sorrow to Sheol.[†] [32] For your servant became collateral for the boy to my father, saying, 'If I don't bring him to you, then I will bear the blame to my father forever.' [33] Now therefore, please let your servant stay instead of the boy, my lord's slave; and let the boy go up with his brothers. [34] For how will I go up to my father, if the boy isn't with me?—lest I see the evil that will come on my father."

45

[1] Then Joseph couldn't control himself before all those who stood before him, and he called out, "Cause everyone to go out from me!" No one else stood with him, while Joseph made himself known to his brothers.[2] He wept aloud. The Egyptians heard, and the house of Pharaoh heard. [3] Joseph said to his brothers, "I am Joseph! Does my father still live?"

His brothers couldn't answer him; for they were terrified at his presence. [4] Joseph said to his brothers, "Come near to me, please."

They came near. He said, "I am Joseph, your brother, whom you sold into Egypt. [5] Now don't be grieved, nor angry with yourselves, that you sold me here, for God sent me before you to preserve life. ⁶ For these two years the famine has been in the land, and there are yet five years, in which there will be no plowing and no harvest. ⁷ God sent me before you to preserve for you a remnant in the earth, and to save you alive by a great deliverance. ⁸ So now it wasn't you who sent me here, but God, and he has made me a father to Pharaoh, lord of all his house, and ruler over all the land of Egypt. ⁹ Hurry, and go up to my father, and tell him, 'This is what your son Joseph says, "God has made me lord of all Egypt. Come down to me. Don't wait. ¹⁰ You shall dwell in the land of Goshen, and you will be near to me, you, your children, your children's children, your flocks, your herds, and all that you have. ¹¹ There I will provide for you; for there are yet five years of famine; lest you come to poverty, you, and your household, and all that you have." ' ¹² Behold, your eyes see, and the eyes of my brother Benjamin, that it is my mouth that speaks to you. ¹³ You shall tell my father of all my glory in Egypt, and of all that you have seen. You shall hurry and bring my father down here." ¹⁴ He fell on his brother Benjamin's neck and wept, and Benjamin wept on his neck. ¹⁵ He kissed all his brothers, and wept on them. After that his brothers talked with him.

¹⁶ The report of it was heard in Pharaoh's house, saying, "Joseph's brothers have come." It pleased Pharaoh well, and his servants. ¹⁷ Pharaoh said to Joseph, "Tell your brothers, 'Do this: Load your animals, and go, travel to the land of Canaan. ¹⁸ Take your father and your households, and come to me, and I will give you the good of the land of Egypt, and you will eat the fat of the land.' ¹⁹ Now you are commanded to do this: Take wagons out of the land of Egypt for your little ones, and for your wives, and bring your father, and come. ²⁰ Also, don't concern yourselves about your belongings, for the good of all the land of Egypt is yours."

²¹ The sons of Israel did so. Joseph gave them wagons, according to the commandment of Pharaoh, and gave them provision for the way. ²² He gave each one of them changes of clothing, but to Benjamin he gave three hundred pieces of silver and five changes of clothing. ²³ He sent the following to his father: ten donkeys loaded with the good things of Egypt, and ten female donkeys loaded with grain and bread and provision for his father by the way. ²⁴ So he sent his brothers away, and they departed. He said to them, "See that you don't quarrel on the way."

²⁵ They went up out of Egypt, and came into the land of Canaan, to Jacob their father. ²⁶ They told him, saying, "Joseph is still alive, and he is ruler over all the land of Egypt." His heart fainted, for he didn't believe them. ²⁷ They told him all the words of Joseph, which he had said to them. When he saw the wagons which Joseph had sent to carry him, the spirit of Jacob, their father, revived. ²⁸ Israel said, "It is enough. Joseph my son is still alive. I will go and see him before I die."

46

¹ Israel traveled with all that he had, and came to Beersheba, and offered sacrifices to the God of his father, Isaac. ² God spoke to Israel in the visions of the night, and said, "Jacob, Jacob!"

He said, "Here I am."

³ He said, "I am God, the God of your father. Don't be afraid to go down into Egypt, for there I will make of you a great nation. ⁴ I will go with you into Egypt. I will also surely bring you up again. Joseph's hand will close your eyes."

⁵ Jacob rose up from Beersheba, and the sons of Israel carried Jacob, their father, their little ones, and their wives, in the wagons which Pharaoh had sent to carry him. ⁶ They took their livestock, and their goods, which they had gotten in the land of Canaan, and came into Egypt—Jacob, and all his offspring with him, ⁷ his sons, and his sons' sons with him, his daughters, and his sons' daughters, and he brought all his offspring with him into Egypt.

⁸ These are the names of the children of Israel, who came into Egypt, Jacob and his sons: Reuben, Jacob's firstborn. ⁹ The sons of Reuben: Hanoch, Pallu, Hezron, and Carmi. ¹⁰ The sons of Simeon: Jemuel, Jamin, Ohad, Jachin, Zohar, and Shaul the son of a Canaanite woman. ¹¹ The sons of Levi: Gershon, Kohath, and Merari. ¹² The sons of Judah: Er, Onan, Shelah, Perez, and Zerah; but Er and Onan died in the land of Canaan. The sons of Perez were Hezron and Hamul. ¹³ The sons of Issachar: Tola, Puvah, Iob, and Shimron. ¹⁴ The sons of Zebulun: Sered, Elon, and Jahleel. ¹⁵ These are the sons of Leah, whom she bore to Jacob in Paddan Aram, with his daughter Dinah. All the souls of his sons and his daughters were thirty-three. ¹⁶ The sons of Gad: Ziphion, Haggi, Shuni, Ezbon, Eri, Arodi, and Areli. ¹⁷ The sons of Asher: Imnah, Ishvah, Ishvi, Beriah, and Serah their sister. The sons of Beriah: Heber and Malchiel. ¹⁸ These are the sons of Zilpah, whom Laban gave to Leah, his daughter, and these she bore to Jacob, even sixteen souls. ¹⁹ The sons of Rachel, Jacob's wife: Joseph and Benjamin. ²⁰ To Joseph in the land of Egypt were born Manasseh and Ephraim, whom Asenath, the daughter of Potiphera, priest of On, bore to him. ²¹ The sons of Benjamin: Bela, Becher, Ashbel, Gera, Naaman, Ehi, Rosh, Muppim, Huppim, and Ard. ²² These are the sons of Rachel, who were born to Jacob: all the souls were fourteen. ²³ The son of Dan: Hushim. ²⁴ The sons of Naphtali: Jahzeel, Guni, Jezer, and Shillem. ²⁵ These are the sons of Bilhah, whom Laban gave to Rachel, his daughter,

and these she bore to Jacob: all the souls were seven. ²⁶ All the souls who came with Jacob into Egypt, who were his direct offspring, in addition to Jacob's sons' wives, all the souls were sixty-six. ²⁷ The sons of Joseph, who were born to him in Egypt, were two souls. All the souls of the house of Jacob, who came into Egypt, were seventy.

²⁸ Jacob sent Judah before him to Joseph, to show the way before him to Goshen, and they came into the land of Goshen. ²⁹ Joseph prepared his chariot, and went up to meet Israel, his father, in Goshen. He presented himself to him, and fell on his neck, and wept on his neck a good while. ³⁰ Israel said to Joseph, "Now let me die, since I have seen your face, that you are still alive."

³¹ Joseph said to his brothers, and to his father's house, "I will go up, and speak with Pharaoh, and will tell him, 'My brothers, and my father's house, who were in the land of Canaan, have come to me. ³² These men are shepherds, for they have been keepers of livestock, and they have brought their flocks, and their herds, and all that they have.' ³³ It will happen, when Pharaoh summons you, and will say, 'What is your occupation?' ³⁴ that you shall say, 'Your servants have been keepers of livestock from our youth even until now, both we, and our fathers:' that you may dwell in the land of Goshen; for every shepherd is an abomination to the Egyptians."

47

¹ Then Joseph went in and told Pharaoh, and said, "My father and my brothers, with their flocks, their herds, and all that they own, have come out of the land of Canaan; and behold, they are in the land of Goshen."² From among his brothers he took five men, and presented them to Pharaoh. ³ Pharaoh said to his brothers, "What is your occupation?"

They said to Pharaoh, "Your servants are shepherds, both we, and our fathers." ⁴ They also said to Pharaoh, "We have come to live as foreigners in the land, for there is no pasture for your servants' flocks. For the famine is severe in the land of Canaan. Now therefore, please let your servants dwell in the land of Goshen."

⁵ Pharaoh spoke to Joseph, saying, "Your father and your brothers have come to you. ⁶ The land of Egypt is before you. Make your father and your brothers dwell in the best of the land. Let them dwell in the land of Goshen. If you know any able men among them, then put them in charge of my livestock."

⁷ Joseph brought in Jacob, his father, and set him before Pharaoh; and Jacob blessed Pharaoh. ⁸ Pharaoh said to Jacob, "How old are you?"

⁹ Jacob said to Pharaoh, "The years of my pilgrimage are one hundred thirty years. The days of the years of my life have been few and evil. They have not attained to the days of the years of the life of my fathers in the days of their pilgrimage." ¹⁰ Jacob blessed Pharaoh, and went out from the presence of Pharaoh.

¹¹ Joseph placed his father and his brothers, and gave them a possession in the land of Egypt, in the best of the land, in the land of Rameses, as Pharaoh had commanded. ¹² Joseph provided his father, his brothers, and all of his father's household with bread, according to the sizes of their families.

¹³ There was no bread in all the land; for the famine was very severe, so that the land of Egypt and the land of Canaan fainted by reason of the famine. ¹⁴ Joseph gathered up all the money that was found in the land of Egypt, and in the land of Canaan, for the grain which they bought: and Joseph brought the money into Pharaoh's house. ¹⁵ When the money was all spent in the land of Egypt, and in the land of Canaan, all the Egyptians came to Joseph, and said, "Give us bread, for why should we die in your presence? For our money fails."

¹⁶ Joseph said, "Give me your livestock; and I will give you food for your livestock, if your money is gone."

¹⁷ They brought their livestock to Joseph, and Joseph gave them bread in exchange for the horses, and for the flocks, and for the herds, and for the donkeys: and he fed them with bread in exchange for all their livestock for that year. ¹⁸ When that year was ended, they came to him the second year, and said to him, "We will not hide from my lord how our money is all spent, and the herds of livestock are my lord's. There is nothing left in the sight of my lord, but our bodies, and our lands. ¹⁹ Why should we die before your eyes, both we and our land? Buy us and our land for bread, and we and our land will be servants to Pharaoh. Give us seed, that we may live, and not die, and that the land won't be desolate."

²⁰ So Joseph bought all the land of Egypt for Pharaoh, for every man of the Egyptians sold his field, because the famine was severe on them, and the land became Pharaoh's. ²¹ As for the people, he moved them to the cities from one end of the border of Egypt even to the other end of it. ²² Only he didn't buy the land of the priests, for the priests had a portion from Pharaoh, and ate their portion which Pharaoh gave them. That is why they didn't sell their land. ²³ Then Joseph said to the people, "Behold, I have bought you and your land today for Pharaoh. Behold, here is seed for you, and you shall sow the land. ²⁴ It will happen at the harvests, that you shall give a fifth to Pharaoh, and four parts will be your own, for seed of the field, for your food, for them of your households, and for food for your little ones."

²⁵ They said, "You have saved our lives! Let us find favor in the sight of my lord, and we will be Pharaoh's servants."

26 Joseph made it a statute concerning the land of Egypt to this day, that Pharaoh should have the fifth. Only the land of the priests alone didn't become Pharaoh's.

27 Israel lived in the land of Egypt, in the land of Goshen; and they got themselves possessions therein, and were fruitful, and multiplied exceedingly. 28 Jacob lived in the land of Egypt seventeen years. So the days of Jacob, the years of his life, were one hundred forty-seven years. 29 The time came near that Israel must die, and he called his son Joseph, and said to him, "If now I have found favor in your sight, please put your hand under my thigh, and deal kindly and truly with me. Please don't bury me in Egypt, 30 but when I sleep with my fathers, you shall carry me out of Egypt, and bury me in their burying place."

Joseph said, "I will do as you have said."

31 Israel said, "Swear to me," and he swore to him. Then Israel bowed himself on the bed's head.

48

1 After these things, someone said to Joseph, "Behold, your father is sick." He took with him his two sons, Manasseh and Ephraim. 2 Someone told Jacob, and said, "Behold, your son Joseph comes to you," and Israel strengthened himself, and sat on the bed. 3 Jacob said to Joseph, "God Almighty appeared to me at Luz in the land of Canaan, and blessed me, 4 and said to me, 'Behold, I will make you fruitful, and multiply you, and I will make of you a company of peoples, and will give this land to your offspring after you for an everlasting possession.' 5 Now your two sons, who were born to you in the land of Egypt before I came to you into Egypt, are mine; Ephraim and Manasseh, even as Reuben and Simeon, will be mine. 6 Your offspring, whom you become the father of after them, will be yours. They will be called after the name of their brothers in their inheritance. 7 As for me, when I came from Paddan, Rachel died beside me in the land of Canaan on the way, when there was still some distance to come to Ephrath, and I buried her there on the way to Ephrath (also called Bethlehem)."

8 Israel saw Joseph's sons, and said, "Who are these?"

9 Joseph said to his father, "They are my sons, whom God has given me here."

He said, "Please bring them to me, and I will bless them." 10 Now the eyes of Israel were dim for age, so that he couldn't see well. Joseph brought them near to him; and he kissed them, and embraced them. 11 Israel said to Joseph, "I didn't think I would see your face, and behold, God has let me see your offspring also." 12 Joseph brought them out from between his knees, and he bowed himself with his face to the earth. 13 Joseph took them both, Ephraim in his right hand toward Israel's left hand, and Manasseh in his left hand toward Israel's right hand, and brought them near to him. 14 Israel stretched out his right hand, and laid it on Ephraim's head, who was the younger, and his left hand on Manasseh's head, guiding his hands knowingly, for Manasseh was the firstborn. 15 He blessed Joseph, and said,

"The God before whom my fathers Abraham and Isaac walked,
the God who has fed me all my life long to this day,
16 the angel who has redeemed me from all evil, bless the lads,
and let my name be named on them,
and the name of my fathers Abraham and Isaac.
Let them grow into a multitude upon the earth."

17 When Joseph saw that his father laid his right hand on the head of Ephraim, it displeased him. He held up his father's hand, to remove it from Ephraim's head to Manasseh's head. 18 Joseph said to his father, "Not so, my father, for this is the firstborn. Put your right hand on his head."

19 His father refused, and said, "I know, my son, I know. He also will become a people, and he also will be great. However, his younger brother will be greater than he, and his offspring will become a multitude of nations." 20 He blessed them that day, saying, "Israel will bless in you, saying, 'God make you as Ephraim and as Manasseh'" He set Ephraim before Manasseh. 21 Israel said to Joseph, "Behold, I am dying, but God will be with you, and bring you again to the land of your fathers. 22 Moreover I have given to you one portion above your brothers, which I took out of the hand of the Amorite with my sword and with my bow."

49

1 Jacob called to his sons, and said: "Gather yourselves together, that I may tell you that which will happen to you in the days to come.

2 Assemble yourselves, and hear, you sons of Jacob.
Listen to Israel, your father.

3 "Reuben, you are my firstborn, my might, and the beginning of my strength;
excelling in dignity, and excelling in power.
4 Boiling over like water, you shall not excel;
because you went up to your father's bed,
then defiled it. He went up to my couch.

5 "Simeon and Levi are brothers.
Their swords are weapons of violence.
6 My soul, don't come into their council.

My glory, don't be united to their assembly;
for in their anger they killed men.
In their self-will they hamstrung cattle.
⁷ Cursed be their anger, for it was fierce;
and their wrath, for it was cruel.
I will divide them in Jacob,
and scatter them in Israel.

⁸ "Judah, your brothers will praise you.
Your hand will be on the neck of your enemies.
Your father's sons will bow down before you.
⁹ Judah is a lion's cub.
From the prey, my son, you have gone up.
He stooped down, he crouched as a lion,
as a lioness.
Who will rouse him up?
¹⁰ The scepter will not depart from Judah,
nor the ruler's staff from between his feet,
until he comes to whom it belongs.
To him will the obedience of the peoples be.
¹¹ Binding his foal to the vine,
his donkey's colt to the choice vine;
he has washed his garments in wine,
his robes in the blood of grapes.
¹² His eyes will be red with wine,
his teeth white with milk.

¹³ "Zebulun will dwell at the haven of the sea.
He will be for a haven of ships.
His border will be on Sidon.

¹⁴ "Issachar is a strong donkey,
lying down between the saddlebags.
¹⁵ He saw a resting place, that it was good,
the land, that it was pleasant.
He bows his shoulder to the burden,
and becomes a servant doing forced labor.

¹⁶ "Dan will judge his people,
as one of the tribes of Israel.
¹⁷ Dan will be a serpent on the trail,
an adder in the path,
That bites the horse's heels,
so that his rider falls backward.
¹⁸ I have waited for your salvation, Yahweh.

¹⁹ "A troop will press on Gad,
but he will press on their heel.

²⁰ "Asher's food will be rich.

He will produce royal dainties.

²¹ "Naphtali is a doe set free,
who bears beautiful fawns.

²² "Joseph is a fruitful vine,
a fruitful vine by a spring.
His branches run over the wall.
²³ The archers have severely grieved him,
shot at him, and persecuted him:
²⁴ But his bow remained strong.
The arms of his hands were made strong,
by the hands of the Mighty One of Jacob,
(from there is the shepherd, the stone of Israel),
²⁵ even by the God of your father, who will help you,
by the Almighty, who will bless you,
with blessings of heaven above,
blessings of the deep that lies below,
blessings of the breasts, and of the womb.
²⁶ The blessings of your father have prevailed above the blessings of your ancestors,
above the boundaries of the ancient hills.
They will be on the head of Joseph,
on the crown of the head of him who is separated from his brothers.

²⁷ "Benjamin is a ravenous wolf.
In the morning he will devour the prey.
At evening he will divide the plunder."

²⁸ All these are the twelve tribes of Israel, and this is what their father spoke to them, and blessed them. He blessed everyone according to his own blessing. ²⁹ He instructed them, and said to them, "I am to be gathered to my people. Bury me with my fathers in the cave that is in the field of Ephron the Hittite, ³⁰ in the cave that is in the field of Machpelah, which is before Mamre, in the land of Canaan, which Abraham bought with the field from Ephron the Hittite as a burial place. ³¹ There they buried Abraham and Sarah, his wife. There they buried Isaac and Rebekah, his wife, and there I buried Leah: ³² the field and the cave that is therein, which was purchased from the children of Heth." ³³ When Jacob finished charging his sons, he gathered up his feet into the bed, breathed his last breath, and was gathered to his people.

50

¹ Joseph fell on his father's face, wept on him, and kissed him. ² Joseph commanded his servants, the physicians, to embalm his father; and the physicians embalmed Israel. ³ Forty

days were used for him, for that is how many the days it takes to embalm. The Egyptians wept for Israel for seventy days.

⁴ When the days of weeping for him were past, Joseph spoke to Pharaoh's staff, saying, "If now I have found favor in your eyes, please speak in the ears of Pharaoh, saying, ⁵ 'My father made me swear, saying, "Behold, I am dying. Bury me in my grave which I have dug for myself in the land of Canaan." Now therefore, please let me go up and bury my father, and I will come again.' "

⁶ Pharaoh said, "Go up, and bury your father, just like he made you swear."

⁷ Joseph went up to bury his father; and with him went up all the servants of Pharaoh, the elders of his house, all the elders of the land of Egypt, ⁸ All the house of Joseph, his brothers, and his father's house. Only their little ones, their flocks, and their herds, they left in the land of Goshen. ⁹ There went up with him both chariots and horsemen. It was a very great company. ¹⁰ They came to the threshing floor of Atad, which is beyond the Jordan, and there they lamented with a very great and severe lamentation. He mourned for his father seven days. ¹¹ When the inhabitants of the land, the Canaanites, saw the mourning in the floor of Atad, they said, "This is a grievous mourning by the Egyptians." Therefore its name was called Abel Mizraim, which is beyond the Jordan. ¹² His sons did to him just as he commanded them, ¹³ for his sons carried him into the land of Canaan, and buried him in the cave of the field of Machpelah, which Abraham bought with the field, as a possession for a burial site, from Ephron the Hittite, near Mamre. ¹⁴ Joseph returned into Egypt—he, and his brothers, and all that went up with him to bury his father, after he had buried his father.

¹⁵ When Joseph's brothers saw that their father was dead, they said, "It may be that Joseph will hate us, and will fully pay us back for all the evil which we did to him." ¹⁶ They sent a message to Joseph, saying, "Your father commanded before he died, saying, ¹⁷ 'You shall tell Joseph, "Now please forgive the disobedience of your brothers, and their sin, because they did evil to you." ' Now, please forgive the disobedience of the servants of the God of your father." Joseph wept when they spoke to him. ¹⁸ His brothers also went and fell down before his face; and they said, "Behold, we are your servants." ¹⁹ Joseph said to them, "Don't be afraid, for am I in the place of God? ²⁰ As for you, you meant evil against me, but God meant it for good, to save many people alive, as is happening today. ²¹ Now therefore don't be afraid. I will provide for you and your little ones." He comforted them, and spoke kindly to them.

²² Joseph lived in Egypt, he, and his father's house. Joseph lived one hundred ten years. ²³ Joseph saw Ephraim's children to the third generation. The children also of Machir, the son of Manasseh, were born on Joseph's knees. ²⁴ Joseph said to his brothers, "I am dying, but God will surely visit you, and bring you up out of this land to the land which he swore to Abraham, to Isaac, and to Jacob." ²⁵ Joseph took an oath from the children of Israel, saying, "God will surely visit you, and you shall carry up my bones from here." ²⁶ So Joseph died, being one hundred ten years old, and they embalmed him, and he was put in a coffin in Egypt.

Text Twenty-two

Exodus

1

[1] Now these are the names of the sons of Israel, who came into Egypt (every man and his household came with Jacob): [2] Reuben, Simeon, Levi, and Judah, [3] Issachar, Zebulun, and Benjamin, [4] Dan and Naphtali, Gad and Asher. [5] All the souls who came out of Jacob's body were seventy souls, and Joseph was in Egypt already. [6] Joseph died, as did all his brothers, and all that generation. [7] The children of Israel were fruitful, and increased abundantly, and multiplied, and grew exceedingly mighty; and the land was filled with them.

[8] Now there arose a new king over Egypt, who didn't know Joseph. [9] He said to his people, "Behold, the people of the children of Israel are more and mightier than we. [10] Come, let's deal wisely with them, lest they multiply, and it happen that when any war breaks out, they also join themselves to our enemies and fight against us, and escape out of the land." [11] Therefore they set taskmasters over them, to afflict them with their burdens. They built storage cities for Pharaoh: Pithom and Raamses. [12] But the more they afflicted them, the more they multiplied and the more they spread out. They started to dread the children of Israel. [13] The Egyptians ruthlessly made the children of Israel serve, [14] and they made their lives bitter with hard service in mortar and in brick, and in all kinds of service in the field, all their service, in which they ruthlessly made them serve.

[15] The king of Egypt spoke to the Hebrew midwives, of whom the name of the one was Shiphrah, and the name of the other Puah, [16] and he said, "When you perform the duty of a midwife to the Hebrew women, and see them on the birth stool, if it is a son, then you shall kill him; but if it is a daughter, then she shall live." [17] But the midwives feared God,† and didn't do what the king of Egypt commanded them, but saved the baby boys alive. [18] The king of Egypt called for the midwives, and said to them, "Why have you done this thing and saved the boys alive?"

[19] The midwives said to Pharaoh, "Because the Hebrew women aren't like the Egyptian women; for they are vigorous and give birth before the midwife comes to them."

[20] God dealt well with the midwives, and the people multiplied, and grew very mighty. [21] Because the midwives feared God, he gave them families. [22] Pharaoh commanded all his people, saying, "You shall cast every son who is born into the river, and every daughter you shall save alive."

2

[1] A man of the house of Levi went and took a daughter of Levi as his wife. [2] The woman conceived and bore a son. When she saw that he was a fine child, she hid him three months. [3] When she could no longer hide him, she took a papyrus basket for him, and coated it with tar and with pitch. She put the child in it, and laid it in the reeds by the river's bank. [4] His sister stood far off, to see what would be done to him. [5] Pharaoh's daughter came down to bathe at the river. Her maidens walked along by the riverside. She saw the basket among the reeds, and sent her servant to get it. [6] She opened it, and saw the child, and behold, the baby cried. She had compassion on him, and said, "This is one of the Hebrews' children."

[7] Then his sister said to Pharaoh's daughter, "Should I go and call a nurse for you from the Hebrew women, that she may nurse the child for you?"

[8] Pharaoh's daughter said to her, "Go."

The young woman went and called the child's mother. [9] Pharaoh's daughter said to her, "Take this child away, and nurse him for me, and I will give you your wages."

The woman took the child, and nursed it. [10] The child grew, and she brought him to Pharaoh's daughter, and he became her son. She named him Moses,* and said, "Because I drew him out of the water."

[11] In those days, when Moses had grown up, he went out to his brothers and saw their burdens. He saw an Egyptian striking a Hebrew, one of his brothers. [12] He looked this way and that way, and when he saw that there was no one, he killed the Egyptian, and hid him in the sand.

[13] He went out the second day, and behold, two men of the Hebrews were fighting with each other. He said to him who did the wrong, "Why do you strike your fellow?"

[14] He said, "Who made you a prince and a judge over us? Do you plan to kill me, as you killed the Egyptian?"

Moses was afraid, and said, "Surely this thing is known." [15] Now when Pharaoh heard this thing, he sought to kill Moses. But Moses fled from the face of Pharaoh, and lived in the land of Midian, and he sat down by a well.

[16] Now the priest of Midian had seven daughters. They came and drew water, and filled the troughs to water their father's flock. [17] The shepherds came and drove them away; but Moses stood up and helped them, and watered their flock. [18] When they came to Reuel, their father, he said, "How is it that you have returned so early today?"

[19] They said, "An Egyptian delivered us out of the hand of the shepherds, and moreover he drew water for us, and watered the flock."

[20] He said to his daughters, "Where is he? Why is it that you have left the man? Call him, that he may eat bread."

[21] Moses was content to dwell with the man. He gave Moses Zipporah, his daughter. [22] She bore a son, and he named him Gershom,† for he said, "I have lived as a foreigner in a foreign land."

[23] In the course of those many days, the king of Egypt died, and the children of Israel sighed because of the bondage, and they cried, and their cry came up to God because of the bondage. [24] God heard their groaning, and God remembered his covenant with Abraham, with Isaac, and with Jacob. [25] God saw the children of Israel, and God was concerned about them.

3

[1] Now Moses was keeping the flock of Jethro, his father-in-law, the priest of Midian, and he led the flock to the back of the wilderness, and came to God's mountain, to Horeb. [2] Yahweh's* angel appeared to him in a flame of fire out of the middle of a bush. He looked, and behold, the bush burned with fire, and the bush was not consumed. [3] Moses said, "I will go now, and see this great sight, why the bush is not burned."

[4] When Yahweh saw that he came over to see, God called to him out of the middle of the bush, and said, "Moses! Moses!"

He said, "Here I am."

[5] He said, "Don't come close. Take off your sandals, for the place you are standing on is holy ground."[6] Moreover he said, "I am the God of your father, the God of Abraham, the God of Isaac, and the God of Jacob."

Moses hid his face because he was afraid to look at God.

[7] Yahweh said, "I have surely seen the affliction of my people who are in Egypt, and have heard their cry because of their taskmasters, for I know their sorrows. [8] I have come down to deliver them out of the hand of the Egyptians, and to bring them up out of that land to a good and large land, to a land flowing with milk and honey; to the place of the Canaanite, the Hittite, the Amorite, the Perizzite, the Hivite, and the Jebusite. [9] Now, behold, the cry of the children of Israel has come to me. Moreover I have seen the oppression with which the Egyptians oppress them. [10] Come now therefore, and I will send you to Pharaoh, that you may bring my people, the children of Israel, out of Egypt."

[11] Moses said to God, "Who am I, that I should go to Pharaoh, and that I should bring the children of Israel out of Egypt?"

[12] He said, "Certainly I will be with you. This will be the token to you, that I have sent you: when you have brought the people out of Egypt, you shall serve God on this mountain."

[13] Moses said to God, "Behold, when I come to the children of Israel, and tell them, 'The God of your fathers has sent me to you,' and they ask me, 'What is his name?' what should I tell them?"

[14] God said to Moses, "I AM WHO I AM," and he said, "You shall tell the children of Israel this: 'I AM has sent me to you.'" [15] God said moreover to Moses, "You shall tell the children of Israel this, 'Yahweh, the God of your fathers, the God of Abraham, the God of Isaac, and the God of Jacob, has sent me to you.' This is my name forever, and this is my memorial to all generations. [16] Go and gather the elders of Israel together, and tell them, 'Yahweh, the God of your fathers, the God of Abraham, of Isaac, and of Jacob, has appeared to me, saying, "I have surely visited you, and seen that which is done to you in Egypt. [17] I have said, I will bring you up out of the affliction of Egypt to the land of the Canaanite, the Hittite, the Amorite, the Perizzite, the Hivite, and the Jebusite, to a land flowing with milk and honey." ' [18] They will listen to your voice. You shall come, you and the elders of Israel, to the king of Egypt, and you shall tell him, 'Yahweh, the God of the Hebrews, has met with us. Now please let us go three days' journey into the wilderness, that we may sacrifice to Yahweh, our God.' [19] I

know that the king of Egypt won't give you permission to go, no, not by a mighty hand. ²⁰ I will reach out my hand and strike Egypt with all my wonders which I will do among them, and after that he will let you go. ²¹ I will give this people favor in the sight of the Egyptians, and it will happen that when you go, you shall not go empty-handed. ²² But every woman shall ask of her neighbor, and of her who visits her house, jewels of silver, jewels of gold, and clothing. You shall put them on your sons, and on your daughters. You shall plunder the Egyptians."

4

¹ Moses answered, "But, behold, they will not believe me, nor listen to my voice; for they will say, 'Yahweh has not appeared to you.'"

² Yahweh said to him, "What is that in your hand?"

He said, "A rod."

³ He said, "Throw it on the ground."

He threw it on the ground, and it became a snake; and Moses ran away from it.

⁴ Yahweh said to Moses, "Stretch out your hand, and take it by the tail."

He stretched out his hand, and took hold of it, and it became a rod in his hand.

⁵ "This is so that they may believe that Yahweh, the God of their fathers, the God of Abraham, the God of Isaac, and the God of Jacob, has appeared to you." ⁶ Yahweh said furthermore to him, "Now put your hand inside your cloak."

He put his hand inside his cloak, and when he took it out, behold, his hand was leprous, as white as snow.

⁷ He said, "Put your hand inside your cloak again."

He put his hand inside his cloak again, and when he took it out of his cloak, behold, it had turned again as his other flesh.

⁸ "It will happen, if they will not believe you or listen to the voice of the first sign, that they will believe the voice of the latter sign. ⁹ It will happen, if they will not believe even these two signs or listen to your voice, that you shall take of the water of the river, and pour it on the dry land. The water which you take out of the river will become blood on the dry land."

¹⁰ Moses said to Yahweh, "O Lord, I am not eloquent, neither before now, nor since you have spoken to your servant; for I am slow of speech, and of a slow tongue."

¹¹ Yahweh said to him, "Who made man's mouth? Or who makes one mute, or deaf, or seeing, or blind? Isn't it I, Yahweh? ¹² Now therefore go, and I will be with your mouth, and teach you what you shall speak."

¹³ Moses said, "Oh, Lord, please send someone else."

¹⁴ Yahweh's anger burned against Moses, and he said, "What about Aaron, your brother, the Levite? I know that he can speak well. Also, behold, he is coming out to meet you. When he sees you, he will be glad in his heart. ¹⁵ You shall speak to him, and put the words in his mouth. I will be with your mouth, and with his mouth, and will teach you what you shall do. ¹⁶ He will be your spokesman to the people. It will happen that he will be to you a mouth, and you will be to him as God. ¹⁷ You shall take this rod in your hand, with which you shall do the signs."

¹⁸ Moses went and returned to Jethro his father-in-law, and said to him, "Please let me go and return to my brothers who are in Egypt, and see whether they are still alive."

Jethro said to Moses, "Go in peace."

¹⁹ Yahweh said to Moses in Midian, "Go, return into Egypt; for all the men who sought your life are dead."

²⁰ Moses took his wife and his sons, and set them on a donkey, and he returned to the land of Egypt. Moses took God's rod in his hand. ²¹ Yahweh said to Moses, "When you go back into Egypt, see that you do before Pharaoh all the wonders which I have put in your hand, but I will harden his heart and he will not let the people go. ²² You shall tell Pharaoh, 'Yahweh says, Israel is my son, my firstborn, ²³ and I have said to you, "Let my son go, that he may serve me;" and you have refused to let him go. Behold, I will kill your firstborn son.'"

²⁴ On the way at a lodging place, Yahweh met Moses and wanted to kill him. ²⁵ Then Zipporah took a flint, and cut off the foreskin of her son, and cast it at his feet; and she said, "Surely you are a bridegroom of blood to me."

²⁶ So he let him alone. Then she said, "You are a bridegroom of blood," because of the circumcision.

²⁷ Yahweh said to Aaron, "Go into the wilderness to meet Moses."

He went, and met him on God's mountain, and kissed him. ²⁸ Moses told Aaron all Yahweh's words with which he had sent him, and all the signs with which he had instructed him. ²⁹ Moses and Aaron went and gathered together all the elders of the children of Israel. ³⁰ Aaron spoke all the words which Yahweh had spoken to Moses, and did the signs in the sight of the people. ³¹ The people believed, and when they heard that Yahweh had visited the children of Israel, and that he had seen their affliction, then they bowed their heads and worshiped.

5

¹ Afterward Moses and Aaron came, and said to Pharaoh, "This is what Yahweh, the God of Israel, says,

'Let my people go, that they may hold a feast to me in the wilderness.' "

² Pharaoh said, "Who is Yahweh, that I should listen to his voice to let Israel go? I don't know Yahweh, and moreover I will not let Israel go."

³ They said, "The God of the Hebrews has met with us. Please let us go three days' journey into the wilderness, and sacrifice to Yahweh, our God, lest he fall on us with pestilence, or with the sword."

⁴ The king of Egypt said to them, "Why do you, Moses and Aaron, take the people from their work? Get back to your burdens!" ⁵ Pharaoh said, "Behold, the people of the land are now many, and you make them rest from their burdens." ⁶ The same day Pharaoh commanded the taskmasters of the people and their officers, saying, ⁷ "You shall no longer give the people straw to make brick, as before. Let them go and gather straw for themselves. ⁸ You shall require from them the number of the bricks which they made before. You shall not diminish anything of it, for they are idle. Therefore they cry, saying, 'Let's go and sacrifice to our God.' ⁹ Let heavier work be laid on the men, that they may labor in it. Don't let them pay any attention to lying words."

¹⁰ The taskmasters of the people went out, and their officers, and they spoke to the people, saying, "This is what Pharaoh says: 'I will not give you straw. ¹¹ Go yourselves, get straw where you can find it, for nothing of your work shall be diminished.'" ¹² So the people were scattered abroad throughout all the land of Egypt to gather stubble for straw. ¹³ The taskmasters were urgent saying, "Fulfill your work quota daily, as when there was straw!" ¹⁴ The officers of the children of Israel, whom Pharaoh's taskmasters had set over them, were beaten, and were asked, "Why haven't you fulfilled your quota both yesterday and today, in making brick as before?"

¹⁵ Then the officers of the children of Israel came and cried to Pharaoh, saying, "Why do you deal this way with your servants? ¹⁶ No straw is given to your servants, and they tell us, 'Make brick!' and behold, your servants are beaten; but the fault is in your own people."

¹⁷ But Pharaoh said, "You are idle! You are idle! Therefore you say, 'Let's go and sacrifice to Yahweh.' ¹⁸ Go therefore now, and work; for no straw shall be given to you; yet you shall deliver the same number of bricks!"

¹⁹ The officers of the children of Israel saw that they were in trouble when it was said, "You shall not diminish anything from your daily quota of bricks!"

²⁰ They met Moses and Aaron, who stood along the way, as they came out from Pharaoh. ²¹ They said to them, "May Yahweh look at you and judge, because you have made us a stench to be abhorred in the eyes of Pharaoh, and in the eyes of his servants, to put a sword in their hand to kill us!"

²² Moses returned to Yahweh, and said, "Lord, why have you brought trouble on this people? Why is it that you have sent me? ²³ For since I came to Pharaoh to speak in your name, he has brought trouble on this people. You have not rescued your people at all!"

6

¹ Yahweh said to Moses, "Now you shall see what I will do to Pharaoh, for by a strong hand he shall let them go, and by a strong hand he shall drive them out of his land."

² God spoke to Moses, and said to him, "I am Yahweh. ³ I appeared to Abraham, to Isaac, and to Jacob, as God Almighty; but by my name Yahweh I was not known to them. ⁴ I have also established my covenant with them, to give them the land of Canaan, the land of their travels, in which they lived as aliens. ⁵ Moreover I have heard the groaning of the children of Israel, whom the Egyptians keep in bondage, and I have remembered my covenant. ⁶ Therefore tell the children of Israel, 'I am Yahweh, and I will bring you out from under the burdens of the Egyptians, and I will rid you out of their bondage, and I will redeem you with an outstretched arm, and with great judgments. ⁷ I will take you to myself for a people. I will be your God; and you shall know that I am Yahweh your God, who brings you out from under the burdens of the Egyptians. ⁸ I will bring you into the land which I swore to give to Abraham, to Isaac, and to Jacob; and I will give it to you for a heritage: I am Yahweh.' "

⁹ Moses spoke so to the children of Israel, but they didn't listen to Moses for anguish of spirit, and for cruel bondage.

¹⁰ Yahweh spoke to Moses, saying, ¹¹ "Go in, speak to Pharaoh king of Egypt, that he let the children of Israel go out of his land."

¹² Moses spoke before Yahweh, saying, "Behold, the children of Israel haven't listened to me. How then shall Pharaoh listen to me, when I have uncircumcised lips?" ¹³ Yahweh spoke to Moses and to Aaron, and gave them a command to the children of Israel, and to Pharaoh king of Egypt, to bring the children of Israel out of the land of Egypt.

¹⁴ These are the heads of their fathers' houses. The sons of Reuben the firstborn of Israel: Hanoch, and Pallu, Hezron, and Carmi; these are the families of Reuben. ¹⁵ The sons of Simeon: Jemuel, and Jamin, and Ohad, and Jachin, and Zohar, and Shaul the son of a Canaanite woman; these are the families of Simeon. ¹⁶ These are the names of the sons of Levi according to their generations: Gershon, and Kohath, and Merari; and the years of the life of Levi were one hundred thirty-seven years. ¹⁷ The sons of Gershon: Libni and Shimei, according to their families. ¹⁸ The sons of Kohath: Amram,

and Izhar, and Hebron, and Uzziel; and the years of the life of Kohath were one hundred thirty-three years. ¹⁹ The sons of Merari: Mahli and Mushi. These are the families of the Levites according to their generations. ²⁰ Amram took Jochebed his father's sister to himself as wife; and she bore him Aaron and Moses. The years of the life of Amram were one hundred thirty-seven years. ²¹ The sons of Izhar: Korah, and Nepheg, and Zichri. ²² The sons of Uzziel: Mishael, and Elzaphan, and Sithri. ²³ Aaron took Elisheba, the daughter of Amminadab, the sister of Nahshon, as his wife; and she bore him Nadab and Abihu, Eleazar and Ithamar. ²⁴ The sons of Korah: Assir, and Elkanah, and Abiasaph; these are the families of the Korahites. ²⁵ Eleazar Aaron's son took one of the daughters of Putiel as his wife; and she bore him Phinehas. These are the heads of the fathers' houses of the Levites according to their families. ²⁶ These are that Aaron and Moses to whom Yahweh said, "Bring out the children of Israel from the land of Egypt according to their armies." ²⁷ These are those who spoke to Pharaoh king of Egypt, to bring out the children of Israel from Egypt. These are that Moses and Aaron.

²⁸ On the day when Yahweh spoke to Moses in the land of Egypt, ²⁹ Yahweh said to Moses, "I am Yahweh. Tell Pharaoh king of Egypt all that I tell you."

³⁰ Moses said before Yahweh, "Behold, I am of uncircumcised lips, and how shall Pharaoh listen to me?"

7

¹ Yahweh said to Moses, "Behold, I have made you as God to Pharaoh; and Aaron your brother shall be your prophet. ² You shall speak all that I command you; and Aaron your brother shall speak to Pharaoh, that he let the children of Israel go out of his land. ³ I will harden Pharaoh's heart, and multiply my signs and my wonders in the land of Egypt. ⁴ But Pharaoh will not listen to you, so I will lay my hand on Egypt, and bring out my armies, my people the children of Israel, out of the land of Egypt by great judgments. ⁵ The Egyptians shall know that I am Yahweh when I stretch out my hand on Egypt, and bring the children of Israel out from among them."

⁶ Moses and Aaron did so. As Yahweh commanded them, so they did. ⁷ Moses was eighty years old, and Aaron eighty-three years old, when they spoke to Pharaoh.

⁸ Yahweh spoke to Moses and to Aaron, saying, ⁹ "When Pharaoh speaks to you, saying, 'Perform a miracle!' then you shall tell Aaron, 'Take your rod, and cast it down before Pharaoh, and it will become a serpent.'"

¹⁰ Moses and Aaron went in to Pharaoh, and they did so, as Yahweh had commanded. Aaron cast down his rod before Pharaoh and before his servants, and it became a serpent. ¹¹ Then Pharaoh also called for the wise men and the sorcerers. They also, the magicians of Egypt, did the same thing with their enchantments. ¹² For they each cast down their rods, and they became serpents; but Aaron's rod swallowed up their rods. ¹³ Pharaoh's heart was hardened, and he didn't listen to them, as Yahweh had spoken.

¹⁴ Yahweh said to Moses, "Pharaoh's heart is stubborn. He refuses to let the people go. ¹⁵ Go to Pharaoh in the morning. Behold, he is going out to the water. You shall stand by the river's bank to meet him. You shall take the rod which was turned to a serpent in your hand. ¹⁶ You shall tell him, 'Yahweh, the God of the Hebrews, has sent me to you, saying, "Let my people go, that they may serve me in the wilderness. Behold, until now you haven't listened."' ¹⁷ Yahweh says, "In this you shall know that I am Yahweh. Behold: I will strike with the rod that is in my hand on the waters which are in the river, and they shall be turned to blood. ¹⁸ The fish that are in the river will die and the river will become foul. The Egyptians will loathe to drink water from the river."'" ¹⁹ Yahweh said to Moses, "Tell Aaron, 'Take your rod, and stretch out your hand over the waters of Egypt, over their rivers, over their streams, and over their pools, and over all their ponds of water, that they may become blood. There will be blood throughout all the land of Egypt, both in vessels of wood and in vessels of stone.'"

²⁰ Moses and Aaron did so, as Yahweh commanded; and he lifted up the rod, and struck the waters that were in the river, in the sight of Pharaoh, and in the sight of his servants; and all the waters that were in the river were turned to blood. ²¹ The fish that were in the river died. The river became foul. The Egyptians couldn't drink water from the river. The blood was throughout all the land of Egypt. ²² The magicians of Egypt did the same thing with their enchantments. So Pharaoh's heart was hardened, and he didn't listen to them, as Yahweh had spoken. ²³ Pharaoh turned and went into his house, and he didn't even take this to heart. ²⁴ All the Egyptians dug around the river for water to drink; for they couldn't drink the river water. ²⁵ Seven days were fulfilled, after Yahweh had struck the river.

8

¹ Yahweh spoke to Moses, "Go in to Pharaoh, and tell him, 'This is what Yahweh says, "Let my people go, that they may serve me. ² If you refuse to let them go, behold, I will plague all your borders with frogs. ³ The river will swarm with frogs, which will go up and come into your house, and into your bedroom, and on your bed, and into the house of your servants, and on your people, and into your ovens, and into

your kneading troughs. ⁴The frogs shall come up both on you, and on your people, and on all your servants." ' " ⁵Yahweh said to Moses, "Tell Aaron, 'Stretch out your hand with your rod over the rivers, over the streams, and over the pools, and cause frogs to come up on the land of Egypt.' " ⁶Aaron stretched out his hand over the waters of Egypt; and the frogs came up, and covered the land of Egypt. ⁷The magicians did the same thing with their enchantments, and brought up frogs on the land of Egypt.

⁸Then Pharaoh called for Moses and Aaron, and said, "Entreat Yahweh, that he take away the frogs from me and from my people; and I will let the people go, that they may sacrifice to Yahweh."

⁹Moses said to Pharaoh, "I give you the honor of setting the time that I should pray for you, and for your servants, and for your people, that the frogs be destroyed from you and your houses, and remain in the river only."

¹⁰Pharaoh said, "Tomorrow."

Moses said, "Let it be according to your word, that you may know that there is no one like Yahweh our God. ¹¹The frogs shall depart from you, and from your houses, and from your servants, and from your people. They shall remain in the river only."

¹²Moses and Aaron went out from Pharaoh, and Moses cried to Yahweh concerning the frogs which he had brought on Pharaoh. ¹³Yahweh did according to the word of Moses, and the frogs died out of the houses, out of the courts, and out of the fields. ¹⁴They gathered them together in heaps, and the land stank. ¹⁵But when Pharaoh saw that there was a respite, he hardened his heart, and didn't listen to them, as Yahweh had spoken.

¹⁶Yahweh said to Moses, "Tell Aaron, 'Stretch out your rod, and strike the dust of the earth, that it may become lice throughout all the land of Egypt.' " ¹⁷They did so; and Aaron stretched out his hand with his rod, and struck the dust of the earth, and there were lice on man, and on animal; all the dust of the earth became lice throughout all the land of Egypt. ¹⁸The magicians tried with their enchantments to produce lice, but they couldn't. There were lice on man, and on animal. ¹⁹Then the magicians said to Pharaoh, "This is God's finger;" but Pharaoh's heart was hardened, and he didn't listen to them, as Yahweh had spoken.

²⁰Yahweh said to Moses, "Rise up early in the morning, and stand before Pharaoh; behold, he comes out to the water; and tell him, 'This is what Yahweh says, "Let my people go, that they may serve me. ²¹Else, if you will not let my people go, behold, I will send swarms of flies on you, and on your servants, and on your people, and into your houses. The houses of the Egyptians shall be full of swarms of flies, and also the ground they are on. ²²I will set apart in that day the land of Goshen, in which my people dwell, that no swarms of flies shall be there, to the end you may know that I am Yahweh on the earth. ²³I will put a division between my people and your people. This sign shall happen by tomorrow." ' " ²⁴Yahweh did so; and there came grievous swarms of flies into the house of Pharaoh, and into his servants' houses. In all the land of Egypt the land was corrupted by reason of the swarms of flies.

²⁵Pharaoh called for Moses and for Aaron, and said, "Go, sacrifice to your God in the land!"

²⁶Moses said, "It isn't appropriate to do so; for we shall sacrifice the abomination of the Egyptians to Yahweh our God. Behold, if we sacrifice the abomination of the Egyptians before their eyes, won't they stone us? ²⁷We will go three days' journey into the wilderness, and sacrifice to Yahweh our God, as he shall command us."

²⁸Pharaoh said, "I will let you go, that you may sacrifice to Yahweh your God in the wilderness, only you shall not go very far away. Pray for me."

²⁹Moses said, "Behold, I am going out from you. I will pray to Yahweh that the swarms of flies may depart from Pharaoh, from his servants, and from his people, tomorrow; only don't let Pharaoh deal deceitfully any more in not letting the people go to sacrifice to Yahweh." ³⁰Moses went out from Pharaoh, and prayed to Yahweh. ³¹Yahweh did according to the word of Moses, and he removed the swarms of flies from Pharaoh, from his servants, and from his people. There remained not one. ³²Pharaoh hardened his heart this time also, and he didn't let the people go.

9

¹Then Yahweh said to Moses, "Go in to Pharaoh, and tell him, 'This is what Yahweh, the God of the Hebrews, says: "Let my people go, that they may serve me. ²For if you refuse to let them go, and hold them still, ³behold, Yahweh's hand is on your livestock which are in the field, on the horses, on the donkeys, on the camels, on the herds, and on the flocks with a very grievous pestilence. ⁴Yahweh will make a distinction between the livestock of Israel and the livestock of Egypt; and nothing shall die of all that belongs to the children of Israel." ' " ⁵Yahweh appointed a set time, saying, "Tomorrow Yahweh shall do this thing in the land." ⁶Yahweh did that thing on the next day; and all the livestock of Egypt died, but of the livestock of the children of Israel, not one died. ⁷Pharaoh sent, and, behold, there was not so much as one of the livestock of the Israelites dead. But the heart of Pharaoh was stubborn, and he didn't let the people go.

⁸Yahweh said to Moses and to Aaron, "Take handfuls of ashes of the furnace, and let Moses sprinkle it toward the

sky in the sight of Pharaoh. ⁹ It shall become small dust over all the land of Egypt, and shall be a boils and blisters breaking out on man and on animal, throughout all the land of Egypt."

¹⁰ They took ashes of the furnace, and stood before Pharaoh; and Moses sprinkled it up toward the sky; and it became boils and blisters breaking on man and on animal. ¹¹ The magicians couldn't stand before Moses because of the boils; for the boils were on the magicians and on all the Egyptians. ¹² Yahweh hardened the heart of Pharaoh, and he didn't listen to them, as Yahweh had spoken to Moses.

¹³ Yahweh said to Moses, "Rise up early in the morning, and stand before Pharaoh, and tell him, 'This is what Yahweh, the God of the Hebrews, says: "Let my people go, that they may serve me. ¹⁴ For this time I will send all my plagues against your heart, against your officials, and against your people; that you may know that there is no one like me in all the earth. ¹⁵ For now I would have stretched out my hand, and struck you and your people with pestilence, and you would have been cut off from the earth; ¹⁶ but indeed for this cause I have made you stand: to show you my power, and that my name may be declared throughout all the earth, ¹⁷ because you still exalt yourself against my people, that you won't let them go. ¹⁸ Behold, tomorrow about this time I will cause it to rain a very grievous hail, such as has not been in Egypt since the day it was founded even until now. ¹⁹ Now therefore command that all of your livestock and all that you have in the field be brought into shelter. The hail will come down on every man and animal that is found in the field, and isn't brought home, and they will die."'"

²⁰ Those who feared Yahweh's word among the servants of Pharaoh made their servants and their livestock flee into the houses. ²¹ Whoever didn't respect Yahweh's word left his servants and his livestock in the field.

²² Yahweh said to Moses, "Stretch out your hand toward the sky, that there may be hail in all the land of Egypt, on man, and on animal, and on every herb of the field, throughout the land of Egypt."

²³ Moses stretched out his rod toward the heavens, and Yahweh sent thunder and hail; and lightning flashed down to the earth. Yahweh rained hail on the land of Egypt. ²⁴ So there was very severe hail, and lightning mixed with the hail, such as had not been in all the land of Egypt since it became a nation. ²⁵ The hail struck throughout all the land of Egypt all that was in the field, both man and animal; and the hail struck every herb of the field, and broke every tree of the field. ²⁶ Only in the land of Goshen, where the children of Israel were, there was no hail.

²⁷ Pharaoh sent and called for Moses and Aaron, and said to them, "I have sinned this time. Yahweh is righteous, and I and my people are wicked. ²⁸ Pray to Yahweh; for there

has been enough of mighty thunderings and hail. I will let you go, and you shall stay no longer."

²⁹ Moses said to him, "As soon as I have gone out of the city, I will spread abroad my hands to Yahweh. The thunders shall cease, and there will not be any more hail; that you may know that the earth is Yahweh's. ³⁰ But as for you and your servants, I know that you don't yet fear Yahweh God."

³¹ The flax and the barley were struck, for the barley had ripened and the flax was blooming. ³² But the wheat and the spelt were not struck, for they had not grown up. ³³ Moses went out of the city from Pharaoh, and spread abroad his hands to Yahweh; and the thunders and hail ceased, and the rain was not poured on the earth. ³⁴ When Pharaoh saw that the rain and the hail and the thunders had ceased, he sinned yet more, and hardened his heart, he and his servants. ³⁵ The heart of Pharaoh was hardened, and he didn't let the children of Israel go, just as Yahweh had spoken through Moses.

10

¹ Yahweh said to Moses, "Go in to Pharaoh, for I have hardened his heart and the heart of his servants, that I may show these my signs among them; ² and that you may tell in the hearing of your son, and of your son's son, what things I have done to Egypt, and my signs which I have done among them; that you may know that I am Yahweh."

³ Moses and Aaron went in to Pharaoh, and said to him, "This is what Yahweh, the God of the Hebrews, says: 'How long will you refuse to humble yourself before me? Let my people go, that they may serve me. ⁴ Or else, if you refuse to let my people go, behold, tomorrow I will bring locusts into your country, ⁵ and they shall cover the surface of the earth, so that one won't be able to see the earth. They shall eat the residue of that which has escaped, which remains to you from the hail, and shall eat every tree which grows for you out of the field. ⁶ Your houses shall be filled, and the houses of all your servants, and the houses of all the Egyptians, as neither your fathers nor your fathers' fathers have seen, since the day that they were on the earth to this day.'" He turned, and went out from Pharaoh.

⁷ Pharaoh's servants said to him, "How long will this man be a snare to us? Let the men go, that they may serve Yahweh, their God. Don't you yet know that Egypt is destroyed?"

⁸ Moses and Aaron were brought again to Pharaoh, and he said to them, "Go, serve Yahweh your God; but who are those who will go?"

⁹ Moses said, "We will go with our young and with our old. We will go with our sons and with our daughters, with

our flocks and with our herds; for we must hold a feast to Yahweh."

¹⁰ He said to them, "Yahweh be with you if I let you go with your little ones! See, evil is clearly before your faces. ¹¹ Not so! Go now you who are men, and serve Yahweh; for that is what you desire!" Then they were driven out from Pharaoh's presence.

¹² Yahweh said to Moses, "Stretch out your hand over the land of Egypt for the locusts, that they may come up on the land of Egypt, and eat every herb of the land, even all that the hail has left." ¹³ Moses stretched out his rod over the land of Egypt, and Yahweh brought an east wind on the land all that day, and all night; and when it was morning, the east wind brought the locusts. ¹⁴ The locusts went up over all the land of Egypt, and rested in all the borders of Egypt. They were very grievous. Before them there were no such locusts as they, nor will there ever be again. ¹⁵ For they covered the surface of the whole earth, so that the land was darkened, and they ate every herb of the land, and all the fruit of the trees which the hail had left. There remained nothing green, either tree or herb of the field, through all the land of Egypt. ¹⁶ Then Pharaoh called for Moses and Aaron in haste, and he said, "I have sinned against Yahweh your God, and against you. ¹⁷ Now therefore please forgive my sin again, and pray to Yahweh your God, that he may also take away from me this death."

¹⁸ Moses went out from Pharaoh, and prayed to Yahweh. ¹⁹ Yahweh turned an exceedingly strong west wind, which took up the locusts, and drove them into the Red Sea. There remained not one locust in all the borders of Egypt. ²⁰ But Yahweh hardened Pharaoh's heart, and he didn't let the children of Israel go.

²¹ Yahweh said to Moses, "Stretch out your hand toward the sky, that there may be darkness over the land of Egypt, even darkness which may be felt." ²² Moses stretched out his hand toward the sky, and there was a thick darkness in all the land of Egypt for three days. ²³ They didn't see one another, and nobody rose from his place for three days; but all the children of Israel had light in their dwellings.

²⁴ Pharaoh called to Moses, and said, "Go, serve Yahweh. Only let your flocks and your herds stay behind. Let your little ones also go with you."

²⁵ Moses said, "You must also give into our hand sacrifices and burnt offerings, that we may sacrifice to Yahweh our God. ²⁶ Our livestock also shall go with us. Not a hoof shall be left behind, for of it we must take to serve Yahweh our God; and we don't know with what we must serve Yahweh, until we come there."

²⁷ But Yahweh hardened Pharaoh's heart, and he wouldn't let them go. ²⁸ Pharaoh said to him, "Get away from

me! Be careful to see my face no more; for in the day you see my face you shall die!"

²⁹ Moses said, "You have spoken well. I will see your face again no more."

11

¹ Yahweh said to Moses, "I will bring yet one more plague on Pharaoh, and on Egypt; afterwards he will let you go. When he lets you go, he will surely thrust you out altogether. ² Speak now in the ears of the people, and let every man ask of his neighbor, and every woman of her neighbor, jewels of silver, and jewels of gold."³ Yahweh gave the people favor in the sight of the Egyptians. Moreover, the man Moses was very great in the land of Egypt, in the sight of Pharaoh's servants, and in the sight of the people.

⁴ Moses said, "This is what Yahweh says: 'About midnight I will go out into the middle of Egypt, ⁵ and all the firstborn in the land of Egypt shall die, from the firstborn of Pharaoh who sits on his throne, even to the firstborn of the female servant who is behind the mill, and all the firstborn of livestock. ⁶ There will be a great cry throughout all the land of Egypt, such as there has not been, nor will be any more. ⁷ But against any of the children of Israel a dog won't even bark or move its tongue, against man or animal, that you may know that Yahweh makes a distinction between the Egyptians and Israel. ⁸ All these servants of yours will come down to me, and bow down themselves to me, saying, "Get out, with all the people who follow you;" and after that I will go out.'" He went out from Pharaoh in hot anger.

⁹ Yahweh said to Moses, "Pharaoh won't listen to you, that my wonders may be multiplied in the land of Egypt." ¹⁰ Moses and Aaron did all these wonders before Pharaoh, but Yahweh hardened Pharaoh's heart, and he didn't let the children of Israel go out of his land.

12

¹ Yahweh spoke to Moses and Aaron in the land of Egypt, saying, ² "This month shall be to you the beginning of months. It shall be the first month of the year to you. ³ Speak to all the congregation of Israel, saying, 'On the tenth day of this month, they shall take to them every man a lamb, according to their fathers' houses, a lamb for a household; ⁴ and if the household is too little for a lamb, then he and his neighbor next to his house shall take one according to the number of the souls. You shall make your count for the lamb according to what everyone can eat. ⁵ Your lamb shall be without defect, a male a year old. You shall take it from the sheep, or from

the goats. ⁶ You shall keep it until the fourteenth day of the same month; and the whole assembly of the congregation of Israel shall kill it at evening. ⁷ They shall take some of the blood, and put it on the two door posts and on the lintel, on the houses in which they shall eat it. ⁸ They shall eat the meat in that night, roasted with fire, and unleavened bread. They shall eat it with bitter herbs. ⁹ Don't eat it raw, nor boiled at all with water, but roasted with fire; with its head, its legs and its inner parts. ¹⁰ You shall let nothing of it remain until the morning; but that which remains of it until the morning you shall burn with fire. ¹¹ This is how you shall eat it: with your belt on your waist, your shoes on your feet, and your staff in your hand; and you shall eat it in haste: it is Yahweh's Passover. ¹² For I will go through the land of Egypt in that night, and will strike all the firstborn in the land of Egypt, both man and animal. I will execute judgments against all the gods of Egypt. I am Yahweh. ¹³ The blood shall be to you for a token on the houses where you are. When I see the blood, I will pass over you, and no plague will be on you to destroy you when I strike the land of Egypt. ¹⁴ This day shall be a memorial for you. You shall keep it as a feast to Yahweh. You shall keep it as a feast throughout your generations by an ordinance forever.

¹⁵ " 'Seven days you shall eat unleavened bread; even the first day you shall put away yeast out of your houses, for whoever eats leavened bread from the first day until the seventh day, that soul shall be cut off from Israel. ¹⁶ In the first day there shall be to you a holy convocation, and in the seventh day a holy convocation; no kind of work shall be done in them, except that which every man must eat, only that may be done by you. ¹⁷ You shall observe the feast of unleavened bread; for in this same day I have brought your armies out of the land of Egypt. Therefore you shall observe this day throughout your generations by an ordinance forever. ¹⁸ In the first month, on the fourteenth day of the month at evening, you shall eat unleavened bread, until the twenty first day of the month at evening. ¹⁹ There shall be no yeast found in your houses for seven days, for whoever eats that which is leavened, that soul shall be cut off from the congregation of Israel, whether he is a foreigner, or one who is born in the land. ²⁰ You shall eat nothing leavened. In all your habitations you shall eat unleavened bread.' "

²¹ Then Moses called for all the elders of Israel, and said to them, "Draw out, and take lambs according to your families, and kill the Passover. ²² You shall take a bunch of hyssop, and dip it in the blood that is in the basin, and strike the lintel and the two door posts with the blood that is in the basin. None of you shall go out of the door of his house until the morning. ²³ For Yahweh will pass through to strike the Egyptians; and when he sees the blood on the lintel, and on the two door posts, Yahweh will pass over the door, and will not allow the destroyer to come in to your houses to strike you. ²⁴ You shall observe this thing for an ordinance to you and to your sons forever. ²⁵ It shall happen when you have come to the land which Yahweh will give you, as he has promised, that you shall keep this service. ²⁶ It will happen, when your children ask you, 'What do you mean by this service?' ²⁷ that you shall say, 'It is the sacrifice of Yahweh's Passover, who passed over the houses of the children of Israel in Egypt, when he struck the Egyptians, and spared our houses.' "

The people bowed their heads and worshiped. ²⁸ The children of Israel went and did so; as Yahweh had commanded Moses and Aaron, so they did.

²⁹ At midnight, Yahweh struck all the firstborn in the land of Egypt, from the firstborn of Pharaoh who sat on his throne to the firstborn of the captive who was in the dungeon, and all the firstborn of livestock. ³⁰ Pharaoh rose up in the night, he, and all his servants, and all the Egyptians; and there was a great cry in Egypt, for there was not a house where there was not one dead. ³¹ He called for Moses and Aaron by night, and said, "Rise up, get out from among my people, both you and the children of Israel; and go, serve Yahweh, as you have said! ³² Take both your flocks and your herds, as you have said, and be gone; and bless me also!"

³³ The Egyptians were urgent with the people, to send them out of the land in haste, for they said, "We are all dead men." ³⁴ The people took their dough before it was leavened, their kneading troughs being bound up in their clothes on their shoulders. ³⁵ The children of Israel did according to the word of Moses; and they asked of the Egyptians jewels of silver, and jewels of gold, and clothing. ³⁶ Yahweh gave the people favor in the sight of the Egyptians, so that they let them have what they asked. They plundered the Egyptians.

³⁷ The children of Israel traveled from Rameses to Succoth, about six hundred thousand on foot who were men, in addition to children. ³⁸ A mixed multitude went up also with them, with flocks, herds, and even very much livestock. ³⁹ They baked unleavened cakes of the dough which they brought out of Egypt; for it wasn't leavened, because they were thrust out of Egypt, and couldn't wait, and they had not prepared any food for themselves. ⁴⁰ Now the time that the children of Israel lived in Egypt was four hundred thirty years. ⁴¹ At the end of four hundred thirty years, to the day, all of Yahweh's armies went out from the land of Egypt. ⁴² It is a night to be much observed to Yahweh for bringing them out from the land of Egypt. This is that night of Yahweh, to be much observed by all the children of Israel throughout their generations.

⁴³ Yahweh said to Moses and Aaron, "This is the ordinance of the Passover. No foreigner shall eat of it, ⁴⁴ but

every man's servant who is bought for money, when you have circumcised him, then shall he eat of it.⁴⁵ A foreigner and a hired servant shall not eat of it. ⁴⁶ It must be eaten in one house. You shall not carry any of the meat outside of the house. Do not break any of its bones. ⁴⁷ All the congregation of Israel shall keep it.⁴⁸ When a stranger lives as a foreigner with you, and would like to keep the Passover to Yahweh, let all his males be circumcised, and then let him come near and keep it. He shall be as one who is born in the land; but no uncircumcised person shall eat of it. ⁴⁹ One law shall be to him who is born at home, and to the stranger who lives as a foreigner among you." ⁵⁰ All the children of Israel did so. As Yahweh commanded Moses and Aaron, so they did. ⁵¹ That same day, Yahweh brought the children of Israel out of the land of Egypt by their armies.

13

¹ Yahweh spoke to Moses, saying, ² "Sanctify to me all the firstborn, whatever opens the womb among the children of Israel, both of man and of animal. It is mine."

³ Moses said to the people, "Remember this day, in which you came out of Egypt, out of the house of bondage; for by strength of hand Yahweh brought you out from this place. No leavened bread shall be eaten.⁴ Today you go out in the month Abib. ⁵ It shall be, when Yahweh brings you into the land of the Canaanite, and the Hittite, and the Amorite, and the Hivite, and the Jebusite, which he swore to your fathers to give you, a land flowing with milk and honey, that you shall keep this service in this month. ⁶ Seven days you shall eat unleavened bread, and in the seventh day shall be a feast to Yahweh. ⁷ Unleavened bread shall be eaten throughout the seven days; and no leavened bread shall be seen with you. No yeast shall be seen with you, within all your borders. ⁸ You shall tell your son in that day, saying, 'It is because of that which Yahweh did for me when I came out of Egypt.' ⁹ It shall be for a sign to you on your hand, and for a memorial between your eyes, that Yahweh's law may be in your mouth; for with a strong hand Yahweh has brought you out of Egypt.¹⁰ You shall therefore keep this ordinance in its season from year to year.

¹¹ "It shall be, when Yahweh brings you into the land of the Canaanite, as he swore to you and to your fathers, and will give it you, ¹² that you shall set apart to Yahweh all that opens the womb, and every firstborn that comes from an animal which you have. The males shall be Yahweh's. ¹³ Every firstborn of a donkey you shall redeem with a lamb; and if you will not redeem it, then you shall break its neck; and you shall redeem all the firstborn of man among your sons. ¹⁴ It shall be,

when your son asks you in time to come, saying, 'What is this?' that you shall tell him, 'By strength of hand Yahweh brought us out from Egypt, from the house of bondage. ¹⁵ When Pharaoh stubbornly refused to let us go, Yahweh killed all the firstborn in the land of Egypt, both the firstborn of man, and the firstborn of livestock. Therefore I sacrifice to Yahweh all that opens the womb, being males; but all the firstborn of my sons I redeem.' ¹⁶ It shall be for a sign on your hand, and for symbols between your eyes; for by strength of hand Yahweh brought us out of Egypt."

¹⁷ When Pharaoh had let the people go, God didn't lead them by the way of the land of the Philistines, although that was near; for God said, "Lest perhaps the people change their minds when they see war, and they return to Egypt"; ¹⁸ but God led the people around by the way of the wilderness by the Red Sea; and the children of Israel went up armed out of the land of Egypt. ¹⁹ Moses took the bones of Joseph with him, for he had made the children of Israel swear, saying, "God will surely visit you, and you shall carry up my bones away from here with you." ²⁰ They took their journey from Succoth, and encamped in Etham, in the edge of the wilderness. ²¹ Yahweh went before them by day in a pillar of cloud, to lead them on their way, and by night in a pillar of fire, to give them light, that they might go by day and by night: ²² the pillar of cloud by day, and the pillar of fire by night, didn't depart from before the people.

14

¹ Yahweh spoke to Moses, saying, ² "Speak to the children of Israel, that they turn back and encamp before Pihahiroth, between Migdol and the sea, before Baal Zephon. You shall encamp opposite it by the sea.³ Pharaoh will say of the children of Israel, 'They are entangled in the land. The wilderness has shut them in.' ⁴ I will harden Pharaoh's heart, and he will follow after them; and I will get honor over Pharaoh, and over all his armies; and the Egyptians shall know that I am Yahweh." They did so.

⁵ The king of Egypt was told that the people had fled; and the heart of Pharaoh and of his servants was changed towards the people, and they said, "What is this we have done, that we have let Israel go from serving us?" ⁶ He prepared his chariot, and took his army with him; ⁷ and he took six hundred chosen chariots, and all the chariots of Egypt, with captains over all of them. ⁸ Yahweh hardened the heart of Pharaoh king of Egypt, and he pursued the children of Israel; for the children of Israel went out with a high hand. ⁹ The Egyptians pursued them. All the horses and chariots of Pharaoh, his horsemen, and his army overtook them encamping by the

sea, beside Pihahiroth, before Baal Zephon.

¹⁰ When Pharaoh came near, the children of Israel lifted up their eyes, and behold, the Egyptians were marching after them; and they were very afraid. The children of Israel cried out to Yahweh. ¹¹ They said to Moses, "Because there were no graves in Egypt, have you taken us away to die in the wilderness? Why have you treated us this way, to bring us out of Egypt? ¹² Isn't this the word that we spoke to you in Egypt, saying, 'Leave us alone, that we may serve the Egyptians?' For it would have been better for us to serve the Egyptians than to die in the wilderness."

¹³ Moses said to the people, "Don't be afraid. Stand still, and see the salvation of Yahweh, which he will work for you today; for you will never again see the Egyptians whom you have seen today. ¹⁴ Yahweh will fight for you, and you shall be still."

¹⁵ Yahweh said to Moses, "Why do you cry to me? Speak to the children of Israel, that they go forward. ¹⁶ Lift up your rod, and stretch out your hand over the sea and divide it. Then the children of Israel shall go into the middle of the sea on dry ground. ¹⁷ Behold, I myself will harden the hearts of the Egyptians, and they will go in after them. I will get myself honor over Pharaoh, and over all his armies, over his chariots, and over his horsemen. ¹⁸ The Egyptians shall know that I am Yahweh when I have gotten myself honor over Pharaoh, over his chariots, and over his horsemen." ¹⁹ The angel of God, who went before the camp of Israel, moved and went behind them; and the pillar of cloud moved from before them, and stood behind them. ²⁰ It came between the camp of Egypt and the camp of Israel. There was the cloud and the darkness, yet gave it light by night. One didn't come near the other all night.

²¹ Moses stretched out his hand over the sea, and Yahweh caused the sea to go back by a strong east wind all night, and made the sea dry land, and the waters were divided. ²² The children of Israel went into the middle of the sea on the dry ground, and the waters were a wall to them on their right hand, and on their left. ²³ The Egyptians pursued, and went in after them into the middle of the sea: all of Pharaoh's horses, his chariots, and his horsemen. ²⁴ In the morning watch, Yahweh looked out on the Egyptian army through the pillar of fire and of cloud, and confused the Egyptian army. ²⁵ He took off their chariot wheels, and they drove them heavily; so that the Egyptians said, "Let's flee from the face of Israel, for Yahweh fights for them against the Egyptians!"

²⁶ Yahweh said to Moses, "Stretch out your hand over the sea, that the waters may come again on the Egyptians, on their chariots, and on their horsemen." ²⁷ Moses stretched out his hand over the sea, and the sea returned to its strength when the morning appeared; and the Egyptians fled against it. Yahweh overthrew the Egyptians in the middle of the sea. ²⁸ The waters returned, and covered the chariots and the horsemen, even all Pharaoh's army that went in after them into the sea. There remained not so much as one of them. ²⁹ But the children of Israel walked on dry land in the middle of the sea, and the waters were a wall to them on their right hand, and on their left. ³⁰ Thus Yahweh saved Israel that day out of the hand of the Egyptians; and Israel saw the Egyptians dead on the seashore. ³¹ Israel saw the great work which Yahweh did to the Egyptians, and the people feared Yahweh; and they believed in Yahweh and in his servant Moses.

15

¹ Then Moses and the children of Israel sang this song to Yahweh, and said,
"I will sing to Yahweh, for he has triumphed gloriously.
He has thrown the horse and his rider into the sea.
² Yah is my strength and song.
He has become my salvation.
This is my God, and I will praise him;
my father's God, and I will exalt him.
³ Yahweh is a man of war.
Yahweh is his name.
⁴ He has cast Pharaoh's chariots and his army into the sea.
His chosen captains are sunk in the Red Sea.
⁵ The deeps cover them.
They went down into the depths like a stone.
⁶ Your right hand, Yahweh, is glorious in power.
Your right hand, Yahweh, dashes the enemy in pieces.
⁷ In the greatness of your excellency, you overthrow those who rise up against you.
You send out your wrath. It consumes them as stubble.
⁸ With the blast of your nostrils, the waters were piled up.
The floods stood upright as a heap.
The deeps were congealed in the heart of the sea.
⁹ The enemy said, 'I will pursue. I will overtake. I will divide the plunder.
My desire will be satisfied on them.
I will draw my sword. My hand will destroy them.'
¹⁰ You blew with your wind.
The sea covered them.
They sank like lead in the mighty waters.
¹¹ Who is like you, Yahweh, among the gods?
Who is like you, glorious in holiness,
fearful in praises, doing wonders?
¹² You stretched out your right hand.
The earth swallowed them.
¹³ "You, in your loving kindness, have led the people that you have redeemed.

You have guided them in your strength to your holy habitation.
¹⁴ The peoples have heard.
They tremble.
Pangs have taken hold of the inhabitants of Philistia.
¹⁵ Then the chiefs of Edom were dismayed.
Trembling takes hold of the mighty men of Moab.
All the inhabitants of Canaan have melted away.
¹⁶ Terror and dread falls on them.
By the greatness of your arm they are as still as a stone,
until your people pass over, Yahweh,
until the people you have purchased pass over.
¹⁷ You will bring them in, and plant them in the mountain of your inheritance,
the place, Yahweh, which you have made for yourself to dwell in;
the sanctuary, Lord, which your hands have established.
¹⁸ Yahweh will reign forever and ever.”

¹⁹ For the horses of Pharaoh went in with his chariots and with his horsemen into the sea, and Yahweh brought back the waters of the sea on them; but the children of Israel walked on dry land in the middle of the sea. ²⁰ Miriam the prophetess, the sister of Aaron, took a tambourine in her hand; and all the women went out after her with tambourines and with dances. ²¹ Miriam answered them,
“Sing to Yahweh, for he has triumphed gloriously.
The horse and his rider he has thrown into the sea.”

²² Moses led Israel onward from the Red Sea, and they went out into the wilderness of Shur; and they went three days in the wilderness, and found no water. ²³ When they came to Marah, they couldn’t drink from the waters of Marah, for they were bitter. Therefore its name was called Marah. ²⁴ The people murmured against Moses, saying, “What shall we drink?” ²⁵ Then he cried to Yahweh. Yahweh showed him a tree, and he threw it into the waters, and the waters were made sweet. There he made a statute and an ordinance for them, and there he tested them. ²⁶ He said, “If you will diligently listen to Yahweh your God’s voice, and will do that which is right in his eyes, and will pay attention to his commandments, and keep all his statutes, I will put none of the diseases on you, which I have put on the Egyptians; for I am Yahweh who heals you.”

²⁷ They came to Elim, where there were twelve springs of water, and seventy palm trees. They encamped there by the waters.

16

¹ They took their journey from Elim, and all the congregation of the children of Israel came to the wilderness of Sin, which is between Elim and Sinai, on the fifteenth day of the second month after their departing out of the land of Egypt. ² The whole congregation of the children of Israel murmured against Moses and against Aaron in the wilderness; ³ and the children of Israel said to them, “We wish that we had died by Yahweh’s hand in the land of Egypt, when we sat by the meat pots, when we ate our fill of bread, for you have brought us out into this wilderness to kill this whole assembly with hunger.”

⁴ Then Yahweh said to Moses, “Behold, I will rain bread from the sky for you, and the people shall go out and gather a day’s portion every day, that I may test them, whether they will walk in my law or not. ⁵ It shall come to pass on the sixth day, that they shall prepare that which they bring in, and it shall be twice as much as they gather daily.”

⁶ Moses and Aaron said to all the children of Israel, “At evening, you shall know that Yahweh has brought you out from the land of Egypt. ⁷ In the morning, you shall see Yahweh’s glory; because he hears your murmurings against Yahweh. Who are we, that you murmur against us?” ⁸ Moses said, “Now Yahweh will give you meat to eat in the evening, and in the morning bread to satisfy you, because Yahweh hears your murmurings which you murmur against him. And who are we? Your murmurings are not against us, but against Yahweh.” ⁹ Moses said to Aaron, “Tell all the congregation of the children of Israel, ‘Come close to Yahweh, for he has heard your murmurings.’ ” ¹⁰ As Aaron spoke to the whole congregation of the children of Israel, they looked toward the wilderness, and behold, Yahweh’s glory appeared in the cloud. ¹¹ Yahweh spoke to Moses, saying, ¹² “I have heard the murmurings of the children of Israel. Speak to them, saying, ‘At evening you shall eat meat, and in the morning you shall be filled with bread. Then you will know that I am Yahweh your God.’ ”

¹³ In the evening, quail came up and covered the camp; and in the morning the dew lay around the camp. ¹⁴ When the dew that lay had gone, behold, on the surface of the wilderness was a small round thing, small as the frost on the ground. ¹⁵ When the children of Israel saw it, they said to one another, “What is it?” For they didn’t know what it was. Moses said to them, “It is the bread which Yahweh has given you to eat. ¹⁶ “This is the thing which Yahweh has commanded: ‘Gather of it everyone according to his eating; an omer a head, according to the number of your persons, you shall take it, every man for those who are in his tent.’ ” ¹⁷ The children of Israel did so, and some gathered more, some less. ¹⁸ When they measured it with an omer, he who gathered much had nothing over, and he who gathered little had no lack. They each gathered according to his eating. ¹⁹ Moses said to them, “Let no one leave of it until the

morning." [20] Notwithstanding they didn't listen to Moses, but some of them left of it until the morning, so it bred worms and became foul; and Moses was angry with them. [21] They gathered it morning by morning, everyone according to his eating. When the sun grew hot, it melted. [22] On the sixth day, they gathered twice as much bread, two omers for each one; and all the rulers of the congregation came and told Moses. [23] He said to them, "This is that which Yahweh has spoken, 'Tomorrow is a solemn rest, a holy Sabbath to Yahweh. Bake that which you want to bake, and boil that which you want to boil; and all that remains over lay up for yourselves to be kept until the morning.'" [24] They laid it up until the morning, as Moses ordered, and it didn't become foul, and there were no worms in it. [25] Moses said, "Eat that today, for today is a Sabbath to Yahweh. Today you shall not find it in the field. [26] Six days you shall gather it, but on the seventh day is the Sabbath. In it there shall be none." [27] On the seventh day, some of the people went out to gather, and they found none. [28] Yahweh said to Moses, "How long do you refuse to keep my commandments and my laws? [29] Behold, because Yahweh has given you the Sabbath, therefore he gives you on the sixth day the bread of two days. Everyone stay in his place. Let no one go out of his place on the seventh day." [30] So the people rested on the seventh day.

[31] The house of Israel called its name "Manna",[†] and it was like coriander seed, white; and its taste was like wafers with honey. [32] Moses said, "This is the thing which Yahweh has commanded, 'Let an omer-full of it be kept throughout your generations, that they may see the bread with which I fed you in the wilderness, when I brought you out of the land of Egypt.'" [33] Moses said to Aaron, "Take a pot, and put an omer-full of manna in it, and lay it up before Yahweh, to be kept throughout your generations." [34] As Yahweh commanded Moses, so Aaron laid it up before the Testimony, to be kept. [35] The children of Israel ate the manna forty years, until they came to an inhabited land. They ate the manna until they came to the borders of the land of Canaan. [36] Now an omer is one tenth of an ephah.[‡]

17

[1] All the congregation of the children of Israel traveled from the wilderness of Sin, starting according to Yahweh's commandment, and encamped in Rephidim; but there was no water for the people to drink. [2] Therefore the people quarreled with Moses, and said, "Give us water to drink."

Moses said to them, "Why do you quarrel with me? Why do you test Yahweh?"

[3] The people were thirsty for water there; so the people murmured against Moses, and said, "Why have you brought us up out of Egypt, to kill us, our children, and our livestock with thirst?"

[4] Moses cried to Yahweh, saying, "What shall I do with these people? They are almost ready to stone me."

[5] Yahweh said to Moses, "Walk on before the people, and take the elders of Israel with you, and take the rod in your hand with which you struck the Nile, and go. [6] Behold, I will stand before you there on the rock in Horeb. You shall strike the rock, and water will come out of it, that the people may drink." Moses did so in the sight of the elders of Israel. [7] He called the name of the place Massah,[*] and Meribah,[†] because the children of Israel quarreled, and because they tested Yahweh, saying, "Is Yahweh among us, or not?"

[8] Then Amalek came and fought with Israel in Rephidim. [9] Moses said to Joshua, "Choose men for us, and go out, fight with Amalek. Tomorrow I will stand on the top of the hill with God's rod in my hand." [10] So Joshua did as Moses had told him, and fought with Amalek; and Moses, Aaron, and Hur went up to the top of the hill. [11] When Moses held up his hand, Israel prevailed. When he let down his hand, Amalek prevailed. [12] But Moses' hands were heavy; so they took a stone, and put it under him, and he sat on it. Aaron and Hur held up his hands, the one on the one side, and the other on the other side. His hands were steady until sunset. [13] Joshua defeated Amalek and his people with the edge of the sword. [14] Yahweh said to Moses, "Write this for a memorial in a book, and rehearse it in the ears of Joshua: that I will utterly blot out the memory of Amalek from under the sky." [15] Moses built an altar, and called its name "Yahweh our Banner".[‡] [16] He said, "Yah has sworn: 'Yahweh will have war with Amalek from generation to generation.'"

18

[1] Now Jethro, the priest of Midian, Moses' father-in-law, heard of all that God had done for Moses, and for Israel his people, how Yahweh had brought Israel out of Egypt. [2] Jethro, Moses' father-in-law, received Zipporah, Moses' wife, after he had sent her away, [3] and her two sons. The name of one son was Gershom,[*] for Moses said, "I have lived as a foreigner in a foreign land". [4] The name of the other was Eliezer,[†] for he said, "My father's God was my help and delivered me from Pharaoh's sword." [5] Jethro, Moses' father-in-law, came with Moses' sons and his wife to Moses into the wilderness where he was encamped, at the Mountain of God. [6] He said to Moses, "I, your father-in-law Jethro, have come to you with your wife, and her two sons with her."

[7] Moses went out to meet his father-in-law, and bowed and kissed him. They asked each other of their welfare, and

they came into the tent. ⁸ Moses told his father-in-law all that Yahweh had done to Pharaoh and to the Egyptians for Israel's sake, all the hardships that had come on them on the way, and how Yahweh delivered them. ⁹ Jethro rejoiced for all the goodness which Yahweh had done to Israel, in that he had delivered them out of the hand of the Egyptians. ¹⁰ Jethro said, "Blessed be Yahweh, who has delivered you out of the hand of the Egyptians, and out of the hand of Pharaoh; who has delivered the people from under the hand of the Egyptians. ¹¹ Now I know that Yahweh is greater than all gods because of the way that they treated people arrogantly." ¹² Jethro, Moses' father-in-law, took a burnt offering and sacrifices for God. Aaron came with all the elders of Israel, to eat bread with Moses' father-in-law before God.

¹³ On the next day, Moses sat to judge the people, and the people stood around Moses from the morning to the evening. ¹⁴ When Moses' father-in-law saw all that he did to the people, he said, "What is this thing that you do for the people? Why do you sit alone, and all the people stand around you from morning to evening?"

¹⁵ Moses said to his father-in-law, "Because the people come to me to inquire of God. ¹⁶ When they have a matter, they come to me, and I judge between a man and his neighbor, and I make them know the statutes of God, and his laws." ¹⁷ Moses' father-in-law said to him, "The thing that you do is not good. ¹⁸ You will surely wear away, both you, and this people that is with you; for the thing is too heavy for you. You are not able to perform it yourself alone. ¹⁹ Listen now to my voice. I will give you counsel, and God be with you. You represent the people before God, and bring the causes to God. ²⁰ You shall teach them the statutes and the laws, and shall show them the way in which they must walk, and the work that they must do. ²¹ Moreover you shall provide out of all the people able men which fear God: men of truth, hating unjust gain; and place such over them, to be rulers of thousands, rulers of hundreds, rulers of fifties, and rulers of tens. ²² Let them judge the people at all times. It shall be that every great matter they shall bring to you, but every small matter they shall judge themselves. So shall it be easier for you, and they shall share the load with you. ²³ If you will do this thing, and God commands you so, then you will be able to endure, and all these people also will go to their place in peace."

²⁴ So Moses listened to the voice of his father-in-law, and did all that he had said. ²⁵ Moses chose able men out of all Israel, and made them heads over the people, rulers of thousands, rulers of hundreds, rulers of fifties, and rulers of tens. ²⁶ They judged the people at all times. They brought the hard causes to Moses, but every small matter they judged

themselves. ²⁷ Moses let his father-in-law depart, and he went his way into his own land.

19

¹ In the third month after the children of Israel had gone out of the land of Egypt, on that same day they came into the wilderness of Sinai. ² When they had departed from Rephidim, and had come to the wilderness of Sinai, they encamped in the wilderness; and there Israel encamped before the mountain. ³ Moses went up to God, and Yahweh called to him out of the mountain, saying, "This is what you shall tell the house of Jacob, and tell the children of Israel: ⁴ 'You have seen what I did to the Egyptians, and how I bore you on eagles' wings, and brought you to myself. ⁵ Now therefore, if you will indeed obey my voice, and keep my covenant, then you shall be my own possession from among all peoples; for all the earth is mine; ⁶ and you shall be to me a kingdom of priests, and a holy nation.' These are the words which you shall speak to the children of Israel."

⁷ Moses came and called for the elders of the people, and set before them all these words which Yahweh commanded him. ⁸ All the people answered together, and said, "All that Yahweh has spoken we will do."

Moses reported the words of the people to Yahweh. ⁹ Yahweh said to Moses, "Behold, I come to you in a thick cloud, that the people may hear when I speak with you, and may also believe you forever." Moses told the words of the people to Yahweh. ¹⁰ Yahweh said to Moses, "Go to the people, and sanctify them today and tomorrow, and let them wash their garments, ¹¹ and be ready for the third day; for on the third day Yahweh will come down in the sight of all the people on Mount Sinai. ¹² You shall set bounds to the people all around, saying, 'Be careful that you don't go up onto the mountain, or touch its border. Whoever touches the mountain shall be surely put to death. ¹³ No hand shall touch him, but he shall surely be stoned or shot through; whether it is animal or man, he shall not live.' When the trumpet sounds long, they shall come up to the mountain."

¹⁴ Moses went down from the mountain to the people, and sanctified the people; and they washed their clothes. ¹⁵ He said to the people, "Be ready by the third day. Don't have sexual relations with a woman."

¹⁶ On the third day, when it was morning, there were thunders and lightnings, and a thick cloud on the mountain, and the sound of an exceedingly loud trumpet; and all the people who were in the camp trembled. ¹⁷ Moses led the people out of the camp to meet God; and they stood at the lower part of the mountain. ¹⁸ All of Mount Sinai

smoked, because Yahweh descended on it in fire; and its smoke ascended like the smoke of a furnace, and the whole mountain quaked greatly. ¹⁹ When the sound of the trumpet grew louder and louder, Moses spoke, and God answered him by a voice. ²⁰ Yahweh came down on Mount Sinai, to the top of the mountain. Yahweh called Moses to the top of the mountain, and Moses went up.

²¹ Yahweh said to Moses, "Go down, warn the people, lest they break through to Yahweh to gaze, and many of them perish. ²² Let the priests also, who come near to Yahweh, sanctify themselves, lest Yahweh break out on them."

²³ Moses said to Yahweh, "The people can't come up to Mount Sinai, for you warned us, saying, 'Set bounds around the mountain, and sanctify it.'"

²⁴ Yahweh said to him, "Go down! You shall bring Aaron up with you, but don't let the priests and the people break through to come up to Yahweh, lest he break out against them."

²⁵ So Moses went down to the people, and told them.

20

¹ God* spoke all these words, saying, ² "I am Yahweh your God, who brought you out of the land of Egypt, out of the house of bondage.

³ "You shall have no other gods before me.

⁴ "You shall not make for yourselves an idol, nor any image of anything that is in the heavens above, or that is in the earth beneath, or that is in the water under the earth: ⁵ you shall not bow yourself down to them, nor serve them, for I, Yahweh your God, am a jealous God, visiting the iniquity of the fathers on the children, on the third and on the fourth generation of those who hate me, ⁶ and showing loving kindness to thousands of those who love me and keep my commandments.

⁷ "You shall not misuse the name of Yahweh your God,† for Yahweh will not hold him guiltless who misuses his name.

⁸ "Remember the Sabbath day, to keep it holy. ⁹ You shall labor six days, and do all your work, ¹⁰ but the seventh day is a Sabbath to Yahweh your God. You shall not do any work in it, you, nor your son, nor your daughter, your male servant, nor your female servant, nor your livestock, nor your stranger who is within your gates; ¹¹ for in six days Yahweh made heaven and earth, the sea, and all that is in them, and rested the seventh day; therefore Yahweh blessed the Sabbath day, and made it holy.

¹² "Honor your father and your mother, that your days may be long in the land which Yahweh your God gives you.

¹³ "You shall not murder.

¹⁴ "You shall not commit adultery.

¹⁵ "You shall not steal.

¹⁶ "You shall not give false testimony against your neighbor.

¹⁷ "You shall not covet your neighbor's house. You shall not covet your neighbor's wife, nor his male servant, nor his female servant, nor his ox, nor his donkey, nor anything that is your neighbor's."

¹⁸ All the people perceived the thunderings, the lightnings, the sound of the trumpet, and the mountain smoking. When the people saw it, they trembled, and stayed at a distance. ¹⁹ They said to Moses, "Speak with us yourself, and we will listen; but don't let God speak with us, lest we die."

²⁰ Moses said to the people, "Don't be afraid, for God has come to test you, and that his fear may be before you, that you won't sin." ²¹ The people stayed at a distance, and Moses came near to the thick darkness where God was.

²² Yahweh said to Moses, "This is what you shall tell the children of Israel: 'You yourselves have seen that I have talked with you from heaven. ²³ You shall most certainly not make gods of silver or gods of gold for yourselves to be alongside me. ²⁴ You shall make an altar of earth for me, and shall sacrifice on it your burnt offerings and your peace offerings, your sheep and your cattle. In every place where I record my name I will come to you and I will bless you. ²⁵ If you make me an altar of stone, you shall not build it of cut stones; for if you lift up your tool on it, you have polluted it. ²⁶ You shall not go up by steps to my altar, that your nakedness may not be exposed to it.'

21

¹ "Now these are the ordinances which you shall set before them:

² "If you buy a Hebrew servant, he shall serve six years, and in the seventh he shall go out free without paying anything. ³ If he comes in by himself, he shall go out by himself. If he is married, then his wife shall go out with him. ⁴ If his master gives him a wife and she bears him sons or daughters, the wife and her children shall be her master's, and he shall go out by himself. ⁵ But if the servant shall plainly say, 'I love my master, my wife, and my children. I will not go out free;' ⁶ then his master shall bring him to God, and shall bring him to the door or to the doorpost, and his master shall bore his ear through with an awl, and he shall serve him forever.

⁷ "If a man sells his daughter to be a female servant, she shall not go out as the male servants do. ⁸ If she doesn't

please her master, who has married her to himself, then he shall let her be redeemed. He shall have no right to sell her to a foreign people, since he has dealt deceitfully with her. ⁹ If he marries her to his son, he shall deal with her as a daughter. ¹⁰ If he takes another wife to himself, he shall not diminish her food, her clothing, and her marital rights. ¹¹ If he doesn't do these three things for her, she may go free without paying any money.

¹² "One who strikes a man so that he dies shall surely be put to death, ¹³ but not if it is unintentional, but God allows it to happen; then I will appoint you a place where he shall flee. ¹⁴ If a man schemes and comes presumptuously on his neighbor to kill him, you shall take him from my altar, that he may die.

¹⁵ "Anyone who attacks his father or his mother shall be surely put to death.

¹⁶ "Anyone who kidnaps someone and sells him, or if he is found in his hand, he shall surely be put to death.

¹⁷ "Anyone who curses his father or his mother shall surely be put to death.

¹⁸ "If men quarrel and one strikes the other with a stone, or with his fist, and he doesn't die, but is confined to bed; ¹⁹ if he rises again and walks around with his staff, then he who struck him shall be cleared; only he shall pay for the loss of his time, and shall provide for his healing until he is thoroughly healed.

²⁰ "If a man strikes his servant or his maid with a rod, and he dies under his hand, the man shall surely be punished. ²¹ Notwithstanding, if his servant gets up after a day or two, he shall not be punished, for the servant is his property.

²² "If men fight and hurt a pregnant woman so that she gives birth prematurely, and yet no harm follows, he shall be surely fined as much as the woman's husband demands and the judges allow. ²³ But if any harm follows, then you must take life for life, ²⁴ eye for eye, tooth for tooth, hand for hand, foot for foot, ²⁵ burning for burning, wound for wound, and bruise for bruise.

²⁶ "If a man strikes his servant's eye, or his maid's eye, and destroys it, he shall let him go free for his eye's sake. ²⁷ If he strikes out his male servant's tooth, or his female servant's tooth, he shall let the servant go free for his tooth's sake.

²⁸ "If a bull gores a man or a woman to death, the bull shall surely be stoned, and its meat shall not be eaten; but the owner of the bull shall not be held responsible. ²⁹ But if the bull had a habit of goring in the past, and this has been testified to its owner, and he has not kept it in, but it has killed a man or a woman, the bull shall be stoned, and its owner shall also be put to death. ³⁰ If a ransom is imposed on him, then he shall give for the redemption of his life whatever is imposed. ³¹ Whether it has gored a son or has gored a daughter, according to this judgment it shall be done to him. ³² If the bull gores a male servant or a female servant, thirty shekels of silver shall be given to their master, and the ox shall be stoned.

³³ "If a man opens a pit, or if a man digs a pit and doesn't cover it, and a bull or a donkey falls into it, ³⁴ the owner of the pit shall make it good. He shall give money to its owner, and the dead animal shall be his.

³⁵ "If one man's bull injures another's, so that it dies, then they shall sell the live bull, and divide its price; and they shall also divide the dead animal. ³⁶ Or if it is known that the bull was in the habit of goring in the past, and its owner has not kept it in, he shall surely pay bull for bull, and the dead animal shall be his own.

22

¹ "If a man steals an ox or a sheep, and kills it or sells it, he shall pay five oxen for an ox, and four sheep for a sheep. ² If the thief is found breaking in, and is struck so that he dies, there shall be no guilt of bloodshed for him. ³ If the sun has risen on him, he is guilty of bloodshed. He shall make restitution. If he has nothing, then he shall be sold for his theft. ⁴ If the stolen property is found in his hand alive, whether it is ox, donkey, or sheep, he shall pay double.

⁵ "If a man causes a field or vineyard to be eaten by letting his animal loose, and it grazes in another man's field, he shall make restitution from the best of his own field, and from the best of his own vineyard.

⁶ "If fire breaks out, and catches in thorns so that the shocks of grain, or the standing grain, or the field are consumed; he who kindled the fire shall surely make restitution.

⁷ "If a man delivers to his neighbor money or stuff to keep, and it is stolen out of the man's house, if the thief is found, he shall pay double. ⁸ If the thief isn't found, then the master of the house shall come near to God, to find out whether or not he has put his hand on his neighbor's goods. ⁹ For every matter of trespass, whether it is for ox, for donkey, for sheep, for clothing, or for any kind of lost thing, about which one says, 'This is mine,' the cause of both parties shall come before God. He whom God condemns shall pay double to his neighbor.

Text Twenty-two: EXODUS

Text Twenty-three
The Prophet Isaiah

1

¹ The vision of Isaiah the son of Amoz, which he saw concerning Judah and Jerusalem, in the days of Uzziah, Jotham, Ahaz, and Hezekiah, kings of Judah.
² Hear, heavens,
and listen, earth; for Yahweh˚ has spoken:
"I have nourished and brought up children,
and they have rebelled against me.
³ The ox knows his owner,
and the donkey his master's crib;
but Israel doesn't know,
my people don't consider."
⁴ Ah sinful nation,
a people loaded with iniquity,
offspring† of evildoers,
children who deal corruptly!
They have forsaken Yahweh.
They have despised the Holy One of Israel.
They are estranged and backward.
⁵ Why should you be beaten more,
that you revolt more and more?
The whole head is sick,
and the whole heart faint.
⁶ From the sole of the foot even to the head there is no soundness in it:
wounds, welts, and open sores.
They haven't been closed, neither bandaged, neither soothed with oil.
⁷ Your country is desolate.
Your cities are burned with fire.
Strangers devour your land in your presence,
and it is desolate,
as overthrown by strangers.
⁸ The daughter of Zion is left like a shelter in a vineyard,
like a hut in a field of melons,
like a besieged city.
⁹ Unless Yahweh of Armies had left to us a very small remnant,
we would have been as Sodom;
we would have been like Gomorrah.

¹⁰ Hear Yahweh's word, you rulers of Sodom!
Listen to the law of our God,‡ you people of Gomorrah!
¹¹ "What are the multitude of your sacrifices to me?", says Yahweh.
"I have had enough of the burnt offerings of rams,
and the fat of fed animals.
I don't delight in the blood of bulls,
or of lambs,
or of male goats.
¹² When you come to appear before me,
who has required this at your hand, to trample my courts?
¹³ Bring no more vain offerings.
Incense is an abomination to me;
new moons, Sabbaths, and convocations:
I can't stand evil assemblies.
¹⁴ My soul hates your New Moons and your appointed feasts.
They are a burden to me.
I am weary of bearing them.
¹⁵ When you spread out your hands, I will hide my eyes from you.
Yes, when you make many prayers, I will not hear.
Your hands are full of blood.
¹⁶ Wash yourselves, make yourself clean.
Put away the evil of your doings from before my eyes.
Cease to do evil.
¹⁷ Learn to do well.
Seek justice.
Relieve the oppressed.
Judge the fatherless.

Plead for the widow."

[18] "Come now, and let's reason together," says Yahweh:
"Though your sins be as scarlet, they shall be as white as snow.
Though they be red like crimson, they shall be as wool.
[19] If you are willing and obedient,
you shall eat the good of the land;
[20] but if you refuse and rebel, you shall be devoured with the sword;
for the mouth of Yahweh has spoken it."

[21] How the faithful city has become a prostitute!
She was full of justice; righteousness lodged in her,
but now murderers.
[22] Your silver has become dross,
your wine mixed with water.
[23] Your princes are rebellious, and companions of thieves.
Everyone loves bribes, and follows after rewards.
They don't judge the fatherless,
neither does the cause of the widow come to them.

[24] Therefore the Lord,[§] Yahweh of Armies,
the Mighty One of Israel, says:

"Ah, I will get relief from my adversaries,
and avenge myself on my enemies;
[25] and I will turn my hand on you,
thoroughly purge away your dross,
and will take away all your tin.
[26] I will restore your judges as at the first,
and your counselors as at the beginning.
Afterward you shall be called 'The city of righteousness,
a faithful town.'
[27] Zion shall be redeemed with justice,
and her converts with righteousness.
[28] But the destruction of transgressors and sinners shall be together,
and those who forsake Yahweh shall be consumed.
[29] For they shall be ashamed of the oaks which you have desired,
and you shall be confounded for the gardens that you have chosen.
[30] For you shall be as an oak whose leaf fades,
and as a garden that has no water.
[31] The strong will be like tinder,
and his work like a spark.
They will both burn together,
and no one will quench them."

Text 24. The Torah

1. Define the Oral Torah and its function. [See TEXT 24]

2. What is the Jewish conception of the afterlife? [see TEXT 25]

Text Twenty-four

The Oral Torah and the Practices of the Torah

V. THE ORAL TORAH

A fundamental issue with the Rabbis was the acceptance of a traditional Torah, transmitted from one generation to another by word of mouth, side by side with the written text. It was claimed that the Oral Torah, equally with the Written Torah, goes back to the Revelation on Sinai, if not in detail at least in principle. Forty-two enactments, which find no record in the Pentateuch, are described by the Talmud as 'laws given to Moses on Sinai.' The rest of the Oral Torah was implied in the Scriptural text and was deducible from it by certain rules of exegesis.

This claim on behalf of the Oral Torah met with strenuous opposition from the Sadducees,[1] and naturally had the effect of making the Rabbis lay exceptional stress on its importance and validity. Hence we get declarations such as these: 'What means that which is written, "And I will give thee the tables of stone, and the law and the commandment, which I have written, that thou mayest teach them" (Exod. xxiv. 12)? "Tables of stone, i.e. the Decalogue; "law," i.e. the Pentateuch; "commandment," i.e. the Mishnah; "which I have written," i.e. the Prophets and Hagiographa; "that thou mayest teach them," i.e. the Gemara. The verse teaches that all of them were given to Moses on Sinai' (Ber. 5a). 'At the time when the Holy One, blessed be He, revealed Himself on Sinai to give the Torah to Israel, He delivered it to Moses in order--Scripture, Mishnah, Talmud, and Haggadah' (Exod. R. XLVII. 1). The Rabbis went so far as to assert, 'The Holy One, blessed be He, only made a covenant with Israel on account of the Oral Torah; as it is said, "For after the tenor of these words[2] I have made a covenant with thee and with Israel" (Exod. xxxiv. 27)' (Git. 60b).

The existence of this dual Revelation is mentioned in conversations about Judaism with non-Jews. For instance, it is related: Roman governor Quietus asked R. Gamaliel, "How many toroth were given to Israel?" He answered, "Two--one in writing and the other orally"' (Sifre Dent. Sec. 351; 145a). It figures in the story about Hillil and the would-be proselyte, and incidentally dwells upon the essential purpose of tradition as a medium for interpreting the text. 'It happened with a heathen that he came before Shammai and asked him, 'How many Toroth have you?" he answered, "Two--the written and the oral." He said, "With respect to the Written Torah I will believe you, but not with respect to the oral Torah. Accept me as a convert on condition that you teach me the former only." Shammai rebuked him and move him out with contempt. He came before Hillel with the same request and he accepted him. The first day he taught him the alphabet in the correct order, but the next day he reversed it. The heathen said to him, "Yesterday you taught it me differently!" Hillel replied, "Have you not to depend upon me for the letters of the alphabet? So must you likewise depend upon me for the interpretation of the Torah"' (Shab. 31a).

Why, however, was it necessary for the Torah to be given in this twofold form? An answer suggested to the question is: 'The Holy One, blessed be He, gave Israel two Toroth, the written and the oral. He gave them the Written Torah in which are six hundred thirteen commandments in order to fill them with precepts whereby they could earn merit. He gave them the Oral Torah whereby they could be distinguished from the other nations. This was not given in writing, so that the Ishmaelites should not fabricate it as they

Source: The Rev. Dr. A Cohen, *Everyman's Talmud* (New York, 1949), pp. 346–389.

have done the Written Torah and say that they were Israel' (Num. R. XIV. 10). In the word 'Ishmaelites' we must detect one of the substitutions which were employed in the Middle Ages to circumvent the censor. Obviously Christians are meant. Since the Church adopted the Hebrew Scriptures, they ceased to be the peculiar possession of Jews. Therefore the Oral Torah, which was not accepted by the Church, safeguarded the distinctiveness of the Jewish people living in a Christian environment.

Another explanation is indicated in this passage: 'It is stated, "Write thou these words" (Exod. xxxiv. 27), and it is also stated, "For after the tenor of these words"[3] (ibid.). How is this to be accounted for? Words of Torah which are written must not be quoted orally, and words which are to be transmitted orally must not be committed to writing. The School of R. Ishmael explained, "Write thou *these* words'--that means these words you are to write but you must not write down traditional dicta' (Git. 60*b*)

In this objection to the Oral Torah being put into writing we see one of its most important functions. The ordinances of the Written Torah were eternal and immutable; only when circumstances made them impossible of fulfilment--as with the sacrifices when the Temple was destroyed and the agrarian laws when the people went into captivity--were they temporarily suspended until the time they could be re-enacted. The Oral Torah which, being unwritten, remained in a flexible state, allowed the written ordinance to be adapted as the conditions of succeeding ages changed. In other words, the Oral Torah prevented the religious legislation of the community from being a fixed system, incapable of progress.

We see this purpose very clearly defined in the following citation: 'If the Torah had been given in a fixed form, the foot would have had no standing.[4] What is the meaning of the oft-recurring phrase, "The Lord spoke unto Moses"? Moses said before Him, "Sovereign of the Universe! cause me to know what the final decision is on each matter of law." He replied, "The majority must be followed. When the majority declare a thing permitted it is permissible, when the majority declare it forbidden it is not allowed; so that the Torah may be capable of interpretation with forty-nine points *pro* and forty-nine points *contra*"' (p. Sanh. 22*a*).

Accordingly the religious leaders of each generation were empowered through the Oral Torah to legislate for their own time in the light of contemporary circumstances. This important principle is deduced by a curious piece of exegesis: 'It is stated, "The Lord sent Jerubbaal and Bedan and Jephthah" (I Sam. xii. 11), and it is further stated, "Moses and Aaron among His priests and Samuel among them that call upon His name" (Ps. xcix. 6). The Scripture makes three of the least important men in the world equal in weight to three of the most important, in order to teach, that Jerubbaal in his generation is like Moses in his, Bedan in his generation like Aaron in his, and Jephthah in his generation like Samuel in his. This indicates that when the most insignificant person is appointed leader over the community he is to be treated as the equal of the most eminent of persons. It is also said, "Thou shalt come unto the priests the Levites, and unto the judge that shall be in those days" (Dent. xvii. 9). Could it possibly enter your mind that a person would go to a judge who was not in his days? The meaning is, You are to go only to a contemporary authority; as the text declares, "Say not thou, What is the cause that the former days were better than these?" (Eccles. Vii. 10)' (R.H. 25*a*, *b*).

In the light of such ideas the statement becomes intelligible: "Even that which a distinguished disciple was destined to teach in the presence of his master was already said to Moses on Sinai' (p. Peah 17*a*). The doctrines of the Rabbis were the harvest from seed which was sown at the time of the original Revelation.

NOTES
1. Priestly families.
2. i.e. spoken, not written, words.
3. The Hebrew is literally: "For by the *mouth* of these words."
4. An idiomatic phrase, meaning the position would have been intolerable.

Sec. VI. THE PRACTICE OF TORAH

The basic purpose of the Talmud was to provide the Jewish people with a body of teaching which should be more than a creed, but also a guide of life in every phase. It created the world in which the Jew moved and had his being. From the roots of the six hundred and thirteen precepts contained in the Pentateuch there grew a tree with numerous branches, the fruits of which provided the daily spiritual sustenance of whoever cared to avail himself of them.

The criticism is often made that the Talmud entangled the Jew in the bonds of legalism so that he was bound hand and foot, and lost all sense of freedom and spirituality. That is merely the outsider's view which receives not the slightest corroboration from the Talmud itself. Instead, it affords conclusive testimony to the spirit of joy and love which animated those who subjected themes to 'the yoke of the Torah.'

'The Holy One, blessed be He, was pleased to make Israel acquire merit; therefore He multiplied for them Torah and commandments; as it is said, "The Lord was well pleased for His righteousness' sake to magnify the Torah and make it honourable" (Is. Xlii, 21)' (Mak. III. 16). This citation, appended by the Prayer Book to the chapters of the Tractate *Aboth* when they are read in the Synagogue on certain Sabbaths, admirably summarizes the Rabbinic attitude towards the life under the Torah. Far from being considered a bondage, it was looked upon as a privilege and a mark of favour from God, to be appreciated with love and gratitude. The words of the Psalmist, 'O how I love Thy Torah' (Ps. Cxix, 97), called forth the comment: 'Solomon said, "a loving bind" (Prov. v. 19)--such is the Torah, all love it; and whoever loves the Torah loves nothing but life. David professed his love for it in the words, "O how I love Thy Torah." Wherever I go it is with me; when I sleep it is with me. Never have I abandoned it in the slightest degree; and since I never abandoned it, it was not a burden upon me but a source of singing; as it is said, "Thy statutes have been my songs in the house of my pilgrimage" (Ps. cxix. 54)' (Midrash ad loc.; 249*b*).

These benedictions, which occur in the Talmud, have become part of the daily liturgy and reflect the true feeling towards the Torah: 'Blessed art Thou, O Lord our God, King of the Universe. Who hast sanctified us by Thy commandments and commanded us to occupy ourselves with the words of Torah. Make pleasant, therefore, we beseech Thee, O Lord our God, the words of Thy Torah in our mouth, and in the mouth of Thy people, the house of Israel, so that we with our offspring and the offspring of Thy people, the house of Israel, may all know Thy name and occupy ourselves with Thy Torah. Blessed art Thou, O Lord, Who teachest Torah to Thy people Israel. Blessed art Thou, O Lord our God, King of the Universe, Who hast chosen us from all nations and given us Thy Torah. Blessed art Thou, O Lord, Who givest the Torah' (Ber. 11*b*).

A guiding principle of action was: 'Greater is he who performs (the commandments) from love than he who performs them from fear' (Sot. 31*a*). One manifestation of this love for the Torah was the erection of a 'fence' around it as a protection against its violation. It was therefore recommended that one should not carry out a religious precept with just the exactitude necessary for compliance with the law, but should add to it for the purpose of being quite certain that the duty had been fulfilled. 'To what is the matter like? To a man who is guarding an orchard. If he guards it from the outside, the whole of it is protected; if he guards it from within, what is in front of him is protected and what is behind him is unprotected' (Jab. 21*a*). As an illustration there is the rule of 'adding from the non-holy to the holy' (R.H. 9*a*), in connection with the sacred days of the calendar; i.e. work is suspended before the actual time that the Sabbath or Festival commences so as not to encroach upon the sanctity of the day inadvertently.

This desire to safeguard the religious duties is exemplified in another way. 'The Sages made a "fence" to their words, so that a man shall not come from the field in the evening and say, "I will go home, eat a little, drink a little, and after that I will offer my prayers." Slumber may overcome him, and as a result he may sleep through all the night. Rather should a man come from the field in the evening and enter a Synagogue; if he is accustomed to read the Scriptures let him read; if he is accustomed to study more advanced branches of learning, let him study. Then let him offer his prayers; after that he should eat his meal and say Grace. Whosoever transgresses the words of the Sages in this matter is worthy of death (Ber. 4*b*).

Another rule which displays devotion to the Torah is *Hiddur Mitzvah* (the embellishment of the commandment), i.e. carrying it out with additional touches beyond what is required by the strict letter of the law, in order to fulfil the command in the best manner one's means allow. It is based on the words of Exod. xv. 2, 'He is my God and I will beautify (*sic*) Him,' which are treated thus: 'Beautify yourself with the precepts of the Torah. Make before Him a beautiful booth (Lev. xxiii. 42), a beautiful palm-branch (ibid. 40), a beautiful ram's horn to be sounded on the New Year (ibid. 24), a beautiful fringe (Num. xv. 38), a beautiful scroll of the Torah written in His honour with the finest ink, with the best pen, by the most competent scribe, and wrapped in the purest silks' (Shab. 133*b*). The ordinances of Judaism must therefore, not be performed in a perfunctory manner, but should be infused with the spirit of enthusiasm and love. It was recognized, on the other hand, that this desire to do honour to God may lead to harmful excess. It might, for example, result in impoverishment. Consequently the rule was laid down, '*Hiddur Mitzvah* may only extend to a third of the value' (B.K. 9*b*), i.e. only a third may be added to the average cost in order to 'embellish the commandment.'

Such, then, was the spirit in which the obligations of the Torah were expected to be discharged. Instead of being an oppressive servitude, it was a joyous service of God which led to the sanctification of the individual life. Indeed, the entire purpose of the Torah was to purify and elevate human existence. The phrase, "The word of the Lord is tried"[1] (Ps. xviii. 30), was made the Support for the doctrine: 'The commandments were only given for the purpose of refining human beings. What, for example, does it matter to the Holy One, blessed be He, whether an animal's neck is cut from the front or the rear?[2] But the ordinances He gave have as their object the purification of human beings' (Gen. R. XLIV. I).

A whole series of commandments was intended to act as reminders of the divine omnipresence and to keep the mind directed to His will at all times. The principal of these are the *Mezuzah* affixed to the door-post, the fringe on the garment and the phylacteries on the arm and forehead. In connection with these we have the statement: 'Beloved are Israel, seeing that the Holy One, blessed be He, has surrounded them with precepts. They have phylacteries on their heads and on their arms, a fringe on their garments and the *Mezuzah* on their doors; and concerning these, said David, "Seven times a day do I praise Thee because of Thy righteous precepts" (Ps. cxix. 164)' (Men. 43*b*). Each will be briefly treated in turn.

The Mezuzah is the literal fulfilment of the command: 'Thou shalt write them upon the posts (*Mezuzah*) of thy house and on thy gates' (Deut. vi. 9). In its traditional form it consists of piece of parchment inscribed with the two passages Deut. Vi. 4-8 and xi.13-21, placed in a case and affixed to the right door post as one enters. On the outside the word *Shaddai* (Almighty) is visible. The original purpose, as already stated, was to provide the Jew with a continuous reminder that he lived even in the privacy of his home under the all-seeing eye of God, and was dependent upon His grace.[3] Therefore it was said, 'Whoever has phylacteries on his head and arm, the fringe on his garment and the *Mezuzah* on his door will presumably not commit a sin' (Men. 43*b*).

In the popular mind, however, the *Mezuzah* became an amulet which assured one of the Divine protection. Two anecdotes illustrate this quite distinctly. 'King Artaban (of Parthia) sent R. Judah the Holy a pearl of great value, with the request that he should return him something equally costly. He sent him a *Mezuzah*. The king said to him, "I sent you something that is priceless and you return me something worth a trifling amount!" He replied, "Your valuable object and mine are quite dissimilar. You sent me something which I have to guard, but I sent you something which will guard you when you are asleep"' (p. Peah 15*a*).

The other story concerns Onkelos (i.e. Akylas), a member of the Roman royal family, who became a convert to Judaism. On hearing of this, the emperor sent a succession of troops to arrest him, but they also were won over to Judaism by his words. Finally the emperor gave his soldiers strict instructions not to converse with him, and they effected his arrest. 'As they left the house," the story continues, 'he looked at the *Mezuzah* which was fixed to the door-post, placed his hand upon it and said to them, "I will tell you what this is. The universal custom is for a human king to sit inside a room and his servants guard him from without. With the Holy One, blessed be He, His servants are inside a room and He guards them from without; as it is said, "The Lord shall keep thy going out and thy coming in, from this time forth and even for evermore" (Ps. cxxi. 8)' (A Z. 11*a*).

Tephillin or phylacteries consist of two small leather cases with straps attached, in each of which is inserted parchment inscribed with four Biblical passages: Exod. xiii. 1-10, 11-16; Deut. vi. 4-9, xi, 13-21. That is the traditional method of fulfilling the law: 'Thou shalt bind them for a sign upon thine hand, and they shall be for frontlets between thine eyes' (Deut. Vi. 8). Their purpose was to make the pprecepts of the Torah a controlling and guiding force in life, so that the ideals of Judaism should mould the thoughts and direct the actions of man. This may be seen from what is narrated of a Talmudic Sage named Rabbah. 'Abbai was sitting in the presence of Rabbah, and noticed that he was very merry. He said to him, "It is written, 'Rejoice with trembling'" (Ps. ii. 11). He relied, "I have laid the phylacteries'" (Ber. 30*b*). He implied by his retort that having them during the day, they would have a sobering influence which would prevent him from exceeding due bounds. The commandment, "Thou shalt not bear (so *lit.*) the name of the Lord they God in vain' (Exod. xx. 7), was interpreted: 'Do not put on the phylacteries, bearing God's name, and then go and sin' (Pesikta, 111*b).*

Text Twenty-four: **THE TORAH**

The purpose of the fringe is described in the verse, "That ye may look upon, it and remember all the commandments of the Lord and do them' (Num. xv. 39), on which the Talmud remarks, "This ordinance is equal to all the precepts, because seeing leads to remembering and remembering to performing' (Men. 43*b*). An instance is quoted in the context of a man who was saved from acting immorally by the reminder he received from the fringe on his garment (ibid. 44*a*). Hence it was taught: 'Whoever is particular with this ordinance is worthy of receiving the presence of the *Shechinah*' (ibid. 43*b*). 'The text does not read "Ye may look upon them," but "look upon Him,"[4] thus declaring that whoever fulfils the law of the fringe is accounted as though he had received the presence of the *Shechinah*, since the colour of the blue thread resembled the colour of the sea which is like that of the firmament and in turn is like that of the Throne of Glory'[5] (Sifre Num. Sec. 115; 34*b*). The meaning is that the understanding use of the fringe kept a person's life pure, and so brought him into closer communion with God.

Here, too, we find a superstitious value attached to the religious rite as a protective force. The neglect of the wearing of the fringe, as well as the omission to fasten the *Mezuzah* to the doorpost, caused death among one's children (Shab. 32*b*); and conversely, 'Whoever scrupulously observed the law of the fringe was worthy that two thousand eight hundred servants should attend upon him; as it is written, "Thus saith the Lord of hosts, In those days shell ten men of all the languages of the nations take hold of the skirt of him that is a Jew, saying, We will go with you for we have heard that God is with you" (Zech. viii, 23)' (ibid.).[6]

Perhaps the most striking example that could be selected of the manner in which the Rabbis developed a Biblical ordinance is the Sabbath. Whereas Scripture merely lays down the general law that no manner of work is to be performed on that day, a whole Talmudic tractate is devoted to the study of what does or does not constitute a desecration of the Sabbath. The prohibited acts were classified under thirty-nine headings: 'Sowing, ploughing, reaping, binding sheaves, threshing, winnowing, selecting, grinding, sifting, kneading, baking; shearing the wool, bleaching, carding, dyeing, spinning, warping, making two thrums, weaving two threads, separating two threads (in the warp), knotting, unknotting, sewing two stitches, tearing for the purpose of sewing two stitches; hunting the stag, slaughtering it, flaying, salting (the flesh), preparing the bide, scraping (the hair), cutting it into pieces; writing two

letters of the alphabet, erasing for the purpose of writing two letters; building, demolishing; kindling a fire, extinguishing it; striking with a hammer; transferring an object from one domain to another' (Shab. VII. 2).

Each item in this classification suggested various problems of definition, and infinite scope for discussion was afforded by questions as to whether a particular act came within one of the categories or not. To give but one illustration. The last-mentioned heading led to two lines of investigation. The first considered the point what involved an act of transference which was a violation of the holy day. That is the subject treated in the first chapter of Tractate *Shabbath*. The first clause of the Mishnah reads: There are two acts of transferring objects (from one domain to another), and these are enlarged to four as affecting the inside (of the premises) and four as affecting the outside. How is this? The beggar, for example, stands outside and the householder inside, and the beggar stretches forth his hand into the interior and places something in the householder's hand or takes it from his hand and draws it outside. In that event the beggar is guilty (or an infraction of the Sabbath law) and the householder is free of guilt. If the householder stretched forth his hand and put something into the beggar's hand or drew from it and brought it into the house, then the householder is guilty and the beggar is free of guilt. If the beggar stretched forth his hand into the interior, and householder takes something out of it or puts something into it, they are both free of guilt. If the householder stretched forth his hand outside and the beggar took something from it or put something into it which the former draws into the house, both are guilty.' It will be gathered from this specimen how complicated the question became under the treatment of the Rabbis.

The second question involved the point what constituted a burden which was forbidden to be carried on the Sabbath. For example, there was a ruling upon what part of a woman's attire was apparel and what an ornament, the latter being considered an unnecessary burden. 'A woman may go out on the Sabbath wearing plaits of hair, whether of her own hair or of another woman or of an animal; or with frontlets or other kinds of ornaments sewn to her headgear; or with a hair-net or false curl, in the courtyard (of her house);[7] or with wadding in her ear or shoe or prepared for a sanitary purpose; or with a pellet of pepper or a grain of salt or anything she is accustomed to keep in her mouth, provided she did not first insert it there on the Sabbath, and if it falls out she must not replace it. As for a tooth which has been re-inserted, or a gold tooth, R. Judah permits it while the Sages forbid it' (Shab. vi. 5).

This is typical of a large number of laws relating to the Sabbath, and it seems to justify the oft-made criticism that under the casuistry of the Rabbis the holy day was turned into a crushing incubus upon the Jews and was robbed of all its joy and spirituality. The truth, however, is that the people who experienced these laws in all their rigour not only failed to notice the supposed crippling burden, but joyfully proclaimed the Sabbath to be a day of light and beauty and godliness.

Here is a brief prayer which was composed by a Rabbi for recital on the Sabbath-eve: 'From Thy love, O Lord our God, wherewith Thou didst love Thy people Israel, and from the compassion, O Lord our King, which Thou didst feel for the children of Thy covenant, Thou didst give us, O Lord our God, this great and holy seventh day in love' (Tosifta Ber. III. xx). Only one to whom the Sabbath was a boon and a delight could have uttered those words, and that is precisely how it was considered. On the text, 'That ye may know what I am the Lord that doth sanctify you' (Exod. xxxi. 13), we have this statement: 'The Holy One, blessed be He, said to Moses, I have a precious gift in My treasury, named Sabbath, and I wish to present it to Israel; go and inform them' (Shab. 10b).

Nor was there the slightest austerity about its observance. Public manifestations of mourning, which extended for a week after the burial of a deceased relative, had to be suspended on the Sabbath. A favourite text in this connection was, 'Call the Sabbath a delight' (Is. lviii, 13), on the basis of which it was recommended that a lamp should be kindled in the home (Shab. 25b), the best clothes worn (ibid. 113a) and three good meals provided (ibid. 117b). To spend freely on honouring the Sabbath was held to be a praiseworthy act, and the assurance was given that 'whoever lends to the Sabbath is well repaid' (ibid. 119a). A story is told of a Rabbi who paid a visit to a colleague's house on the Sabbath, and a bounteous supply of cooked dishes was set before him. 'Did you know I was coming, that you have provided so liberally?' the guest asked; to which the host retorted, 'Are you more esteemed by me than the Sabbath?' (ibid.). This custom of doing honour to the Sabbath gave rise to this application of the words, 'I am black but comely' (Cant. i. 5); 'I (Israel) am black on the weekdays but comely on the Sabbath' (Midrash ad loc.).

What loving devotion was displayed by two Rabbis of whom it, is related: 'R. Channina used to don his best clothes, and towards sunset on Friday exclaim, "Come, let us go forth to meet Queen Sabbath." R. Jannai used to don his best clothes on the Sabbath eve and exclaim, "Enter, O bride; enter, O bride!"' (Shab. 119a).

The Sabbath had for its object the hallowing of life. "For it is holy unto you" (Exod. xxxi. 14)--this teaches that the Sabbath increases holiness for Israel' (Mech. ad loc.; 104a). As we have seen, there was a current belief that the holy day endowed him who honoured it with an 'additional soul.'[8]

Two variants of the same story indicate the special flavour which the Sabbath introduced into the life of the people. 'The emperor asked R. Joshua b. Chananya, "How is it that the Sabbath food has so pleasant an odour?" He answered, "We possess a spice, named Sabbath,[9] which we include in it and that gives it its fragrance." The emperor requested to be presented with some of the spice; but he was told, "It only avails him who observes the Sabbath"' (Shab. 119a). 'R. Judah entertained Antoninus on a Sabbath when all the dishes were served cold.[10] He ate and enjoyed the food. R. Judah entertained him on another occasion, but on a weekday, when the dishes were served hot. Antoninus said, "The dishes on the previous occasion pleased me better." His host answered, "They lack a certain spice." "Does, then, the king's treasury lack anything?" he asked. "The dishes lack the Sabbath," was the reply, "and have you the Sabbath?"' (Gen. R. xi. 4).

If the Sabbath is the most noteworthy instance of the elaboration of a Biblical ordinance by the Talmud, the chapter may be concluded by inquiry how an important piece of Scriptural legislation fared when circumstances rendered its performance impossible. The Temple and its ritual played a very prominent part in the life of the people, and much space is devoted in the Talmud to their description. For the Rabbis the sacrifices were divinely enacted. What, then, was their attitude when the Temple ceased to exist?

The answer is best indicated in the story told of R. Jochanan b. Zakkai and his disciple R. Joshua. 'On one occasion, when they were leaving Jerusalem, the latter gazed upon the destroyed Temple cried out, "Woe to us! The place where Israel obtained atonement for sins is in ruins!" R. Jochanan said to him, "My son, be not distressed. We still have an atonement equally efficacious, and that is the practice of benevolence'" (ARN IV). God is likewise depicted as announcing. 'More beloved by Me are the justice and righteousness which you perform than sacrifices" (p. Ber. 4*b*). Another statement which He is represented as having made to David was, 'Better to Me is one day spent in occupation with the Torah than a thousand burnt-offerings which your son Solomon will sacrifice before Me upon the altar' (Shab. 30*a*).

The greatest accomplishment which the teaching of the Talmud achieved for the Jewish people was to make them feel that the end of the Temple did not imply an end to their religion. Severe as the loss was, the way of approach to God was kept open. In addition to charity, justice, and Torah-study there was also prayer, which was declared to be even 'greater than sacrifices' (Ber. 32*b*). On the basis of the words, 'We will render the calves of our lips (Hos. xiv. 2), the doctrine was taught, 'What can be a substitue for the bulls which we used to offer before Thee? Our lips, with the prayer which we pray unto Thee' (Pesikta 165*b*).

In this chapter only an outline sketch could be attempted of an exposition of the Rabbinic theory of Torah. A whole volume would be required to treat it with anything like adequate completeness.[11] The wrong way to view the subject, is from the standpoint of modern religious conceptions. It can only be justly appraised from the premises of the Rabbis themselves, and the only fair test is the pragmatic one. By their interpretation of Torah they enabled Judaism to continue in existence after the ritual of the altar had stopped and the State been broken up, whereas their opponents, the Sadducees, disappeared from history. The preservation of Israel's religion was their aim, and the fact that it was realized was to them all the proof they required of the truth what they taught.

NOTES
1. The Hebrew word means 'refined.'
2. When it is slaughtered for food; see pp. 237 f.
3. This explanation is found in Josephus: 'They are also to inscribe the, pincipal blessings they have received from God upon their doors, and show the same on their arms; as also they are to bear inscribed on their head and arm whatever can declare the power of God and His good will towards them, that God's readiness to bless them may appear everywhere conspicuous about them' (Antiq. IV. viii. 13).
4. The suffix can mean 'it' or 'Him.' For homiletic purposes the latter is adopted.
5. See Ezek. 1 25.
6. The number 2,800 is obtained in this way. There are seventy nations, and since ten of each are concerned, we have 700. This number will hold each of the four corners of the garment, and therefore it must be multiplied by four.
7. i.e. a private domain; but she may not go into a public street.
8. See p. 78.
9. Point is added to the two stories by the fact that the Hebrew word for 'dill' is *Shebeth* and has the same consonants as *Shabbath*, 'Sabbath.'
10. Cooking is forbidden on the Sabbath and food has to be prepared before its advent.
11. The reader is recommended to study R. T. Seaford, *The Pharisees* (1924) where the subject is excellently treated.

Text Twenty-five

The Hereafter

Sec. I. THE MESSIAH

WHEREAS other peoples of antiquity placed their Golden Age in the dim and remote past, the Jews relegated it to the future. The prophets of Israel repeatedly allude to 'the latter days,' still unborn, as the period when the national greatness would reach its zenith. This hope took a firm grip of the popular mind and grew not only in its intensity but, as time proceeded, likewise in the marvels which its realization would bring to the world. The glorious future centred around the person of a *Mashiach*, 'an anointed one,' who would be deputed by God to inaugurate this new and wonderful era.

The Talmud has hundreds of references to the Messiah and his mission, but we find only one teacher sounding a skeptical note. A fourth century Rabbi, Hillel, declared: 'Israel has no Messiah (yet to come) since he already enjoyed him in the days of Hezekiah' (Sanh. 98*b*). He was taken to task for his remark. There may, however, have been a section of the people who believed that the splendid reign of that king witnessed the fulfillment of Isaiah's Messianic prophecies, because the Talmud expressly repudiates the thought, 'Why has the word *lemarbeh* "the increase" (Is. ix. 7) in the Hebrew, 6) a final *m* as a middle letter![1] The Holy One, blessed be He, wished to make Hezekiah the Messiah and Senna-cherib Gog and Magog;[2] but the attribute of justice spoke before Him, "Sovereign of the Universe! David, king of Israel, who composed so many songs and praises in Thy honour. Thou hast not made the Messiah, and wilt Thou make Hezekiah the Messiah for whom Thou hast performed so many miracles and yet he did not compose one song for Thee?"' (Sanh. 94*a*). Nevertheless, in the farewell scene between Jochanan b. Zakklai and his disciples, he addressed the cryptic remark to them on his death-bed: 'Prepare a seat for Hezekiah, king of Judah, who is coming' (Ber.28*b*). His words are usually understood as foreshadowing the advent of the Messiah; and if that be so, this eminent Rabbi of the first century identified him with Hezekiah. As will be seen, there was considerable variety of opinion about the identity of the future Redeemer.

The belief was general that the sending of the Messiah was part of the Creator's plan at the inception of the Universe. 'Seven things were created before the world was created: Torah, repentance, the Garden of Eden (i.e. Paradise), Gehinnom, the Throne of Glory, he Temple, and the name of the Messiah' (Pes. 54*a*). In a later work there is the observation: 'From the beginning of the creation of the world king Messiah was born, for he entered the mind (of God) before even the world was Created' (Pesikta Rab. 152*b*).

Naturally speculation was rife as to who the Messiah would be, and Scriptural texts were studied for enlightenment. On one point the Rabbis were unanimous, viz. he would be just a human being divinely appointed to carry out an allotted task. The Talmud nowhere indicates a belief in a superhuman Deliverer as the Messiah.

Some authorities identified him with David. The verse, 'Afterward shall the children of Israel return and seek the Lord their God and David their king' (Hos. iii. 5), was interpreted thus: 'The Rabbis declare, That is king Messiah. If he is born from among the living, David is his name; and if he be from among the dead, David is his name' (p; Ber.

Source: The Rev. Dr. A Cohen, *Everyman's Talmud* (New York, 1949), pp. 146–158.

5a). This opinion was sharply challenged by the citation of another passage: "Great deliverance giveth He to His king, and sheweth lovingkindness to His anointed (Heb. *Messiah*), to David and to his seed, for evermore" (Ps. xviii. 50)--it is not written here "to David" but "to David and to his seed'" (Lament. R. I. 51). The prevailing belief was that the Messiah would be a descendant of the king, and a common designation for him in Rabbinic literature is 'the son of David.'

Biblical passages which were interpreted in a Messianic sense afforded a variety of names by which he would be called. Certain Rabbinic students even exercised their ingenuity to discover for him a name similar to that borne by their teacher. 'What is the Messiah's name? The School of R. Sheila said, "Shiloh, as it is written, 'Until Shiloh come' (Gen. xlix. 10)." The School of R. Jannai declared, "Jinnon, as it is said, 'His name shall be continued (Heb. *jinnon*) as long as the sun' (Ps. lxxii. 17)." The School of R. Channina declared, "Chaninah, as it is said, 'I will show you no favour' (Heb. *chaninah*) (Jer. xvi. 13)." Others contend that his name is Menachem son of Hezekiah, as it is said, "The comforter (Heb. *menachem*) that should refresh my soul is far from me" (Lament. i, 16). The Rabbis maintain that his name is "the leprous one of the School of R. Judah the Prince," as it is said, "Surely he hath borne our griefs, and carried our sorrows; yet we did esteem him stricken, smitten of God, and afflicted"[3] (Is. liii. 4). Rab declared, The Holy One, blessed be He, will hereafter raise up for Israel another David, as it is said, "They shall serve the Lord their God and David their king, whom I will raise up unto them" (Jer. Xxx. 9). It is not stated "has raised" but "will raise'" (Sanh. 98b).

Other designations suggested for him are given in these extracts: 'R. Joshua, b. Levi said, His name is *Tsemach* ("the branch," cf. Zech. Vi. 12). R. Judan said, It is Menachem. R. Aibu said, The two are identical since the numerical value of the letters forming their names is the same' (p. Ber. 5a). 'R. Nachman asked R. Isaac, "Have you heard when *Bar Naphle* ('son of the fallen') will come?" He said to him, "Who is *Bar Naphle?*" He answered, "The Messiah." The other asked, "Do you call the Messiah *Bar Naphle?*" He replied, "I do, because it is written, 'In that day will I raise up the tabernacle of David that is fallen' (Amos ix., 11)'" (Sanh. 96b).

Mention is once made of a rather mysterious figure called Messiah son of Joseph. The passage reads: 'Messiah son of

Joseph was slain, as it is written, "They shall look unto me whom they have pierced; and they shall mourn for him as one mourneth for his only son" (Zech. Xii. 10)' (Suk, 52a). 'Son of Joseph,' like 'son of David,' means a descendant of the ancestor of that name; and its origin seems to be indicated in this citation: 'Our father Jacob foresaw that the seed of Esau would only be delivered into the hand of the seed of Joseph, as it is said, "The house of Jacob shall be a fire, and the house of Joseph a flame, and the house of Esau for stubble, and they shall burn among them and devour them" (Obad. 18)' (b.B. 123b).[4]

The hope for the coming of the Messiah naturally became more fervent in the time of severe national eclipse. When the oppression of the conqueror grew intolerable, the Jews instinctively turned to the Messianic predictions contained in their Scriptures. Josephus records how, in the years immediately preceding the destruction of the Temple, men came forward claiming to be the Redeemer foretold by the prophets.[5] A notable instance is afforded in the following century by Bar Kochba, or, as some named him, Bar Koziba, who led the revolt against Rome and was hailed by R. Akiba as the Messiah. We are informed: 'R. Akiba expounded, "There shall come forth a star (Heb. *hochab*) out of Jacob" (Num. xxiv. 17) in the sense, "There shall come forth Koziba from Jacob." When R. Akiba beheld Bar Koziba he exclaimed, "This is king Messiah"; but R. Jochanan b. Torta remarked, "Akiba, grass will grow in your cheeks and still the son of David will not have come'" (p. Taan. 68d).

To hearten the people in their misery and encourage them to persevere in the face of the severest hardships, the Rabbis preached the doctrine that there will be 'the travail of the Messiah,' i.e. his coming will be attended by pangs of suffering in the same manner that a child is born at the cost of much pain to its mother. On the principle that the night is darkest before the dawn, they taught that the world would show signs of utter demoralization before his arrival and the conditions of life prove well-nigh unbearable.

Statements to this effect are: 'In the generation in which the son of David will come youths will insult their elders, the old will have to stand up before the young, daughter will revolt against her mother, daughter-in-law against her mother-in-law, the face of the generation will be like the face of the dog (for impudence), and a son will feel no shame in the presence of his father' (Sanh. 97a). 'Meeting-places for study will be turned into brothels, the learning of the scribes will decay and sin-fearing men will be contemned' (ibid). 'The son of David will only come in a generation which is wholly innocent or wholly guilty--wholly innocent, as it is said, "Thy people also shall be all righteous, they shall inherit the land for ever" (Is. lx. 21); and wholly guilty, as it is said, "He saw that there was no man and wondered that there was no intercessor; therefore His own arm brought salvation unto him" (ibid. lix. 16), and it is written, "For Mine own sake, for Mine own sake,[6] will I do it" (ibid. xiviii, 11)' (Sanh. 98a).

A tradition relates: 'During the period of seven years in which the son of David will come, in the first year the verse will be fulfilled, "I caused it to rain upon one city and caused it not to rain upon another city" (Amos iv. 7). In the second year the arrows of famine will be let loose. In the third year famine will be severe, and men, women, and children, and pious and saintly men will perish, and Torah will be forgotten by its, students. In the fourth year there will be plenty and not plenty.[7] In the fifth year there will be great abundance; people will eat, drink, and be merry, and Torah will return to its students. In the sixth year there will be voices (from heaven). In the seventh year wars will occur, and at the conclusion of this seven-year period the son of David will come' (Sanh. 97a).

The time of his advent will be particularly marked by political unrest, culminating in bitter warfare. 'If you see the kingdoms contending with each other, look for the foot of the Messiah. Know that it will be so, because it happened thus in the days of Abraham. When the kingdoms strove with each other (Gen. xiv), redemption came to Abraham' (Gen. R. XLII. 4).

This strife is symbolized under the term 'wars of Gog and Magog' (see Ezek. xxxviii).[8] "Arise, O Lord, confront him, cast him down" (Ps. xvii. 13). Five petitions to "arise" did David address to the Holy One, blessed be He, in the Book of Psalms.[9] Four of them are in connection with the four kingdoms which he foresaw by the Holy Spirit would enslave Israel, and he besought Him to arise against each of them. The fifth concerned the kingdom of Gog and Magog which he foresaw would advance against Israel in might; and he said to the Holy One, blessed be He, "Arise, O Lord; O God, lift up Thine hand" (Ps. x. 12), for we have no ruler but Thee to contend with it' (Midrash ad loc.; 66b). The four kingdoms alluded to are specified in this extract: "When they, be in the land of their enemies, I will not reject them, neither will I abhor them, to destroy them utterly, and to break My covenant with them, for I am the Lord their God" (Lev. xxvi. 44)--"I will not reject them" in the days of the Greeks, "neither will I abhor them" in the days of Nebuchadnezzar, "to destroy them utterly" in the days of Haman (i.e. Persia), "to break My covenant with them" in the days of the Romans,[10] "for I am the Lord their God" in the days of Gog. and Magog' (Meg. 11a).

An interesting reference to the subject occurs in this anecdote. 'R. Chanan b. Tachlipha sent this message to R. Joseph: I met a man holding a scroll written in the Hebrew square characters in the holy tongue. I asked him, "Where did you get this?" He answered, "I was a mercenary in the Roman army and I discovered it among the Roman archives." There was written in it, "After 4,291 years from the creation of the world (i.e. A.D. 531), the world will be destroyed, partly by the wars of the sea-monsters, partly by the wars of Gog and Magog, and then will the days of the Messiah occur; and the Holy One, blessed be He, will not renew the world until after seven thousand years' (Sanh. 97b).

Other calculations of the time of his advent are found in the Talmud, most of them indicating a date about the end of the fifth century. For example, Elijah told a Rabbi, "The world will endure for at least eight-five Jubilees (i.e. 4,250 years) and in the last Jubilee the son of David will come.' The Rabbi asked him, 'Will he come at the beginning or end of the Jubilee?' He answered, 'I do not know' (ibid.). This yields a date between 440 and 490. 'If a person, four hundred years after the destruction of the Temple (which occurred in A.D. 70), should ask you to purchase a field worth a thousand denarii for one denarius, do not buy it. There is a Rabbinic teaching: After 4,231 years from the creation of the world (i.e. A.D. 471) if a field worth a thousand denarii is offered for one denarius, do not buy it' (A.Z. 9b), because the Messiah will then come and land will cease to have value.

Attempts to calculate 'the end,' i.e. the time of the Messiah's coming, were deprecated, by the majority of the Rabbis on the ground that they raised hopes which were ultimately falsified. There is the emphatic warning: 'Cursed be they who calculate "the end," because they argue that since "the end" has arrived and the Messiah has not come, he never will come; but wait for him, as it is said, "Though it (the appointed time) tarry, wait for it" (Hab. ii. 3)' (Sanh. 97b). According to one opinion, 'Israel will be redeemed in *Tishri*; another opinion is, they were redeemed (from Egypt) in *Nisan* and in *Nisan* they will be redeemed' (R.H. 11*a*).

As against the belief that God had determined an exact date for the dawn of the Messianic era, there grew up another doctrine that the date was not fixed but would be affected by the conduct of the people. That thought was read into the words, 'I the Lord will hasten it in its time' (Is. lx. 22), which were explained in this sense: 'If you are worthy I will hasten it; if you are not worthy it will be in its time' (Sanh. 98*a*).

We likewise read such utterances as: 'Great is repentance because it brings the Redemption near' (Joma 86*b*); 'All "the ends" have passed (and the Messiah has not come); it depends only upon repentance and good deeds' (Sanh, 97*b*); 'If Israel repented a single day, immediately would the son of David come. If Israel observed a single Sabbath properly, immediately would the son of David come' (p. Taan, 64*a*); 'If Israel were to keep two Sabbaths according to the law, they would be redeemed forthwith' (Shab. 118*b*).

Imagination ran riot in the attempt to envisage the world as it will appear under the transforming hand of the Messiah. The productivity of nature will be increased to a marvelous degree. 'Not like this world will be the World to Come.[12] In this world one has the trouble to harvest the grapes and press them; but in the World to Come a person will bring a single grape in a wagon or a ship, store it in the corner of his house, and draw from it enough wine to fill a large flagon, and its stalk will be used as fuel under the pot. There will not be a grape which will not yield thirty measures of wine' (Keth. 111*b*). 'As in this world grain is produced after six months and trees grow fruit after twelve months, in the Hereafter grain will be produced after one month and trees will grow fruit after two months. R. Jose said, In the Hereafter grain will be produced after fifteen days and trees will grow fruit after one month' (p. Taan, 64*a*). Still more extravagant are the remarks: 'In the Hereafter the land of Israel will grow loaves of the finest flour and garments of the finest wool; and the soil will produce wheat the ears of which will be the size of two kidneys of a large ox' (Keth. 111*b*); and 'In the Hereafter women will bear children daily and trees will produce fruit daily' (Shab. 30*b*).

An elaborate description of the effect which the Messianic era will have upon the state of the world is contained in this extract: 'Ten things will the Holy One, blessed be He, renew in the Hereafter: (i) He will illumine the world; as it is said, "The sun shall be no more thy light by day, neither for brightness shall the moon give light unto thee; but the Lord shall be unto thee an everlasting light" (Is. lx. 19). Is, then, man able to gaze upon the Holy One, blessed be he! But what will He do to the sun? He will illumine it with forty-nine parts of light;[13] as it is said, "The light of the moon shall be as the light of the sun, and the light of the sun shall be seven-fold the light of seven days" (ibid. xxx. 26). Even when a person is ill, the Holy One, blessed be He, will order the sun to bring him healing; as it is said, "Unto you that fear My name shall the sun of righteousness arise with healing in his wings" (Mal. Iv.2). (ii) He will cause running water to issue from Jerusalem, and whoever has an ailment will find healing there; as it is said, "Every thing shall live whithersoever the river cometh" (Ezek. Xivii. 9). (iii) He will cause trees to produce their fruit every month and all persons will eat of them and be healed; as it is said, "It shall bring forth new fruit every month . . . and the fruit thereof shall be for food, and the leaf thereof for healing" (ibid. 12). (iv) All ruined cities will be rebuilt and no waste place will remain in the world. Even Sodom and Gomorrah will be rebuilt in the Hereafter; as it is said, "Thy sisters Sodom and her daughters shall return to their former estate" (ibid. xvi. 55). (v) He will rebuild Jerusalem with sapphires; as it is said, "I will lay thy foundations with sapphires" (Is. liv. Ii) and "I will make thy pinnacles of rubies" (ibid. 12), and those stones will shine like the sun so that idolaters will come and look upon the glory of Israel, as it is said, "Nations shall come to thy light" (ibid. ix. 3). (vi) (Peace will reign throughout nature), as it is said, "The cow and the bear shall feed together" (ibid. xi. 7). (vii) He will assemble all beasts, birds, and reptiles, and make a covenant between them and all Israel; as it is said, "In that day (Hos. li. 18). (viii) Weeping and wailing will cease in the world; as it is said, "The voice of weeping shall be no more heard in her" (Is. lxv. 19). (ix) Death will cease in the world; as it is said, "He hath swallowed up death for ever" (ibid. xxv. 8). (x) There will be no more sighing, groaning, or anguish, but all will be happy; as it is said, "The ransomed of the Lord shall return and come with signing to Zion" (ibid. xxxv. 10)' (Exod. R. xv. 21).

That the Messiah will inaugurate a time of abiding peace and happiness and contentment is naturally stressed. 'Not like this world is the World to Come. In this world, on hearing good tidings one utters the benediction, "Blessed is He Who is good and doeth good," and on hearing bad tidings, "Blessed be the true Judge;" "Blessed is He Who is good and doeth good"' (Pes.

50*a*). 'While in this world one man builds and another uses it out, one man plants and another eats the fruit, with regard to the Hereafter what is written? "They shall not build and another inhabit, they shall not plant and another eat . . . they shall not labour in vain, nor bring forth for calamity" (Is. lxv. 22 f.)' (Lev. R. xxv. 8). 'Come and see: all whom the Holy One, blessed be He, smote in this world He will heal in the Hereafter. The blind will be cured; as it is said, "Then the eyes of the blind shall be opened" (Is. xxxv. 5) The lame will be cured; as it is said, "Then shall the lame man leap as a hart" (ibid. 6)' (Gen. R. xcv. 1). 'The Holy One, blessed be He, said, In this world through the evil impulse My creatures have split up and become divided into seventy languages, but in the World to Come they will all combine to call upon My name and serve Me; as it is said, "For then will I turn to the peoples a pure language, that they may all call upon the name of the lord, to serve Him with one consent" (Zeph. iii. 9)' (Tanchuma Noach Sec. 19).

Chief of all will Israel be blessed by the coming of the Messiah. His oppression by a hostile world will end and he will be restored to the position of eminence designed for him by God. ' "Thou broughtest a vine out of Egypt" (Ps. lxxx. 8). As the vine is the lowliest of trees and yet rules over all the trees, so Israel is made to appear lowly in this world but will in the Hereafter inherit the world from end to end. As the vine is at first trodden under the foot but is afterwards brought upon the table of kings, so Israel is made to appear contemptible in this world, as it is said, "I am become a derision to all my people" (Lament, iii. 14); but in the Hereafter the Lord will set him on high, as it is said, "Kings shall be thy nursing fathers" (Is. xlix. 23)' (Lev. R. xxxvi. 2). 'The Holy One, blessed be He, said to Israel, In this world I set before you blessings and curses, good fortune and disasters, but in the World to Come I will remove from you the curses and disasters and bless you, so that all who behold you will declare you to be a people of the blessed' (Tanchuma Reeh Sec. 4).

So striking will be the change in Israel's fortune that many non-Jews will attempt to join the Community, but will have to be rejected because their motive is not disinterested. 'In the Hereafter the gentile peoples will come to be made proselytes, but we will not accept any of them; for there is a Rabbinic dictum. No proselytes are to be accepted in the days of the Messiah' (A.Z. 3*b*).

Another confirmed belief was that the Messiah would effect the reunion of the tribes of Israel. While we find the teaching,

'The ten tribes will have no share in the World to Come' (Tosifta Sanh. Xiii. 12), the Talmud usually takes the opposite view. By appealing to such texts as Is. xxvii. 13 and Jer. Iii, 12, the Rabbis enunciated the doctrine of the return of the lost ten tribes (Sanh. 110*b*). 'Great will be the day when the exiles of Israel will be reassembled as the day when heaven and earth were created' (Pes. 88*a*). A law of nature will even be miraculously suspended to assist this great reunion. 'In the present world when the wind blows in the north it does not blow in the south, and vice versa; but in the Hereafter, with reference to the gathering together of the exiles of Israel, the Holy One, blessed be He, said, I will bring a north-west wind into the world which will affect both directions; as it is written, "I will say to the north, Give up; and to the south, Keep not back; brings My sons from afar, and My daughters from the end of the earth" (Is. xliii, 6)' (Midrash to. Esth. i. 8).

The regathering of the tribes will be preceded by another wondrous event, viz. the restoration of the Holy City. 'If a man tells you that the scattered exiles of Israel have been gathered together without Jerusalem having been rebuilt, do not believe him, for Thus is it written, "The Lord doth build up Jerusalem" (Ps. cxlvii, 2), and then "He gathereth together the outcasts of Israel" (ibid.). The Israelites spoke before the Holy One, blessed be He, "'Lord of the Universe! Was not Jerusalem previously built and then destroyed?" He said to them, "On account of your iniquities it was laid waste and you were exiled from it; but in the Hereafter I will rebuild and never destroy it again"' (Tanchuma Noach Sec. 11).

Included in the rebuilding of Jerusalem will be the re-establishment of the Temple. This belief was deduced from several texts: '"The beloved of the Lord shall dwell in safety by Him" (Deut. xxxiii. 12), i.e. the rebuilding of the first Temple; "He covereth him all the day long," i.e. the building of the second Temple; "and he dwelleth between His shoulders, i.e. the Temple rebuilt and, perfected in the Hereafter' (Sifre Deut. Sec. 352; 145*b*). "That I may tell, you that which shall befall you in the latter days" (Gen. xlix. 1). Jacob showed his sons the rebuilding of the Temple' (Gen. R. xcviii. 2). We likewise have the observation: 'The Holy One, blessed be He, said, I am He that made the Temple into a heap of ruins in this world, and I am He that will make it a thing of beauty in the World to Come. . . . He will rebuild the Temple and cause His *Shechinah* to abide there' (Midresh to Cant. iv. 4).

The new Temple will not play quite the same part in the life of the people as did the previous structures, because, sin having been abolished, there will be no need for expiatory sacrifices. The feeling of gratitude which will fill all hearts will make at least one class of sacrifice necessary. In the Hereafter all offerings will cease except the thanksgiving offering which will never come to an end' (Pesikta 79a).

Since the Messianic era will bring such great happiness, it is only right that the good who have passed away should be allowed to participate in it and the wicked excluded. Consequently the belief grew that the coming of the Messiah would be distinguished by the resurrection of the dead if they had been worthy of this reward. This subject will be treated in the next section. As for them who live unworthily, 'Near to the days of the Messiah a great pestilence will come upon the world in which the wicked will perish' (Cant. R. to ii. 13).

There seems, however, to have been a reaction to these imaginative dreams, and we have the view expressed that the Messiah will only produce one result, viz. the freeing of Israel from his oppressors; and for the abolition of the various ills to which man is heir he will have to wait until he departs from this life. 'There is no difference between this world and the days of the Messiah except the servitude of the heathen kingdoms alone; as it is said, "For the poor shall never cease out of the land" (Deut. Xv. 11)' (Ber. 34b), i.e. not even in the Messianic era.

Many Rabbis believed that the period of the Messiah was to be only a transitionary stage between this world and the World to Come, and opinions differed on the time of its duration. 'How long will the days of the Messiah last? R. Akiba said, Forty years, as long as the Israelites were in the wilderness. R. Eliezer (b. Jose) said, A hundred years. R. Berechya said in the name of R. Dosa, Six hundred years. R. Judah the Prince said, Four hundred years, as long as the Israelites were in Egypt. R. Eliezer (b. Hyrcanus) said, A thousand years. R. Abbahu said, Seven thousand years; and the Rabbis generally declared, Two thousand years' (Tanchuma Ekeb Sec. 7). Other versions read: 'R. Eliezer said, The days of the Messiah will be forty years. R. Eleazar b, Azariah said, Seventy years, R. Judah the Prince said, Three generations' (Sanh. 99a). 'R. Eliezer said, The days of the Messiah will be forty years. R. Dosa said, Four hundred years. R. Judah the Prince said, Three hundred and sixty-five years. R. Abimi b. Abbahu said, Seven thousand years. R. Judah said in the name of Rab, As long as the world has already lasted. R. Nachman b. Isaac said, As long as from the days of Noah up to the present' (ibid). 'It was taught in

the School of Elijah, The world will endure six thousand years--two thousand years in chaos,[14] two thousand with Torah, and two thousand years will be the days of the Messiah' (ibid. 97a).

NOTES
1. Five letters of the Hebrew alphabet, including *m,* have a different shape when they occur at the end of a word. In *lemarbeh,* although the *m* is not a final letter, the traditional text gives it that form.
2. The allusion to Gog and Magog as the fomentors of strife before the coming of the Messiah will be explained below, pp. 350 f.
3. The Rabbis interpreted 'stricken' in the sense of 'leprous.' The verse therefore foreshadowed a Messiah who would suffer from leprosy. It is told of R. Judah the Prince that though he was grievously smitten with illness of R. Judah the Prince that though he was grievously smitten with illness for thirteen years, yet he used to say, 'Beloved are sufferings,' as a sign of God's mercy (B.M. 85a). Accordingly it was remarked that the Messiah, as prophesied by Isiah, would belong to the type exemplified by this Rabbi.
4. The conception of a Messiah son of Joseph only came into existence after the failure of Bar Kochba's revolt in A.D. 135 (see Klausner, *Jesus of Nazareth,* p. 201). He figures prominently in later Jewish legends. One of them identifies him with the child restored to life by Elijah (*Seder Elijahu Rabba,* xvii. Ed. Friedmann, pp. 97 f.).
5. See p. 124.
6. Not for the sake of the righteous, because there are none.
7. In effect, although there will be plenty, people will be discontented.
8. Cf. also Rusk. xxxix. 11, and Rev. xx. 8.
9. See also iii 7; vii. 6; ix. 10; x. 12.
10. The text reads 'Persians,' but the substitution was occasioned by the medieval censors who detected allusions to the Church in references to Rome.
11. The seventh month of the Jewish calendar in which the New Year occurs. *Nisan* is the first month in which the Passover is observed.
12. Here, and often elsewhere, the phrase 'World to Come' denotes the Messianic era.
13. In effect, make its light forty-nine times more brilliant.
14. That is, the period from the Creation to the Revelation at Sinai.

Sec. II. RESURRECTION OF THE DEAD
No aspect of the subject of the Hereafter has so important a

Place in the religious teaching of the Rabbis as the doctrine of the Resurrection. It became with them an article of faith the denial of which was condemned as sinful; and they declared: 'Since, a person repudiated belief in the Resurrection of the dead, he will have no share in the Resurrection' (Sanh. 90*a*).

The prominence which this dogma assumed was the effect of religious controversy. It was one of the differences between the Pharisees and Sadducees. The latter, as we know from other sources,[1] taught that the soul became extinct when the body died and death was the final end of the human being. This denial of a Hereafter involved the doctrine of reward and punishment to which the Pharisees attached great importance, and for that reason they fought it strenuously. They made it the theme of one of the Eighteen Benedictions which formed part of the daily service of prayer: 'Thou sustainest the living with loving kindness, revivest the dead with great mercy, supportest the falling, healest the sick, loosest the bound, and keepest Thy faith to them that sleep in the dust. Who is like unto Thee, Lord of mighty acts, and who resembleth Thee, O king, Who killest and revivest, and causest salvation to spring forth? Yea, faithful art Thou to revive the dead. Blessed art Thou, O Lord, Who revivest the dead.'[2]

We are informed that the disputation on this matter led to an alteration in the wording of the liturgy used in the Temple. 'At the conclusion of every benediction in the Sanctuary they used to say, "For ever;"[3] but when the Sadducees perverted the truth and declared that there is only one world, it was ordained that the wording should be "From everlasting to everlasting"' (Ber. Ix. 5).

An apparent reason why the Sadducees rejected the doctrine was that it was not taught, so they alleged, in the Pentateuch, and was therefore part of the Oral Torah which they repudiated. This view was strongly controverted by the Rabbis. The Talmud even remarks: 'There is no section of the (written) Torah which does not imply the doctrine of Resurrection, but we have not the capacity to expound it in this sense' (Sifre Deut. Sec. 306; 132*a*). Much ingenuity was therefore expended to demonstrate that the Torah does teach, it. A selection of these proofs will here be given.

'Whence is the doctrine of the Resurrection derived from the Torah? As it is said, 'Ye shall give the Lord's heave-offering to Aaron the priest' (Num. xviii. 28). But did Aaron live for ever to receive the offering? Is it not true that

he did not enter the land of Israel? Consequently the text teaches that he is to be restored to life (in the Hereafter) and will receive the heave-offering. Hence the Resurrection is deducible from the Torah' (Sanh. go*b*).

'The Sadducees asked R. Gamaliel, "Whence is it known that the Holy One, blessed be He, revives the dead?" He, answered, "From the Pentateuch, the Prophets, and Hagiographa;" but they did not accept his proofs. "From the Pentateuch, for it is written, 'Behold, thou shalt sleep with thy fathers and rise up' (*sic* Deut. Xxxi. 16)." They replied, "The meaning is rather, 'This people will rise up and go a-whoring after the strange gods.'" "From the Prophets, for it is written, 'Thy dead shall live; my dead bodies shall arise. Awake and sing, ye that dwell in the dust, for thy dew is as the dew of herbs, and the earth shall cast forth the dead' (Is. xxvi. 19)." They replied, "Perhaps this passage refers to the revival of the dead described in Ezek. xxxvii."[4] "From the Hagiographa, for it is written, 'Thy mouth is like the best wine, that goeth down smoothly for my beloved, gliding through the lips of those that are asleep'[5] (Cant. vii. 9)." They replied, "Perhaps the reference is here to ordinary movement of the lips;" in accordance with the statement of R. Jochanan who said in the name of R. Simeon b. Jehotzedek: When a legal decision of a departed authority is quoted in this world, his lips move in the grave, as it is said, "Gliding through the lips of those that are asleep." Finally he quoted for them, "The land which the Lord sware unto your fathers to give unto them" (Deut. xi. 9). It is not stated "unto you," but "unto them;" hence the doctrine of the Resurrection is deducible from the Torah.[6] Others maintain that it can be derived from, "Ye that did cleave unto the Lord your God are alive every one of you this day" (ibid. iv. 4)--obviously "Ye are alive, every one of you this day;" therefore the meaning must be, even on the day when people in general are dead you will live, and as you are all alive this day so will you all live in the World to Come' (Sanh. 90*b*).

'It is written, "I kill and I make alive" (Dent. xxxii. 39). It is possible to think that death is caused by one Power and life by another, as is the usual way of the world; therefore the text continues, "I have wounded and I heal." As both wounding and healing are in the hands of the same Power, so are killing and reviving in the hands of the same Power. This is a refutation of those who declare that the Resurrection is not taught in the Torah. R. Meir asked, Whence is the Resurrection derived from the Torah? As it is said, "Then will[7] Moses and the children of Israel sing this song unto the Lord" (Exod. xv. 1). It is not said "sang" but "will sing;" hence the Resurrection is deducible from the Torah. R. Joshua b. Levi asked, Whence is the Resurrection derived from the Torah? As it is said, "Blessed are they that dwell in Thy house, they will be still praising Thee" (Ps. lxxxiv. 4). It is not stated, "They have praised Thee" but "will be still praising Thee" (in the Hereafter); hence the Resurrection is deducible from the Torah. Raba asked, Whence is the Resurrection derived from the Torah? As it is said, "Let Reuben live and not die" (Deut. xxxiii. 6)--"let Reuben live" in this world, "and not die in the World to Come. Rabina declared that it may be deduced from, "Many of them that sleep in the dust of the earth shall awake, some to everlasting life and some to shame and everlasting contempt" (Dan. xii. 2). R. Ashe deduced it from, "Go thou thy way till the end be, for thou shalt rest, and shalt stand in thy lot at the end of the days" (ibid. 13)' (Sanh. 91*b* et seq.).

In addition to the Sadducees, another sect denied this dogma, viz. the Samaritans. A polemic against them is contained in this passage: 'R. Eliezer b. Jose said, In this matter I proved the books of the Samaritans[8] who declared that the Resurrection is not taught in the Torah to be false. I told them, You have falsified your recension of the Torah but it has availed you nothing in your contention that the Resurrection is not taught in the Torah, because it is there stated, "That soul shall be utterly cut off, his iniquity shall be upon him" (Num. xv. 31)--"shall be utterly cut off" must refer to this world;[9] when, then, "shall his iniquity be upon him"? Must it not be in the World to Come?' (Sanh. 90*b*).

'What means that which is written, "There are three things that are never satisfied . . . the grave and the barren womb" (Prov. xxx. 15 f.)? What is the connection between "the grave" and "the barren womb"? The intention is to tell you that as the womb receives and yields up, so the grave receives and yields up. And may we not use the *a fortiori* argument? As the womb receives the seed in silence and yields up the child with loud cries, how much more so will the grave, which receives the body with loud cries of lament, yield up with loud cries! Hence a refutation of those who assert that the Resurrection is not taught in the Torah' (Ber. 15*b*).

Other arguments, apart from Scriptural exegesis, were employed to establish the doctrine. 'Should any one tell you that the dead will not live again, cite to him the instance of Elijah' (Num. R. XIV. 1). 'A heretic said to R. Gamaliel,

"You declare that the dead will live again; but they have become dust and can dust come to life?' The Rabbi's daughter said to her father, "Leave him to me and I will answer him. In our city are two potters, one who forms pots out of water, and the other out of clay; who of them is the more praiseworthy?" The heretic replied, "The one who formed them from water." She retorted, "He who formed the human being from a liquid drop, shall He not the more easily be able to form him from clay?"' (Sanh. 90*b* et seq.).

'A Sadducee said to Gebiha b. Pesisa, "Woe to you guilty ones (the Pharisees) who declare that the dead will live; since the living die, shall the dead revive? He replied, "Woe to guilty ones (the Sadducees) who declare that the dead will not live; since those who were not in existence come to life, how much more will they who have lived come to life again!"' (ibid. 91*a*).

'It happened that a man who resided in Sepphoris lost his son and a heretic was sitting with him. R. Jose b. Chalaphta went to pay him a visit; and on seeing him, he sat down and laughed. The bereaved father asked, "Why do you laugh?" He answered, "We trust in the Lord of Heaven that you will again see your son in the World to Come." The heretic said to him, "Has not this man suffered enough anguish that you come to inflict further pain upon him? Can pieces of potsherd be mended? And is it not written, 'Thou shalt dash them in pieces like a potter's vessel'[10] (Ps. ii. 9)?" He replied, "With an earthenware vessel, its creation is from water and its completion in fire; with a glass vessel, both its creation and completion are in fire. If the former is broken, can it be mended?[11] But if the latter is broken, can it not be repaired?" The heretic answered, "Glass can be repaired because it is made by the process of blowing." The Rabbi retorted, "Let your ears take note of what your mouth utters. If something which is made by the blowing of a human being can be repaired, how much more so with that which is made by the breath of the Holy One, blessed be He!"' (Gen. R. XIV. 7).

A question, debated by several Rabbis, was: Who will enjoy the privilege of living again after death? Their opinion will be cited more fully in the sections on the World to Come and the Last Judgment. The passages which deal more generally with the subject of Resurrection display a lack of unanimity. On the one hand we read such statements as: 'They that are born are destined to die, and the dead to be brought to life again' (Aboth IV. 29); and "'They (i.e. the Lord's mercies) are new every morning; great is Thy faithfulness" (Lament. iii. 23)--since

Text Twenty-five: THE HEREAFTER

Thou art He that renewest us every morning, we know that "great is Thy faithfulness" for the revival of the dead' (Midrash ad loc.)--which seem to have a universal application.[12] On the other hand, there is the opposite extreme expressed, 'The Resurrection is reserved for Israel' (Gen. R. XIII. 6).

Other teachers held that the future life was a reward granted only to those who deserve it. 'More important is a day of rain than the Resurrection of the dead, since the Resurrection is for the righteous and not the wicked, whereas rain is for both the righteous and the wicked' (Taan. 7a). The analogy appears to indicate that the author of this dictum did not restrict 'the righteous' to his own people, inasmuch as the rain descends upon all, irrespective of race or creed. The following utterance excludes even Israelites who have not earned the privilege: 'They who are ignorant of Torah will not live again; as it is said, "They are dead, they shall not live" (Is. xxvi. 14). It is possible to argue that this applies to all (Israel); therefore the text continues, "They are deceased, they shall not rise." These words allude to one who relaxes[13] himself from words of Torah. Whoever makes use of the light of Torah, the light of Torah will revive (after death); and whoever does not make use of the light of Torah, the light of Torah will not revive' (Keth. 111b).

The Talmud records speculations on various matters connected with the process of Resurrection. There was a firm belief that the momentous event would, take place in the Holy Land. Some Rabbis took the extreme view that only they who were interred there would share in the future life. 'Those who die outside the land of Israel will not live again; as it is said, "I will set delight in the land of the living" (Ezek. xxvi. 20)--those who die in the land of My delight will live again, but they who do not die there will not' (Keth. 111a). 'Even a Canaanite maidservant in the land of Israel is assured of inheriting the World to Come' (ibid.).

Other Rabbis, while admitting that the Resurrection will occur in the Holy Land, do not go so far as to affirm that they who are buried elsewhere are to be excluded, but their bodies will have to be transported there before they come to life again. '"Thy dead shall live; my dead bodies shall arise" (Is. xxvi. 19). The first clause, refers to those who die in the land of Israel, the second to those, who die outside its borders' (Keth. 111a). This thought gave rise to a curious piece of folk-lore. '"I will walk before the Lord. In the land of the living" (Ps. cxvi. 9), i.e. the land whose dead will be revived first in the days of the Messiah. What is the reason?

It is stated, "He giveth breath unto the people upon it"[14] (Is. xlii. 5). Then our Rabbis who reside in Babylon will be at a disadvantage! The Holy One, blessed be He, will burrow the earth before them, and their bodies will roll through the excavation like bottles, and when they arrive at the land of Israel their souls will be reunited to them' (p. Keth. 35b).

One of the points of dispute between the Schools of Hillel and Shammai related to the order in which the human body will be reformed. 'The School of Shammai said, Not like the formation of the human being in this world will be his formation in the World to Come. In this world, it begins with skin and flesh and ends with sinews and bones; but in the Hereafter it will begin with sinews and bones and end with skin and flesh. For it is so stated with regard to the dead in the vision of Ezekiel, "And I beheld, and lo, there were sinews upon them, and flesh came up, and skin covered them above" (Ezek. xxxvii. 8). R. Jonathan said, We draw no inferences from the dead in the vision of Ezekiel. To what were they like? To a person who entered a bath-house; what he strips off first he afterwards puts on last. The School of Hillel said, Similar to the formation in this world will be the formation in the World to Come. In this world it begins with skin and flesh and ends with sinews and bones, and it will be the same in the Hereafter; for thus declared Job, "Wilt Thou not pour me out as milk and curdle me like cheese?" (x. 10). It is not written, "Hast Thou not poured me out?" but "Wilt Thou not pour me out?"[15] Nor is it written "curdled me like cheese" but "wilt curdle." It is not written, "Thou hast clothed me with skin and flesh" (ibid. 11) but "Thou wilt clothe;" nor is it written, "And Thou hast knit me together with bones and sinews" but "And Thou wilt knit me together." It is like a bowl full of milk; until one places rennet therein the milk keeps fluid, but after rennet is inserted the milk curdles and sets' (Gen. R. XIV. 5).

Will the bodies arise clothed or naked? The answer is 'As man goes (into the grave) clothed, so he will return clothed. This may be learnt from the example of Samuel whom Saul beheld. He asked the witch of Endor, "What form is he of? And, she said, An old man cometh up and he is covered with a robe" (I Sam. xxviii. 14)' (Gen. R. XCV. 1). An argument in favour of this view is given in this anecdote: 'Queen Cleopatra[16] asked R. Meir, "I know that the dead will revive, for it is written, 'They of the city shall flourish like grass of the earth' (Ps. lxxii. 16). But when they arise (from the grave), will they stand up naked or clothed?" He replied, "An argument may be based on the analogy of wheat:[17]

As wheat is buried in the soil naked and comes forth with various garbs, how much more so with the righteous who are buried in their garments!"' (Sanh. 90*b*). The reference is to the custom of burying the dead enwrapped in shrouds.

Another problem is dealt with in this story: 'Hadrian asked R. Joshua b. Chananya, "From what will the Holy One, blessed be He, cause the human being to grow in the Hereafter?"[18] He said, "From a bone in the spinal column called *Lus*." He asked, "How do you know this?" He answered, "Have it brought to me and I will show you." When this bone was fetched, they tried to grind it in a mill but it could not be ground; they tried to burn it in fire but it could not be consumed; they put it in water but it did not dissolve; they set it upon an anvil and began to strike it with a hammer, but the anvil was split and the hammer shattered without a piece of the bone having been broken off' (Gen. R. XXVIII. 3).

The last question relates to whether the defects of the living body will .reappear in the Resurrection. ' "One generation goeth' and another generation cometh" (Eccles. i. 4); as a generation goes so it will come back. He who goes lame comes back lame; he who goes blind comes back blind; so that people shall not say that He put to death persons different from those He restored to life. For it is written, "I kill and I make alive" (Deut. xxxii. 39), He Who declared His power to do the more difficult task is He Who declared the lighter. "I kill and I make alive" is the more .difficult task; "I have wounded and I heal" (ibid.) is the lighter. As I (God) raise up the dead with their physical blemishes, so that people shall not say, "He put to death persons different from those He restored to life," it is I that killeth and reviveth, and I who have wounded (in this world) will restore and heal them (after they have been revived)' (Eccles. R. to 1. 4). The divinely appointed agent for the accomplishment of the Resurrection is Elijah. 'The Resurrection of the dead will come through Elijah' (Sot. IX. 15), who will likewise act as the herald to announce the advent of the Messiah (see Mal. iv. 5). The reawakened life will be of endless duration. 'The righteous whom the Holy One, blessed be He, will restore to life will never return to their dust' (Sanh. 92*a*).

NOTES

1. See Josephus, Antiq. Xviii. i. 4; War, II. Viii. 14; and in the New Testament, Acts xxiii. 8.

2. *Authorised Daily Prayer Book,* ed. Singer, p. 45. This prayer is referred to in Ber. V. 2. See also the prayer to be said on waking in the morning, quoted above, p. 87.

3. Lit. 'for *a* world.' The amended form means 'from a world to a world,' i.e. from this world to the World to Come.

4. And consequently it would have no bearing on the question of the Resurrection of the dead in the Hereafter.

5. He understood the sleep to refer to the sleep of death.

6. Since the 'fathers' were dead, it was necessary for them to live again if the divine promise was to be fulfilled.

7. The verb in the Hebrew has the future form in accordance with the idiom that as, 'then,' is followed by the verb in the imperfect tense to denote a completed action.

8. The Talmudic text has 'Sadducees,' but it must be corrected.

9. The Rabbis understood the phrase to mean a premature death; see p. 322.

10. This verse proves that Scripture teaches a broken vessel cannot be repaired.

11. Because its creation and completion take place in different elements, it cannot be put together again. Broken glass, on the other hand, can be remelted and then blown into another vessel.

12. There was agreement that there was no Hereafter for animals (see Midrash to Ps. xix. 1; 81*b*).

13. The word for 'relaxes' is connected in the Hebrew with the word for 'deceased.'

14. viz. upon the land of Israel.

15. This is the literal rendering of the Hebrew, although the English version translates in the past tense.

16. Since this queen lived nearly two centuries before R. Meir, the mention of her is an anachronism. The text is doubtless corrupt and the true reading is: 'The patriarch of the Samaritans.'

17. Cf. 1 Cor. xv. 37.

18. Since the body crumbles to dust in the grave, what distinguishable relic is there from which the resurrected person can be reconstructed?

Sec. III. THE WORLD TO COME

In the eschatological doctrine of the Talmud a clear divergence of opinion may be traced. The earlier generations of the Rabbis identified the Messianic era with the World to Come. The promised Redeemer would bring the existing world-order to an end and inaugurate the timeless sphere in which the righteous would lead a purely spiritual existence freed from the trammels of the flesh. Subsequent teachers regarded the Messianic period as but a transitory stage between this world and the next.

That this life is only preliminary to another and higher life was universally accepted by the Rabbis. They would have

Text Twenty-five: THE HEREAFTER

given unanimous assent to the aphorism, 'This world is like a vestibule before the World to Come; prepare yourself in the vestibule that you may enter into the hall' (Aboth IV. 21). But what is to be experienced by those who will be privileged to enter 'the hall' has not been disclosed even to the seers of Israel. 'Every prophet only prophesied for the days of the Messiah; but as for the World to Come, "No eye hath seen what God, and nobody but Thee, will work for him that waiteth for Him" (*sic* Is. lxiv. 4)' (Ber. 34*b*). 'All Israel assembled by Moses and said to Him, "Our master, Moses, tell us what goodness the Holy One, blessed be He, will give us in the World to Come." He replied to them, "I do not know what I can tell you. Happy are ye for what is prepared for you"' (Sifre Deut. Sec. 356; 148*b*).

Despite this reticence, teachers were not deterred from creating their own picture of the Hereafter. Their reflections on the problems of life compelled them to postulate a new world where the inequalities of the present world would be redressed and the divine justice made evident. That solution, to the mystery of evil coloured their whole conception of the World to Come.

According to one anecdote; their theory was corroborated by experience. 'R. Joseph, the son of R. Joshua b. Levi, was ill and fell into a state of coma. When he recovered, his father asked him, "What did you see?" He replied, "I beheld a world the reverse of this one; those who are on top here were below there, and vice versa." He said to him, "My son, you have seen a corrected world. But what is the position of us students of the Torah there?" He answered, "We are there the same as here. I heard it stated, Happy is he who comes here possessed of learning; and I further heard it said that martyrs occupy an eminence which nobody else can attain"' (Pes. 50*a*).

It followed, therefore, that sufferings which were innocently incurred and privations voluntarily assumed in this world must help to gain admittance into the World to Come. 'R. Judah the Prince said, Whoever accepts the delights of this world will be deprived of the delights of the World to Come, and whoever declines the delights of this world will receive the delights of the World to Come' (ARN XXVIII). It was even remarked, 'Three precious gifts did the Holy One, blessed be He, give to Israel, and all of them He gave only through the medium of suffering; they are: Torah, the land of Israel, and the World to Come' (Ber. 5*a*). A common saying among the people was, 'Not every one has the merit

of two tables' (ibid. 5b), i.e. happiness here and bliss in the Hereafter.

The great distinguishing feature between the two worlds is the revaluation of values. Things which are estimated here so highly that they are the main pursuit of man's efforts cease to exist when the bridge is crossed into the World to Come. This thought is summarized in the aphorism of a Rabbi: 'Not like this world is the World to Come. In the World to Come there is neither eating nor drinking; nor procreation of children or business transactions; no envy or hatred or rivalry; but the righteous sit enthroned, their crowns on their heads, and enjoy the lustre of the *Shechinah*' (Ber. 17*a*). Life will be conducted on an entirely different plane, 'Physical desires will no longer obtrude, and the sway of the spiritual nature of man will be dominant. What the holy day of the week is to man on this earth as compared with the working days, such will the World to Come be on a vastly enhanced scale. 'The Sabbath is a sixtieth of the World to Come' (ibid. 57*b*).[1]

A saying of doubtful interpretation runs: 'Better is one hour of repentance and good deeds in this world than the whole life of the World to Come; and better is one hour of blissfulness of spirit in the World to Come than the whole life of this world' (Aboth IV, 22). The most satisfactory explanation is that offered by R. T. Herford, who sees in the teaching a contrast between the changefulness of the present life and the changelessness of the future life. In this world man is able to repent and perform meritorious acts, and these bring him a joy superior even to 'an eternity of static bliss' which characterizes the World to Come. 'On the other hand, in a world where there is no change, the highest and best form of existence is that of perfect peace in the beholding of God. One hour of such bliss is better, under the conditions of such a world, than all "the changes and chances of this mortal, life."'[2]

Man best qualifies himself in the vestibule for the pure, spiritual atmosphere of 'the hall' by devoting himself to the study and practice of the precepts revealed by God. 'He who has acquired for himself words of Torah has acquired for himself life in the World to Come' (Aboth II. 8). Of the Torah it was said: "When thou liest down it shall watch over thee" (Prov. vi. 22), i.e. at the time of death; "when thou awakest," i.e. in the days of the Messiah; "it shall talk with thee," i.e. in the World to Come' (Sifre Deut, Sec. 34; 74*b*). More explicit still is the declaration: 'In the hour of man's departure from the world neither silver nor gold nor precious stones nor pearls accompany him, but only Torah and good works; as it is said, "When thou walkest it shall lead thee when thou liest down it shall watch over thee; and when thou awakest it shall talk with thee;" "when thou walkest it shall lead thee" in this world; "when thou liest down it shall watch over thee" in the grave; "and when thou awakest it shall talk with thee"" in the World to Come' (Aboth VI. 9).

Other utterances expressive of the same thought are, 'What means, "I shall be satisfied, when I awake, with Thy likeness" (Ps. xvii. 15)? It alludes to the disciples of the Sages who banish sleep from their eyes in this world, and the Holy One, blessed be He, will satisfy them with the lustre of the *Shechinah* in the World to Come' (B.B. 10*a*). R. Nechunya b, Hakkanah, a saintly teacher of the first century, used to offer this prayer on departing from the House of Study: 'I give thanks before Thee, O Lord my God, that Thou hast set my portion with those who sit in the House of Study and not with those who sit at street corners;[3] for I and they rise early--I to words of Torah but they to vain matters; I and they labour, but I labour to receive a reward, whereas they labour and receive no reward; I and they hasten--I to the life of the World to Come, but they to the pit of destruction' (Ber. 28*b*).

'When R. Eliezer was ill, his disciples went in to visit him. They said to him, "Master, teach us the ways of life whereby we may be worthy of the life of the World to Come." He said to them, "Be careful of the honour of your colleagues; restrain your children from recitation,[4] and seat them between the knees of the disciples of the Sages; and when you pray, know before Whom you stand; and on that account will you be worthy of the life of the World to Come' (ibid.).

Since there are ever higher degrees of spirituality to scale we find it stated: 'The disciples of the Sages have rest neither in this world nor in the World to Come; as it is said, "They go from strength to strength, every one of them appeareth before God in Zion" (Ps. lxxxiv. 7)' (Ber. 64*a*).

Much attention was devoted by the Rabbis to the question of who will be admitted to, or excluded from, the joys of the Hereafter. Many *obiter dicta* occur in the Talmud declaring that the person who performs a certain action will, or will not, have a share in the World to Come. Some instances are: 'With regard to him who enjoys the fruit of his labour it is

written, "When thou eatest the labour of thy hands, happy shalt thou be and it shall be well with thee" (Ps. cxxviii. 2); "happy shalt thou be" in this world, "and it shall be well with thee" in the World to Come' (Ber. 8*a*). 'Who will inherit the World to Come? He who joins the benediction "Blessed art Thou Who hast redeemed Israel" to the Eighteen Benedictions' (ibid. 4*b*).[5] 'Whoever recites Ps. cxlv thrice daily may be assured that he is a son of the World to Come. The reason is that it contains the verse, "Thou openest Thy hand and satisfiest every living thing with favour" (verse 16)' (Ber. 4*b*).[6] 'Whoever says the benediction (in the Grace after meals) over a full cup of wine will be granted a boundless inheritance and will be worthy to inherit two worlds, this world and the World to Come' (ibid. 51*a*).[7]

'Among those who will inherit the World to Come are: who resides in the land of Israel and who rears his son in the study of the Torah' (Pes. 113*a*). 'Whoever walks a distance of four cubits in the land of Israel is assured of being a son of the World to Come' (Keth. 111*a*). 'He who studies the laws of Judaism is assured of being a son of the World to Come' (Meg. 28*b*). 'They sent a question from Palestine to the Rabbis in Babylon, "Who will be a son of the World to Come?" They answered, "He who is meek and humble, walks about with a lowly demeanour, studies the Torah constantly, and takes no credit to himself"' (Sanh. 88*b*).

As for those who are to be excluded, we are told: 'Whoever crosses a stream behind a woman will have no share in the World to Come' (Ber. 61*a*). 'Who puts his fellow-man to shame in public will have no share in the World to Come' (B.M. 59*a*). 'Seven classes of persons will have no share in the World to Come: a scribe, a teacher of children, the best of physicians, the judge of a city, an enchanter, a synagogue beadle, and a butcher' (ARN XXXVI).[8]

It must be obvious that in these utterances we cannot have a dogmatic verdict on the eternal fate of the persons concerned. They are nothing more than a hyberbolical expression of approval or disapproval. More importance must, however, be attached to this extract: 'All Israel has a share in the World to Come, as it is said, "Thy people shall be all righteous, they shall inherit the land for ever" (Is. lx. 21). The following have no share in the World to Come: He who says that the doctrine of the Resurrection is not deducible from the Torah, who maintains that the Torah does not come from Heaven, and the epicurean.[9] R. Akiba says, Also he who reads non-canonical books,[10] who utters a spell over a wound, citing,

"I will put none of the diseases upon thee which I have put upon the Egyptians, for I am the Lord that healeth thee" (Exod. XV. 26). Abba Saul says, Also he who pronounces the Tetragrammaton as it is written'[11] (Sanh, x. 1).

It is an error to read into the first sentence of this declaration any idea of favouritism on the part of God for Israel. If construed in its historical context, the intention was probably to encourage the Jews to persevere in the struggle to maintain their identity against intense pressure. Two forces were tending to obliterate the community, oppression by gentile powers and the influence of contemporary thought, both Hellenistic and Christian. Only by a determined and conscious effort, usually at a costly sacrifice, could the Jew maintain a successful resistance; and the Rabbis helped him with the teaching that he would receive his reward in the Hereafter. The survivors of the contest, who refused to succumb, constituted a 'people all righteous,' and God would recognize them as such by granting them an inheritance in the World to Come. On the question whether Gentiles will share in the Hereafter there was not an agreed opinion. 'R. Eliezer declared, "No Gentiles will have a share in the World to Come; as it is said, 'The. wicked shall return to the nether world, even all the nations that forget God' (Ps. ix. 17)--'the wicked' refers to the evil among Israel." R. Joshua said to him, "If the verse had stated, 'The wicked shall return to the nether world and all the nations,' and had stopped there, I should have agreed with you. Since, however, the text adds, 'that forget God,' behold, there must be righteous men among the nations who will have a share in the World to Come"' (Tosifta Sank. XIII. 2).[12]

On the assumption that righteous Gentiles will enjoy the bliss of the Hereafter and the wicked will not, a point arises as to what will be the fate of the children of the latter who were too young to be charged with moral responsibility. Here, too, a similar divergence of opinion occurs. 'The children of the wicked Gentiles will have no share in the World to Come; as it is said, "For behold, the day cometh, it burneth as a furnace; and all the proud, and all that work wickedness shall be stubble" (Mal. iv. 1). This is the statement of R. Gamaliel. R. Joshua said, They will enter the World to Come; for it, is written, "The Lord preserveth the simple" [13] (Ps. cxvi. 6), and "Hew down the tree and cut off his branches[14] . . . nevertheless leave the stump of his roots in the earth" (Dan. iv. 14 f.)' (Tosifta Sanh. XIII. 1). The same discussion is held in connection with the children of the wicked of Israel and opposite sides taken on the

identical texts, and the remark is added: With respect to the children of the wicked Gentiles all agree that they will not enter the World to Come' (Sanh. 110*b*). If they are excluded from the blessings of the Hereafter, they will not be held to account in the matter of punishment: 'The children of the wicked of the Gentiles will not revive (in the Resurrection) nor be judged' (Tosifta Sanh. XIII. 2).

There is likewise a discussion on the stage in its life at which an Israelite child qualifies for admission to the World to Come. 'From what point of time does a minor become entitled to the World to Come? One Rabbi answered, From the hour of birth, as it is said, "They shall declare His righteousness unto a people that is born" (Ps. xxii. 31). Another declared, From the tune it can speak; as it is said, "A seed shall serve Him, it shall be told of the Lord unto the generation" (ibid. 30). Other opinions are: From the time of conception; for it is written, "A seed shall serve Him." From the time of circumcision; for it is written, "I am afflicted and ready to die from my youth up" (ibid. lxxxviii. 15). From the time that it utters Amen; as it is said, "Open ye the gates, that the righteous nation which keepeth truth may enter in" (Is. xxvi. 2)--read not "which keepeth truth" but "which uttereth Amen"'[15] (Sanh. 110*b*)

NOTES

1. Cf. Matt. xxii. 30.
2. R. T. Herford, *Pirhe Aboth*, pp. 116 f.
3. The Palestinian Talmud reads instead, 'with those who frequent theatres and circuses.'
4. An obscure phrase which has been variously explained as the parading of a superficial knowledge of the Scriptures by verbal memorization, or philosophical speculation (the word is the term in medieval Hebrew for 'logic'), or reading apocryphal literature.
5. See *Prayer Book*, ed. Singer, p. 99. The meaning is that there must be no interruption between the two prayers. The saying was probably intended to abolish a custom which was then growing up of introducing petitions of a personal nature at this point, the practice being deprecated because it tended to destroy the congregational character of the Service.
6. By reciting this Psalm, therefore, a man would be thrice daily acknowledging his dependence upon the Divine mercy.
7. The use of a full cup would indicate a sense of gratitude for the divine bounty which had been enjoyed during the meal.
8. These persons were supposed to be generally unconscientious in the discharge of their duties.

Text Twenty-five: THE HEREAFTER

9. See p. 3.

10. See p. 145

11. See p. 25.

12. This may be fairly considered to be the official Jewish doctrine. Maimonides, in his digest of Rabbinic law, declared: 'The pious of the Gentiles will have a share in the World to Come' (Hil. Teshubah III. 5).

13. The Hebrew word, translated 'simple,' is explained in the Talmud to mean 'child' (Sanh. 110*b*, Gen. R. LXXXVII. 1).

14. Typifying the wicked of the Gentiles, whereas 'the stump of his roots' represents the children.

Sec. IV. THE LAST JUDGMENT

The doctrine of Retribution, we have seen, was a cardinal belief of the Rabbis.[1] Apart from the fact that it was a necessary corollary of their trust in Divine justice, it afforded the only solution to the problem which was created by the unhappy plight of their people. Gentile nations could not oppress God's elect with impunity, and a day of reckoning had to come. '"Thou overthrowest them that rise up against Thee" (Exod. XV. 7). Who are they that rise up against Thee? They are they who rise up against Thy children. It is not written, "Thou overthrowest them that rise up against us" but "against Thee"--teaching that whoever rises up against Israel is as though he rises up against the Holy One, blessed be He' (Mechilta, ad loc.; 39*a*). That being so, God must arraign the nations for their cruel treatment of Israel.

Accordingly, besides the Tribunal before which the individual will have to appear after death, a Day of Judgment will be appointed when the gentile peoples will be placed on trial. This will happen at the beginning of the Messianic era when righteousness will be vindicated. '"The Lord of Hosts will be exalted in judgment" (Is. v. 16). When will the Holy One, blessed be He, be raised on high in His Universe? When He executes judgment on the gentile nations; as it is said, "The Lord standeth up to plead, and standeth to judge the peoples." (ibid. iii. 13); and also, "I beheld till thrones were placed" (Dan. Vii. 9). Are there, then, many celestial thrones? Is it not written, "I saw the Lord sitting upon a throne high and lifted up" (Is. vi. 1), and also, "A king that sitteth on the throne of judgment" (Prov. xx. 8)? What, then, means "thrones?" R. Jose of Galilee declared, The term implies the Throne and its footstool. R. Akiba declared, It refers to the thrones of the gentile nations which He will overturn; as it is said, "I will overthrow the thrones of kingdoms" (Hag. ii. 22). The Rabbis declared, In the Hereafter the Holy One, blessed

be He, will sit, and the angels will set thrones for the great men of Israel who will be seated upon them; the Holy One, blessed be He, will sit with the Elders of Israel like a President of a *Beth Din* and judge the gentile nations; as it is said, "The Lord will enter into judgment with the elders of His people" (Is. iii. 14). It is not written "against the elders" but "with the elders," which indicates that the Holy One, blessed be He, will sit with them and judge the gentile nations. What means, "The hair of His head like pure wool" (Dan. vii. 9)? The Holy One, blessed be He, dears Himself with respect to the gentile nations by giving them their reward for the minor precepts which they observed in this world so as to judge and sentence them in the World to Come, that they may have no plea to make and no merit can be found on their behalf' (Tanchuma Kedoshim Sec. 1).

Here follows a description of the trial of the nations. 'In the Hereafter, the Holy One, blessed be He, will take a Scroll of the Torah, set it upon His lap and say, "Let him who occupied himself therewith come and receive his reward." Immediately the nations of the world gather together and come in disorder. The Holy One," blessed be He, says to them, "Do not enter before Me in disorder, but let each nation present itself together with its teachers." First comes the kingdom of Rome because it is the most important; and the Holy One, blessed be He, asks, "With what have you occupied yourself?" It answers, "Lord of the Universe! many market-places have we instituted, many baths have we erected, gold and silver in abundance have we accumulated; and we only did all this for the sake of Israel that he might devote himself to the Torah." The Holy One, blessed be He, replies, "You most foolish people in the world! All that you did was for your own benefit; you instituted market-places as a resort of harlots; you erected baths for your own enjoyment; while the silver and gold belong to Me." It at once departs in despair and is followed by the kingdom of Persia, which is next in importance. The Holy One, blessed be He, asks, "With what have you occupied yourself?" It answers, "Lord of the Universe! many bridges have we constructed, many cities have we conquered, many wars have we waged; and we only did all this for the sake of Israel that he might devote himself to the Torah." The Holy One, blessed be He, replies, "All that you did was for your own benefit. You constructed bridges to receive toll from them; you conquered cities to force the inhabitants to labour for you; and as for wars I wage them." It at once departs in despair. But since the Persian kingdom saw that it availed the Roman kingdom nothing, why did it enter? Because it

Text Twenty-five: **THE HEREAFTER**

said, "They destroyed the Temple, whereas we helped to restore it."[2] Similarly the other nations went in one after the other; but why did they enter when they saw that it availed their predecessors nothing? They thought, "Rome and Persia enslaved Israel but we did not." What is the difference between the first two kingdoms that they are considered of importance and the remainder are not so esteemed? Because they continue in their sovereignty until judged, rightly hast Thou acquitted, rightly hast Thou condemned, Messiah comes. They will then plead before Him, "Lord of the Universe! Didst Thou give us the Torah and we rejected it?" But how can they use such a plea, seeing that the Holy One, blessed be he, offered it to every people and they declined to receive it until He came to Israel who accepted it?' (A.Z. 2a,b)[3] They put forward various other arguments in their defence which are proved to be invalid; and so the trial ends in their discomfiture and the glorification of Israel.

As for individuals, God has ordained 'the day of the Great Judgment' (Mechilta to xvi. 25; 50b), which will take place after death. Talmudic law prescribes: 'Who beholds the graves of Israelites says, "Blessed be He Who formed you in judgment, Who nourished you in judgment, sustained you in judgment, and gathered you in judgment, and will hereafter raise you in judgment"' (Ber. 58b): Not only Israelites, however, but every human being is called to account. The following extract is quite general in its scope: 'They that are born are destined to die; and the dead to be brought to life again; and the living to be judged, to know, to make known, and to be made conscious that He is God, He the Maker, He the Creator, 'He the discerner, He the Judge, He the witness, He the complainant; He it is that will in the Hereafter judge, blessed be with Whom there is no unrighteousness, nor forgetfulness, nor respect of persons, nor taking of bribes. Know also that everything is according to the reckoning. And let not your imagination give you hope that the grave will be a place of refuge for you; for perforce were you formed, and perforce were you born, and it perforce you live, and perforce you die, and perforce you will in the Hereafter have to give account and reckoning before the supreme King of kings, the Holy One, blessed be He' (Aboth IV. 29).

In many other passages the terms used are 'righteous' and 'wicked' without restriction of creed or nationality. "Passing through the valley of weeping, they make it a place of springs; yea the early rain covereth it with blessings" (Ps. lxxxiv, 6)--"passing," i.e. the men who transgress the will of the Holy One, blessed be He; "valley," i.e. they make Gehinnom deep for themselves; "weeping," i.e. they cry and shed tears like the well by the side of the Temple-altar; "yea the early rain covereth it with blessings," i.e. they acknowledge the justice of the sentence passed upon them, saying, "Lord of the Universe! rightly hast Thou judged, rightly has Thou acquitted, rightly has Thou condemned, rightly hast Thou instituted Gehinnom for the wicked and Gan Eden for the righteous"' (Erub. 19a).

'The matter may be likened to a king who arranged a banquet and invited guests to it. The king issued a decree, saying, "Each guest must bring that on which he will recline." Some brought carpets; others brought mattresses or bolsters or cushions or stools, while still others brought logs of wood or stones. The king observed what they had done, and said, "Let each man sit on what he brought." They who had to sit on wood or stone murmured against the kind and said, "Is that honourable to a king that we, his guests, should be seated on wood and stone?" When the king heard this, he said to them, "Not enough that you have disgraced with your stone and wood the palace which was erected for me at great cost, but you dare to invent a complaint against me! (The lack of) respect paid to you is the consequence of your own action." Similarly in the Hereafter the wicked will be sentenced to Gehinnom and will murmur against the Holy One, blessed be He, saying, "Lo, we looked for His salvation, and such a fate should befall us!" He answers them, "When you were on earth did you not quarrel and slander and do all kinds of evil? Were you not responsible for strife and violence? That is what is written, 'Behold, all ye that kindle a fire, that gird yourselves about with firebrands' (Is. l. 11). That being so, 'Walk ye in the flame of your fire and among the brands that ye have kindled' (ibid). Should you say, 'This have ye of Mine hand,' it is not so; you have done it for yourselves, and hence 'ye shall lie down in sorrow' (ibid.)"' (Eccles. R. to iii. 9).

Other extracts deal specifically with the judgment of Israelites. As recipients of the Torah, their responsibility was heavier. While obedience of the precepts would bring a rich reward, disobedience would ensue in a correspondingly severe punishment. 'In the Hereafter the Holy One, blessed be He, will judge the righteous and wicked of Israel. To the righteous He will grant a permit for them to enter Gan Eden and the wicked He will send back to Gehinnom. He will subsequently take them out of Gehinnom and set them in Gan Eden with the righteous, saying to them, "Lo, this is the place of the righteous (and there is still unoccupied space amongst them, so that you should not say, Even if we had repented, there would have been no room for us in Gan Eden among the righteous).' He will then remove the righteous from Gan Eden take them into Gehinnom, saying to them, "Lo, this is the place of the wicked, and there is still unoccupied space amongst them (so that you should not say, Even if we had sinned, there would have been no room for us in Gehinnom);[4] but the wicked inherit their and your Gehinnom." That is the meaning of the verse, "For your shame ye shall have double . . . therefore in their land they shall possess double" (Is. lxi. 7). After that He will restore me the righteous to Gan Eden and the wicked to Gehinn om' (Midrash to Ps. xxxi; 120a).

The intention of the phrase, 'the wicked inherit their and your Gehinnom,' is elucidated by this citation: 'After Elisha b. Abuyah became an infidel, he asked R. Meir, "What is the meaning of 'God hath made the one side by side with the other' (Eccles, vii. 14)?" He replied, "Whatever the Holy One, blessed be he created, He made an opposite to it; e.g. mountains and yell oceans and rivers." He said to him, "Your teacher, Akiba, did not give you that interpretation, but (so he explained it) God created the righteous and wicked, Gan Eden and Gehinnom. Each person has two portions, one in Gan Eden and the other in Gehinnom. If a person is meritorious and righteous, he takes his share and that of his fellow in Gan Eden; and if he incurred guilt and is wicked, he makes his share and that of his fellow in Gehinnom"' (Chag. 15a).

In preparation for the Day of Judgment a record is kept of all that the human being does while on earth. 'All your deeds are written in a book' (Aboth II. 1). 'At the time of a man's departure from the world, all his actions are detailed before him, and he is told, "So and so have you done in such a place on such a day." He assents and is then ordered to sign the record, which he does. Not only that, but he admits the justice of the verdict and says, "Rightly hast Thou judged me"' (Taan. 11a). 'Even superfluous remarks that pass between husband and wife are recorded against him in the hour of death' (Chag. 5b). 'The Holy One, blessed be He will sit in judgment with the righteous and wicked. He will judge the righteous and conduct them to Gan Eden. He will judge the wicked and condemn them to Gehinnom. The wicked say, "he has not judged us fairly; He acquits whomever He likes and convicts whomever He likes." The Holy One, blessed be He, replies, "I did not desire to expose you." So what does He do? He reads out their record and they descend to Gehinnom' (Midrash to Ps. i; 12b).

Then standing his trial, man will have brought up against him many misdeeds which he at the time thought too trivial to worry about. 'What does the text mean, "When iniquity at my heels compasseth me about" (Ps. xlix. 5)? The iniquities which a man treads down with his heels[5] in this world will compass him about the Day of Judgment' (A.Z. 18a).

Among the questions addressed to him are: 'Did you transact your business honestly? Did you fix times for the study of Torah? Did you fulfil your duty with respect to establishing a family? Did you hope for the salvation (of the Messiah)? Did you search for wisdom? Did you try to deduce one thing from another (in study)? Even should all these questions be answered affirmatively, only if "the tear of the Lord is his treasure" (Is. xxxiii. 6)[6] will avail, otherwise it will not' (Shab. 31a).

The question whether punishment is exacted of both body and soul was the theme of a parable which has, already been quoted.[7] The moral was that as body and soul are equally concerned in the comission of sin, they are alike penalized. Another parable reaches the opposite conclusion. 'A priest married two wives, one a priest's daughter and the other a lay-Israelite's daughter.

He handed to them flour of an offering which they defiled, and each blamed the other for it. What did the priest do? He ignored the wife who was a layman's daughter and began to chide the priest's daughter. She said to him, "my lord, why do you ignore the other and rebuke me?" He answered, "She is the daughter of a layman and was not taught in her father's house (the sanctity of the flour of an offering); but you are a priest's daughter, and you were taught this in your father's house. That is the reason why I overlook her and reprimand you." Similarly in the Hereafter, the soul and body will stand in judgment. What will the Holy One, blessed be He, do? He will overlook the body and censure the soul, and when it pleads, "Lord of the Universe! The two of us sinned alike, so why dost Thou overlook the body and censure me?" He answers, "The body comes from below where people sin; but you come from above where sin is not committed. Therefore I overlook the body and censure you"' (Lev. R. IV. 5).

The opinion generally adopted was that the soul is rejoined to the body for the purpose of judgment, and is expressed in this statement: "Throughout twelve months (after death in Gehinnom) the body exists and the soul ascends and descends; after twelve months the body ceases to exist and the soul ascends without descending' (Shab. 152b et seq.).

Text Twenty-five: **THE HEREAFTER**

What is the duration of the penalty meted out to the sinful? Does the Talmud teach eternal punishment? There is at least one passage where such a doctrine seems to be implied. 'When R. Jochanan b. Zakkai was ill his disciples went in to visit him. On beholding them he began to weep. They said to him, "O lamp of Israel, right-hand pillar, mighty, hammer! wherefore do you weep?" He replied to them, "If I was being led into the presence of a human king who today is here and tomorrow in the grave, who if he were wrathful against me his anger would not be eternal, who if he imprisoned me the imprisonment would not be everlasting, who if he condemned me to death the death would not be for ever, and whom I can appease with words and bribe with money--even then I would weep; but now, when I am being led into the presence of the King of kings, the Holy One, blessed be He, Who lives and endures for all eternity, who if He be wrathful against me His anger is eternal, Who if He imprisoned me the imprisonment would be everlasting, Who if He condemned me to death the death would be for ever, and Whom I cannot appease with words nor bribe with money--nay more, when before me lie two ways, one of Gan Eden and the other of Gehinnom, and I know not to which I am to be led--shall I not weep?"' (Ber. 28b).

It would, however, be precarious to deduce from a rhetorical utterance like this that the Rabbi actually believed in eternal punishment. The contrast between the earthly ruler and the supreme King is merely worked out to its fullest extent. The authoritative doctrine is enunciated by R. Akiba in these terms: 'The judgment on the generation of the Flood was for twelve months, on Job for twelve months, on the Egyptians for twelve months, on Gog and Magog in the Hereafter for twelve months, and on the wicked in Gehinnom for twelve months. R. Jochanan b. Nun said, It endures only the space of time between Passover and Pentecost' (Eduy. II. 10), viz. a period of seven weeks.

Although it is definitely stated, 'The generation of the Flood will have no share in the World to Come,' and there is difference of opinion whether it will or will not 'arise for judgment' (Sanh. x. 3), we also find the, remark, 'The sentence of the generation of the Flood is for twelve months. When they have endured this term they will have a share in the World to Come' (Gen. R. XXVIII. 9). This is evidence of the reluctance on the part of the Rabbis to think of an endless punishment. One authority declared: 'All who descend to Gehinnom will ascend except three: he who has intercourse with another man's wife, he who puts his fellow to shame in public, and he who calls his fellow by an opprobrious nickname'[8] (B.M. 58b). The first-mentioned offence is omitted by some teachers (ibid. 59a).

The *locus classicus* on the subject reads: 'The School of Shammai declared, There are three classes with respect to the Day of Judgment: the perfectly righteous, the completely wicked, and the average people. Those in the first class are forthwith inscribed and sealed for eternal life. Those in the second Glass are forthwith inscribed and sealed for Gehinnom; as it is said, "Many of them that sleep in the dust of the earth shall awake, some to everlasting life and some to shame and everlasting contempt" (Dan. xii. 2). The third class will descend to Gehinnom and cry out (from the pains endured there) and then ascend; as it is said, "I will bring the third part through fire, and will refine them as silver is refined, and will try them as gold is tried; they shall call on My name and I will hear them" (Zech. xiii. 9). Concerning them Hannah said, "The Lord killeth and maketh alive, He bringeth down to Sheol and bringeth up" (1 Sam. ii. 6). The School of Hillel quoted, "He is plenteous in mercy" (Exod. xxxiv. 6); He inclines towards mercy; and concerning them said David, "I love the Lord, because He hath heard my voice and my supplications" (Ps. csvi. 1). The whole of that Psalm was composed by David about them: "I was brought low and He saved me" (ibid. 6). The sinners of Israel with their bodies and the sinners of the Gentiles with their bodies descend to Gehinom and are judged there for twelve months. After twelve months their bodies are destroyed, and their souls burnt and scattered by a wind under the soles of the feet of the righteous; as it is said, "Ye shall tread down the wicked, for they shall be ashes under the soles of your feet" (Mal. iv. 3). But the sectaries, informers, epicureans who denied the Torah[9] and denied the Resurrection, they who separated themselves from the ways of the community, they who set their dread in the land of the living,[10] and they who, like Jeroboam the son of Nebat and his associates, sinned and caused the multitude to sin (cf. 1 Kings xiv. 16), will descend to Gehinnom and be judged there generations on generations; as it is said, "They shall go forth and look upon the carcasses of the men that have transgressed against Me; for their worm shall not die, neither shall their fire be quenched" (Is. lxvi. 24). Gehinnom will cease but, they will not cease (to suffer); as it is said, "Their form shall be for Sheol to consume that there be no habitation for it" (Ps. xlix. 14). Concerning them said Hannah, "They that strive with the Lord shall be broken to pieces" (1 Sam. Ii. 10). R. Isaac b. Abin said, Their faces will be black like the bottom of a pot' (R.H. 16b et seq.)

We gather from this extract that in the first century one of the principal Schools, influenced by a verse from Daniel, assigned the utterly, wicked to eternal punishment; but the other School found such a doctrine incompatible with Divine mercy. Sinners must be penalized. They undergo twelve months of pain and then suffer annihilation because they are unworthy of entrance into Gan Eden. They who have, been exceptionally wicked stay in Gehinnom for generations on generations. That this expression does not signify eternity is clear from the statement that Gehinnom will cease.' They will not, after their sufferings there, undergo extinction, but will continue in existence as conscious entities--how and where is not explained--in a perpetual state of remorse.

NOTES

1. There is a play of words here. 'Which keepeth truth' is in Hebrew *shomer omunim,* and 'which uttereth Amen' is *she-omer amen.*
2. At the instigation of the Persian king Cyrus (Ezra i. 1 ff.).
3. See p. 61.
4. The words in brackets do not occur in Buber's edition but must be to complete the sense.
5. An idiomatic expression meaning to disregard as of no importance.
6. i.d. the fear of God had been his controlling motive in all his pursuits.
7. See p. 238.
8. Cf. Matt. V. 22.
9. i.e. its heavenly origin; see p. 146.
10. The phrase is defined in the Talmud as 'a president who instilled excessive fear into the community he governed, but not for the sake of Heaven,' i.e. he did it for personal motives.

Sec. V. GEHINNOM

The fate of the wicked, as the reader has already learnt, is to descend into a place of punishment called Gehinnom. 'A Roman lady asked R. Jose b. Chalaphta, "What is the meaning of the text 'Who knoweth the spirit of man that goeth upward' (Eccles. iii. 21)?" He answered, "It refers to the souls of the righteous which are deposited in the Divine treasury; as Abigail told David through the medium of the Holy Spirit, 'The soul of my lord shall be bound in the bundle of life with the Lord thy God' (1 Sam. xxv. 29). It is possible to think that the same destiny awaits the wicked; therefore the verse continues, 'And the souls of thine enemies, them shall He sling out as from the hollow of a sling.'" The Roman lady further asked, "What is the meaning of the text, 'And the spirit of the beast that it goeth downward to the earth'?" He

answered, "It refers to the souls of the wicked which descend below to Gehinnom'" (Eccles. R. to iii. 21).

Its origin predates the creation of the Universe;[1] but according to another view the pre-existence of Gehinnom only applies to its room and not to its contents. 'The space of Gehinnom was created before the Universe but its fire on the eve of the first Sabbath. It has, however, been taught, Why does not Scripture add "God saw that it was good" to the account of the second day? Because on that day the fire of Gehinnom was created? The fact is that the space of Gehinnom was created before the Universe, its fire on the second day, and the plan of creating ordinary fire entered His thought on the eve of the Sabbath, but it was not actually created until the termination of the Sabbath' (Pes. 54a).

A number of names was discovered in Scripture for the place of punishment. 'Gehinnom is called by seven designations: Sheol (Jonah ii: 2), Abaddon or Destruction (Ps. lxxxviii. 11), Corruption (ibid. xvi. 10), Horrible Pit and Miry Clay (ibid. xl. 2), Shadow of Death (ibid. cvii. 10), and the Nether world which is a tradition.[2] Are there not other names? For instance, Gehinnom--i.e. *Ge'*, a deep "valley" into which all descend on account of "lusts" (*Hinnom*), and Topheth (Is. xxx. 33), which is so called because every one who is led astray (*mithpatteh*) by his passions falls therein' (Erub. 19a).

While the regular use of the verb 'descend' in connection with Gehinnom points to the common belief that it lies below the earth, there is also a statement, 'Gehinnom is above the firmament; others say it lies behind the mountains of darkness' (Tamid 32b). These mysterious mountains were supposed to be located in the extreme west of the world. A similar view is found in this extract: 'The sun is red in the morning and evening--in the morning because it passes over (and catches the reflection of) the roses of Gan Eden, and in the evening because it passes over the entrance of Gehinnon' (B.B. 84a). Accordingly Gan Eden is in the east and Gehinnom in the west.

On the matter of its dimensions we are informed: 'The world is a sixtieth part of Gan Eden and Gan Eden a sixtieth part of Gehinnon; consequently the whole world is in comparison to Gehinnom like the lid of a pot. Some declare that Gan Eden is limitless in extent and others say the same of Gehinnom' (Taan. 10a).

With regard to its entrances the Talmud states: 'It has three--one in the wilderness, a second in the sea, and a third in

Text Twenty-five: THE HEREAFTER

Jerusalem. Another tradition tells, There are two date-palms in the valley of Ben-Hinnom from between which smoke ascends and that is the entrance of Gehinnom' (Erub. 19a).

It is divided into seven storeys, and the more wicked the person the lower is his place of accommodation. 'Each of the seven classes in Gan Eden has a dwelling for itself, and correspondingly there are seven storeys for the wicked in Gehinnom, their names being: Sheol, Abaddon, Shadow of Death, Nether world, Land of Forgetfulness (Ps. lxxxviii, 12), Gehinnom, and Silence (ibid. csv. 17)' (Midrash to Ps. xi. 7; 51a). From Ps. xi. 6 the deduction was drawn that there were seven storeys, viz. Snares,[3] Fire, Brimstone, Wind, and Flames (Midrash ad loc.; 50b). 'At the time that absalom's hair was caught on the tree, Sheol was split asunder beneath him. Why did David in his lament over him exclaim "my son" eight times?[4] Seven for the purpose of bringing him up from the seven storeys of Gehinnom, and the eighth to unite his head (which had been decapitated) to his body; or, according to others, to make him enter the World to Come' (Sot. 10b).

The principal element which exists there for the torment of the sinful is fire, but a fire of abnormal intensity. '(Ordinary) fire is a sixtieth of (the fire of) Behinnom' (Ber. 57b). '"a fiery stream issued and came forth before Him" (Dan. Vii. 10). Whence does it originate? From the sweat of the holy *Chayyoth*. And where does it empty itself? Upon the heads of the wicked in Gehinnom; as it is said, "It shall burst upon the head of the wicked" (Jer. Xxiii. 19)' (Chag. 13b). A Rabbi relates how an Arab met him in the desert and said, '"Come I will show you where Korah was swallowed up." I saw two cracks in the ground from which smoke issued forth. He took a ball of wool, steeped it in water, set it on the end of his spear, inserted it into the hole, and when he drew it out it was completely scorched' (B.B. 74a).

There is a teaching, 'The fire of Gehinnom will never be extinguished' (Tosifta Ber. VI. 7), but it conflicts with the doctrine of the School of Hillel that Gehinnom will, cease.[5] It is also stated that 'Gehinnom is half fire and half hail' (Exod. R. L.I. 7), while, according to another opinion, snow is likewise found there: 'The Holy One, blessed be He, judges the wicked in Gehinnom for twelve months. At first he afflicts them with itching; after that with fire, at which they cry out "O! O!" and then with snow, at which they cry out "Woe! Woe!"' (p. Sanh. 29b).

Another element which abounds there is brimstone. 'Why does man's soul shrink from the odour of brimstone? Because it knows that it will be judged therein in the Hereafter' (Gen. R. L.I. 3). Finally it is full of smoke. 'Gehinnom is narrow on top and wide below' (Sifrê Deut. Sec. 357; 149b). The reason why it has that shape is, 'Its mouth is narrow so that its smoke may be retained therein' (Men. 99b). Legend tells that 'smoke issued from the grave of Acher' (Chag. 15b). It is likewise a place of darkness. 'The wicked are darkness, Gehinnom is darkness, the depths are darkness. I lead the wicked to Gehinnom and cover them with the depths' (Gen. R. XXXIII. 1). 'Gehinnom is (black) like the night' (Jeb. 109b). 'They who descend to Gehinnom will be judged by nothing else than darkness; as it is said, "A land of thick darkness, as darkness itself" (Job x. 22)' (Tanchuma Noach Sec. 1). "And Moses stretched forth his hand toward heaven, and there was thick darkness" (Exod. x. 22). Whence did the darkness originate? From the darkness of Gehinnom' (Tanchuma Bo Sec. 2).

The severities of Gehinnom may be mitigated, or even altogether escaped, by various means. Prominent among them is the fact that a person has undergone circumcision, unless he had been exceptionally wicked. 'In the Hereafter Abraham will sit at the entrance of Gehinnom and will not allow any circumcised Israelite to descend into it. As for those who sinned unduly, what does he do to them? He removes the foreskin from children who had died before circumcision, places it upon them and sends them down to Gehinnom' (Gen. R. XLVIII. 8). 'Israelites who are circumcised will not descend to Gehinnom. So that heretics and the sinners in Israel shall not say, "Inasmuch as we are circumcised we will not go down to Gehinnom," what does the Holy One, blessed be He, do? He sends an angel who extends the foreskin and they descend to Gehinnom' (Exod. R. xix. 4).

The patriarch helps the release of those who had been condemned. '"Passing through the valley of weeping" (Ps. lxxxiv. 6), i.e. they who are sentenced for a time in Gehinnom; and Abraham our father comes and takes them out and receives them, with the exception of an Israelite who had intercourse with a gentile woman or disguised his circumcision for the purpose of concealing his identity' (Erub. 19a).

The recitation of certain prayers is another means of gaining immunity. 'Whoever reads the *Shema* with distinct pronunciation of its letters, Gehinnom is cooled for him' (Ber. 15b). That is an effect which originally belonged to the altar in the Temple. 'What means the word for altar (*Mizbeaeh*)? M=*mechilah* "forgiveness," because the altar secures pardon for the sins of Israel. Z=*sachath* "merit," because it secures for them merit for the World to Come, B=*berachah* "blessing," because the Holy One, blessed be He, brings a blessing upon the work of their hands. CH=*chayyim* "life," since they become worthy of the life of the World to Come. He who is helped by these four things and then goes and serves idolatry will be consumed by the great fire; as it is said, "The Lord thy God is a devouring fire, a jealous God" (Deut. iv. 24). But should he repent, the fire which burns on the altar will bring him atonement and nullify the fire of Gehinnom' (Tanchuma Tzab Sec. 14).

The principal safeguard, however, is the study of Torah. "The fire of Gehinnom has no power over the disciples of the Sages. This may be reasoned from the salamander. If a person is anointed with the blood of a salamander, which originates in fire, he cannot be harmed by fire; how much more immune are the disciples of the Sages whose body is fire; as it is said, "Is not My word like a fire, saith the Lord?" (Jer. xxiii. 29). The fire of Gehinnom has no power over the sinners in Israel. This may be reasoned from the golden altar. If this altar, which was only covered with a plating of gold the thickness of a gold *denarius,* endured so many years and was not overcome by the fire upon it, how much more will the Israelites resist the fire who are filled, even the most empty of them, with the precepts (of the Torah) as a pomegranate is filled with seeds!' (Chag. 27*a*).

A tradition existed to the effect that the sufferers in Gehinnom enjoyed a respite every Sabbath. It is mentioned in a dialogue between the Roman governor, Tineius Rufus, and R. Akiba. 'The Roman asked, "How is the Sabbath different from any other day?" The Rabbi retorted, "How are you (a Roman official) different from any other man?" Rufus said, "The Emperor was pleased to honour me"; and Akiba replied, "Similarly the Holy One, blessed be He, was pleased to honour the Sabbath." "How can you prove that to me?" "Behold the River Sabbatyon[6] carries stones as it flows[7] all the days of the week, but it rests on the Sabbath." "To a distant place you lead me!"[8] Akiba said, "Behold, a necromancer can prove it, because the dead ascend all the days of the week but not on the Sabbath. You can test my statement by your father." Later on Rufus had occasion to call up his father's spirit; it ascended every day of the week but not on the Sabbath. On Sunday he caused him to ascend and asked, "Have you become a Jew since your death? Why did you come up every day of the week but

not on the Sabbath?" He replied, "Whoever does not observe the Sabbath with you (on earth) does so voluntarily, but here he is compelled to keep the Sabbath." The son asked, "Is there, then, work where you are that you toil on the weekdays and rest on the Sabbath?" He answered, "All the days of the week we are under sentence but not on the Sabbath"' (Gen. R. XI. 5).

Noteworthy is the fact that at least one Rabbi denied the objective reality of a special place reserved for the punishment of the wicked. R. Simeon b. Lakish, who lived in the third century, declared: 'There is no Gehinnom in the Hereafter; but the Holy One, blessed be He, will remove the sun from its sheath and blacken (the world with its fierce rays). The wicked will be punished and the righteous healed thereby' (A.Z. 3*b*).

NOTES
1. See p. 347.
2. In effect, it is not Scriptural.
3. The plural, as also of 'Flames,' indicates two.
4. See a Sam. xviii. 33 and xix. 4.
5. See p. 378.
6. A legendary river, the name being derived from 'Sabbath.'
7. By the force of its current.
8. That means, your evidence is far-fetched.

Sec. VI. GAN EDEN
The place of happiness allocated to the righteous is called Gan Eden, 'the Garden of Eden.' It was usually regarded as distinct from the abode of that name which had been prepared for Adam. What is the meaning of "No eye hath seen what God, and nobody but Thee, will work for him that waiteth for Him" (*sic* Is. lxiv. 4)? It refers to Eden, upon which the eye of no creature has gazed. Perhaps you will ask, Where, then, was Adam? In the Garden. But perhaps you will say that the Garden is the same as Eden! Therefore a text teaches, "A river went out of Eden to water the garden" (Gen. ii. 10). Hence the Garden and Eden are distinct' (Ber. 34*b*).

Its exact site was a matter of doubt. 'If Gan Eden is located in the land of Israel its entrance is Beth-Shean; if in Arabia its entrance is Beth-Gerem; if between the rivers (Mesopotamia) its entrance is Damascus' (Erub. 19*a*). This evidently refers to the terrestrial Garden, the Paradise of the righteous being thought of as located in heaven.[1]

As with Gehinnorn, Gan Eden was supposed to consist of seven divisions for the seven degrees into which those

Text Twenty-five: **The Hereafter**

who merit it are capable of being classified. 'There are seven classes of righteous in Gan Eden, one higher than the other. The first class is alluded to in the text, "Surely the righteous shall give thanks unto Thy name; the upright shall dwell in Thy presence" (Ps. cxl. 13). The second is alluded to in, "Blessed is the man whom Thou choosest and causest to approach that he may dwell in Thy courts" (ibid. lxv. 4). The third is alluded to in, "Blessed are they that dwell in Thy house" (ibid. lxxxiv. 4). The fourth is alluded to in, "Lord, who shall sojourn in Thy tabernacle?" (ibid. xv. 1). The fifth is alluded to in, "Who shall dwell in Thy holy hill?" (ibid.). The sixth is alluded to in, "Who shall ascend into the hill of the Lord?" (ibid. xxiv. 3), and the seventh in, "Who shall stand in His holy place?" (ibid.)' (Sire Deut. Sec. 10; 67*b*). The seven divisions, counting downward, are therefore designated as: Presence, Courts, House, Tabernacle, Holy Hill, Hill of the Lord, and Holy Place.

Another version reads: 'Seven classes will stand before the Holy One, blessed be He, in the Hereafter. Which is the highest of them to receive the presence of the *Shechinah?* It is the class of the upright; as it is said, "The upright shall behold their face' (Ps. xi. 7). It is not written "His face" but "their face," i.e. the presence of the *Shechinah* and His retinue.[2] The first class sits in the company of the King and beholds His presence; as it is said, "The upright shall dwell in Thy presence." The second dwells in the house of the King; as it is said, "Blessed are they that dwell in Thy house." The third ascends the hill to meet the King, as it is said, "Who shall ascend into the hill of the Lord?" The fourth is in the court of the King; as it is said, "Happy is the man whom Thou choosest and causest to approach that he may dwell in Thy courts." The fifth is in the Tabernacle of the King; as it is said, Lord, who shall sojourn in Thy tabernacle?" The sixth is in the holy hill of the King; as it is said, "Who shall dwell in Thy holy hill?" The seventh is in the place of the King; as it is said, "Who shall stand in His holy place?"' (Midrash to Ps. xi. 7; 51*a*).

They who are admitted into Gan Eden are adjudged so that they may be accommodated in the division to which they are entitled. 'Each righteous person will be assigned a dwelling in accordance with the honour due to him. Parable of a human king who entered a city with his servants. Although they all enter through the one gate, when they take up their quarters each is allotted a dwelling according to his rank' (Shab. 152*a*).

The main characteristic of this heavenly abode is that the pious, who suffered privation while on earth, will now come into their own. 'In this world the wicked are rich and enjoy comfort and rest, white the righteous are poor. But in the Hereafter, when the Holy One, blessed be He, will open for the righteous the treasures of Gan Eden, the wicked, who extorted usury, will bite their flesh with their teeth; as it is said, "The fool foldeth his hands together and eateth his own flesh" (Eccles. iv. 5); and they will exclaim, "Would that we were labourers or carriers or slaves, and our fate were like theirs!" As it is said, "Better is a handful with quietness than two handfuls with labour and striving after wind" (ibid. 6)' (Exod. R. XXXI. 5).

The happiness which is in store for those who merit Gan Eden is symbolized as a wonderful banquet. The Bible makes mention of a monster called Leviathan which God slew and gave 'as meat to the people inhabiting the wilderness' (Ps. lxxiv. 14).[3] Popular fancy seized upon this and constituted it the principal course in the banquet which was to be arranged for the worthy. 'The Holy One, blessed be He, created one (Leviathan) a male and another a female; but had they mated they would have destroyed the whole world. What did He do? He emasculated the male, killed the female and preserved its flesh in brine for the righteous in the Hereafter' (B.B. 74*b*). 'In the Hereafter the Holy One, blessed be He, will make a banquet for the righteous from the flesh of Leviathan, and the remainder they will divide and sell as merchandise in the streets of Jerusalem.'[4] Its skin will be made by Him into a booth for the pious (ibid. 75*a*). For drink they will have 'wine preserved in the grape from the six days of Creation' (Ber. 34*b*).

The chief joy they will experience is being in the actual presence of God. In the Hereafter the Holy One, blessed be He, will prepare a banquet for the righteous in Gan Eden and there will be no need to provide balsam or perfumes, because a north wind and a south wind will sweep through and sprinkle all the aromatic plants of Gan Eden so that they yield their fragrance. The Israelites will say before the Holy One, blessed be He, "Does a host arrange a meal for wayfarers and not recline with them? Does a bridegroom prepare a banquet for guests and not sit with them? If it be Thy will, 'Let my Beloved come into His garden and eat His precious fruits' (Cant. iv. 16)." The Holy One, blessed be He, replies to them, "I will do as you desire." Then he enters Gan Eden; as it is written, "I am come into My garden, My sister, My bride" (ibid. v. 1)' (Num. R. XIII. 2).

Still bolder in expression are these extracts: 'In the Hereafter the Holy One, blessed be He, will arrange a dance for the

Text Twenty-five: **THE HEREAFTER**

righteous in Gan Eden, He sitting in their midst; and each one will point to Him with his finger, exclaiming, "Lo, this is our God, we have waited for Him and He will save us; this is the Lord, we have waited for Him, we will be glad and rejoice in His salvation" (Is. xxv. 9)' (Taan. 31*a*). "'I will walk among you" (Lev. xxvi. 12). To what is this like? To a king who went out to walk with his tenant in his orchard; but the tenant hid himself from him. The king called to him, "Why do you hide from me? See, I am just the same as you!" Similarly the Holy One, blessed be He, will walk with the righteous in Gan Eden in the Hereafter; and the righteous, on beholding Him, will retreat in terror before Him. But He will call to them, 'See, I am the same as you!" Since, however, it is possible to imagine that My fear should no longer be upon you, the text declares, "I will be your God, and ye shall be My people" (ibid.)' (Sifra ad loc.).[5]

Since the study of Torah leads to piety it opens the road to Gan Eden, and they who have devoted themselves to its acquisition will be specially welcomed there. 'R. Jochanan b. Zakkai said to R. Jose the Priest, In my dream I saw the two of us reclining upon Mount Sinai, and a *Bath Kol* issued from Heaven concerning us, "Ascend hither! Ascend hither! Large banqueting couches and beautiful coverlets are prepared for you. You, your disciples, and the disciples of your disciples are invited into the third class"'[6] (Chag. 14*b*). Their particular reward is the solution of the intellectual difficulties which had beset them on earth. 'As for the disciples of the Sages who wrinkle their foreheads with study of Torah in this world, the Holy One, blessed be He, will reveal to them its mysteries in the World to Come' (ibid. 14*a*).

In the Talmud and older Midrashim there is no attempt, beyond what has been cited, to give an elaborate description of the interior of Gan Eden and the life there. In later works this restraint is lacking and detailed accounts occur. One very striking verbal picture is found in the *Jalkut Shimeoni* (Genesis Sec. 20), a collection of Rabbinic material which was compiled about the thirteenth century. The authorship of the passage is ascribed to R. Joshua b. Levi, a Rabbi of the third century, who is known to have had a tendency towards mysticism. For that reason it is included here, although it must remain a matter of doubt whether he is the author.

'Gan Eden has two gates of ruby, by which stand sixty myriads of ministering angels. The lustre of the face of each of them glistens like the splendour of the firmament. When a righteous person arrives, they divest him of the garments in which he arose from the grave, clothe him in eight robes of the clouds of glory, set two crowns upon his head, one made of gems and pearls and the other of gold from Parvaim (see 2 Chron. iii. 6), place eight myrtles in his hand, and praise him, saying, "Go, eat your food in joy." They take him into a place where are brooks of water, surrounded by eight hundred varieties of roses and myrtles. Each person has a chamber allotted to him by himself according to the honour due to him. From it issue four streams, one of milk, one of wine, one of balsam, and one of honey; and above every chamber there is a golden vine studded with thirty pearls; each of them glistening like the brilliance of the planet Venus. In every chamber there is a table of gems and pearls, and sixty angels attending upon each righteous man, saying to him, "Go, eat honey in joy, since you occupied yourself with Torah which is compared to honey; and drink wine which has been preserved in the grape from the six days of Creation, since you occupied yourself with Torah which is compared to wine." The ugliest of the inhabitants of Gan Eden will be like Joseph and R. Jochanan.[7] There is no night for them, and the period (which would normally have been night) is renewed for them in three watches. In the first watch, the righteous person becomes like a child, enters the department of children and plays their games. In the second watch, he becomes a young man, enters the department of young men and plays their games. In the third watch, he becomes an old man, enters the department of old men and plays their games.

In every corner of Gan Eden there are eighty myriad species of trees, the most inferior of them being finer than all the aromatic plants (of this world); and in each corner are sixty myriads of ministering angels singing in pleasant tones. In the centre is the Tree of Life, its branches covering the whole of Gan Eden, containing five hundred thousand varieties of fruit all differing in appearance and taste. Above it are the clouds of glory, and it is smitten by the four winds so that its odour is wafted from one end of the world to, the other. Beneath it are the disciples of the Sages who expounded the Torah, each of them possessing two chambers, one of the stars and the other of the sun and moon. Between every chamber hangs a curtain of clouds of glory, behind which lies Eden. Inside it are three hundred and ten worlds,[9] and in it are seven classes of the righteous. The first consists of martyrs,[10] such as it Akiba and his colleagues. The second consists of those drowned at sea.[11] In the third are R. Jochanan b. Zakkai and his disciples. Such was his might (in scholarship) that he said of himself, "If all the heaven were parchment, all human beings scribes, and all the trees of the forests pens, it would be insufficient to write what I have learnt from my teachers; and yet I only took away from them as much as a dog laps from the ocean!"[12] In the fourth class are they upon whom the cloud descended as a covering.[13] In the fifth class are the penitents and where they stand not even the perfectly righteous stand. In the sixth class are the unmarried who never tasted sin (and remained chaste). In the seventh class are the poor who are possessed of knowledge of Scripture and Mishnah and were engaged in a worldly occupation. Concerning them it is written, "Let all those that put their trust in Thee rejoice" (Ps. v. 11). The Holy One, blessed be He, sits in their midst and expounds the Torah to them; as it is said, "Mine eyes shall be upon the faithful of the land, that they may dwell with Me" (ibid. ci. 6).'

NOTES

1. Or in the extreme east of the world; see p. 380.

2. The suffix in the Hebrew is unusual and can be translated 'His' or 'their.'

3. See also Ps. civ. 26; Is. xxvii. 1; and Job xli. 1.

4. The mention of the sale of the flesh makes it doubtful whether the Hereafter in this passage is to be understood as the period after death or the Messianic era. The term has both connotations and they are sometimes confused.

5. We detect here the anxiety of the Rabbis to insist that there must always be an unbridgeable gulf between man, even in his highest spiritual development, and God. The two cannot ever be absolutely identical. Even in the Hereafter, although human beings will enjoy the closest possible communion with Him, He will still be God and they will still be His 'people,' i.e. human.

6. The third of the seven classes in Paradise was reserved for the great scholars; see p. 388.

7. See p. 134.

8. Both were famed for their beauty; see pp. 137, 274.

9. This is based on the Talmudic homily: 'R. Joshua b. Levi said, The Holy One, blessed be He, will give each righteous person three hundred and ten worlds as an inheritance; as it is said, 'That I may cause those that love Me to inherit substance"(Prov. viii. (Uktz. III. 12). The letters of the Hebrew word for 'substance' have the numerical value of three hundred and ten.

10. The information that martyrs occupy a pre-eminent position. in Gan Eden was communicated to R. Joshua b. Levi by his son after recovery from a state of coma. See p. 365.

11. viz. the Jewish youths and maidens who sacrificed their lives rather than be dishonoured. See p. 45.

12. This version of this well-known hyperbole is taken partly from Sopherim XVI. 8, and partly from Sanh. 68a.

13. It is not certain to whom allusion is made here. Possibly the reference is to great men whom God distinguished either during their lifetime or at their death by enveloping them with the cloud of glory. When Moses ascended Sinai to receive the Torah, God protected him from the envy of the angels by spreading a cloud over him (Shah. 88b). As Moses stripped Aaron of his vestments before his death a cloud covered him (Jalkut Num. Sec. 787). Josephus also tells: As he (Moses) was embracing Eleazar and Joshua and was still conversing with them, a cloud stood over him on a sudden, and he disappeared in a certain ravine' (Antiq. IV. Viii. 48).

Christianity

Mosaic of Jesus Christ Found in the Former Greek Basilica of Hagia Sophia in Istanbul, Turkey

Shutterstock © Taiga, 2012. Used under license of Shutterstock, Inc.

Mary and Jesus (Tikhvin Church, Kazan, Tatarstan, Russian Federation)

Photo Courtesy Agnes Kefeli

Photo Courtesy Agnes Kefeli

Christian Tatar Cemetery, Tatarstan. Russian Federation.

Photo Courtesy Agnes Kefeli

Tikhvin Church, Eastern Orthodox Church, Tatarstan. Russian Federation

CHRISTIANITY

Beginnings
Demography
- 2.3 billion Christians on earth
- 1 of every 3 persons on earth is Christian

Basic Info About Christianity
- Faith in Jesus of Nazareth
- Jesus is the Christ (Messiah = Anointed)
- God became human in Christ to save humanity
- Jesus provided a new interpretation of the Torah
- "Sabbath was made for man."
  – Jesus picked grain
  – Jesus healed
- Jesus rose from the dead

Christianity was the second response to the fall of the second temple (rabbical judisum was as well)

Rituals Shared by Most Branches of Christianity
- Baptism → ONE TIME
- Eucharist

- Babtism is a Jewish ritual (mikvah) → continual

Unique Christian Concept of Original Sin
- Sin = Failure to live in harmony with God
- Original Sin
  – Human will has become corrupted
  – Adam's disobedience brought
    - Sin
    - Death
- Jesus = Savior (Messiah)
  – Recreated a good will
  – Repaired the world through his sacrifice

Why did Jews bring sacrifices to the Temple?
- To thank God
- To praise Him
- To cleanse their sins (Atonement)
- Christians believe that Jesus was God's sacrifice + fulfillment of Hebrew prophecy

Jesus = Fulfillment of Hebrew Prophecy
- In Matthew's Gospel ← *most Jewish gospel*
- Jesus = son of David, son of Abraham = Messiah
- Virgin birth

- Matthew quotes *Isaiah*: "Behold, a virgin shall conceive and bear a son, and his name shall be called Emmanuel (which means, 'God with us')"
- Jesus' family escapes from the slaughter of infants by King Herod = Exodus account of Israelites' escape from Egypt
- Jesus = "New Moses"
  - Sermon on Mount = Torah on Mount Sinai

RABBINICAL JUDAISM AND CHRISTIANITY
= TWO DIFFERENT RESPONSES TO DESTRUCTION OF SECOND TEMPLE IN 70 CE

- Both are two developments of Ancient Judaism
- Both reflected on destruction of temple
- Judaism developed the TORAH (teaching)
- Christianity developed CHRISTOLOGY

The Jesus Movement

- Christianity began as a Jewish movement
- Jesus was a Jew
- Jesus' followers were Jews
- Jesus taught as a Rabbi [master], a teacher of Jewish law

The Jesus Movement: A Form of Judaism

- Jesus' followers
  - Were initially all Jews
  - Worshiped with other Jews in the Temple
  - Observed the Torah and Jewish feasts
- Jesus' followers came to believe
  - Jesus was the promised Messiah
  - Jesus had risen from the dead

Jesus' Passion and Resurrection

- Friday—executed by Pontius Pilate
  - His body was placed in a rock tomb
- Sunday morning—women found tomb empty
- Jesus had been raised from the dead
- Over 40 days Jesus appeared to his disciples
- Ascension Thursday—ascended to Heaven

Early Christian Rituals

- Based on Jewish rituals
- Baptism = *mikveh* [ritual bath]
  - Christian rite of initiation

- Eucharist = "Thanksgiving"
  - Re-enactment of Jesus' last meal with disciples
  - Similar to Passover meal

Passion of Jesus
- Setting—Jerusalem at Passover time
- Institution of Eucharist
- Last Supper
  - Bread = Jesus' body
    - "Take, eat: This is my Body, which is given for you. Do this for the remembrance of me."
  - Wine = Blood of the new covenant
    - "Drink this, all of you: This is my Blood of the new Covenant, which is shed for you and for many for the forgiveness of sins. Whenever you drink it, do this for the remembrance of me."
- Jesus = Passover lamb

Early Christian Festivals
- Easter, Pascha = Resurrection of Jesus
  - Similar to Jewish Passover (Pesach)
  - Passover = Exodus from Egypt
- Pentecost = Reception of Holy Spirit
  - Descent of Holy Spirit on Apostles
  - Similar to Jewish Shavuot (Feast of Weeks)
  - Shavuot celebrates Reception of Torah by Moses

How did Christianity Separate from Judaism?
- "God-Fearing" Gentiles enter Christian community (30s)
- Council of Jerusalem (48 CE)
  - Circumcision unnecessary for Christians
- Destruction of Second Temple (70 CE)

Before the Destruction of Second Temple—
Paul of Tarsus, Apostle to Gentiles
- Learned Jew
- Roman citizen
- He initially persecuted Christians
- Dramatic conversion after vision of Jesus
- Became itinerant Christian missionary
- Letters to churches became part of New Testament

Council of Jerusalem (48 CE)
- Critical issue = status of Gentile converts
- Conservative Christians argued that Gentiles must
  - Be circumcised
  - Follow Mosaic law

- Paul argued
  - Faith in Jesus Christ—not obedience to Torah—saves
  - Gentiles should be exempt from circumcision
  - But still keep moral commandments of Mosaic covenant
- Conclusion—Gentile Christians did not need to be circumcised

Problem of the Destruction of Second Temple
- Jewish sacrificial system is at an end
- How is it possible to reach God?
- Christians develop CHRISTOLOGY
  - Four gospels are written after 70
  - Jesus = sacrifice
  - Destruction = God's punishment of non-Christian Jews
- Jews develop TORAH

Church Became Increasingly Gentile
- New Testament is in Greek, not Aramaic

The New Testament
- Testament = covenant
- Old Testament = Hebrew Bible

The New Testament has 27 books
- 4 gospels
- Apostle Paul's letters (earliest documents)
- Other letters
- History of early church (Acts)
- Prophecy of the end of times (Revelation)

Organization of Church
- Christians initially expected imminent return of Christ
- When Christ tarried, Christians organized Church (*ekklesia* = gathering, convocation)

Episcopal Organization
- Bishop (episkopos, overseer)
  - Leader of urban Christian community
- Bishop of Rome ➔ principal bishop
  - Apostle Peter = 1st Bishop of Rome
  - By 4th century, bishop of Rome is called Pope (father)

Roman Persecution
- After Rome burnt in 64 CE, Nero accused Christians of starting the fire and labeled them enemies of the state

Institutionalization of the Church
- Emperor Constantine (r. 306-337)
- 313—Edict of Milan or Edict of Toleration
  - Legalized Christianity
- Made Sunday a legal holiday
- 330—Moved capital to Byzantium

Constantine
- Sought to unify empire through religion
- Called the first ecumenical council to resolve church conflicts
  - Ecumenical = "from the whole world"
- Later emperors called similar councils

Concept of Trinity = ONE GOD
- What did Jesus mean when He said:
  "No one can come to the father except through me." (John 14:6)
  Or "I and the father are one" (John 10:30)
- What is the relationship between
  - God, the Father
  - Jesus, the Son
  - and the Holy Spirit?
- How can polytheism be avoided?

What does God do in Judaism, Christianity, and Islam?
- Creates
- Redeems
- Reveals

In Christianity
- God the Father = Creator
- Son Jesus = the Redeemer
- Holy Spirit = the Revelator

TRINITY
- The Trinity refers to God's activity in relation to humanity
- It explains how God works through Christ
- Metaphor used by early Christians to explain Trinity: The Sun is light and heat

Who is the Holy Spirit?
- He is the relationship between God and Jesus
- He lives in the heart of all believers
- He is the One who testifies about Christ
- He is a continuing source of inspiration, guidance, and comfort

Important Early Ecumenical Councils
- 1st Ecumenical Council—Nicea, 325
  - Declared that Christ is fully God
  - Arius lost: he believed that Jesus was not eternal but created within time
  - Bishop Athanasius won
  - The Father and the Son were co-eternal
  - Only God could repair the world
- 2nd Ecumenical Council in Constantinople, 381
  - Formulated Doctrine of Trinity
  - God has 3 Persons
  - Persons are NOT beings
  - Persons = God's activities or manifestations
  - Trinity = Monotheism
  - Jews and Muslims misunderstand concept of Trinity as form of polytheism
- 4th Ecumenical Council—Chalcedon, 451
  - Declared that Christ is fully human and fully God

Two Major Splits
- The Great Schism
  - 11th century (1054)
  - Split between Orthodox and Catholic
  - Mutual Excommunication
    - The Pope (Leo IX) excommunicated Patriarch of Constantinople
    - Patriarch of Constantinople returned the favor
- The Reformation
  - 16th century
  - Split between Catholic and Protestant

Great Schism = What caused the divorce?
- 330—Constantine moved capital to Constantinople
- Two halves of Roman Empire grew apart

Differences between East and West
- Language
- Church-State relations
- Episcopal authority
- Procession of the Holy Spirit (*filioque*)
- Liturgical practices

Language
- West—Latin
  - Rome had ONE sacred language, Latin
  - Until 1960s, Rome promoted ONE language

- East—Linguistic diversity
  – Primary Christian language in East was Greek
  – Other Christian liturgical language = Syriac
  – Orthodox Church always used several sacred languages
    - Greek Orthodox use Greek
    - Slavic Orthodox use Slavonic
    - Arabic Orthodox use Arabic

Church-State Relations

- Byzantine empire lasted much longer in East
  – 476: last emperor in Rome
  – 1453: last emperor in Constantinople
- Byzantium
  – Emperor ruled over both church and state in the name of Christ
- Western Europe
  – Pope took on greater authority

Papal Primacy

- Orthodox—All bishops are equal
- Catholic—Pope is vicar of Christ, above all other

Procession of Holy Spirit

- West
  – Spirit proceeds from the Father and the Son (*filioque*)
- East
  – The Father is the source from which everything issues

Different Liturgical Practices

Catholic

- Altar in full view
- 3-dimensional statues
- Secular artists
  – Development of realist style
- Baptism by sprinkling
- Left-to-right cross
- Parish priests are celibate
- Unleavened bread in Eucharist

Orthodox

- Icon-screen hides altar
- 2-dimensional icons
- Monastic artists
  – Rejection of realist style

- Baptism by immersion
- Right-to-left cross
- Married parish priests
- Leavened bread in Eucharist

Orthodoxy Today
- There are different orthodox churches (Greek, Russian, Coptic). All the Eastern churches together probably have about 200 million adherents.

Missionary Outreach
- 9th century: Cyril and Methodius lead mission to Slavs
- 10th century: Conversion of Vladimir of Kiev
- 16th century: Moscow becomes Patriarchate

Protestantism (16th century)
Causes of the Reformation?
- Growing middle class
- Corruption of Church
- Sale of indulgences
- Printing

Martin Luther (1483-1546)
- Monk, priest, professor at U. of Wittenberg
- Salvation by grace through faith
- Luther revived the Pauline doctrine of justification by faith
- Challenged mediating role of church
  - Papacy
  - Sacraments

Luther's Ideas
- Authority of scripture
  - Availability of scripture in vernacular
  - German Bible
- Priesthood of all believers
  - All professions are sacred

Political Support for Reformation
- Luther won the support of German princes
- German princes wanted to end the drain of their country's resources to Rome

John Calvin (1509-1564)
- Emphasized God's sovereignty
- Iconoclastic
- Austere

Calvinist Movements

- Puritans
- Huguenots
- Presbyterians

Protestantism Takes Many Forms

- Anglicans
- Anabaptists
- Baptists
- Society of Friends
- Methodists
- Pentecostals

Catholic Reformation or Counterreformation: Council of Trent in Italy (1545-1563)

- Affirmed Church tradition
- Authority of popes
- 7 sacraments
- Celebration of the Mass in Latin
- Transubstantiation
- Salvation by good works and faith

Society of Jesus (Jesuits)

- Ignatius Loyola, a former Spanish soldier
- Highly disciplined order
- Approved by Pope in 1540
- Founded schools all over Europe
- Sent missionaries to Europe, Asia, and Americas

Vatican II

- Pope John XXIII (1881-1963)
- Decentralized church
- Introduced use of vernacular in worship
- Endorse dialogue with other religions
- Consult with lay people
- Permitted modern approaches to Bible
- Simplify decorations
- Reformed liturgy
- Encouraged religious to participate in world

EXTRA NOTES

CHRISTIANITY

From Jesus to Christ: The First Christians

1. Why do scholars have difficulty in describing the historical Jesus?

2. When was Jesus born?

3. What was Jesus' social background? How did the scholars in the film interpret the evidence about his social background? What were their disagreements?

4. Who was Herod the Great? When did he die? What was the great port city that he built? What did he do to the Temple?

5. Where was Sephoris? What have recent archeological excavations of this town told us about the context of Jesus' life?

6. What does the term "apocalyptic" mean? What were the two apocalyptic movements of 1st-century Judaism mentioned in the video?

7. Why do historians think that Jesus was a disciple of John the Baptist?

8. According to the Dead Sea Scrolls, what kind of messiah(s) did the Qumran community expect?

9. What kind of metaphors did Jesus use to describe the kingdom of God?

10. Why was Jesus' message interpreted as a threat by the Romans?

11. Who was Pontius Pilate? (Dates)

12. What did Jesus do in Jerusalem?

13. How did Jesus get into trouble?

14. What role did the priests play in his arrest?

15. Who was responsible for Jesus' execution?

16. Which of the Hebrew scriptures did the writers of the Gospel allude to when they described the crucifixion?

17. Why was Jesus executed?

Constantine

1. Who was Constantine?

2. What kind of vision did he have?

3. When did it occur?

4. What is the evidence that Constantine genuinely converted to Christianity?

5. What is the evidence against his conversion?

6. How did the conversion of Constantine affect Christianity and the Roman Empire?

Eastern Orthodox Christianity in Russia

The first two questions are general questions on the film. Answers to these questions may be found throughout the film. Questions 3–13 follow the film sequence closely.

1. What was the status of the Christian church during the Soviet Union (Communist rule) – 1917-1985? What were the consequences of the Communist rule? How did believers maintain their Christian identity during the Communist rule?

2. There is a revival of Christianity in Russia since Perestroika (led by Gorbachev). How is it expressed?

3. What is an icon? What are the major iconic themes?

4. What is an iconostasis? What does it represent?

5. What is the purpose of icons?

6. What is confession?

7. How do people worship in Eastern Orthodox churches? Do you notice any differences with the Western Catholic churches?

8. How do Eastern Orthodox Christians call their service?

9. Describe the service. What does it commemorate?

10. What is the Holy Communion?

11. What is the meaning of baptism?

12. What is Chrismation? What is its meaning?

13. After watching the film, list the sacraments (or mysteries) shown in the film.

The Reformation: Age of Revolt

1. What are indulgences?

2. Who was Luther?

3. What did Luther oppose?

4. What did Luther stand for?

5. What technology helped the spread of Luther's ideas?

6. In what language did Luther write?

7. Who was Charles the V (r. 1519-56)?

8. Who was Thomas Muntzer (c. 1490-1525)?

9. Was Luther a social revolutionary?

10. Who was Huldrych Zwingli (1484-1531)? Why is he important?

11. Who was John Calvin? Why is he important?

First task: Give a title to each picture

A

© jonsvo, 2013. Used under license from Shutterstock, Inc.

The crucifiction

B

© jonsvo, 2013. Used under license from Shutterstock, Inc.

The Last Supper

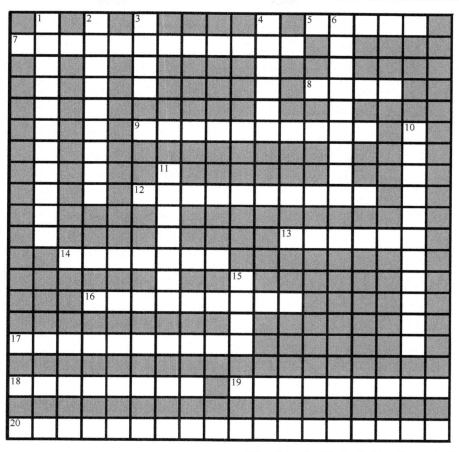

ACROSS

5. List of authoritative scriptures
7. The appearance of an angel to the Virgin Mary to tell her that she would bear a son, conceived by the Holy Spirit to save the world
8. Preparatory period before Easter; it lasts 40 days
9. Revelation
12. Greek translation of the Hebrew Bible, made in Alexandria
13. Month of spiritual preparation leading up to Christmas
14. Concept of God as having three "persons" or three manifestations as Father (Creator), Son (Redeemer) and Holy Spirit (Revelator)
16. Eastern branch of Christianity; it also means "correct belief"
17. Remission of time spent in purgatory in Catholicism
18. Refers to three similar books of the Gospels: Matthew, Mark, and Luke
19. Intermediate after-death state in which souls are purified from sin

20. Idea in Catholicism (but not Protestantism) that wine and bread are mystically transformed into the blood and flesh of Christ during the Lord's Supper

DOWN

1. God became flesh in Jesus
2. The Lord's Supper
3. Sacred image in Eastern Orthodox Christian church
4. Good News
6. The ascent of Jesus to heaven 40 days after his resurrection
10. Attempt to understand the nature of Jesus and his relationship with God
11. The "anointed," the expected king and deliverer of the Jews; a term applied by Christians to Jesus
15. It means "father" literally and designates the bishop of Rome and head of the Roman Catholic Church

Questions on the New Testament

1. Most scholars agree that Mark was the first Gospel to be composed. Would you say that the Gospel of Mark constitutes a thorough biography of Jesus' life? What is missing? [See TEXT 26]

2. Scholars argue that the Gospel of Matthew is the most Jewish of the four Gospels and that it was originally composed for the Pharisaic community of Jamnia. Explain why. [See TEXT 27]

3. Who is Jesus in Mark? What is his mission? [See TEXT 26]

4. What is the "Good News" in Mark? [See TEXT 26]

5. Did Jesus face opposition in Mark? Did his miracles convince people that he was the Messiah? What is the ultimate proof that he is the Messiah according to Mark? [See TEXT 26]

6. What did Jesus instruct his disciples about in John, 13-17? Are these instructions present in Mark's Gospel? [See TEXTS 26 and 28]

7. What is the relationship between God and Jesus in John? [See TEXT 28]

8. How different is Jesus in Mark, John, and Revelation? [See TEXTS 26, 28, and 30]

9. What is the general tone of Paul's letter to the Galatians? What can you say about Paul's personality? [See TEXT 29]

10. According to Paul, what is the relationship between Law and Faith? [See TEXT 29]

11. On the basis of the information provided by Paul, why was circumcision such a big deal? [See TEXT 29]

12. Compare Jesus in your booklet's excerpts from the New Testament and in Surah 19 of the Qur'an (Mary or Maryam: 17-38). How does the nativity story in Matthew differ from the Qur'an's? How does the Qur'an view Jesus and Christians? Why does the same Surah refer to Abraham and his father? On the basis of John, why do you think Christians would object to the Qur'an's understanding of Jesus? [See TEXTS 26-30 and 35]

Text Twenty-six

The Gospel According to Mark

1

¹ The beginning of the Good News of Jesus Christ, the Son of God. ² As it is written in the prophets,
"Behold,* I send my messenger before your face,
who will prepare your way before you:
³ the voice of one crying in the wilderness,
'Make ready the way of the Lord!
Make his paths straight!' "

⁴ John came baptizing† in the wilderness and preaching the baptism of repentance for forgiveness of sins.⁵ All the country of Judea and all those of Jerusalem went out to him. They were baptized by him in the Jordan river, confessing their sins. ⁶ John was clothed with camel's hair and a leather belt around his waist. He ate locusts and wild honey. ⁷ He preached, saying, "After me comes he who is mightier than I, the thong of whose sandals I am not worthy to stoop down and loosen. ⁸ I baptized you in‡ water, but he will baptize you in the Holy Spirit."

⁹ In those days, Jesus came from Nazareth of Galilee, and was baptized by John in the Jordan.¹⁰ Immediately coming up from the water, he saw the heavens parting, and the Spirit descending on him like a dove. ¹¹ A voice came out of the sky, "You are my beloved Son, in whom I am well pleased."

¹² Immediately the Spirit drove him out into the wilderness. ¹³ He was there in the wilderness forty days tempted by Satan. He was with the wild animals; and the angels were serving him.

¹⁴ Now after John was taken into custody, Jesus came into Galilee, preaching the Good News of God's Kingdom, ¹⁵ and saying, "The time is fulfilled, and God's Kingdom is at hand! Repent, and believe in the Good News."

¹⁶ Passing along by the sea of Galilee, he saw Simon and Andrew the brother of Simon casting a net into the sea, for they were fishermen. ¹⁷ Jesus said to them, "Come after me, and I will make you into fishers for men."

¹⁸ Immediately they left their nets, and followed him. ¹⁹ Going on a little further from there, he saw James the son of Zebedee, and John, his brother, who were also in the boat mending the nets. ²⁰ Immediately he called them, and they left their father, Zebedee, in the boat with the hired servants, and went after him. ²¹ They went into Capernaum, and immediately on the Sabbath day he entered into the synagogue and taught. ²² They were astonished at his teaching, for he taught them as having authority, and not as the scribes. ²³ Immediately there was in their synagogue a man with an unclean spirit, and he cried out, ²⁴ saying, "Ha! What do we have to do with you, Jesus, you Nazarene? Have you come to destroy us? I know you who you are: the Holy One of God!"

²⁵ Jesus rebuked him, saying, "Be quiet, and come out of him!"

²⁶ The unclean spirit, convulsing him and crying with a loud voice, came out of him. ²⁷ They were all amazed, so that they questioned among themselves, saying, "What is this? A new teaching? For with authority he commands even the unclean spirits, and they obey him!" ²⁸ The report of him went out immediately everywhere into all the region of Galilee and its surrounding area.

²⁹ Immediately, when they had come out of the synagogue, they came into the house of Simon and Andrew, with James and John. ³⁰ Now Simon's wife's mother lay sick with a fever, and immediately they told him about her. ³¹ He came and took her by the hand, and raised her up. The fever left her, and she served them.³² At evening, when the sun had set, they brought to him all who were sick, and those who were possessed by demons. ³³ All the city was gathered together at the door. ³⁴ He healed many who were sick with various diseases, and cast out many demons. He didn't allow the demons to speak, because they knew him.

[35] Early in the morning, while it was still dark, he rose up and went out, and departed into a deserted place, and prayed there. [36] Simon and those who were with him searched for him. [37] They found him and told him, "Everyone is looking for you."

[38] He said to them, "Let's go elsewhere into the next towns, that I may preach there also, because I came out for this reason." [39] He went into their synagogues throughout all Galilee, preaching and casting out demons.

[40] A leper came to him, begging him, kneeling down to him, and saying to him, "If you want to, you can make me clean."

[41] Being moved with compassion, he stretched out his hand, and touched him, and said to him, "I want to. Be made clean." [42] When he had said this, immediately the leprosy departed from him, and he was made clean. [43] He strictly warned him, and immediately sent him out, [44] and said to him, "See you say nothing to anybody, but go show yourself to the priest, and offer for your cleansing the things which Moses commanded, for a testimony to them."

[45] But he went out, and began to proclaim it much, and to spread about the matter, so that Jesus could no more openly enter into a city, but was outside in desert places. People came to him from everywhere.

2

[1] When he entered again into Capernaum after some days, it was heard that he was in the house. [2] Immediately many were gathered together, so that there was no more room, not even around the door; and he spoke the word to them. [3] Four people came, carrying a paralytic to him. [4] When they could not come near to him for the crowd, they removed the roof where he was. When they had broken it up, they let down the mat that the paralytic was lying on. [5] Jesus, seeing their faith, said to the paralytic, "Son, your sins are forgiven you."

[6] But there were some of the scribes sitting there, and reasoning in their hearts, [7] "Why does this man speak blasphemies like that? Who can forgive sins but God alone?"

[8] Immediately Jesus, perceiving in his spirit that they so reasoned within themselves, said to them, "Why do you reason these things in your hearts? [9] Which is easier, to tell the paralytic, 'Your sins are forgiven;' or to say, 'Arise, and take up your bed, and walk?' [10] But that you may know that the Son of Man has authority on earth to forgive sins"—he said to the paralytic— [11] "I tell you, arise, take up your mat, and go to your house."

[12] He arose, and immediately took up the mat, and went out in front of them all; so that they were all amazed, and glorified God, saying, "We never saw anything like this!"

[13] He went out again by the seaside. All the multitude came to him, and he taught them. [14] As he passed by, he saw Levi, the son of Alphaeus, sitting at the tax office, and he said to him, "Follow me." And he arose and followed him.

[15] He was reclining at the table in his house, and many tax collectors and sinners sat down with Jesus and his disciples, for there were many, and they followed him. [16] The scribes and the Pharisees, when they saw that he was eating with the sinners and tax collectors, said to his disciples, "Why is it that he eats and drinks with tax collectors and sinners?"

[17] When Jesus heard it, he said to them, "Those who are healthy have no need for a physician, but those who are sick. I came not to call the righteous, but sinners to repentance."

[18] John's disciples and the Pharisees were fasting, and they came and asked him, "Why do John's disciples and the disciples of the Pharisees fast, but your disciples don't fast?"

[19] Jesus said to them, "Can the groomsmen fast while the bridegroom is with them? As long as they have the bridegroom with them, they can't fast. [20] But the days will come when the bridegroom will be taken away from them, and then they will fast in that day. [21] No one sews a piece of unshrunk cloth on an old garment, or else the patch shrinks and the new tears away from the old, and a worse hole is made. [22] No one puts new wine into old wineskins, or else the new wine will burst the skins, and the wine pours out, and the skins will be destroyed; but they put new wine into fresh wineskins."

[23] He was going on the Sabbath day through the grain fields, and his disciples began, as they went, to pluck the ears of grain. [24] The Pharisees said to him, "Behold, why do they do that which is not lawful on the Sabbath day?"

[25] He said to them, "Did you never read what David did, when he had need, and was hungry—he, and those who were with him? [26] How he entered into God's house at the time of Abiathar the high priest, and ate the show bread, which is not lawful to eat except for the priests, and gave also to those who were with him?" [27] He said to them, "The Sabbath was made for man, not man for the Sabbath. [28] Therefore the Son of Man is lord even of the Sabbath."

3

[1] He entered again into the synagogue, and there was a man there who had his hand withered. [2] They watched him, whether he would heal him on the Sabbath day, that they might accuse him. [3] He said to the man who had his hand withered, "Stand up." [4] He said to them, "Is it lawful on the Sabbath day to do good, or to do harm? To save a life, or to kill?" But they were silent. [5] When he had looked around at them with anger, being grieved at the hardening of

their hearts, he said to the man, "Stretch out your hand." He stretched it out, and his hand was restored as healthy as the other. ⁶ The Pharisees went out, and immediately conspired with the Herodians against him, how they might destroy him.

⁷ Jesus withdrew to the sea with his disciples, and a great multitude followed him from Galilee, from Judea, ⁸ from Jerusalem, from Idumaea, beyond the Jordan, and those from around Tyre and Sidon. A great multitude, hearing what great things he did, came to him. ⁹ He spoke to his disciples that a little boat should stay near him because of the crowd, so that they wouldn't press on him. ¹⁰ For he had healed many, so that as many as had diseases pressed on him that they might touch him. ¹¹ The unclean spirits, whenever they saw him, fell down before him, and cried, "You are the Son of God!" ¹² He sternly warned them that they should not make him known.

¹³ He went up into the mountain, and called to himself those whom he wanted, and they went to him. ¹⁴ He appointed twelve, that they might be with him, and that he might send them out to preach, ¹⁵ and to have authority to heal sicknesses and to cast out demons: ¹⁶ Simon (to whom he gave the name Peter); ¹⁷ James the son of Zebedee; and John, the brother of James, (whom he called Boanerges, which means, Sons of Thunder);¹⁸ Andrew; Philip; Bartholomew; Matthew; Thomas; James, the son of Alphaeus; Thaddaeus; Simon the Zealot;¹⁹ and Judas Iscariot, who also betrayed him.

Then he came into a house. ²⁰ The multitude came together again, so that they could not so much as eat bread. ²¹ When his friends heard it, they went out to seize him; for they said, "He is insane." ²² The scribes who came down from Jerusalem said, "He has Beelzebul," and, "By the prince of the demons he casts out the demons."

²³ He summoned them, and said to them in parables, "How can Satan cast out Satan? ²⁴ If a kingdom is divided against itself, that kingdom cannot stand. ²⁵ If a house is divided against itself, that house cannot stand. ²⁶ If Satan has risen up against himself, and is divided, he can't stand, but has an end. ²⁷ But no one can enter into the house of the strong man to plunder unless he first binds the strong man; then he will plunder his house. ²⁸ Most certainly I tell you, all sins of the descendants of man will be forgiven, including their blasphemies with which they may blaspheme; ²⁹ but whoever may blaspheme against the Holy Spirit never has forgiveness, but is subject to eternal condemnation.'" ³⁰ — because they said, "He has an unclean spirit."

³¹ His mother and his brothers came, and standing outside, they sent to him, calling him. ³² A multitude was sitting around him, and they told him, "Behold, your mother, your brothers, and your sisters† are outside looking for you."

³³ He answered them, "Who are my mother and my brothers?" ³⁴ Looking around at those who sat around him, he said, "Behold, my mother and my brothers! ³⁵ For whoever does the will of God is my brother, my sister, and mother."

4

¹ Again he began to teach by the seaside. A great multitude was gathered to him, so that he entered into a boat in the sea, and sat down. All the multitude were on the land by the sea. ² He taught them many things in parables, and told them in his teaching, ³ "Listen! Behold, the farmer went out to sow, ⁴ and as he sowed, some seed fell by the road, and the birds' came and devoured it. ⁵ Others fell on the rocky ground, where it had little soil, and immediately it sprang up, because it had no depth of soil. ⁶ When the sun had risen, it was scorched; and because it had no root, it withered away. ⁷ Others fell among the thorns, and the thorns grew up, and choked it, and it yielded no fruit. ⁸ Others fell into the good ground, and yielded fruit, growing up and increasing. Some produced thirty times, some sixty times, and some one hundred times as much." ⁹ He said, "Whoever has ears to hear, let him hear."

¹⁰ When he was alone, those who were around him with the twelve asked him about the parables. ¹¹ He said to them, "To you is given the mystery of God's Kingdom, but to those who are outside, all things are done in parables, ¹² that 'seeing they may see, and not perceive; and hearing they may hear, and not understand; lest perhaps they should turn again, and their sins should be forgiven them.'"

¹³ He said to them, "Don't you understand this parable? How will you understand all of the parables? ¹⁴ The farmer sows the word. ¹⁵ The ones by the road are the ones where the word is sown; and when they have heard, immediately Satan comes, and takes away the word which has been sown in them. ¹⁶ These in the same way are those who are sown on the rocky places, who, when they have heard the word, immediately receive it with joy. ¹⁷ They have no root in themselves, but are short-lived. When oppression or persecution arises because of the word, immediately they stumble. ¹⁸ Others are those who are sown among the thorns. These are those who have heard the word, ¹⁹ and the cares of this age, and the deceitfulness of riches, and the lusts of other things entering in choke the word, and it becomes unfruitful. ²⁰ Those which were sown on the good ground are those who hear the word, and accept it, and bear fruit, some thirty times, some sixty times, and some one hundred times."

²¹ He said to them, "Is the lamp brought to be put under a basket † or under a bed? Isn't it put on a stand? ²² For there is nothing hidden, except that it should be made known; neither was anything made secret, but that it should come to light. ²³ If any man has ears to hear, let him hear."

24 He said to them, "Take heed what you hear. With whatever measure you measure, it will be measured to you, and more will be given to you who hear. 25 For whoever has, to him more will be given, and he who doesn't have, even that which he has will be taken away from him."

26 He said, "God's Kingdom is as if a man should cast seed on the earth, 27 and should sleep and rise night and day, and the seed should spring up and grow, though he doesn't know how. 28 For the earth bears fruit: first the blade, then the ear, then the full grain in the ear. 29 But when the fruit is ripe, immediately he puts in the sickle, because the harvest has come."

30 He said, "How will we liken God's Kingdom? Or with what parable will we illustrate it? 31 It's like a grain of mustard seed, which, when it is sown in the earth, though it is less than all the seeds that are on the earth, 32 yet when it is sown, grows up, and becomes greater than all the herbs, and puts out great branches, so that the birds of the sky can lodge under its shadow."

33 With many such parables he spoke the word to them, as they were able to hear it. 34 Without a parable he didn't speak to them; but privately to his own disciples he explained everything.

35 On that day, when evening had come, he said to them, "Let's go over to the other side." 36 Leaving the multitude, they took him with them, even as he was, in the boat. Other small boats were also with him. 37 A big wind storm arose, and the waves beat into the boat, so much that the boat was already filled. 38 He himself was in the stern, asleep on the cushion, and they woke him up, and told him, "Teacher, don't you care that we are dying?"

39 He awoke, and rebuked the wind, and said to the sea, "Peace! Be still!" The wind ceased, and there was a great calm. 40 He said to them, "Why are you so afraid? How is it that you have no faith?"

41 They were greatly afraid, and said to one another, "Who then is this, that even the wind and the sea obey him?"

5

1 They came to the other side of the sea, into the country of the Gadarenes. 2 When he had come out of the boat, immediately a man with an unclean spirit met him out of the tombs. 3 He lived in the tombs. Nobody could bind him any more, not even with chains, 4 because he had been often bound with fetters and chains, and the chains had been torn apart by him, and the fetters broken in pieces. Nobody had the strength to tame him. 5 Always, night and day, in the tombs and in the mountains, he was crying out, and cutting himself with stones. 6 When he saw Jesus from afar, he ran

and bowed down to him, 7 and crying out with a loud voice, he said, "What have I to do with you, Jesus, you Son of the Most High God? I adjure you by God, don't torment me." 8 For he said to him, "Come out of the man, you unclean spirit!"

9 He asked him, "What is your name?"

He said to him, "My name is Legion, for we are many." 10 He begged him much that he would not send them away out of the country. 11 Now on the mountainside there was a great herd of pigs feeding. 12 All the demons begged him, saying, "Send us into the pigs, that we may enter into them."

13 At once Jesus gave them permission. The unclean spirits came out and entered into the pigs. The herd of about two thousand rushed down the steep bank into the sea, and they were drowned in the sea. 14 Those who fed them fled, and told it in the city and in the country.

The people came to see what it was that had happened. 15 They came to Jesus, and saw him who had been possessed by demons sitting, clothed, and in his right mind, even him who had the legion; and they were afraid. 16 Those who saw it declared to them what happened to him who was possessed by demons, and about the pigs. 17 They began to beg him to depart from their region.

18 As he was entering into the boat, he who had been possessed by demons begged him that he might be with him. 19 He didn't allow him, but said to him, "Go to your house, to your friends, and tell them what great things the Lord has done for you, and how he had mercy on you."

20 He went his way, and began to proclaim in Decapolis how Jesus had done great things for him, and everyone marveled.

21 When Jesus had crossed back over in the boat to the other side, a great multitude was gathered to him; and he was by the sea. 22 Behold, one of the rulers of the synagogue, Jairus by name, came; and seeing him, he fell at his feet, 23 and begged him much, saying, "My little daughter is at the point of death. Please come and lay your hands on her, that she may be made healthy, and live."

24 He went with him, and a great multitude followed him, and they pressed upon him on all sides. 25 A certain woman, who had a discharge of blood for twelve years, 26 and had suffered many things by many physicians, and had spent all that she had, and was no better, but rather grew worse, 27 having heard the things concerning Jesus, came up behind him in the crowd, and touched his clothes. 28 For she said, "If I just touch his clothes, I will be made well." 29 Immediately the flow of her blood was dried up, and she felt in her body that she was healed of her affliction.

30 Immediately Jesus, perceiving in himself that the power had gone out from him, turned around in the crowd, and asked, "Who touched my clothes?"

³¹ His disciples said to him, "You see the multitude pressing against you, and you say, 'Who touched me?' "

³² He looked around to see her who had done this thing. ³³ But the woman, fearing and trembling, knowing what had been done to her, came and fell down before him, and told him all the truth.

³⁴ He said to her, "Daughter, your faith has made you well. Go in peace, and be cured of your disease."

³⁵ While he was still speaking, people came from the synagogue ruler's house saying, "Your daughter is dead. Why bother the Teacher any more?"

³⁶ But Jesus, when he heard the message spoken, immediately said to the ruler of the synagogue, "Don't be afraid, only believe." ³⁷ He allowed no one to follow him, except Peter, James, and John the brother of James.³⁸ He came to the synagogue ruler's house, and he saw an uproar, weeping, and great wailing. ³⁹ When he had entered in, he said to them, "Why do you make an uproar and weep? The child is not dead, but is asleep."

⁴⁰ They ridiculed him. But he, having put them all out, took the father of the child, her mother, and those who were with him, and went in where the child was lying. ⁴¹ Taking the child by the hand, he said to her, "Talitha cumi!" which means, being interpreted, "Girl, I tell you, get up!" ⁴² Immediately the girl rose up and walked, for she was twelve years old. They were amazed with great amazement. ⁴³ He strictly ordered them that no one should know this, and commanded that something should be given to her to eat.

6

¹ He went out from there. He came into his own country, and his disciples followed him. ² When the Sabbath had come, he began to teach in the synagogue, and many hearing him were astonished, saying, "Where did this man get these things?" and, "What is the wisdom that is given to this man, that such mighty works come about by his hands? ³ Isn't this the carpenter, the son of Mary, and brother of James, Joses, Judah, and Simon? Aren't his sisters here with us?" They were offended at him.

⁴ Jesus said to them, "A prophet is not without honor, except in his own country, and among his own relatives, and in his own house." ⁵ He could do no mighty work there, except that he laid his hands on a few sick people, and healed them. ⁶ He marveled because of their unbelief.

He went around the villages teaching. ⁷ He called to himself the twelve, and began to send them out two by two; and he gave them authority over the unclean spirits. ⁸ He commanded them that they should take nothing for their journey, except a staff only: no bread, no wallet, no money

in their purse, ⁹ but to wear sandals, and not put on two tunics. ¹⁰ He said to them, "Wherever you enter into a house, stay there until you depart from there. ¹¹ Whoever will not receive you nor hear you, as you depart from there, shake off the dust that is under your feet for a testimony against them. Assuredly, I tell you, it will be more tolerable for Sodom and Gomorrah in the day of judgment than for that city!"

¹² They went out and preached that people should repent. ¹³ They cast out many demons, and anointed many with oil who were sick, and healed them. ¹⁴ King Herod heard this, for his name had become known, and he said, "John the Baptizer has risen from the dead, and therefore these powers are at work in him." ¹⁵ But others said, "He is Elijah." Others said, "He is a prophet, or like one of the prophets." ¹⁶ But Herod, when he heard this, said, "This is John, whom I beheaded. He has risen from the dead." ¹⁷ For Herod himself had sent out and arrested John, and bound him in prison for the sake of Herodias, his brother Philip's wife, for he had married her. ¹⁸ For John said to Herod, "It is not lawful for you to have your brother's wife." ¹⁹ Herodias set herself against him, and desired to kill him, but she couldn't, ²⁰ for Herod feared John, knowing that he was a righteous and holy man, and kept him safe. When he heard him, he did many things, and he heard him gladly.

²¹ Then a convenient day came, that Herod on his birthday made a supper for his nobles, the high officers, and the chief men of Galilee. ²² When the daughter of Herodias herself came in and danced, she pleased Herod and those sitting with him. The king said to the young lady, "Ask me whatever you want, and I will give it to you." ²³ He swore to her, "Whatever you shall ask of me, I will give you, up to half of my kingdom."

²⁴ She went out, and said to her mother, "What shall I ask?"

She said, "The head of John the Baptizer."

²⁵ She came in immediately with haste to the king, and asked, "I want you to give me right now the head of John the Baptizer on a platter."

²⁶ The king was exceedingly sorry, but for the sake of his oaths, and of his dinner guests, he didn't wish to refuse her. ²⁷ Immediately the king sent out a soldier of his guard, and commanded to bring John's head, and he went and beheaded him in the prison, ²⁸ and brought his head on a platter, and gave it to the young lady; and the young lady gave it to her mother.

²⁹ When his disciples heard this, they came and took up his corpse, and laid it in a tomb.

³⁰ The apostles gathered themselves together to Jesus, and they told him all things, whatever they had done, and whatever they had taught. ³¹ He said to them, "You come

apart into a deserted place, and rest awhile." For there were many coming and going, and they had no leisure so much as to eat. [32] They went away in the boat to a deserted place by themselves. [33] They* saw them going, and many recognized him and ran there on foot from all the cities. They arrived before them and came together to him. [34] Jesus came out, saw a great multitude, and he had compassion on them, because they were like sheep without a shepherd, and he began to teach them many things. [35] When it was late in the day, his disciples came to him, and said, "This place is deserted, and it is late in the day. [36] Send them away, that they may go into the surrounding country and villages, and buy themselves bread, for they have nothing to eat."

[37] But he answered them, "You give them something to eat."

They asked him, "Shall we go and buy two hundred denarii[†] worth of bread, and give them something to eat?"

[38] He said to them, "How many loaves do you have? Go see."

When they knew, they said, "Five, and two fish."

[39] He commanded them that everyone should sit down in groups on the green grass. [40] They sat down in ranks, by hundreds and by fifties. [41] He took the five loaves and the two fish, and looking up to heaven, he blessed and broke the loaves, and he gave to his disciples to set before them, and he divided the two fish among them all. [42] They all ate, and were filled. [43] They took up twelve baskets full of broken pieces and also of the fish. [44] Those who ate the loaves were[‡] five thousand men.

[45] Immediately he made his disciples get into the boat, and to go ahead to the other side, to Bethsaida, while he himself sent the multitude away. [46] After he had taken leave of them, he went up the mountain to pray.

[47] When evening had come, the boat was in the middle of the sea, and he was alone on the land. [48] Seeing them distressed in rowing, for the wind was contrary to them, about the fourth watch of the night he came to them, walking on the sea, and he would have passed by them, [49] but they, when they saw him walking on the sea, supposed that it was a ghost, and cried out; [50] for they all saw him, and were troubled. But he immediately spoke with them, and said to them, "Cheer up! It is I![§] Don't be afraid." [51] He got into the boat with them; and the wind ceased, and they were very amazed among themselves, and marveled; [52] for they hadn't understood about the loaves, but their hearts were hardened.

[53] When they had crossed over, they came to land at Gennesaret, and moored to the shore. [54] When they had come out of the boat, immediately the people recognized him, [55] and ran around that whole region, and began to bring those who were sick, on their mats, to where they heard he was. [56] Wherever he entered, into villages, or into cities, or into the country, they laid the sick in the marketplaces, and begged him that they might just touch the fringe* of his garment; and as many as touched him were made well.

7

[1] Then the Pharisees and some of the scribes gathered together to him, having come from Jerusalem. [2] Now when they saw some of his disciples eating bread with defiled, that is unwashed, hands, they found fault. [3] (For the Pharisees and all the Jews don't eat unless they wash their hands and forearms, holding to the tradition of the elders. [4] They don't eat when they come from the marketplace unless they bathe themselves, and there are many other things, which they have received to hold to: washings of cups, pitchers, bronze vessels, and couches.) [5] The Pharisees and the scribes asked him, "Why don't your disciples walk according to the tradition of the elders, but eat their bread with unwashed hands?"

[6] He answered them, "Well did Isaiah prophesy of you hypocrites, as it is written,
'This people honors me with their lips,
but their heart is far from me.
[7] But they worship me in vain,
teaching as doctrines the commandments of men.'

[8] "For you set aside the commandment of God, and hold tightly to the tradition of men—the washing of pitchers and cups, and you do many other such things." [9] He said to them, "Full well do you reject the commandment of God, that you may keep your tradition. [10] For Moses said, 'Honor your father and your mother;' and, 'He who speaks evil of father or mother, let him be put to death.' [11] But you say, 'If a man tells his father or his mother, "Whatever profit you might have received from me is Corban,* that is to say, given to God",' [12] then you no longer allow him to do anything for his father or his mother, [13] making void the word of God by your tradition, which you have handed down. You do many things like this."

[14] He called all the multitude to himself, and said to them, "Hear me, all of you, and understand. [15] There is nothing from outside of the man, that going into him can defile him; but the things which proceed out of the man are those that defile the man. [16] If anyone has ears to hear, let him hear!"[†]

[17] When he had entered into a house away from the multitude, his disciples asked him about the parable. [18] He said to them, "Are you also without understanding? Don't you perceive that whatever goes into the man from outside can't defile him, [19] because it doesn't go into his heart, but into his stomach, then into the latrine, thus purifying all

foods‡?" 20 He said, "That which proceeds out of the man, that defiles the man. 21 For from within, out of the hearts of men, proceed evil thoughts, adulteries, sexual sins, murders, thefts, 22 covetings, wickedness, deceit, lustful desires, an evil eye, blasphemy, pride, and foolishness. 23 All these evil things come from within, and defile the man."

24 From there he arose, and went away into the borders of Tyre and Sidon. He entered into a house, and didn't want anyone to know it, but he couldn't escape notice. 25 For a woman, whose little daughter had an unclean spirit, having heard of him, came and fell down at his feet. 26 Now the woman was a Greek, a Syrophoenician by race. She begged him that he would cast the demon out of her daughter. 27 But Jesus said to her, "Let the children be filled first, for it is not appropriate to take the children's bread and throw it to the dogs."

28 But she answered him, "Yes, Lord. Yet even the dogs under the table eat the children's crumbs."

29 He said to her, "For this saying, go your way. The demon has gone out of your daughter."

30 She went away to her house, and found the child having been laid on the bed, with the demon gone out.

31 Again he departed from the borders of Tyre and Sidon, and came to the sea of Galilee, through the middle of the region of Decapolis. 32 They brought to him one who was deaf and had an impediment in his speech. They begged him to lay his hand on him. 33 He took him aside from the multitude, privately, and put his fingers into his ears, and he spat, and touched his tongue. 34 Looking up to heaven, he sighed, and said to him, "Ephphatha!" that is, "Be opened!" 35 Immediately his ears were opened, and the impediment of his tongue was released, and he spoke clearly. 36 He commanded them that they should tell no one, but the more he commanded them, so much the more widely they proclaimed it. 37 They were astonished beyond measure, saying, "He has done all things well. He makes even the deaf hear, and the mute speak!"

8

1 In those days, when there was a very great multitude, and they had nothing to eat, Jesus called his disciples to himself, and said to them, 2 "I have compassion on the multitude, because they have stayed with me now three days, and have nothing to eat. 3 If I send them away fasting to their home, they will faint on the way, for some of them have come a long way."

4 His disciples answered him, "From where could one satisfy these people with bread here in a deserted place?"

5 He asked them, "How many loaves do you have?"

They said, "Seven."

6 He commanded the multitude to sit down on the ground, and he took the seven loaves. Having given thanks, he broke them, and gave them to his disciples to serve, and they served the multitude. 7 They had a few small fish. Having blessed them, he said to serve these also. 8 They ate, and were filled. They took up seven baskets of broken pieces that were left over. 9 Those who had eaten were about four thousand. Then he sent them away.

10 Immediately he entered into the boat with his disciples, and came into the region of Dalmanutha. 11 The Pharisees came out and began to question him, seeking from him a sign from heaven, and testing him. 12 He sighed deeply in his spirit, and said, "Why does this generation * seek a sign? Most certainly I tell you, no sign will be given to this generation."

13 He left them, and again entering into the boat, departed to the other side. 14 They forgot to take bread; and they didn't have more than one loaf in the boat with them. 15 He warned them, saying, "Take heed: beware of the yeast of the Pharisees and the yeast of Herod."

16 They reasoned with one another, saying, "It's because we have no bread."

17 Jesus, perceiving it, said to them, "Why do you reason that it's because you have no bread? Don't you perceive yet, neither understand? Is your heart still hardened? 18 Having eyes, don't you see? Having ears, don't you hear? Don't you remember? 19 When I broke the five loaves among the five thousand, how many baskets full of broken pieces did you take up?"

They told him, "Twelve."

20 "When the seven loaves fed the four thousand, how many baskets full of broken pieces did you take up?"

They told him, "Seven."

21 He asked them, "Don't you understand yet?"

22 He came to Bethsaida. They brought a blind man to him, and begged him to touch him. 23 He took hold of the blind man by the hand, and brought him out of the village. When he had spat on his eyes, and laid his hands on him, he asked him if he saw anything.

24 He looked up, and said, "I see men; for I see them like trees walking."

25 Then again he laid his hands on his eyes. He looked intently, and was restored, and saw everyone clearly. 26 He sent him away to his house, saying, "Don't enter into the village, nor tell anyone in the village."

27 Jesus went out, with his disciples, into the villages of Caesarea Philippi. On the way he asked his disciples, "Who do men say that I am?"

28 They told him, "John the Baptizer, and others say Elijah, but others: one of the prophets."

²⁹ He said to them, "But who do you say that I am?" Peter answered, "You are the Christ."

³⁰ He commanded them that they should tell no one about him. ³¹ He began to teach them that the Son of Man must suffer many things, and be rejected by the elders, the chief priests, and the scribes, and be killed, and after three days rise again. ³² He spoke to them openly. Peter took him, and began to rebuke him. ³³ But he, turning around, and seeing his disciples, rebuked Peter, and said, "Get behind me, Satan! For you have in mind not the things of God, but the things of men."

³⁴ He called the multitude to himself with his disciples, and said to them, "Whoever wants to come after me, let him deny himself, and take up his cross, and follow me. ³⁵ For whoever wants to save his life will lose it; and whoever will lose his life for my sake and the sake of the Good News will save it. ³⁶ For what does it profit a man, to gain the whole world, and forfeit his life? ³⁷ For what will a man give in exchange for his life? ³⁸ For whoever will be ashamed of me and of my words in this adulterous and sinful generation, the Son of Man also will be ashamed of him, when he comes in his Father's glory, with the holy angels."

9

¹ He said to them, "Most certainly I tell you, there are some standing here who will in no way taste death until they see God's Kingdom come with power."

² After six days Jesus took with him Peter, James, and John, and brought them up onto a high mountain privately by themselves, and he was changed into another form in front of them. ³ His clothing became glistening, exceedingly white, like snow, such as no launderer on earth can whiten them. ⁴ Elijah and Moses appeared to them, and they were talking with Jesus.

⁵ Peter answered Jesus, "Rabbi, it is good for us to be here. Let's make three tents: one for you, one for Moses, and one for Elijah." ⁶ For he didn't know what to say, for they were very afraid.

⁷ A cloud came, overshadowing them, and a voice came out of the cloud, "This is my beloved Son. Listen to him."

⁸ Suddenly looking around, they saw no one with them any more, except Jesus only.

⁹ As they were coming down from the mountain, he commanded them that they should tell no one what things they had seen, until after the Son of Man had risen from the dead. ¹⁰ They kept this saying to themselves, questioning what the "rising from the dead" meant.

¹¹ They asked him, saying, "Why do the scribes say that Elijah must come first?"

¹² He said to them, "Elijah indeed comes first, and restores all things. How is it written about the Son of Man, that he should suffer many things and be despised? ¹³ But I tell you that Elijah has come, and they have also done to him whatever they wanted to, even as it is written about him."

¹⁴ Coming to the disciples, he saw a great multitude around them, and scribes questioning them. ¹⁵ Immediately all the multitude, when they saw him, were greatly amazed, and running to him, greeted him. ¹⁶ He asked the scribes, "What are you asking them?"

¹⁷ One of the multitude answered, "Teacher, I brought to you my son, who has a mute spirit; ¹⁸ and wherever it seizes him, it throws him down, and he foams at the mouth, and grinds his teeth, and wastes away. I asked your disciples to cast it out, and they weren't able."

¹⁹ He answered him, "Unbelieving generation, how long shall I be with you? How long shall I bear with you? Bring him to me."

²⁰ They brought him to him, and when he saw him, immediately the spirit convulsed him, and he fell on the ground, wallowing and foaming at the mouth.

²¹ He asked his father, "How long has it been since this has come to him?"

He said, "From childhood. ²² Often it has cast him both into the fire and into the water to destroy him. But if you can do anything, have compassion on us, and help us."

²³ Jesus said to him, "If you can believe, all things are possible to him who believes."

²⁴ Immediately the father of the child cried out with tears, "I believe. Help my unbelief!"

²⁵ When Jesus saw that a multitude came running together, he rebuked the unclean spirit, saying to him, "You mute and deaf spirit, I command you, come out of him, and never enter him again!"

²⁶ After crying out and convulsing him greatly, it came out of him. The boy became like one dead, so much that most of them said, "He is dead." ²⁷ But Jesus took him by the hand, and raised him up; and he arose.

²⁸ When he had come into the house, his disciples asked him privately, "Why couldn't we cast it out?" ²⁹ He said to them, "This kind can come out by nothing, except by prayer and fasting."

³⁰ They went out from there, and passed through Galilee. He didn't want anyone to know it. ³¹ For he was teaching his disciples, and said to them, "The Son of Man is being handed over to the hands of men, and they will kill him; and when he is killed, on the third day he will rise again."

³² But they didn't understand the saying, and were afraid to ask him.

33 He came to Capernaum, and when he was in the house he asked them, "What were you arguing among yourselves on the way?"

34 But they were silent, for they had disputed with one another on the way about who was the greatest.

35 He sat down, and called the twelve; and he said to them, "If any man wants to be first, he shall be last of all, and servant of all." 36 He took a little child, and set him in the middle of them. Taking him in his arms, he said to them, 37 "Whoever receives one such little child in my name, receives me, and whoever receives me, doesn't receive me, but him who sent me."

38 John said to him, "Teacher, we saw someone who doesn't follow us casting out demons in your name; and we forbade him, because he doesn't follow us."

39 But Jesus said, "Don't forbid him, for there is no one who will do a mighty work in my name, and be able quickly to speak evil of me. 40 For whoever is not against us is on our side. 41 For whoever will give you a cup of water to drink in my name, because you are Christ's, most certainly I tell you, he will in no way lose his reward. 42 Whoever will cause one of these little ones who believe in me to stumble, it would be better for him if he were thrown into the sea with a millstone hung around his neck. 43 If your hand causes you to stumble, cut it off. It is better for you to enter into life maimed, rather than having your two hands to go into Gehenna,* into the unquenchable fire, 44 'where their worm doesn't die, and the fire is not quenched.' † 45 If your foot causes you to stumble, cut it off. It is better for you to enter into life lame, rather than having your two feet to be cast into Gehenna, ‡ into the fire that will never be quenched— 46 'where their worm doesn't die, and the fire is not quenched.' § 47 If your eye causes you to stumble, cast it out. It is better for you to enter into God's Kingdom with one eye, rather than having two eyes to be cast into the Gehenna* of fire, 48 'where their worm doesn't die, and the fire is not quenched.' 49 For everyone will be salted with fire, and every sacrifice will be seasoned with salt. 50 Salt is good, but if the salt has lost its saltiness, with what will you season it? Have salt in yourselves, and be at peace with one another."

10

1 He arose from there and came into the borders of Judea and beyond the Jordan. Multitudes came together to him again. As he usually did, he was again teaching them. 2 Pharisees came to him testing him, and asked him, "Is it lawful for a man to divorce his wife?"

3 He answered, "What did Moses command you?"

4 They said, "Moses allowed a certificate of divorce to be written, and to divorce her."

5 But Jesus said to them, "For your hardness of heart, he wrote you this commandment. 6 But from the beginning of the creation, God made them male and female. 7 For this cause a man will leave his father and mother, and will join to his wife, 8 and the two will become one flesh, so that they are no longer two, but one flesh. 9 What therefore God has joined together, let no man separate."

10 In the house, his disciples asked him again about the same matter. 11 He said to them, "Whoever divorces his wife, and marries another, commits adultery against her. 12 If a woman herself divorces her husband, and marries another, she commits adultery."

13 They were bringing to him little children, that he should touch them, but the disciples rebuked those who were bringing them. 14 But when Jesus saw it, he was moved with indignation, and said to them, "Allow the little children to come to me! Don't forbid them, for God's Kingdom belongs to such as these. 15 Most certainly I tell you, whoever will not receive God's Kingdom like a little child, he will in no way enter into it." 16 He took them in his arms, and blessed them, laying his hands on them.

17 As he was going out into the way, one ran to him, knelt before him, and asked him, "Good Teacher, what shall I do that I may inherit eternal life?"

18 Jesus said to him, "Why do you call me good? No one is good except one—God. 19 You know the commandments: 'Do not murder,' 'Do not commit adultery,' 'Do not steal,' 'Do not give false testimony,' 'Do not defraud,' 'Honor your father and mother.' "

20 He said to him, "Teacher, I have observed all these things from my youth."

21 Jesus looking at him loved him, and said to him, "One thing you lack. Go, sell whatever you have, and give to the poor, and you will have treasure in heaven; and come, follow me, taking up the cross."

22 But his face fell at that saying, and he went away sorrowful, for he was one who had great possessions. 23 Jesus looked around, and said to his disciples, "How difficult it is for those who have riches to enter into God's Kingdom!"

24 The disciples were amazed at his words. But Jesus answered again, "Children, how hard it is for those who trust in riches to enter into God's Kingdom! 25 It is easier for a camel to go through a needle's eye than for a rich man to enter into God's Kingdom."

26 They were exceedingly astonished, saying to him, "Then who can be saved?"

27 Jesus, looking at them, said, "With men it is impossible, but not with God, for all things are possible with God."

28 Peter began to tell him, "Behold, we have left all, and have followed you."

²⁹ Jesus said, "Most certainly I tell you, there is no one who has left house, or brothers, or sisters, or father, or mother, or wife, or children, or land, for my sake, and for the sake of the Good News, ³⁰ but he will receive one hundred times more now in this time: houses, brothers, sisters, mothers, children, and land, with persecutions; and in the age to come eternal life. ³¹ But many who are first will be last; and the last first."

³² They were on the way, going up to Jerusalem; and Jesus was going in front of them, and they were amazed; and those who followed were afraid. He again took the twelve, and began to tell them the things that were going to happen to him. ³³ "Behold, we are going up to Jerusalem. The Son of Man will be delivered to the chief priests and the scribes. They will condemn him to death, and will deliver him to the Gentiles. ³⁴ They will mock him, spit on him, scourge him, and kill him. On the third day he will rise again."

³⁵ James and John, the sons of Zebedee, came near to him, saying, "Teacher, we want you to do for us whatever we will ask."

³⁶ He said to them, "What do you want me to do for you?"

³⁷ They said to him, "Grant to us that we may sit, one at your right hand, and one at your left hand, in your glory."

³⁸ But Jesus said to them, "You don't know what you are asking. Are you able to drink the cup that I drink, and to be baptized with the baptism that I am baptized with?"

³⁹ They said to him, "We are able."

Jesus said to them, "You shall indeed drink the cup that I drink, and you shall be baptized with the baptism that I am baptized with; ⁴⁰ but to sit at my right hand and at my left hand is not mine to give, but for whom it has been prepared."

⁴¹ When the ten heard it, they began to be indignant towards James and John.

⁴² Jesus summoned them, and said to them, "You know that they who are recognized as rulers over the nations lord it over them, and their great ones exercise authority over them. ⁴³ But it shall not be so among you, but whoever wants to become great among you shall be your servant. ⁴⁴ Whoever of you wants to become first among you, shall be bondservant of all. ⁴⁵ For the Son of Man also came not to be served, but to serve, and to give his life as a ransom for many."

⁴⁶ They came to Jericho. As he went out from Jericho, with his disciples and a great multitude, the son of Timaeus, Bartimaeus, a blind beggar, was sitting by the road. ⁴⁷ When he heard that it was Jesus the Nazarene, he began to cry out, and say, "Jesus, you son of David, have mercy on me!" ⁴⁸ Many rebuked him, that he should be quiet, but he cried out much more, "You son of David, have mercy on me!"

⁴⁹ Jesus stood still, and said, "Call him."

They called the blind man, saying to him, "Cheer up! Get up. He is calling you!"

⁵⁰ He, casting away his cloak, sprang up, and came to Jesus.

⁵¹ Jesus asked him, "What do you want me to do for you?"

The blind man said to him, "Rabboni,* that I may see again."

⁵² Jesus said to him, "Go your way. Your faith has made you well." Immediately he received his sight, and followed Jesus on the way.

11

¹ When they came near to Jerusalem, to Bethsphage* and Bethany, at the Mount of Olives, he sent two of his disciples, ² and said to them, "Go your way into the village that is opposite you. Immediately as you enter into it, you will find a young donkey tied, on which no one has sat. Untie him, and bring him. ³ If anyone asks you, 'Why are you doing this?' say, 'The Lord needs him;' and immediately he will send him back here."

⁴ They went away, and found a young donkey tied at the door outside in the open street, and they untied him. ⁵ Some of those who stood there asked them, "What are you doing, untying the young donkey?" ⁶ They said to them just as Jesus had said, and they let them go.

⁷ They brought the young donkey to Jesus, and threw their garments on it, and Jesus sat on it. ⁸ Many spread their garments on the way, and others were cutting down branches from the trees, and spreading them on the road. ⁹ Those who went in front, and those who followed, cried out, "Hosanna! [†] Blessed is he who comes in the name of the Lord! ¹⁰ Blessed is the kingdom of our father David that is coming in the name of the Lord! Hosanna in the highest!"

¹¹ Jesus entered into the temple in Jerusalem. When he had looked around at everything, it being now evening, he went out to Bethany with the twelve.

¹² The next day, when they had come out from Bethany, he was hungry. ¹³ Seeing a fig tree afar off having leaves, he came to see if perhaps he might find anything on it. When he came to it, he found nothing but leaves, for it was not the season for figs. ¹⁴ Jesus told it, "May no one ever eat fruit from you again!" and his disciples heard it.

¹⁵ They came to Jerusalem, and Jesus entered into the temple, and began to throw out those who sold and those who bought in the temple, and overthrew the money changers' tables, and the seats of those who sold the doves. ¹⁶ He would not allow anyone to carry a container through the temple. ¹⁷ He taught, saying to them, "Isn't it written, 'My

house will be called a house of prayer for all the nations?' But you have made it a den of robbers!"

¹⁸ The chief priests and the scribes heard it, and sought how they might destroy him. For they feared him, because all the multitude was astonished at his teaching.

¹⁹ When evening came, he went out of the city. ²⁰ As they passed by in the morning, they saw the fig tree withered away from the roots. ²¹ Peter, remembering, said to him, "Rabbi, look! The fig tree which you cursed has withered away."

²² Jesus answered them, "Have faith in God. ²³ For most certainly I tell you, whoever may tell this mountain, 'Be taken up and cast into the sea,' and doesn't doubt in his heart, but believes that what he says is happening; he shall have whatever he says. ²⁴ Therefore I tell you, all things whatever you pray and ask for, believe that you have received them, and you shall have them. ²⁵ Whenever you stand praying, forgive, if you have anything against anyone; so that your Father, who is in heaven, may also forgive you your transgressions. ²⁶ But if you do not forgive, neither will your Father in heaven forgive your transgressions."‡

²⁷ They came again to Jerusalem, and as he was walking in the temple, the chief priests, the scribes, and the elders came to him, ²⁸ and they began saying to him, "By what authority do you do these things? Or who gave you this authority to do these things?"

²⁹ Jesus said to them, "I will ask you one question. Answer me, and I will tell you by what authority I do these things. ³⁰ The baptism of John—was it from heaven, or from men? Answer me."

³¹ They reasoned with themselves, saying, "If we should say, 'From heaven;' he will say, 'Why then did you not believe him?' ³² If we should say, 'From men' "—they feared the people, for all held John to really be a prophet. ³³ They answered Jesus, "We don't know."

Jesus said to them, "Neither do I tell you by what authority I do these things."

12

¹ He began to speak to them in parables. "A man planted a vineyard, put a hedge around it, dug a pit for the wine press, built a tower, rented it out to a farmer, and went into another country. ² When it was time, he sent a servant to the farmer to get from the farmer his share of the fruit of the vineyard. ³ They took him, beat him, and sent him away empty. ⁴ Again, he sent another servant to them; and they threw stones at him, wounded him in the head, and sent him away shamefully treated. ⁵ Again he sent another; and they killed him; and many others, beating some, and killing

some. ⁶ Therefore still having one, his beloved son, he sent him last to them, saying, 'They will respect my son.' ⁷ But those farmers said among themselves, 'This is the heir. Come, let's kill him, and the inheritance will be ours.' ⁸ They took him, killed him, and cast him out of the vineyard. ⁹ What therefore will the lord of the vineyard do? He will come and destroy the farmers, and will give the vineyard to others. ¹⁰ Haven't you even read this Scripture:
'The stone which the builders rejected
was made the head of the corner.
¹¹ This was from the Lord.
It is marvelous in our eyes'?"

¹² They tried to seize him, but they feared the multitude; for they perceived that he spoke the parable against them. They left him, and went away. ¹³ They sent some of the Pharisees and the Herodians to him, that they might trap him with words. ¹⁴ When they had come, they asked him, "Teacher, we know that you are honest, and don't defer to anyone; for you aren't partial to anyone, but truly teach the way of God. Is it lawful to pay taxes to Caesar, or not? ¹⁵ Shall we give, or shall we not give?"

But he, knowing their hypocrisy, said to them, "Why do you test me? Bring me a denarius, that I may see it."

¹⁶ They brought it.

He said to them, "Whose is this image and inscription?"

They said to him, "Caesar's."

¹⁷ Jesus answered them, "Render to Caesar the things that are Caesar's, and to God the things that are God's."

They marveled greatly at him.

¹⁸ Some Sadducees, who say that there is no resurrection, came to him. They asked him, saying, ¹⁹ "Teacher, Moses wrote to us, 'If a man's brother dies, and leaves a wife behind him, and leaves no children, that his brother should take his wife, and raise up offspring for his brother.' ²⁰ There were seven brothers. The first took a wife, and dying left no offspring. ²¹ The second took her, and died, leaving no children behind him. The third likewise; ²² and the seven took her and left no children. Last of all the woman also died. ²³ In the resurrection, when they rise, whose wife will she be of them? For the seven had her as a wife."

²⁴ Jesus answered them, "Isn't this because you are mistaken, not knowing the Scriptures, nor the power of God? ²⁵ For when they will rise from the dead, they neither marry, nor are given in marriage, but are like angels in heaven. ²⁶ But about the dead, that they are raised; haven't you read in the book of Moses, about the Bush, how God spoke to him, saying, 'I am the God of Abraham, the God of Isaac, and the God of Jacob'? ²⁷ He is not the God of the dead, but of the living. You are therefore badly mistaken."

28 One of the scribes came, and heard them questioning together. Knowing that he had answered them well, asked him, "Which commandment is the greatest of all?"

29 Jesus answered, "The greatest is, 'Hear, Israel, the Lord our God, the Lord is one: 30 you shall love the Lord your God with all your heart, and with all your soul, and with all your mind, and with all your strength.' This is the first commandment. 31 The second is like this, 'You shall love your neighbor as yourself.' There is no other commandment greater than these."

32 The scribe said to him, "Truly, teacher, you have said well that he is one, and there is none other but he, 33 and to love him with all the heart, and with all the understanding, with all the soul, and with all the strength, and to love his neighbor as himself, is more important than all whole burnt offerings and sacrifices."

34 When Jesus saw that he answered wisely, he said to him, "You are not far from God's Kingdom."

No one dared ask him any question after that. 35 Jesus responded, as he taught in the temple, "How is it that the scribes say that the Christ is the son of David? 36 For David himself said in the Holy Spirit,

'The Lord said to my Lord,
"Sit at my right hand,
until I make your enemies the footstool of your feet." '

37 Therefore David himself calls him Lord, so how can he be his son?"

The common people heard him gladly. 38 In his teaching he said to them, "Beware of the scribes, who like to walk in long robes, and to get greetings in the marketplaces, 39 and the best seats in the synagogues, and the best places at feasts: 40 those who devour widows' houses, and for a pretense make long prayers. These will receive greater condemnation."

41 Jesus sat down opposite the treasury, and saw how the multitude cast money into the treasury. Many who were rich cast in much. 42 A poor widow came, and she cast in two small brass coins, which equal a quadrans coin.† 43 He called his disciples to himself, and said to them, "Most certainly I tell you, this poor widow gave more than all those who are giving into the treasury, 44 for they all gave out of their abundance, but she, out of her poverty, gave all that she had to live on."

13

1 As he went out of the temple, one of his disciples said to him, "Teacher, see what kind of stones and what kind of buildings!"

2 Jesus said to him, "Do you see these great buildings? There will not be left here one stone on another, which will not be thrown down."

3 As he sat on the Mount of Olives opposite the temple, Peter, James, John, and Andrew asked him privately, 4 "Tell us, when will these things be? What is the sign that these things are all about to be fulfilled?"

5 Jesus, answering, began to tell them, "Be careful that no one leads you astray. 6 For many will come in my name, saying, 'I am he!' and will lead many astray.

7 "When you hear of wars and rumors of wars, don't be troubled. For those must happen, but the end is not yet. 8 For nation will rise against nation, and kingdom against kingdom. There will be earthquakes in various places. There will be famines and troubles. These things are the beginning of birth pains. 9 But watch yourselves, for they will deliver you up to councils. You will be beaten in synagogues. You will stand before rulers and kings for my sake, for a testimony to them. 10 The Good News must first be preached to all the nations. 11 When they lead you away and deliver you up, don't be anxious beforehand, or premeditate what you will say, but say whatever will be given you in that hour. For it is not you who speak, but the Holy Spirit.

12 "Brother will deliver up brother to death, and the father his child. Children will rise up against parents, and cause them to be put to death. 13 You will be hated by all men for my name's sake, but he who endures to the end will be saved. 14 But when you see the abomination of desolation, spoken of by Daniel the prophet, standing where it ought not (let the reader understand), then let those who are in Judea flee to the mountains, 15 and let him who is on the housetop not go down, nor enter in, to take anything out of his house. 16 Let him who is in the field not return back to take his cloak. 17 But woe to those who are with child and to those who nurse babies in those days! 18 Pray that your flight won't be in the winter. 19 For in those days there will be oppression, such as there has not been the like from the beginning of the creation which God created until now, and never will be. 20 Unless the Lord had shortened the days, no flesh would have been saved; but for the sake of the chosen ones, whom he picked out, he shortened the days. 21 Then if anyone tells you, 'Look, here is the Christ!' or, 'Look, there!' don't believe it. 22 For there will arise false christs and false prophets, and will show signs and wonders, that they may lead astray, if possible, even the chosen ones. 23 But you watch.

"Behold, I have told you all things beforehand. 24 But in those days, after that oppression, the sun will be darkened, the moon will not give its light, 25 the stars will be falling from the sky, and the powers that are in the heavens will be shaken. 26 Then they will see the Son of Man coming in clouds with great power and glory. 27 Then he will send out his angels, and will gather together his chosen ones from the four winds, from the ends of the earth to the ends of the sky.

[28] "Now from the fig tree, learn this parable. When the branch has now become tender, and produces its leaves, you know that the summer is near; [29] even so you also, when you see these things coming to pass, know that it is near, at the doors. [30] Most certainly I say to you, this generation† will not pass away until all these things happen. [31] Heaven and earth will pass away, but my words will not pass away. [32] But of that day or that hour no one knows, not even the angels in heaven, nor the Son, but only the Father. [33] Watch, keep alert, and pray; for you don't know when the time is.

[34] "It is like a man, traveling to another country, having left his house, and given authority to his servants, and to each one his work, and also commanded the doorkeeper to keep watch. [35] Watch therefore, for you don't know when the lord of the house is coming, whether at evening, or at midnight, or when the rooster crows, or in the morning; [36] lest coming suddenly he might find you sleeping. [37] What I tell you, I tell all: Watch."

14

[1] It was now two days before the feast of the Passover and the unleavened bread, and the chief priests and the scribes sought how they might seize him by deception, and kill him. [2] For they said, "Not during the feast, because there might be a riot among the people."

[3] While he was at Bethany, in the house of Simon the leper, as he sat at the table, a woman came having an alabaster jar of ointment of pure nard—very costly. She broke the jar, and poured it over his head. [4] But there were some who were indignant among themselves, saying, "Why has this ointment been wasted? [5] For this might have been sold for more than three hundred denarii, * and given to the poor." So they grumbled against her.

[6] But Jesus said, "Leave her alone. Why do you trouble her? She has done a good work for me. [7] For you always have the poor with you, and whenever you want to, you can do them good; but you will not always have me. [8] She has done what she could. She has anointed my body beforehand for the burying. [9] Most certainly I tell you, wherever this Good News may be preached throughout the whole world, that which this woman has done will also be spoken of for a memorial of her."

[10] Judas Iscariot, who was one of the twelve, went away to the chief priests, that he might deliver him to them. [11] They, when they heard it, were glad, and promised to give him money. He sought how he might conveniently deliver him. [12] On the first day of unleavened bread, when they sacrificed the Passover, his disciples asked him, "Where do you want us to go and prepare that you may eat the Passover?"

[13] He sent two of his disciples, and said to them, "Go into the city, and there you will meet a man carrying a pitcher of water. Follow him, [14] and wherever he enters in, tell the master of the house, 'The Teacher says, "Where is the guest room, where I may eat the Passover with my disciples?" ' [15] He will himself show you a large upper room furnished and ready. Get ready for us there."

[16] His disciples went out, and came into the city, and found things as he had said to them, and they prepared the Passover.

[17] When it was evening he came with the twelve. [18] As they sat and were eating, Jesus said, "Most certainly I tell you, one of you will betray me—he who eats with me."

[19] They began to be sorrowful, and to ask him one by one, "Surely not I?" And another said, "Surely not I?"

[20] He answered them, "It is one of the twelve, he who dips with me in the dish. [21] For the Son of Man goes, even as it is written about him, but woe to that man by whom the Son of Man is betrayed! It would be better for that man if he had not been born."

[22] As they were eating, Jesus took bread, and when he had blessed, he broke it, and gave to them, and said, "Take, eat. This is my body."

[23] He took the cup, and when he had given thanks, he gave to them. They all drank of it. [24] He said to them, "This is my blood of the new covenant, which is poured out for many. [25] Most certainly I tell you, I will no more drink of the fruit of the vine, until that day when I drink it anew in God's Kingdom." [26] When they had sung a hymn, they went out to the Mount of Olives.

[27] Jesus said to them, "All of you will be made to stumble because of me tonight, for it is written, 'I will strike the shepherd, and the sheep will be scattered.' [28] However, after I am raised up, I will go before you into Galilee."

[29] But Peter said to him, "Although all will be offended, yet I will not."

[30] Jesus said to him, "Most certainly I tell you, that you today, even this night, before the rooster crows twice, you will deny me three times."

[31] But he spoke all the more, "If I must die with you, I will not deny you." They all said the same thing.

[32] They came to a place which was named Gethsemane. He said to his disciples, "Sit here, while I pray." [33] He took with him Peter, James, and John, and began to be greatly troubled and distressed. [34] He said to them, "My soul is exceedingly sorrowful, even to death. Stay here, and watch."

[35] He went forward a little, and fell on the ground, and prayed that, if it were possible, the hour might pass away from him. [36] He said, "Abba,† Father, all things are possible to you. Please remove this cup from me. However, not what I desire, but what you desire."

[37] He came and found them sleeping, and said to Peter, "Simon, are you sleeping? Couldn't you watch one hour? [38] Watch and pray, that you may not enter into temptation. The spirit indeed is willing, but the flesh is weak."

[39] Again he went away, and prayed, saying the same words. [40] Again he returned, and found them sleeping, for their eyes were very heavy, and they didn't know what to answer him. [41] He came the third time, and said to them, "Sleep on now, and take your rest. It is enough. The hour has come. Behold, the Son of Man is betrayed into the hands of sinners. [42] Arise! Let's get going. Behold: he who betrays me is at hand."

[43] Immediately, while he was still speaking, Judas, one of the twelve, came—and with him a multitude with swords and clubs, from the chief priests, the scribes, and the elders. [44] Now he who betrayed him had given them a sign, saying, "Whomever I will kiss, that is he. Seize him, and lead him away safely." [45] When he had come, immediately he came to him, and said, "Rabbi! Rabbi!" and kissed him. [46] They laid their hands on him, and seized him. [47] But a certain one of those who stood by drew his sword, and struck the servant of the high priest, and cut off his ear.

[48] Jesus answered them, "Have you come out, as against a robber, with swords and clubs to seize me? [49] I was daily with you in the temple teaching, and you didn't arrest me. But this is so that the Scriptures might be fulfilled."

[50] They all left him, and fled. [51] A certain young man followed him, having a linen cloth thrown around himself over his naked body. The young men grabbed him, [52] but he left the linen cloth, and fled from them naked. [53] They led Jesus away to the high priest. All the chief priests, the elders, and the scribes came together with him.

[54] Peter had followed him from a distance, until he came into the court of the high priest. He was sitting with the officers, and warming himself in the light of the fire. [55] Now the chief priests and the whole council sought witnesses against Jesus to put him to death, and found none. [56] For many gave false testimony against him, and their testimony didn't agree with each other. [57] Some stood up, and gave false testimony against him, saying, [58] "We heard him say, 'I will destroy this temple that is made with hands, and in three days I will build another made without hands.'" [59] Even so, their testimony didn't agree.

[60] The high priest stood up in the middle, and asked Jesus, "Have you no answer? What is it which these testify against you?" [61] But he stayed quiet, and answered nothing. Again the high priest asked him, "Are you the Christ, the Son of the Blessed?"

[62] Jesus said, "I am. You will see the Son of Man sitting at the right hand of Power, and coming with the clouds of the sky."

[63] The high priest tore his clothes, and said, "What further need have we of witnesses? [64] You have heard the blasphemy! What do you think?" They all condemned him to be worthy of death. [65] Some began to spit on him, and to cover his face, and to beat him with fists, and to tell him, "Prophesy!" The officers struck him with the palms of their hands.

[66] As Peter was in the courtyard below, one of the maids of the high priest came, [67] and seeing Peter warming himself, she looked at him, and said, "You were also with the Nazarene, Jesus!"

[68] But he denied it, saying, "I neither know, nor understand what you are saying." He went out on the porch, and the rooster crowed.

[69] The maid saw him, and began again to tell those who stood by, "This is one of them." [70] But he again denied it. After a little while again those who stood by said to Peter, "You truly are one of them, for you are a Galilean, and your speech shows it." [71] But he began to curse, and to swear, "I don't know this man of whom you speak!" [72] The rooster crowed the second time. Peter remembered the word, how that Jesus said to him, "Before the rooster crows twice, you will deny me three times." When he thought about that, he wept.

15

[1] Immediately in the morning the chief priests, with the elders and scribes, and the whole council, held a consultation, bound Jesus, carried him away, and delivered him up to Pilate. [2] Pilate asked him, "Are you the King of the Jews?"

He answered, "So you say."

[3] The chief priests accused him of many things. [4] Pilate again asked him, "Have you no answer? See how many things they testify against you!"

[5] But Jesus made no further answer, so that Pilate marveled.

[6] Now at the feast he used to release to them one prisoner, whom they asked of him. [7] There was one called Barabbas, bound with his fellow insurgents, men who in the insurrection had committed murder. [8] The multitude, crying aloud, began to ask him to do as he always did for them. [9] Pilate answered them, saying, "Do you want me to release to you the King of the Jews?" [10] For he perceived that for envy the chief priests had delivered him up. [11] But the chief priests stirred up the multitude, that he should release Barabbas to them instead. [12] Pilate again asked them, "What then should I do to him whom you call the King of the Jews?"

[13] They cried out again, "Crucify him!"

[14] Pilate said to them, "Why, what evil has he done?"

But they cried out exceedingly, "Crucify him!"

[15] Pilate, wishing to please the multitude, released Barabbas to them, and handed over Jesus, when he had flogged him, to be crucified. [16] The soldiers led him away within the court, which is the Praetorium; and they called together the whole cohort. [17] They clothed him with purple, and weaving a crown of thorns, they put it on him. [18] They began to salute

him, "Hail, King of the Jews!" [19] They struck his head with a reed, and spat on him, and bowing their knees, did homage to him. [20] When they had mocked him, they took the purple off him, and put his own garments on him. They led him out to crucify him. [21] They compelled one passing by, coming from the country, Simon of Cyrene, the father of Alexander and Rufus, to go with them, that he might bear his cross. [22] They brought him to the place called Golgotha, which is, being interpreted, "The place of a skull." [23] They offered him wine mixed with myrrh to drink, but he didn't take it.

[24] Crucifying him, they parted his garments among them, casting lots on them, what each should take. [25] It was the third hour, [*] and they crucified him. [26] The superscription of his accusation was written over him, "THE KING OF THE JEWS." [27] With him they crucified two robbers; one on his right hand, and one on his left. [28] The Scripture was fulfilled, which says, "He was counted with transgressors." [†]

[29] Those who passed by blasphemed him, wagging their heads, and saying, "Ha! You who destroy the temple, and build it in three days, [30] save yourself, and come down from the cross!"

[31] Likewise, also the chief priests mocking among themselves with the scribes said, "He saved others. He can't save himself. [32] Let the Christ, the King of Israel, now come down from the cross, that we may see and believe him." [‡] Those who were crucified with him also insulted him.

[33] When the sixth hour [§] had come, there was darkness over the whole land until the ninth hour. [*] [34] At the ninth hour Jesus cried with a loud voice, saying, "Eloi, Eloi, lama sabachthani?" which is, being interpreted, "My God, my God, why have you forsaken me?"

[35] Some of those who stood by, when they heard it, said, "Behold, he is calling Elijah."

[36] One ran, and filling a sponge full of vinegar, put it on a reed, and gave it to him to drink, saying, "Let him be. Let's see whether Elijah comes to take him down."

[37] Jesus cried out with a loud voice, and gave up the spirit. [38] The veil of the temple was torn in two from the top to the bottom. [39] When the centurion, who stood by opposite him, saw that he cried out like this and breathed his last, he said, "Truly this man was the Son of God!"

[40] There were also women watching from afar, among whom were both Mary Magdalene, and Mary the mother of James the less and of Joses, and Salome; [41] who, when he was in Galilee, followed him and served him; and many other women who came up with him to Jerusalem.

[42] When evening had now come, because it was the Preparation Day, that is, the day before the Sabbath, [43] Joseph of Arimathaea, a prominent council member who also himself was looking for God's Kingdom, came. He boldly went in to Pilate, and asked for Jesus' body. [44] Pilate marveled if he were already dead; and summoning the centurion, he asked him whether he had been dead long. [45] When he found out from the centurion, he granted the body to Joseph. [46] He bought a linen cloth, and taking him down, wound him in the linen cloth, and laid him in a tomb which had been cut out of a rock. He rolled a stone against the door of the tomb. [47] Mary Magdalene and Mary, the mother of Joses, saw where he was laid.

16

[1] When the Sabbath was past, Mary Magdalene, and Mary the mother of James, and Salome, bought spices, that they might come and anoint him. [2] Very early on the first day of the week, they came to the tomb when the sun had risen. [3] They were saying among themselves, "Who will roll away the stone from the door of the tomb for us?" [4] for it was very big. Looking up, they saw that the stone was rolled back.

[5] Entering into the tomb, they saw a young man sitting on the right side, dressed in a white robe, and they were amazed. [6] He said to them, "Don't be amazed. You seek Jesus, the Nazarene, who has been crucified. He has risen. He is not here. Behold, the place where they laid him! [7] But go, tell his disciples and Peter, 'He goes before you into Galilee. There you will see him, as he said to you.'"

[8] They went out, [*] and fled from the tomb, for trembling and astonishment had come on them. They said nothing to anyone; for they were afraid. [†] [9] [‡] Now when he had risen early on the first day of the week, he appeared first to Mary Magdalene, from whom he had cast out seven demons. [10] She went and told those who had been with him, as they mourned and wept. [11] When they heard that he was alive, and had been seen by her, they disbelieved. [12] After these things he was revealed in another form to two of them, as they walked, on their way into the country. [13] They went away and told it to the rest. They didn't believe them, either.

[14] Afterward he was revealed to the eleven themselves as they sat at the table, and he rebuked them for their unbelief and hardness of heart, because they didn't believe those who had seen him after he had risen. [15] He said to them, "Go into all the world, and preach the Good News to the whole creation. [16] He who believes and is baptized will be saved; but he who disbelieves will be condemned. [17] These signs will accompany those who believe: in my name they will cast out demons; they will speak with new languages; [18] they will take up serpents; and if they drink any deadly thing, it will in no way hurt them; they will lay hands on the sick, and they will recover."

[19] So then the Lord, [§] after he had spoken to them, was received up into heaven, and sat down at the right hand of God. [20] They went out, and preached everywhere, the Lord working with them, and confirming the word by the signs that followed. Amen.

Text Twenty-seven
The Gospel According to Matthew

1

[1] The book of the genealogy of Jesus Christ,* the son of David, the son of Abraham. [2] Abraham became the father of Isaac. Isaac became the father of Jacob. Jacob became the father of Judah and his brothers. [3] Judah became the father of Perez and Zerah by Tamar. Perez became the father of Hezron. Hezron became the father of Ram. [4] Ram became the father of Amminadab. Amminadab became the father of Nahshon. Nahshon became the father of Salmon. [5] Salmon became the father of Boaz by Rahab. Boaz became the father of Obed by Ruth. Obed became the father of Jesse. [6] Jesse became the father of King David. David became the father of Solomon by her who had been Uriah's wife. [7] Solomon became the father of Rehoboam. Rehoboam became the father of Abijah. Abijah became the father of Asa. [8] Asa became the father of Jehoshaphat. Jehoshaphat became the father of Joram. Joram became the father of Uzziah. [9] Uzziah became the father of Jotham. Jotham became the father of Ahaz. Ahaz became the father of Hezekiah. [10] Hezekiah became the father of Manasseh. Manasseh became the father of Amon. Amon became the father of Josiah. [11] Josiah became the father of Jechoniah and his brothers, at the time of the exile to Babylon. [12] After the exile to Babylon, Jechoniah became the father of Shealtiel. Shealtiel became the father of Zerubbabel. [13] Zerubbabel became the father of Abiud. Abiud became the father of Eliakim. Eliakim became the father of Azor. [14] Azor became the father of Zadok. Zadok became the father of Achim. Achim became the father of Eliud. [15] Eliud became the father of Eleazar. Eleazar became the father of Matthan. Matthan became the father of Jacob. [16] Jacob became the father of Joseph, the husband of Mary, from whom was born Jesus,† who is called Christ. [17] So all the generations from Abraham to David are fourteen generations; from David to the exile to Babylon fourteen generations; and from the carrying away to Babylon to the Christ, fourteen generations.

[18] Now the birth of Jesus Christ was like this: After his mother, Mary, was engaged to Joseph, before they came together, she was found pregnant by the Holy Spirit. [19] Joseph, her husband, being a righteous man, and not willing to make her a public example, intended to put her away secretly. [20] But when he thought about these things, behold,‡ an angel of the Lord appeared to him in a dream, saying, "Joseph, son of David, don't be afraid to take to yourself Mary, your wife, for that which is conceived in her is of the Holy Spirit. [21] She shall give birth to a son. You shall call his name Jesus,§ for it is he who shall save his people from their sins."

[22] Now all this has happened, that it might be fulfilled which was spoken by the Lord through the prophet, saying, [23] "Behold, the virgin shall be with child, and shall give birth to a son. They shall call his name Immanuel;" which is, being interpreted, "God with us."

[24] Joseph arose from his sleep, and did as the angel of the Lord commanded him, and took his wife to himself; [25] and didn't know her sexually until she had given birth to her firstborn son. He named him Jesus.

2

[1] Now when Jesus was born in Bethlehem of Judea in the days of King Herod, behold, wise men* from the east came to Jerusalem, saying, [2] "Where is he who is born King of the Jews? For we saw his star in the east, and have come to worship him." [3] When King Herod heard it, he was troubled, and all Jerusalem with him. [4] Gathering together all the chief priests and scribes of the people, he asked them where the Christ would be born. [5] They said to him, "In

Bethlehem of Judea, for this is written through the prophet,
[6] 'You Bethlehem, land of Judah,
are in no way least among the princes of Judah:
for out of you shall come a governor,
who shall shepherd my people, Israel.' "

[7] Then Herod secretly called the wise men, and learned from them exactly what time the star appeared. [8] He sent them to Bethlehem, and said, "Go and search diligently for the young child. When you have found him, bring me word, so that I also may come and worship him."

[9] They, having heard the king, went their way; and behold, the star, which they saw in the east, went before them, until it came and stood over where the young child was. [10] When they saw the star, they rejoiced with exceedingly great joy. [11] They came into the house and saw the young child with Mary, his mother, and they fell down and worshiped him. Opening their treasures, they offered to him gifts: gold, frankincense, and myrrh. [12] Being warned in a dream not to return to Herod, they went back to their own country another way.

[13] Now when they had departed, behold, an angel of the Lord appeared to Joseph in a dream, saying, "Arise and take the young child and his mother, and flee into Egypt, and stay there until I tell you, for Herod will seek the young child to destroy him."

[14] He arose and took the young child and his mother by night, and departed into Egypt, [15] and was there until the death of Herod; that it might be fulfilled which was spoken by the Lord through the prophet, saying, "Out of Egypt I called my son."

[16] Then Herod, when he saw that he was mocked by the wise men, was exceedingly angry, and sent out, and killed all the male children who were in Bethlehem and in all the surrounding countryside, from two years old and under, according to the exact time which he had learned from the wise men. [17] Then that which was spoken by Jeremiah the prophet was fulfilled, saying,
[18] "A voice was heard in Ramah,
lamentation, weeping and great mourning,
Rachel weeping for her children;
she wouldn't be comforted,
because they are no more."

[19] But when Herod was dead, behold, an angel of the Lord appeared in a dream to Joseph in Egypt, saying, [20] "Arise and take the young child and his mother, and go into the land of Israel, for those who sought the young child's life are dead."

[21] He arose and took the young child and his mother, and came into the land of Israel. [22] But when he heard that Archelaus was reigning over Judea in the place of his father, Herod, he was afraid to go there. Being warned in a dream, he withdrew into the region of Galilee, [23] and came and lived in a city called Nazareth; that it might be fulfilled which was spoken through the prophets: "He will be called a Nazarene."

3

[1] In those days, John the Baptizer came, preaching in the wilderness of Judea, saying, [2] "Repent, for the Kingdom of Heaven is at hand!" [3] For this is he who was spoken of by Isaiah the prophet, saying,
"The voice of one crying in the wilderness,
make ready the way of the Lord.
Make his paths straight."

[4] Now John himself wore clothing made of camel's hair, with a leather belt around his waist. His food was locusts and wild honey. [5] Then people from Jerusalem, all of Judea, and all the region around the Jordan went out to him. [6] They were baptized by him in the Jordan, confessing their sins. [7] But when he saw many of the Pharisees and Sadducees coming for his baptism, he said to them, "You offspring of vipers, who warned you to flee from the wrath to come? [8] Therefore produce fruit worthy of repentance! [9] Don't think to yourselves, 'We have Abraham for our father,' for I tell you that God is able to raise up children to Abraham from these stones.

[10] "Even now the ax lies at the root of the trees. Therefore every tree that doesn't produce good fruit is cut down, and cast into the fire. [11] I indeed baptize you in water for repentance, but he who comes after me is mightier than I, whose shoes I am not worthy to carry. He will baptize you in the Holy Spirit.[*] [12] His winnowing fork is in his hand, and he will thoroughly cleanse his threshing floor. He will gather his wheat into the barn, but the chaff he will burn up with unquenchable fire."

[13] Then Jesus came from Galilee to the Jordan[†] to John, to be baptized by him. [14] But John would have hindered him, saying, "I need to be baptized by you, and you come to me?"

[15] But Jesus, answering, said to him, "Allow it now, for this is the fitting way for us to fulfill all righteousness." Then he allowed him. [16] Jesus, when he was baptized, went up directly from the water: and behold, the heavens were opened to him. He saw the Spirit of God descending as a dove, and coming on him. [17] Behold, a voice out of the heavens said, "This is my beloved Son, with whom I am well pleased."

Text Twenty-eight

The Gospel of John

13

¹ Now before the feast of the Passover, Jesus, knowing that his time had come that he would depart from this world to the Father, having loved his own who were in the world, he loved them to the end. ² During supper, the devil having already put into the heart of Judas Iscariot, Simon's son, to betray him, ³ Jesus, knowing that the Father had given all things into his hands, and that he came from God, and was going to God, ⁴ arose from supper, and laid aside his outer garments. He took a towel and wrapped a towel around his waist. ⁵ Then he poured water into the basin, and began to wash the disciples' feet and to wipe them with the towel that was wrapped around him. ⁶ Then he came to Simon Peter. He said to him, "Lord, do you wash my feet?"

⁷ Jesus answered him, "You don't know what I am doing now, but you will understand later."

⁸ Peter said to him, "You will never wash my feet!"

Jesus answered him, "If I don't wash you, you have no part with me."

⁹ Simon Peter said to him, "Lord, not my feet only, but also my hands and my head!"

¹⁰ Jesus said to him, "Someone who has bathed only needs to have his feet washed, but is completely clean. You are clean, but not all of you." ¹¹ For he knew him who would betray him, therefore he said, "You are not all clean." ¹² So when he had washed their feet, put his outer garment back on, and sat down again, he said to them, "Do you know what I have done to you? ¹³ You call me, 'Teacher' and 'Lord.' You say so correctly, for so I am. ¹⁴ If I then, the Lord and the Teacher, have washed your feet, you also ought to wash one another's feet. ¹⁵ For I have given you an example, that you also should do as I have done to you. ¹⁶ Most certainly I tell you, a servant is not greater than his lord, neither one who is sent greater than he who sent him. ¹⁷ If you know these things, blessed are you if you do them. ¹⁸ I don't speak concerning all

of you. I know whom I have chosen. But that the Scripture may be fulfilled, 'He who eats bread with me has lifted up his heel against me.' ¹⁹ From now on, I tell you before it happens, that when it happens, you may believe that I am he. ²⁰ Most certainly I tell you, he who receives whomever I send, receives me; and he who receives me, receives him who sent me."

²¹ When Jesus had said this, he was troubled in spirit, and testified, "Most certainly I tell you that one of you will betray me."

²² The disciples looked at one another, perplexed about whom he spoke. ²³ One of his disciples, whom Jesus loved, was at the table, leaning against Jesus' breast. ²⁴ Simon Peter therefore beckoned to him, and said to him, "Tell us who it is of whom he speaks."

²⁵ He, leaning back, as he was, on Jesus' breast, asked him, "Lord, who is it?"

²⁶ Jesus therefore answered, "It is he to whom I will give this piece of bread when I have dipped it." So when he had dipped the piece of bread, he gave it to Judas, the son of Simon Iscariot. ²⁷ After the piece of bread, then Satan entered into him.

Then Jesus said to him, "What you do, do quickly."

²⁸ Now no man at the table knew why he said this to him. ²⁹ For some thought, because Judas had the money box, that Jesus said to him, "Buy what things we need for the feast," or that he should give something to the poor. ³⁰ Therefore having received that morsel, he went out immediately. It was night.

³¹ When he had gone out, Jesus said, "Now the Son of Man has been glorified, and God has been glorified in him. ³² If God has been glorified in him, God will also glorify him in himself, and he will glorify him immediately. ³³ Little children, I will be with you a little while longer. You will seek me, and as I said to the Jews, 'Where I am going, you can't come,' so now I tell you. ³⁴ A new commandment I give to you, that you love one another. Just as I have loved you, you

also love one another. ³⁵ By this everyone will know that you are my disciples, if you have love for one another."

³⁶ Simon Peter said to him, "Lord, where are you going?"

Jesus answered, "Where I am going, you can't follow now, but you will follow afterwards."

³⁷ Peter said to him, "Lord, why can't I follow you now? I will lay down my life for you."

³⁸ Jesus answered him, "Will you lay down your life for me? Most certainly I tell you, the rooster won't crow until you have denied me three times.

14

¹ "Don't let your heart be troubled. Believe in God. Believe also in me. ² In my Father's house are many homes. If it weren't so, I would have told you. I am going to prepare a place for you. ³ If I go and prepare a place for you, I will come again, and will receive you to myself; that where I am, you may be there also. ⁴ You know where I go, and you know the way."

⁵ Thomas said to him, "Lord, we don't know where you are going. How can we know the way?"

⁶ Jesus said to him, "I am the way, the truth, and the life. No one comes to the Father, except through me.⁷ If you had known me, you would have known my Father also. From now on, you know him, and have seen him."

⁸ Philip said to him, "Lord, show us the Father, and that will be enough for us."

⁹ Jesus said to him, "Have I been with you such a long time, and do you not know me, Philip? He who has seen me has seen the Father. How do you say, 'Show us the Father?' ¹⁰ Don't you believe that I am in the Father, and the Father in me? The words that I tell you, I speak not from myself; but the Father who lives in me does his works. ¹¹ Believe me that I am in the Father, and the Father in me; or else believe me for the very works' sake. ¹² Most certainly I tell you, he who believes in me, the works that I do, he will do also; and he will do greater works than these, because I am going to my Father. ¹³ Whatever you will ask in my name, I will do it, that the Father may be glorified in the Son. ¹⁴ If you will ask anything in my name, I will do it. ¹⁵ If you love me, keep my commandments. ¹⁶ I will pray to the Father, and he will give you another Counselor,˟ that he may be with you forever: ¹⁷ the Spirit of truth, whom the world can't receive; for it doesn't see him and doesn't know him. You know him, for he lives with you, and will be in you. ¹⁸ I will not leave you orphans. I will come to you. ¹⁹ Yet a little while, and the world will see me no more; but you will see me. Because I live, you will live also. ²⁰ In that day you will know that I am in my Father, and you in me, and I in you. ²¹ One who has my commandments and keeps them, that person is one who loves me. One who loves me will be loved by my Father, and I will love him, and will reveal myself to him."

²² Judas (not Iscariot) said to him, "Lord, what has happened that you are about to reveal yourself to us, and not to the world?"

²³ Jesus answered him, "If a man loves me, he will keep my word. My Father will love him, and we will come to him, and make our home with him. ²⁴ He who doesn't love me doesn't keep my words. The word which you hear isn't mine, but the Father's who sent me. ²⁵ I have said these things to you while still living with you. ²⁶ But the Counselor, the Holy Spirit, whom the Father will send in my name, will teach you all things, and will remind you of all that I said to you. ²⁷ Peace I leave with you. My peace I give to you; not as the world gives, I give to you. Don't let your heart be troubled, neither let it be fearful. ²⁸ You heard how I told you, 'I go away, and I come to you.' If you loved me, you would have rejoiced, because I said 'I am going to my Father;' for the Father is greater than I. ²⁹ Now I have told you before it happens so that when it happens, you may believe. ³⁰ I will no more speak much with you, for the prince of the world comes, and he has nothing in me. ³¹ But that the world may know that I love the Father, and as the Father commanded me, even so I do. Arise, let's go from here.

15

¹ "I am the true vine, and my Father is the farmer. ² Every branch in me that doesn't bear fruit, he takes away. Every branch that bears fruit, he prunes, that it may bear more fruit. ³ You are already pruned clean because of the word which I have spoken to you. ⁴ Remain in me, and I in you. As the branch can't bear fruit by itself unless it remains in the vine, so neither can you, unless you remain in me. ⁵ I am the vine. You are the branches. He who remains in me and I in him bears much fruit, for apart from me you can do nothing. ⁶ If a man doesn't remain in me, he is thrown out as a branch and is withered; and they gather them, throw them into the fire, and they are burned. ⁷ If you remain in me, and my words remain in you, you will ask whatever you desire, and it will be done for you.

⁸ "In this my Father is glorified, that you bear much fruit; and so you will be my disciples. ⁹ Even as the Father has loved me, I also have loved you. Remain in my love. ¹⁰ If you keep my commandments, you will remain in my love; even as I have kept my Father's commandments, and remain in his love. ¹¹ I have spoken these things to you, that my joy may remain in you, and that your joy may be made full.

¹² "This is my commandment, that you love one another, even as I have loved you. ¹³ Greater love has no one than this, that someone lay down his life for his friends. ¹⁴ You are my

Text Twenty-eight: **THE GOSPEL OF JOHN**

friends, if you do whatever I command you. ¹⁵ No longer do I call you servants, for the servant doesn't know what his lord does. But I have called you friends, for everything that I heard from my Father, I have made known to you. ¹⁶ You didn't choose me, but I chose you and appointed you, that you should go and bear fruit, and that your fruit should remain; that whatever you will ask of the Father in my name, he may give it to you.

¹⁷ "I command these things to you, that you may love one another. ¹⁸ If the world hates you, you know that it has hated me before it hated you. ¹⁹ If you were of the world, the world would love its own. But because you are not of the world, since I chose you out of the world, therefore the world hates you. ²⁰ Remember the word that I said to you: 'A servant is not greater than his lord.' If they persecuted me, they will also persecute you. If they kept my word, they will also keep yours. ²¹ But they will do all these things to you for my name's sake, because they don't know him who sent me. ²² If I had not come and spoken to them, they would not have had sin; but now they have no excuse for their sin. ²³ He who hates me, hates my Father also. ²⁴ If I hadn't done among them the works which no one else did, they wouldn't have had sin. But now they have seen and also hated both me and my Father. ²⁵ But this happened so that the word may be fulfilled which was written in their law, 'They hated me without a cause.'

²⁶ "When the Counselor* has come, whom I will send to you from the Father, the Spirit of truth, who proceeds from the Father, he will testify about me. ²⁷ You will also testify, because you have been with me from the beginning.

16

¹ "I have said these things to you so that you wouldn't be caused to stumble. ² They will put you out of the synagogues. Yes, the time comes that whoever kills you will think that he offers service to God. ³ They will do these things* because they have not known the Father, nor me. ⁴ But I have told you these things, so that when the time comes, you may remember that I told you about them. I didn't tell you these things from the beginning, because I was with you. ⁵ But now I am going to him who sent me, and none of you asks me, 'Where are you going?' ⁶ But because I have told you these things, sorrow has filled your heart. ⁷ Nevertheless I tell you the truth: It is to your advantage that I go away, for if I don't go away, the Counselor won't come to you. But if I go, I will send him to you. ⁸ When he has come, he will convict the world about sin, about righteousness, and about judgment; ⁹ about sin, because they don't believe in me; ¹⁰ about righteousness, because I am going to my Father, and you won't see me any more; ¹¹ about judgment, because the prince of this world has been judged.

¹² "I still have many things to tell you, but you can't bear them now. ¹³ However when he, the Spirit of truth, has come, he will guide you into all truth, for he will not speak from himself; but whatever he hears, he will speak. He will declare to you things that are coming. ¹⁴ He will glorify me, for he will take from what is mine, and will declare it to you. ¹⁵ All things that the Father has are mine; therefore I said that he takes† of mine and will declare it to you. ¹⁶ A little while, and you will not see me. Again a little while, and you will see me."

¹⁷ Some of his disciples therefore said to one another, "What is this that he says to us, 'A little while, and you won't see me, and again a little while, and you will see me;' and, 'Because I go to the Father'?" ¹⁸ They said therefore, "What is this that he says, 'A little while'? We don't know what he is saying."

¹⁹ Therefore Jesus perceived that they wanted to ask him, and he said to them, "Do you inquire among yourselves concerning this, that I said, 'A little while, and you won't see me, and again a little while, and you will see me?' ²⁰ Most certainly I tell you that you will weep and lament, but the world will rejoice. You will be sorrowful, but your sorrow will be turned into joy. ²¹ A woman, when she gives birth, has sorrow because her time has come. But when she has delivered the child, she doesn't remember the anguish any more, for the joy that a human being is born into the world. ²² Therefore you now have sorrow, but I will see you again, and your heart will rejoice, and no one will take your joy away from you.

²³ "In that day you will ask me no questions. Most certainly I tell you, whatever you may ask of the Father in my name, he will give it to you. ²⁴ Until now, you have asked nothing in my name. Ask, and you will receive, that your joy may be made full. ²⁵ I have spoken these things to you in figures of speech. But the time is coming when I will no more speak to you in figures of speech, but will tell you plainly about the Father. ²⁶ In that day you will ask in my name; and I don't say to you that I will pray to the Father for you, ²⁷ for the Father himself loves you, because you have loved me, and have believed that I came from God. ²⁸ I came from the Father, and have come into the world. Again, I leave the world, and go to the Father."

²⁹ His disciples said to him, "Behold, now you are speaking plainly, and using no figures of speech. ³⁰ Now we know that you know all things, and don't need for anyone to question you. By this we believe that you came from God."

³¹ Jesus answered them, "Do you now believe? ³² Behold, the time is coming, yes, and has now come, that you will be scattered, everyone to his own place, and you will leave me alone. Yet I am not alone, because the Father is with me. ³³ I have told you these things, that in me you may have peace. In the world you have trouble; but cheer up! I have overcome the world."

17

¹ Jesus said these things, then lifting up his eyes to heaven, he said, "Father, the time has come. Glorify your Son, that your Son may also glorify you; ² even as you gave him authority over all flesh, so he will give eternal life to all whom you have given him. ³ This is eternal life, that they should know you, the only true God, and him whom you sent, Jesus Christ. ⁴ I glorified you on the earth. I have accomplished the work which you have given me to do. ⁵ Now, Father, glorify me with your own self with the glory which I had with you before the world existed. ⁶ I revealed your name to the people whom you have given me out of the world. They were yours, and you have given them to me. They have kept your word. ⁷ Now they have known that all things whatever you have given me are from you, ⁸ for the words which you have given me I have given to them, and they received them, and knew for sure that I came from you. They have believed that you sent me. ⁹ I pray for them. I don't pray for the world, but for those whom you have given me, for they are yours. ¹⁰ All things that are mine are yours, and yours are mine, and I am glorified in them. ¹¹ I am no more in the world, but these are in the world, and I am coming to you. Holy Father, keep them through your name which you have given me, that they may be one, even as we are. ¹² While I was with them in the world, I kept them in your name. I have kept those whom you have given me. None of them is lost except the son of destruction, that the Scripture might be fulfilled. ¹³ But now I come to you, and I say these things in the world, that they may have my joy made full in themselves. ¹⁴ I have given them your word. The world hated them, because they are not of the world, even as I am not of the world. ¹⁵ I pray not that you would take them from the world, but that you would keep them from the evil one. ¹⁶ They are not of the world even as I am not of the world. ¹⁷ Sanctify them in your truth. Your word is truth. ¹⁸ As you sent me into the world, even so I have sent them into the world. ¹⁹ For their sakes I sanctify myself, that they themselves also may be sanctified in truth. ²⁰ Not for these only do I pray, but for those also who will believe in me through their word, ²¹ that they may all be one; even as you, Father, are in me, and I in you, that they also may be one in us; that the world may believe that you sent me. ²² The glory which you have given me, I have given to them; that they may be one, even as we are one; ²³ I in them, and you in me, that they may be perfected into one; that the world may know that you sent me and loved them, even as you loved me. ²⁴ Father, I desire that they also whom you have given me be with me where I am, that they may see my glory, which you have given me, for you loved me before the foundation of the world. ²⁵ Righteous Father, the world hasn't known you, but I knew you; and these knew that you

sent me. ²⁶ I made known to them your name, and will make it known; that the love with which you loved me may be in them, and I in them."

18

¹ When Jesus had spoken these words, he went out with his disciples over the brook Kidron, where there was a garden, into which he and his disciples entered. ² Now Judas, who betrayed him, also knew the place, for Jesus often met there with his disciples. ³ Judas then, having taken a detachment of soldiers and officers from the chief priests and the Pharisees, came there with lanterns, torches, and weapons. ⁴ Jesus therefore, knowing all the things that were happening to him, went out, and said to them, "Who are you looking for?"

⁵ They answered him, "Jesus of Nazareth."

Jesus said to them, "I am he."

Judas also, who betrayed him, was standing with them. ⁶ When therefore he said to them, "I am he," they went backward, and fell to the ground.

⁷ Again therefore he asked them, "Who are you looking for?"

They said, "Jesus of Nazareth."

⁸ Jesus answered, "I told you that I am he. If therefore you seek me, let these go their way," ⁹ that the word might be fulfilled which he spoke, "Of those whom you have given me, I have lost none."

¹⁰ Simon Peter therefore, having a sword, drew it, struck the high priest's servant, and cut off his right ear. The servant's name was Malchus. ¹¹ Jesus therefore said to Peter, "Put the sword into its sheath. The cup which the Father has given me, shall I not surely drink it?"

¹² So the detachment, the commanding officer, and the officers of the Jews seized Jesus and bound him, ¹³ and led him to Annas first, for he was father-in-law to Caiaphas, who was high priest that year. ¹⁴ Now it was Caiaphas who advised the Jews that it was expedient that one man should perish for the people. ¹⁵ Simon Peter followed Jesus, as did another disciple. Now that disciple was known to the high priest, and entered in with Jesus into the court of the high priest; ¹⁶ but Peter was standing at the door outside. So the other disciple, who was known to the high priest, went out and spoke to her who kept the door, and brought in Peter. ¹⁷ Then the maid who kept the door said to Peter, "Are you also one of this man's disciples?"

He said, "I am not."

¹⁸ Now the servants and the officers were standing there, having made a fire of coals, for it was cold. They were warming themselves. Peter was with them, standing and warming himself. ¹⁹ The high priest therefore asked Jesus about his disciples and about his teaching. ²⁰ Jesus answered him, "I spoke openly to the world. I always taught in

synagogues, and in the temple, where the Jews always meet. I said nothing in secret. ²¹ Why do you ask me? Ask those who have heard me what I said to them. Behold, these know the things which I said."

²² When he had said this, one of the officers standing by slapped Jesus with his hand, saying, "Do you answer the high priest like that?"

²³ Jesus answered him, "If I have spoken evil, testify of the evil; but if well, why do you beat me?"

²⁴ Annas sent him bound to Caiaphas, the high priest. ²⁵ Now Simon Peter was standing and warming himself. They said therefore to him, "You aren't also one of his disciples, are you?"

He denied it and said, "I am not."

²⁶ One of the servants of the high priest, being a relative of him whose ear Peter had cut off, said, "Didn't I see you in the garden with him?"

²⁷ Peter therefore denied it again, and immediately the rooster crowed.

²⁸ They led Jesus therefore from Caiaphas into the Praetorium. It was early, and they themselves didn't enter into the Praetorium, that they might not be defiled, but might eat the Passover. ²⁹ Pilate therefore went out to them, and said, "What accusation do you bring against this man?"

³⁰ They answered him, "If this man weren't an evildoer, we wouldn't have delivered him up to you."

³¹ Pilate therefore said to them, "Take him yourselves, and judge him according to your law."

Therefore the Jews said to him, "It is illegal for us to put anyone to death," ³² that the word of Jesus might be fulfilled, which he spoke, signifying by what kind of death he should die.

³³ Pilate therefore entered again into the Praetorium, called Jesus, and said to him, "Are you the King of the Jews?"

³⁴ Jesus answered him, "Do you say this by yourself, or did others tell you about me?"

³⁵ Pilate answered, "I'm not a Jew, am I? Your own nation and the chief priests delivered you to me. What have you done?"

³⁶ Jesus answered, "My Kingdom is not of this world. If my Kingdom were of this world, then my servants would fight, that I wouldn't be delivered to the Jews. But now my Kingdom is not from here."

³⁷ Pilate therefore said to him, "Are you a king then?"

Jesus answered, "You say that I am a king. For this reason I have been born, and for this reason I have come into the world, that I should testify to the truth. Everyone who is of the truth listens to my voice."

³⁸ Pilate said to him, "What is truth?"

When he had said this, he went out again to the Jews, and said to them, "I find no basis for a charge against him. ³⁹ But you have a custom, that I should release someone to you at the Passover. Therefore, do you want me to release to you the King of the Jews?"

⁴⁰ Then they all shouted again, saying, "Not this man, but Barabbas!" Now Barabbas was a robber.

19

¹ So Pilate then took Jesus, and flogged him. ² The soldiers twisted thorns into a crown, and put it on his head, and dressed him in a purple garment. ³ They kept saying, "Hail, King of the Jews!" and they kept slapping him.

⁴ Then Pilate went out again, and said to them, "Behold, I bring him out to you, that you may know that I find no basis for a charge against him."

⁵ Jesus therefore came out, wearing the crown of thorns and the purple garment. Pilate said to them, "Behold, the man!"

⁶ When therefore the chief priests and the officers saw him, they shouted, saying, "Crucify! Crucify!"

Pilate said to them, "Take him yourselves, and crucify him, for I find no basis for a charge against him."

⁷ The Jews answered him, "We have a law, and by our law he ought to die, because he made himself the Son of God."

⁸ When therefore Pilate heard this saying, he was more afraid. ⁹ He entered into the Praetorium again, and said to Jesus, "Where are you from?" But Jesus gave him no answer. ¹⁰ Pilate therefore said to him, "Aren't you speaking to me? Don't you know that I have power to release you and have power to crucify you?"

¹¹ Jesus answered, "You would have no power at all against me, unless it were given to you from above. Therefore he who delivered me to you has greater sin."

¹² At this, Pilate was seeking to release him, but the Jews cried out, saying, "If you release this man, you aren't Caesar's friend! Everyone who makes himself a king speaks against Caesar!"

¹³ When Pilate therefore heard these words, he brought Jesus out and sat down on the judgment seat at a place called "The Pavement", but in Hebrew, "Gabbatha." ¹⁴ Now it was the Preparation Day of the Passover, at about the sixth hour.* He said to the Jews, "Behold, your King!"

¹⁵ They cried out, "Away with him! Away with him! Crucify him!"

Pilate said to them, "Shall I crucify your King?"

The chief priests answered, "We have no king but Caesar!"

¹⁶ So then he delivered him to them to be crucified. So they took Jesus and led him away. ¹⁷ He went out, bearing his cross, to the place called "The Place of a Skull", which is called in Hebrew, "Golgotha", ¹⁸ where they crucified him, and with him two others, on either side one, and Jesus in the

middle. ¹⁹ Pilate wrote a title also, and put it on the cross. There was written, "JESUS OF NAZARETH, THE KING OF THE JEWS." ²⁰ Therefore many of the Jews read this title, for the place where Jesus was crucified was near the city; and it was written in Hebrew, in Latin, and in Greek. ²¹ The chief priests of the Jews therefore said to Pilate, "Don't write, 'The King of the Jews,' but, 'he said, "I am King of the Jews.""'"

²² Pilate answered, "What I have written, I have written."

²³ Then the soldiers, when they had crucified Jesus, took his garments and made four parts, to every soldier a part; and also the coat. Now the coat was without seam, woven from the top throughout. ²⁴ Then they said to one another, "Let's not tear it, but cast lots for it to decide whose it will be," that the Scripture might be fulfilled, which says,
"They parted my garments among them.
For my cloak they cast lots."

Therefore the soldiers did these things. ²⁵ But standing by Jesus' cross were his mother, his mother's sister, Mary the wife of Clopas, and Mary Magdalene. ²⁶ Therefore when Jesus saw his mother, and the disciple whom he loved standing there, he said to his mother, "Woman, behold, your son!" ²⁷ Then he said to the disciple, "Behold, your mother!" From that hour, the disciple took her to his own home.

²⁸ After this, Jesus, seeing† that all things were now finished, that the Scripture might be fulfilled, said, "I am thirsty." ²⁹ Now a vessel full of vinegar was set there; so they put a sponge full of the vinegar on hyssop, and held it at his mouth. ³⁰ When Jesus therefore had received the vinegar, he said, "It is finished." He bowed his head, and gave up his spirit.

³¹ Therefore the Jews, because it was the Preparation Day, so that the bodies wouldn't remain on the cross on the Sabbath (for that Sabbath was a special one), asked of Pilate that their legs might be broken, and that they might be taken away. ³² Therefore the soldiers came, and broke the legs of the first, and of the other who was crucified with him; ³³ but when they came to Jesus, and saw that he was already dead, they didn't break his legs. ³⁴ However one of the soldiers pierced his side with a spear, and immediately blood and water came out.³⁵ He who has seen has testified, and his testimony is true. He knows that he tells the truth, that you may believe. ³⁶ For these things happened that the Scripture might be fulfilled, "A bone of him will not be broken." ³⁷ Again another Scripture says, "They will look on him whom they pierced."

³⁸ After these things, Joseph of Arimathaea, being a disciple of Jesus, but secretly for fear of the Jews, asked of Pilate that he might take away Jesus' body. Pilate gave him permission. He came therefore and took away his body. ³⁹ Nicodemus, who at first came to Jesus by night, also came bringing a mixture of myrrh and aloes, about a hundred Roman pounds.‡ ⁴⁰ So they took Jesus' body, and bound it in linen cloths with the spices, as the custom of the Jews is to bury. ⁴¹ Now in the place where he was crucified there was a garden. In the garden was a new tomb in which no man had ever yet been laid. ⁴² Then because of the Jews' Preparation Day (for the tomb was near at hand) they laid Jesus there.

20

¹ Now on the first day of the week, Mary Magdalene went early, while it was still dark, to the tomb, and saw the stone taken away from the tomb. ² Therefore she ran and came to Simon Peter and to the other disciple whom Jesus loved, and said to them, "They have taken away the Lord out of the tomb, and we don't know where they have laid him!"

³ Therefore Peter and the other disciple went out, and they went toward the tomb. ⁴ They both ran together. The other disciple outran Peter, and came to the tomb first. ⁵ Stooping and looking in, he saw the linen cloths lying, yet he didn't enter in. ⁶ Then Simon Peter came, following him, and entered into the tomb. He saw the linen cloths lying, ⁷ and the cloth that had been on his head, not lying with the linen cloths, but rolled up in a place by itself. ⁸ So then the other disciple who came first to the tomb also entered in, and he saw and believed. ⁹ For as yet they didn't know the Scripture, that he must rise from the dead. ¹⁰ So the disciples went away again to their own homes.

¹¹ But Mary was standing outside at the tomb weeping. So as she wept, she stooped and looked into the tomb, ¹² and she saw two angels in white sitting, one at the head, and one at the feet, where the body of Jesus had lain. ¹³ They asked her, "Woman, why are you weeping?"

She said to them, "Because they have taken away my Lord, and I don't know where they have laid him." ¹⁴ When she had said this, she turned around and saw Jesus standing, and didn't know that it was Jesus.

¹⁵ Jesus said to her, "Woman, why are you weeping? Who are you looking for?"

She, supposing him to be the gardener, said to him, "Sir, if you have carried him away, tell me where you have laid him, and I will take him away."

¹⁶ Jesus said to her, "Mary."

She turned and said to him, "Rabboni!" which is to say, "Teacher!"†

¹⁷ Jesus said to her, "Don't hold me, for I haven't yet ascended to my Father; but go to my brothers and tell them, 'I am ascending to my Father and your Father, to my God and your God.'"

¹⁸ Mary Magdalene came and told the disciples that she had seen the Lord, and that he had said these things to her. ¹⁹ When therefore it was evening on that day, the first day of the week, and when the doors were locked where the disciples were assembled, for fear of the Jews, Jesus came and stood in the middle, and said to them, "Peace be to you."

²⁰ When he had said this, he showed them his hands and his side. The disciples therefore were glad when they saw the Lord. ²¹ Jesus therefore said to them again, "Peace be to you. As the Father has sent me, even so I send you." ²² When he had said this, he breathed on them, and said to them, "Receive the Holy Spirit! ²³ If you forgive anyone's sins, they have been forgiven them. If you retain anyone's sins, they have been retained."

²⁴ But Thomas, one of the twelve, called Didymus, wasn't with them when Jesus came. ²⁵ The other disciples therefore said to him, "We have seen the Lord!"

But he said to them, "Unless I see in his hands the print of the nails, put my finger into the print of the nails, and put my hand into his side, I will not believe."

²⁶ After eight days again his disciples were inside and Thomas was with them. Jesus came, the doors being locked, and stood in the middle, and said, "Peace be to you." ²⁷ Then he said to Thomas, "Reach here your finger, and see my hands. Reach here your hand, and put it into my side. Don't be unbelieving, but believing."

²⁸ Thomas answered him, "My Lord and my God!"

²⁹ Jesus said to him, "Because you have seen me,‡ you have believed. Blessed are those who have not seen, and have believed."

³⁰ Therefore Jesus did many other signs in the presence of his disciples, which are not written in this book; ³¹ but these are written, that you may believe that Jesus is the Christ, the Son of God, and that believing you may have life in his name.

21

¹ After these things, Jesus revealed himself again to the disciples at the sea of Tiberias. He revealed himself this way. ² Simon Peter, Thomas called Didymus, Nathanael of Cana in Galilee, and the sons of Zebedee, and two others of his disciples were together. ³ Simon Peter said to them, "I'm going fishing."

They told him, "We are also coming with you." They immediately went out, and entered into the boat. That night, they caught nothing. ⁴ But when day had already come, Jesus stood on the beach, yet the disciples didn't know that it was Jesus. ⁵ Jesus therefore said to them, "Children, have you anything to eat?"

They answered him, "No."

⁶ He said to them, "Cast the net on the right side of the boat, and you will find some."

They cast it therefore, and now they weren't able to draw it in for the multitude of fish. ⁷ That disciple therefore whom Jesus loved said to Peter, "It's the Lord!"

So when Simon Peter heard that it was the Lord, he wrapped his coat around himself (for he was naked), and threw himself into the sea. ⁸ But the other disciples came in the little boat (for they were not far from the land, but about

two hundred cubits* away), dragging the net full of fish. ⁹ So when they got out on the land, they saw a fire of coals there, with fish and bread laid on it. ¹⁰ Jesus said to them, "Bring some of the fish which you have just caught."

¹¹ Simon Peter went up, and drew the net to land, full of one hundred fifty-three great fish. Even though there were so many, the net wasn't torn.

¹² Jesus said to them, "Come and eat breakfast!"

None of the disciples dared inquire of him, "Who are you?" knowing that it was the Lord.

¹³ Then Jesus came and took the bread, gave it to them, and the fish likewise. ¹⁴ This is now the third time that Jesus was revealed to his disciples after he had risen from the dead. ¹⁵ So when they had eaten their breakfast, Jesus said to Simon Peter, "Simon, son of Jonah, do you love me more than these?"

He said to him, "Yes, Lord; you know that I have affection for you."

He said to him, "Feed my lambs." ¹⁶ He said to him again a second time, "Simon, son of Jonah, do you love me?"

He said to him, "Yes, Lord; you know that I have affection for you."

He said to him, "Tend my sheep." ¹⁷ He said to him the third time, "Simon, son of Jonah, do you have affection for me?"

Peter was grieved because he asked him the third time, "Do you have affection for me?" He said to him, "Lord, you know everything. You know that I have affection for you."

Jesus said to him, "Feed my sheep. ¹⁸ Most certainly I tell you, when you were young, you dressed yourself and walked where you wanted to. But when you are old, you will stretch out your hands, and another will dress you and carry you where you don't want to go."

¹⁹ Now he said this, signifying by what kind of death he would glorify God. When he had said this, he said to him, "Follow me."

²⁰ Then Peter, turning around, saw a disciple following. This was the disciple whom Jesus loved, the one who had also leaned on Jesus' breast at the supper and asked, "Lord, who is going to betray you?" ²¹ Peter seeing him, said to Jesus, "Lord, what about this man?"

²² Jesus said to him, "If I desire that he stay until I come, what is that to you? You follow me." ²³ This saying therefore went out among the brothers,† that this disciple wouldn't die. Yet Jesus didn't say to him that he wouldn't die, but, "If I desire that he stay until I come, what is that to you?" ²⁴ This is the disciple who testifies about these things, and wrote these things. We know that his witness is true. ²⁵ There are also many other things which Jesus did, which if they would all be written, I suppose that even the world itself wouldn't have room for the books that would be written.

Text Twenty-nine

Paul's Letter to the Galatians

1

¹ Paul, an apostle—not from men, nor through man, but through Jesus Christ, and God the Father, who raised him from the dead— ² and all the brothers* who are with me, to the assemblies of Galatia: ³ Grace to you and peace from God the Father and our Lord Jesus Christ, ⁴ who gave himself for our sins, that he might deliver us out of this present evil age, according to the will of our God and Father— ⁵ to whom be the glory forever and ever. Amen.

⁶ I marvel that you are so quickly deserting him who called you in the grace of Christ to a different "good news", ⁷ but there isn't another "good news." Only there are some who trouble you and want to pervert the Good News of Christ. ⁸ But even though we, or an angel from heaven, should preach to you any "good news" other than that which we preached to you, let him be cursed. ⁹ As we have said before, so I now say again: if any man preaches to you any "good news" other than that which you received, let him be cursed. ¹⁰ For am I now seeking the favor of men, or of God? Or am I striving to please men? For if I were still pleasing men, I wouldn't be a servant of Christ.

¹¹ But I make known to you, brothers, concerning the Good News which was preached by me, that it is not according to man. ¹² For I didn't receive it from man, nor was I taught it, but it came to me through revelation of Jesus Christ. ¹³ For you have heard of my way of living in time past in the Jews' religion, how that beyond measure I persecuted the assembly of God and ravaged it. ¹⁴ I advanced in the Jews' religion beyond many of my own age among my countrymen, being more exceedingly zealous for the traditions of my fathers. ¹⁵ But when it was the good pleasure of God, who separated me from my mother's womb and called me through his grace ¹⁶ to reveal his Son in me, that I might preach him among the Gentiles, I didn't immediately confer with flesh and blood, ¹⁷ nor did I go up to Jerusalem to those who were apostles before me, but I went away into Arabia. Then I returned to Damascus.

¹⁸ Then after three years I went up to Jerusalem to visit Peter, and stayed with him fifteen days. ¹⁹ But of the other apostles I saw no one except James, the Lord's brother. ²⁰ Now about the things which I write to you, behold,† before God, I'm not lying. ²¹ Then I came to the regions of Syria and Cilicia. ²² I was still unknown by face to the assemblies of Judea which were in Christ, ²³ but they only heard: "He who once persecuted us now preaches the faith that he once tried to destroy." ²⁴ So they glorified God in me.

2

¹ Then after a period of fourteen years I went up again to Jerusalem with Barnabas, taking Titus also with me. ² I went up by revelation, and I laid before them the Good News which I preach among the Gentiles, but privately before those who were respected, for fear that I might be running, or had run, in vain. ³ But not even Titus, who was with me, being a Greek, was compelled to be circumcised. ⁴ This was because of the false brothers secretly brought in, who stole in to spy out our liberty which we have in Christ Jesus, that they might bring us into bondage, ⁵ to whom we gave no place in the way of subjection, not for an hour, that the truth of the Good News might continue with you. ⁶ But from those who were reputed to be important— whatever they were, it makes no difference to me; God doesn't show partiality to man—they, I say, who were respected imparted nothing to me, ⁷ but to the contrary, when they saw that I had been entrusted with the Good News for the uncircumcised, even as Peter with the Good News for the circumcised— ⁸ for he who worked through

Peter in the apostleship with the circumcised also worked through me with the Gentiles— ⁹ and when they perceived the grace that was given to me, James and Cephas and John, those who were reputed to be pillars, gave to Barnabas and me the right hand of fellowship, that we should go to the Gentiles, and they to the circumcision. ¹⁰ They only asked us to remember the poor—which very thing I was also zealous to do.

¹¹ But when Peter came to Antioch, I resisted him to his face, because he stood condemned. ¹² For before some people came from James, he ate with the Gentiles. But when they came, he drew back and separated himself, fearing those who were of the circumcision. ¹³ And the rest of the Jews joined him in his hypocrisy, so that even Barnabas was carried away with their hypocrisy. ¹⁴ But when I saw that they didn't walk uprightly according to the truth of the Good News, I said to Peter before them all, "If you, being a Jew, live as the Gentiles do, and not as the Jews do, why do you compel the Gentiles to live as the Jews do?

¹⁵ "We, being Jews by nature, and not Gentile sinners, ¹⁶ yet knowing that a man is not justified by the works of the law but through faith in Jesus Christ, even we believed in Christ Jesus, that we might be justified by faith in Christ, and not by the works of the law, because no flesh will be justified by the works of the law.¹⁷ But if while we sought to be justified in Christ, we ourselves also were found sinners, is Christ a servant of sin? Certainly not! ¹⁸ For if I build up again those things which I destroyed, I prove myself a law-breaker. ¹⁹ For I, through the law, died to the law, that I might live to God. ²⁰ I have been crucified with Christ, and it is no longer I that live, but Christ lives in me. That life which I now live in the flesh, I live by faith in the Son of God, who loved me, and gave himself up for me. ²¹ I don't reject the grace of God. For if righteousness is through the law, then Christ died for nothing!"

3

¹ Foolish Galatians, who has bewitched you not to obey the truth, before whose eyes Jesus Christ was openly portrayed among you as crucified? ² I just want to learn this from you: Did you receive the Spirit by the works of the law, or by hearing of faith? ³ Are you so foolish? Having begun in the Spirit, are you now completed in the flesh? ⁴ Did you suffer so many things in vain, if it is indeed in vain? ⁵ He therefore who supplies the Spirit to you and does miracles among you, does he do it by the works of the law, or by hearing of faith? ⁶ Even as Abraham "believed God, and it was counted to him for righteousness." ⁷ Know therefore

that those who are of faith are children of Abraham. ⁸ The Scripture, foreseeing that God would justify the Gentiles by faith, preached the Good News beforehand to Abraham, saying, "In you all the nations will be blessed." ⁹ So then, those who are of faith are blessed with the faithful Abraham. ¹⁰ For as many as are of the works of the law are under a curse. For it is written, "Cursed is everyone who doesn't continue in all things that are written in the book of the law, to do them." ¹¹ Now that no man is justified by the law before God is evident, for, "The righteous will live by faith." ¹² The law is not of faith, but, "The man who does them will live by them."

¹³ Christ redeemed us from the curse of the law, having become a curse for us. For it is written, "Cursed is everyone who hangs on a tree," ¹⁴ that the blessing of Abraham might come on the Gentiles through Christ Jesus, that we might receive the promise of the Spirit through faith.

¹⁵ Brothers, speaking of human terms, though it is only a man's covenant, yet when it has been confirmed, no one makes it void or adds to it. ¹⁶ Now the promises were spoken to Abraham and to his offspring. He doesn't say, "To descendants†", as of many, but as of one, "To your offspring", which is Christ. ¹⁷ Now I say this: A covenant confirmed beforehand by God in Christ, the law, which came four hundred thirty years after, does not annul, so as to make the promise of no effect. ¹⁸ For if the inheritance is of the law, it is no more of promise; but God has granted it to Abraham by promise.

¹⁹ Then why is there the law? It was added because of transgressions, until the offspring should come to whom the promise has been made. It was ordained through angels by the hand of a mediator. ²⁰ Now a mediator is not between one, but God is one. ²¹ Is the law then against the promises of God? Certainly not! For if there had been a law given which could make alive, most certainly righteousness would have been of the law. ²² But the Scripture imprisoned all things under sin, that the promise by faith in Jesus Christ might be given to those who believe.

²³ But before faith came, we were kept in custody under the law, confined for the faith which should afterwards be revealed. ²⁴ So that the law has become our tutor to bring us to Christ, that we might be justified by faith. ²⁵ But now that faith has come, we are no longer under a tutor. ²⁶ For you are all children of God, through faith in Christ Jesus. ²⁷ For as many of you as were baptized into Christ have put on Christ. ²⁸ There is neither Jew nor Greek, there is neither slave nor free man, there is neither male nor female; for you are all one in Christ Jesus. ²⁹ If you are Christ's, then you are Abraham's offspring and heirs according to promise.

4

¹ But I say that so long as the heir is a child, he is no different from a bondservant, though he is lord of all,² but is under guardians and stewards until the day appointed by the father. ³ So we also, when we were children, were held in bondage under the elemental principles of the world. ⁴ But when the fullness of the time came, God sent out his Son, born to a woman, born under the law, ⁵ that he might redeem those who were under the law, that we might receive the adoption of children. ⁶ And because you are children, God sent out the Spirit of his Son into your hearts, crying, "Abba,˙ Father!" ⁷ So you are no longer a bondservant, but a son; and if a son, then an heir of God through Christ.

⁸ However at that time, not knowing God, you were in bondage to those who by nature are not gods. ⁹ But now that you have come to know God, or rather to be known by God, why do you turn back again to the weak and miserable elemental principles, to which you desire to be in bondage all over again? ¹⁰ You observe days, months, seasons, and years. ¹¹ I am afraid for you, that I might have wasted my labor for you.

¹² I beg you, brothers, become as I am, for I also have become as you are. You did me no wrong, ¹³ but you know that because of weakness in the flesh I preached the Good News to you the first time. ¹⁴ That which was a temptation to you in my flesh, you didn't despise nor reject; but you received me as an angel of God, even as Christ Jesus.

¹⁵ What was the blessing you enjoyed? For I testify to you that, if possible, you would have plucked out your eyes and given them to me. ¹⁶ So then, have I become your enemy by telling you the truth? ¹⁷ They zealously seek you in no good way. No, they desire to alienate you, that you may seek them. ¹⁸ But it is always good to be zealous in a good cause, and not only when I am present with you.

¹⁹ My little children, of whom I am again in travail until Christ is formed in you— ²⁰ but I could wish to be present with you now, and to change my tone, for I am perplexed about you.

²¹ Tell me, you that desire to be under the law, don't you listen to the law? ²² For it is written that Abraham had two sons, one by the servant, and one by the free woman. ²³ However, the son by the servant was born according to the flesh, but the son by the free woman was born through promise. ²⁴ These things contain an allegory, for these are two covenants. One is from Mount Sinai, bearing children to bondage, which is Hagar.²⁵ For this Hagar is Mount Sinai in Arabia, and answers to the Jerusalem that exists now, for she is in bondage with her children. ²⁶ But the Jerusalem that is above is free, which is the mother of us all. ²⁷ For it is written,
"Rejoice, you barren who don't bear.
Break out and shout, you who don't travail.
For the desolate have more children than her who has a husband."

²⁸ Now we, brothers, as Isaac was, are children of promise. ²⁹ But as then, he who was born according to the flesh persecuted him who was born according to the Spirit, so also it is now. ³⁰ However what does the Scripture say? "Throw out the servant and her son, for the son of the servant will not inherit with the son of the free woman." ³¹ So then, brothers, we are not children of a servant, but of the free woman.

5

¹ Stand firm therefore in the liberty by which Christ has made us free, and don't be entangled again with a yoke of bondage.

² Behold, I, Paul, tell you that if you receive circumcision, Christ will profit you nothing. ³ Yes, I testify again to every man who receives circumcision that he is a debtor to do the whole law. ⁴ You are alienated from Christ, you who desire to be justified by the law. You have fallen away from grace. ⁵ For we, through the Spirit, by faith wait for the hope of righteousness. ⁶ For in Christ Jesus neither circumcision amounts to anything, nor uncircumcision, but faith working through love. ⁷ You were running well! Who interfered with you that you should not obey the truth? ⁸ This persuasion is not from him who calls you. ⁹ A little yeast grows through the whole lump. ¹⁰ I have confidence toward you in the Lord that you will think no other way. But he who troubles you will bear his judgment, whoever he is.

¹¹ But I, brothers, if I still preach circumcision, why am I still persecuted? Then the stumbling block of the cross has been removed. ¹² I wish that those who disturb you would cut themselves off.

¹³ For you, brothers, were called for freedom. Only don't use your freedom for gain to the flesh, but through love be servants to one another. ¹⁴ For the whole law is fulfilled in one word, in this: "You shall love your neighbor as yourself." ¹⁵ But if you bite and devour one another, be careful that you don't consume one another.

¹⁶ But I say, walk by the Spirit, and you won't fulfill the lust of the flesh. ¹⁷ For the flesh lusts against the Spirit, and the Spirit against the flesh; and these are contrary to one another, that you may not do the things that you desire. ¹⁸ But if you are led by the Spirit, you are not under the law. ¹⁹ Now

the deeds of the flesh are obvious, which are: adultery, sexual immorality, uncleanness, lustfulness, [20] idolatry, sorcery, hatred, strife, jealousies, outbursts of anger, rivalries, divisions, heresies, [21] envy, murders, drunkenness, orgies, and things like these; of which I forewarn you, even as I also forewarned you, that those who practice such things will not inherit God's Kingdom.

[22] But the fruit of the Spirit is love, joy, peace, patience, kindness, goodness, faith,* [23] gentleness, and self-control. Against such things there is no law. [24] Those who belong to Christ have crucified the flesh with its passions and lusts.

[25] If we live by the Spirit, let's also walk by the Spirit. [26] Let's not become conceited, provoking one another, and envying one another.

6

[1] Brothers, even if a man is caught in some fault, you who are spiritual must restore such a one in a spirit of gentleness; looking to yourself so that you also aren't tempted. [2] Bear one another's burdens, and so fulfill the law of Christ. [3] For if a man thinks himself to be something when he is nothing, he deceives himself. [4] But let each man examine his own work, and then he will have reason to boast in himself, and not in someone else.[5] For each man will bear his own burden.

[6] But let him who is taught in the word share all good things with him who teaches. [7] Don't be deceived. God is not mocked, for whatever a man sows, that he will also reap. [8] For he who sows to his own flesh will from the flesh reap corruption. But he who sows to the Spirit will from the Spirit reap eternal life. [9] Let's not be weary in doing good, for we will reap in due season, if we don't give up. [10] So then, as we have opportunity, let's do what is good toward all men, and especially toward those who are of the household of the faith.

[11] See with what large letters I write to you with my own hand. [12] As many as desire to make a good impression in the flesh compel you to be circumcised; just so they may not be persecuted for the cross of Christ. [13] For even they who receive circumcision don't keep the law themselves, but they desire to have you circumcised, that they may boast in your flesh. [14] But far be it from me to boast, except in the cross of our Lord Jesus Christ, through which the world has been crucified to me, and I to the world. [15] For in Christ Jesus neither is circumcision anything, nor uncircumcision, but a new creation. [16] As many as walk by this rule, peace and mercy be on them, and on God's Israel.

[17] From now on, let no one cause me any trouble, for I bear the marks of the Lord Jesus branded on my body.

[18] The grace of our Lord Jesus Christ be with your spirit, brothers. Amen.

Text Thirty

Revelation

1

¹ This is the Revelation of Jesus Christ, which God gave him to show to his servants the things which must happen soon, which he sent and made known by his angel* to his servant, John, ² who testified to God's word and of the testimony of Jesus Christ, about everything that he saw.

³ Blessed is he who reads and those who hear the words of the prophecy, and keep the things that are written in it, for the time is at hand.

⁴ John, to the seven assemblies that are in Asia: Grace to you and peace from God, who is and who was and who is to come; and from the seven Spirits who are before his throne; ⁵ and from Jesus Christ, the faithful witness, the firstborn of the dead, and the ruler of the kings of the earth. To him who loves us, and washed us from our sins by his blood— ⁶ and he made us to be a Kingdom, priests to his God and Father—to him be the glory and the dominion forever and ever. Amen.

⁷ Behold,† he is coming with the clouds, and every eye will see him, including those who pierced him. All the tribes of the earth will mourn over him. Even so, Amen.

⁸ "I am the Alpha and the Omega,‡" says the Lord God,§ "who is and who was and who is to come, the Almighty."

⁹ I John, your brother and partner with you in the oppression, Kingdom, and perseverance in Christ Jesus, was on the isle that is called Patmos because of God's Word and the testimony of Jesus Christ. ¹⁰ I was in the Spirit on the Lord's day, and I heard behind me a loud voice, like a trumpet ¹¹ saying, "'What you see, write in a book and send to the seven assemblies:† to Ephesus, Smyrna, Pergamum, Thyatira, Sardis, Philadelphia, and to Laodicea."

¹² I turned to see the voice that spoke with me. Having turned, I saw seven golden lamp stands. ¹³ And among the lamp stands was one like a son of man, clothed with a robe reaching down to his feet, and with a golden sash around his chest. ¹⁴ His head and his hair were white as white wool, like snow. His eyes were like a flame of fire. ¹⁵ His feet were like burnished brass, as if it had been refined in a furnace. His voice was like the voice of many waters. ¹⁶ He had seven stars in his right hand. Out of his mouth proceeded a sharp two-edged sword. His face was like the sun shining at its brightest. ¹⁷ When I saw him, I fell at his feet like a dead man.

He laid his right hand on me, saying, "Don't be afraid. I am the first and the last, ¹⁸ and the Living one. I was dead, and behold, I am alive forever and ever. Amen. I have the keys of Death and of Hades.‡ ¹⁹ Write therefore the things which you have seen, and the things which are, and the things which will happen hereafter. ²⁰ The mystery of the seven stars which you saw in my right hand, and the seven golden lamp stands is this: The seven stars are the angels§ of the seven assemblies. The seven lamp stands are seven assemblies.

Protestantism (16th century): Martin Luther [TEXT 31]

1. What are the three walls? How does Martin Luther attack the three walls?

2. How does Luther use the Bible to prove his points?

3. Why do you think that this text was revolutionary for its time?

Text Thirty-one

Martin Luther: The Reformation

The Romanists have very cleverly surrounded themselves with three walls, which have protected them till now in such a way that no one could reform them. As a result, the whole of Christendom has suffered woeful corruption. In the first place, when under the threat of secular force, they have stood firm and declared that secular force had no jurisdiction over them; rather the opposite was the case, and the spiritual was superior to the secular. In the second place, when the Holy Scriptures have been, used to reprove them, they have responded that no one except the pope was competent to expound Scripture. In the third place, when threatened with a council, they have pretended that no one but the pope could summon a council. In this way, they have adroitly nullified these three means, of correction, and avoided punishment. Thus they still remain in secure possession of these three walls, and practise all the villainy and wickedness we see today. When they have been compelled to hold a council, they have made it nugatory by compelling the princes to swear in advance that the present position shall remain undisturbed. In addition they have given the pope full authority over all the decisions of a council, till it is a matter of indifference whether there be many councils or none, for they only deceive with make-believes and sham-fights. So terribly fearful are they for their skins, if a truly free council were held. Further, the Romanists have overawed kings and princes till the latter believe it would be impious not to obey them in spite of all the deceitful and cunning dodges of theirs.

May God now help us, and give us one of those trumpets with which the walls of Jericho were overthrown; that we may blow away these walls of paper and straw, and set free the Christian, corrective measures to punish sin, and to bring the devil's deceits and wiles to the light of day. In this way, may we be reformed through suffering and again receive God's blessing.

Let us begin by attacking the first wall. To call popes, bishops, priests, monks, and nuns, the religious class, but princes, lords, artisans, and farmworkers the secular class, is a specious device invented by certain timeservers; but no one ought to be frightened by it; and for good reason. For all Christians whatsoever really and truly belong to the religious class, and there is no difference among them except in so far as they do different work That is St. Paul's meaning in I Corinthians 12:12f., when he says: "We are all one body, yet each member hath his own work for serving others." This applies to us all, because we have one baptism, one gospel, one faith, and are all equally Christian. For baptism, gospel, and faith alone make men religious and create a Christian people. When a pope or bishop anoints, grants tonsures, ordains, consecrates, dresses differently from laymen, he may make a hypocrite of a man, or an anointed image, but never a Christian or a spiritually-minded man. The fact is that our baptism consecrates us all without exception, and makes us all priests: As St. Peter says, I Pet 2 [:9], "You are a royal priesthood and a realm of priests," and Revelation, "Thou hast made us priests and kings by Thy blood" [Rev. 5:9 f.]. If we ourselves as Christians did not receive a higher consecration than that given by pope or bishop, then no one would be made priest even by consecration at the hands of pope or bishop; nor would anyone be authorized to celebrate Eucharist, or preach, or pronounce absolution.

"The Three Walls" by Martin Luther from *The Reformation Writings of Martin Luther, Volume 1, The Basis of the Protestant Reformation*, translated and edited by Bertram Lee Woolf, 1953, James Clarke & Co., Lutterworth Press. Reprinted by permission.

When a bishop consecrates, he simply acts on behalf of the entire congregation, all of whom have the same authority. They may select one of their number and command him to exercise this authority on behalf of the others. It would be similar if ten brothers, king's sons and equal heirs, were to choose one of themselves to rule the kingdom for them. All would be kings and of equal authority, although one was appointed to rule. To put it more plainly, suppose a small group of earnest Christian laymen were taken prisoner and settled in the middle of a desert without any episcopally ordained priest among them; and they then agreed to choose one of themselves, whether married or not, and endow him with the office of baptizing, administering the sacrament, pronouncing absolution, and preaching; that would be as truly a priest as if he had been ordained by all the bishops and the popes. It follows that; if needs be, anyone may baptize or pronounce absolution, an impossible Bible situation if we were not all priests. The fact that baptism, and the Christian status which it confers, possess such great grace and authority, is what the Romanists have overridden by their canon law, and kept us in ignorance thereof. But, in former days, Christians used to choose their bishops and priests from their own members, and these were afterwards confirmed by other bishops without any of the pomp of present custom. St. Augustine, Ambrose, and Cyprian each became bishops in this way.

Those who exercise secular authority have been baptized like the rest of us, and have the same faith and the same gospel; therefore we must admit that they are priests and bishops. They discharge their office as an office of the Christian community, and for the benefit of that community. Every one who has been baptized may claim that he has already been consecrated priest or bishop, or pope, even though it is not seemly for any particular person arbitrarily to exercise the office just because we are all priests of equal standing, no one must push himself forward and, without the consent and choice of the rest, presume to do that for which we all have equal authority. Only by the consent and command of the community should any individual person claim for himself what belongs equally to all. If it should happen that anyone abuses an office for which he has been chosen, and is dismissed for that reason, he would resume his former status. It follows that the status of a priest among Christians is merely that of an office-bearer; while he holds the office he exercises it; if he be deposed he resumes his status in the community and becomes like the rest. Certainly a priest is no longer a priest after being unfrocked. Yet the Romanists have devised the claim to *characteres indelebiles*, and assert that a

priest, even if deposed, is different from a mere layman. They even hold the illusion that a priest can never be anything else than a priest, and therefore never a layman again. All these are human inventions and regulations.

Hence we deduce that there is, at bottom, really no other difference between laymen, priests, princes, bishops, or, in Romanist terminology, between religious and secular, than that of office or occupation, and not that of Christian status. All have spiritual status, and all are truly priests, bishops, and popes. But Christians do not all follow the same occupation. Similarly, priests and monks do not all work at the same task. . . .

Therefore those now called "the religious," i.e., priests, bishops, and popes, possess no further or greater dignity than other Christians, except that their duty is to expound the word of God and administer the sacraments--that being their office. In the same way, the secular authorities "hold the sword and the rod," their function being to punish evil-doers and protect the law-abiding. A shoemaker, a smith, a farmer, each has his manual occupation and work; and yet, at the same time, all are eligible to act as priests and bishops. Every one of them in his occupation or handicraft ought to be useful to his fellows, and serve them in such a way that the various trades are all directed to the best advantage of the community, and promote the well-being of body and soul, just as all the organs of the body serve each other. . . .

ii

The second wall is more loosely built and less indefensible. The Romanists profess to be the only interpreters of Scripture, even though they never learn anything contained in it their lives long. They claim authority for themselves alone, juggle with words shamelessly before our eyes, saying that the pope cannot err as to the faith, whether he be bad or good; although they cannot quote a single letter of Scripture to support their claim. Thus it comes about that so many heretical, unchristian, and even unnatural laws are contained in the canon law--matters of which there is no need for discussion at the present juncture. Just because the Romanists profess to believe that the Holy Spirit has not abandoned them, no matter if they are as ignorant and bad as they could be, they presume to assert whatever they please. In such a case, what is the need or the value of Holy Scripture? Let it be burned, and let us be content with the ignorant gentlemen at Rome who "possess the Holy Spirit within," who, however, in fact, dwells in pious souls only.

Text Thirty-one: **MARTIN LUTHER**

Had I not read it, I should have thought it incredible that the devil should have produced such ineptitudes at Rome, and have gained adherents to them. But, lest we fight them with mere words, let us adduce Scripture. St Paul says, I Corinthians 14 [:30], "If something superior be revealed to any one sitting, there and listening to another speaking God's word, the first speaker must be silent and give place." What would be the virtue of this commandment if only the speaker, or the person in the highest position, were to be believed? Christ Himself says, John 6 [:45], "that all Christians shall be taught by God." Then if the pope and his adherents were bad men, and not true Christians, i.e., not taught by God to have: a true understanding; and if, on the other hand, a humble person should have the true understanding, why ever should we not follow him? Has not the pope made many errors? Who could enlighten Christian people if the pope erred, unless someone else, who had the support of Scriptum, were more to be believed than he? . . .

iii

The third wall falls without more ado when the first two are demolished; for, even if the pope acts contrary to Scripture, we ourselves are bound to abide by Scripture. We must punish him and constrain him, according to the passage, "If thy brother sin against thee, go and tell it him between thee and him alone; but if he hear thee not, take with thee one or two more; and if he hear them not, tell it to the church; and if he hear not the church, let him be unto thee as a Gentile" [Matt. 18:15-17]. This passage commands each member to exercise concern for his fellow; much more is it our duty when the wrongdoer is one who rules over us all alike, and who causes much harm and offence to the rest by his conduct. And if I am to lay a charge against him before the church, then I must call it together.

Romanists have no Scriptural basis for their contention that the pope alone has the right to summon or sanction a council. This is their own ruling, and only valid as long as it is not harmful to Christian well-being or contrary to God's laws. If, however, the pope is in the wrong, this ruling becomes invalid, because it is harmful to Christian well-being not to punish him through a council. . . .

It is empty talk when the Romanists boast of possessing an authority such as cannot properly be contested. No one in Christendom has authority to do evil, or to forbid evil front being resisted. The church has no authority except to promote the greater good. Hence, if the pope should exercise

his authority to prevent a free council, and so hinder the reform of the church, we ought to pay no regard to him and his authority. If he should excommunicate and fulminate, that ought to be despised as the proceedings of a foolish man. Trusting in God's protection, we ought to excommunicate him in return, and manage as best we can; for this authority of his would be presumptuous and empty. He does not possess it, and he would fall an easy victim to a passage of Scripture; for Paul says to the Corinthians, "For God gave us authority; not to cast down Christendom, but to build it up" [II Cor. 10:8]. Who would pretend to ignore this text? Only the power of the devil and the Antichrist attempting to arrest whatever serves the reform of Christendom. Wherefore, we must resist that power with life and limb, and might and main.

Even if some supernatural sign should be given, and appear to support the pope against the secular authority; e.g., if a plague were to strike someone down, as they boast has happened sometimes, we ought only to regard it as caused by the devil on account of our lack of faith in God. It is what Christ proclaimed, "False Christs and false prophets will come in my name, and will do signs and wonders, so as to lead astray, if possible, even the elect" [Matt. 24:24]. St. Paul says to the Thessalonians [II Thess. 2:9] that the Antichrist shall, through Satan, be mighty in false, miraculous signs.

Therefore, let us firmly maintain that no Christian authority is valid when exercised contrary to Christ. St. Paul says, "We can do nothing against Christ, but only for Christ" [II Cor. 13:8]. But if an authority does anything against Christ, it is due to the power of the Antichrist and of the devil, even if that authority makes it rain and hail miracles and plagues. Miracles and plagues prove nothing, especially in these latter days of evil, for specious miracles of this kind are foretold everywhere in Scripture. Therefore, we must hold to God's Word with firm faith. The devil will soon abandon his miracles.

And now, I hope that I have laid these false and deceptive terrors, though the Romanists have long used them to make us diffident and of a fearful conscience. It is obvious to all that they like us, are subject to the authority of the state, that they have no warrant to expound Scripture arbitrarily and without special knowledge. They are not empowered to prohibit a council or, according to their pleasure, to determine its decisions in advance, to bind it and to rob it of freedom. But if they do so, I hope I have shown that of a truth they belong to the community of Antichrist and the devil, and have nothing in common with Christ except the name.

Text Thirty-one: **MARTIN LUTHER**

Little Girl Reads the Holy Koran (Qur'an)

© 2012 Orhan Cam. Used under license of Shutterstock, Inc.

Photo Courtesy Agnes Kefeli

Qol Sharif, Kazan, Tatarstan, Russian Federation

Photo Courtesy Agnes Kefeli

Muslim Cemetery, Elyshevo, Tatarstan, Russian Federation

ISLAM

What do these words mean?
- Islam is a word that means "submission to God"
- The followers of Islam are called Muslims. The word Muslim means "one who submits to Allah"
- Allah is the Arabic word for GOD

Judaism, Christianity, Islam
Similar Beliefs — middle east
- ONE GOD
- Patriarch Abraham
- Universal prophetic message
- Angels
- Satan
- Divine Judgment

Differences
- Muslims believe that Jews and Christians have gone astray
- God sent Muhammad to restore the true faith of Abraham

→ Jews did not recognize muhammad

Islam → Jesus ≠ divine

Arabia at the Time of the Prophet
- Urbanized, trading community in the Saudi desert
- Polytheistic
- Allah, high God of the Ka`ba
- Exposed to Jewish, Christian, and Zoroastrian influences

Shahada —
witness of faith

Prophet Muhammad
- 570—Birth in Mecca
- 610—First revelation (Night of Power and Excellence)
- 622—Hijra (flight from Mecca to Medina)
- 630—Capitulation of Mecca [destruction of idols at Ka`ba (Kaaba)]
- 632—Death of Muhammad in Medina

Hadith reports on what the profit did

Revelation of Qur'an
← 7th c. CE
- 610 CE—Muhammad was 40
- Received 1st revelation in a cave at Mount Hira
- Jibreel (Gabriel) appeared and ordered Muhammad to recite
- "The Night of Power and Excellence"
  - Celebrated during Ramadan (Sawm)
  - Muhammad became Messenger of God

Development of Qur'an
- Prophet received divine revelations over 22 years (610-632)
- Ca. 650 CE, after Prophet's death, 3rd caliph (Uthman) established authoritative text
- Uthman's text is the one still used

Composition of Qur'an
- Qur'an = Word of God = recitation
- 114 chapters of 6,000 verses
- Chapters arranged according to length, not to chronology
- Earliest suras (chapters), revealed in Mecca, are shortest
- Earliest suras at end

Themes of Early Message in MECCA
- God is just, all-powerful, majestic, and holy
- God's judgment of humanity at end of the world
- Resurrection of dead to
  – Eternal felicity
  – Eternal punishment

God's Demands
- Worship, praise, gratitude
- Moral behavior
- God condemns female infanticide
- God emphasizes generosity toward others, particularly the poor, the outcast
- God is merciful and compassionate

Meccan versus Medinan Suras
- Consequence of Hijra
- Opposition in Mecca forced Muhammad and followers to retreat to Medina
- In Medina, Muhammad combined the role of
  – Religious prophet
  – Political ruler

Themes in MEDINA
- Revelations become longer
- Revelations include legislation, community affairs
- In early Qur'anic revelations, umma = community of a prophet
- In Medina, umma = community of Muhammad

Views of the Qur'an
- Uncreated (= Eternal) Word of God
- Untranslatable
- Only undistorted revelation

- Restoration, not reformation
  - Adam was the first prophet
  - Every child is Muslim
  - No "original sin"

Judaism versus Islam
- Until 624, Muslims prayed toward Jerusalem
- Muslims and Jews shared same fasts and prayed same number of times (3)
- But Jews denied Muhammad's prophethood
- Muslims started praying toward Mecca
- Ka`ba understood as originally built by Abraham + Ishmael
- Muslims celebrated Ramadan + prayed 5 times

The Rightly Guided Caliphs (632-661)
- 632—Muhammad died
- No clear successor to Muhammad
- Muslim elders created institution of caliphate
- Caliph (Khalifah) = representative of another (Muhammad)
- Caliphate modeled on tribal shaykh or chief
  - First among equals
  - Moral authority

Shiite → minority / blood successor

Suni → majority / no chosen successor

Questions of Succession
- Should caliph be member of Prophet's tribe, the Quraysh?
- Should caliph be chosen from Muhammad's immediate family? [Ali, cousin of Prophet who had married his daughter]

Shiite beleif:

Rightly Guided Caliphs (632-61)
- Abu Bakr — *tried to consolidate rule of Islam in Arabic Pennisula*
- Umar
- Uthman
- Ali

Achievements
- Abu Bakr: conquest of Arabia
- Umar and Uthman: conquests beyond Arabia (parts of Byzantine Empire + Persia)
- Definitive edition of Qur'an under Uthman
- Development of lunar liturgical calendar

Civil War and Schism of Sunni and Shiite Muslims
- Civil war broke out after Uthman's assassination
- Uthman belonged to Umayyad clan of Quraysh tribe
- Umayyad clan of the Quraysh tribe against Ali's party

Ali
- Muhammad's cousin
- He had also married Fatima, Muhammad's daughter
- So his sons Hasan and Husayn were Muhammad's grandsons

Shiites
- Party of the House of Ali — Shi'i
- Sunni = those who follow the Prophet's example
- Shiites emphasized the authority of genetic connection to Prophet

Tragic Event at Karbala (Iraq) = Final Divorce
- 680 CE
- Husayn, Ali's son, i.e. Muhammad's grandson, was killed
- Ashura (the Tenth) commemorates martyrdom of Husayn
- Umayyad dynasty triumphs

Shiite Views of Leadership
- Leader should be descendant of Ali and Husayn
- Leadership vested in Imam (leader)
- Imam is not a prophet
- Imam is
  - Divinely inspired
  - Sinless
  - Infallible
  - Religio-political leader
  - Direct descendant of the Prophet
  - Final authoritative interpreter of God's will

IMAMS
- In Sunni Islam = prayer leader
- In Shiite Islam = descendant of Muhammad

Imams are NOT Ayatollahs

Ayatollahs = scholars of Islam = interpret sacred texts in the name of "Hidden Imam"

Where can Shiites be found?
- Iran
- Iraq
- Syria
- Lebanon
- Saudi Arabia
- Yemen
- Pakistan

Major Accomplishments under Umayyads
- 661-750 CE
- Conquered north Africa + Southern Spain
- Capital city: Damascus

Abbasids
- 750-1258 CE
- Capital city: Baghdad
- Development of Islamic Law
- + Islamic Philosophy
- + Sufism

Islam Spread in Different Ways
- Conquest
- Trade
- Teaching
- Marriage

Shariah (Islamic Law)
- Guide, path
- Sources
  - Qur'an
  - Sunna of Prophet (contained in Hadith)
  - Analogy
  - Consensus
- Four Madhabs (legal schools). The Hanbalite school is most conservative.

SUNNA
- In pre-Islamic times, it referred to customs and usages of elders
- At the death of the Prophet, it referred to the "life-example" of Muhammad's word and deed
- Principal source: Hadith literature (hadith = "recollection," remembrance of act and sayings of Prophet Muhammad)   *example of the prophet*
- Guide of proper conduct for all Muslims

Islamic Intellectual Contributions
- Islamic Philosophy
- Preserved the works of Greek philosophers
  - Transmitted them to Europeans
- Ibn Sina (d. 1037) [Avicenna]

Islamic Mysticism (Sufism)

- Sufi = "rough wool"— garment worn by early Sufis as part of ascetic practice
- Goal of Sufism: Unity with God
- Sufi practices to achieve this goal
  - Zikr = communal recitation of Names of God
  - *TARIQA* = Sufi order

Five Pillars of Islam

- Statement of Faith [shahada]
- Prayer [salat, namaz]
- Alms [zakat]
- Sawm [Fast]— ramadan
- Pilgrimage [hajj]

Alms/zakat — portion of weath (not income) that is donated

EXTRA NOTES

Yathrib - migrated/yasbey Mecca → medina (Old name of medina)

Sharia - Islamic law 1) Qur'an 2) Haddith

Umma - community of the prophet

Hijra - Jamey from Meea → medina (marks begining of muslim calandar)

Sura - chapter of Qur'an

ALIM (plural: ULAMA) - a Scholar of Islam

ISLAM

Islam: Empire of Faith

THE PROPHET MUHAMMAD'S LIFE AND BACKGROUND

1. How many times does the call for prayer sound? What does the muezzin (the caller for prayer) say?

   5 x

2. How many people on earth are Muslim?

   1.6 billion   1/4 people on earth

3. What were some of Islam's contributions to Western civilization?

   - reclaimed wisdom of greeks - medicine, numbers
   - seeds of renaissance

4. Who was the founder of Islam?

   Mahamad

5. Gather as much biographical data as you can about the Prophet from the video. (When was he born? Where? What was his profession? Who was the Prophet's first wife? Why was he called the Trusted One? What happened in a cave near Mecca?)

   born 570 AD , parents died

6. What can you say about pre-Islamic Arab society and religions?

7. What was the spiritual and economic importance of the Kaaba?

   sancuary - provided peace
   facilitated trading

8. What was the Prophet's message? What were the social implications of his message?

   - only one god
   - one people / no more tribal divisions
         poor / unprotected = better
   social justice

9. Was Muhammad a poet? What does the Qur'an say?

"not a poet, poets speak through desire;
not desire / word of god"

10. What is the Qur'an? How was the Qur'an put together? What was it about? How is God represented in the Qur'an?

preserve muhammad's message / ethical & social guidance
power + tenderness   no image of god

11. How is Muhammad represented in Islam? Are the miniatures you saw devotional images?

no - as a historical figure

12. Was Muhammad immediately accepted? If not, who challenged him and why?

No, arabies - afterlife, durre, speaking one god   of "fire" / apocalyptic

he was a threat

13. Why was Muhammad invited to Yathrib? What is the current name of Yathrib and what does this mean?

help settle their disputes in exchange for safe refuge

14. What does the word Hijra mean? When did it occur? And why?

15. What distinguished the Prophet's first community?

16. Did Islam challenge other religions?

They don't

17. How do Muslims pray and what does this form of worship symbolize?

physical gestures → body + mind + soul
together → sense of community

18. When was Mecca conquered? What did Muhammad do when he entered Mecca?

630 AD   - did not carry out bloody revenge
- embraced them

THE EXPANSION OF ISLAM (Abbasid Empire)

1. Baghdad (currently capital of Iraq). In 750, the Abbasid dynasty moved the capital of the empire from Damascus to Baghdad. Describe the city:

2. What were the needs of the new Empire?

3. What were the Islamic original contributions to the world and, in particular, to the West?

MUSLIM FESTIVALS: Eid al-Adha

1. Where does the film take place?

2. What is Eid al-Adha? What does it celebrate?

3. How many times do Muslims pray per day? In what direction do they pray?

4. How does this family celebrate Eid al-Adha?

5. What are the five pillars of Islam?

6. What do they watch on TV?

Let's Learn Arabic in One Day (Matching Game)

SHAHADA •

ZAKAT •

HAJJ •

HIJRA •

SHARIA •

SURA •

SUNNA •

UMMA •

ZIKR •

ULAMA •

MADHAB •

HADITH •

• Community of the Prophet

• Pilgrimage to Mecca

• Scholars of Islam

• Islamic Law

• The Prophet's migration from Mecca to Yathrib (Medina)

• Remembering God's Name in Sufi Rituals

• The Prophet's Deeds and Sayings

• Alms

• Legal School

• The Example of the Prophet

• Chapter of the Qur'an

• Witness of Faith

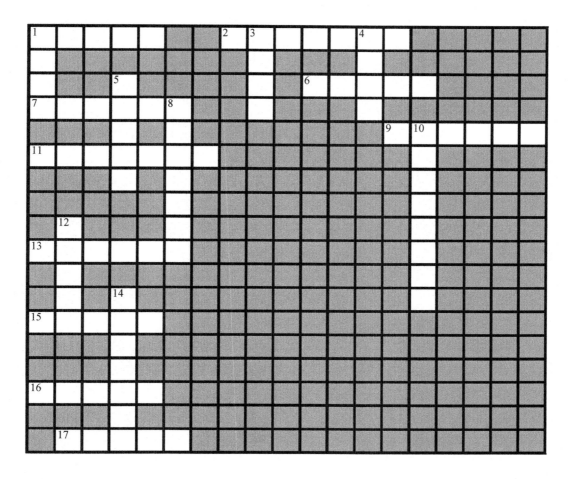

ACROSS

1. Submission to God
2. Muhammad's tribe
6. Prophet's miraculous ascent to Heaven
7. A person who submits to God and follower of Islam
9. Religious and political leaders of the Muslim community after the death of Muhammad
11. Tower used by a chanter who calls people to pray
13. Islam's holy book meaning "recitation." It is understood as the direct Word of God.
15. Ritual prayer, an act of adoration of God
16. The migration of Muhammad and his followers from Mecca to Medina in 622
17. The direction of the prayer toward Mecca

DOWN

1. Prayer leader in Sunni Islam; one of the hereditary successors of Muhammad in Shiite Islam
3. Community of the Prophet
4. Chapter of the Qur'an
5. Arabic word meaning "the God" and used as a proper name for God
8. Person who calls people to prayer
10. First caliph or successor to Muhammad (also called "Rightly Guided")
12. "Well-trodden path" or the way of the ancestors in pre-Islamic Arabia. After Muhammad, it designated Muhammad's behavior and the pattern of life he established. It is one of the sources of Islamic law.
14. The city of Medina before the Emigration

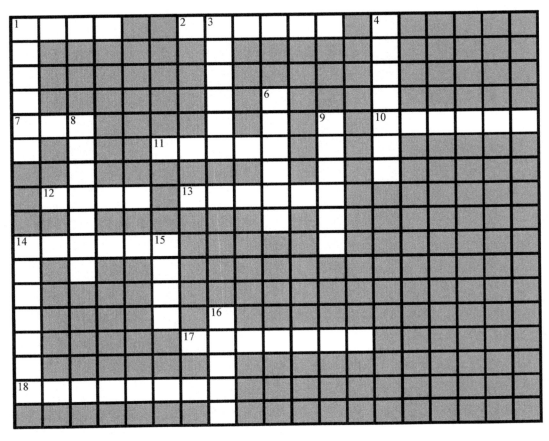

ACROSS

1. Second caliph
2. Muhammad's daughter
7. Fourth caliph, Muhammad's cousin and son-in-law and husband of Muhammad's daughter Fatima
10. Sufi brotherhood
11. Jurists and scholars of Islam
12. Devotional remembrance or repetition of God's names. It is one of the favorite meditation practices of Sufis
13. Sayings and deeds of the Prophet Muhammad
14. Sufi master
17. Fast during the ninth month of the Islamic calendar. The Qur'an was revealed to the Prophet in one of the last ten nights of this month.
18. Central Asian famous philosopher and physician (980-1037) whose books served as textbooks in medieval European universities until the 17th century

DOWN

1. Third caliph
3. Annual Shiite festival to commemorate the martyrdom of Husayn
4. Partisans of Ali. They separated from the Sunnis over the status of Ali as the immediate successor to Muhammad.
6. Islamic law as a whole (lit. the way to the water hole)
8. Independent interpretation or personal reasoning applied to the development of legal opinions
9. School of jurisprudence
14. Islamic profession of faith: "There is no God, but God (ALLAH), and Muhammad is the messenger." It is one of the five pillars of Islam.
15. Pilgrimage to Mecca—one of the five pillars of Islam
16. Almsgiving equivalent to 2.5 percent of people's wealth (it is one of the five pillars of Islam)

Questions on the Qur'an translated (interpreted) by Abdullah Yusuf Ali

1. After reading all the Surahs cited in this workbook, which characters did you recognize from the Hebrew and Christian Bibles? Have you noticed any similarities or differences between the Biblical and Qur'anic narratives? What accounts for these differences and similarities? [See TEXTS 20-22, 26-28, and 33-36]

2. In the Cow (Surah 2: 2:30-37), how does the story of Adam and his wife differ from the Genesis account? [See TEXTS 33 and 20]

3. Name God's qualities in the Qur'an (Surahs 1 and 2). Are they different from God's qualities in the Bible? [See TEXTS 20-23 and 32-33]

4. What are humankind's responsibilities in the Qur'an (Surahs 1 and 2)? Are they different from humanity's responsibilities in the Hebrew Bible? [See TEXTS 20- 23 and 32-33]

5. How different is the Qur'anic narrative structure from the Christian Biblical one? What does it tell us about the Qur'an's audience (at the time of the book's revelation or compilation)? [See TEXTS 20-23, 26-28, and 32-36]

6. How does the second Surah (2:62-145) deal with Judaism and Christianity and their theological disputes? [See TEXT 33]

7. As in the Hebrew Bible (see Exodus, 20-22), the Qur'an contains all kinds of regulations. After reading Surah 2:170-286, create a thematic list of these regulations (for example: diet, marriage, divorce, women, debts, witness, etc.) [See TEXTS 22 and 33]

8. What are the believers' religious duties in Surahs 1 and 2? [See TEXTS 32 and 33]

9. How did the Qur'an seek to protect the rights of men and women of 7th-century Arabia in Surah 2:170-286? [See TEXT 33]

10. Are women absent in the Qur'anic story? What role do they play in the development of the Qur'anic story? Can they be models of faith? Think about unnamed Eve in the Qur'anic story of the fall: was she responsible for the fall? What about Mary (whose name is also the title of Surah 19) and the unnamed woman who sought to seduce Joseph in Surah 12? [See TEXTS 33-36]

Text Thirty-two

Surah 1

Al-Fatiha or the Opening

1. In the name of Allah, the Most Beneficent, the Most Merciful.

2. Praise be to Allah, the Cherisher and Sustainer of the worlds;

3. Most Gracious, Most Merciful;

4. Master of the Day of Judgment.

5. Thee do we worship, and Thine aid we seek.

6. Show us the straight way,

7. The way of those on whom Thou hast bestowed Thy Grace, those whose (portion) is not wrath, and who go not astray.

Text Thirty-three

Surah 2

Al-Baqara Or the Heifer

Total Verses: 286 Revealed At: MADINA

In the name of Allah, the Most Beneficent, the Most Merciful.

1. A.L.M.

2. This is the Book; in it is guidance sure, without doubt, to those who fear Allah;

3. Who believe in the Unseen, are steadfast in prayer, and spend out of what We have provided for them;

4.z And who believe in the Revelation sent to thee, and sent before thy time, and (in their hearts) have the assurance of the Hereafter.

5. They are on (true) guidance, from their Lord, and it is these who will prosper.

6. As to those who reject Faith, it is the same to them whether thou warn them or do not warn them; they will not believe.

7. Allah hath set a seal on their hearts and on their hearing, and on their eyes is a veil; great is the penalty they (incur).

8. Of the people there are some who say: "We believe in Allah and the Last Day;" but they do not (really) believe.

9. Fain would they deceive Allah and those who believe, but they only deceive themselves, and realise (it) not!

10. In their hearts is a disease; and Allah has increased their disease: And grievous is the penalty they (incur), because they are false (to themselves).

11. When it is said to them: "Make not mischief on the earth," they say: "Why, we only Want to make peace!"

12. Of a surety, they are the ones who make mischief, but they realise (it) not.

13. When it is said to them: "Believe as the others believe:" They say: "Shall we believe as the fools believe?" Nay, of a surety they are the fools, but they do not know.

14. When they meet those who believe, they say: "We believe;" but when they are alone with their evil ones, they say: "We are really with you: We (were) only jesting."

15. Allah will throw back their mockery on them, and give them rope in their trespasses; so they will wander like blind ones (To and fro).

16. These are they who have bartered Guidance for error: But their traffic is profitless, and they have lost true direction,

17. Their similitude is that of a man who kindled a fire; when it lighted all around him, Allah took away their light and left them in utter darkness. So they could not see.

18. Deaf, dumb, and blind, they will not return (to the path).

19. Or (another similitude) is that of a rain-laden cloud from the sky: In it are zones of darkness, and thunder and lightning: They press their fingers in their ears to keep out the stunning thunder-clap, the while they are in terror of death. But Allah is ever round the rejecters of Faith!

20. The lightning all but snatches away their sight; every time the light (Helps) them, they walk therein, and when the darkness grows on them, they stand still. And if Allah willed, He could take away their faculty of hearing and seeing; for Allah hath power over all things.

21. O ye people! Adore your Guardian-Lord, who created you and those who came before you, that ye may have the chance to learn righteousness;

22. Who has made the earth your couch, and the heavens your canopy; and sent down rain from the heavens; and brought forth therewith Fruits for your sustenance; then set not up rivals unto Allah when ye know (the truth).

23. And if ye are in doubt as to what We have revealed from time to time to Our servant, then produce a Sura like thereunto; and call your witnesses or helpers (If there are any) besides Allah, if your (doubts) are true.

24. But if ye cannot—and of a surety ye cannot— then fear the Fire whose fuel is men and stones,—which is prepared for those who reject Faith.

25. But give glad tidings to those who believe and work righteousness, that their portion is Gardens, beneath which rivers flow. Every time they are fed with fruits therefrom, they say: "Why, this is what we were fed with before," for they are given things in similitude; and they have therein companions pure (and holy); and they abide therein (for ever).

26. Allah disdains not to use the similitude of things, lowest as well as highest. Those who believe know that it is truth from their Lord; but those who reject Faith say: "What means Allah by this similitude?" By it He causes many to stray, and many He leads into the right path; but He causes not to stray, except those who forsake (the path),—

27. Those who break Allah's Covenant after it is ratified, and who sunder what Allah has ordered to be joined, and do mischief on earth: These cause loss (only) to themselves.

28. How can ye reject the faith in Allah?—seeing that ye were without life, and He gave you life; then will He cause you to die, and will again bring you to life; and again to Him will ye return.

29. It is He Who hath created for you all things that are on earth; Moreover His design comprehended the heavens, for He gave order and perfection to the seven firmaments; and of all things He hath perfect knowledge.

30. Behold, thy Lord said to the angels: "I will create a vicegerent on earth." They said: "Wilt Thou place therein one who will make mischief therein and shed blood?— whilst we do celebrate Thy praises and glorify Thy holy (name)?" He said: "I know what ye know not."

31. And He taught Adam the names of all things; then He placed them before the angels, and said: "Tell me the names of these if ye are right."

32. They said: "Glory to Thee, of knowledge We have none, save what Thou Hast taught us: In truth it is Thou Who art perfect in knowledge and wisdom."

33. He said: "O Adam! Tell them their names." When he had told them, Allah said: "Did I not tell you that I know the secrets of heaven and earth, and I know what ye reveal and what ye conceal?"

34. And behold, We said to the angels: "Bow down to Adam" and they bowed down. Not so Iblis: he refused and was haughty: He was of those who reject Faith.

35. We said: "O Adam! dwell thou and thy wife in the Garden; and eat of the bountiful things therein as (where and when) ye will; but approach not this tree, or ye run into harm and transgression."

36. Then did Satan make them slip from the (garden), and get them out of the state (of felicity) in which they had been. We said: "Get ye down, all (ye people), with enmity between yourselves. On earth will be your dwelling-place and your means of livelihood—for a time."

37. Then learnt Adam from his Lord words of inspiration, and his Lord Turned towards him; for He is Oft-Returning, Most Merciful.

38. We said: "Get ye down all from here; and if, as is sure, there comes to you Guidance from me," whosoever follows My guidance, on them shall be no fear, nor shall they grieve.

39. "But those who reject Faith and belie Our Signs, they shall be companions of the Fire; they shall abide therein."

40. O Children of Israel! call to mind the (special) favour which I bestowed upon you, and fulfil your covenant with Me as I fulfil My Covenant with you, and fear none but Me.

41. And believe in what I reveal, confirming the revelation which is with you, and be not the first to reject Faith therein, nor sell My Signs for a small price; and fear Me, and Me alone.

42. And cover not Truth with falsehood, nor conceal the Truth when ye know (what it is).

43. And be steadfast in prayer; practise regular charity; and bow down your heads with those who bow down (in worship).

Text Thirty-three: **SURAH 2**

44. Do ye enjoin right conduct on the people, and forget (To practise it) yourselves, and yet ye study the Scripture? Will ye not understand?

45. Nay, seek (Allah's) help with patient perseverance and prayer: It is indeed hard, except to those who bring a lowly spirit,—

46. Who bear in mind the certainty that they are to meet their Lord, and that they are to return to Him.

47. Children of Israel! call to mind the (special) favour which I bestowed upon you, and that I preferred you to all other (for My Message).

48. Then guard yourselves against a day when one soul shall not avail another nor shall intercession be accepted for her, nor shall compensation be taken from her, nor shall anyone be helped (from outside).

49. And remember, We delivered you from the people of Pharaoh: They set you hard tasks and punishments, slaughtered your sons and let your women-folk live; therein was a tremendous trial from your Lord.

50. And remember We divided the sea for you and saved you and drowned Pharaoh's people within your very sight.

51. And remember We appointed forty nights for Moses, and in his absence ye took the calf (for worship), and ye did grievous wrong.

52. Even then We did forgive you; there was a chance for you to be grateful.

53. And remember We gave Moses the Scripture and the Criterion (Between right and wrong): There was a chance for you to be guided aright.

54. And remember Moses said to his people: "O my people! Ye have indeed wronged yourselves by your worship of the calf: So turn (in repentance) to your Maker, and slay yourselves (the wrong-doers); that will be better for you in the sight of your Maker." Then He turned towards you (in forgiveness): For He is Oft-Returning, Most Merciful.

55. And remember ye said: "O Moses! We shall never believe in thee until we see Allah manifestly," but ye were dazed with thunder and lighting even as ye looked on.

56. Then We raised you up after your death: Ye had the chance to be grateful.

57. And We gave you the shade of clouds and sent down to you Manna and quails, saying: "Eat of the good things We have provided for you:" (But they rebelled); to us they did no harm, but they harmed their own souls.

58. And remember We said: "Enter this town, and eat of the plenty therein as ye wish; but enter the gate with humility, in posture and in words, and We shall forgive you your faults and increase (the portion of) those who do good."

59. But the transgressors changed the word from that which had been given them; so We sent on the transgressors a plague from heaven, for that they infringed (Our command) repeatedly.

60. And remember Moses prayed for water for his people; We said:

"Strike the rock with thy staff." Then gushed forth therefrom twelve springs. Each group knew its own place for water. So eat and drink of the sustenance provided by Allah, and do no evil nor mischief on the (face of the) earth.

61. And remember ye said: "O Moses! we cannot endure one kind of food (always); so beseech thy Lord for us to produce for us of what the earth groweth,—its pot-herbs, and cucumbers, its garlic, lentils, and onions." He said: "Will ye exchange the better for the worse? Go ye down to any town, and ye shall find what ye want!" They were covered with humiliation and misery; they drew on themselves the wrath of Allah. This because they went on rejecting the Signs of Allah and slaying His Messengers without just cause. This because they rebelled and went on transgressing.

62. Those who believe (in the Qur'an), and those who follow the Jewish (scriptures), and the Christians and the Sabians,—any who believe in Allah and the Last Day, and work righteousness, shall have their reward with their Lord; on them shall be no fear, nor shall they grieve.

63. And remember We took your covenant and We raised above you (The towering height) of Mount (Sinai) (Saying): "Hold firmly to what We have given you and bring (ever) to remembrance what is therein: Perchance ye may fear Allah."

64. But ye turned back thereafter: Had it not been for the Grace and Mercy of Allah to you, ye had surely been among the lost.

65. And well ye knew those amongst you who transgressed in the matter of the Sabbath: We said to them: "Be ye apes, despised and rejected."

66. So We made it an example to their own time and to their posterity, and a lesson to those who fear Allah.

67. And remember Moses said to his people: "Allah commands that ye sacrifice a heifer." They said: "Makest thou a laughing-stock of us?" He said: "Allah save me from being an ignorant (fool)!"

68. They said: "Beseech on our behalf Thy Lord to make plain to us what (heifer) it is!" He said; "He says: The heifer should be neither too old nor too young, but of middling age. Now do what ye are commanded!"

69. They said: "Beseech on our behalf Thy Lord to make plain to us Her colour." He said: "He says: A fawn-coloured heifer, pure and rich in tone, the admiration of beholders!"

70. They said: "Beseech on our behalf Thy Lord to make plain to us what she is: To us are all heifers alike: We wish indeed for guidance, if Allah wills."

71. He said: "He says: A heifer not trained to till the soil or water the fields; sound and without blemish." They said: "Now hast thou brought the truth." Then they offered her in sacrifice, but not with good-will.

72. Remember ye slew a man and fell into a dispute among yourselves as to the crime: But Allah was to bring forth what ye did hide.

73. So We said: "Strike the (body) with a piece of the (heifer)." Thus Allah bringeth the dead to life and showeth you His Signs: Perchance ye may understand.

74. Thenceforth were your hearts hardened: They became like a rock and even worse in hardness. For among rocks there are some from which rivers gush forth; others there are which when split asunder send forth water; and others which sink for fear of Allah. And Allah is not unmindful of what ye do.

75. Can ye (O ye men of Faith) entertain the hope that they will believe in you?—Seeing that a party of them heard the Word of Allah, and perverted it knowingly after they understood it.

76. Behold! when they meet the men of Faith, they say: "We believe": But when they meet each other in private, they say: "Shall you tell them what Allah hath revealed to you, that they may engage you in argument about it before your Lord?"—Do ye not understand (their aim)?

77. Know they not that Allah knoweth what they conceal and what they reveal?

78. And there are among them illiterates, who know not the Book, but (see therein their own) desires, and they do nothing but conjecture.

79. Then woe to those who write the Book with their own hands, and then say: "This is from Allah," to traffic with it for miserable price!—Woe to them for what their hands do write, and for the gain they make thereby.

80. And they say: "The Fire shall not touch us but for a few numbered days:" Say: "Have ye taken a promise from Allah, for He never breaks His promise? or is it that ye say of Allah what ye do not know?"

81. Nay, those who seek gain in evil, and are girt round by their sins,- they are companions of the Fire: Therein shall they abide (For ever).

P: Nay, but whosoever hath done evil and his sin surroundeth him; such are rightful owners of the Fire; they will abide therein.

S: Yea, whoever earns evil and his sins beset him on every side, these are the inmates of the fire; in it they shall abide.

82. But those who have faith and work righteousness, they are companions of the Garden: Therein shall they abide (For ever).

83. And remember We took a covenant from the Children of Israel (to this effect): Worship none but Allah; treat with kindness your parents and kindred, and orphans and those in need; speak fair to the people; be steadfast in prayer; and practise regular charity. Then did ye turn back, except a few among you, and ye backslide (even now).

84. And remember We took your covenant (to this effect): Shed no blood amongst you, nor turn out your own people from your homes: and this ye solemnly ratified, and to this ye can bear witness.

85. After this it is ye, the same people, who slay among yourselves, and banish a party of you from their homes; assist (Their enemies) against them, in guilt and rancour; and if they come to you as captives, ye ransom them, though it was not lawful for you to banish them. Then is it only a part of the Book that ye believe in, and do ye reject the rest? but what is the reward for those among you who behave like

this but disgrace in this life?—and on the Day of Judgment they shall be consigned to the most grievous penalty. For Allah is not unmindful of what ye do.

86. These are the people who buy the life of this world at the price of the Hereafter: their penalty shall not be lightened nor shall they be helped.

87. We gave Moses the Book and followed him up with a succession of messengers; We gave Jesus the son of Mary Clear (Signs) and strengthened him with the holy spirit. Is it that whenever there comes to you a messenger with what ye yourselves desire not, ye are puffed up with pride?—Some ye called impostors, and others ye slay!

88. They say, "Our hearts are the wrappings (which preserve Allah's Word: we need no more)." Nay, Allah's curse is on them for their blasphemy: Little is it they believe.

89. And when there comes to them a Book from Allah, confirming what is with them,—although from of old they had prayed for victory against those without Faith,—when there comes to them that which they (should) have recognised, they refuse to believe in it but the curse of Allah is on those without Faith.

90. Miserable is the price for which they have sold their souls, in that they deny (the revelation) which Allah has sent down, in insolent envy that Allah of His Grace should send it to any of His servants He pleases: Thus have they drawn on themselves Wrath upon Wrath. And humiliating is the punishment of those who reject Faith.

91. When it is said to them: "Believe in what Allah Hath sent down," they say, "We believe in what was sent down to us": yet they reject all besides, even if it be Truth confirming what is with them. Say: "Why then have ye slain the prophets of Allah in times gone by, if ye did indeed believe?"

92. There came to you Moses with clear (Signs); yet ye worshipped the calf (Even) after that, and ye did behave wrongfully.

93. And remember We took your covenant and We raised above you (the towering height) of Mount (Sinai): (Saying): "Hold firmly to what We have given you, and hearken (to the Law)": They said: "We hear, and we disobey": And they had to drink into their hearts (of the taint) of the calf because of their Faithlessness. Say: "Vile indeed are the behests of your Faith if ye have any faith!"

94. Say: "If the last Home, with Allah, be for you specially, and not for anyone else, then seek ye for death, if ye are sincere."

95. But they will never seek for death, on account of the (sins) which their hands have sent on before them. And Allah is well-acquainted with the wrong-doers.

96. Thou wilt indeed find them, of all people, most greedy of life,—even more than the idolaters: Each one of them wishes He could be given a life of a thousand years: But the grant of such life will not save him from (due) punishment. For Allah sees well all that they do.

97. Say: Whoever is an enemy to Gabriel—for he brings down the (revelation) to thy heart by Allah's will, a confirmation of what went before, and guidance and glad tidings for those who believe,—

98. Whoever is an enemy to Allah and His angels and messengers, to Gabriel and Michael,—Lo! Allah is an enemy to those who reject Faith.

99. We have sent down to thee Manifest Signs (ayat); and none reject them but those who are perverse.

100. Is it not (the case) that every time they make a covenant, some party among them throw it aside?—Nay, most of them are faithless.

101. And when there came to them a messenger from Allah, confirming what was with them, a party of the people of the Book threw away the Book of Allah behind their backs, as if (it had been something) they did not know!

102. They followed what the evil ones gave out (falsely) against the power of Solomon: the blasphemers Were, not Solomon, but the evil ones, teaching men Magic, and such things as came down at Babylon to the angels Harut and Marut. But neither of these taught anyone (Such things) without saying: "We are only for trial; so do not blaspheme." They learned from them the means to sow discord between man and wife. But they could not thus harm anyone except by Allah's permission. And they learned what harmed them, not what profited them. And they knew that the buyers of (magic) would have no share in the happiness of the Hereafter. And vile was the price for which they did sell their souls, if they but knew!

103. If they had kept their Faith and guarded themselves from evil, far better had been the reward from their Lord, if they but knew!

Text Thirty-three: SURAH 2

104. O ye of Faith! Say not (to the Messenger) words of ambiguous import, but words of respect; and hearken (to him): To those without Faith is a grievous punishment.

105. It is never the wish of those without Faith among the People of the Book, nor of the Pagans, that anything good should come down to you from your Lord. But Allah will choose for His special Mercy whom He will —for Allah is Lord of grace abounding.

106. None of Our revelations do We abrogate or cause to be forgotten, but We substitute something better or similar: Knowest thou not that Allah Hath power over all things?

107. Knowest thou not that to Allah belongeth the dominion of the heavens and the earth? And besides Him ye have neither patron nor helper.

108. Would ye question your Messenger as Moses was questioned of old? but whoever changeth from Faith to Unbelief, Hath strayed without doubt from the even way.

109. Quite a number of the People of the Book wish they could Turn you (people) back to infidelity after ye have believed, from selfish envy, after the Truth hath become Manifest unto them: But forgive and overlook, Till Allah accomplish His purpose; for Allah Hath power over all things.

110. And be steadfast in prayer and regular in charity: And whatever good ye send forth for your souls before you, ye shall find it with Allah: for Allah sees Well all that ye do.

111. And they say: "None shall enter Paradise unless he be a Jew or a Christian." Those are their (vain) desires. Say: "Produce your proof if ye are truthful."

112. Nay,—whoever submits His whole self to Allah and is a doer of good,—He will get his reward with his Lord; on such shall be no fear, nor shall they grieve.

113. The Jews say: "The Christians have naught (to stand) upon"; and the Christians say: "The Jews have naught (To stand) upon." Yet they (Profess to) study the (same) Book. Like unto their word is what those say who know not; but Allah will judge between them in their quarrel on the Day of Judgment.

114. And who is more unjust than he who forbids that in places for the worship of Allah, Allah's name should be celebrated?—whose zeal is (in fact) to ruin them? It was not fitting that such should themselves enter them except in fear. For them there is nothing but disgrace in this world, and in the world to come, an exceeding torment.

115. To Allah belong the east and the West: Whithersoever ye turn, there is the presence of Allah. For Allah is All-Pervading, All-Knowing.

116. They say: "Allah hath begotten a son": Glory be to Him.—Nay, to Him belongs all that is in the heavens and on earth: everything renders worship to Him.

117. To Him is due the primal origin of the heavens and the earth: When He decreeth a matter, He saith to it: "Be," and it is.

118. Say those without knowledge: "Why speaketh not Allah unto us? or why cometh not unto us a Sign?" So said the people before them words of similar import. Their hearts are alike. We have indeed made clear the Signs unto any people who hold firmly to Faith (in their hearts).

119. Verily We have sent thee in truth as a bearer of glad tidings and a warner: But of thee no question shall be asked of the Companions of the Blazing Fire.

120. Never will the Jews or the Christians be satisfied with thee unless thou follow their form of religion. Say: "The Guidance of Allah,—that is the (only) Guidance." Wert thou to follow their desires after the knowledge which hath reached thee, then wouldst thou find neither Protector nor helper against Allah.

121. Those to whom We have sent the Book study it as it should be studied: They are the ones that believe therein: Those who reject faith therein,—the loss is their own.

122. O Children of Israel! call to mind the special favour which I bestowed upon you, and that I preferred you to all others (for My Message).

123. Then guard yourselves against a-Day when one soul shall not avail another, nor shall compensation be accepted from her nor shall intercession profit her nor shall anyone be helped (from outside).

124. And remember that Abraham was tried by his Lord with certain commands, which he fulfilled: He said: "I will make thee an Imam to the Nations." He pleaded: "And also (Imams) from my offspring!" He answered:

125. Remember We made the House a place of assembly for men and a place of safety; and take ye the station of Abraham as a place of prayer; and We covenanted with

Abraham and Isma'il, that they should sanctify My House for those who compass it round, or use it as a retreat, or bow, or prostrate themselves (therein in prayer).

126. And remember Abraham said: "My Lord, make this a City of Peace, and feed its people with fruits,—such of them as believe in Allah and the Last Day." He said: "(Yea), and such as reject Faith,—for a while will I grant them their pleasure, but will soon drive them to the torment of Fire,- an evil destination (indeed)!"

127. And remember Abraham and Isma'il raised the foundations of the House (With this prayer): "Our Lord! Accept (this service) from us: For Thou art the All-Hearing, the All-Knowing."

128. "Our Lord! make of us Muslims, bowing to Thy (Will), and of our progeny a people Muslim, bowing to Thy (will); and show us our place for the celebration of (due) rites; and turn unto us (in Mercy); for Thou art the Oft-Returning, Most Merciful."

129. "Our Lord! send amongst them a Messenger of their own, who shall rehearse Thy Signs to them and instruct them in scripture and wisdom, and sanctify them: For Thou art the Exalted in Might, the Wise."

130. And who turns away from the religion of Abraham but such as debase their souls with folly? Him We chose and rendered pure in this world: And he will be in the Hereafter in the ranks of the Righteous.

131. Behold! his Lord said to him: "Bow (thy will to Me):" He said: "I bow (my will) to the Lord and Cherisher of the Universe."

132. And this was the legacy that Abraham left to his sons, and so did Jacob; "Oh my sons! Allah hath chosen the Faith for you; then die not except in the Faith of Islam."

133. Were ye witnesses when death appeared before Jacob? Behold, he said to his sons: "What will ye worship after me?" They said: "We shall worship Thy god and the god of thy fathers, of Abraham, Isma'il and Isaac,—the one (True) Allah: To Him we bow (in Islam)."

134. That was a people that hath passed away. They shall reap the fruit of what they did, and ye of what ye do! Of their merits there is no question in your case!

135. They say: "Become Jews or Christians if ye would be guided (To salvation)." Say thou: "Nay! (I would rather) the Religion of Abraham the True, and he joined not gods with Allah."

136. Say ye: "We believe in Allah, and the revelation given to us, and to Abraham, Isma'il, Isaac, Jacob, and the Tribes, and that given to Moses and Jesus, and that given to (all) prophets from their Lord: We make no difference between one and another of them: And we bow to Allah (in Islam)."

137. So if they believe as ye believe, they are indeed on the right path; but if they turn back, it is they who are in schism; but Allah will suffice thee as against them, and He is the All-Hearing, the All-Knowing.

138. (Our religion is) the Baptism of Allah: And who can baptize better than Allah? And it is He Whom we worship.

139. Say: Will ye dispute with us about Allah, seeing that He is our Lord and your Lord; that we are responsible for our doings and ye for yours; and that We are sincere (in our faith) in Him?

140. Or do ye say that Abraham, Isma'il Isaac, Jacob and the Tribes were Jews or Christians? Say: Do ye know better than Allah? Ah! who is more unjust than those who conceal the testimony they have from Allah? but Allah is not unmindful of what ye do!

141. That was a people that hath passed away. They shall reap the fruit of what they did, and ye of what ye do! Of their merits there is no question in your case:

142. The fools among the people will say: "What hath turned them from the Qibla to which they were used?" Say: To Allah belong both east and West: He guideth whom He will to a Way that is straight.

143. Thus, have We made of you an Ummat justly balanced, that ye might be witnesses over the nations, and the Messenger a witness over yourselves; and We appointed the Qibla to which thou wast used, only to test those who followed the Messenger from those who would turn on their heels (From the Faith). Indeed it was (A change) momentous, except to those guided by Allah. And never would Allah Make your faith of no effect. For Allah is to all people most surely full of kindness, Most Merciful.

144. We see the turning of thy face (for guidance) to the heavens: now Shall We turn thee to a Qibla that shall please thee. Turn then Thy face in the direction of the sacred Mosque: Wherever ye are, turn your faces in that direction.

The people of the Book know well that that is the truth from their Lord. Nor is Allah unmindful of what they do.

145. Even if thou wert to bring to the people of the Book all the Signs (together), they would not follow Thy Qibla; nor art thou going to follow their Qibla; nor indeed will they follow each other's Qibla. If thou after the knowledge hath reached thee, Wert to follow their (vain) desires,-then wert thou Indeed (clearly) in the wrong.

146. The people of the Book know this as they know their own sons; but some of them conceal the truth which they themselves know.

147. The Truth is from thy Lord; so be not at all in doubt.

148. To each is a goal to which Allah turns him; then strive together (as in a race) Towards all that is good. Wheresoever ye are, Allah will bring you Together. For Allah Hath power over all things.

149. From whencesoever Thou startest forth, turn Thy face in the direction of the sacred Mosque; that is indeed the truth from the Lord. And Allah is not unmindful of what ye do.

150. So from whencesoever Thou startest forth, turn Thy face in the direction of the sacred Mosque; and wheresoever ye are, Turn your face thither: that there be no ground of dispute against you among the people, except those of them that are bent on wickedness; so fear them not, but fear Me; and that I may complete My favours on you, and ye May (consent to) be guided;

151. A similar (favour have ye already received) in that We have sent among you a Messenger of your own, rehearsing to you Our Signs, and sanctifying you, and instructing you in Scripture and Wisdom, and in new knowledge.

152. Then do ye remember Me; I will remember you. Be grateful to Me, and reject not Faith.

153. O ye who believe! seek help with patient perseverance and prayer; for Allah is with those who patiently persevere.

154. And say not of those who are slain in the way of Allah: "They are dead." Nay, they are living, though ye perceive (it) not.

155. Be sure we shall test you with something of fear and hunger, some loss in goods or lives or the fruits (of your toil), but give glad tidings to those who patiently persevere,

156. Who say, when afflicted with calamity: "To Allah We belong, and to Him is our return":—

157. They are those on whom (Descend) blessings from Allah, and Mercy, and they are the ones that receive guidance.

158. Behold! Safa and Marwa are among the Symbols of Allah. So if those who visit the House in the Season or at other times, should compass them round, it is no sin in them. And if any one obeyeth his own impulse to good,—be sure that Allah is He Who recogniseth and knoweth.

159. Those who conceal the clear (Signs) We have sent down, and the Guidance, after We have made it clear for the people in the Book,—on them shall be Allah's curse, and the curse of those entitled to curse,—

160. Except those who repent and make amends and openly declare (the Truth): To them I turn; for I am Oft-Returning, Most Merciful.

161. Those who reject Faith, and die rejecting,—on them is Allah's curse, and the curse of angels, and of all mankind;

162. They will abide therein: Their penalty will not be lightened, nor will respite be their (lot).

163. And your Allah is One Allah: There is no god but He, Most Gracious, Most Merciful.

164. Behold! in the creation of the heavens and the earth; in the alternation of the night and the day; in the sailing of the ships through the ocean for the profit of mankind; in the rain which Allah Sends down from the skies, and the life which He gives therewith to an earth that is dead; in the beasts of all kinds that He scatters through the earth; in the change of the winds, and the clouds which they Trail like their slaves between the sky and the earth;—(Here) indeed are Signs for a people that are wise.

165. Yet there are men who take (for worship) others besides Allah, as equal (with Allah): They love them as they should love Allah. But those of Faith are overflowing in their love for Allah. If only the unrighteous could see, behold, they would see the penalty: that to Allah belongs all power, and Allah will strongly enforce the penalty.

166. Then would those who are followed clear themselves of those who follow (them): They would see the penalty, and all relations between them would be cut off.

167. And those who followed would say: "If only We had one more chance, We would clear ourselves of them, as they have cleared themselves of us." Thus will Allah show them (The

fruits of) their deeds as (nothing but) regrets. Nor will there be a way for them out of the Fire.

168. O ye people! Eat of what is on earth, Lawful and good; and do not follow the footsteps of the evil one, for he is to you an avowed enemy.

169. For he commands you what is evil and shameful, and that ye should say of Allah that of which ye have no knowledge.

170. When it is said to them: "Follow what Allah hath revealed:" They say: "Nay! we shall follow the ways of our fathers." What! even though their fathers Were void of wisdom and guidance?

171. The parable of those who reject Faith is as if one were to shout Like a goat-herd, to things that listen to nothing but calls and cries: Deaf, dumb, and blind, they are void of wisdom.

172. O ye who believe! Eat of the good things that We have provided for you, and be grateful to Allah, if it is Him ye worship.

173. He hath only forbidden you dead meat, and blood, and the flesh of swine, and that on which any other name hath been invoked besides that of Allah. But if one is forced by necessity, without wilful disobedience, nor transgressing due limits,—then is he guiltless. For Allah is Oft-Forgiving Most Merciful.

174. Those who conceal Allah's revelations in the Book, and purchase for them a miserable profit,—they swallow into themselves naught but Fire; Allah will not address them on the Day of Resurrection. Nor purify them: Grievous will be their penalty.

175. They are the ones who buy Error in place of Guidance and Torment in place of Forgiveness. Ah! what boldness (They show) for the Fire!

176. (Their doom is) because Allah sent down the Book in truth but those who seek causes of dispute in the Book are in a schism Far (from the purpose).

177. It is not righteousness that ye turn your faces Towards east or West; but it is righteousness—to believe in Allah and the Last Day, and the Angels, and the Book, and the Messengers; to spend of your substance, out of love for Him, for your kin, for orphans, for the needy, for the wayfarer, for those who ask, and for the ransom of slaves; to be steadfast in prayer, and practice regular charity; to fulfil the contracts which ye have made; and to be firm and patient, in pain (or suffering) and adversity, and throughout all periods of panic. Such are the people of truth, the Allah-fearing.

178. O ye who believe! the law of equality is prescribed to you in cases of murder: the free for the free, the slave for the slave, the woman for the woman. But if any remission is made by the brother of the slain, then grant any reasonable demand, and compensate him with handsome gratitude, this is a concession and a Mercy from your Lord. After this whoever exceeds the limits shall be in grave penalty.

179. In the Law of Equality there is (saving of) Life to you, O ye men of understanding; that ye may restrain yourselves.

180. It is prescribed, when death approaches any of you, if he leave any goods that he make a bequest to parents and next of kin, according to reasonable usage; this is due from the Allah-fearing.

181. If anyone changes the bequest after hearing it, the guilt shall be on those who make the change. For Allah hears and knows all things.

182. But if anyone fears partiality or wrong-doing on the part of the testator, and makes peace between (The parties concerned), there is no wrong in him: For Allah is Oft-Forgiving, Most Merciful.

183. O ye who believe! Fasting is prescribed to you as it was prescribed to those before you, that ye may (learn) self-restraint,—

184. (Fasting) for a fixed number of days; but if any of you is ill, or on a journey, the prescribed number (Should be made up) from days later. For those who can do it (With hardship), is a ransom, the feeding of one that is indigent. But he that will give more, of his own free will,—it is better for him. And it is better for you that ye fast, if ye only knew.

185. Ramadhan is the (month) in which was sent down the Qur'an, as a guide to mankind, also clear (Signs) for guidance and judgment (Between right and wrong). So every one of you who is present (at his home) during that month should spend it in fasting, but if any one is ill, or on a journey, the prescribed period (Should be made up) by days later. Allah intends every facility for you; He does not want to put to difficulties. (He wants you) to complete the

prescribed period, and to glorify Him in that He has guided you; and perchance ye shall be grateful.

186. When My servants ask thee concerning Me, I am indeed close (to them): I listen to the prayer of every suppliant when he calleth on Me: Let them also, with a will, Listen to My call, and believe in Me: That they may walk in the right way.

187. Permitted to you, on the night of the fasts, is the approach to your wives. They are your garments and ye are their garments. Allah knoweth what ye used to do secretly among yourselves; but He turned to you and forgave you; so now associate with them, and seek what Allah Hath ordained for you, and eat and drink, until the white thread of dawn appear to you distinct from its black thread; then complete your fast Till the night appears; but do not associate with your wives while ye are in retreat in the mosques. Those are Limits (set by) Allah: Approach not nigh thereto. Thus doth Allah make clear His Signs to men: that they may learn self-restraint.

188. And do not eat up your property among yourselves for vanities, nor use it as bait for the judges, with intent that ye may eat up wrongfully and knowingly a little of (other) people's property.

189. They ask thee concerning the New Moons. Say: They are but signs to mark fixed periods of time in (the affairs of) men, and for Pilgrimage. It is no virtue if ye enter your houses from the back: It is virtue if ye fear Allah. Enter houses through the proper doors: And fear Allah: That ye may prosper.

190. Fight in the cause of Allah those who fight you, but do not transgress limits; for Allah loveth not transgressors.

191. And slay them wherever ye catch them, and turn them out from where they have Turned you out; for tumult and oppression are worse than slaughter; but fight them not at the Sacred Mosque, unless they (first) fight you there; but if they fight you, slay them. Such is the reward of those who suppress faith.

192. But if they cease, Allah is Oft-Forgiving, Most Merciful.

193. And fight them on until there is no more Tumult or oppression, and there prevail justice and faith in Allah; but if they cease, Let there be no hostility except to those who practise oppression.

194. The prohibited month for the prohibited month,—and so for all things prohibited,—there is the law of equality. If then any one transgresses the prohibition against you, Transgress ye likewise against him. But fear Allah, and know that Allah is with those who restrain themselves.

195. And spend of your substance in the cause of Allah, and make not your own hands contribute to (your) destruction; but do good; for Allah loveth those who do good.

196. And complete the Hajj or 'umra in the service of Allah. But if ye are prevented (From completing it), send an offering for sacrifice, such as ye may find, and do not shave your heads until the offering reaches the place of sacrifice. And if any of you is ill, or has an ailment in his scalp, (Necessitating shaving), (He should) in compensation either fast, or feed the poor, or offer sacrifice; and when ye are in peaceful conditions (again), if any one wishes to continue the 'umra on to the hajj, He must make an offering, such as he can afford, but if he cannot afford it, He should fast three days during the hajj and seven days on his return, Making ten days in all. This is for those whose household is not in (the precincts of) the Sacred Mosque. And fear Allah, and know that Allah Is strict in punishment.

197. For Hajj are the months well known. If any one undertakes that duty therein, Let there be no obscenity, nor wickedness, nor wrangling in the Hajj. And whatever good ye do, (be sure) Allah knoweth it. And take a provision (With you) for the journey, but the best of provisions is right conduct. So fear Me, O ye that are wise.

198. It is no crime in you if ye seek of the bounty of your Lord (during pilgrimage). Then when ye pour down from (Mount) Arafat, celebrate the praises of Allah at the Sacred Monument, and celebrate His praises as He has directed you, even though, before this, ye went astray.

199. Then pass on at a quick pace from the place whence it is usual for the multitude so to do, and ask for Allah's forgiveness. For Allah is Oft-Forgiving, Most Merciful.

200. So when ye have accomplished your holy rites, celebrate the praises of Allah, as ye used to celebrate the praises of your fathers,—yea, with far more Heart and soul. There are men who say: "Our Lord! Give us (Thy bounties) in this world!" but they will have no portion in the Hereafter.

201. And there are men who say: "Our Lord! Give us good in this world and good in the Hereafter, and defend us from the torment of the Fire!"

202. To these will be allotted what they have earned; and Allah is quick in account.

203. Celebrate the praises of Allah during the Appointed Days. But if any one hastens to leave in two days, there is no blame on him, and if any one stays on, there is no blame on him, if his aim is to do right. Then fear Allah, and know that ye will surely be gathered unto Him.

204. There is the type of man whose speech about this world's life May dazzle thee, and he calls Allah to witness about what is in his heart; yet is he the most contentious of enemies.

205. When he turns his back, His aim everywhere is to spread mischief through the earth and destroy crops and cattle. But Allah loveth not mischief.

206. When it is said to him, "Fear Allah", He is led by arrogance to (more) crime. Enough for him is Hell;—An evil bed indeed (To lie on)!

207. And there is the type of man who gives his life to earn the pleasure of Allah: And Allah is full of kindness to (His) devotees.

208. O ye who believe! Enter into Islam whole-heartedly; and follow not the footsteps of the evil one; for he is to you an avowed enemy.

209. If ye backslide after the clear (Signs) have come to you, then know that Allah is Exalted in Power, Wise.

210. Will they wait until Allah comes to them in canopies of clouds, with angels (in His train) and the question is (thus) settled? but to Allah do all questions go back (for decision).

211. Ask the Children of Israel how many clear (Signs) We have sent them. But if any one, after Allah's favour has come to him, substitutes (something else), Allah is strict in punishment.

212. The life of this world is alluring to those who reject faith, and they scoff at those who believe. But the righteous will be above them on the Day of Resurrection; for Allah bestows His abundance without measure on whom He will.

213. Mankind was one single nation, and Allah sent Messengers with glad tidings and warnings; and with them He sent the Book in truth, to judge between people in matters wherein they differed; but the People of the Book, after the clear Signs came to them, did not differ among themselves, except through selfish contumacy. Allah by His Grace Guided the believers to the Truth, concerning that wherein they differed. For Allah guided whom He will to a path that is straight.

214. Or do ye think that ye shall enter the Garden (of bliss) without such (trials) as came to those who passed away before you? they encountered suffering and adversity, and were so shaken in spirit that even the Messenger and those of faith who were with him cried: "When (will come) the help of Allah?" Ah! Verily, the help of Allah is (always) near!

215. They ask thee what they should spend (In charity). Say: Whatever ye spend that is good, is for parents and kindred and orphans and those in want and for wayfarers. And whatever ye do that is good,—Allah knoweth it well.

216. Fighting is prescribed for you, and ye dislike it. But it is possible that ye dislike a thing which is good for you, and that ye love a thing which is bad for you. But Allah knoweth, and ye know not.

217. They ask thee concerning fighting in the Prohibited Month. Say: "Fighting therein is a grave (offence); but graver is it in the sight of Allah to prevent access to the path of Allah, to deny Him, to prevent access to the Sacred Mosque, and drive out its members." Tumult and oppression are worse than slaughter. Nor will they cease fighting you until they turn you back from your faith if they can. And if any of you turn back from their faith and die in unbelief, their works will bear no fruit in this life and in the Hereafter; they will be companions of the Fire and will abide therein.

218. Those who believed and those who suffered exile and fought (and strove and struggled) in the path of Allah,- they have the hope of the Mercy of Allah: And Allah is Oft—Forgiving, Most Merciful.

219. They ask thee concerning wine and gambling. Say: "In them is great sin, and some profit, for men; but the sin is greater than the profit." They ask thee how much they are to spend; Say: "What is beyond your needs." Thus doth Allah Make clear to you His Signs: In order that ye may consider—

220. (Their bearings) on this life and the Hereafter. They ask thee concerning orphans. Say: "The best thing to do is

what is for their good; if ye mix their affairs with yours, they are your brethren; but Allah knows the man who means mischief from the man who means good. And if Allah had wished, He could have put you into difficulties: He is indeed Exalted in Power, Wise."

221. Do not marry unbelieving women (idolaters), until they believe: A slave woman who believes is better than an unbelieving woman, even though she allures you. Nor marry (your girls) to unbelievers until they believe: A man slave who believes is better than an unbeliever, even though he allures you. Unbelievers do (but) beckon you to the Fire. But Allah beckons by His Grace to the Garden (of bliss) and forgiveness, and makes His Signs clear to mankind: That they may celebrate His praise.

222. They ask thee concerning women's courses. Say: They are a hurt and a pollution: So keep away from women in their courses, and do not approach them until they are clean. But when they have purified themselves, ye may approach them in any manner, time, or place ordained for you by Allah. For Allah loves those who turn to Him constantly and He loves those who keep themselves pure and clean.

223. Your wives are as a tilth unto you; so approach your tilth when or how ye will; but do some good act for your souls beforehand; and fear Allah. And know that ye are to meet Him (in the Hereafter), and give (these) good tidings to those who believe.

224. And make not Allah's (name) an excuse in your oaths against doing good, or acting rightly, or making peace between persons; for Allah is One Who heareth and knoweth all things.

225. Allah will not call you to account for thoughtlessness in your oaths, but for the intention in your hearts; and He is Oft-Forgiving, Most Forbearing.

226. For those who take an oath for abstention from their wives, a waiting for four months is ordained; if then they return, Allah is Oft-Forgiving, Most Merciful.

227. But if their intention is firm for divorce, Allah heareth and knoweth all things.

228. Divorced women shall wait concerning themselves for three monthly periods. Nor is it lawful for them to hide what Allah Hath created in their wombs, if they have faith in Allah and the Last Day. And their husbands have the better right to take them back in that period, if they wish for reconciliation. And women shall have rights similar to the rights against them, according to what is equitable; but men have a degree (of advantage) over them. And Allah is Exalted in Power, Wise.

229. A divorce is only permissible twice: after that, the parties should either hold Together on equitable terms, or separate with kindness. It is not lawful for you, (Men), to take back any of your gifts (from your wives), except when both parties fear that they would be unable to keep the limits ordained by Allah. If ye (judges) do indeed fear that they would be unable to keep the limits ordained by Allah, there is no blame on either of them if she give something for her freedom. These are the limits ordained by Allah; so do not transgress them if any do transgress the limits ordained by Allah, such persons wrong (Themselves as well as others).

230. So if a husband divorces his wife (irrevocably), He cannot, after that, re-marry her until after she has married another husband and He has divorced her. In that case there is no blame on either of them if they re-unite, provided they feel that they can keep the limits ordained by Allah. Such are the limits ordained by Allah, which He makes plain to those who understand.

231. When ye divorce women, and they fulfil the term of their ('Iddat), either take them back on equitable terms or set them free on equitable terms; but do not take them back to injure them, (or) to take undue advantage; if any one does that; He wrongs his own soul. Do not treat Allah's Signs as a jest, but solemnly rehearse Allah's favours on you, and the fact that He sent down to you the Book and Wisdom, for your instruction. And fear Allah, and know that Allah is well acquainted with all things.

232. When ye divorce women, and they fulfil the term of their ('Iddat), do not prevent them from marrying their (former) husbands, if they mutually agree on equitable terms. This instruction is for all amongst you, who believe in Allah and the Last Day. That is (the course Making for) most virtue and purity amongst you and Allah knows, and ye know not.

233. The mothers shall give suck to their offspring for two whole years, if the father desires to complete the term. But he shall bear the cost of their food and clothing on equitable terms. No soul shall have a burden laid on it greater than it

Text Thirty-three: SURAH 2

can bear. No mother shall be Treated unfairly on account of her child. Nor father on account of his child, an heir shall be chargeable in the same way. If they both decide on weaning, by mutual consent, and after due consultation, there is no blame on them. If ye decide on a foster-mother for your offspring, there is no blame on you, provided ye pay (the mother) what ye offered, on equitable terms. But fear Allah and know that Allah sees well what ye do.

234. If any of you die and leave widows behind, they shall wait concerning themselves four months and ten days: When they have fulfilled their term, there is no blame on you if they dispose of themselves in a just and reasonable manner. And Allah is well acquainted with what ye do.

235. There is no blame on you if ye make an offer of betrothal or hold it in your hearts. Allah knows that ye cherish them in your hearts: But do not make a secret contract with them except in terms honourable, nor resolve on the tie of marriage till the term prescribed is fulfilled. And know that Allah Knoweth what is in your hearts, and take heed of Him; and know that Allah is Oft-Forgiving, Most Forbearing.

236. There is no blame on you if ye divorce women before consummation or the fixation of their dower; but bestow on them (A suitable gift), the wealthy according to his means, and the poor according to his means;—A gift of a reasonable amount is due from those who wish to do the right thing.

237. And if ye divorce them before consummation, but after the fixation of a dower for them, then the half of the dower (Is due to them), unless they remit it or (the man's half) is remitted by him in whose hands is the marriage tie; and the remission (of the man's half) is the nearest to righteousness. And do not forget Liberality between yourselves. For Allah sees well all that ye do.

238. Guard strictly your (habit of) prayers, especially the Middle Prayer; and stand before Allah in a devout (frame of mind).

239. If ye fear (an enemy), pray on foot, or riding, (as may be most convenient), but when ye are in security, celebrate Allah's praises in the manner He has taught you, which ye knew not (before).

240. Those of you who die and leave widows should bequeath for their widows a year's maintenance and residence; but if they leave (The residence), there is no blame on you for what they do with themselves, provided it is reasonable. And Allah is Exalted in Power, Wise.

241. For divorced women Maintenance (should be provided) on a reasonable (scale). This is a duty on the righteous.

242. Thus doth Allah Make clear His Signs to you: In order that ye may understand.

243. Didst thou not Turn by vision to those who abandoned their homes, though they were thousands (In number), for fear of death? Allah said to them: "Die": Then He restored them to life. For Allah is full of bounty to mankind, but most of them are ungrateful.

244. Then fight in the cause of Allah, and know that Allah Heareth and knoweth all things.

245. Who is he that will loan to Allah a beautiful loan, which Allah will double unto his credit and multiply many times? It is Allah that giveth (you) Want or plenty, and to Him shall be your return.

246. Hast thou not Turned thy vision to the Chiefs of the Children of Israel after (the time of) Moses? they said to a prophet (That was) among them: "Appoint for us a king, that we May fight in the cause of Allah." He said: "Is it not possible, if ye were commanded to fight, that that ye will not fight?" They said: "How could we refuse to fight in the cause of Allah, seeing that we were turned out of our homes and our families?" but when they were commanded to fight, they turned back, except a small band among them. But Allah Has full knowledge of those who do wrong.

247. Their Prophet said to them: "Allah hath appointed Talut as king over you." They said: "How can he exercise authority over us when we are better fitted than he to exercise authority, and he is not even gifted, with wealth in abundance?" He said: "Allah hath Chosen him above you, and hath gifted him abundantly with knowledge and bodily prowess: Allah Granteth His authority to whom He pleaseth. Allah careth for all, and He knoweth all things."

248. And (further) their Prophet said to them: "A Sign of his authority is that there shall come to you the Ark of the covenant, with (an assurance) therein of security from your Lord, and the relics left by the family of Moses and the family of Aaron, carried by angels. In this is a symbol for you if ye indeed have faith."

Text Thirty-three: SURAH 2

249. When Talut set forth with the armies, he said: "Allah will test you at the stream: if any drinks of its water, He goes not with my army: Only those who taste not of it go with me: A mere sip out of the hand is excused." but they all drank of it, except a few. When they crossed the river,—He and the faithful ones with him,—they said: "This day We cannot cope with Goliath and his forces." but those who were convinced that they must meet Allah, said: "How oft, by Allah's will, Hath a small force vanquished a big one? Allah is with those who steadfastly persevere."

250. When they advanced to meet Goliath and his forces, they prayed: "Our Lord! Pour out constancy on us and make our steps firm: Help us against those that reject faith."

251. By Allah's will they routed them; and David slew Goliath; and Allah gave him power and wisdom and taught him whatever (else) He willed. And did not Allah Check one set of people by means of another, the earth would indeed be full of mischief: But Allah is full of bounty to all the worlds.

252. These are the Signs of Allah: we rehearse them to thee in truth: verily Thou art one of the messengers.

253. Those messengers We endowed with gifts, some above others: To one of them Allah spoke; others He raised to degrees (of honour); to Jesus the son of Mary We gave clear (Signs), and strengthened him with the holy spirit. If Allah had so willed, succeeding generations would not have fought among each other, after clear (Signs) had come to them, but they (chose) to wrangle, some believing and others rejecting. If Allah had so willed, they would not have fought each other; but Allah Fulfilleth His plan.

254. O ye who believe! Spend out of (the bounties) We have provided for you, before the Day comes when no bargaining (Will avail), nor friendship nor intercession. Those who reject Faith they are the wrong-doers.

255. Allah! There is no god but He,—the Living, the Self-subsisting, Eternal. No slumber can seize Him nor sleep. His are all things in the heavens and on earth. Who is there can intercede in His presence except as He permitteth? He knoweth what (appeareth to His creatures as) before or after or behind them. Nor shall they compass aught of His knowledge except as He willeth. His Throne doth extend over the heavens and the earth, and He feeleth no fatigue in guarding and preserving them for He is the Most High, the Supreme (in glory).

256. Let there be no compulsion in religion: Truth stands out clear from Error: whoever rejects evil and believes in Allah hath grasped the most trustworthy hand-hold, that never breaks. And Allah heareth and knoweth all things.

257. Allah is the Protector of those who have faith: from the depths of darkness He will lead them forth into light. Of those who reject faith the patrons are the evil ones: from light they will lead them forth into the depths of darkness. They will be companions of the fire, to dwell therein (For ever).

258. Hast thou not Turned thy vision to one who disputed with Abraham About his Lord, because Allah had granted him power? Abraham said: "My Lord is He Who giveth life and death." He said: "I give life and death." Said Abraham: "But it is Allah that causeth the sun to rise from the east: Do thou then cause him to rise from the West." Thus was he confounded who (in arrogance) rejected faith. Nor doth Allah Give guidance to a people unjust.

259. Or (take) the similitude of one who passed by a hamlet, all in ruins to its roofs. He said: "Oh! how shall Allah bring it (ever) to life, after (this) its death?" but Allah caused him to die for a hundred years, then raised him up (again). He said: "How long didst thou tarry (thus)?" He said: "(Perhaps) a day or part of a day." He said: "Nay, thou hast tarried thus a hundred years; but look at thy food and thy drink; they show no signs of age; and look at thy donkey: And that We may make of thee a sign unto the people, Look further at the bones, how We bring them together and clothe them with flesh." When this was shown clearly to him, he said: "I know that Allah hath power over all things."

260. When Abraham said: "Show me, Lord, how You will raise the dead," He replied: "Have you no faith?" He said "Yes, but just to reassure my heart." Allah said, "Take four birds, draw them to you, and cut their bodies to pieces. Scatter them over the mountain-tops, then call them back. They will come swiftly to you. Know that Allah is Mighty, Wise."

261. The parable of those who spend their substance in the way of Allah is that of a grain of corn: it groweth seven ears, and each ear Hath a hundred grains. Allah giveth manifold increase to whom He pleaseth: And Allah careth for all and He knoweth all things.

262. Those who spend their substance in the cause of Allah, and follow not up their gifts with reminders of their

Text Thirty-three: **SURAH 2**

generosity or with injury,—for them their reward is with their Lord: on them shall be no fear, nor shall they grieve.

263. Kind words and the covering of faults are better than charity followed by injury. Allah is free of all wants, and He is Most-Forbearing.

264. O ye who believe! cancel not your charity by reminders of your generosity or by injury,- like those who spend their substance to be seen of men, but believe neither in Allah nor in the Last Day. They are in parable like a hard, barren rock, on which is a little soil: on it falls heavy rain, which leaves it (Just) a bare stone. They will be able to do nothing with aught they have earned. And Allah guideth not those who reject faith.

265. And the likeness of those who spend their substance, seeking to please Allah and to strengthen their souls, is as a garden, high and fertile: heavy rain falls on it but makes it yield a double increase of harvest, and if it receives not Heavy rain, light moisture sufficeth it. Allah seeth well whatever ye do.

266. Does any of you wish that he should have a garden with date-palms and vines and streams flowing underneath, and all kinds of fruit, while he is stricken with old age, and his children are not strong (enough to look after themselves)— that it should be caught in a whirlwind, with fire therein, and be burnt up? Thus doth Allah make clear to you (His) Signs; that ye may consider.

267. O ye who believe! Give of the good things which ye have (honourably) earned, and of the fruits of the earth which We have produced for you, and do not even aim at getting anything which is bad, in order that out of it ye may give away something, when ye yourselves would not receive it except with closed eyes. And know that Allah is Free of all wants, and worthy of all praise.

268. The Evil one threatens you with poverty and bids you to conduct unseemly. Allah promiseth you His forgiveness and bounties. And Allah careth for all and He knoweth all things.

269. He granteth wisdom to whom He pleaseth; and he to whom wisdom is granted receiveth indeed a benefit overflowing; but none will grasp the Message but men of understanding.

270. And whatever ye spend in charity or devotion, be sure Allah knows it all. But the wrong-doers have no helpers.

271. If ye disclose (acts of) charity, even so it is well, but if ye conceal them, and make them reach those (really) in need, that is best for you: It will remove from you some of your (stains of) evil. And Allah is well acquainted with what ye do.

272. It is not required of thee (O Messenger), to set them on the right path, but Allah sets on the right path whom He pleaseth. Whatever of good ye give benefits your own souls, and ye shall only do so seeking the "Face" of Allah. Whatever good ye give, shall be rendered back to you, and ye shall not Be dealt with unjustly.

273. (Charity is) for those in need, who, in Allah's cause are restricted (from travel), and cannot move about in the land, seeking (For trade or work): the ignorant man thinks, because of their modesty, that they are free from want. Thou shalt know them by their (Unfailing) mark: They beg not importunately from all the sundry. And whatever of good ye give, be assured Allah knoweth it well.

274. Those who (in charity) spend of their goods by night and by day, in secret and in public, have their reward with their Lord: on them shall be no fear, nor shall they grieve.

275. Those who devour usury will not stand except as stand one whom the Evil one by his touch Hath driven to madness. That is because they say: "Trade is like usury," but Allah hath permitted trade and forbidden usury. Those who after receiving direction from their Lord, desist, shall be pardoned for the past; their case is for Allah (to judge); but those who repeat (The offence) are companions of the Fire: They will abide therein (for ever).

276. Allah will deprive usury of all blessing, but will give increase for deeds of charity: For He loveth not creatures ungrateful and wicked.

277. Those who believe, and do deeds of righteousness, and establish regular prayers and regular charity, will have their reward with their Lord: on them shall be no fear, nor shall they grieve.

278. O ye who believe! Fear Allah, and give up what remains of your demand for usury, if ye are indeed believers.

279. If ye do it not, Take notice of war from Allah and His Messenger: But if ye turn back, ye shall have your capital sums: Deal not unjustly, and ye shall not be dealt with unjustly.

280. If the debtor is in a difficulty, grant him time Till it is easy for him to repay. But if ye remit it by way of charity, that is best for you if ye only knew.

Text Thirty-three: **SURAH 2**

281. And fear the Day when ye shall be brought back to Allah. Then shall every soul be paid what it earned, and none shall be dealt with unjustly.

282. O ye who believe! When ye deal with each other, in transactions involving future obligations in a fixed period of time, reduce them to writing Let a scribe write down faithfully as between the parties: let not the scribe refuse to write: as Allah has taught him, so let him write. Let him who incurs the liability dictate, but let him fear His Lord Allah, and not diminish aught of what he owes. If they party liable is mentally deficient, or weak, or unable Himself to dictate, Let his guardian dictate faithfully, and get two witnesses, out of your own men, and if there are not two men, then a man and two women, such as ye choose, for witnesses, so that if one of them errs, the other can remind her. The witnesses should not refuse when they are called on (For evidence). Disdain not to reduce to writing (your contract) for a future period, whether it be small or big: it is juster in the sight of Allah, More suitable as evidence, and more convenient to prevent doubts among yourselves but if it be a transaction which ye carry out on the spot among yourselves, there is no blame on you if ye reduce it not to writing. But take witness whenever ye make a commercial contract; and let neither scribe nor witness suffer harm. If ye do (such harm), it would be wickedness in you. So fear Allah; For it is Good that teaches you. And Allah is well acquainted with all things. If ye are on a journey, and cannot find a scribe, a pledge with possession (may serve the purpose). And if one of you deposits a thing on trust with another, let the trustee (faithfully) discharge his trust, and let him Fear his

Lord conceal not evidence; for whoever conceals it,—his heart is tainted with sin. And Allah knoweth all that ye do.

283. If ye are on a journey, and cannot find a scribe, a pledge with possession (may serve the purpose). And if one of you deposits a thing on trust with another, Let the trustee (Faithfully) discharge His trust, and let him fear his Lord. Conceal not evidence; for whoever conceals it,—His heart is tainted with sin. And Allah Knoweth all that ye do.

284. To Allah belongeth all that is in the heavens and on earth. Whether ye show what is in your minds or conceal it, Allah Calleth you to account for it. He forgiveth whom He pleaseth, and punisheth whom He pleaseth, for Allah hath power over all things.

285. The Messenger believeth in what hath been revealed to him from his Lord, as do the men of faith. Each one (of them) believeth in Allah, His angels, His books, and His messengers. "We make no distinction (they say) between one and another of His messengers." And they say: "We hear, and we obey: (We seek) Thy forgiveness, our Lord, and to Thee is the end of all journeys."

286. On no soul doth Allah Place a burden greater than it can bear. It gets every good that it earns, and it suffers every ill that it earns. (Pray:) "Our Lord! Condemn us not if we forget or fall into error; our Lord! Lay not on us a burden Like that which Thou didst lay on those before us; Our Lord! Lay not on us a burden greater than we have strength to bear. Blot out our sins, and grant us forgiveness. Have mercy on us. Thou art our Protector; Help us against those who stand against faith."

Text Thirty-four

Surah 12

Yusuf or Joseph

In the name of Allah, the Most Beneficent, the Most Merciful.

1. A.L.R. These are the symbols (or Verses) of the perspicuous Book.

2. We have sent it down as an Arabic Qur'an, in order that ye may learn wisdom.

3. We do relate unto thee the most beautiful of stories, in that We reveal to thee this (portion of the) Qur'an: before this, thou too was among those who knew it not.

4. Behold! Joseph said to his father: "O my father! I did see eleven stars and the sun and the moon: I saw them prostrate themselves to me!"

5. Said (the father): "My (dear) little son! relate not thy vision to thy brothers, lest they concoct a plot against thee: for Satan is to man an avowed enemy!"

6. "Thus will thy Lord choose thee and teach thee the interpretation of stories (and events) and perfect His favour to thee and to the posterity of Jacob—even as He perfected it to thy fathers Abraham and Isaac aforetime! for Allah is full of knowledge and wisdom."

7. Verily in Joseph and his brethren are signs (or symbols) for seekers (after Truth).

8. They said: "Truly Joseph and his brother are loved more by our father than we: But we are a goodly body! really our father is obviously wandering (in his mind)!"

9. "Slay ye Joseph or cast him out to some (unknown) land, that so the favour of your father may be given to you alone: (there will be time enough) for you to be righteous after that!"

10. Said one of them: "Slay not Joseph, but if ye must do something, throw him down to the bottom of the well: he will be picked up by some caravan of travellers."

11. They said: "O our father! why dost thou not trust us with Joseph,—seeing we are indeed his sincere well-wishers?"

12. "Send him with us tomorrow to enjoy himself and play, and we shall take every care of him."

13. (Jacob) said: "Really it saddens me that ye should take him away: I fear lest the wolf should devour him while ye attend not to him."

14. They said: "If the wolf were to devour him while we are (so large) a party, then should we indeed (first) have perished ourselves!"

15. So they did take him away, and they all agreed to throw him down to the bottom of the well: and We put into his heart (this Message): 'Of a surety thou shalt (one day) tell them the truth of this their affair while they know (thee) not'

16. Then they came to their father in the early part of the night, weeping.

17. They said: "O our father! We went racing with one another, and left Joseph with our things; and the wolf devoured him…. But thou wilt never believe us even though we tell the truth."

18. They stained his shirt with false blood. He said: "Nay, but your minds have made up a tale (that may pass) with you, (for me) patience is most fitting: Against that which ye assert, it is Allah (alone) Whose help can be sought".

19. Then there came a caravan of travellers: they sent their water-carrier (for water), and he let down his bucket (into

the well)…He said: "Ah there! Good news! Here is a (fine) young man!" So they concealed him as a treasure! But Allah knoweth well all that they do!

20. The (Brethren) sold him for a miserable price, for a few dirhams counted out: in such low estimation did they hold him!

21. The man in Egypt who bought him, said to his wife: "Make his stay (among us) honourable: may be he will bring us much good, or we shall adopt him as a son." Thus did We establish Joseph in the land, that We might teach him the interpretation of stories (and events). And Allah hath full power and control over His affairs; but most among mankind know it not.

22. When Joseph attained His full manhood, We gave him power and knowledge: thus do We reward those who do right.

23. But she in whose house he was, sought to seduce him from his (true) self: she fastened the doors, and said: "Now come, thou (dear one)!" He said: "Allah forbid! truly (thy husband) is my lord! he made my sojourn agreeable! truly to no good come those who do wrong!"

24. And (with passion) did she desire him, and he would have desired her, but that he saw the evidence of his Lord: thus (did We order) that We might turn away from him (all) evil and shameful deeds: for he was one of Our servants, sincere and purified.

25. So they both raced each other to the door, and she tore his shirt from the back: they both found her lord near the door. She said: "What is the (fitting) punishment for one who formed an evil design against thy wife, but prison or a grievous chastisement?"

26. He said: "It was she that sought to seduce me— from my (true) self." And one of her household saw (this) and bore witness, (thus):—"If it be that his shirt is rent from the front, then is her tale true, and he is a liar!"

27. "But if it be that his shirt is torn from the back, then is she the liar, and he is telling the truth!"

28. So when he saw his shirt,—that it was torn at the back,—(her husband) said: "Behold! It is a snare of you women! truly, mighty is your snare!"

29. "O Joseph, pass this over! (O wife), ask forgiveness for thy sin, for truly thou hast been at fault!"

30. Ladies said in the City: "The wife of the (great) 'Aziz is seeking to seduce her slave from his (true) self: Truly hath he inspired her with violent love: we see she is evidently going astray."

31. When she heard of their malicious talk, she sent for them and prepared a banquet for them: she gave each of them a knife: and she said (to Joseph), "Come out before them." When they saw him, they did extol him, and (in their amazement) cut their hands: they said, "Allah preserve us! no mortal is this! this is none other than a noble angel!"

32. She said: "There before you is the man about whom ye did blame me! I did seek to seduce him from his (true) self but he did firmly save himself guiltless!…. And now, if he doth not my bidding, he shall certainly be cast into prison, and (what is more) be of the company of the vilest!"

33. He said: "O my Lord! the prison is more to my liking than that to which they invite me: Unless Thou turn away their snare from me, I should (in my youthful folly) feel inclined towards them and join the ranks of the ignorant."

34. So his Lord hearkened to him (in his prayer), and turned away from him their snare: Verily He heareth and knoweth (all things).

35. Then it occurred to the men, after they had seen the signs, (that it was best) to imprison him for a time.

36. Now with him there came into the prison two young men. Said one of them: "I see myself (in a dream) pressing wine." said the other: "I see myself (in a dream) carrying bread on my head, and birds are eating, thereof." "Tell us" (they said) "The truth and meaning thereof: for we see thou art one that doth good (to all)."

37. He said: "Before any food comes (in due course) to feed either of you, I will surely reveal to you the truth and meaning of this ere it befall you: that is part of the (duty) which my Lord hath taught me. I have (I assure you) abandoned the ways of a people that believe not in Allah and that (even) deny the Hereafter."

38. "And I follow the ways of my fathers,—Abraham, Isaac, and Jacob; and never could we attribute any partners whatever to Allah: that (comes) of the grace of Allah to us and to mankind: yet most men are not grateful."

39. "O my two companions of the prison! (I ask you): are many lords differing among themselves better, or the One Allah, Supreme and Irresistible?"

40. "If not Him, ye worship nothing but names which ye have named,—ye and your fathers,—for which Allah hath sent down no authority: the command is for none but Allah: He hath commanded that ye worship none but Him: that is the right religion, but most men understand not…"

41. "O my two companions of the prison! As to one of you, he will pour out the wine for his lord to drink: as for the other, he will hang from the cross, and the birds will eat from off his head. (So) hath been decreed that matter whereof ye twain do enquire…"

42. And of the two, to that one whom he consider about to be saved, he said: "Mention me to thy lord." But Satan made him forget to mention him to his lord: and (Joseph) lingered in prison a few (more) years.

P: And he said unto him of the twain who he knew would be released: Mention me in the presence of thy lord. But Satan caused him to forget to mention it to his lord, so he (Joseph) stayed in prison for some years.

S: And he said to him whom he knew would be delivered of the two: Remember me with your lord; but the Shaitan caused him to forget mentioning (it) to his lord, so he remained in the prison a few years.

43. The king (of Egypt) said: "I do see (in a vision) seven fat kine, whom seven lean ones devour, and seven green ears of corn, and seven (others) withered. O ye chiefs! Expound to me my vision if it be that ye can interpret visions."

44. They said: "A confused medley of dreams: and we are not skilled in the interpretation of dreams."

45. But the man who had been released, one of the two (who had been in prison) and who now bethought him after (so long) a space of time, said: "I will tell you the truth of its interpretation: send ye me (therefore)."

46. "O Joseph!" (he said) "O man of truth! Expound to us (the dream) of seven fat kine whom seven lean ones devour, and of seven green ears of corn and (seven) others withered: that I may return to the people, and that they may understand."

47. (Joseph) said: "For seven years shall ye diligently sow as is your wont: and the harvests that ye reap, ye shall leave them in the ear,—except a little, of which ye shall eat."

48. "Then will come after that (period) seven dreadful (years), which will devour what ye shall have laid by in advance for them,—(all) except a little which ye shall have (specially) guarded."

49. "Then will come after that (period) a year in which the people will have abundant water, and in which they will press (wine and oil)."

50. So the king said: "Bring ye him unto me." But when the messenger came to him, (Joseph) said: "Go thou back to thy lord, and ask him, 'What is the state of mind of the ladies who cut their hands'? For my Lord is certainly well aware of their snare."

51. (The king) said (to the ladies): "What was your affair when ye did seek to seduce Joseph from his (true) self?" The ladies said: "Allah preserve us! no evil know we against him!" Said the 'Aziz's wife: "Now is the truth manifest (to all): it was I who sought to seduce him from his (true) self: He is indeed of those who are (ever) true (and virtuous)."

52. "This (say I), in order that He may know that I have never been false to him in his absence, and that Allah will never guide the snare of the false ones."

53. "Nor do I absolve my own self (of blame): the (human) soul is certainly prone to evil, unless my Lord do bestow His Mercy: but surely my Lord is Oft-Forgiving, Most Merciful."

54. So the king said: "Bring him unto me; I will take him specially to serve about my own person." Therefore when he had spoken to him, he said: "Be assured this day, thou art, before our own presence, with rank firmly established, and fidelity fully proved!"

55. (Joseph) said: "Set me over the store-houses of the land: I will indeed guard them, as one that knows (their importance)."

56. Thus did We give established power to Joseph in the land, to take possession therein as, when, or where he pleased. We bestow of our Mercy on whom We please, and We suffer not, to be lost, the reward of those who do good.

57. But verily the reward of the Hereafter is the best, for those who believe, and are constant in righteousness.

58. Then came Joseph's brethren: they entered his presence, and he knew them, but they knew him not.

59. And when he had furnished them forth with provisions (suitable) for them, he said: "Bring unto me a brother ye have, of the same father as yourselves, (but a different mother): see ye not that I pay out full measure, and that I do provide the best hospitality?"

60. "Now if ye bring him not to me, ye shall have no measure (of corn) from me, nor shall ye (even) come near me."

61. They said: "We shall certainly seek to get our wish about him from his father: Indeed we shall do it."

62. And (Joseph) told his servants to put their stock-in-trade (with which they had bartered) into their saddle-bags, so they should know it only when they returned to their people, in order that they might come back.

Text Thirty-four: SURAH 12

63. Now when they returned to their father, they said: "O our father! No more measure of grain shall we get (unless we take our brother): So send our brother with us, that we may get our measure; and we will indeed take every care of him."

64. He said: "Shall I trust you with him with any result other than when I trusted you with his brother aforetime? But Allah is the best to take care (of him), and He is the Most Merciful of those who show mercy!"

65. Then when they opened their baggage, they found their stock-in-trade had been returned to them. They said: "O our father! What (more) can we desire? this our stock-in-trade has been returned to us: so we shall get (more) food for our family; We shall take care of our brother; and add (at the same time) a full camel's load (of grain to our provisions). This is but a small quantity."

66. (Jacob) said: "Never will I send him with you until ye swear a solemn oath to me, in Allah's name, that ye will be sure to bring him back to me unless ye are yourselves hemmed in (and made powerless)." And when they had sworn their solemn oath, he said: "Over all that we say, be Allah the witness and guardian!"

67. Further he said: "O my sons! enter not all by one gate: enter ye by different gates. Not that I can profit you aught against Allah (with my advice): None can command except Allah: On Him do I put my trust: and let all that trust put their trust on Him."

68. And when they entered in the manner their father had enjoined, it did not profit them in the least against (the plan of) Allah: It was but a necessity of Jacob's soul, which he discharged. For he was, by our instruction, full of knowledge (and experience): but most men know not.

69. Now when they came into Joseph's presence, he received his (full) brother to stay with him. He said (to him): "Behold! I am thy (own) brother; so grieve not at aught of their doings."

70. At length when he had furnished them forth with provisions (suitable) for them, he put the drinking cup into his brother's saddle-bag. Then shouted out a crier: "O ye (in) the caravan! behold! ye are thieves, without doubt!"

71. They said, turning towards them: "What is it that ye miss?"

72. They said: "We miss the great beaker of the king; for him who produces it, is (the reward of) a camel load; I will be bound by it."

73. (The brothers) said: "By Allah! well ye know that we came not to make mischief in the land, and we are no thieves!"

74. (The Egyptians) said: "What then shall be the penalty of this, if ye are (proved) to have lied?"

75. They said: "The penalty should be that he in whose saddle-bag it is found, should be held (as bondman) to atone for the (crime). Thus it is we punish the wrong-doers!"

76. So he began (the search) with their baggage, before (he came to) the baggage of his brother: at length he brought it out of his brother's baggage. Thus did We plan for Joseph. He could not take his brother by the law of the king except that Allah willed it (so). We raise to degrees (of wisdom) whom We please: but over all endued with knowledge is one, the All-Knowing.

77. They said: "If he steals, there was a brother of his who did steal before (him)." But these things did Joseph keep locked in his heart, revealing not the secrets to them. He (simply) said (to himself): "Ye are the worse situated; and Allah knoweth best the truth of what ye assert!"

78. They said: "O exalted one! Behold! he has a father, aged and venerable, (who will grieve for him); so take one of us in his place; for we see that thou art (gracious) in doing good."

79. He said: "Allah forbid that we take other than him with whom we found our property: indeed (if we did so), we should be acting wrongfully."

80. Now when they saw no hope of his (yielding), they held a conference in private. The leader among them said: "Know ye not that your father did take an oath from you in Allah's name, and how, before this, ye did fail in your duty with Joseph? Therefore will I not leave this land until my father permits me, or Allah commands me; and He is the best to command."

81. "Turn ye back to your father, and say, 'O our father! behold! thy son committed theft! we bear witness only to what we know, and we could not well guard against the unseen!'

82. "'Ask at the town where we have been and the caravan in which we returned, and (you will find) we are indeed telling the truth.'"

83. Jacob said: "Nay, but ye have yourselves contrived a story (good enough) for you. So patience is most fitting (for me). Maybe Allah will bring them (back) all to me (in the end). For He is indeed full of knowledge and wisdom."

84. And he turned away from them, and said: "How great is my grief for Joseph!" And his eyes became white with sorrow, and he fell into silent melancholy.

Text Thirty-four: **SURAH 12**

85. They said: "By Allah! (never) wilt thou cease to remember Joseph until thou reach the last extremity of illness, or until thou die!"

86. He said: "I only complain of my distraction and anguish to Allah, and I know from Allah that which ye know not…"

87. "O my sons! go ye and enquire about Joseph and his brother, and never give up hope of Allah's Soothing Mercy: truly no one despairs of Allah's Soothing Mercy, except those who have no faith."

88. Then, when they came (back) into (Joseph's) presence they said: "O exalted one! distress has seized us and our family: we have (now) brought but scanty capital: so pay us full measure, (we pray thee), and treat it as charity to us: for Allah doth reward the charitable."

89. He said: "Know ye how ye dealt with Joseph and his brother, not knowing (what ye were doing)?"

90. They said: "Art thou indeed Joseph?" He said, "I am Joseph, and this is my brother: Allah has indeed been gracious to us (all): behold, he that is righteous and patient,—never will Allah suffer the reward to be lost, of those who do right."

91. They said: "By Allah! indeed has Allah preferred thee above us, and we certainly have been guilty of sin!"

92. He said: "This day let no reproach be (cast) on you: Allah will forgive you, and He is the Most Merciful of those who show mercy!"

93. "Go with this my shirt, and cast it over the face of my father: he will come to see (clearly). Then come ye (here) to me together with all your family."

94. When the caravan left (Egypt), their father said: "I do indeed scent the presence of Joseph: Nay, think me not a dotard."

95. They said: "By Allah! truly thou art in thine old wandering mind."

96. Then when the bearer of the good news came, He cast (the shirt) over his face, and he forthwith regained clear sight. He said: "Did I not say to you, 'I know from Allah that which ye know not?'"

97. They said: "O our father! ask for us forgiveness for our sins, for we were truly at fault."

98. He said: "Soon will I ask my Lord for forgiveness for you: for he is indeed Oft-Forgiving, Most Merciful."

99. Then when they entered the presence of Joseph, he provided a home for his parents with himself, and said: "Enter ye Egypt (all) in safety if it please Allah."

100. And he raised his parents high on the throne (of dignity), and they fell down in prostration, (all) before him. He said: "O my father! this is the fulfilment of my vision of old! Allah hath made it come true! He was indeed good to me when He took me out of prison and brought you (all here) out of the desert, (even) after Satan had sown enmity between me and my brothers. Verily my Lord understandeth best the mysteries of all that He planneth to do, for verily He is full of knowledge and wisdom."

101. "O my Lord! Thou hast indeed bestowed on me some power, and taught me something of the interpretation of dreams and events,—O Thou Creator of the heavens and the earth! Thou art my Protector in this world and in the Hereafter. Take Thou my soul (at death) as one submitting to Thy will (as a Muslim), and unite me with the righteous."

102. Such is one of the stories of what happened unseen, which We reveal by inspiration unto thee; nor wast thou (present) with them then when they concerted their plans together in the process of weaving their plots.

103. Yet no faith will the greater part of mankind have, however ardently thou dost desire it.

104. And no reward dost thou ask of them for this: it is no less than a message for all creatures.

105. And how many Signs in the heavens and the earth do they pass by? Yet they turn (their faces) away from them!

106. And most of them believe not in Allah without associating (other as partners) with Him!

107. Do they then feel secure from the coming against them of the covering veil of the wrath of Allah,— or of the coming against them of the (final) Hour all of a sudden while they perceive not?

108. Say thou: "This is my way: I do invite unto Allah,—on evidence clear as the seeing with one's eyes,—I and whoever follows me. Glory to Allah! and never will I join gods with Allah!"

109. Nor did We send before thee (as messengers) any but men, whom we did inspire,—(men) living in human habitations. Do they not travel through the earth, and see what was the end of those before them? But the home of the hereafter is best, for those who do right. Will ye not then understand?

110. (Respite will be granted) until, when the messengers give up hope (of their people) and (come to) think that they were treated as liars, there reaches them Our help, and those whom We will are delivered into safety. But never will be warded off our punishment from those who are in sin.

111. There is, in their stories, instruction for men endued with understanding. It is not a tale invented, but a confirmation of what went before it,—a detailed exposition of all things, and a guide and a mercy to any such as believe.

Text Thirty-five

Surah 19

Maryam or Mary

In the name of Allah, the Most Beneficent, the Most Merciful.

1. Kaf. Ha. Ya. 'Ain. Sad.

2. (This is) a recital of the Mercy of thy Lord to His servant Zakariya.

3. Behold! he cried to his Lord in secret,

4. Praying: "O my Lord! infirm indeed are my bones, and the hair of my head doth glisten with grey: but never am I unblest, O my Lord, in my prayer to Thee!"

5. "Now I fear (what) my relatives (and colleagues) (will do) after me: but my wife is barren: so give me an heir as from Thyself,"—

6. "(One that) will (truly) represent me, and represent the posterity of Jacob; and make him, O my Lord! one with whom Thou art well-pleased!"

7. (His prayer was answered): "O Zakariya! We give thee good news of a son: His name shall be Yahya: on none by that name have We conferred distinction before."

8. He said: "O my Lord! How shall I have a son, when my wife is barren and I have grown quite decrepit from old age?"

9. He said: "So (it will be) thy Lord saith, 'that is easy for Me: I did indeed create thee before, when thou hadst been nothing!'"

10. (Zakariya) said: "O my Lord! give me a Sign." "Thy Sign," was the answer, "Shall be that thou shalt speak to no man for three nights, although thou art not dumb."

11. So Zakariya came out to his people from him chamber: He told them by signs to celebrate Allah's praises in the morning and in the evening.

12. (To his son came the command): "O Yahya! take hold of the Book with might": and We gave him Wisdom even as a youth,

13. And piety (for all creatures) as from Us, and purity: He was devout,

14. And kind to his parents, and he was not overbearing or rebellious.

15. So Peace on him the day he was born, the day that he dies, and the day that he will be raised up to life (again)!

16. Relate in the Book (the story of) Mary, when she withdrew from her family to a place in the East.

17. She placed a screen (to screen herself) from them; then We sent her our angel, and he appeared before her as a man in all respects.

18. She said: "I seek refuge from thee to (Allah) Most Gracious: (come not near) if thou dost fear Allah."

19. He said: "Nay, I am only a messenger from thy Lord, (to announce) to thee the gift of a holy son."

20. She said: "How shall I have a son, seeing that no man has touched me, and I am not unchaste?"

21. He said: "So (it will be): Thy Lord saith, 'that is easy for Me: and (We wish) to appoint him as a Sign unto men and a Mercy from Us': It is a matter (so) decreed."

22. So she conceived him, and she retired with him to a remote place.

23. And the pains of childbirth drove her to the trunk of a palm-tree: She cried (in her anguish): "Ah! would that I had died before this! would that I had been a thing forgotten and out of sight!"

24. But (a voice) cried to her from beneath the (palm-tree): "Grieve not! for thy Lord hath provided a rivulet beneath thee;"

25. "And shake towards thyself the trunk of the palm-tree: It will let fall fresh ripe dates upon thee."

26. "So eat and drink and cool (thine) eye. And if thou dost see any man, say, 'I have vowed a fast to (Allah) Most Gracious, and this day will I enter into not talk with any human being'"

27. At length she brought the (babe) to her people, carrying him (in her arms). They said: "O Mary! truly an amazing thing hast thou brought!"

28. "O sister of Aaron! Thy father was not a man of evil, nor thy mother a woman unchaste!"

29. But she pointed to the babe. They said: "How can we talk to one who is a child in the cradle?"

30. He said: "I am indeed a servant of Allah: He hath given me revelation and made me a prophet;"

31. "And He hath made me blessed wheresoever I be, and hath enjoined on me Prayer and Charity as long as I live;"

32. "(He) hath made me kind to my mother, and not overbearing or miserable;"

33. "So peace is on me the day I was born, the day that I die, and the day that I shall be raised up to life (again)"!

34. Such (was) Jesus the son of Mary: (it is) a statement of truth, about which they (vainly) dispute.

35. It is not befitting to (the majesty of) Allah that He should beget a son. Glory be to Him! when He determines a matter, He only says to it, "Be", and it is.

36. Verily Allah is my Lord and your Lord: Him therefore serve ye: this is a Way that is straight.

37. But the sects differ among themselves: and woe to the unbelievers because of the (coming) Judgment of a Momentous Day!

38. How plainly will they see and hear, the Day that they will appear before Us! but the unjust today are in error manifest!

39. But warn them of the Day of Distress, when the matter will be determined: for (behold,) they are negligent and they do not believe!

40. It is We Who will inherit the earth, and all beings thereon: to Us will they all be returned.

41. (Also) mention in the Book (the story of) Abraham: He was a man of Truth, a prophet.

42. Behold, he said to his father: "O my father! why worship that which heareth not and seeth not, and can profit thee nothing?"

43. "O my father! to me hath come knowledge which hath not reached thee: so follow me: I will guide thee to a way that is even and straight."

44. "O my father! serve not Satan: for Satan is a rebel against (Allah) Most Gracious."

45. "O my father! I fear lest a Penalty afflict thee from (Allah) Most Gracious, so that thou become to Satan a friend."

46. (The father) replied: "Dost thou hate my gods, O Abraham? If thou forbear not, I will indeed stone thee: Now get away from me for a good long while!"

47. Abraham said: "Peace be on thee: I will pray to my Lord for thy forgiveness: for He is to me Most Gracious."

48. "And I will turn away from you (all) and from those whom ye invoke besides Allah: I will call on my Lord: perhaps, by my prayer to my Lord, I shall be not unblest."

49. When he had turned away from them and from those whom they worshipped besides Allah, We bestowed on him Isaac and Jacob, and each one of them We made a prophet.

50. And We bestowed of Our Mercy on them, and We granted them lofty honour on the tongue of truth.

51. Also mention in the Book (the story of) Moses: for he was specially chosen, and he was a messenger (and) a prophet.

52. And we called him from the right side of Mount (Sinai), and made him draw near to Us, for mystic (converse).

53. And, out of Our Mercy, We gave him his brother Aaron, (also) a prophet.

54. Also mention in the Book (the story of) Isma'il: He was (strictly) true to what he promised, and he was a messenger (and) a prophet.

55. He used to enjoin on his people Prayer and Charity, and he was most acceptable in the sight of his Lord.

Text Thirty-six

Surah 71

Nuh or Noah

In the name of Allah, the Most Beneficent, the Most Merciful.

1. We sent Noah to his People (with the Command): "Do thou warn thy People before there comes to them a grievous Penalty."

2. He said: "O my People! I am to you a Warner, clear and open:"

3. "That ye should worship Allah, fear Him and obey me:"

4. "So He may forgive you your sins and give you respite for a stated Term: for when the Term given by Allah is accomplished, it cannot be put forward: if ye only knew."

5. He said: "O my Lord! I have called to my People night and day:"

6. "But my call only increases (their) flight (from the Right)."

7. "And every time I have called to them, that Thou mightest forgive them, they have (only) thrust their fingers into their ears, covered themselves up with their garments, grown obstinate, and given themselves up to arrogance."

8. "So I have called to them aloud;"

9. "Further I have spoken to them in public and secretly in private,"

10. "Saying, 'Ask forgiveness from your Lord; for He is Oft-Forgiving;'"

11. "'He will send rain to you in abundance;'"

071. "'Give you increase in wealth and sons; and bestow on you gardens and bestow on you rivers (of flowing water).'"

13. "'What is the matter with you, that ye place not your hope for kindness and long-suffering in Allah,'"—

14. "'Seeing that it is He that has created you in diverse stages?'"

15. "'See ye not how Allah has created the seven heavens one above another,'"

16. "'And made the moon a light in their midst, and made the sun as a (Glorious) Lamp?'"

17. "'And Allah has produced you from the earth growing (gradually),'"

18. "'And in the End He will return you into the (earth), and raise you forth (again at the Resurrection)?'"

19. "'And Allah has made the earth for you as a carpet (spread out),'"

20. "'That ye may go about therein, in spacious roads.'"

21. Noah said: "O my Lord! They have disobeyed me, but they follow (men) whose wealth and children give them no increase but only Loss."

22. "And they have devised a tremendous Plot."

23. "And they have said (to each other), 'Abandon not your gods: Abandon neither Wadd nor Suwa', neither Yaguth nor Ya'uq, nor Nasr';"—

24. "They have already misled many; and grant Thou no increase to the wrong-doers but in straying (from their mark)."

25. Because of their sins they were drowned (in the flood), and were made to enter the Fire (of Punishment): and they found—in lieu of Allah—none to help them.

26. And Noah, said: "O my Lord! Leave not of the Unbelievers, a single one on earth!"

27. "For, if Thou dost leave (any of) them, they will but mislead Thy devotees, and they will breed none but wicked ungrateful ones."

28. "O my Lord! Forgive me, my parents, all who enter my house in Faith, and (all) believing men and believing women: and to the wrong-doers grant Thou no increase but in perdition!"

Example of Hadith: The Night Journey

What is the religious meaning of the Night Journey? [TEXT 37]

Text Thirty-seven

The Night Journey in the Hadith

Narrated Anas ibn Malik from Malik ibn Sa'sa'a that Allah's Apostle described to them his Night Journey saying, While I was lying in Al-Hatim or Al-Hijr, suddenly someone came to me and cut my body open from here to here (across the chest). He then took out my heart. Then a gold tray full of Belief was brought to me and my heart was washed and was filled (with Belief) and then returned to its original place. Then a white animal which was smaller than a mule and bigger than a donkey was brought to me . . . The animal's step (was so wide that it) reached the nearest heaven. Then he asked for the gate to be opened it was asked, "Who is it?" Gabriel answered, "Gabriel." It was asked, "Who was accompanying you?" Gabriel replied, "Muhammad." It was asked, "Has Muhammad been called?" Gabriel replied in the affirmative. Then it was said, "He is welcomed. What an excellent visit his is!" The gate was opened and when I went over the first heaven. I saw Adam there. Gabriel said (to me), "This is your father, Adam; pay him your greetings." So I greeted him and he returned the greeting to me and said," You are welcomed, o pious son and pious Prophet." Then Gabriel ascended with me till we reached the second heaven. . . .There I saw Yahya (i.e., John) and 'Isa (i.e., Jesus) who were cousins of each other. . . .Then Gabriel ascended with me to the third heaven and . . . there I saw Joseph . . . then Gabriel ascended with me to the fourth heaven and . . . there I saw Idris.

Then Gabriel ascended with me to the first heaven and . . . there I saw Harun (i.e., Aaron). Then Gabriel ascended with me to the sixth heaven and . . . there I saw Moses . . . When I left him (i.e., Moses) he wept. Someone asked him, "What makes you weep?" Moses said, "I weep because after me there has been sent (as Prophet) a young man whose followers will enter Paradise in greater numbers than my followers." Then Gabriel ascended with me to the seventh heaven and . . . there I saw Abraham . . . Then I was made to ascend to Sidratul-Muntaha (i.e., the Lote Tree of the farthest limit). Behold! Its fruits were like the jars of Har (i.e., a place near Medina) and its leaves were as big as the ears of elephants. Gabriel said, "This is the Lote Tree of the farthest limit," Behold! There ran four rivers, two were hidden and two were visible. I asked, "What are these two kinds of rivers, O Gabriel?" He replied, "As for the hidden rivers, they are two rivers in Paradise, and the visible rivers are the Nile and the Euphrates. Then Al-Bait-ul-Ma'mur (i.e., the Sacred House) was shown to me and a container full of wine and another full of milk and a third full of honey were brought to me. I took the milk. Gabriel remarked, "This is the Islamic religion which you and your followers are following." Then the prayers were enjoined on me: They were fifty prayers a day.

When I returned, I passed by Moses who asked (me), "What have you been ordered to do?" I replied, "I have been ordered to offer fifty prayers a day." Moses said, Your followers cannot bear fifty prayers a day, and by Allah, I have tested people before you, and I have tried my level best with Bani Israil (in vain). Go back to your Lord and ask for reducing your followers' burden." So I went back, and Allah reduced ten prayers for me. Then again I went back to Allah and he reduced ten more prayers. When I came back to Moses he said the same, I went back to Allah and he ordered me to observe ten prayers a day. When I came back to Moses, he repeated the same advice, so I went back to Allah and was ordered to observe five prayers a day. When I came back to Moses, he said . . . go back to your Lord and ask for reducing your followers' burden." I said, "I have requested so much of my Lord that I feel ashamed, but I am satisfied now and surrender to Allah's Order." When I left, I heard a voice saying, "I have passed My Order and have reduced the burden of My Worshippers."

"The Night Journey" (Sahih al-Bukhari, 5:227) from *The Translation of the Meanings of Sahib al-Bukhari,* 9 Volumes, translated by Muhammad Muhsin Khan, 1979. Reprinted by permission of Dar-us-Salam Publications.

Reading Glossary

Please note that this glossary will help you read the primary documents for Hinduism, Buddhism, and Sikhism.

HINDUISM

Agni = fire god

Ahimsa = non-violence

Ambika = different name and form of Devi, the main Hindu female deity. Ambika in this account is the Goddess Durga.

Angiras = ancient family of priests, sages

Arjuna = warrior, one of the five Pandava brothers in the *Bhagavad Gita* (Song of God)

Asuras = demons, titans

Bhishma = grandfather of Arjuna, the warrior

Brahmanas = priests

Camunda = different name and form of Devi, the main Hindu female deity

Canda = demon

Chandika = different name and form of Devi, the main Hindu female deity

Daityas = demons

Daiva = godly

Daksha = ancient king

Danavas = demons

Dharma = duty, justice

Drona = teacher of Arjuna, the warrior

Gandharvas = demi-gods

Himsa = violence

Indra = head of the Vedic gods

Kali = "the Black one" or warrior goddess

Kalpa = era

Karma = the concept that good and bad actions carry consequences in this life and in the next reincarnation

Krishna = avatar of great Hindu God Vishnu

Kubera = Lord of wealth

Mahakali = different name and form of Devi, the main Hindu female deity

Manu = ancient king

Matsyas and Pancalas = people living in Northern India along the Ganges river

Munda = demon

Nisumbha = demon

Prithu = ancient king

Purusha = primeval man

Rakhasas = demons

Sanjaya = character in the epic of Mahabharata who narrates the events happening on the battlefield of Kuru-
shetra to the blind king Dhritarashtra

Sapinda = close relative, cousin

Srotriya = Brahmins of highest level

Sumbha = demon

Varuna = god of night and waters

Vena = ancient and evil king

Viraj = manifest and all-powerful deity or active female creative principle

Yama = god of death and king of justice (dharma)

BUDDHISM

Ameno minaka = a primordial kami

Amenominakanushi-no-Okami = in this context, creator god of the entire universe, all knowing

Ananda = perfect bliss; a disciple of Buddha

Arhat = one who is worthy; in Theravada Buddhism, someone who has attained enlightenment through his/
her own effort

Bhikkhus = beggars or monks

Bodhi = awakening

Bodhicitta = compassionate aspiration

Bodhidharma = enlightenment and first patriarch of Zen Buddhism

Bodhisattva = one who vows to achieve buddhahood to free everyone from suffering

Brahman = the one Supreme

Devas = gods, divinities

Dharma = teachings of Buddha and/or phenomena

Dharmadhatu = ultimate nature of reality

Dojo = art of self defense

Dokusan = private audience with one's master

Gong = rimmed metal disk hit with a mallet to produce loud noise

Hara = lower abdominal region of the human body where qi (primordial breath of life) is collected. It is the
center of mental and physical energy

Hekigan = collection of koan

Hokkaido = a place in Japan

Kageki = theater (much like an operetta)

Kami = Shinto (Japanese) divinity

Kensho = enlightenment

Koan = word puzzle, a story inaccessible to rational understanding

Kotoshiro-nushi-no-kami = god of fishermen

Makyo = unpleasant thoughts

Mandala = chart, representation of the cosmos

Mara = tempter of the Buddha

Maya = illusion

Miko = Japanese "Shaman woman"

Misogi = ritual purification

Mu = usually translated by "no" or "does not have"

Mumonkan = collection of koans

Nagas = a member of a race of spirits

Nirvana = cessation of suffering

Parinirvana = see nirvana

Pratyekabuddhas = "individually enlightened ones" or disciples of the Buddha devoted to solitary practice (Theravada Buddhism)

Roshi = spiritual leader in Zen Buddhism

Samsara = "wandering"; wheel of birth, death, and rebirth

Sangha = community of monks

Satori = sudden spiritual awakening

Sesshin = a Zen retreat

Shoyoroku = a classic koan collection

Shuddhohana = a scion of the solar race; the Buddha's father

Skanda = skandha = physical/mental constituents (aggregates) of a person

Sravakas = listeners, disciples of the Buddha in Theravada Buddhism. Their goal is to become arhat.

Stupa = a reliquary containing the remains of the Buddha

Sugata = well gone; epithet of a Buddha

Takuhotsu = Buddhist's alms-begging

Tatami = mat rice straw Japanese floor covering

Tathagata = one who has thus come; another epithet or title of the Buddha

Teisho = a demonstration by a Zen master

Waka = classic verse form of Japanese poetry of thirty one syllables

Zazen = Zen sitting meditation

SIKHISM

Akaashic ethers = akasha is "sky" in Sanskrit

Amrit Vaylaa = early morning meditation

Chitr = angel who records deeds

Dharma = in Hinduism, the fundamental order of the Universe; in Buddhism, Buddha's teachings

Gupt = angel who records deeds

Guru Nanak = the founder of Sikhism and the first of the ten Gurus of the Sikhs

Hukam = a random verse read from the sacred scripture of Guru Granth

Koran = Islam's holiest book

Lakhshmi = Lakshmi = consort of Vishnu and Hindu goddess of health and prosperity

Maya = the illusory appearance of the sensible world

Mohini = the only female avatar of the Hindu god Vishnu

Naam = Nam: name of God in Sikhism

Paarvati = Parvati = Hindu goddess and consort of Shiva

Pandits = religious scholars

Puraanas = Puranas = ancient Hindu poems considered part of the smriti (tradition) literature

Qazi = Qadi = Muslim judge who renders decisions according to the Sharia, the canon law of Islam

Ragas = a traditional melodic type in Hindu music, consisting of a theme that expresses an aspect of religious feeling

Saadhu = Sidhu = an ascetic holy man

Samaadhi = Samadhi = advance state of mental awareness as a result of intense meditation

Shaastras = rules, teachings

Shaykh = religious official or Sufi master in Islam

Siddhas = "one who has attained perfection and bliss" or spiritual leaders

Simritees = smriti = tradition, memory, or category of Hindu sacred writings that are authoritative (for example: *Puranas* or *Laws of Manu*) but secondary to shruti ("that which is heard," canon) literature (for example: *Vedas + Upanishads*)

Sufism = mystical movement in Islam

Reading Glossary

References

Beckerlegge, Gwilym, ed. *The World Religions Reader*. London and New York: Routledge, 1998.

Carmody, Denise L. and T. L. Brink. *Ways to the Center: An Introduction to World Religions*. 5th edition. Belmont, CA: Thompson Wadsworth, 2002.

Esposito, John, Darrell J. Fasching, and Todd Lewis. *World Religions Today*. New York: Oxford University Press, 2006.

Fisher, Mary Pat. *Living Religions*. 8th edition. Upper Saddle River, NJ: Prentice Hall, 2011.

Forman, Robert K. C., Niels Nielsen, Norvin Hein, Frank E. Reynolds, Alan L. Miller, Samuel E. Karff, Alice C. Cowan, Paul McLean, Grace G. Burford, John Y. Fenton, Laura Grillo, Elizabeth Leeper. *Religions of the World*. 3rd edition. New York: St. Martin Press, 1993.

Kessler, Gary E. *Ways of Being Religious*. New York: McGraw Hill, 2000.

Matthews, Warren. *World Religions*. 4th edition. Belmont, CA: Thompson Wadsworth, 2004.

Molloy, Michael. *Experiencing the World Religions: Tradition, Challenge, and Change*. 5th edition. New York: McGraw Hill, 2010.

Noss, David S. *A History of the World's Religions*. 11th edition. Upper Saddle River, NJ: Prentice Hall, 2003.

Oxtoby, Willard G. and Alan F. Segal. *A Concise Introduction to World Religions*. Oxford: University Press, 2007.

Schmidt, Roger, Gene C. Sager, Gerald T. Carney, Albert Charles Muller, Kenneth J. Zanca, Julius J. Jackson, Jr., C. Wayne Mayhall, and Jeffrey C. Burke. *Patterns of Religion*. 2nd edition. Belmont, CA: Thompson Wadsworth, 2005.

Young, William. *The World's Religions: Worldviews and Contemporary Issues*. 2nd edition. Upper Saddle River, NJ: Prentice Hall, 2005.

CPSIA information can be obtained
at www.ICGtesting.com
Printed in the USA
LVOW02s0927140216

474943LV00005B/15/P